**HRM** NELSON SERIES IN
HUMAN RESOURCES MANAGEMENT

# STRATEGIC COMPENSATION IN CANADA

SEVENTH EDITION

**Parbudyal Singh**

York University

**Richard J. Long**

University of Saskatchewan

**Series Editor:**
**Monica Belcourt**

York University

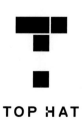

**TOP HAT**      **NELSON**

# TOP HAT

**Strategic Compensation in Canada, Seventh Edition**
by Parbudyal Singh and Richard J. Long

**Content Portfolio Manager:**
Lindsay Bradac

**Content Manager:**
Elke Price

**Photo and Permissions Researcher:**
Carrie McGregor

**Production Project Manager:**
Shannon Martin

**Production Service:**
SPi Global

**Copy Editor:**
Jessie Coffey

**Proofreader:**
SPi Global

**Indexer:**
SPi Global

**Design Project Manager:**
Pamela Johnston

**Interior Design:**
Cathy Mayer

**Cover Design:**
Courtney Hellam

**Cover Image:**
uniqdes/Shutterstock.com

**Compositor:**
SPi Global

ISBN-13: 978-1-77412-844-2
ISBN-10: 1-77412-844-6

*This book is dedicated to the memory of Richard Long.*
*—Parbudyal Singh*

# BRIEF CONTENTS

# CONTENTS

## PART 5   IMPLEMENTING, MANAGING, EVALUATING, AND ADAPTING THE COMPENSATION SYSTEM   441

# ABOUT THE SERIES

The management of human resources has become an important source of innovation, competitive advantage, and productivity for organizations. More than ever, human resources management (HRM) professionals need the knowledge and skills to design HRM policies and practices that not only meet legal requirements but also are effective in supporting organizational strategy as well as improving the work lives of employees. Increasingly, these professionals turn to published research and books on best practices for assistance in the development of effective HR strategies. The books in the *Nelson Series in Human Resources Management* are the best source in Canada for reliable, valid, and current knowledge about practices in HRM.

The texts in this series include:

- Managing Performance through Training and Development
- Management of Occupational Health and Safety
- Recruitment and Selection in Canada
- Strategic Compensation in Canada
- Strategic Human Resources Planning
- Industrial Relations in Canada

The *Nelson Series in Human Resources Management* represents a significant development in the field of HRM for many reasons. Each book in the series is the first, and now bestselling, text in the functional area. Furthermore, HR professionals in Canada must work with Canadian laws, statistics, policies, and values. This series serves their needs. It is the only opportunity that students and practitioners have to access a complete set of HRM books, standardized in presentation, which enables them to access information quickly across many HRM disciplines. Students who are pursuing the HR professional designation through their provincial HR associations will find the books in this series invaluable in preparing for the knowledge exams. This one-stop resource will prove useful to anyone looking for solutions for the effective management of people.

The publication of this series is one more step on the road to the professionalization of the HRM field where theory and applied research guide practice. The books in the series present the best and most current research in the functional areas of HRM. Research is supplemented with examples of the best practices used by Canadian companies that are leaders in HRM. Each text begins with a general model of the discipline, and then describes the implementation of effective strategies. The books serve as an introduction to the functional area for the new student of HR and as a validation source for the more experienced HRM practitioner. Cases, exercises, and endnotes provide opportunities for further discussion and analysis.

As you read and consult the books in this series, I hope you share my excitement in being involved and knowledgeable about a profession that has such a significant impact on the achievement of organizational goals and on employees' lives.

*Monica Belcourt, PhD, FCHRL*
*Series Editor*
*May 2020*

# PREFACE

The premise of this book is that an organization's compensation system can have a major impact on its success. An effective compensation system may be very different from one organization to the next and may even differ over time for the same organization. However, as there is no single compensation system that fits all organizations, this makes life very complicated for those who manage organizations.

This book provides a systematic framework for identifying and designing the compensation system that will add the most value to the organization. Chapter 1 lays out a road map for how this book will do that. The first half of the book focuses on developing the compensation strategy and the second half focuses on how to transform the compensation strategy into an operating compensation system.

Achieving an effective compensation system requires a diagnostic approach. That is, to identify the most effective compensation system for a given organization it is first necessary to understand that organization, its strategy, and its people.

Part One of the book focuses on developing these understandings by first providing a road map to effective compensation (Chapter 1), a strategic framework for compensation (Chapter 2), and then a behavioural framework for compensation (Chapter 3).

Part Two provides the ingredients and processes for formulating a compensation strategy. The three main components of a compensation system are examined, along with the choices to be made in determining the most appropriate compensation mix for a given firm (Chapter 4). Next, the available choices of performance pay plans is presented (Chapter 5), along with the key factors in deciding which of these choices are suitable for inclusion in the compensation mix. After identifying factors that constrain compensation choices, Chapter 6 provides a process that should result in the formulation of the most appropriate compensation strategy for a given firm.

However, the formulation of the compensation strategy does not mark the end of the compensation process. Compensation strategy needs to be translated into an operating compensation system that results in an actual dollar value of compensation for every employee. Determining a compensation value for a given employee depends on a combination of the relative value of that employee's job to the employer (as determined through job evaluation), the value the labour market places on that job (as determined by compensation surveys), and the value of that employee's performance (as determined by performance appraisal). Part Three covers the many technical processes necessary to convert the compensation strategy into a compensation system, including those for evaluating jobs (Chapters 7 and 8), for evaluating the market (Chapter 9), and for evaluating individual employees (Chapter 10).

Part Four provides detailed guidance on the key issues in designing performance pay plans (Chapter 11) and indirect pay plans (Chapter 12). Finally, Part Five provides detailed guidance on the key issues in implementing a new compensation system and its ongoing operation (Chapter 13).

This book was written for two main purposes: to help those wishing to learn how to create effective compensation systems, and to serve as a useful source of information for practitioners. In so doing, it fills a gap in the textual resources available in Canada. Other

Canadian books on compensation have lacked an integrated strategic framework and have tended to focus on either the behavioural principles in compensation or the technical details of compensation. Both of these are important, but what is needed is a balanced, comprehensive, and integrated presentation of strategic, behavioural, and technical principles. That is what this book seeks to provide.

The content of this book is based on a foundation of scientific research, informed by relevant theoretical principles and verified by actual organizational experiences. The Compensation Today cases help to illustrate these principles, research, and practice. Although there is still much to learn about the design of effective reward and compensation systems, our knowledge about compensation has advanced to the point where effective use of the available knowledge will significantly increase the likelihood of organizational success.

This book can stand alone as the principal resource for a course. Student learning can be further enhanced by accompanying it with *Strategic Compensation: A Simulation Workbook,* Seventh Edition, and the ABC Inc. case, which provide students with the opportunity to design an entire compensation system, right from formulation of compensation strategy to implementation of the new compensation system, complete with market-based actual dollars attached to the pay ranges. This simulation and case have been specifically designed by the authors to use all the steps required to develop an effective compensation system.

To maximize its value as an effective learning tool, this book incorporates several features. Its content is based on a scientific foundation and is enhanced by a variety of pedagogical tools, but its writing style is informal to smooth the road to effective learning. A key feature is the overall framework for the book—the "road map" to effective compensation. Getting to any destination is facilitated by a conceptual map of how to get there. The entire book is organized around this conceptual road map.

Features retained from the previous edition include chapter learning objectives, opening vignettes, "Compensation Today" boxes to put issues into real-life context, "Compensation Notebook" features to highlight key points in the chapter, extensive use of Canadian examples, margin definitions of key concepts, chapter summaries, listings of key terms, discussion questions, exercises, compensation exercises, and questions for case analysis.

As a part of the process needed to earn a professional HR designation, granted by the HR provincial associations, applicants must undergo two assessments: one is a knowledge-based exam, and the second assessment is based on experience. Because the competencies required for the knowledge exams may differ by province, we have not provided lists or links in this edition. Those interested in obtaining an HR designation should consult the HR association in their province.

## NEW TO THIS EDITION

One purpose of this revision of *Strategic Compensation in Canada* is to present current, relevant content and every new edition of the book brings changes and updates. This edition benefitted from a comprehensive update of the relevant research. In addition to some new discussion questions and exercises in the end-of-chapter material and references on recent publications, the following list highlights some of the new key and updated topics and examples that have been included in this edition.

## CHAPTER 1: A ROAD MAP TO EFFECTIVE COMPENSATION

- Updated and expanded the opening vignette, "A Whopping Salary Increase for Everyone! Does It Work?"
- New examples added throughout chapter include Wells Fargo, Edward Jones, and TTC
- Updated "Compensation Today, Internships: Paid or Unpaid?" discusses proposed federal laws

## CHAPTER 2: A STRATEGIC FRAMEWORK FOR COMPENSATION

- New example, ArcelorMittal Dofasco, highlighted in the opening vignette
- Added discussion of Fujifilm successfully responding to external changes in "Compensation Today, Did Human Relations Sink Kodak?"
- Updated "Compensation Today, Involvement Flies High at WestJet" includes coverage of some of the recent challenges faced by the company

## CHAPTER 3: A BEHAVIOURAL FRAMEWORK FOR COMPENSATION

- New opening vignette, "Fair Processes? Don't Bank On It," discusses how a culture of pressure, fear, and unrealistic sales expectations at Wells Fargo demanded employees to defraud customers
- New and updated coverage in "Compensation Today, Violating the Psychological Contract at CAMI" describes how the company violated the trust of its employees who wanted job security
- Expanded coverage in "Causes of Membership Behaviour" section includes a recent HRM study on continuance commitment and its subcomponents

## CHAPTER 4: COMPONENTS OF COMPENSATION STRATEGY

- New coverage of merit budgets and compensation planning statistics in the opening vignette, "Pay Systems Are Changing"
- Expanded coverage includes new research in "Disadvantages of Performance Pay and Indirect Pay"
- New coverage of compensable factors in job evaluations in "Disadvantages of Job Evaluation"

## CHAPTER 5: PERFORMANCE PAY CHOICES

- Added coverage of a recent study comparing sales professional quota-bonus compensation plans to quota-commission sales plans in "Applicability of Commissions"
- Expanded coverage of performance ratings and merit pay for teachers in "Compensation Today, Grade the Teachers?"
- New "Compensation Today, A Slice of The Business" illustrates a gain-sharing plan in a Parisian restaurant
- Added coverage of unions and gain-sharing plans

## CHAPTER 6: FORMULATING THE REWARD AND COMPENSATION STRATEGY

- Updated opening vignette, "Compensation Strategy at WestJet Airlines," highlights how volatile economic conditions affect the culture at the company
- Expanded coverage to reflect current conditions related to contingent workers
- New "Compensation Today, Walking Away with $62 million" highlights fired CEO compensation at Boeing

## CHAPTER 7: EVALUATING JOBS: THE JOB EVALUATION PROCESS

- Expanded coverage in "Compensation Today, Would I Be Treated This Way If I Were A Man?" discusses a recent study on the earnings of transsexuals
- Added coverage of a recent case about independent contractors who work for Uber Technologies Inc.
- New section, "Pay Equity in the Federal Jurisdiction," provides comprehensive coverage of pay equity legislation

## CHAPTER 8: EVALUATING JOBS: THE POINT METHOD OF JOB EVALUATION

- New "Compensation Today, Strike Two for Job Evaluations" covers job evaluation and pay for city workers in Cambridge
- Expanded coverage of living wages and includes discussion of a newly released report

## CHAPTER 9: EVALUATING THE MARKET

- New "Compensation Today, The Dirt on Compensation" discusses sanitation workers and compensating differentials
- New "Compensation Today, Nursing Homes Need More than Market" discusses the proxy method and pay-equity in female-dominated workplaces

## CHAPTER 10: EVALUATING INDIVIDUALS

- New section, "Continuous Performance Management," covers a new approach to traditional employee reviews
- New coverage of "720-degree Feedback" added

## CHAPTER 11: DESIGNING PERFORMANCE PAY PLANS

- New "Compensation Today, A Gain Sharing Plan for Neurosurgeons"
- Expanded coverage in "Compensation Today, Profit Sharing at Two Prominent Canadian Companies" includes CPSP, DCPP, and SRIP at ArcelorMittal and Canadian Tire
- New "Compensation Today, Not Only Money at Google" covers employee rewards and recognition programs

## CHAPTER 12: DESIGNING INDIRECT PAY PLANS

- Expanded coverage of hybrid plans, pension plans, and disability insurance
- Updated discussion of child and elder care services
- New "Compensation Today, Flexible Benefits at KPMG Canada"

## CHAPTER 13: ACTIVATING AND MAINTAINING AN EFFECTIVE COMPENSATION SYSTEM

- Updated opening vignette, "Thousands of Federal Employees Plagued by Problems," includes a recent report on Phoenix pay problems
- New "Compensation Today, Ontario Energy Board Declared Reductions to the Nuclear Budget" covers the impact of compensation costs
- New "Compensation Today, Media Companies Cut Costs Amid COVID-19" discusses the impact of coronavirus on advertising

# INSTRUCTOR RESOURCES

## TOP HAT

Top Hat's all-in-one teaching platform enables professors to connect with students inside and outside the classroom with engaging content, tools, and activities and has been used by over 3 million students.

Only Top Hat can power any course with active learning. Professors can use the platform to create engaging real-time and self-paced learning experiences for students. Students benefit from more active participation and increased comprehension with polls, quizzes, and discussion questions embedded in synchronous class presentations, homework assignments, and course readings. Top Hat also enables professors to perform secure and reliable summative assessments, such as tests and exams, with students in-person and remotely.

The Top Hat platform works on both mobile devices and laptops and features a number of enhanced accessibility features to support an equitable learning experience.

The **Nelson Education Teaching Advantage (NETA)** program delivers research-based instructor resources that promote student engagement and higher-order thinking to enable the success of Canadian students and educators.

The following instructor resources have been created for *Strategic Compensation in Canada*, Seventh Edition.

## NETA TEST BANK

This resource includes over 390 multiple-choice questions written according to NETA guidelines for effective construction and development of higher-order questions. Also included are 130 true/false and over 65 short-answer questions.

## NETA POWERPOINT

Microsoft® PowerPoint® lecture slides have been created for every chapter. There is an average of 35 slides per chapter, many featuring key figures, tables, and photographs from *Strategic Compensation in Canada*, Seventh Edition. NETA principles of clear design and engaging content have been incorporated throughout, making it simple for instructors to customize the deck for their courses.

## NETA INSTRUCTOR GUIDE

This resource is organized according to the textbook chapters and addresses key educational concerns, such as typical stumbling blocks students face and how to address them. Other features include notes for End-of-Chapter Discussion Questions, Exercises and Case Questions, and Sources of Lecture Enrichment.

## STUDENT ANCILLARIES
## STRATEGIC COMPENSATION: A SIMULATION

*Strategic Compensation: A Simulation*, Seventh Edition, offers students the opportunity to design a comprehensive system from beginning to end—from strategy to implementation. The result is a complete compensation system with pay grades and pay ranges, performance pay, and benefits—expressed in actual dollar values—for employees at a Canadian firm. By giving students an opportunity to apply the conceptual knowledge of compensation they have gained from their text and classes, this simulation offers a richer understanding of both the concepts and the practical realities of compensation. Students also gain practical skills that employers value. Instructors have a choice of two firms for which student teams can design a compensation system.

The simulation has been designed by Richard Long and Henry S. Ravichander to accompany the seventh edition of *Strategic Compensation in Canada*.

## CONTACT THE AUTHOR

The objectives for this book are ambitious, and it is up to readers to judge how effectively they have been achieved. The first author would welcome any suggestions, comments, or other feedback from you, the reader. You can use email (singhp@yorku.ca), telephone (416-736-2100, ext. 30100), or postal mail (Parbudyal Singh, School of Human Resource Management, York University, Toronto, M3J 1P3). I look forward to hearing from you!

*Parbudyal Singh, Ph.D.*
*School of Human Resource Management*
*York University*

# ABOUT THE AUTHORS

## Parbudyal Singh

Parbudyal Singh is a Professor of Human Resource Management at York University, Toronto. He completed his PhD from McMaster University. Prior to York University, he was the Associate Dean of the School of Business at the University of New Haven, Connecticut. Dr. Singh has more than 100 refereed publications, many of which are in top-tier journals such as *Industrial Relations*, *Journal of Business Ethics*, *The Leadership Quarterly*, *Human Resource Management*, *International Journal of Human Resource Management*, and *Human Resource Management Review*. He is a co-author of one of the leading human resource management textbooks in Canada (*Managing Human Resources*, Ninth Canadian Edition, Nelson Canada). Over his career, Dr. Singh has won numerous scholastic awards, several national research grants, and teaching and research awards.

Dr. Singh was a member of the committee appointed by the Ontario government in 2015 to study, consult, and make recommendations on closing the gender wage gap in Ontario. In 2018, he was awarded the first Distinguished Human Resource Professional designation by the Human Resource Professional Association of Ontario for his achievements in the field. He has also served as an advisor/consultant for many leading Canadian firms, as well as public sector organizations, on their compensation systems. Prior to being a university professor, Dr. Singh was a personnel manager at a large manufacturing firm.

## Richard J. Long

Richard J. Long was Professor of Human Resources and Organizational Behaviour at the Edwards School of Business at the University of Saskatchewan. He held B.Com. and MBA degrees from the University of Alberta and a PhD from Cornell University and was a Certified Human Resources Professional (CHRP).

Dr. Long taught, conducted research, and consulted in human resources management for more than 35 years and produced over 100 publications based on his research and experience. He was the author of two books, *New Office Information Technology: Human and Managerial Implications* and the textbook *Strategic Compensation in Canada*. He served on the editorial boards of *International Journal of Human Resource Management* and *Relations Industrielles/Industrial Relations*. He received the University of Saskatchewan's coveted Master Teacher award in 2014.

# ACKNOWLEDGEMENTS

Many people have contributed to this book in a variety of ways. A project such as this draws on the knowledge, experience, and insights of a large number of researchers, scholars, and practitioners, each of whom has played a role in developing the body of knowledge reflected in this book.

I am very grateful for the excellent research assistance provided by Marlee Mercer, a graduate student at York University. Over the years, I have learned with my students at York University and elsewhere. I thank them for their insights.

I would also like to acknowledge those reviewers who assisted in reviewing earlier editions of this textbook: Stan Arnold of Humber College, Bob Barnetson of Athabasca University, Judy Benevides of Kwantlen Polytechnic University, Julie Bulmash of George Brown College, Roger Gunn of NAIT, Sean MacDonald of the University of Manitoba, Ted Mock of Seneca College, John Pucic of Humber College, Stephen Risavy of Wilfrid Laurier University, Kristen Rosen of Seneca College, and Carol Ann Samhaber of Algonquin College. And for their useful suggestions and thoughtful comments on this edition, I am grateful to the following reviewers: Rupinder Gill of Fanshawe Colle, Ann Hrabok of NAIT, Patricia Hull of Mount Royal University, Gary Mearns of University of Saskatchewan, John Pucic of Humber College, and Wayne Rawcliffe of University of British Columbia.

I would like to express my gratitude to the team at Nelson, especially Alexis Hood, Jackie Wood, and Elke Price, for their feedback and guidance. I am also indebted to Monica Belcourt, the series editor and a colleague, for her confidence in my ability and her feedback in this edition. Finally, I am eternally grateful to my wife, Nirmala, and three children (Alysha, Amelia, and Aren) for all their encouragement and support.

My sincere thanks to the many who use our text in both academic and professional settings.

Parbudyal Singh, PhD
School of Human Resource Management
York University

# CHAPTER 1

# A ROAD MAP TO EFFECTIVE COMPENSATION

## Learning Outcomes

AFTER READING THIS CHAPTER, YOU SHOULD BE ABLE TO:

- Describe the key purpose of a compensation system.
- Explain why an effective compensation system is important to most organizations.
- Distinguish between extrinsic and intrinsic rewards.
- Distinguish between a reward system and a compensation system.
- Describe the key aspects of a compensation strategy.
- Explain why a compensation system must be viewed in the context of the total reward system, and the broader environment of the organization.
- Understand the key criteria for evaluating the success of a compensation system.
- Describe the steps along the road to effective compensation and explain how this book will facilitate that journey.

## A WHOPPING SALARY INCREASE FOR EVERYONE! DOES IT WORK?

Just imagine working for $40 000 a year as a compensation analyst in your organization. Then one day the boss calls a meeting and announces that the minimum pay for everyone would be $70 000! How would you react? How do you think those working above $70 000 will react? How would the competition react?

Well, this actually happened at Gravity Payments, a Seattle-based credit card processing firm in 2015. It is reported that the CEO of Gravity Payments, Dan Price, was challenged by an employee about his pay. The employee was making $35 000 a year, while Dan Price was making over $1 million. Shortly after this encounter, and after reviewing research that suggested employees are not happy until they earn a significant salary, the CEO raised the minimum pay of everyone in his 120-employee firm to $70 000, over a three-year period. To help pay for the increase, he took a pay cut to $70 000. The news made global headlines. Most of the employees at Gravity Payments reacted with joy; however, a few did not. In fact, two senior employees left the firm soon thereafter, complaining that those earning above $70 000 were not equitably compensated in the new pay system and that many of those who were now getting this increase did not deserve it, as they were just "clocking time" at work.

So, what have been the effects of the pay increase over time? Consequences to date are very encouraging from the organization's perspective. Applications for jobs with Gravity soared, which allowed the firm to be more selective in its new hires. One Yahoo executive actually took a pay cut to work for Gravity because she wanted to work in an environment that was "fun and meaningful." The media frenzy surrounding the pay increase resulted in free publicity for the firm and demand for its services grew. This new business has helped to compensate for the pay increase. Profits doubled in the six months following the pay hike and customer retention rates increased from 91 to 95 percent. Dan Price insists that the move is not intended to generate profits but is the morally right thing to do for his employees.

There were reports, however, that some businesses in the Seattle area were not very happy because of the pressures to match Gravity's new pay, and some commentators were calling the move a business gimmick to seek free publicity.

One radio personality even called Dan Price a "socialist" and predicted that Gravity will fail.

Gravity's revenues continue to grow. In 2018, the company processed $10.2 billion in payments. In 2014, before the wage increases, the company had processed $3.8 billion. The amount of independent businesses that Gravity now serves has increased by over 80 percent. Gravity has expanded and moved into a new building. The number of employees has increased by 40 percent, to more than 200 workers. Attrition rates are low. Employees can better contribute to their retirement plans and can afford housing that promises a shorter commute. Furthermore, now that the new wage has successfully been implemented, Gravity's board is determining the appropriate time to start paying the traditional CEO salary.

Some businesses have heard Dan Price speak and followed suit. For example, the CEO of Pharmalogics Recruiting, Megan Driscoll, increased employee base pay by 33 percent. Over two years, the company's revenue increased from $6.7 million to $15 million. Their retention rate increased from 40 percent to 84 percent.

CEO Dan Price takes a pay cut at Gravity Payments

Sources: Paul Keegan, "Here's What Really Happened at That Company That Set a $70,000 Minimum Wage," *Inc.com*, October 21, 2015; Karen Weise, "The CEO Paying Everyone $70,000 Salaries Has Something to Hide," *Bloomberg*, December 1, 2015; Christine Wang, "$70K CEO: I Wasn't Ready for the Surge of Attention," *CNBC*, April 18, 2016; Robin Levinson King, "Forget the Minimum Wage. Gravity Payments CEO Dan Price sets $70K 'Happiness' Wage," *Thestar.com*, April 17, 2015;

Peter Georgescu, "What Are We Waiting For?" *Forbes*, January 24, 2018; Michael Wheeler, "3 Years Ago This Boss Set a $70,000 Minimum Wage for His Employees—and the Move is Still Paying Off," *CNBC*, August 29, 2017; Nicholas Kristof, "The $70,000 a Year Minimum Wage," *The New York Times*, March 30, 2019; Jim Ludema & Amber Johnson, "Gravity Payment's Dan Price On How He Measures Success After His $70k Experiment," *Forbes*, August 28, 2018; Gaby Hinsliff, "This CEO Took a Pay Cut to Give Employees $70,000 a Year. Now He's Battling Amazon," *HuffPost*, May 19, 2018; Hana Kim, "How Much Buys Happiness in Western Washington?" *Q13Fox*, November 16, 2017; Katie Herzog, "Is Amazon's Minimum Wage Increase a Step Forward or Just a Savvy PR Move?" *The Stranger*, October 4, 2018.

## THE IMPORTANCE OF COMPENSATION SYSTEMS

Why is the compensation system important?

The debate on the role of compensation has spanned decades. Compensation means different things to different people. As the pay increase at Gravity Payments shows, it often depends on your perspective. For employers, the compensation system can be used to help the organization achieve its strategy and objectives; it can help to attract, retain, and motivate employees. It can also have philosophical and moral implications. For employees, pay influences their standard of living. For some, it may mean going hungry or not. For shareholders, the financial value of the pay system to the organization's bottom line is important. The wider society tends to view compensation from an equity perspective, and questions on justice are often included in the narratives. Often, the focus is on executive pay and the discussion tends to revolve around fairness when compared to employee pay. Regardless of your perspective, the compensation system is extremely important.

At the time this book was being revised for this edition, the COVID-19 pandemic was creating havoc in society. While the core medical issues related to testing, flattening the curve, immune systems, and vaccines, a core organizational and societal issue was how to incentivize and reward those on the frontlines, including essential workers. The debate revolved around the fairness and motivational effects of pay. Should organizations pay an additional $2/hour for grocery workers, or more? Was a $500 bonus the way to go? Are employees in long-term care residences paid fairly? Should nurses get more pay? Should these pay increases be permanent or be paid as some sort of "hazard" or "hero" pay? These were only some of the questions that added another dimension on the importance of pay systems.

While well-thought out pay systems can have positive implications for organizations, employees, and society, poorly designed compensation systems can have undesirable consequences, as the examples below illustrate.

- Green Giant wanted to improve the quality of its canned vegetables, so it decided to give a bonus to each worker depending on the number of insect parts each plucked from the processing line. The plan seemed to be enormously successful—hundreds and hundreds of insect parts were turned in, and large bonuses were paid. The only problem was that most of the additional insect parts were coming from the workers' backyards, where they were much easier to find, rather than from the canning line.

- To encourage high productivity among its computer programmers, IBM rewarded each programmer on the number of lines of computer code they produced. It took the company years to notice that IBM computer programs tended to be much longer and more inefficiently written than those of other companies.

- Wells Fargo placed intense pressure on retail bank employees. The company had extremely high sales targets and bonuses that tied into opening an unrealistic amount of customer accounts. For the employees to meet their targets and receive their bonuses, the employees opened accounts without customers' knowledge, charged auto finance customers for insurance policies of which they were unaware, and charged mortgage customers over $100 million in indefensible fees. Most of these fake accounts didn't even generate profit, while the rest of the accounts generated around $2.4 million in fees. This profit is not substantial for a bank that generates $88 billion annually. Furthermore, it is insubstantial when you consider the $185 million in fines and penalties that Wells Fargo was ordered to pay, plus the approximately $2.7 billion in civil and criminal suits.[1]

These examples show that reward systems can have powerful effects on behaviour, but it may not always be the behaviour we want. How can we design reward and compensation systems that produce the behaviour we want, while avoiding the behaviour we don't want? How can we predict whether a proposed reward and compensation system is likely to lead to the behaviour we want?

Answering these questions is what this book is all about; however, there are no simple answers. First, in many fields, the employee behaviour that companies need has become more complex, and a higher level of performance is required than in the past. In general, the more complex the behaviour and the higher the level of performance required, the more complex the compensation system needs to be. Second, there are now more choices of compensation practices available than ever before and choosing among these is no simple task.

There is no "one best" compensation system that fits all firms. For every successful compensation practice described in Compensation Today 1.1, examples can be found where the same practice was a complete failure. Understanding why the same compensation system that is successful in one firm yet fails at another is an essential requirement to successful compensation design.

---

## COMPENSATION TODAY 1.1

### COMPENSATION SUPPORTS STRATEGY

Many organizations regard their compensation system as a cost to be minimized while others believe that compensation can help the company carry out its strategies and achieve its goals. Here are some examples:

- At Adobe Systems Canada, a market-leading software firm, all employees participate in profit-sharing and employee share purchase plans; they also receive family-friendly benefits such as flexible working hours, telecommuting, and maternity leave top-up payments. The point is to recognize the high degree of commitment that Adobe employees display.

- At Boeing Canada's Winnipeg Division, which produces components for Boeing's new 787 Dreamliner aircraft, unionized employees participate in a gain-sharing program, under which they share in any cost savings they help generate. The company believes that this program cuts waste and boosts productivity.

- At Canadian Tire, management attributes a great deal of the firm's success to its employee profit-sharing plan, which it believes has led to a more committed and motivated workforce than is usual in the retail business.

- At Edward Jones, the company offers high earning potential with support at the preliminary stages in an employees' career. Financial Advisors studying for their exams are paid a salary, and the company also pays for their licensing. Edward Jones offers a higher base salary and New Asset Compensation for an employee's first four years with the expectation that their commission will be minimal. Within those four years, their fixed pay will decrease, as expected commissions will increase. Additionally, the company offers profitability bonuses, travel, profit sharing, and partnership opportunities. The company's strategy involves attention to long-term investing in quality. That doesn't seem to be far off from their people strategy.[2]

- At Herman Miller, a large manufacturer of office furniture, the centrepiece of the compensation strategy is a gain-sharing plan under which employees share in company productivity gains. This plan supports the company strategy of delegating a high amount of responsibility to employees.

- At RBC Financial, management is integrating performance pay elements into compensation packages for all employees to support the firm's increased focus on customers and performance. In the past, virtually all employees in the banking industry were paid fixed salaries.

- At Shell Canada's chemical plant in Sarnia, Ontario, pay is based not on the specific job an employee does, but on the number of jobs the worker is qualified to perform. The company believes that this radical departure from tradition has resulted in a more flexible and efficient workforce.

- At Starbucks, all employees—including part-time baristas—are given stock options. This supports the company strategy of committed service from employees. In most organizations, stock options are limited to a few top executives.

- At Toronto Transit Commission (TTC), the company created a rewards and recognition program that identifies employees who have contributed innovative solutions that save time and money but do not infringe on safety or quality. This recognition program supports the five-year plan to create a workforce that is empowered, reliable, and customer-focused. Furthermore, the company has been rated one of the top companies to work for in terms of salary, benefits, and pensions.[3]

- At Vanderpol's Eggs in Surrey, British Columbia, management regards employee share ownership as vital to its managerial strategy, which is to create a partnership between owners and employees. Management believes that employee-owners are more committed and productive.

- At WestJet Airlines, the profit-sharing and stock plans have made employees "owners." This pay strategy is aligned with the firm's strategy to develop employees' commitment and increase their participation and engagement. It has also spawned a culture that fosters teamwork.

- At Zappos, an online retailer of shoes and other consumer products, the company works hard to create a culture of involvement and commitment among its 1500 employees. The extrinsic rewards are not high (except for health care benefits); instead, the company relies on intrinsic rewards such as job autonomy and wide latitude for employees to make job decisions. For example, the amount of time that employees spend on a customer call is not monitored, so employees can spend as much time as they see fit with each customer.

## WHY STUDY COMPENSATION?

For many students, this is a required course in a degree, diploma, and certificate program. It is a key component of the national and provincial certification examinations. Compensation may also be a key aspect of the jobs that some do; thus, they study it. And a career in compensation is very rewarding. There are several jobs and career paths within the compensation field, including job evaluation specialists, payroll administrators, benefits specialists, and executive compensation consultants (see Compensation Today 1.3 for details on pay for some of these jobs). The pay varies for these jobs in Canada (and you will learn why this is the case as you progress through this text). On average, compensation professionals tend to be among the highest paid human resource practitioners.

## COMPENSATION SYSTEM: DOES IT HELP OR HURT YOUR ORGANIZATION?

Canadian firms typically spend 40–70 percent of their operating budgets to compensate their employees. For many firms, compensation is the single largest operating expenditure. According to Statistics Canada, employers in Canada are now spending around *a trillion* dollars on wages, salaries, and benefits (imagine a stack of $100 bills 1112 kilometres high).[4] Are they getting their money's worth? Is this money being well spent?

In many cases, it is not. Some firms are spending too much. Others are spending too little. But while the amount being spent is important, it is not the key issue. The real question is this: What is the organization receiving for its investment in wages, salaries, and benefits? Are the compensation system and the money devoted to it contributing to the achievement of organizational objectives in the fullest possible way? Does the firm's compensation system add the greatest possible value to the company after costs are taken into account?

A compensation system is one of the most powerful tools available for shaping employee behaviour and influencing company performance, yet many organizations waste this potential by viewing compensation as a cost to be minimized. Even worse, some compensation systems actually promote unproductive or counterproductive behaviour. As we will see in the following chapters, unmotivated employees, poor job performance, high turnover, irresponsible behaviour, and even employee dishonesty often have their roots in the compensation system. Other problems such as organizational rigidity, inability to adapt to change, lack of innovation, conflict between organizational units, and poor customer service may also stem, in part, from the reward system.

What complicates matters further is that without any obvious warning signs, a compensation system that has worked well in the past can become a serious liability when circumstances change. Failure to adapt reward systems to changing circumstances can cause new strategies to falter, new organizational structures to collapse, new technologies to malfunction, and entire companies to struggle. Ironically, because the reward system often affects behaviour in very subtle ways, many firms never identify their reward system as a major contributor to these problems.

## THE PREMISE OF THIS BOOK

Organizations that treat their reward system as a key strategic variable and use it to support their corporate and managerial strategies receive more value from their compensation system than those that do not, resulting in superior company performance and higher achievement of organizational objectives. This book's purpose is to help you learn to design and implement a reward and compensation strategy that best fits your circumstances—one that will add the greatest possible value to your organization. For those of you who are not directly involved in the design of compensation systems, the knowledge gained by learning the material in this text should help you better understand an organization's reward systems, as well as your own pay. This chapter begins by explaining some essential concepts and presenting a road map of the steps along the path to effective compensation.

# ROLE AND PURPOSE OF THE COMPENSATION SYSTEM

*How do you get organization members to do what the organization wants and needs them to do?* This is a central problem that has challenged those in charge of organizations since their creation. And it is a problem that is growing more complex, especially for organizations whose products, services, and technologies are becoming increasingly complicated, whose environments are more dynamic and competitive, who operate in democratic and relatively affluent societies, and who require complicated behaviours and high performance levels from their members. Compensation is normally a key part of the solution, although there are many other important parts, all which must fit together if the desired results are to be fully achieved.

The **purpose of a compensation system** is to help create a willingness among qualified persons to join the organization and to perform the tasks the organization needs. What this means is that employees must perceive that accepting a job with a given employer will help them satisfy some of their own important needs. These include economic needs for the basic necessities of life but may also include needs for security, social interaction, status, achievement, recognition, and growth and development.

**purpose of a compensation system**
To help create a willingness among qualified persons to join the organization and to perform the tasks needed by the organization.

## EXTRINSIC VS. INTRINSIC REWARDS

An early theory of motivation by Abraham Maslow contended that humans have a hierarchy of needs, and that each need is satisfied through different behaviours. Maslow proposed that humans have five levels of needs, with the most basic being physiological needs (such as the need for food and shelter), followed by safety and security (e.g., protection from physical and emotional harm), social needs (e.g., affection, belongingness), respect and self-esteem (e.g., status and recognition), and self-actualization (e.g., growth and self-fulfillment). This hierarchy is usually captured diagrammatically with a pyramid, with the physiological needs at the base and self-actualization at the top. The theory suggests that humans tend to first satisfy their basic needs (such as physiological and safety) before the higher-order needs such as self-actualization. Each level in the hierarchy must be fairly well satisfied before the next level motivates human behaviour; that is, once a lower-order need is satisfied, then the next level takes precedence and dominates human behaviour. Rewards are linked to this theory.

Anything provided by the organization that satisfies one or more of an employee's needs can be considered a **reward**. The types of organizational rewards can be divided into two main categories: extrinsic and intrinsic. **Extrinsic rewards** satisfy basic needs for survival and security, as well as social needs and needs for recognition. They derive from factors surrounding the job—the job *context*—such as pay, supervisory behaviour, coworkers, and general working conditions. **Intrinsic rewards** satisfy higher level needs for self-esteem, achievement, growth, and development. They derive from factors inherent in the work itself—the job *content*—such as the amount of challenge or interest the job provides, the degree of variety in the job, and the extent to which it provides feedback and allows autonomy, as well as the meaning or significance of the work.

**reward**
Anything provided by the job or the organization that satisfies an employee need.

**extrinsic rewards**
Factors that satisfy basic human needs for survival and security, as well as social needs and needs for recognition.

**intrinsic rewards**
Factors that satisfy higher-order human needs for self-esteem, achievement, growth, and development.

## REWARDS VS. INCENTIVES

Although the terms "rewards" and "incentives" are often used interchangeably, it is important to understand that they are not synonymous. Rewards are the positive consequences of performing behaviours desired by the organization, and employees normally receive these

**incentive**
A promise that a specified reward will be provided if a specified employee behaviour is performed.

**reward system**
The mix of intrinsic and extrinsic rewards that an organization provides to its members.

**compensation system**
The economic or monetary part of the reward system.

**total rewards**
A compensation philosophy that considers the entire spectrum of rewards that an organization may offer to employees.

**reward strategy**
The plan for the mix of rewards to be provided to members, along with the means through which they will be provided.

**base pay**
The foundation pay component for most employees, usually based on some unit of time worked.

**performance pay**
Relates employee monetary rewards to some measure of individual, group, or organizational performance.

**indirect pay**
Noncash items or services that satisfy a variety of specific employee needs, sometimes known as "employee benefits."

rewards either subsequent to performing the behaviour (in the case of extrinsic rewards) or during performance of the behaviour (in the case of intrinsic rewards). An **incentive** is a promise that a specified reward will be provided if the employee performs a specified behaviour. Incentives are offered to induce employees to perform behaviours that they might not otherwise perform, or to perform these behaviours at a higher level than they otherwise would. Incentives are intended to *induce* valued behaviour, while rewards serve to *recognize* valued behaviour. However, the two concepts can merge over time; this is because rewards, when used consistently to recognize a desired behaviour, are often seen as an implied promise for performing that behaviour in the future—in other words, as an incentive.

## REWARD VS. COMPENSATION STRATEGY

Both extrinsic and intrinsic rewards are important to people and, if used effectively, each can produce important benefits for the organization. As captured in **Figure 1.1**, the mix of these rewards provided by an organization is termed its **reward system**. The **compensation system** deals only with the economic or monetary part of the reward system. But because behaviour is affected by the total spectrum of rewards provided by the organization and not just by compensation, the compensation system can never be regarded in isolation from the overall reward system. This practice of looking at the total spectrum of rewards—which include career advancement opportunities, intrinsic characteristics of the job, work/life balance, employee recognition programs, and a positive workplace culture, as well as compensation—is known as the **total rewards** approach to compensation.[5] This approach is becoming increasingly common in Canada[6] and is the approach adopted in this book.

Under the total rewards approach, before a company starts developing its compensation system, it needs to establish a reward strategy. The **reward strategy** is the plan for the mix of rewards, both extrinsic and intrinsic, that the organization intends to provide to its members—along with the means through which they will be provided—in order to elicit the behaviours necessary for the organization's success. The reward strategy is the blueprint for creating the reward system.

The compensation system has three main components: (1) base pay, (2) performance pay, and (3) indirect pay. **Base pay** is the foundation pay component for most employees and is generally based on some unit of time—an hour, a week, a month, or a year. **Performance pay** relates employee monetary rewards to some measure of individual, group, or organizational performance. **Indirect pay**, sometimes known as "employee benefits," consists of

**FIGURE 1.1**

Components of the Rewards and Compensation Strategies

| Total Rewards | |
| --- | --- |
| **Compensation** | **Examples of Broader Rewards** |
| • Base Pay | • Career Advancement |
| • Performance Pay | • Recognition Programs |
| • Indirect Pay | • Positive Workplace Culture |
| | • Work/life Balance |

Rewards include work/life balance.

Show me the money.

noncash items or services that satisfy a variety of specific employee needs, such as health protection (e.g., extended medical and dental plans) or retirement security (e.g., pension plans).

There are two key aspects of a compensation strategy. One aspect is the mix of the three compensation components, and whether and how this mix will vary for different employee groups. The other is the total amount of compensation to be provided to individuals and groups. In short, "*How* should compensation be paid?" and "*How much* compensation should be paid?" are the two key questions for compensation strategy. While simple to state, these questions are extremely complex to answer.

The optimal choices for these two aspects of compensation strategy ultimately depend on the organizational context, but the most immediate determinant is the reward strategy. At one extreme, the reward strategy may include none of the three compensation components; at the other extreme, compensation may be the only appreciable reward provided by an organization.

Therefore, the first step in formulating a compensation strategy is to determine the role that compensation will play in the reward system. Assuming organizations wish to minimize compensation costs whenever possible, we must first identify what other rewards are being provided by the organization and determine whether these alone are sufficient to elicit the necessary behaviour from organization members. For example, some volunteer organizations receive thousands of hours of labour from their members for no pay; intrinsic rewards alone are sufficient to motivate the needed behaviour.

Most work organizations cannot expect to get away with providing no compensation to their members, even though some may try. See Compensation Today 1.2 for a discussion on interns. The key point is that the amount of pay needed to attract and retain the appropriate workforce varies with the other rewards that the organization can offer.

Some organizations, such as banks, have traditionally offered high job security. This has enabled them to pay less than other organizations that do not offer job security while still attracting the same calibre of employee. However, if job security is no longer a reward that banks can provide, they may need to increase pay or other rewards to attract and retain the same calibre of employee. In fact, because bank jobs are no longer as secure as they once were, and because the needs for bank employee behaviour have changed, most Canadian banks have radically changed their compensation structures in recent years.

**compensation strategy**
The plan for the mix and total amount of base pay, performance pay, and indirect pay to be paid to various categories of employees.

Some organizations provide jobs that have high intrinsic rewards that may attract employees more easily than those that do not. Similarly, firms that enjoy a high level of prestige and public esteem often find it less necessary to offer as much pay as firms that do not enjoy such prestige. Firms that offer opportunities for learning and development may be able to offer less pay than those that do not.

Firms that offer many noncompensation rewards may also choose to provide relatively high levels of compensation to attract high calibre employees and elicit high commitment and performance. The key point is that various combinations of intrinsic and extrinsic rewards need to be considered when developing the optimal reward strategy. It is only in this context that the most appropriate compensation strategy can be determined.

## COMPENSATION TODAY 1.2

### INTERNSHIPS: PAID OR UNPAID?

Unpaid internships have increasingly come under fire in Canada in recent years. There are reports that there are about 300 000 interns working in Canada—some of them in leading organizations—for free. These interns are often expected to be on time for work, perform the same responsibilities as paid employees, and do their work efficiently. Some are even paying for this opportunity because, to participate in the internship, they must pay for the post-secondary semester's tuition.

The use of unpaid interns has led to much debate in Canada and was, in fact, a contested issue in the previous national elections. It was seen a hot issue for youths and has resulted in various protests throughout the country, including an event in Quebec where 35 000 post-secondary students participated in a week-long walkout. Eliminating unpaid internships was a liberal campaign promise that has since been delayed almost four years, in preparation for the next election. While some regard unpaid internships as a good opportunity for training, "on-the-job" experience, and a form of "hope labour" that promises future employment, others view it as exploitation. Those against unpaid internships argue that the process advantages the wealthy, devalues young workers' labour efforts, violates minimum wage laws, and results in workers having low confidence in employers. Additionally, unpaid internships are typical in industries that are traditionally "feminine." As stipulated by labour and employment standards legislation across Canada, unpaid internships are legally allowed only under certain conditions. The laws vary across provinces. In Ontario, an intern is considered an employee if he or she is trained by the employer or trained in a skill that is used by employees. The only exemption to this rule is if the intern is working under a program that is approved by a college of applied arts and technology or university or is approved by a private career college.

There are, however, many organizations, some well known, where interns work for no pay, but these conditions are not met. This has led to a crackdown on employers in Canada. One investigation by the government revealed that of 123 workplaces that used interns in Ontario, one-quarter did not meet the requirements under the employment standards legislation. As a result of the investigation, many interns received pay owing to them.

The federal government has proposed laws that provide paid interns in federally regulated industries (such as banking and telecommunications) the same rights as those of paid employees. These rights include 40-hour work weeks, holidays, breaks, maternity-related reassignments, and

When should interns be paid?

protected leaves. Furthermore, the proposition states that unpaid internships will only be allowed for placements to fulfill the requirements of educational courses. An employer would have to obtain paperwork from the school explaining how the work placement ties into the educational program and the expected number of hours. Though unpaid internships are only comprised of around 2346 interns in federally regulated industries, the hope is to set a precedent that those working under the federal jurisdiction are paid for their work.

Sources: Peter Henderson, "Unpaid Internships Are a Major Concern for Canadian Youth: NDP and Liberals," *CTV News*, October 15, 2015; "Unpaid Interns to See Thousands in Pay After Ontario Blitz of Employers," *Huffington Post*, April 29, 2016; *CBC News*, "Unpaid Internships Focus of Growing Backlash," *The Canadian Press*, March 2, 2014; "New Rules Released to Govern Unpaid Interns in Federally Regulated Sectors," *Global News*, June 11, 2019; Christian Paas-Lang, "New Rules Governing Unpaid Interns in Federally-Regulated Sectors Released," *The Globe and Mail*, June 11, 2019; Nicole S. Cohen and Greig de Peuter, "Interns Talk Back: Disrupting Media Narratives about Unpaid Work," *The Political Economy of Communication* 6, no. 2 (2018): 3–24; "Gatineau Student Teachers Protest Unpaid Internships," *CBC News*, November 21, 2018; Your guide to the Employment Standards Act: Employee Status," *Government of Ontario*; Kori Allan, "Volunteering As Hope Labour: The Potential Value of Unpaid Work Experience For The Un-and Under-Employed," *Culture, Theory and Critique* 60, no. 1 (2019): 66–83; Kalina Laframboise, "Quebec Students March to Education Ministry Over Unpaid Internships," *Global News,* March 21, 2019.

For example, if a firm is experiencing high employee turnover because employees find their jobs mind-numbingly dull, one solution might be to increase pay to make employees more reluctant to quit. Another approach might be to enrich the jobs by making them more interesting, thereby increasing intrinsic rewards. Of course, it may even be possible to automate these jobs, which would eliminate the reward issue.

The best choice depends on the relative costs and benefits of each approach. It is possible that the most cost-effective approach is to do nothing—that is, if the cost of turnover is less than the cost of increasing extrinsic or intrinsic rewards or of automating the jobs. However, other factors come into play in this decision-making process. For example, job enrichment may not only reduce turnover but may also increase work quality. This may tip the scales toward job enrichment or a combination approach, rather than simply increased pay. The philosophy of the organization's leadership is also important.

# CRITERIA FOR SUCCESS: GOALS FOR THE COMPENSATION SYSTEM

What should an optimal reward and compensation system achieve? There are eight main criteria, as shown in Compensation Notebook 1.1. First and foremost, a reward system must help the organization achieve its goals. Second, it must fit with the organization's strategy for achieving its goals and support its structure for implementing that strategy. Third, it must attract and retain individuals who possess the attributes necessary to perform the required task behaviours. Fourth, it should promote the entire spectrum of desired task behaviour for every organization member. Fifth, it should be seen as equitable by all organization members. Sixth, it must comply with all relevant laws within the jurisdictions in which the firm operates. Seventh, it must achieve all this at a cost that is within the financial means of the organization. Eighth, it should achieve these objectives in the most cost-effective manner possible.

## GOALS OF THE REWARD AND COMPENSATION SYSTEM

1. Promote achievement of the organization's goals.
2. Fit with and support the organization's strategy and structure.
3. Attract and retain qualified individuals.
4. Promote desired employee behaviour.
5. Be seen as equitable.
6. Comply with the law.
7. Be within the financial means of the organization.
8. Achieve the above goals in the most cost-effective manner.

**optimal reward system**
The reward system that adds the most value to the organization, after considering all its costs.

In general, the optimal reward system will be the one that adds the most value to the organization, after considering all its costs. However, this does not necessarily mean that the optimal compensation system is the cheapest one. For example, for some firms, a high-wage compensation strategy may be the one that maximizes overall company effectiveness. Resource constraints may prevent a company from adopting an optimal reward strategy. Overall, an effective reward system maximizes the value added relative to the resources devoted to the reward system.

The objective of this book is to help readers learn how to create a reward system that will satisfy the criteria outlined in Compensation Notebook 1.1.

But wait a minute! These goals sound very nice in theory, but is it really necessary for a firm to achieve all of them? We probably know of successful organizations that violate several of these criteria. In fact, there are some successful organizations where it would be difficult to find *anyone* who believes that their reward system is equitable. Does this mean that an equitable reward system may be desirable from a social and ethical viewpoint, but not from the viewpoint of organizational performance?

Not necessarily. As we will see in Chapter 3, an inequitable reward system creates undesirable consequences for an employer, such as increased employee turnover and reduced work motivation. But the costs of these consequences vary dramatically across employers. For some firms, these costs and consequences may be tolerable, while for others they may not be. As will be discussed, a variety of factors determine how important an equitable reward system is to a given employer.

In Canada, the circumstances under which an organization can afford an inequitable reward system are disappearing and, for most organizations, an equitable reward system is a competitive advantage, if not a business necessity. Organizations vary greatly in terms of how much reward and compensation systems affect their performance, as Chapter 2 will discuss.

Is it realistic to expect a reward system to achieve all eight criteria? Probably not. But these criteria still serve as goals and measures of progress. In today's rapidly changing work environment, ongoing evaluation of the effectiveness of the reward and compensation system is crucial for most organizations.

As firms struggle to find the right answers to the compensation puzzle, the field of compensation is attracting more and more interest in the business and popular media. Firms with comprehensive and attractive reward and compensation systems may even find themselves included among "Canada's 100 Top Employers"—a significant advantage when it comes to employee recruitment.[7]

# A ROAD MAP TO EFFECTIVE COMPENSATION

What are the steps along the road to an effective compensation system? **Figure 1.2** provides a road map with links to the chapters that provide guidance for each step. Chapters 1 through 6 focus on the first two steps. These chapters provide the tools you need to develop a compensation *strategy*. Chapters 7 through 13 focus on the last three steps, which provide you with the tools and knowledge needed to transform your compensation strategy into an operating compensation *system*.

## STEP 1: UNDERSTAND YOUR ORGANIZATION AND YOUR PEOPLE

The first step in creating an effective compensation system is to understand the organizational context within which it will operate. The reward system is just one part of the total organizational system, and each part must fit with and support the other parts. There are three viable patterns into which these parts can be arranged, and each pattern constitutes one type of managerial strategy.

Each successful managerial strategy relies on a different reward and compensation strategy. The most appropriate managerial strategy is determined by several key contextual factors, such as the firm's environment, its corporate strategy, its technology, its size, and, of

**FIGURE 1.2**

A Road Map to Effective Compensation

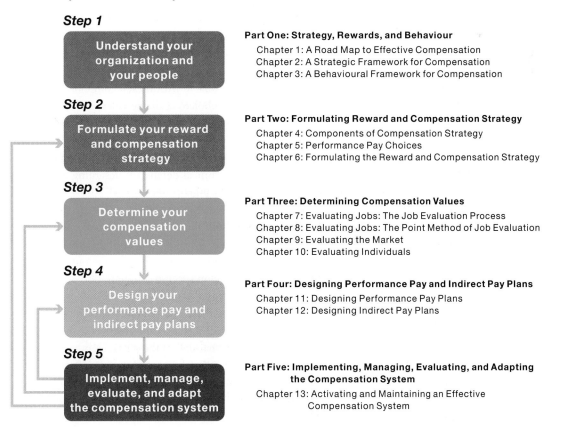

**Step 1**

Understand your organization and your people

**Part One: Strategy, Rewards, and Behaviour**
Chapter 1: A Road Map to Effective Compensation
Chapter 2: A Strategic Framework for Compensation
Chapter 3: A Behavioural Framework for Compensation

**Step 2**

Formulate your reward and compensation strategy

**Part Two: Formulating Reward and Compensation Strategy**
Chapter 4: Components of Compensation Strategy
Chapter 5: Performance Pay Choices
Chapter 6: Formulating the Reward and Compensation Strategy

**Step 3**

Determine your compensation values

**Part Three: Determining Compensation Values**
Chapter 7: Evaluating Jobs: The Job Evaluation Process
Chapter 8: Evaluating Jobs: The Point Method of Job Evaluation
Chapter 9: Evaluating the Market
Chapter 10: Evaluating Individuals

**Step 4**

Design your performance pay and indirect pay plans

**Part Four: Designing Performance Pay and Indirect Pay Plans**
Chapter 11: Designing Performance Pay Plans
Chapter 12: Designing Indirect Pay Plans

**Step 5**

Implement, manage, evaluate, and adapt the compensation system

**Part Five: Implementing, Managing, Evaluating, and Adapting the Compensation System**
Chapter 13: Activating and Maintaining an Effective Compensation System

course, its people. A key implication of these factors is that they are all related—whenever one factor changes, it can create a need for many other organizational changes, including changes to the reward and compensation system. Chapter 2 ("A Strategic Framework for Compensation") provides a conceptual toolkit for understanding the organizational context and identifying the compensation system that best fits that context.

Another essential concept is the link between reward systems and human behaviour. Three main behaviours are desirable to an organization—*membership behaviour*, *task behaviour*, and *citizenship behaviour*—but the importance of each can vary dramatically for different organizations. It is crucial to understand what specific attitudes and behaviours are needed by your organization and the role the reward system can play in eliciting these behaviours.

Besides understanding how reward systems can promote desired behaviours, it is also important to understand how reward systems can unintentionally generate *undesirable* attitudes and behaviours. As Chapter 3 explains, this is a surprisingly common phenomenon. Chapter 3 ("A Behavioural Framework for Compensation") provides a conceptual toolkit for understanding the process through which compensation affects employee behaviour.

## STEP 2: FORMULATE YOUR REWARD AND COMPENSATION STRATEGY

The next step in creating an effective compensation system is to formulate your reward and compensation strategy—to determine the mix of compensation components to include in your system and the total level of compensation to provide, relative to other employers. To determine the compensation mix, you must understand what compensation options are available, their advantages and disadvantages, and the consequences each produces.

There are three main compensation components—base pay, performance pay, and indirect pay. Chapter 4 ("Components of Compensation Strategy") examines these components, along with the key elements and choices available within each component. Chapter 5 ("Performance Pay Choices") examines the key choices available when performance pay is being incorporated into compensation strategy. Chapters 4 and 5 describe the available choices in sufficient detail to allow you to decide the mix of components and elements to include in a reward strategy that best fits your organization. To allow you to focus on the strategic aspects of these choices, most of the technical details for designing and implementing these components are deferred to later chapters in the book.

Based on the concepts provided in the first five chapters, you can identify the kinds of behaviour your organization needs and then choose the most appropriate combination of rewards (the reward strategy) to elicit this behaviour. A major purpose of the reward strategy is to define the role that compensation is expected to play in bringing about the desired behaviour. From this reward strategy, you will develop specific compensation objectives.

You can then formulate a compensation strategy that defines the mix of compensation components (along with the specific elements of these components) and the compensation level strategy that best fits your organization. But to do this effectively, you must first understand the constraints on your organization that define the parameters within which choices can be made. These include legal constraints, labour market constraints, product/service market constraints, and constraints on the financial resources available to the organization. Chapter 6 ("Formulating the Reward and Compensation Strategy") guides you through this process.

## STEP 3: DETERMINE YOUR COMPENSATION VALUES

By this point, you will have developed a compensation *strategy*, but you don't yet have a compensation *system*. Once you have formulated the compensation strategy, you must next establish the processes for determining actual dollar values for jobs and for individual employees. The dollar value of compensation to be provided to a specific employee is typically determined by a combination of three factors.

1. The value of the employee's assigned job relative to other jobs in the firm, usually determined by a process called *job evaluation*.

2. The value of the employee's job relative to what other firms are paying for this job, usually determined through a process known as *labour market surveys*.

3. The value of the employee's job performance relative to other employees performing the same job, usually determined by a process called *performance appraisal*.

The first and third factors deal with achieving *internal pay equity* (equity of pay among employees within the firm), while the second factor deals with achieving *external pay equity* (equity with what comparable employees are being paid in other firms). Note that equity is not the same as equality; giving equal pay to employees who make a lesser contribution to the firm than other employees is in fact very inequitable. When developing a pay system, pay equity (fairness) is our goal, not pay equality.

In Step 2, you decided which of these three processes would play a role in your compensation strategy. For compensation strategies in which job evaluation plays a role, Chapter 7 ("Evaluating Jobs: The Job Evaluation Process") and Chapter 8 ("Evaluating Jobs: The Point Method of Job Evaluation") provide a description of the key steps and procedures in the job evaluation process. For compensation strategies in which compensation is calibrated to the "going market rates," Chapter 9 ("Evaluating the Market") describes how to gather and apply labour market data to determine these rates. Finally, for those compensation strategies that include performance appraisals as a basis for determining pay, Chapter 10 ("Evaluating Individuals") describes how to design these systems.

## STEP 4: DESIGN YOUR PERFORMANCE PAY AND INDIRECT PAY PLANS

Your compensation strategy probably contains some performance pay and some indirect pay. What you need to do now is actually design your performance pay and indirect pay plans. Chapter 11 ("Designing Performance Pay Plans") focuses on design issues for the specific performance pay plans you have chosen, and Chapter 12 ("Designing Indirect Pay Plans") focuses on the key issues for designing indirect pay plans that will serve company needs.

## STEP 5: IMPLEMENT, MANAGE, EVALUATE, AND ADAPT THE COMPENSATION SYSTEM

The final step involves implementing and managing your compensation system on an ongoing basis. The key issues include procedures for implementing the system, communicating information about the system, dealing with compensation problems, budgeting, and controlling compensation costs.

After the compensation system is implemented, it must be continually evaluated to determine whether it is accomplishing the company's objectives in the most cost-effective manner. If it is not, then some of the technical aspects of the compensation system may need to be changed, or the compensation and rewards strategy may need to be reworked, as the feedback loops in Figure 1.2 illustrate.

Furthermore, if the circumstances change, or if the technology, strategy, or structure of the organization changes, these may trigger a need for changes to the compensation strategy or system. The organization must have a way of detecting unintended negative consequences generated by the compensation system. The final chapter, Chapter 13 ("Activating and Maintaining an Effective Compensation System"), provides guidance on how to deal with these issues.

## MANAGING COMPENSATION IN ORGANIZATIONS

Except for voluntary organizations, all organizations—whether large or small—must deal with compensation issues.

In small organizations, the responsibility for compensation strategy usually resides with the owner or chief executive officer, and compensation administration is often contracted out to firms that specialize in payroll management.

In larger organizations, the compensation function normally resides within the Human Resources Department, with the head of that department bearing ultimate responsibility for the successful operation of the compensation system. Typically, compensation strategy is formulated by the head of HR, based on the recommendations of the manager of compensation, but because it is such a crucial issue for most organizations, the approval of top management (and often the board of directors) is always required for major changes to compensation strategy.

Within a large firm, there are many specialized roles for compensation specialists. For example, *job analysts* develop job descriptions and conduct job evaluations, *benefits specialists* oversee benefits plans, *compensation analysts* evaluate market data, and *compensation managers* oversee the administration of the compensation system and recommend, design, and implement compensation policies. Compensation Today 1.3 gives three examples of HR jobs that require extensive knowledge of compensation, along with their pay levels.

Responsibility for specialized aspects of compensation (e.g., evaluating the market or managing benefits plans) is often contracted to compensation consulting firms. Compensation consulting firms have grown in number due to the increasing complexity of compensation systems and have become an important source of employment for compensation professionals.

In recognition of its importance in the Human Resources field, compensation has been designated as one of the main categories of professional capabilities required for the certification as a human resource professional in Canada. In nine provinces and three territories across Canada (not including Ontario), successful candidates are approved for the Chartered Professional in Human Resources (CPHR) designation. In Ontario, they are awarded the Certified Human Resources Professional (CHRP) designation. In general, to receive this designation, a candidate must demonstrate expertise in several capabilities through a testing process conducted by the Human Resources Professionals Association of Ontario and/or the Canadian Council of Human Resources Associations.

As a part of the process needed to earn a professional HR designation, granted by the HR provincial associations, applicants generally undergo two assessments: one is a knowledge-based exam, and the second assessment is based on experience. Those interested in obtaining an HR designation should consult the HR association in their province on the specific requirements.

# SUMMARY

Chapter 1 sets the stage for the study of compensation and the rest of the text by explaining the importance of effective compensation systems to firm success, by defining key reward and compensation concepts, and by providing you with a map to guide you along the road to the development of an effective compensation system. This "road map" is used as the organizing framework for everything that is to come, and links specific text chapters to each step along the road to effective compensation. An understanding of the key concepts underpinning compensation design, and an understanding of the process for design of effective compensation systems, will make it much easier for you to put the following chapters in context, and will facilitate your comprehension and understanding.

# KEY TERMS

base pay

compensation strategy

compensation system

extrinsic rewards

incentive

indirect pay

intrinsic rewards

optimal reward system

performance pay

purpose of a compensation system

reward

reward strategy

reward system

total rewards

# DISCUSSION QUESTIONS

1. Discuss why an effective compensation system is so important to most organizations.
2. Discuss why a compensation system must be viewed in the context of the total reward system.
3. Should "hero" pay for essential workers during the COVID-19 pandemic be considered a reward or an incentive? Why?
4. Discuss the five steps in designing an effective compensation system.

# EXERCISES

1. Using the *Job Bank* (https://www.jobbank.gc.ca/trend-analysis/search-wages), what conclusions can you draw about variations in pay level in different parts of Canada? Pick two or three different jobs to make your comparisons across the country.
2. Again using the *Job Bank*, check how much the pay ranges for the jobs in Compensation Today 1.3 have changed since 2019, the year in which this book's salary data were collected.
3. In a small group, describe to one another the compensation system at your most recent job, in terms of base pay, performance pay, and indirect pay. Then discuss your reactions to this system. Do you believe it was equitable? What impact did it have on your motivation and commitment to the organization? How could it have been improved? Of the compensation systems described by your group members, which appeared to be the most effective, and why?
4. In a small group, discuss your experiences (or the experiences of someone you know) with an internship. Was it for free? Do you believe that the unpaid internship met the legal criteria for identified in Compensation Today 1.2? What are your thoughts on unpaid internships?

## CASE QUESTION

1. Read *Case 1—Henderson Printing* in the Appendix. Assess the compensation system in place at the company. Do you think it meets the criteria for an effective compensation system as set out in Compensation Notebook 1.1? Which criteria does it meet, and which criteria does it violate?

## SIMULATION CROSS-REFERENCE

If you are using *Strategic Compensation: A Simulation* in conjunction with this text, you will find that the concepts in Chapter 1 are helpful in preparing the simulation.

# ENDNOTES

1. Matt Levine, "Fake Accounts Still Haunt Wells Fargo," *Bloomberg.com*, www.bloomberg.com/opinion/articles/2018-10-23/fake-accounts-still-haunt-wells-fargo; Bill Chappell, "Wells Fargo Fined $185 Million Over Creation of Fake Accounts For Bonuses," *NPR*, September 8, 2016, www.npr.org/sections/thetwo-way/2016/09/08/493130449/wells-fargo-to-pay-around-190-million-over-fake-accounts-that-sparked-bonuses; Josh Shapiro, "Attorney General Shapiro Announces $575 Million 50-State Settlement with Wells Fargo Bank for Opening Unauthorized Accounts and Charging Consumers for Unnecessary Auto Insurance, Mortgage Fees," *Pennsylvania Office of Attorney General*, December 2018.

2. Edward Jones-Compensation. *Edward Jones Careers Site*, careers.edwardjones.ca/explore-opportunities/new-financial-advisors/compensation/compensation.html.

3. Chief Executive Officer, *TTC Corporate Plan 2018-2022*. TTC Board. (January 25, 2018). Retrieved August 7, 2019, from https://www.ttc.ca/Coupler/PDFs/1_Corporate_Plan_2018-2022.pdf.

4. *Statistics Canada*, "Individuals by Total Income Level, by Province and Territory (Canada)." Retrieved August 10, 2019, from www.statcan.gc.ca/tables-tableaux/sum-som/l01/cst01/famil105a-eng.htm.

5. Edward E. Lawler, "Creating a New Employment Deal," *Organizational Dynamics* 40, no. 4 (2011): 302–309; See also World at Work, *The World at Work Handbook of Compensation, Benefits, and Total Rewards: A Comprehensive Guide for HR Professionals* (Hoboken: Wiley, 2007); Shabnum Durrani and Parbudyal Singh, "Women, Private Practice and Billable Hours," *Compensation & Benefits Review* 43, no. 5, (2011): 300–05; Duncan Brown, "The Future of Reward Management," *Compensation & Benefits Review* 46, no. 3, (2014): 147–51; Alessandro M. Peluso, Laura Innocenti, Massimo Pilati, "Pay Is Not Everything," *Evidence-Based HRM: A Global Forum for Empirical Scholarship* 5, no. 3 (2017): 311–327.

6. Todd Humber, "Total Rewards: One Concept, Many Monikers," *Canadian HR Reporter*, February 14, 2005, R3. See also Gail Evans, "Figuring out Total Rewards in a Rocky Economy," *Canadian HR Reporter*, August 10, 2015. Retrieved from www.hrreporter.com/news/hr-news/figuring-out-total-rewards-in-a-rocky-economy/281138; Marcel Vander Wier, "Pay Raises Expected to Stay Steady for 2019," *Canadian HR Reporter*, Canadian HR Reporter, November 1, 2018. Retrieved from www.hrreporter.com/focus-areas/compensation-and-benefits/pay-raises-expected-to-stay-steady-for-2019/283459.

7. See "Canada's Top 100 Employers" at www.CanadasTop100.com.

8. For the Salary Wizard, see https://swz.salary.com/CanadaSalary-wizard/layoutscripts/cswzl_newsearch.aspx.

# A STRATEGIC FRAMEWORK FOR COMPENSATION

- Understand the concept of "fit" and explain why a compensation system that is a success in one firm can be a failure in another.

- Explain how the strategic framework for compensation can be used as a tool for designing effective reward and compensation systems.

- Describe the main elements in the strategic compensation framework and explain how they relate to one another.

- Describe the three main managerial strategies that organizations can adopt and explain their implications for compensation systems.

- Describe the key determinants of managerial strategy and explain how they can be used to select the most appropriate managerial strategy.

- Analyze an organization to determine the most appropriate managerial strategy for that organization to adopt.

- Discuss how conditions in North America changed during the 20th century and explain how this has affected today's managerial and compensation strategies.

ArcelorMittal Dofasco is a leading Canadian manufacturing company located in Hamilton, Ontario. It started its operations in the early 1900s. The company produces and ships 4.5 million net tons of steel every year for the automotive, energy, construction, and packaging industries. Their products include steel car parts (such as armrests, handles, and brakes), steel appliances (such as refrigerators, freezers, and dryers), construction pieces (such as residential roofing and garage doors), consumer packaging (such as steel cans), and hundreds of other products. The company's motto is, "Our product is steel. Our strength is people." According to the firm, the secret to their success is their people and this is the reason why they created the first profit-sharing program in Canada. Today, Dofasco offers employees competitive compensation with the market. In addition to competitive salaries, the company also provides a variable compensation plan and a profit-sharing program. Both are created to allow employees higher incomes with the company's increasing profitability. Variable compensation is approximately 10 percent of the employees' salary. Profit sharing is 14 percent of Dofasco's pre-tax net profit. Dofasco also offers a great pension plan and group supplemental benefits.

Many people at Dofasco have been employed most of their working lives there; around 50 percent of the organization has recently retired. Over the past few years, the company hired 2000 of the 5000 employees currently working at Dofasco as part of an ongoing hiring campaign. Finding qualified people to fill positions has been an industry challenge; therefore, the compensation system must assist in attracting the right people.

By contrast, Koch Foods operates a plant in Morton, Mississippi, that converts live chickens into packages of chicken parts. All work is centred around the "chain" on which the live chickens are hung, which rattles past line workers at a rate of 90 birds per minute. Workers posted along the chain perform various operations on the chickens as they pass by, such as snipping their heads off or reaching in and yanking out their innards. Unlike Dofasco, and although the company's annual sales figure is around $3 billion, Koch Foods hasn't implemented any pay innovations. Koch Foods simply pays workers an hourly wage not much above the legal minimum. Employee benefits are minimal. The firm has no fixed pension plan, other than a savings plan to which the company contributes, but only when the firm is profitable.

The company's compensation system has been the cause of several lawsuits. A female plant worker sued the company for pay discrimination when she was paid less than her male counterpart in the same position. Another lawsuit entailed two workers alleging that employees must work more than 40 hours a week to meet their quota for chickens but were never reimbursed for overtime nor for travel time between farms. Are you surprised to learn that employee turnover often exceeds 100 percent a year in plants like these?

Sources: Elliot C. McLaughlin, "Targeted in Mississippi Immigration Raids, Poultry Company Holds Job Fair Just Down the Road," *CNN*, August 12, 2019; Robert Channick, "Mississippi ICE Raids Hit Koch Foods, A Large Suburban Poultry Processor That Mostly Flies Under the Radar," *Chicago Tribune*, August 8, 2019; Press Release, "EEOC Sues Koch Foods of Mississippi for Pay Discrimination," *Equal Employment Opportunity Commission*, September 30, 2016; "Chicken Catchers Sue Koch Foods," *Meat + Poultry*, June 24, 2016; "Benefits and Pay at Arcelormittal Dofasco," *Arcelor Mittal*; Mark McNeil, "ArcelorMittal Dofasco Hosting Job Fair to Hire Hundreds," *The Hamilton Spectator*, October 25, 2018.

# INTRODUCTION TO EFFECTIVE COMPENSATION SYSTEMS

Let us start this chapter with a little contest. The reward for winning? Strictly intrinsic. As you noticed, the two firms discussed above have completely different compensation systems. Here's your skill-testing question: Which compensation system is more effective? Note that this question does not ask you to pick the system that you like the most, but the one that best fits our definition of an effective compensation system. As we discussed in Chapter 1, the most effective compensation system for a given firm is the one that adds the most value to the organization, after considering all its costs.

So back to the question. Which of these compensation systems do you think is the most effective? Dofasco sounds like an excellent place to work. But how can the company stay competitive when it pays its workers so well? And while Koch Foods certainly can't be accused of overpaying its workers, wouldn't their turnover rate cause serious problems?

Aha, you think. Maybe this is a trick question and neither system is effective! In fact, despite being so different, *both* compensation systems are effective. How can this be? The answer is that they each *fit* the organization and its strategy. If these firms were to trade compensation systems, they would both soon be as dead as the Koch chickens.

How can a compensation system that is a great success in one organization be a miserable flop in another? And how do you know in advance whether a particular type of compensation system will succeed for your organization? These are puzzles that must be solved if you want to successfully design or redesign a compensation system.

## A STRATEGIC FRAMEWORK FOR COMPENSATION

*Pay is a "red phone." When it rings, employees want to find out who is on the other end and what is being said. The goal is to wire the red phone to company strategy.*[1]

Sounds good. So how exactly do you do that? Properly wiring the "red phone" is more complex than it sounds. Fortunately, this chapter develops a tool to do just that. Be prepared, though—initially, this tool will seem to only make things more complicated! But once you invest the effort necessary to understand it, you should find it an indispensable part of your conceptual toolkit for building effective compensation systems.

### STRATEGY AND THE CONCEPT OF FIT

An organization's vision, mission, and/or values provide the basis for its strategies. The **vision** of an organization refers to the long-term, optimal desired state; it's like "what you want to be when you grow up" or your aspirational goal. Its **mission** is more immediate; that is, the present state or purpose of the organization, or "who you are today." It gives the reason for the organization's existence. Organizational **values** refer to its underlying guiding principles, beliefs, and attitudes that guide behaviour; for instance, "teamwork" and "integrity" can be organizational values.

Fit is an important concept in strategic management.[2] It refers to the alignment of strategies at various levels in an organization. There are two related concepts: vertical and horizontal fit, or vertical and horizontal integration.[3] **Vertical fit** refers to the alignment between an organization's mission, vision, and/or values, and the various supportive strategies that cascade down an organization. A tight fit means that human resource management (HRM) strategies, for instance, are closely aligned with the strategic thrust of the organization; that is, the HRM strategies support the organizational strategy. For instance, 3M and Apple are widely known for their innovative organizational strategies. Compensation strategies that support innovation imply that there is some level of vertical fit. **Horizontal fit** refers to the alignment between and among strategies at the same level; for instance, HRM strategies such as performance management and compensation are aligned or support each other.

The organization's strategy helps it to achieve its mission, vision, values, and goals. The **business strategy** (sometimes known as the "competitive strategy" or "corporate strategy")

**vision**
An organization's desired future state.

**mission**
An organization's reason for existence.

**values**
Principles, beliefs, and attitudes that drive behaviour.

**vertical fit**
Alignment of strategies at different levels.

**horizontal fit**
Alignment of strategies at the same level.

**business strategy**
An organization's plan for how it will achieve its goals.

is the organization's plan for how it will achieve its goals. The **organization structure** is the vehicle for executing this strategy and has several structural dimensions or variables. The purpose of the organization structure is to generate the behaviours necessary to carry out the organization's strategy.

For the organizational system to be effective, the business strategy and organization structure must also fit with other key variables, including the type of environment in which the organization operates, the type of technology it uses, the size of the organization, and the characteristics of the people employed. This is known as the **contingency approach to organizational design**,[4] and it is the foundation for the strategic framework presented in this chapter.

Ultimately, the success or failure of any reward system depends on how well it fits the organization's context and its system as a whole. Therefore, to successfully design, manage, and modify any reward system, you must understand this context and how it links to the reward system.

But what are the key aspects of the organizational context, and exactly how do they relate to reward strategy? This chapter addresses that question by developing a framework that identifies the key aspects of the organizational context and then illustrates how each affects the reward system. This framework describes three managerial strategies that an organization can adopt and shows how each relates to an organization's structure and its best-fit reward system. The framework then identifies the determinants of managerial strategy, as these will ultimately determine the most appropriate reward strategy. The chapter ends with a discussion of trends in managerial strategies and compensation systems.

**Figure 2.1** shows the two main sets of variables—contextual and structural—and the link with managerial strategy. As the diagram shows, the reward system is only one of the variables that make up the organization's structure. To be effective, the reward system must fit with the other structural variables, as well as with the managerial strategy, which must in turn fit with the contextual variables. But what do all the double-sided arrows mean? Simply that all the structural variables are interrelated and must fit with one another if the organization is to be effective. The same is true for the contextual variables.

**organization structure**
The means through which an organization generates the behaviours necessary to execute its business strategy.

**contingency approach to organizational design**
An approach to organization design based on the premise that the best type of structure for an organization depends on the key contingencies (contextual variables) associated with that organization.

---

**FIGURE 2.1**

A Strategic Framework for Compensation

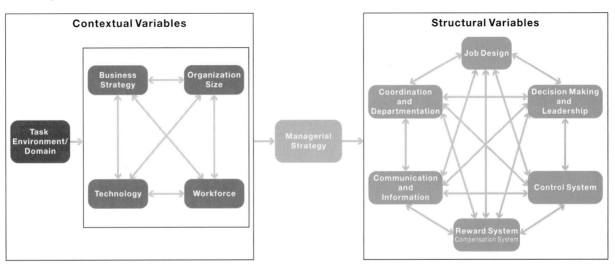

## STRUCTURAL VARIABLES

**job design**
A dimension of organization structure that describes the manner in which the total task of an organization is divided into separate jobs.

**coordination and departmentation**
A dimension of organization structure that describes the methods used to coordinate the work of individual employees and subunits in an organization.

**decision-making and leadership structure**
A dimension of organization structure that describes the nature of the decision-making and leadership processes used in an organization.

**communication and information structure**
A dimension of organization structure that describes the nature of and methods for communication in an organization.

**control structure**
A dimension of organization structure that describes the nature of the processes used to control employee behaviour in an organization.

**managerial strategy**
One of three main patterns or combinations of structural variables that can be adopted by an organization—namely, classical, human relations, or high involvement.

**contextual variables**
Factors in the firm's context that indicate the most appropriate managerial strategy and organizational structure.

The first step in understanding how to use this framework is to understand each of these components.

## STRUCTURAL VARIABLES

To generate the behaviours necessary to execute a corporate strategy, an organization structure needs to do two main things: it first needs to *divide* the total task into manageable subtasks (a process sometimes known as "differentiation"), and then it needs to *coordinate* the completion of these subtasks so that they fit together to accomplish the organization's total task (a process sometimes known as "integration").

An effective organization structure reduces internal and external uncertainty for the organization. It reduces internal uncertainty by structuring and directing employee behaviour; it reduces external uncertainty by creating specialized units to interpret and deal with key aspects of the firm's environment and bring appropriate information to organizational decision makers. For example, a firm may create a marketing department to learn about and deal with its customers, a purchasing department to learn about and deal with its suppliers, and an economic forecasting unit to help understand economic trends and how they affect the organization.

The organization structure has several separate variables or dimensions. These variables are the *levers* that are used to produce the behaviour the organization desires. Besides the reward system, there are five other structural variables. Job design describes the manner in which the total amount of work to be done is divided into subtasks that can be handled by individual workers. Coordination and departmentation mechanisms are the methods used to ensure that the work of individual employees fits together such that the overall task is accomplished.

The decision-making and leadership structure comprises the mechanisms through which the organization's decisions are made and the type of leadership role played by those in managerial positions. The communication and information structure describes the methods used to communicate information throughout the organization and the amount and kinds of information to be transmitted. The control structure is the means used to ensure that organization members are actually doing what they are supposed to do.

## MANAGERIAL STRATEGY

The structural variables described above can be arranged in a virtually limitless number of ways. However, over time, three main patterns of structural variables, known as "managerial strategies," have emerged: (1) the classical managerial strategy, (2) the human relations managerial strategy, and (3) the high-involvement managerial strategy.[5] Each of these managerial strategies represents a particular combination of structural variables that has proved to be successful in the right circumstances. The particular managerial strategy used by a given firm is the most important single determinant of what will or will not be a successful reward system for that firm. The specific linkages between managerial strategies and the structural variables, including reward systems, are discussed in more detail later in the chapter.

## CONTEXTUAL VARIABLES

So what determines the most appropriate managerial strategy for an organization to adopt? The five main contextual variables are shown in Figure 2.1: the organization's environment, business strategy, technology, size, and workforce. Each of these is discussed in more detail later in the chapter, along with its relationship to managerial strategy.

But if contextual variables differ between organizations, how are the contextual variables themselves determined? It all starts with organizational goals. When founders create an organization, they have certain goals for their organization. In a business enterprise, the goals may include making money and/or providing employment for the owner. In a governmental organization, the goal may be to satisfy some collective need, such as the need for fire or police protection, or for education. In a not-for-profit enterprise, the goal may be to address some important need not currently being met. For example, the Canadian Cancer Society was created to serve the needs of those who have cancer and to find a way to cure or prevent cancer. UNICEF was created to help serve the needs of children in poverty-stricken areas.

From the interaction between the goals of the founders and the general environment in which the firm will be situated, the organization's *domain* emerges. The **domain** defines the specific products or services to be offered by the organization. The domain also defines the **task environment**, which is the specific slice of the general environment of particular relevance to the organization. Key elements of the task environment include the customers or clients of the organization, as well as competitors, suppliers, and regulatory agencies.

Once a firm has established its goals and defined its domain, it needs to formulate a plan for achieving its goals (its *business strategy*). Decisions can then be made about the most appropriate type of technology to produce the product or service, the most appropriate size for the organization, and the nature of the workforce needed. These decisions need to be seen as interrelated because changes in one variable affect each of the others. For example, a change in the firm's technology may necessitate changes to its business strategy and its workforce, as well as to the size of the firm.

The key point about contextual variables is that a change in any of them may trigger a need for a change in the reward system. Thus, a company that changes its business strategy, implements a new technology, grows in size, or experiences a change in its workforce may need a new reward strategy. A company attempting to introduce work teams or flexible production almost always needs to change its reward system. A firm striving to change its managerial strategy usually needs to change its reward system. As discussed earlier, failure to make the right changes to the reward system in the light of these other changes may have dire consequences. Because organizations are systems, change in one aspect of the organization almost inevitably has implications for other parts of the organization.

**domain**
Describes the specific products or services offered by a given organization.

**task environment**
The portion of the general environment that has direct relevance to a given organization.

## MANAGERIAL STRATEGIES AND REWARD SYSTEMS

Each of the three main managerial strategies has different implications for how the reward and compensation systems should be designed. Each of these strategies also reflects different assumptions about employees and how they should be managed. To understand how each managerial strategy links to rewards and compensation, you first need to understand the assumptions on which each is based.

Adherents of the **classical managerial strategy** believe that people are inherently lazy, dislike work, and would prefer to get as much as they possibly can from a work relationship while giving as little as possible. According to this perspective, the only way to get people to work is to create circumstances under which satisfaction of their economic needs becomes threatened if they do not behave as the organization wants them to. Essentially, this school of thought views employees as potentially dishonest shirkers who need to be tightly controlled if the organization is going to be sure of getting any work out of them.

**classical managerial strategy**
An approach to management that assumes most employees inherently dislike work but can be induced to work in order to satisfy their economic needs.

Adherents of the **human relations managerial strategy** agree with the classical managers that people inherently dislike work, but they differ in that they believe people can be motivated by appealing to their social needs. They have observed that the classical school of thought often creates an adversarial and unpleasant relationship between management and workers and that peer groups of workers often form within the firm in order to satisfy human needs that are unmet or threatened by the formal organization.

These peer groups often have more influence than management over the workers and often work against management. But by treating employees with fairness and consideration and supporting and encouraging peer groups (rather than trying to break them up, which would be the classical approach), human relations managers believe that positive employee norms can develop. Employees work loyally and comply with these norms out of gratitude for the satisfying social environment the firm provides. The human relations view of employees tends toward paternalism—the organization is like a family, in which employees are like children who need to be treated kindly but firmly by a benevolent employer who knows what is best for them and the organization.

The **high-involvement managerial strategy**[6] differs from the previous two schools in its belief that if jobs are structured correctly, people can actually enjoy and be motivated intrinsically by their work. Adherents believe that people are motivated by needs for interesting work, challenge, autonomy, personal growth, and professional development, and that employees can exercise self-control if the organization provides these conditions while treating employees fairly and equitably. (You should be aware that the high-involvement managerial strategy has several labels. The "mutual gains enterprise,"[7] the "high-performance work system,"[8] "open book management,"[9] and "high commitment management"[10] are all very similar to the high-involvement managerial strategy described here.)

Given the disparate assumptions that each of the three managerial strategies holds about employees, it is not surprising that organizations will be structured very differently, depending on their managerial strategy. Compensation Notebook 2.1 summarizes how each of the three managerial strategies compares in terms of the six main dimensions of organization structure.

## CLASSICAL MANAGERIAL STRATEGY

Under the classical managerial strategy, thinking is completely separated from doing. Jobs are designed with only a few basic elements so that they can be supervised closely and so that employees can be replaced easily if they quit or are dismissed. The specific duties and work methods for each job are planned and defined in detail by management because employees cannot be trusted to perform effectively without doing so. Jobs are arranged in strict, hierarchical, pyramidal fashion because of the overriding need for accountability. Coordination is always handled vertically by a common superior. Employees are organized by function; for example, all engineers are put into one department, all marketers into another department, and all production staff into another department.

Monty Rakusen/Getty Images

Narrow jobs still exist on many production assembly lines.

## COMPARISON OF THE THREE MANAGERIAL STRATEGIES AND THEIR STRUCTURAL IMPLICATIONS

| Structural Variable | Classical Managerial Strategy | Human Relations Managerial Strategy | High-Involvement Managerial Strategy |
|---|---|---|---|
| **Job Design** | Thinking separate from doing; narrow, fragmented jobs | Similar to classical, but job design may allow more social contact | Joint planning and goal setting; broader, more meaningful jobs |
| **Coordination and Departmentation** | Strict, formalized pyramidal hierarchy emphasizing accountability; vertical coordination (by superiors); departmentation by function | Similar to classical; possibly use of some work teams | Horizontal coordination (by employees) in addition to vertical coordination; use of work teams; departmentation by product, customer, project, or matrix |
| **Control** | External—through supervision, rules, punishments, and some extrinsic rewards | External—through use of social or peer pressure, rules, some extrinsic rewards | Internal—through intrinsic rewards from the work itself, self-control through internalized commitment |
| **Communication** | Formal and vertical; restricted | Use of formal and informal (grapevine) communication; some restriction | High amount of vertical and horizontal communication; less formal; climate of open communication |
| **Decision Making and Leadership** | Autocratic decision making; task-oriented; controlling supervisory role | Autocratic decision making with minor consultation; employee-oriented; controlling supervisory role | Participative or democratic decision style; both task- and employee-oriented; facilitator supervisory role |
| **Reward systems** | Extrinsic economic rewards related to individual output (e.g., piece rates, commissions) or to time worked (e.g., hourly pay) | Extrinsic economic rewards, unrelated to performance; liberal fringe benefits (indirect pay) and loyalty rewards; social rewards | Intrinsic rewards from job itself; pay for knowledge; extrinsic rewards focusing on group/organization performance (e.g., gain sharing, profit sharing, stock ownership) |

The major role of the supervisor is to control and evaluate subordinates who, according to this theory's assumptions, will try to shirk and goof off if given the opportunity. Decisions are made at a relatively high level in the organization, and the main leadership role is autocratic, with a high emphasis on tasks. Essentially, senior management makes the decisions, middle management transmits them, and first-line management (supervisors) enforces them.

Control is exercised through close supervision and the threat of punitive action should the employee deviate from organizational policies. There is often a large body of formal rules and procedures that are strictly enforced. Control is also frequently embedded in the technology or the work process itself, as in the case of assembly lines, which do not allow deviation from the standard procedures.

Communication is quite low, with an emphasis on a downward vertical flow, and tends to be formal. Informal communication (i.e., the "grapevine") is discouraged, although, ironically, the grapevine usually flourishes as employees attempt to fill in the information gaps. Generally, management disseminates as little information as possible, in the belief that information is power. Communication upward from employees is not generally sought, and when sought is likely minimal and distorted, due to the adversarial relations.

Because management's key task is to minimize variations in employee behaviour from the specified behaviour, the reward system is quite simple—an extrinsic (economic) reward. Wherever feasible, a system that ties pay directly to output—such as piece rates or sales commissions—is used. Where this is not feasible, pay is tied directly to hours of work. In both cases, pay is no higher than absolutely necessary to attract a sufficient flow of job applicants. Little indirect pay is used, because it is not tied to individual performance, and management does not see much value in incurring large benefits costs in order to promote loyalty and reduce turnover. This is because classical organizations are structured to minimize the cost of turnover: with narrow job categorizations, workers are easy to replace, train, and supervise. Compensation Today 2.1 illustrates how one firm, Foxconn, uses a classical strategy.

One exception to the general rule about poor compensation in classical organizations arises in unionized classical firms. Because of the low consideration for workers' needs in most classical firms and their adversarial worker–management relations, workers in these organizations often form unions in an attempt to protect their interests. These unions often win substantially higher compensation packages than management would wish to provide—packages that include extensive benefits. As a result, non-union classical firms often provide more compensation than they would wish, in order to attract employees and as a union avoidance tactic. Ironically, these classical firms may end up paying very well indeed, which is precisely the opposite of their compensation goal.

### CLASSICAL ORGANIZATIONS IN THE 21ST CENTURY

If you use an iPhone, or one of many other brand name smart phones, it is very likely to have been made in China by Foxconn. Foxconn is the largest contract manufacturer of electronics, the largest assembler of Apple products, and employs around 1.2 million people around the world with manufacturing facilities in 24 countries. The company employs 350 000 people in China and has created a mini city that residents refer to as "IPhone City." Foxconn is considered the most valuable technology company in China.

For most of the manufacturing workers at Foxconn, a typical work day looks like this: you enter a multi-storey concrete building in the morning, put on the uniform (a plastic jacket, hat, and booties); for the next 10–12 hours, you may be sitting or standing on a production line with many others for most of your shift; your tasks may be to grab components from a bin and slot them into circuit boards as they move down a conveyer, or to feed a machine with tapes that hold tiny microprocessors like candy on paper spools, or to check a component under a magnifying glass, or to place completed cell phone circuit boards into lead-lined boxes to test each piece for electromagnetic interference. You raise your hand when you need to go to the washroom and wait for someone to take your spot. You get an hour for lunch and two 10-minute breaks. So far it is probably the same or similar to factory work anywhere in the world, a 21st-century version of Charlie Chaplin's *Modern Times* with some variation. After work, you walk or take a shuttle back to your company-provided dormitory, where you share a room with up to seven other employees. While this may seem less than ideal to Westerners, it is much better than many workers in other factories experience; they have to find shelter in dodgy slums or sleep on the assembly line. After you eat in the company cafeteria, you can watch television in a common room, play videogames, or check email in one of the on-campus cyber-cafés. If you are dating, there are a few "couples' booths" that you can use. The next morning, you clean yourself up in the communal sinks or showers, then head to the production line to do it all over again. The hourly pay is around US$2.26 per hour but provides you an opportunity to save and send home money to help your family, often in the rural areas. Fifty-hour workweeks or 10–12-hour shifts are typical, but up to 100-hour workweeks during peak production can be possible. You like some overtime work because it gives you the opportunity to make some extra money to send home. Optimizing work design to minimize task variation and leveraging low labour cost provided by geographical differentials (many workers are from rural areas) is how Foxconn can deliver flexibility and scale at rock-bottom prices.

While this industrialization process may have benefited many Chinese workers, it was not without problems. Seventeen worker suicides were reported by 2011. The situation became so severe that the company had to place nettings on the building to catch employees when they jumped off the roof. As Foxconn expanded into the interior of China, strikes and riots were reported. With the increasing public attention and audits by customers like Apple, Foxconn claimed that they would make improvements, including increases in wages to keep up, in part, with minimum wages in China, and committed to limiting overtime work to keep within the Chinese legal maximum of 49 hours a week, total hours worked.

A 2017–18 investigation revealed that Foxconn had continued to force workers to work an illegal amount of overtime and that the conditions even further worsened. Workers had more overtime hours and lower wages from the previous year. During the off-season, employees worked between 60–80 overtime hours a month, and during peak season, employees worked 80–140 overtime hours a month. Some workers had two days off in the entire month of July 2018.

The situation for interns was an increasing concern. Interns, who make up 21 percent of the 7,400 workers in the inspected facility, had to work overtime and nightshifts, did not have living stipends, were not offered bonuses, and earned US$1.42 an hour. Intern pay was decreased from 2018. Interns had to work 10 hours a day, six days a week with their heads in the same position with a frequency of motion of over 50 times per minute. The physical requirements violated the law which specified that young workers are not to keep their heads down, in uncomfortable, strained positions, for an extended period nor have a frequency of motion over 50 times per minute. If an intern refused overtime or night shifts, teachers would be encouraged to fire them. Teachers were found to physically and verbally abuse interns.

Furthermore, the company hired an illegal number of temporary workers who earned US$2.06 an hour. These workers did not receive sick pay or holiday pay and could be laid off without wages.

Due to the decreasing profitability of iPhones, Foxconn has made recent cuts in "workers' benefits." Shuttle buses between facilities and dorms have closed, and now workers must walk 40 minutes each way. Workers now must pay US$1 for laundry and US$2.70 for dry cleaning, a service previously offered for free. Workers who were promised to be compensated 80 percent of their regular pay for a sick day had three days' pay reduced from their paycheck. Workers were promised medical coverage but had to pay all medical expenses out of pocket. Many people on the assembly line were found sleeping, their hands grew numb, and their vision significantly impaired. However, Foxconn workers claim that these conditions are not better nor worse than other factories in which they have worked in China.

Sources: Joel Johnson, "1 Million Workers. 90 Million iPhones. 17 Suicides. Who's to Blame?" *Wired*, February 28, 2011; Ross Perlin, "Chinese Workers Foxconned," *Dissent*, Spring 2013; Jane Wakefield, "Foxconn Replaces '60,000 Factory Workers with Robots'," *BBC News*, May 25, 2016; Foxconn website, "Competitive Advantages," http://www.foxconn.com/GroupProfile_En/CompetitiveAdvantages.html, accessed September 20, 2016; Rick Rommell, "Facing Possible Trade War, Foxconn Says It May Broaden Range of Products Made at Wisconsin Factory," *Milwaukee Journal Sentinel*, June 11, 2019; "Foxconn Said to Begin Assembling Top-End Apple iPhone in India in 2019," *Reuters*, December 28, 2018; Katie Schoolov, "Foxconn Says in Rare Interview That It Remains Committed to Massive Wisconsin Factory," *CNBC*, June 29, 2019; "Amazon's Supplier Factory Foxconn Recruits Illegally: Interns Forced to Work Overtime," *China Labour Watch*, August 8, 2019; Harrison Jacobs and Annie Zheng, "Tens of Thousands of Chinese People Live at the Mercy of Apple's Factories—And They Don't Even Work There," *Business Insider*, May 15, 2018; "Foxconn Unit Becomes Most Valuable China-Listed Tech Company," June 8, 2018; Malcolm Owen, "Foxconn Employees Endure Reduced Salaries and Benefits in Wake of Reduced Chinese iPhone Demand," *Apple Insider*, March 1, 2019; Gethin Chamberlain, "Workers Not Paid Legally by Amazon Contractor in China," *The Guardian*, June 9, 2019; Alec Anderson, "Report Documents Abuse of Chinese Workers at Foxconn Supplier Plant for Amazon," *World Socialist Web Site*, June 16, 2018.

## HUMAN RELATIONS MANAGERIAL STRATEGY

The human relations approach is similar to the classical approach in terms of job design, although management attempts to arrange jobs to allow social interaction among employees. This approach is also like the classical school in the way it coordinates employees. But the supervisor's role is much more complicated than it is in the classical school. Leadership is still autocratic in the sense that senior management makes all the important decisions, but there is a much greater attempt to "sell" the decisions, something the classical manager does not bother with.

Human relations managers understand that people like to feel they have some control over their work lives, so they attempt to provide employees with the *feeling* that they have some influence over company decisions (although employees typically have little *real* influence). Therefore, employees are sometimes asked for their opinions on decisions, or they are permitted to make a number of minor, inconsequential decisions. Besides attempting to sell decisions, the supervisor has the added task of exhibiting a high concern for people and fostering a pleasant atmosphere. Overall, the leader plays a controlling but employee-oriented role.

In the human relations school of thought, control is still external but is preferably exercised through the work group. The human relations organization devotes considerable effort toward developing loyal employees who are dedicated to the norms of the organization. Pressure from the work group is expected to make individual members conform to the organization's expectations. If this fails, the supervisor is then expected to step in. However, punishments are not used extensively, out of fear that they will disrupt the social harmony.

Communication within informal work groups is encouraged, and management often attempts to use the grapevine for communication. Management also makes considerable effort to facilitate social communication (such as when an employee marries or has a baby). However, the flow of work-related communication tends to be low, whether up or down the hierarchy. As in the classical school, management still tries to restrict the flow of what it considers to be important information. But unlike in the classical school, they often make use of suggestion systems and newsletters.

The human relations strategy calls for rewards that are mainly extrinsic and that focus on loyalty to the organization. Salaries (rather than hourly pay) are often used to foster a feeling of permanence. To encourage workforce stability, seniority increases are also likely provided. In addition, liberal employee benefits may also be provided to develop employee loyalty. Noneconomic rewards, such as five-year pins and employee-of-the-month citations, also show that the organization is interested in its employees. Management expects employees to find the positive social environment in these firms rewarding.

Kodak was famous for its human relations strategy (see Compensation Today 2.2), although the firm attempted to adopt a more high-involvement strategy in the 1990s in response to its increasingly dynamic task environment. Unfortunately, this change failed, and the company slid into bankruptcy in 2012.

## HIGH-INVOLVEMENT MANAGERIAL STRATEGY

Under the high-involvement model, job design is very different from what we saw in the previous two strategies. Here, a strong effort is made to create jobs that are both interesting and challenging and to provide workers with considerable autonomy when it comes to planning and executing the work activity, as well as with job-based feedback on how well

## DID HUMAN RELATIONS SINK KODAK?

Eastman Kodak, the well-known photographic products firm, was the largest innovator in the industry for over 100 years. The company had been renowned for the fierce loyalty it generated among its employees. But this didn't happen by accident. Historically, Kodak's management practices included rigid adherence to a "promote from within" policy, an excellent compensation package with large profit-sharing bonuses, and a "no layoff" policy to maintain employment security. Its benefits package was truly remarkable, including everything from an excellent pension plan to generous sick leave entitlements and even free noontime movies. As a result, Kodak attracted top-notch employees.

Although most companies in its industry were unionized, there was never any interest in unionization among Kodak employees, and the company always remained non-union. The company had many long-term employees who were committed to the traditional "Kodak way" of doing things, which had proved successful for many years. A classic illustration of Kodak's traditional mentality was the case of a supervisor who had recently retired. When he left, it was discovered that he had kept employment records from as far back as the 1930s in his office drawer "because they had always been there."

The company had a traditional hierarchical structure. Management style at Kodak could best be described as patient and paternalistic, with an extensive system of written rules, policies, and procedures. Even minor decisions percolated to the top. For instance, the head of photographic and information products could be called on to make a decision about any one of 50,000 products.

Although the company had many years of success with this human relations managerial strategy, ultimately dominating the world market for many photographic products, it started to encounter problems in the 1980s, resulting in financial difficulties by the end of the decade. Profit-sharing bonuses shrank to nothing, and the company was forced to sell divisions, close plants, and lay off thousands of employees, the first such layoffs in the company's history. From 1996 onwards, profitability steadily declined. What happened?

Several things. Kodak continuously failed to predict where the industry was going. New competitors, such as Fuji, had entered the film market, a high-margin market dominated by Kodak for decades. In addition, technological change in the photographic business had increased dramatically, and Kodak wasn't able to keep up, despite spending billions on research and development. For example, Kodak didn't believe that 35 mm cameras or video cameras would amount to much and delayed entry into these products until they were dominated by others. When Kodak did introduce new products, such as the disc camera and a CD system for viewing snapshots on a television screen, these new products flopped.

In late 1993, Kodak brought in a new CEO, George Fisher, who had been head of Motorola (a highly innovative and effective producer of communications technology) to try to get the company back on track. Shortly after his arrival, Fisher attempted to move toward a high-involvement managerial strategy in those areas of the business that depended on innovation. However, Kodak's problems continued, resulting in layoffs in 1998 that reduced the company's workforce from 100 000 to about 84 000 employees; continuing reductions decreased total employment to 80 000 by mid-2000. While this did improve the company's bottom line, it didn't seem to make the firm any more flexible or innovative. That prompted some commentators to argue that Kodak should give up on innovation entirely and hive off the innovative portions of its business—such as digital imaging—into a separate business not under the control of Kodak management.

Instead, in 2003, Kodak launched a four-year downscoping program to focus on digital photography products and printers, during which time the firm reduced employment to about 27 000 employees. However, as seems typical for Kodak, it was considered "late in the game" to get into digital products and services. In 2003, for the first time, digital cameras overtook film cameras in sales. The printer and digital markets were already saturated. Kodak was now competing against a vast array of companies in the low-margin business of digital cameras. But Kodak continued to chase and invest in this unprofitable market, divesting its other areas of business, such as chemical technology, to focus purely on the imaging business. In 2005 and onwards, the company's revenues and net incomes were alarmingly low and steadily decreasing. In 2009, Kodak froze employee pay for the year and cut another 4,500 employees. In 2012, the firm declared bankruptcy. Kodak had failed to update their business model to external changes.

Fujifilm faced the same obstacles but came out of the situation more successful than before. The way the company

(*continued*)

did so was by acting quickly and changing its business model. In 2004, the company created a six-year plan to save Fujifilm from external changes. Management decreased production lines and closed redundant facilities. Research and development employees were asked to keep a record of the company's current technologies and compare them with the international market's demands. Fujifilm created a plan of their pre-existing technologies that may be aligned with future markets. With the realization that film had an ill-fated future, the company diversified into other profitable markets. Fujifilm invested in pharmaceuticals, chemical technologies, and cosmetics. If a gap existed between a market and their innovations, the company would close this gap by buying other companies that already had success in a market. In 2000, around 67 percent of Fujifilm's profit was from film, but by 2010 film accounted for below 16 percent of the company's profits. The company succeeded by reorganization and diversification.

Sources: Sanford M. Jacoby, *Modern Manors: Welfare Capitalism Since the New Deal* (Princeton: Princeton University Press, 1997); Stephen P. Robbins, *Organization Theory: Structure, Design, and Applications* (Englewood Cliffs: Prentice-Hall, 1990), 514–15; Mark Maremont, "Kodak's New Focus," *Business Week*, January 30, 1995: 62–68; Peter Coy, "The Myth of Corporate Reinvention," *Business Week*, October 30, 2000: 80–82; Ben Dobbin, "Perez to Replace Carp as Kodak CEO," *Business Week Online*, May 11, 2005; Franklin Paul, "Kodak to Cut Up to 4,500 Jobs," *Reuters*, January 29, 2009; Michael Zhang, "A Brief History of Kodak: The Rise and Fall of a Camera Giant," *Peta Pixel*, June 14, 2018; Oliver Kmia, "Why Kodak Died and Fujifilm Thrived: A Tale of Two Film Companies," *Peta Pixel*, October 19, 2018; Jonathon C. Ho and Hongyi Chen, "Managing the Disruptive and Sustaining the Disrupted: The Case of Kodak and Fujifilm in the Face of Digital Disruption," *Review of Policy Research* 35, no. 3 (2018): 352–71.

they are performing. Efforts are made to include a meaningful cycle of work activity, with the result that jobs are broader and involve more elements. Joint employee–management planning and goal setting are often used. In contrast to the classical approach, a conscious effort is made to *combine* the thinking and the doing.

Coordination is horizontal as well as vertical. In fact, horizontal coordination, whereby workers coordinate directly with one another in task completion, is preferred to vertical coordination. Jobs are often arranged in clusters, with a group of employees responsible for coordinating the completion of a set of tasks. These clusters, or teams, often consist of people from various specialties mingled together. Departmentation is based on the product, customer, or project, not on functional groupings.

The role of the supervisor in a high-involvement organization is very different from that in the other two schools. Rather than being primarily a controller and evaluator, the supervisor is a facilitator. His or her job is to remove barriers to effective performance and to provide adequate resources and other assistance to enable subordinates to perform effectively.

Intrinsic rewards can be motivational.

Because employees are assumed to be able to exercise self-control and self-motivation, the supervisor does not need to perform a control function. Moreover, because employees are assumed to be self-motivated and competent, decisions can be made at the lowest possible level in the organization. The leadership style is participative or democratic in nature.

Control is internal (within the individual). Employees are expected to exercise self-control, because of their identification with the goals of the organization and the intrinsic rewards flowing from the work itself, and because they have sufficient training and knowledge to behave responsibly. Because of this internalized commitment, little supervision is necessary and formalized rules and regulations can be kept to a minimum.

Full disclosure of information is essential because decisions are being made at all levels throughout the organization. Without adequate information, poor decisions would result. The high-involvement firm recognizes this, so communication is a major focus of management attention. Great effort is made for communication to flow vertically (both up and down the organization), horizontally, and diagonally.

A high-involvement organization uses a wide variety of both intrinsic and extrinsic rewards. Employees are expected to receive substantial intrinsic rewards directly from performing their jobs and participating in decision making. Extrinsic rewards are geared toward fostering good performance rather than controlling substandard output, and they tend to focus on the work unit, rather than the individual, because tasks are usually complex and require teamwork.

Base pay tends to be salary, augmented by profit- and gain-sharing plans of various types, as well as employee share ownership. Pay is often person-based (i.e., pay for knowledge) rather than job-based, in order to promote skills acquisition and flexibility within the organization. Because of the complex behaviour and high-performance levels required in high-involvement organizations, reward and compensation systems are usually more complex than those in firms using the other two managerial strategies.

Compensation Today 2.3 illustrates how one high-involvement firm, WestJet, puts all this together.

---

## COMPENSATION TODAY 2.3

### INVOLVEMENT FLIES HIGH AT WESTJET

Founded in Calgary in 1996, WestJet Airlines has enjoyed phenomenal growth in an industry characterized by bankruptcies and failures. In 2000, its share of the Canadian market was seven percent, compared to the 77 percent held by its main rival, Air Canada. By 2011, WestJet's market share had quintupled to 36 percent, while Air Canada's had declined to 56 percent and most other competitors had disappeared entirely. The airline has increased total revenue by five percent year over year from 2014 to 2018. In addition, WestJet has won various awards, such as Best Airline in Canada by Trip Advisor in 2018.

Although once a stable industry, the airline industry has been anything but stable in recent years. Starting with deregulation in the 1980s, the environment for the industry has become turbulent, buffeted by recession and unforeseen events such as the terrorist attacks of September 11, 2001, increased airport taxes and security costs, the SARS epidemic, the H1N1 flu pandemic, and the global COVID-19 pandemic of 2020, all which affected travel. So, in this kind of environment, what has accounted for WestJet's success?

The founders started with the vision of differentiating WestJet from its competitors by establishing a workforce of friendly, upbeat employees committed to customer service and by delivering low ticket prices through operational efficiencies, such as flying only one type of aircraft (the Boeing 737) to reduce maintenance costs. From the beginning, the founders considered the practice of a high-involvement managerial strategy to be the cornerstone to the firm's success. Jobs are defined broadly, with ticket counter staff doubling as baggage handlers when necessary.

Within the guidelines that must be followed for safety and operational reasons, employees are given latitude to do what they can to create an enjoyable flying experience for "guests"—as passengers are known.

Employees (known as "our people" or "WestJetters") are aided in developing their trademark comedic banter by the "WestJesters." This is one of several committees of WestJet flight attendants who meet regularly to discuss everything from customer service to language and culture. This participative approach permeates the entire company. For example, when confronted with the travel plunge caused by the 2008–09 financial meltdown, the firm included rank-and-file employees in consultations about how to see itself through this challenging period.

Why can management expect employees to show as much concern about the firm as the owners do? Well, the intrinsic rewards built into the jobs themselves and the highly participative and satisfying corporate culture certainly help,

(continued)

Employee ownership is emphasized at WestJet.

but the most important reason is that the employees *are* owners. Instead of a conventional defined benefit pension plan (which the firm was not sure it could afford), WestJet has a share purchase plan under which employees can invest up to 20 percent of their earnings in company shares, which the company then matches with free shares. Also, with no employee contributions required, employees receive shares through an employee profit-sharing plan.

In recent years, WestJet has faced challenges. The company's net earnings decreased from $279 million in 2017 to $91 million in 2018, and operating margins had steadily decreased from 14.1 percent in 2015 to 0.3 percent in 2018. WestJet's newly purchased Max 8 planes remain grounded after several fatal crashes. Aircraft fuel costs have been on the increase; in 2017, it cost 64 cents per litre, but in 2018 the price rose to 81 cents per litre. In 2018, profit-sharing expenditures decreased 65.9 percent from the prior year. In 2015, WestJet's profit-share expense was $101 million, and the company had 9211 employees. By 2018, with 11 624 employees, the company had profit-share expenses of $16 million. In 2020 the COVID-19 pandemic impacted airlines and WestJet laid off almost 8000 employees. While most of these employees were re-hired with government assistance, at the time of writing this chapter almost 2000 were still unemployed, including pilots.

As the airline grows, with pressures to become more mainstream, the business model changing and with the airline's expansion into international flights, there are indications that WestJet's culture may be changing. WestJet pilots unionized in 2017 and flight attendants unionized in 2018. Shortly after unionization, 91 percent of WestJet's pilots voted in agreement to strike. Some commentators contend that unionization signalled discontent. And many employees are indeed disgruntled with their workload. There are recent reports that employees are not cracking jokes as before, maybe as a result of increasing job pressures. In poor economic conditions, employees are receiving less payout and therefore, may feel unfairness and a decreased feeling of company commitment.

Changes in compensation can inadvertently be affecting the company's culture. WestJet plans to pay commission to flight attendants on Swoop airlines, a new ultra-low-cost carrier of WestJet, for in-flight purchased food and drinks. Furthermore, flight attendants are complaining that they only earn money when in the air. "In air pay" means that if flight attendants are earning $25 an hour but only spend half an 8-hour day in the air, they are making less than minimum wage because they are only paid for four hours. Other airlines often pay flight attendants for tasks such as preparing the airplanes or deplaning.

There are also issues with customers. By way of example, WestJet began charging US$30 for checked baggage for return flights. Some issued tickets did not convey this new policy and, despite customer complaints, these customers weren't refunded. One passenger remarked, "everyone will know they don't have their customers' interests at heart." The company's growth without consideration of its culture can lead to significant problems.

Competition from Air Canada and other airlines is also increasing. Furthermore, as the company expands internationally, it will face new competition. These are challenges that WestJet will have to effectively manage as it tries to achieve its goal of becoming one of the best airlines in the world.

Sources: Jason Kirby, "WestJet's Plan to Crush Air Canada," *Maclean's*, May 4, 2009, 38–41; Richard W. Yerema, *Canada's Top 100 Employers* (Toronto: Mediacorp, 2005); Andrew Wahl, "Culture Shock: A Survey of Canadian Executives Reveals That Corporate Culture Is in Need of Improvement," *Canadian Business* online, October 10, 2005; Christine Owram, "Losing the WestJet Effect: How the Once Scrappy Upstart is Changing as it Expands Globally," *National Post*, October 2, 2015; Parbudyal Singh, "WestJet Airlines: Clear Skies or Turbulence Ahead?" Case Study, Nelson Canada, August 2013; Kaylen Small, "WestJet Flight Attendants Set to Unionize," *Global News*, July 9, 2018; Ross Marowits, "WestJet Pilots Vow Not To Disrupt Long Weekend as a Goodwill Gesture," *CTV News*, May 10, 2018; Scott Sonenshein, "We're Changing—Or Are We? Untangling the Role of Progressive and Regressive, and Stability Narratives During Strategic Change Implementation," *Academy of Management Journal* 53, no.3 (2010): 477–512; Leon Grunberg, Sarah Moore, and Edward S. Greenberg, "The Changing Workplace and Its Effects: A Longitudinal Examination of Employee Responses at a Large Company," *The Journal of Applied Behavioral Science* 44, no. 2 (2008): 215–36; Sophia Harris, "WestJet Passengers Who Scored $30 U.S. Baggage Fee Refund Want to Spread the Word," *CBC*, April 14, 2019; Kyle Bakx, "WestJet and Air Canada: How Little Separates the Airlines Anymore," *CBC*, May 12, 2018; Amanda Stephenson, "Law Firms Consider Class-Action On Behalf of WestJet Flight Attendants For Unpaid Work," *Calgary Herald*, August 1, 2018; "2019 First Quarter Report," *WestJet*, May 6, 2019.

# INTERRELATIONSHIPS AMONG STRUCTURAL VARIABLES

It should now be apparent that there are strong relationships among the structural variables. Some elements are *complementary*—that is, they must occur together for any of them to be effective. For example, pushing decision making down to lower-level employees in the organization is dangerous if they have not been provided with adequate information with which to make informed decisions, a knowledge base to understand this information, and a reward system that creates a strong sense of identity with the company. But at the same time, creating knowledgeable, well-informed employees with a financial stake in the firm's performance and then not allowing them input into decision making creates employee frustration.

Research has also shown that some structural elements can serve as *substitutes* for others. For example, a Canadian study has shown that profit-sharing and gain-sharing systems can serve as substitutes for managerial control.[11] This study found that firms with profit- or gain-sharing systems (or preferably both) were able to operate with 31 percent fewer managers and supervisors and significantly fewer rules and regulations than firms without these systems. These firms, like WestJet, substitute internal (self-control) for external control.

Organizations that consistently adopt a single managerial strategy, no matter what that managerial strategy is, are usually more effective than those that have an inconsistent mix of structural elements. MacDuffie refers to internally consistent practices as "human resource bundles"[12] and presents evidence that firms that use these "bundles" perform better than those that do not.

It should be noted that even within a given managerial strategy, there are various possible combinations of human resource policies. For example, a firm may choose to hire only experienced workers, or it may hire inexperienced workers and train them. Hiring experienced workers usually costs more in compensation, but hiring inexperienced workers costs more in training costs and there is the risk of losing them once they are trained.

But different managerial perspectives have different preferences. Because of high turnover, classical organizations would prefer not to incur high training costs. So, their tendency is to hire experienced, trained workers, where jobs require training. (Their preferred course of action is to fragment tasks into small pieces so that little training is necessary.)

Other human resource policies, such as recruitment, must fit into the managerial strategy. Because high-involvement organizations need workers who have high potential for growth, self-control, and motivation by higher order needs, they have the most comprehensive selection processes. In contrast, because classical organization demands are simple task performance, they have the least sophisticated recruitment and selection procedures. Human relations organizations fall in between: they want to screen out people who would disrupt the social environment of the firm.

Before we leave organization structure, there is one other concept that is relevant—organizational culture. **Organizational culture** is the set of values, guiding beliefs, understandings, and ways of thinking that are shared by members of an organization."[13] Organizational culture—that is, the organization's informal structure—can help guide employee behaviour.

A strong culture can play a major role in shaping and directing behaviour within the organization. Culture can supplement the organization's formal structure or can substitute for it. For example, because of their need to stay flexible, high-involvement organizations like to use as little formal structure as possible, so a strong organizational culture is important to them. Classical firms, on the other hand, prefer to depend on the formal structure, so they focus very little on organizational culture. Human relations firms use both formal structure and culture to shape behaviour.

**organizational culture**
The set of core values and understandings shared by members of an organization.

A given culture may be beneficial to one organization but detrimental to another, depending on whether it fits with the managerial strategy. However, some cultures are simply detrimental. For example, employees in many classical organizations develop a strong anti-management culture, which may include norms such as "never cooperate with management," "never go beyond your minimum work requirements," and "ignore the rules when the supervisor is gone." In human relations firms, a culture of avoiding conflict, never criticizing the company or a coworker, valuing tradition, and doing things the way they have always been done tends to develop. Remember the Kodak employee who kept 50-year-old employment records in his desk drawer because they "had always been there"? In contrast, key cultural values in high-involvement organizations such as WestJet include honesty, trustworthiness, open communication, and acceptance of risk taking.

An organization shapes culture by its actions. For example, a firm that says it values initiative and risk taking but then punishes every employee initiative that fails teaches employees not to exercise any initiative. The reward system is critical in shaping culture. A firm that says it values cooperation and teamwork but then promotes an employee who isn't a team player is signalling a very different message. If a company's top management is fond of talking about how "we are all partners in this enterprise" but doesn't share gains when the firm is successful and lays off employees at the first sign of trouble, then employees will not feel much like "partners."

Human relations and high-involvement organizations typically spend considerable effort developing their cultures. But culture is most important to high-involvement organizations because they depend on it as a substitute for the formal structure. Organizational culture, as a concept, came to prominence with the rise of high-involvement organizations.

## DETERMINANTS OF THE MOST APPROPRIATE MANAGERIAL STRATEGY

If the most appropriate reward system is determined by the managerial strategy, then it is important to understand the factors that determine the most appropriate managerial strategy. The answer lies in the five key contextual variables identified in Figure 2.1: environment, business strategy, technology, organization size, and nature of the workforce. It is important to know how each variable relates to managerial strategy.

This section begins by showing how each of these contextual variables can be categorized into types, and then how each type relates to managerial strategy. At the end of this section (in Compensation Notebook 2.2), a template is provided as a tool to help identify the most appropriate managerial strategy (and hence, reward strategy) for any given organization.

Of course, just because the contextual variables point to a particular managerial strategy doesn't necessarily mean that the organization has actually adopted that managerial strategy. In some cases, firms may be using a managerial strategy that doesn't match their contextual variables and, in some cases, firms really have no distinct managerial strategy.[14] In either case, company performance will be lower than it should be; indeed, company survival could be threatened if competitors have adopted the most appropriate managerial strategy.

Finally, an organization may have a mixed set of structural dimensions and thus appear to have no definite managerial strategy, but it is actually in a planned transition from one managerial strategy to another. This transition may be very appropriate if the change is being driven by the need to respond to changes in the firm's contextual variables, although successful transitions from one managerial strategy to another (such as from classical to high involvement) are actually very difficult.

## ENVIRONMENT

Of the five contextual variables, the most important is the environment that faces a given firm. The first question to ask is whether the firm's environment is stable or unstable. An unstable (dynamic) environment exists where product or service life cycles are short, where product or service demand is volatile, where customer needs change quickly and unpredictably, where technologies are changing rapidly, where new competitors often enter the field, and where the regulatory environment is unpredictable. Firms generally have little control over the level of stability in the task environment. Because of their rigidity, classical and human relations firms have great difficulty operating successfully in dynamic, unstable environments.

The second question to ask is whether the firm's environment is simple or complex. A firm's environment is complex if the firm has many distinct product or service domains, if the product/service provided is complicated, if the technology is complex, and if a multitude of factors can influence success. While firms do not have much control over the degree of stability in their environments, they do have some control over the *complexity* of their task environments. For example, a firm that chooses to operate in several unrelated product/service domains creates a more complex environment for itself than a firm that operates in only one product/service domain. Thus, the complexity of a firm's environment depends in part on how broadly it defines its domain(s). But note that some domains (e.g., designing microcircuits) are inherently more complex than others (e.g., processing chickens).

However, even if a task environment is complex, *as long as it is stable*, a classical or human relations approach can be effective. If the complexity stems from operating in many domains, either a classical or human relations approach should work. But if the complexity is due to the domain itself, then a human relations approach may work best. This is because complex domains often require high levels of expertise among employees, and the high turnover that typifies a classical organization will be very costly in these circumstances.

By contrast, when task environments are dynamic, complexity compounds the uncertainty facing the organization. Neither classical nor human relations organizations are able to adapt quickly to environmental change. In general, a high-involvement approach is needed whenever environments are highly unstable or dynamic; this is even more essential when the environment is also complex.

## CORPORATE STRATEGY

There are several ways of classifying an organization's business strategy, including one developed by Miles and Snow[15] and the other developed by Porter.[16] Each of these typologies yields useful insights into how business strategy relates to the most appropriate managerial strategy for an organization to adopt. Below we discuss how the Miles and Snow typology can be applied.

## Miles and Snow Typology of Corporate Strategy

Miles and Snow suggest that business strategies are of three main types—defender, prospector, and analyzer—with a residual type reactor—to cover firms that do not practise any distinct overall strategy.

The **defender business strategy** entails taking a narrow product or service segment and excelling in it, based on a combination of product quality and price. A defender firm may not always be the low-cost leader, but it will always try to provide the best possible quality/price tradeoff so that its products offer the best value to customers. The byword for this strategy is *consistency*. The key need is to identify the most efficient process for providing the product or service and then to lock it in. For defenders, the classical or human relations approaches are most suitable. In general, classical works well for manufacturing, and human relations for service enterprises, where there is extensive contact with customers.

The **prospector business strategy** is the complete opposite of the defender strategy. It focuses on identifying new product and market opportunities and being the first to exploit them. Prospectors tend to move on to other new products or services as competitors enter the market. These competitors can copy the product and mass produce it at a lower cost than the prospector can because the competitors do not have to include development costs or costs of failed products in their pricing structures. The byword for the prospector strategy is *speed*. The key needs are for a process to identify new opportunities quickly and for an organization flexible and dynamic enough to get them to market before anybody else. Clearly, a high-involvement approach is essential.

The **analyzer business strategy** is the most complex of the three corporate strategies because it attempts to combine the prospector and defender strategies. This strategy entails identifying and exploiting new product or service opportunities at a relatively early stage—not long after the prospectors—while also maintaining a firm base of traditional products or services. The byword for the analyzer strategy is *balance*. The key need is to balance stability and flexibility. This often requires a hybrid or dual organization structure: one that promotes speed and flexibility for new product development, and one that promotes stability and consistency for established products. Typically, analyzer firms are not the first to offer new products or services, but they do enter these markets early, after the prospectors have identified them. They are generally less efficient in production than defenders, but are able to get their products on the market long before the defenders in the industry get around to doing so.

Analyzers likely operate best with something close to a high-involvement approach for new product development and a classical approach for their traditional products. But because it is very difficult to practise two such divergent managerial strategies in the same firm, analyzers often seem to end up practising a compromise human relations strategy across the board. This can be successful as long as the environment is not too dynamic.

## TECHNOLOGY

An organization's technology is the set of procedures and resources it uses to transform resources to usable products or services. An organization's technology can be classified in a number of ways, such as the type of production processes involved, the degree to which the technology is routine or non-routine, or whether small or large batches are used.

If an organization has a technology orientation, it implements new processes, services, and ideas by aligning its resources, structures, and systems with technology.[17] Because of technological growth and the decreasing life cycle of goods and services, organizations are compelled to improve their technological abilities and knowledge to compete within their market.[18] Technology can serve as a competitive advantage for a variety of reasons. For instance, it increases knowledge transfer, allows for the assimilation of knowledge across business units and develops the social capital required for knowledge integration.[19] The technology used by the organization will have implications for its workforce capabilities, for example, and this will influence the complexity of the firm's environment and the managerial and compensation strategies to be used.

## ORGANIZATION SIZE

Because of the need to coordinate and control large numbers of people, large organizations generally use classical or human relations strategies, although these strategies can be found in organizations of all sizes. In general, it is easier to implement high involvement in a small- to medium-sized organization because the larger the organization, the greater the need for some formal structure. However, some large organizations have resolved this problem by segmenting the organization into a series of relatively small units and then practising high involvement in these units. Hewlett-Packard, the computer products firm, has traditionally used this approach.

Size affects structure in at least one other way. As organizations get larger, the impact of technology on their structure lessens. Some large organizations may use a number of different technologies. This diversification may call for different managerial strategies in different parts of the organization, which can be very difficult to manage as top management tends to prefer one particular managerial strategy (the one consistent with their assumptions about people).

## THE NATURE OF THE WORKFORCE

The nature of the people employed by the organization—their skills, educational characteristics, and expectations—also has a major impact on the choice of managerial strategy. Highly skilled, well-educated, or professional employees are generally more suited to the high-involvement organization. Indeed, a high-involvement strategy *requires* these characteristics because of the broad job and decision-making responsibilities that employees are expected to assume.

Classical organizations are designed specifically to use employees with relatively low skill levels. Because of their approach to motivation and control, these organizations are best suited to workers who badly need the money the job provides. Classical motivational approaches work best in poor economic circumstances and in areas with high unemployment and a low standard of living. (This helps explain why many classical firms move their production operations to less prosperous countries, where living conditions make their managerial strategy effective.) In contrast, human relations organizations can often use relatively low-skilled workers but do not need to depend on poor economic circumstances for their motivational policies because they offer both economic and social rewards.

Unions influence employees' pay.

It is also important to note the role of unions in organizations. Unions can have an effect on employee skills, their tasks and responsibilities, and their expectations. Unions add voice to employees and influence pay in the bargaining unit through collective bargaining. In unionized environments, employees usually receive higher pay and more benefits. Unions also have an effect on managerial autonomy; that is, unions may put restrictions on what management can and cannot do. Overall, unions will have differential effects on managerial strategies, employees' attitudes and behaviours, and organizational outcomes depending on the interaction of all aspects of the organization's context.

## TYING IT ALL TOGETHER

For an organization to maximize its chances of success, the chosen managerial strategy must align with the firm's contextual variables, and those variables must align with one another. For example, using a defender strategy in an unstable environment is courting disaster, because the organization may not be able to respond quickly to change. Compatible combinations would be those that are consistent with a given managerial strategy. Thus, a defender strategy, a stable environment, a relatively low-skilled work-force, and a large organization would be a good combination, well suited for the classical managerial strategy.

Compensation Notebook 2.2 illustrates these combinations and provides a template for selecting the most appropriate managerial strategy for a given organization to adopt.

---

**COMPENSATION NOTEBOOK 2.2**

### TEMPLATE FOR SELECTING THE MOST APPROPRIATE MANAGERIAL STRATEGY FOR AN ORGANIZATION TO ADOPT

| CONTEXTUAL VARIABLE | CLASSICAL | HUMAN RELATIONS | HIGH-INVOLVEMENT |
|---|---|---|---|
| **Environment** | | | |
| • Stability | • Stable | • Stable | |
| • Complexity | • Simple | • Simple or complex | • Unstable complex |
| **Business Strategy** | | | |
| • Miles and Snow typology | • Defender | • Analyzer | • Prospector |
| • Porter's typology | • Low cost | • Focused differentiator | • Differentiator |
| **Technology** | | | |
| • Product transformed | • Things | • People | • Ideas |
| **Size** | | | |
| • Number of employees | • Any size | • Any size | • Small/medium |
| **Workforce** | | | |
| • Skills/education | • Low | • Moderate | • High |
| • Economic circumstances | • Poor | • Moderate | • Good |

---

(Of course, where the contextual variables are out of alignment with one another, there can be no ideal managerial strategy and no ideal reward strategy.) The template also helps solve the mystery of why some firms do quite nicely without adopting pay innovations, and why compensation systems that work well for some firms are completely inadequate in others.

Let us use this template to revisit some of the organizations you learned about earlier in the chapter. Start with Koch chicken processors. But before doing so, you need a little more background on chicken processing, which Compensation Today 2.4 provides. After reading Compensation Today 2.4, you will probably know more about chicken processing than you ever really wanted to know.

Now, compare Koch Foods with the characteristics in the template. Koch Foods has a stable, simple environment, uses a defender strategy (where low-cost production is crucial) and a long-linked technology, requires low-skilled employees, and is located in a region where economic conditions are generally poor. Perfect for a classical structure! Although employee turnover is high, *it doesn't matter* because employees are easy to replace and train. Employee commitment is not needed because control is easy, with the technology itself (the "chain") providing most of the necessary control. Given all this, the sole purpose of the compensation system is to ensure a sufficient flow of applicants so that the chain is always staffed at the lowest possible cost.

Let us take a closer look at ArcelorMittal Dofasco which pays its employees fairly well. Because of overcapacity in its industry and the U.S. now imposing steel tariffs on Canadian companies, the environment can be considered quite unstable, although

---

## COMPENSATION TODAY 2.4

### ANYONE FOR CHICKEN FINGERS?

If chickens don't have fingers, then where do chicken fingers come from? One story is that a marketer was trying to come up with a name for the company's new chicken product when there was an accident on the processing line. An employee had two fingers lopped off, which fell into the boxes of chicken parts. As workers shouted, "Get the fingers from the chicken!" inspiration struck the marketer! Whether or not this story is really true, safety on a chicken-processing line is no joking matter, and accident rates are high in this line of work.

In a chicken-processing plant, all work is centred around the "chain" on which the live birds are first hung by workers dubbed "live hangers." This is considered the worst of all the jobs in the plant, as the angry chickens take every opportunity to peck, claw, and defecate all over the workers, who are expected to clip a desperately struggling bird to the chain every two seconds or so. Because so few workers can handle this job, it pays a bit more than the minimum wage most workers receive.

The birds are then stunned electrically, killed, and mechanically plucked. They then continue along the chain on their way to becoming packages of chicken parts. Many workers play a role in this transformation process as the birds pass by individual workers at up to 90 birds a minute. Part of the transformation process is performed by workers known as "butthole cutters," who open up the bird so that a "gut puller" can reach in and pull out the innards. The process is wet and noisy, with workers in such close quarters that they often cut themselves or other workers. Because any worker who doesn't keep up creates more work for those down the line, the system is basically self-supervising. And all this for minimum wage!

Not surprisingly, turnover is often over 100 percent a year. As the demand for chicken has been growing by leaps and bounds in North America, this is one job you won't find tough to snag even in a down economy!

Source: Based on Tony Horwitz, "9 to Nowhere," *Wall Street Journal*, 1994.

relatively simple because ArcelorMittal Dofasco specializes in a narrow range of products. The firm uses a defender strategy with a focus on high-quality products. Process technology is used. The plant is large, with around 5000 employees. But because of the complexity of the production process, the skill levels required of workers are high. The cost of errors is potentially high, as is the cost of downtime due to equipment failures and other problems. Economic conditions in Hamilton, where the plant is located, is expected to be among Canada's strongest economies (at the time the text was revised in 2019–20).

When you compare these points to the template in Compensation Notebook 2.2, you can see that the ArcelorMittal Dofasco case is not as clear-cut as the chicken plant case: various contextual variables point toward different managerial strategies. You can find examples of each of the three managerial strategies in the steel industry, although the classical approach predominates.

Remember Foxconn in Compensation Today 2.1? Use the strategic template to classify this firm. It uses low-skilled labour and a routine technology. The firm deals with things, not people. The environment is simple and relatively stable because of high demand for its service. We can predict that Foxconn could use a classical managerial strategy very successfully, which of course, it does. The pay system fits the firm's strategy. We may not like Foxconn and we can predict that the employees probably don't either. However, whether by accident or design, Foxconn has created an organizational system, including its pay system, that matches its strategy.

In contrast, Kodak illustrates what can happen when circumstances change and what was once a highly effective management strategy no longer fits these circumstances. Conditions used to fit the human relations strategy well. Kodak always had a complex environment, as evidenced by the vast array of products it made, but the firm's very dominance created a relatively stable environment. In the 1970s and 1980s, it practised a defender strategy for some products and an analyzer strategy for others. Technology was routine for most products. Except in the research and development areas, only moderate employee skills and education were required.

When competitors entered the field and product innovations occurred, Kodak could not change rapidly enough to adjust to these changes. It moved too slow and its overloaded hierarchical decision-making systems were not able to accurately judge its environment.

Kodak's organizational culture of stability, which had once been an asset, became a liability when the firm tried to move toward a prospector strategy. The company undertook several measures to try to deal with these problems, such as reducing environmental complexity (through the sale of noncore divisions) and moving toward a high-involvement strategy in areas of the business that depended on innovation. But as Compensation Today 2.2 suggests, these changes did not bear fruit. Moving from a human relations organization to a high-involvement organization is a difficult and long-term process, especially for large organizations with entrenched cultures.

Finally, consider WestJet. It is an excellent example of fit. Look at how its high-involvement managerial style fits the company's context: unstable, complex environment; differentiator strategy; relatively small size; relatively educated workforce; operating in a relatively prosperous region. Instead of a formal structure, the organization encourages a culture of commitment, egalitarianism, teamwork, and risk taking. And look at how the reward system fits with and supports the company's strategy.

# TRENDS IN MANAGERIAL AND COMPENSATION STRATEGIES

All three managerial strategies can be effective in the right context. But how are circumstances changing in North America, and how will these changes affect the choice of managerial strategy? This is an important question for those designing reward systems, because the most appropriate reward system for a given firm depends on the managerial strategy that is in place at that firm. To get a handle on this question, you need to understand how business conditions and managerial strategies have evolved in Canada. As will be discussed at the end of this section, these changes also help explain some of the current trends in Canadian compensation practices.

## THE EVOLUTION OF MANAGERIAL STRATEGIES

Since the development of classical and human relations managerial strategies in the first half of the 20th century, many fundamental socioeconomic changes have taken place in Canada, and those changes have created conditions that are more suitable for high-involvement organizations and less suitable for classical and human relations organizations. Educational levels have increased, economic security and social security have improved, and social values have become more democratic and egalitarian.

Information technology has allowed for flatter organization structures and more decentralized decision making. At the same time, products and services have become more complex, along with the technologies used to produce them. All of this generally calls for greater skill, initiative, and motivation from employees. Rapid discovery of new knowledge causes older knowledge to quickly become obsolete, and it is not uncommon for new employees in many firms to understand more about the firm's technology than their bosses. All these conditions work against classical and human relations organizations.

While there remains a demand for simple products and services, globalization has allowed much of the work of producing these products and services to be outsourced to developing countries. Because these countries have conditions that better fit classical organizations (such as large unskilled or semiskilled workforces with relatively poor economic circumstances) than the conditions in Canada, many classical firms have found developing countries a much better fit for their preferred managerial strategy and have moved operations there.

While there are still some contexts in which classical and human relations strategies are effective, notably for organizations producing relatively simple products and services and operating in protected or less competitive markets, Canadian firms are finding it increasingly difficult to make these two managerial strategies work for them. For classical firms, besides a problem with poor employee–management relationships, the key problem in changing times is rigidity. Classical organizations spend huge sums to discover the "one best way" of doing something, to develop specialized technology and job structures, and then to lock in employee behaviour. Obviously, employee innovation is discouraged; if a company already has the "best system" then, by definition, any deviation is inefficient. Despite their kinder employee relations, human relations organizations tend to be as rigid and inflexible as classical ones.

To survive, human relations companies have been forced to react to their changing environment in one of three ways. First, some try to become more classical, eliminating job security, cutting wages and benefits, and cutting staff—in other words, undoing the very managerial practices that made them successful in the first place. This "lean and mean" approach may extend their survival, but it does not deal with the fundamental problem: inability to cope with change. Paradoxically, there is considerable evidence that such actions actually make the organization more resistant to and/or incapable of change. The best employees end up feeling betrayed and seek jobs elsewhere, while the remainder try to keep their heads down. Furthermore, the high stress levels caused by the lean-and-mean approach are antithetical to effective change. Interestingly, there is evidence that downsizing generally does not increase future profitability[20] and that it actually decreases worker efficiency.[21]

A second option is to retain the human relations school of thought but attempt to shift to markets that are less dynamic. In other words, if your environment no longer fits your management strategy, find an environment that does. This course of action often requires major surgery, with entire divisions being sold or closed down. However, for those parts of the organization that remain, there are no major changes to managerial strategy or to the reward system. Some organizations have used this approach, known as *downscoping*, and it has been successful in some, but not all, cases. As Compensation Today 2.2 described, downscoping was part of Kodak's strategy for survival, a strategy that did not succeed.

The final option for human relations firms trying to deal with environmental change is to retain the current domain but attempt to become flexible and innovative—that is, to become a high-involvement organization. Converting to the high-involvement approach is in many ways the toughest road, but it is probably the only one that will lead to long-term success if the firm chooses to stay in a dynamic environment. (Indeed, environments that are not dynamic are becoming increasingly scarce.) This approach has major implications for all aspects of the organizational system. As Figure 2.1 showed, virtually every structural variable—including the reward system—must undergo dramatic change to make this conversion.

Classical organizations that find themselves facing a dynamic environment are in an even worse position than human relations organizations. Because they are already "lean and mean," there is not much fat that can be easily trimmed, and tough unions may prevent them from becoming as mean as they would like to be. Seeing unions as a threat to their power, some firms have attempted to destroy or at least weaken their unions. They then have a freer hand to cut costs by cutting pay and benefits, reducing staffing levels, and increasing workloads. Other firms have attempted to circumvent the union by contracting out as much work as possible to non-union or weak-union firms. Another tactic is to shift production to regions or countries where unions are not strong or economic conditions are poor. Sometimes firms find that simply threatening to do so may be sufficient to get the union to agree to various concessions.

Classical firms that have chosen to move to a high-involvement management approach have an even tougher task than human relations organizations because they are starting off with very poor and adversarial employee–management relationships, and the key ingredient for movement to a high-involvement school of thought—trust—is lacking. Furthermore, classical structural characteristics are the exact opposite of what is needed for a high-involvement organization. It often takes a major crisis, coupled with visionary leadership, to successfully make the transition.

A key part—perhaps the most crucial part—of making the transition to high involvement is changing the reward and compensation system. The compensation system can be a powerful tool for change or a powerful inhibitor of change (see Chapter 3). There is considerable evidence that business firms attempting to move to high-involvement management find their success short lived if their reward and compensation system does not support the new managerial strategy.[22] Even when employees value high-involvement management for its intrinsic rewards, failure to spread the extrinsic rewards generated by the new management system to all employees can create a sense of inequity that destroys the foundation of trust and goodwill necessary for high involvement to be successful.

An exception to the need for extrinsic rewards can arise in not-for-profit organizations. Where the organization generates no financial surpluses that can be shared, employees may be willing to accept high-involvement management (and even welcome it) on its intrinsic rewards alone. But even here, it is unlikely that high involvement can survive long unless organization members perceive that whatever extrinsic rewards are available are being distributed equitably. Overall, reward equity, to the extent that it is within the organization's control, is a critical foundation of the high-involvement approach (see Chapter 3).

## TRENDS IN COMPENSATION SYSTEMS

The strategic framework presented in this chapter helps explain some of the trends that took place in Canadian compensation systems during the latter part of the 20th century. The underlying trend has been toward more complicated pay systems. When classical firms dominated in the first half of the 20th century, pay systems were simple, based on output or hourly pay. As human relations firms came to the fore in the second half of the century, indirect pay made extrinsic rewards more complex as more benefits were added to increase employee security and well-being, as illustrated by Kodak. Finally, as some firms began to practise high-involvement management, with a need for complex employee behaviour and high employee performance, compensation systems became even more complex with group or organizational performance pay added to the mix, as illustrated by WestJet.

General compensation trends over the past two or three decades have included an increase in the adoption of pay-for-performance systems—especially those aimed at organizational performance, such as profit-sharing and employee share plans. There has also been an increase in group- or team-based incentive systems, and more firms have also experimented with pay-for-knowledge systems in place of traditional job-based pay systems. Flexible benefit plans have also increased in popularity, and there has been a gradual movement away from hourly pay toward the use of salary. However, many of these trends appear to have stalled in the first two decades of the 21st century.

The global financial crisis of 2008–09 saw wage cuts and rollbacks. Those firms that try to address their financial problems simply by cutting employee compensation tend to be either classical organizations that are attempting to become even leaner and meaner or human relations organizations attempting to survive by shifting toward less generous pay policies. Many firms—not just classical or human relations firms—are moving away from defined benefit pension plans (where the employer guarantees that pension payouts to retirees will be a specified amount) toward defined contribution pension plans (where the employer makes no such guarantees).

Another change with direct implications for compensation was the increased use of part-time, temporary, and contract workers ("contingent workers") during the 1980s and 1990s. While this trend levelled off in the first decade of the 21st century, it may re-emerge as a result of the difficult economic circumstances. There were several reasons for this trend (see Chapter 6). That said, a major advantage of contingent workers is that they are often much cheaper to employ than regular full-time employees because of lower wages and employee benefits. Also, organizations can dismiss contingent workers without demonstrating cause or providing severance pay; this provides flexibility and fits well with the classical management philosophy. Another reason classical organizations prefer these workers is that they are easier to manage because of their economic insecurity. Now that conditions have become more difficult for classical organizations, many are looking to contingent workers as one means to survive.

Some high-involvement organizations have increased their use of contingent workers for different reasons. For example, these workers strengthen employment security for the core workforce by serving as a buffer against demand fluctuations. In many high-involvement firms, though, contingent workers are compensated on the same basis as permanent employees, because the motivation for using them is not to cut costs.

A final trend is noncash employee recognition programs whereby desired employee behaviours are recognized in a variety of ways that do not involve cash bonuses or pay raises. These programs have developed partly in reaction to the perceived deficiencies of cash-based performance recognition programs, and partly because they are relatively inexpensive (see Chapter 3). By the early part of the 21st century, more than half of medium to large Canadian firms reported having noncash employee recognition programs in place.[23] However, rather than substituting noncash recognition for cash-based recognition programs, it appears that most firms are simply supplementing their cash-based performance pay with noncash employee recognition.

## SUMMARY

This chapter has provided you with a strategic framework for identifying the reward and compensation system that will best fit an organization's strategy and structure. The compensation system must be developed in the context of the total reward system which in turn must be developed in the context of the organization's managerial strategy.

The three managerial strategies—classical, human relations, and high involvement—each call for a different reward and compensation system. Because the most appropriate managerial strategy (and therefore the most appropriate reward and compensation system) for a given organization depends on certain key factors in that organization's context, it is important that you understand what these factors are and how they relate to managerial strategy.

Conditions in recent years have become less favourable for classical and human relations managerial strategies, and the shift to high involvement is changing the nature of reward systems. Organizations with a suboptimal managerial strategy can survive for a period of time, but only as long as market conditions are favourable or as long as none of their competitors is managed any better than they are. (Of course, if they have no competitors at all, as in the case of a monopoly, they may be able to survive for an indefinite time even with an inappropriate managerial strategy.)

Not all organizations have a conscious managerial strategy. In most organizations, managerial strategy is implicit rather than explicit. The degree of development and refinement of managerial strategies varies across firms. However, for some firms, there is no consistent managerial strategy at all. This means there is no ideal reward and compensation system for these firms. If there is no coherent managerial strategy, you cannot design a compensation system to support that strategy until you have sorted out the underlying organizational problems.

The next step on your journey to effective compensation systems is to add to your conceptual toolkit a framework that will help you understand how reward systems link to employee behaviour.

## KEY TERMS

analyzer business strategy

business strategy

classical managerial strategy

communication and information structure

contextual variables

contingency approach to organizational design

control structure

coordination and departmentation

decision-making and leadership structure

defender business strategy

domain

high-involvement managerial strategy

horizontal fit

human relations managerial strategy

job design

managerial strategy

mission

organization structure

organizational culture

prospector business strategy

task environment

values

vertical fit

vision

## DISCUSSION QUESTIONS

1. "If a compensation system works well for one business, that same compensation system should also work well for other businesses." Discuss whether this statement is true, and why or why not.

2. Using the concept of fit, discuss the types of compensation and rewards that would work best for each of the three managerial strategies.

3. What are the typical responses to employees' pay when organizations face external crisis such as COVID-19 and recessions? Are these the most effective in the long term? Why or why not?

## EXERCISES

1. Go to the website for the *Canadian HR Reporter* (www.hrreporter.com) and click on *Payroll*. From the stories that have been published in recent months, what seem to be the key themes and concerns in relation to compensation? What were the organizational compensation-related responses to the COVID-19 pandemic?

2. Take an organization that you know well, such as a current or former employer, and apply the template in Compensation Notebook 2.2 to determine the most appropriate managerial strategy for that firm. Does this match the managerial strategy actually in use? If not, why not? Do you agree with what the template indicates to be the best managerial strategy? Would you consider this firm to be an effective organization? Does the organization's reward system match its managerial strategy?

3. In a group of five or six people, share the results of your analysis from Exercise 2. Compare the organizations that were considered to be effective with those that were not. Were the firms that matched strategy with contextual variables rated better than those that did not? Discuss why or why not. If you find some organizations that seem effective despite a poor fit between contextual variables and managerial strategy, discuss why this might be.

1. Read *Case 2—The Fit Stop Ltd.* in the Appendix. Which managerial strategy would be most effective for this firm? Given what you know about Susan Superfit, which managerial strategy do you think she would prefer to use? Does this match your choice?

2. Read *Case 3—Multi-Products Corporation* in the Appendix. Which managerial strategy would be most effective for this firm? What reward and compensation strategy would fit this managerial strategy? What problems might you encounter in using this managerial strategy?

3. Read *Case 4—Patriot Transportation Holding Inc.* in the Appendix. Patriot is having trouble recruiting truck drivers. To get as many ideas as possible for solving this problem, management has hired three different consultants. One is an adherent of the classical managerial strategy, one is an adherent of the human relations managerial strategy, and one is an adherent of the high-involvement managerial strategy. Each consultant works separately and provides a separate set of recommendations for solving the problem. Their recommendations include changes to both the compensation system and employees' work structure, but these changes are all different. Knowing what you do about the three managerial strategies, what do you think the recommendations of each consultant were? Which do you think would be the most effective solution?

## SIMULATION CROSS-REFERENCE

If you are using *Strategic Compensation: A Simulation* in conjunction with this text, you will find that the concepts in Chapter 2 are helpful in preparing the simulation.

## ENDNOTES

1. Ted Turnasella, "Aligning Pay with Business Strategies and Cultural Values," *Compensation and Benefits Review* 26, no. 5 (1994): 65.

2. Al-Karim Samnani and Parbudyal Singh, "Stop Chasing Best Practices: Focus on Fit for Your HR Function," *People and Strategy* 34, no. 1 (2011): 34–36; Mohan Thithe, *e-HRM: Digital Approaches, Directions & Applications* (New York, NY: Routledge, 2019)

3. Al-Karim Samnani and Parbudyal Singh, "Exploring the Fit Perspective: An Ethnographic Approach," *Human Resource Management* 52, no. 1 (2013): 123–44; Mohan Thithe, *e-HRM: Digital Approaches, Directions & Applications* (New York, NY: Routledge, 2019); Mollie Painter, Sareh Pouryousefi, Sally Hibbert, and Jo-Anna Russon, "Sharing Vocabularies: Towards Horizontal Alignment of Values-Driven Business Functions," *Journal of Business Ethics* 155, no. 4 (2019): 965–79.

4. Richard Daft and Ann Armstrong, *Organization Theory and Design*, First Canadian Edition (Toronto: Nelson Education, 2009); Sven Feurer, Monika C. Schuhmacher, and Sabine Kuester, "How Pricing Teams Develop Effective Pricing Strategies for New Products," *Journal of Product Innovation Management* 36, no. 1 (2019): 66–86; Monique Aubry and Melanie Lavoie-Tremblay, "Rethinking Organizational Design for Managing Multiple Projects," *International Journal of Project Management* 36, no. 1 (2018): 12–26.

5. Raymond E. Miles, *Theories of Management: Implications for Organizational Behavior and Development* (New York: McGraw-Hill, 1975); Anne M. Nicotera, *Origins and Traditions of Organizational Communication,* (New York, NY: Routledge, 2019)

6. Edward E. Lawler, *The Ultimate Advantage: Creating the High Involvement Organization* (San Francisco: Jossey-Bass, 1992); Peter Boxall and Keith Macky, "Research and Theory on High-Performance Work Systems: Progressing the High Involvement Stream," *Human Resource Management Journal* 19, no. 1 (2009): 3–23; Stephen Wood and Chidiebere Ogbonnaya, "High-Involvement Management, Economic Recession, Well-Being, and Organizational Performance," *Journal of Management* 44, no. 8 (2018): 3070–95.

7. Thomas A. Kochan and Paul Osterman, *The Mutual Gains Enterprise* (Cambridge, MA: Harvard Business School, 1994).

8. Gordon Betcherman, Kathryn McMullen, Norm Leckie, and Christina Caron, *The Canadian Workplace in Transition* (Kingston: IRC Press, 1994); Mercedes Ubeda-Garcia, Enrique Claver-Cortes, Bartolome Marco-Lajara, Patrocinio Zaragoza-Saez, and Francisco Garcia-Lillo, "High Performance Work System and Performance: Opening the Black Box Through the Organizational Ambidexterity and Human Resource Flexibility," *Journal of Business Research* 88 (2018): 397–406.

9. John Case, *Open Book Management: The Coming Business Revolution* (New York: Harper Business, 1995); Faisal Abdulkarim Alkhamis, "The Mediating Role of Employee Job Performance In the Impact of Open Book Management Dimensions on Customer Satisfaction," *Verslas: Teorija Ir Praktika* 19, no. 1 (2018): 157–65.

10. Stephen Wood, "High Commitment Management and Payment Systems," *Journal of Management Studies* 33, no. 1 (1996): 5–77.

11. Richard J. Long, "Gain Sharing, Hierarchy, and Managers: Are They Substitutes?" *Proceedings of the Annual Conference of the Administrative Sciences of Canada, Organization Theory Division* 15, no. 12 (1994): 5–60.

12. John Paul MacDuffie, "Human Resource Bundles and Manufacturing Performance: Organizational Logic and Flexible Production Systems in the World Automobile Industry," *Industrial and Labor Relations Review* 48, no. 2 (1995): 197–221.

13. Edgar H. Schein, *Organizational Culture and Leadership,* Third Edition (San Francisco, CA: Jossey-Bass, 2010), 17.

14. Randy Hodson, "Disorganized, Unilateral, and Participative Organizations: New Insights from the Ethnographic Literature," *Industrial Relations* 40, no. 2 (2001): 20–30; Donald Sull, Charles Sull, and James Yoder, "No One Knows Your Strategy—Not Even Your Top Leaders," *MIT Sloan Management Review* 59, no. 3 (2018): 1–6.

15. Raymond E. Miles and Charles Snow, *Organizational Strategy, Structure, and Process* (New York: McGraw-Hill, 1978).

16. Michael E. Porter, *Competitive Strategy: Techniques for Analyzing Industries and Competitors* (New York: Free Press, 1980).

17. Jinan Aref Hajir, Bader Obeidat, Mahmoud Al-Dalameh, and Ra'ed Masa'deh, "The Role of Knowledge Management Infrastructure in Enhancing Innovation at Mobile Tele-communications Companies in Jordan," *European Journal of Social Sciences* 50, no. 3 (2015): 313–30.

18. Charles Perroe, "A Framework for Competitive Analysis of Organizations," *American Sociological Review* 32 (1967): 194–208; Rajan Yadav, Sujeet Kumar Sharma, and Ali Tarhini, "A Multi-Analytical Approach to Understand and Predict the Mobile Commerce Adoption," *Journal of Enterprise Information Management* 29, no. 2 (2016): 222–37.

19. Joan Woodward, *Industrial Organization: Theory and Practice* (London: Oxford University Press, 1965). Hongyi Mao, Shan Liu, Jinlong Zhang, and Zhaohua Deng, "Information Technology Resource, Knowledge Management Capability, and Competitive Advantage: The Moderating Role of Resource Commitment," *International Journal of Information Management* 36, no. 6 (2016): 1062–74.

20. Marc S. Mentzer, "Corporate Downsizing and Profitability in Canada," *Canadian Journal of Administrative Sciences* 13, no. 3 (1996): 237–50; Tim Goesaert, Matthias Heinz, and Stijn Vanormelingen, "Downsizing and Firm Performance from German Firm Data," *Industrial and Corporate Change* 24, no. 6 (2015): 1443–72; Norifumi Kawai, "Does Downsizing Really Matter? Evidence from Japanese Multinationals in the European Manufacturing Industry," *The International Journal of Human Resources Management* 26, no. 4 (2015): 501–19; James P. Guthrie and Deepak K. Datta, "Dumb and Dumber: The Impact of Downsizing on Firm Performance as Moderated by Industry Conditions," *Organization Science* 19, no. 1 (2008): 108–23.

21. Terry H. Wagar, "Exploring the Consequences of Workforce Reduction," *Canadian Journal of Administrative Sciences* 15, no. 4 (1997): 300–09; Tim Goesaert, Matthias Heinz, and Stijn Vanormelingen, "Downsizing and Firm Performance from German Firm Data," *Industrial and Corporate Change* 24, no. 6 (2015): 1443–72.

22. Edward E. Lawler, *The Ultimate Advantage: Creating the High Involvement Organization* (San Francisco: Jossey-Bass, 1992); Rebecca R. Kehoe and Patrick M. Wright, "The Impact of High-Performance Human Resources Practices on Employees' Attitudes and Behaviours," *Journal of Management* 39, no. 2 (2013): 366–91.

23. Richard J. Long and John L. Shields, "From Pay to Praise? Non-Cash Employee Recognition in Canadian and Australian Firms," *International Journal of Human Resource Management* 21, no. 8 (2010): 1145–72.

# A BEHAVIOURAL FRAMEWORK FOR COMPENSATION

## Learning Outcomes

AFTER READING THIS CHAPTER, YOU SHOULD BE ABLE TO:

- Identify the types of reward problems that can afflict organizations.
- Define the three key employee behaviours desired by employers.
- Identify three key job attitudes and explain their roles in determining employee behaviour.
- Describe the causes and consequences of reward dissatisfaction.
- Explain how to generate membership behaviour.
- Outline the process through which task behaviour is motivated.
- Explain how to generate organizational citizenship behaviour.
- Discuss the role that managerial strategy plays in determining the types of employee attitudes and behaviour needed by an organization.
- Describe the implications of the behavioural framework for designing effective reward systems.

## FAIR PROCESSES? DON'T BANK ON IT

Wells Fargo faced a rough few years dealing with the repercussions of their fraudulent actions. From 2016 onwards, the bank's misconduct was slowly uncovered.

Bank employees created 3.5 million unauthorized bank and credit card accounts without customers' knowledge. Even though bank accounts were classified as empty and closed, employees were caught transferring funds to new accounts, resulting in overdraft fees and harming credit scores. The bank illegally repossessed cars and charged customers for auto insurance that they didn't require. They defrauded small businesses by overcharging them for credit card transactions. Wells Fargo provided those small businesses with a 63-page contract, knowing that these companies would be ill-prepared to read the agreement in its entirety. Bank employees modified mortgages without approval from customers and illegally fined mortgage clients.

The Consumer Financial Protection Bureau discovered the wrongdoing and the story slowly emerged. The bank alleged that managers had no idea. They blamed low-level employees and fired over 5000 of them. These terminated employees now have a permanent stamp on their forehead when applying to new jobs: fraud.

But why would over 5000 employees individually participate in such unethical behaviour? Social science research claims that ethical behaviour is less about who you are and the values you stand for, and more about the situation to which you are subjected. Any company that has thousands of people partaking in the same behaviour must look at situational factors contributing to that behaviour.

What the bank conveniently didn't mention was their use of job insecurity, poverty-level wages, and unrealistic sales expectations combined with intense pressure. The bank didn't say that in 2010 this extreme pressure had already been an issue. In 2010, the bank urged employees to sell at least eight accounts to every customer. Ten years prior, the bank had encouraged employees to sell only three accounts to every customer.

Former bank employees characterized the atmosphere as a culture of pressure and fear. Wells Fargo used impossible sales expectations to practically demand employees to defraud customers. Workers were rewarded for aggressive sales tactics and written up, demoted, or fired if they did not meet sales targets. The only way to achieve their objectives were to engage in illegal tactics. Employees had to work overtime and weekends to come even close to making what was expected of them.

Furthermore, employees were not given a liveable wage. They were faced with the choice of either making a living or being ethical. They were often told that if they did not reach their sales targets, they would "end up working for McDonald's."

Since this scandal emerged, Wells Fargo has had to pay over $1.7 billion in fines. However, according to the employees, the bank continues to mistreat their employees. Employees are still under intense pressure to receive their bonuses. Employees still feel there is no work–life balance. Although the bank increased the base minimum wage for their U.S. employees to $15 an hour in 2017, shortly afterward the bank terminated 265 000 employees and sent many of these jobs abroad. At the same time the CEO, Tim Sloan, received a $4.6 million raise, resulting in a salary of $17.6 million. His salary is 564 times more than a Wells Fargo bank employee.

Employees have organized a group called the Committee for Better Banks to force Wells Fargo to engage in fair practices. This committee provides actions for employees to take if they have been mistreated. The Committee for Better Banks is especially important considering the banking industry has the lowest rate of unionization in the United States.

The Wells Fargo fiasco is not an isolated incident in the banking industry. Nor is it specific to the United States. Such issues are occurring in Canada as well. There are allegations against TD Bank, for instance. TD employees have described the company culture as "poisoned," "stress-inducing," "insane," and "zero focus on ethics." Many TD workers have claimed they are on medical leave or have severe anxiety or depression as a result of pressure to upsell.

Extreme sales goals lead TD employees to neglect customer needs. It is difficult to help customers find the products they need while meeting sales targets. Managers have

*(continued)*

reportedly told TD employees to sell customers accounts without informing them of the fees associated with such accounts. The managers urge employees to make customers read the paperwork, knowing that they will not entirely read or understand the legal document.

Employees have admitted to breaking the law at the customer's misfortune. It is a frenzied attempt to meet the targets and not get fired. One teller who worked at the bank for over 20 years admitted to having increased customers' overdraft protection without the customers knowing. Another employee confessed to having raised lines of credit by a couple of thousand dollars without telling the customers. Such behaviour is a violation of the federal Bank Act.

Sources: Dave Johnson, "Banks Used Low Wages, Job Insecurity to Force Employees to Commit Fraud," *Huffpost*, August 20, 2016; Michael Sainato, "Wells Fargo Employees Say Little Has Changed Since Fake Accounts Scandal," *The Guardian*, January 4, 2019; Jackie Wattles, "Wells Fargo 20-Month Nightmare," *CNN Business*, April 24, 2018; Anthony Bolante, "How Wells Fargo Encouraged Employees to Commit Fraud," *The Conversation*, October 6, 2016; Eric Johnson, "'We Do It Because Our Jobs Are At Stake': TD Bank Employees Admit to Breaking the Law for Fear of Being Fired," *CBC*, March 10, 2017.

# INTRODUCTION TO REWARD SYSTEMS AND BEHAVIOUR

On the surface, the reward systems for banks, as discussed above, made sense. Employees were encouraged to be aggressive in their deals to attain targets. The financial institutions got what they wanted—high sales. However, there were adverse consequences and unanticipated problems. The reward systems drove undesirable behaviours—and illegalities.

Similar problems occur in other organizations, as the following examples show.

- To boost book sales in its college division, a major Canadian publisher introduced a plan that would pay bonuses to its sales reps if annual sales exceeded a target set by the regional sales manager. Sales reps played no role in setting the targets, which were set high in order "to really motivate employees," according to the vice president of marketing. The plan seemed to have no effect on sales and was eliminated within a year.

- A manufacturer of consumer products had the following system for rewarding its three main units: marketing was evaluated on volume of sales, production was evaluated on production costs, and research and development was evaluated on number of patents registered. Not only did this system cause enormous conflict between the three units, but also the company also found it almost impossible to bring new products to the market on a timely basis. Those that did reach the market either did not achieve customer acceptance or were not profitable.

- For years, purchasing officers at Canadian National Railways (CN Rail) were evaluated on the basis of how much they had reduced item costs in comparison to the previous year. For example, one key part of a boxcar is the axle, a round bar of steel on which the wheels are mounted. Thousands of axles were being used in a year, which meant that a purchasing officer who could reduce the cost of each axle by even two or three percent was regarded as a hero. It turns out that the axles would have lasted much longer had they been ordered slightly thicker and had slightly more been spent on them. Yet under the reward system, any purchasing officer who bought the longer-lasting axles would have been penalized.

- A Canadian auto retailer wanted to create a more cooperative "team" atmosphere among its sales staff by having experienced sales personnel take more responsibility for training new sales staff. Compensation for sales staff was straight commission on volume sold. Management couldn't understand why, despite their exhortations, senior sales personnel showed little interest in training new sales staff.

These examples illustrate that reward systems can have a powerful effect on behaviour and that the behaviour we get is not always the behaviour we want.

Why do people behave as they do? Why do they often not behave as we want them to? How can we get them to behave as the organization needs them to behave? And how can reward systems influence their behaviour? Every manager knows that the answers to these questions are not obvious. But finding those answers is crucial for designing an effective reward system. This chapter develops a conceptual framework that can be used to find the answers.

We will start by identifying three main categories of reward problems: (1) failure to produce desired behaviour, (2) production of desired behaviour but with undesirable consequences, and (3) production of reward dissatisfaction. Then we will look at three types of desired employee behaviour: (1) membership behaviour, (2) task behaviour, and (3) organizational citizenship behaviour.

Because reward systems can generate these desired behaviours only through their impact on employee attitudes, we will focus on the job attitudes that generally lead to these behaviours. We will then examine the causes and potential consequences of reward dissatisfaction.

Next, we will examine each of the three desired employee behaviours and consider how the reward system can help generate these behaviours. The culmination of this will be a set of specific implications for designing reward systems that will generate the employee behaviour the organization needs and wants.

## TYPES OF REWARD PROBLEMS

A multitude of reward problems can arise. To gain a clearer understanding of them, we can organize them into three basic types:

1. failure to produce the desired behaviour,
2. production of the desired behaviour but with undesirable consequences, and
3. production of reward dissatisfaction.

## FAILURE TO PRODUCE DESIRED BEHAVIOUR

A reward system often has no impact on behaviour, as in the case of the publisher described above. (While we don't know the details, a possible cause was that the sales targets were set too high, and we know that unrealistic goals do not motivate behaviour.) Obviously, if the behaviour the organization needs isn't occurring, or if it is occurring only among certain employees, this can be a serious problem. And there is an even more harmful variation of this problem: in some cases, the reward system not only fails to produce the desired behaviour, but also produces undesirable behaviour, or behaviour that has negative consequences. For example, the Green Giant reward system (see Chapter 1) did not result in significantly cleaner product, but it did result in higher costs.

## PRODUCTION OF DESIRED BEHAVIOUR WITH UNDESIRABLE CONSEQUENCES

Another type of problem occurs when the reward system generates the desired behaviour, but with unanticipated negative consequences. CN Rail's reward system reduced per-item purchasing costs, but it also discouraged any search for potentially more valuable approaches to cost savings.

The reward system at the consumer products manufacturer discussed above did motivate marketing to increase sales, production to minimize costs, and research and development (R&D) to develop new products. However, while the R&D department did secure many patents, most of these products either had no market or were difficult to manufacture. The production department did minimize costs, but it did so by using poor-quality materials and oversimplifying the product. Marketing did try to sell these products but found that the only way to do so was by making outlandish promises or by cutting prices, which put even more pressure on the production department to reduce costs. These behaviours resulted in low cooperation and high conflict among the departments. Marketing blamed the R&D department for developing "useless" products and production for producing poor-quality products. R&D blamed production for destroying "good product designs" and blamed marketing for not knowing how to sell. Production accused both R&D and marketing of incompetence.

In short, the more that each department tried to meet its own reward goals, the less successful the company was. By rewarding mutually incompatible goals in a situation where interdependence is high and cooperation is essential, the company was guaranteeing failure. Thus, a reward system that looks reasonable when viewed in a narrow (departmental) context may in fact be very damaging for the organization as a whole.

A slight variation of this problem occurs when the reward system does generate the desired behaviours with no obvious negative consequences but also suppresses other desirable behaviours that are not measured or rewarded. The case of the auto retailer illustrates this problem. If the sales staff are paid only based on their individual sales, why would they want to spend time training possible competitors? When an organization rewards only one aspect of a job, is it really surprising that the other aspects are neglected?

Why, then, do companies reward only certain aspects of a job? As many studies have shown, companies tend to reward job aspects that are easy to measure—aspects that are highly visible and for which objective data are available—while hoping that employees will also perform job tasks that are not measured or rewarded.[1] In fact, some conscientious employees may perform all the desired job aspects, but if they do, it is in spite of the reward system, not because of it.

## PRODUCTION OF REWARD DISSATISFACTION

A final type of problem is not related specifically to any single aspect of the reward system but is potentially very serious. When employees believe the rewards they receive are not consistent with the contributions they are making to the organization, or when they believe the reward system is unfair, they will experience *reward dissatisfaction*. Reward dissatisfaction can have a variety of negative consequences, such as poor work performance, high turnover, poor customer service, and even employee dishonesty. Because reward dissatisfaction can be such a serious problem, its causes and consequences will be examined in depth later in the chapter.

# DESIRED REWARD OUTCOMES

Before examining the causes and consequences of reward dissatisfaction, we need to focus briefly on the other side of the coin—what outcomes *should* the reward system produce, and how can we produce them?

## THREE KEY EMPLOYEE BEHAVIOURS

An effective reward system should not only avoid causing undesirable behaviour but also promote desired behaviour. There are three general sets of behaviours most organizations find desirable.

1. **Membership behaviour** occurs when employees decide to join and remain with a firm.
2. **Task behaviour** occurs when employees perform the specific tasks that have been assigned to them.
3. **Organizational citizenship behaviour** occurs when employees voluntarily undertake special behaviours beneficial to the organization that go beyond simple membership and task behaviour, such as extra effort, high cooperation with others, high initiative, high innovativeness, extra customer service, and a general willingness to make sacrifices for the good of the organization. Organizational citizenship behaviour is sometimes known as "contextual performance" in contrast with "task performance."[2]

## THREE KEY EMPLOYEE ATTITUDES

So how do you create a reward system that will generate these behaviours? This question is complicated by the fact that reward systems do not affect human behaviour directly. They first affect employee perceptions and attitudes, which then drive behaviour. This brings us to another question: What are the key employee attitudes that need to be created to generate the employee behaviour we desire?

The three key attitudes are outlined below.

1. **Job satisfaction**, which can be defined as the attitude one holds toward one's job and workplace, either positive or negative.
2. **Work motivation**, which can be defined as the attitude one holds toward good job performance, either positive or negative. Essentially, it is the strength of an employee's desire to perform his or her duties well.
3. **Organizational identification**, which has three interrelated elements: a sense of shared goals and values with the organization, a sense of membership or belonging, and an intention to remain a member of the organization. The third aspect of organizational identification is sometimes known as *organizational commitment*.

Each of these attitudes can lead to behaviour that is beneficial to the organization in different ways. Job satisfaction leads to membership behaviour, work motivation leads to task behaviour, and organizational identification leads to citizenship behaviour, although it also contributes to the other two behaviours. **Figure 3.1** illustrates these relationships.

**membership behaviour**
Occurs when employees decide to join and remain with a firm.

**task behaviour**
Occurs when employees perform the tasks that have been assigned to them.

**organizational citizenship behaviour**
Occurs when employees voluntarily undertake special behaviours beneficial to the organization.

**job satisfaction**
The attitude one holds toward one's job and workplace.

**work motivation**
The attitude one holds toward good job performance.

**organizational identification**
A sense of shared goals and belonging, and the desire to remain a member of the organization.

FIGURE 3.1

How Rewards Affect Employee Behaviour

You will notice that Figure 3.1 has arrows leading from organizational identification to both job satisfaction and motivation. That is because organizational identification can have a positive impact on each of these elements. For example, a sense of membership and belonging can help satisfy social needs, which then enhances job satisfaction. A sense of shared goals and the positive group norms that develop from shared goals can increase employee motivation.

But wait a minute. Isn't there an arrow missing? Shouldn't job satisfaction also increase motivation and task behaviour? In the past, many people believed that job satisfaction was virtually synonymous with work motivation. But we now know that this is not true.

Satisfied, happy workers are not necessarily more productive workers, but they are less likely to quit, be absent, or submit grievances, and they are more likely to be pleasant with other employees and customers. Satisfied employees also suffer less work stress, which in turn reduces errors and accidents and produces fewer health problems, consequently reducing absenteeism.

Because of low turnover rates, organizations with high job satisfaction have lower recruiting and training costs and more knowledgeable employees, who more often develop cordial relationships with customers than employees in firms with low job satisfaction. So, although high job satisfaction does not automatically bring high productivity, it can bring several real benefits. As with the other two key employee attitudes, the reward system can have a major impact on job satisfaction.

**Figure 3.2** summarizes some of the specific consequences of each job attitude. As discussed, the consequences of job satisfaction include decreased turnover, absenteeism, and grievances; reduced stress; and positive group norms. Work motivation leads to job effort, which should in turn lead to task performance. Organizational identification leads to positive group norms, cooperative behaviour, innovative behaviour, and increased job effort, along with decreased turnover, absenteeism, and grievances.

FIGURE 3.2

**Key Employee Attitudes and their Consequences**

Clearly, all three of these attitudes are desirable. But exactly how important they are to a given firm varies enormously. Consider the example of Koch Foods (Compensation Today 2.4 in Chapter 2). From Koch management's point of view, employee job satisfaction and organizational identification would be nice to have, but certainly not essential. The firm doesn't need innovative or cooperative behaviour from its employees, nor does management care if turnover is high because employee replacement costs are so low. The company doesn't even need particularly high motivation because the "chain" dictates productivity.

The chicken plant needs enough physical job effort from each employee to keep up with the chain. No more, no less. In return for this minimal expectation, the firm provides minimal rewards. The reward system only needs to accomplish a sufficient flow of new employees to replace those who quit. Under current conditions, the company's reward system—while very simple and exclusively extrinsic—appears to be appropriate. It fits the firm's classical managerial strategy, which in turn fits the firm's contextual variables.

Of course, minimal employee contributions are inadequate for firms whose reward systems need to be much more sophisticated to promote the full range of desired behaviours. As a general rule, the more complex the desired behaviour—and the higher the performance level required—the more complex the reward system will have to be.

Compensation Today 3.1 illustrates this point further by describing the multifaceted reward system at Toyota Motors. For Toyota, all three job attitudes are important. High job satisfaction is important because the firm wants to develop a stable and loyal workforce with cohesive work teams. Employee motivation is important because Toyota expects very high employee job performance. Organizational identification is important because the firm depends on employee initiative for constantly improving the production process and on employee self-control to reduce the need for costly inspection and supervision. Positive group norms are also important to motivate and direct employee behaviour. As this example shows, it takes a complex combination of extrinsic and intrinsic rewards to produce the kinds of attitudes and behaviours Toyota needs for its high-involvement managerial strategy to work.

By now it should be apparent that the three managerial strategies will require different behaviours and different attitudes, so let us summarize here. Classical organizations need only provide sufficient rewards to create some degree of membership behaviour. They don't really need job satisfaction because very little membership behaviour is really needed. Motivation for task behaviour can be achieved through rewards tied directly to the needed behaviours, or through the use of control systems, with the underlying threat of dismissal providing the basic motivation. Classical organizations pay a price for not having job and reward satisfaction or organizational identification, but they are structured to minimize this price.

In contrast, human relations organizations rely on job satisfaction and positive work norms and must ensure that they have equitable reward systems that generate job satisfaction and a substantial degree of commitment. They depend on high membership behaviour and adequate task behaviour. Organizational identification, while desirable, is not essential because a high degree of organizational citizenship behaviour is not essential.

Because high-involvement organizations typically require the most complex behaviour from their employees and the highest level of performance, they generally require the most complex reward systems. They need to generate all three job attitudes and behaviours. The key job attitude for them is organizational identification, which generates the organizational citizenship behaviour so important to these firms and plays a major role in generating membership and task behaviour. Work motivation needs to be high. And job satisfaction must also be high enough to help generate the high membership behaviour that the firm needs. Clearly, a key element in maintaining these attitudes is employee satisfaction with the reward system.

### REWARDS SUPPORT STRATEGY AT TOYOTA

At its Kentucky assembly plant, Toyota uses a carefully conceived reward system to support its managerial strategy, which focuses on three central concepts: employee loyalty and commitment to the firm, teamwork, and high performance. So how do you create the attitudes necessary to generate these behaviours?

The reward system includes all three compensation components: base pay, indirect pay, and performance pay. Base pay is reasonable, but not high for the industry. But to create a feeling of cohesion among production workers, all employees receive the same pay once they have completed 18 months of service. A production team member reportedly earns $25 an hour at the plant in Georgetown, Kentucky. Toyota provides an extensive array of benefits to employees, including childcare. The childcare centre offers round the clock accommodations to children of parents who work early mornings or late nights. Kids are offered outdoor learning areas, developmental and vision screening twice a year, and opportunities to learn about healthy eating and exercise. However, these benefits are not out of line for the auto industry, which is famous for the benefits its unions have won.

What is unusual is that benefits are structured identically for all employees, from assembly workers to the plant manager. There are no executive dining rooms, preferred parking, or private offices for executives. The company believes that egalitarianism is necessary to avoid the division between workers and managers that is so common in this highly unionized industry. (Toyota employees have never voted to unionize.)

Toyota purposely deemphasizes cash rewards. Most companies within the United States have much more complex systems of performance evaluation and performance pay. When Toyota uses performance pay, it is not based on the individual. For example, annual bonuses, based on company performance, make up a big chunk of earnings for all employees. As a decentralized strategy to problem solving and empowering workers, special award money is distributed to groups or teams that have made suggestions that result in safety, cost, or quality improvements. This money is distributed equally among group members and usually consists of gift certificates that can be used at local retailers. The purpose of this program is threefold: to make sure this money simply doesn't get lost in the paycheque, to create family involvement, and to make the reward more tangible. For example, every time employees look at their new flat-screen TV, purchased with these certificates, they will be reminded why they received it. In addition, PT (personal touch) money is made available to team leaders to support team social activities, such as a summer picnic, monthly team lunches, or trips to ball games.

As a part of its reward strategy, the company offers numerous rewards beyond compensation, one being job security. Management has fostered a relationship where employees can suggest process improvement ideas because streamlining their work will not eliminate their jobs. According to Terry Besser in a *Journal of Management Studies* article, "Of all the rewards an organization can offer, the one which was seen as most important by nearly all my informants was the job security offered them by Toyota. Every American interviewee mentioned job security in one form or another as either the reason they took a job with Toyota and/or the reason they would remain, even if offered a better paying job."

Another key pillar of the reward system is training and promotion opportunities. Toyota has partnered with Bluegrass Community and Technical College in creating a program where students can earn an associate degree. However, their only classes occur at Toyota's manufacturing plant. Almost all the students receive a job at the plant once they graduate. The company also has a promote-from-within policy and invests heavily in training for its employees. Toyota focuses on bringing in top calibre employees with the potential to grow and develop. However, to keep them interested in what is essentially routine and repetitive work is a challenge. Toyota deals with this challenge by providing job enrichment, cross training, team-based decision making, job rotation, and the possibility of advancement to other jobs.

Finally, there are a number of recognition rewards, such as plaques for a perfect safety record. Toyota hosts a volunteer-of-the-year recognition dinner. These rewards are valued by employees for the symbolic meaning behind them rather than for any economic value. But they must be seen in the context of the total reward system. As one observer notes: "Certainly, these tokens alone would be insufficient, perhaps even insulting to employees. However, in conjunction with the other rewards already discussed, they encourage employees to believe that they will not be 'fools for busting their butts for the company.'" All the components of the reward system tie into the key competitive competency of Toyota: developing employees.

The result of all this? A tight knit, team-oriented workplace, with very low turnover, high productivity, and high quality. These characteristics have served Toyota well, helping the company to survive the financial meltdown of 2008–09 without needing to resort to the taxpayer-funded bailouts that other auto firms needed to survive the economic crisis. In fact, Toyota's U.S. plants have been so successful that by 2013 all of them—including the Kentucky plant—had been expanded. The company invested $1.33 billion in Toyota manufacturing in Kentucky, the second largest in state history. By 2015, the Kentucky plant began production of the first U.S.-assembled Lexus, adding 50 000 vehicles to its current annual capacity of 500 000. In total, approximately 10 million vehicles have rolled off the Kentucky plant assembly line. The plant provides full-time employment to around 10 000 people and has 350 American suppliers with over 100 located in Kentucky. A study by the Center for Automotive Research has determined that Toyota Kentucky supports around 30 000 jobs in the state, either directly or indirectly.

*(continued)*

In 2016, consumers classified Toyota as the number one retail brand for the fifth year in a row. Toyota Camry was the best-selling car in America for 15 consecutive years. In 2016, Toyota also achieved another all time high in North American vehicle production. In 2017, Toyota was named by *Fortune* as one of the world's most admired companies and rated number one motor vehicle company for the third consecutive year. In 2019, the company announced that Toyota would invest an additional $238 million in its Kentucky plant and add two vehicles to the production line. In the end, Toyota will exceed its 2017 promise of a $10 billion investment over five years in the United States.

CEO of Toyota Motor North America, Jim Lentz, claims, "Our success is driven by the talent and dedication of the men and women who manufacture our products here in the U.S."

Adapted from Terry L. Besser, "Rewards Support Strategy at Toyota," *Journal of Management Studies* 34, no. (1995): 383–99. Copyright © 1995 Blackwell Publishing Ltd.; *Toyota Kentucky: The Official Website of TMMK*, toyotageorgetown.com/; "Georgetown/Scott County 2017 Community Profile," *Georgetown/Scott Country Chamber of Commerce*; "Toyota Reports December 2016 and Year-End Sales," *Toyota Kentucky*, January 4, 2017; "Toyota Production in North America Exceeds 2 Million Again in 2016," *Toyota Kentucky*, January 19, 2017; "Toyota Announces Record $1.33 Billion Investment in Kentucky Plant," *Toyota Kentucky*, April 10, 2017; Carolyn Tribble Greer, "Toyota to Invest $238M in Kentucky Plant, Add Two Vehicles," *Louisville Business First*, March 14, 2019; Jeffrey K. Liker and Michael Hoseus, "Human Resource Development in Toyota Culture," *International Journal of Human Resources Development and Management* 10, no. 1 (2009): 34–50; Brad Power, "How Toyota pulls Improvement from the Front Line," *Harvard Business Review*, June 24, 2011; "Toyota North America Salaries in Georgetown, KY," www.glassdoor. ca/Salary/Toyota-North-America-Georgetown-Salaries-EI_IE3544.0,20_IL.21,31_IC1137675.htm?countryRedirect=true; Maricar Santos, "5 Fabulous and Inspiring Onsite Daycares," *Working Mother*, December 16, 2016; Emily Hanford, "A Company Short on Skilled Workers Creates Its Own College-Degree Program," *American Radioworks*, September 17, 2014; Jennifer Peryam, "TMMK Employees Recognized for Volunteer Work," *News-Graphic*, July 31, 2018; Jayanth Jayaram, Ajay Das, and Mariana Nicolae, "Looking beyond the obvious: Unraveling the Toyota production system," *International Journal of Production Economics* 128, no. 1 (2010): 280–91.

# CAUSES AND CONSEQUENCES OF REWARD DISSATISFACTION

Reward dissatisfaction can have many undesirable consequences for organizations. But first, what causes reward dissatisfaction?

## CAUSES OF REWARD DISSATISFACTION

As **Figure 3.3** illustrates, reward dissatisfaction has four main causes:

1. violation of the psychological contract,
2. perceived inequity,
3. relative deprivation, and
4. lack of organizational justice.

### Violation of the Psychological Contract

When people decide to join a firm, they do so based on their expectations about the rewards they will receive and the contributions they will have to make. This is known as their **psychological contract**.[3] Similarly, an organization hires someone based on the expectation that the individual will make certain contributions to the organization, in return for certain rewards. In some cases, these psychological contracts include legally enforceable contracts that spell out the rewards to be provided and the contributions to be made. In most cases, they do not.

**psychological contract**
Expectations about the rewards offered by a given job and the contributions necessary to perform the job.

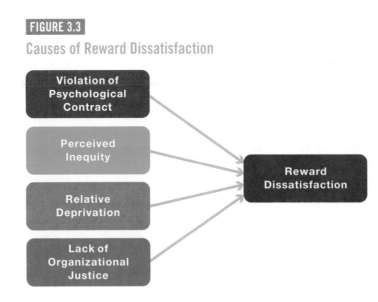

**FIGURE 3.3**

Causes of Reward Dissatisfaction

Violation of Psychological Contract

Perceived Inequity

Relative Deprivation

Lack of Organizational Justice

Reward Dissatisfaction

When an employee accepts an offer and joins a firm, problems with the psychological contract can arise for two main reasons: (1) there has not been accurate communication about the rewards that will be provided and/or the contributions that are required, and these turn out to be different from what the employee expects; and (2) the employer unilaterally changes the "contract" in a way that the employee perceives as detrimental.

Researchers have labelled these two possibilities "incongruence" of expectations and "reneging," and argue that either can lead to a perceived violation of the psychological contract.[4] They cite evidence that perceived violations can cause employees to have less trust in their employer, decreased job satisfaction, reduced citizenship behaviour, decreased work performance, and can lead to increased turnover, theft, or even sabotage.

Psychological contracts are related to reward dissatisfaction in at least two other ways. First, employee perceptions of the fairness of the "contract" may change. That is, employees may come to see the original contract as unfair (even though it is being honoured) in the light of new information they receive. Second, employees may feel compelled to accept a contract even though they believe it to be unfair right from the outset. In each of these cases, reward dissatisfaction will likely occur.

Spurred by the economic recession that began in 2008, many firms reduced aspects of their reward structures (including indirect pay) in violation of longstanding psychological contracts. Not surprisingly, research has shown that their doing so had a negative impact on the psychological contract.[5] However, the impact of these violations depended on the nature of the firm. For human relations firms, the costs of contract violations can be especially high because employee satisfaction and trust in management are the glue that holds these organizations together. These problems will be particularly severe if the cuts appear to be unnecessary—if, for example, cuts are made even in the face of acceptable company profitability.

Compensation Today 3.2 illustrates what can happen when an organization promises a fundamentally new type of psychological contract but is then perceived to be violating these promises.

## VIOLATING THE PSYCHOLOGICAL CONTRACT AT CAMI

Perceived violation of the psychological contract helped derail an attempt to create a collaborative union–management relationship at CAMI Inc., a joint GM–Suzuki venture that was established in 1988 to manufacture small cars in Ingersoll, Ontario. Before the new plant opened, CAMI agreed to a voluntary recognition of the Canadian Auto Workers (CAW) union. The union agreed to accept somewhat lower wages and benefits than were offered by the "big three" North American automakers (GM, Ford, Chrysler) in return for a nonclassical approach from management in which workers would be treated with respect and dignity and their ideas and inputs would be valued.

To reinforce this image of equality, time clocks, executive parking spaces, and executive cafeterias were eliminated, and production was organized into teams. Hourly employees were known as production associates, team leaders, and maintenance associates. However, despite the titles, relatively few changes were made to the nature of the work itself. Perhaps most significantly, no changes were made to the usual reward system for hourly employees, and no rewards were provided for productivity or performance. Part of the reason may have been that CAW is philosophically opposed to performance pay, although it is not clear whether the company actually pushed for group or organizational performance rewards.

Consequently, despite all the symbolic changes, workers soon came to believe that the promise of a fundamentally different relationship was an empty one, and that all the changes were merely superficial, oriented only toward manipulating workers to produce more. Workers pointed to the extremely lean staffing levels which put great pressure on them to produce.

As a result of this perceived violation of the psychological contract and the nonappearance of the intrinsic rewards the employees were expecting, union–management relations became bitter, culminating in 1992 in the first strike at any Japanese "transplant" in North America. Prominent among the strike issues were the demand that workloads be reduced and that the wage/benefit gap between CAMI and other "big three" plants be narrowed. The company made both concessions.

It appears that after the strike, a psychological contract emerged that was more in line with the North American auto industry; workers now believed that the firm was "just another car factory" and did not really expect treatment different from the industry norm. For a period of time, there were no major strikes and, in 1998, CAMI was selected as lead plant for the production of two new sport utility vehicles. However, this decision was likely prompted more by the plant's relatively new production technology than by any special union–management relationship.

The new psychological contract was one that pinned employer against employees. The mentality became "us" against "them." On May 30, 1999, workers refused to report to work in protest over the firing of a union steward involved in an altercation with a supervisor. The company responded by replacing the termination with a suspension, and work resumed.

For a brief period, the company and its employees appeared to have come to a mutual understanding and an acceptance of the psychological contract, and operations ran smoothly at the plant. In 2005, GM announced a $500 million investment in the CAMI plant so that it could retool and expand. In 2009, CAMI was reported to be one of the most efficient auto plants in North America and enjoyed an employee absenteeism rate of less than one percent. By 2012, demand for its products was so high that employees were working mandatory overtime just to keep up.

Since then, however, the relationship between employer and employee has been spiralling downward. The company continues to violate the trust of its employees. The "us" versus "them" mentality has resulted in ongoing discord.

In July 2017, over 400 employees were laid off as part of the production was moved to Mexico. Chairperson of CAMI's union, Mike Van Boekel stated, "Our members are furious, they are pissed off. We have been working six days a week for eight years, and now this. We have done everything they have asked of us. It is terrible."

In September 2017, employees at CAMI walked off the job due to job security issues. This walkout resulted in a 30-day strike. Employees wanted the contract to state that CAMI would have preferred production status for one of the primary vehicles, the Chevrolet Equinox. Employees further wanted job security and a wage increase to $36.12-an-hour for labourers and $42.27-an-hour for skilled trade workers by the end of the new four-year agreement. And finally, employees wanted $6000 in performance bonuses throughout the four-year deal.

Due to this strike, Magna International suspended the supply of parts to the CAMI facility. Sources say that the company was within days of closing the plant permanently before the strike ended. The strike cost CAMI $5 million dollars a day. However, a new four-year collective agreement was established. Employees were not promised salary increases, and the factory was not given preferred production status for the Equinox. (Instead, the job was sent to Mexico). However, the agreement ensured that employees would be strongly remunerated if the plant were to shut down. Furthermore, if a worker had 28 years of experience and the plant were to layoff employees, the employee would be paid until they reach 30 years of experience. Those working with 30 years of experience were entitled to a full pension.

In 2018, 25 laid-off employees were recalled. This recall was seen as a step in the right direction. CAMI also said that they would recall many more employees in 2019; however, this has not yet occurred. Even worse, in August 2019, CAMI announced that the company would have a temporary week-long layoff in the Fall 2019 for 2000 employees. Further "blackout" weeks are to be announced at a later date. Employees are ineligible for employment insurance. Van Boekel again expressed his opinion, "If you're a young family and you're married with kids, and you got a set paycheque, and it's gone, that hurts . . . even for single people." The company is currently not doing well financially.

Maybe the original psychological contract should have been maintained.

Sources: James Rinehart, Christopher Huxley, and David Robertson, *Just Another Car Factory?* (Ithaca: ILR Press, 1997); Norman De Bono, "Ingersoll Plant Ranks Fifth in a CAW Report on Productivity," *London Free Press Online*, January 28, 2009; Norman De Bono, "CAMI Ups Wow Factor with High-End Denali," *London Free Press Online*, March 20, 2012; Heather Rivers, "Twenty-Five Laid Off Cami Workers Recalled to Ingersoll Plant," *The London Free Press*, July 3, 2018; Norman De Bono, "Cami Ingersoll Slashing 600 Jobs, Moving Terrain Production to Mexico," *Chatham Daily News*, January 27, 2017; "Magna International Suspends Supply of Parts to CAMI," *CBC*, September 20, 2017; Jonathan Juha, "Sales Slump Prompts Rare Cami Fall Shutdown," *The London Free Press*, August 1, 2019; Norman De Bono, "GM Was Within Days of Shutting Ingersoll Plant for Good When Strike Ended, Sources Say," *Financial Post*, October 18, 2017; "Cami Deal Approved by Union, Even Without Job Guarantee," *St. Thomas Times Journal*, October 16, 2017; Norman De Bono, "Month-Long Strike Fails to Pry Pledge from GM to Keep Auto Plant Jobs in Canada," *National Post*, October 16, 2017; Geoff Robbins, "GM Workers at Ontario Cami Plant Approve New Contract," *The Globe and Mail*, October 16, 2017; "GM Announces Blackout Weeks at CAMI Plant in Ingersoll," *CBC News*, August 2, 2019.

## Perceived Inequity

Individuals use at least two perceptual screens when deciding whether the rewards/contributions balance is fair. The first is an internal calculus, based on their own valuations of the rewards received and contributions made. The second is a comparison with the rewards/contributions ratio of relevant others, a process explained by equity theory.[6]

Equity theory helps explain why, for example, a person making over $5 million a year doing a job they have coveted all their life may feel under-rewarded and threaten to quit, while another person earning $50 000 a year at a job they never particularly wanted is satisfied with their rewards. Sound far-fetched? Not if the first person is the highest scoring hockey player in the National Hockey League and the second is an accounting clerk with a high school education, employed by a firm that provides high job security. The accounting clerk may look around and see that most people with similar performance, education, and job security are earning less while the hockey player may see six players who scored fewer goals but have higher paycheques.

Equity theory also helps explain why if two employees working side by side at the same job, each making $50 000 per year, one may believe the arrangement is equitable and the other regards it as highly unfair. Why? The dissatisfied employee believes that their contribution is much greater than the contribution of the other employee and yet both are receiving the same rewards.

**equity theory**
Employees' base perceptions of equity (fairness) on a comparison of their rewards/contributions ratio to the ratios of others perceived as being similar.

The essence of equity theory is simple: people compare their own rewards/contributions ratio to the ratios of relevant others, mostly coworkers. When making this comparison, they are often more concerned about fairness than about the actual amount of rewards received. Research has found that employee satisfaction is determined more strongly by relative pay than by the absolute amount of pay[7] (much to the astonishment of economists!).

An important aspect of equity theory is the selection of the comparison "other." For example, the managers of a veterinary hospital at a Canadian university were surprised to learn that their technicians considered themselves underpaid, even though their pay and working conditions were considerably better than those of technicians employed by private veterinary hospitals. It turns out that instead of comparing themselves with their private sector colleagues, they were comparing their pay and working conditions with those of the professors and research scientists with whom they were working.

As another example, the gap between the earnings of rank-and-file employees and top executives has been widening dramatically in recent years. Between 1980 and 1995, executive pay in the United States increased from 42 times the average worker's pay to 141 times.[8] By the first decade of the 21st century, the average compensation of CEOs in publicly traded U.S. corporations was 521 times the average pay of a factory worker.[9] In 2014, Walmart paid its CEO $25.6 million. However, the median salary for an employee in the United States was $23 000. This is a pay ratio of 1133 to 1.[10]

Although workers may recognize that the job of a top executive is not similar to theirs, they may still believe it is inequitable for their CEO to be receiving 521 times as much as they do. This is particularly true when workers are asked to make sacrifices in their rewards while executives receive increases, as was the case toward the end of the first decade of the 21st century.

## Relative Deprivation

Research suggests that employees experience dissatisfaction with their pay level under six conditions.[11]

1. There is a discrepancy between the outcome they want and what they actually receive.
2. They see that a comparison "other" receives more than they do.
3. Past experience has led them to expect more than they now receive.
4. Expectations for achieving better outcomes are low.
5. They feel they are entitled to more.
6. They absolve themselves of personal responsibility for the lack of better outcomes.

To assess the validity of this theory, researchers examined four samples of American employees. While actual pay level did predict pay satisfaction (the higher the pay, the greater the satisfaction), in every sample, Crosby's six conditions were at least three times as important as the pay level in predicting pay satisfaction. Three conditions were of particular importance: social comparisons (condition 2, which is the basis of equity theory), the discrepancy between desired and actual pay (condition 1), and sense of entitlement (condition 5).[12] One's pay relative to a referent group predicts pay satisfaction just as much as actual pay levels. A feeling of significant inequity in pay among employees results in increased disobedience, disloyalty to the organization, disengagement, and intentions to quit.[13]

## Lack of Organizational Justice

The concept of organizational justice[14] is also useful for understanding how people judge the fairness of their rewards. Organizational justice has two main components that can be applied to compensation. **Distributive justice** is the perception that overall reward *outcomes* are fair, which is what equity theory is all about. **Procedural justice** is the perception that the *process* through which rewards are determined is fair. Unless people believe that both are fair, they will not feel that the reward system is fair.[15]

For example, suppose an individual has no faith in the process for determining rewards, regarding it as arbitrary or even capricious. Even if the actual outcome turns out to be fair in a given instance (distributive justice), the employee may still feel dissatisfied with the reward system, because he or she has little confidence that the outcome will be fair next time. On the other hand, if the employee believes that the process is fair (procedural justice), even if the reward outcome is less than the employee believes to be warranted, the employee will be less dissatisfied with that outcome.

Suppose a firm is facing extreme financial pressure and the total salary bill must be cut by 10 percent. Currently, company employees are fairly compensated relative to industry standards. If the employees view the process by which it is determined that a 10 percent cut is necessary as reasonable, and if the cut is distributed fairly, then they will be much less likely to feel reward dissatisfaction.

Research shows that distributive justice and procedural justice both have an impact on employee pay satisfaction but that distributive justice has a much stronger effect.[16] However, these findings are reversed when employee satisfaction with the supervisor is examined: apparently, employees strongly blame their supervisors for unfair pay procedures but only mildly blame them for perceived lack of fairness in the total amount of pay they receive (distributive justice).[17] For *job* satisfaction, both distributive justice and procedural justice also have an effect, but the latter has a stronger effect.[18] And when organizational commitment—the degree of attachment to the firm expressed by employees—is examined, only procedural justice has an impact.

In practical terms, procedural justice can be achieved if the pay system meets the following conditions.[19] The pay system must be:

- *consistent*—procedures are applied uniformly to different jobs and time periods,
- *free of bias*—personal interests do not enter into application of the procedures,
- *flexible*—there must be procedures for employees to appeal pay system decisions,
- *accurate*—the application of procedures must be based on factual information,
- *ethical*—accepted moral principles must guide the application of the procedures, and
- *representative*—all affected employees must have an opportunity to express their concerns, which the organization must consider seriously.

In general, when an organization has no choice but to change the psychological contract in ways that may be unfavourable to employees, it can reduce the negative impact by practising principles of both distributive and procedural justice.

# CONSEQUENCES OF REWARD DISSATISFACTION

What happens when employees experience reward dissatisfaction—when they perceive that the balance between rewards and contributions is unfair? **Figure 3.4** provides an illustration of some of the possible consequences. As can be seen, employees have two main options to redress the imbalance: increase the rewards they receive or reduce the contributions they make.

## Attempt to Increase Rewards

Employees who choose to try to increase their rewards have several options. One is to quit the organization and take a more rewarding job. Of course, this is an option only if a more rewarding job is available to the employee.

Another alternative is to simply demand higher extrinsic rewards, either individually (i.e., by asking for a raise) or collectively through a union (i.e., by demanding wage increases during the next round of collective bargaining). If no union exists, employees may attempt to form one if enough of them perceive an unfair rewards/contributions balance. If more rewards are forthcoming, then reward dissatisfaction is reduced, as Figure 3.4 illustrates. But if more rewards are not forthcoming, employees may simply quit, or they may attempt to even the balance in another way.

Some employees may resort to illicit means to increase their rewards, such as padding their expense accounts or stealing the firm's property or money. Employees may rationalize

**FIGURE 3.4**

Consequences of Reward Dissatisfaction

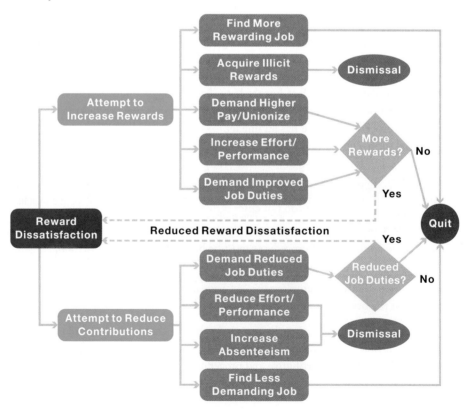

this behaviour by telling themselves that because the company is short-changing them, they are justified in "evening the score." In some sectors where rewards are low and many illicit reward opportunities exist (such as in retailing), employee theft can be a serious problem, as Compensation Today 3.3 and Compensation Today 3.4 show. In other cases, it may be the customer—not the employer—who is the victim, as Compensation Today 3.5 illustrates.

In some instances, employees may actually increase their work performance in response to reward dissatisfaction, but only if they are quite certain this will lead to significantly increased rewards. For example, if a promotion would provide a job in which rewards and contributions are balanced, and if increased performance has a high probability of leading to this promotion, then the employee may attempt to improve performance, even though, in the short run, this worsens the rewards/contributions imbalance. But this is not the most likely response to reward dissatisfaction.

Stealing is not a good way to address perceptions of inequity.

---

## COMPENSATION TODAY 3.3

### THE DEVIL MADE ME DO IT! (OR WAS IT REWARD DISSATISFACTION?)

"The devil made me do it!" This was a trademark line used by an old-time comedian to explain any malfeasance he committed. But it's not a very scientific explanation. The Global Retail Theft Barometer Study surveyed retailers in 24 countries and reported that retail theft cost the industry $128 billion in 2014 and $42 billion in the United States, representing 1.48 percent of sales. Among the loss, employee theft accounted for 42.9 percent, followed by shoplifting at 37.4 percent. American retailers also spent 0.42 percent of their sales in loss prevention programs and equipment. In Canada, retail theft costs businesses around $5 billion per year, according to the Retail Council of Canada. Employee theft alone costs Canadian businesses around $1.4 billion annually. Around 556 000 employee thefts in Canada remain undetected each year.

Rather than the devil, a sense of reward dissatisfaction or inequity can account for this situation. The relationship between reward dissatisfaction and employee theft is supported in academic literature. In an early study by Gerald Greenberg (1990) in manufacturing plants, employee theft was measured before, during, and after a temporary 10-week pay cut caused by a decrease in orders. Greenberg found that theft increased dramatically during the rollback but returned to normal levels once the normal pay level had been restored. Interestingly, the increase in theft was less pronounced in a plant where management explained the need for pay cuts in a candid way, and where they expressed concern for the well-being of employees.

Clara Xiaoling Chen and Tatiana Sandino (2012) studied a sample of retail chains to examine whether high levels of employee compensation can deter employee theft. Their study found that employee theft decreased when employees were paid higher relative to those in competing stores after controlling for employee characteristics, the monitoring environment, and the socioeconomic environment. They also found that coworkers are less likely to collude to steal inventory when they were paid relatively higher than competitors, and more likely to collude to steal inventory when paid lower relative to competitors. Among their findings, the authors discovered that employees were most likely to steal electronic equipment and clothing. They identified the reasons for employee theft as being due to financial need, work stress, and emotional issues. The authors concluded that employers could reduce theft by creating jobs that are challenging and of interest to

*(continued)*

employees, as well as by compensating employees fairly in an amount that employees perceive as equitable.

Art Markman, professor of psychology and marketing at the University of Texas and author of the article "The Psychology Behind Why People Steal Their Coworkers' Stuff" stated, "Generally, people like to think of themselves as basically good, and so they need to have some justification for the crime that allows them to preserve their self-image. One way to do that is to see the company as doing wrong to them in some way. If they feel poorly treated at work or underpaid, then they can justify the crime as a way of balancing the scales."

Sources: Jerald Greenberg, "Employee Theft as a Reaction to Underpayment Inequity: The Hidden Cost of Pay Cuts," *Journal of Applied Psychology* 75 (1990): 561–68; Laura Klepacki, "The High Cost of Retail Theft," *Chain Store Age*, December 30, 2014; Anne Fisher, "U.S. Retail Workers Are No.1 ... in Employee Theft," *Fortune*, January 26, 2015; C.X. Chen and T. Sandino, "Can Wages Buy Honesty? The Relationship Between Relative Wages and Employee Theft," *Journal of Accounting Research* 50, no. 4 (2012): 967–1000; Dana Wilkie, "Why is Workplace Theft on the Rise?" *SHRM*, March 4, 2019.

## COMPENSATION TODAY 3.4

### THAT'S THE WAY THE COOKIE CRUMBLES

Surveillance cameras and empty food wrappers left her red-handed. A Walmart employee in Indiana was charged with felony theft upon being found guilty of snacking on Oreos stolen from the store. The employee admitted that she did eat the cookies that night. She also said she had taken snacks from the shelves every week for four years (she had been working at Walmart for seven years). The employee apologized and said that she would never do this again. However, Walmart chose to terminate her. When police asked the woman why she stole from the store, the woman admitted that she could not afford to purchase the snacks. She had been earning $11.40 an hour.

Sources: Danielle Genet, "Walmart Employee Hit with Felony for Snacking on Store Oreos," *ABC News*, February 22, 2013.

## COMPENSATION TODAY 3.5

### BAD TIPPERS BEWARE!

Stories of what can happen when restaurant customers displease restaurant staff are legendary. While the most common response is tampering with the food (see the movie *Road Trip* for one particularly harrowing example!), one enterprising server at a Florida restaurant found a way of both punishing unreasonable diners and evening out her rewards/contributions balance. This server apparently "used a hand-sized electronic skimming device to scan customers' credit cards without their knowledge or consent." She then passed on this information to associates, who used it to make purchases (most of them relatively small) at nearby retailers.

However, the server was selective in who she scammed. She apparently scammed only those customers she considered to be overly demanding or who tipped too poorly, leaving most customers alone. Although the server must have known that her actions were illegal, in her own mind she probably saw herself as "only being fair," because she scammed only those customers she believed had short-changed her!

Source: Geffner, Marcie, "Waitress Scams Bad Tippers," Credit Card Blog: Bankrate.com, August 9, 2011.

Finally, some employees may seek to even the balance by increasing their intrinsic rewards. For example, they may seek improvements to their job duties such that their work becomes more intrinsically satisfying. Their reasoning may go like this: "I may not be getting the pay I deserve, but at least I will now have a job I enjoy doing."

## Attempt to Reduce Contributions

If rewards cannot be increased in some way that is significant to the employee, the employee may stay with the firm but redress the imbalance by formally or informally reducing his or her contributions. For example, employees may formally request that their job duties be reduced. They may ask to be relieved of duties that require them to spend weekends away from home or that cause them to put in unpaid overtime.

This reduced contribution may also take the form of reduced effort or longer coffee breaks. It may also involve reducing the quality of customer service or eliminating any voluntary work activities. Organizational citizenship behaviour is one of the first things to go when employees seek to reduce their contributions. This is a major reason that reward dissatisfaction can be particularly damaging to high-involvement organizations.

Reduced contributions can also take the form of increased absenteeism or negative employee behaviour, such as sabotage, as a means of evening the balance. Of course, such behaviours can result in dismissal but this may not be seen as much of a loss by the employee.

If the perceived imbalance cannot be evened out, then an employee may seek a less demanding job in a different firm, even if it pays the same as the current job. If able to find such a job, the employee will quit. And even if there are no other employment opportunities available, some employees may still quit, preferring unemployment to an intolerable imbalance and the stress it causes.

## Predicting Employee Reactions

But exactly how will a given employee respond to reward dissatisfaction? Individual reactions to reward dissatisfaction are difficult to predict because they depend on the personal characteristics and circumstances of the employee and on the specific characteristics of the situation. Are alternative jobs readily available? Can the employee afford to be unemployed? Does the employee have strong values about honesty or a strong work ethic that would prevent that person from using illicit rewards or reducing work performance?

In some instances, certain options are simply not available to employees, because organizations deliberately structure themselves to prevent them. For example, how could you reduce work performance at the chicken-processing plant? About the only way would be by not showing up for work. But if you don't show up, you simply don't get paid, so absenteeism doesn't get you very far.

At these classical firms there isn't much employees can do to increase rewards or decrease contributions, other than to threaten to quit. But that probably would not be effective either because these firms pay little price for high turnover. Clearly, classical organizations are much more able to tolerate reward dissatisfaction than are human relations or high-involvement firms.

The employer's response to the concerns the employee raises has a strong influence on what further actions the employee takes. Employee reactions also depend on their tolerance for stress and perceived inequity. For example, some employees have a high level of a personality trait known as **equity sensitivity**. Equity sensitivity is particularly prevalent in Millennials as compared to Baby Boomers and Gen Xers.[20] Such people focus on maximizing their personal rewards and are predisposed to perceiving inequity, be it imagined or real.[21] They are also more likely to resort to drastic action to reduce their perceived reward imbalance.

**equity sensitivity**
A personality trait that entails a high predisposition toward perceiving personal inequity.

The specific factor causing the reward dissatisfaction may help predict an employee's response to it. For example, the addition of new job duties may trigger demands for more pay in recognition of increased employee contribution. A wage cut may lead to increased illicit rewards, reduced job performance, or withdrawal from the organization, depending on the personal values of the employee. Reduction in job security may cause employees to seek employment where greater job security exists, or to seek higher pay to compensate for their increased risk of job loss.

## UNDERSTANDING MEMBERSHIP BEHAVIOUR

Why would anyone choose to pull chicken guts for a living? In fact, why would a person choose to engage in paid employment at all? Not everyone does. Of the potential Canadian labour force (defined as persons aged 15 or older), just under 64 percent are currently engaged in paid employment or self-employment, according to Statistics Canada. Currently, around six percent of the potential labour force are not employed but are seeking employment.[22]

That leaves about 30 percent of the potential labour force who choose not to seek paid employment at this time. Most of these people are retirees, students, stay-at-home spouses, or single parents. Overall, the proportion of adults not choosing employment has been declining steadily over the past 50 years, primarily due to women entering the labour force during the 1960s and 1970s. The proportion of adults not choosing employment may decrease even further now that mandatory retirement has been abolished. Clearly, more people are choosing to engage in paid employment than in the past.

So back to our question: Why do people work? Basically, people accept employment if they (1) have unsatisfied needs, (2) perceive employment as the best means to satisfy those needs, and (3) are able and willing to do the things the employment requires. People will accept a job if the inducements or rewards associated with it exceed the costs of the contributions they must make to secure and retain it. If several jobs are available that fit the above criteria, people tend to choose the one in which the value of the rewards exceeds the cost of the contributions to the greatest extent.

That part is simple. The complicated part is that people can value the same rewards, costs, and contributions differently, depending on their personal characteristics and circumstances. Thus, when three people are each presented with the same two job offers, one person may choose the first offer, another may choose the second, and a third person may reject both. (The model of behaviour presented later in this chapter sheds more light on how people make these decisions.)

### CAUSES OF MEMBERSHIP BEHAVIOUR

Assume that an individual has selected an employer. What factors determine whether she *stays* with that employer? Many factors can play a role, but two job attitudes—job satisfaction and organizational identification—are pivotal, as was discussed earlier in the chapter.

In general, job satisfaction develops when the job satisfies one's important needs. One well-known model suggests that job satisfaction has five main facets: pay, promotion, supervisors, coworkers, and the job itself.[23] Although the weighting of each of these facets varies from person to person, each likely plays some role in overall job satisfaction.

*Satisfaction with pay* means that economic rewards meet employee needs and are considered fair. *Satisfaction with promotion* is the extent to which advancement opportunities are available. *Satisfaction with supervisors* regards whether supervisors are seen as supportive, helpful, and fair in their treatment of employees. *Satisfaction with coworkers* is the extent to which coworkers are viewed as friendly, sociable, helpful, cooperative, and supportive. *Satisfaction with the job itself* is the extent to which the job provides various intrinsic rewards.

But there are other important components such as job security. Researchers have found that for most employees, the degree of job or employment security provided by the organization plays a major role in their level of job satisfaction.[24] Other important employee needs relate to work motivation, which is discussed later in this chapter.

Job satisfaction is a positive contributor to membership behaviour but is not the only factor. The strength of an individual's attachment to an organization is known as his or her level of organizational commitment. There are two main types of commitment: affective commitment and continuance commitment.

With affective commitment, individuals remain with the organization out of a sense of belongingness and loyalty and because they identify with the organization's goals. With continuance commitment, individuals stay with an organization because they would lose too much by quitting: they cannot find another job that would be comparable in terms of the ratio of rewards to contributions. Continuance commitment implies nothing about an employee's emotional attachment to the employer or that employee's job satisfaction. It is simply a hard-headed calculation that "I have no better alternatives available to me." It's possible for an individual to have high continuance commitment but extremely low levels of job satisfaction and affective commitment.

Research shows no relationship between continuance commitment and affective commitment[25] or between continuance commitment and job satisfaction.[26] However, affective commitment and job satisfaction *are* related: affective commitment and job satisfaction both have a significant influence on reducing employee turnover.[27]

Research has also shown that continuance commitment has an additional, separate effect on reducing employee turnover.[28] However, in a Canadian study of Human Resources Management professionals, this relationship must be considered in terms of the type of continuance commitment. Continuance commitment can be broken down into its two subcomponents: (1) the believed sacrifice in leaving the organization and (2) a believed lack of alternatives. In the former, a person will feel stress at the thought of leaving for fear of losing important advantages of the job. If a person has either negative affectivity or is risk aversive, the belief of sacrifice will urge them to stay. However, in the latter, the person will feel stress due to staying because of a sense of affecting one's health and a feeling of entrapment. In this case, if a person has negative affect, this will lead them to quit as stress levels will be comparatively high.[29]

## REWARDS, SATISFACTION, AND COMMITMENT

The key question now is this: What role can the reward system play in generating job satisfaction and organizational commitment? Because a reward is anything provided by the organization that satisfies a person's needs, rewards clearly have a direct impact on job satisfaction. Of the five facets of job satisfaction discussed earlier, four are extrinsic and one (the job itself) is intrinsic. Also, two of the facets are compensation-related: pay satisfaction and promotion satisfaction.

**organizational commitment**
The strength of the individual's attachment to his or her organization.

**affective commitment**
Attachment to an organization based on positive feelings toward the organization.

**continuance commitment**
Attachment to an organization based on perceived lack of better alternatives.

With regard to generating organizational commitment, the key issue is not so much what individuals receive from their jobs, but the relationship between employees and the organization as a whole. Psychological contracts, trust, and organizational justice—especially procedural justice—play a major role in organizational commitment. For example, research has found a strong relationship between procedural justice and affective commitment.[30] Another study found that organizations perceived to be concerned about their employees' welfare had higher affective commitment than other organizations.[31] Employee benefits can help create this perception, and rewards geared to organizational performance, such as profit-sharing and employee share plans, help create a feeling of belongingness and shared goals, leading to organizational identification and affective commitment. Both line managers and Human Resources professionals have been found to have a significant role in fostering affective commitment when they invest in human resources management practices.[32]

Job security has also been found to relate to both job satisfaction and affective commitment. However, the impact of job security varies with its source. For example, some unionized employees have a high level of job security built into their contracts. This should enhance job satisfaction, but it may not enhance affective commitment if the employer is seen to be granting the job security grudgingly. For job security to have a positive impact on affective commitment, it needs to be seen as something granted willingly by the employer. Employees need to feel that "I am a valued and loyal employee and the firm is recognizing this by giving me job security," not "They'd love to fire me, but they can't."

To generate continuance commitment, several types of compensation policies can be used. Seniority-based rewards are a cornerstone; these include seniority increases in pay as well as benefit packages that increase with continued employment (especially if they are not entirely portable). Of course, simply paying better than competitor firms reduces employee turnover by increasing the costs of quitting (thus increasing continuance commitment).[33]

But if a high pay level is the only strategy a firm adopts to decrease turnover, it may be a very costly one.[34] One study found that higher pay levels did decrease quit rates somewhat, but it concluded that "raising wages to reduce turnover would be profitable only if turnover costs were enormous."[35] This finding is not surprising as we have seen that pay level is only one of many factors affecting turnover. In fact, pay may not be the most important factor in controlling for turnover.[36] Though pay satisfaction is related to affective commitment,[37] so too are factors such as advancement opportunities, fringe benefits, rewards for recognition and achievement, manager relationship, and the nature of the work.[38]

Other strategies can be used to reduce turnover. Pay dispersion, meaning substantial differences between the lowest and highest-paid employees, should be reduced to promote equitable treatment. Furthermore, introducing pay schemes such as profit-sharing plans with lengthy vesting periods helps reduce turnover. Clearly communicating compensation procedures is also helpful.

There are also non-monetary related actions that employers could take to reduce turnover. Employees should be assessed in terms of their job satisfaction, commitment, and employee mobility, as these are key indicators of turnover intention. Well-developed measures can be used to do so. As leadership behaviour is an indicator of turnover intention, leadership training should be provided to all managers. Leaders can be trained on subjects such as understanding the relevance in providing role expectations, designing procedures to reduce role conflict, and providing support in succession planning. Also, positive relationships with coworkers will reduce turnover intention. Therefore, managers should support activities that help with relationship building and give new employees opportunities to develop relationships.[39]

# IS LOW TURNOVER ALWAYS GOOD?

You have no doubt noticed that most of the earlier discussion assumes that employee turnover is a bad thing. Turnover can be very costly, but is a very low turnover rate *always* a good thing? Low turnover may not be a sign of organizational health if it is due only to continuance commitment. If a firm focuses on continuance commitment (by, say, providing high wages) but neglects job satisfaction and affective commitment, it risks ending up with a workforce of dissatisfied, disgruntled employees *who will never quit.*

So, turnover rate does not always tell the whole story. Two firms may have identical turnover rates but this does not mean they have equally good reward and compensation systems. The key question is: *Who is quitting?* Are they employees who are not really a good fit with the organization, or are they valuable employees the firm truly needs?

Excessively low turnover can also cause stagnation in an organization, especially when the organization is not expanding. Some firms have launched early-retirement programs specifically to provide opportunities to younger employees. And at the opposite end of the employee spectrum, Compensation Today 3.6 describes a firm that actually offers financial incentives for their newly trained recruits to quit! Their logic is that any new employee who can be enticed to quit because of a financial incentive is not an employee who shows the affective commitment the organization wants.

---

## COMPENSATION TODAY 3.6

### AT ZAPPOS, FINISH YOUR TRAINING AND THEN WE'LL PAY YOU TO QUIT!

Las Vegas–based Zappos has always been an unconventional firm. The company came from a simple start. One of the founders decided to create Zappos because he couldn't find the colour shoe he was looking for. But Zappos turned the unlikely concept of selling shoes over the Internet into a billion-dollar business. A crucial part of its business model is to employ friendly, helpful call centre employees, something that any Internet retailer would like to do. But how can you be sure that every one of your 1600 call centre employees has the right stuff, before unleashing them on your customers?

It's simple: test the commitment of newly trained employees by offering them cash to quit! After prospective call centre employees finish one week of paid training, every one of them is presented with "The Offer"—quit today and receive a $2000 bonus! After the first month of training, employees are continually provided the opportunity to quit, as the amount increases by $1000 every year up to $5000. "The Offer" was conceived by CEO Tony Hsieh, who implemented it at Zappos in 2006. His logic was that any employee willing to quit in return for a financial inducement was not likely the kind of employee who would show the type of affective commitment that the firm wanted and needed. He believes that this strategy will weed out those who are too overwhelmed by the extensive training or company culture and are too afraid to quit on their own accord. Employees are given a lot of latitude in handling calls, and unlike most call centres, the firm does not keep track of the time that employees spend with each customer, so it is important that employees "buy into" company values.

The strategy seems to be working. Customers gush over the customer service at Zappos. This strategy also allows employees to leave the company with a positive experience. Those who leave are thankful that the company understands it may not be the right place for them. Previous employees can continue to speak about the company positively, and the company keeps a good reputation.

CEO Tony Hsieh continued to introduce unconventional management practices. Holacracy, a self-management operating structure, was launched in 2013 as a way of ensuring sustainable growth and productivity. By 2015, he offered generous severance packages to employees who could not commit to embracing Holacracy with the same logic: employees must align their behaviours to the company's culture.

*(continued)*

When Amazon took over Zappos, the company also acquired this strategy. In a memo entitled, "Please Don't Take this Offer," Amazon announced that it would pay full-time employees at the fulfillment centre if they were to quit. They would be paid in the same fashion as Zappos.

But perhaps Amazon may have different motives than Zappos. The warehouse experiences high turnover and places a strong emphasis on efficiency. Amazon continuously struggles in trying to get employees to stay long-term. So why would the company encourage people to quit?

Some analysts contend that this offer may actually be a strategy to allure employees to stay at the company longer than they otherwise would have. If employees refuse the initial enticement of quitting and leaving with money, they, in turn, feel more committed to their work. An employee will attempt to resolve cognitive dissonance (if there are two conflicting beliefs, people will justify one belief to make it cohesive to the other). Workers may not like their work. But if they refused a chance to quit, they'll try to assure themselves that staying was worth it.

Employees may also stay due to an "escalation of commitment." When a person puts a lot of money or effort into a decision, and the situation goes sour, they will often commit even further to that decision. The person feels as though they have already invested too much.

By incentivizing employees to quit, Zappos kept employees that are aligned with their culture, while it seems as if Amazon just intends to keep employees!

Sources: Jennifer Reingold, "The Zappos Experiment," *Fortune*, March 15, 2016; Richard Feloni, "Inside Zappos CEO Tony Hsieh's Radical Management Experiment That Prompted 14% of Employees to Quit," *Business Insider*, May 16, 2015; Tony Hsieh, 2011. "How Zappos Creates Happy Customers and Employees" (2009), Great Place to Work Institute; Rachel Mendleson, "Why Zappos Pays New Hires to Quit," *Maclean's*, June 9, 2008: 52; Ruth Umoh, "Why Amazon Pays Employees $5,000 to Quit," *CNBC*, May 21, 2018; Dan Percival, "Why Zappos Pays People to Quit," *Medium*, August 1, 2017; "Why Zappos.com Pays New Hires $1,000 to Quit," *AMA Articles*, January 24, 2019; Alana Samuels, "Why Amazon Pays Some of Its Workers to Quit," *The Atlantic*, February 14, 2018.

# UNDERSTANDING TASK BEHAVIOUR

Have you ever watched somebody do something and then wondered, "Now, why did that person do that?" To understand a person's behaviour, you need to understand the person's *motivation*. Over the past few decades, two useful sets of motivation theories have emerged—content *theories* and *process theories*—that can help us better understand motivation.

**content theories of motivation**
Theories that focus on understanding motivation by identifying underlying human needs.

**Content theories of motivation** focus on identifying and understanding underlying needs based on the idea that people behave in ways they think will help them satisfy their key needs. For example, a basic human need is the need for survival—for food and shelter. In modern society, this translates into a need for money. But content theories cannot predict the precise behaviours that different people will perform to satisfy their need for money. For example, some people will seek paid employment. Some will buy lottery tickets or go to the racetrack. Some will seek a rich spouse. Some will rob banks.

**process theories of motivation**
Theories that focus on understanding motivation by determining the processes humans use to make choices about the specific actions they will take.

If we all have the same basic needs but can pursue different avenues to satisfy those needs, what determines how each person will go about satisfying them? **Process theories of motivation** help us understand the process through which different people choose different courses of action in pursuit of the same needs.

## CONTENT THEORIES OF MOTIVATION

What are the important needs that human beings seek to satisfy? Using a variety of classification systems, psychologists have identified dozens of specific needs that drive behaviour. However, for our purposes, it is useful to group these needs.

# MASLOW'S HIERARCHY OF NEEDS

We briefly described Maslow's hierarchy of needs in Chapter 1; we will now discuss it in more detail. Maslow suggested that people have five sets of needs, which are arranged in a hierarchy,[40] as shown in **Figure 3.5**. There are two key points to his theory. First, lower order needs must be satisfied before higher order needs come into play. Second, a satisfied need no longer motivates behaviour.

Thus, once a person's immediate physiological (survival) needs—for food and shelter—are satisfied, that person will become concerned about the next level—safety and security needs: that is, how to satisfy his or her survival needs tomorrow and the next day and the day after that. People like the security of knowing that their basic needs will be satisfied in the future.

Once safety and security needs are met, people then become concerned about satisfying their needs for companionship and positive social regard by others, a need to be with and be accepted by other humans. Once these social or belonging needs are met, people then become concerned with ego or esteem needs—for accomplishment, achievement, and mastery or competence. Finally, if these needs are satisfied, the final set of needs is activated—for self-actualization. This is the need to maximize one's human potential, the need for continued learning, growth, and development. Maslow argues that self-actualization is the ultimate motivator, because, unlike the other needs, it can never be satisfied.

But is Maslow correct? Does human motivation really work the way he suggests? So far, research has not been able to confirm the theory precisely as outlined by Maslow. Some researchers have collapsed Maslow's five categories into three: existence (corresponding to Maslow's lower two need levels), relatedness (corresponding to Maslow's middle or social need level), and growth (corresponding to Maslow's upper two levels).[41] Research has shown that lower order needs do not have to be completely satisfied before the other needs come into play, and that people can be motivated by more than one level of needs simultaneously.

To illustrate the possible variation in needs, consider the most basic need—the need for survival. Most people would view the need for survival as the most important need. But even here there are dramatic variations. If the basic need for survival dominates all else, then why did the electrical crew of the *Titanic*—faced with certain death from drowning if they

**Maslow's hierarchy of needs** A content theory of motivation that groups human needs into five main levels and states that humans seek to satisfy the lowest order needs before satisfying higher order needs.

**FIGURE 3.5**

Maslow's Hierarchy of Needs

did not leave—stay at their stations deep in the bowels of the ship to keep the vital electrical system operating even as the ship slid beneath the waves? Of course, it is possible that they believed that the ship really was unsinkable, and that this is why they stayed at their stations. But what about secret service agents who willingly accept the duty to shield their heads of state from an assassin's bullet with their own bodies? And what about those cases where people intentionally take their own lives?

The reality is that people differ greatly in the strength of their needs and these needs may change over time. For example, a single person may have relatively low economic needs but relatively high social needs. Therefore, that person will turn down opportunities to earn overtime in order to socialize with friends. But suppose that person gets married, buys a house, and has children. Economic needs may increase, reducing the importance of social needs. That person will then be more likely to be motivated to work overtime.

But even though Maslow's theory is unable to predict an individual's motive pattern, it is still useful because it describes group or aggregate behaviour. For example, as the income of a group or society increases, there tends to be a greater concern for satisfying higher-order needs. Thus, in a relatively wealthy society, such as Sweden, where the social welfare system ensures that lower-order needs are met, it is difficult to entice people to work at jobs that do not satisfy their higher-order needs.

Compensation Today 3.7 illustrates how personal needs can change with the context of the situation.

---

## COMPENSATION TODAY 3.7

### CHANGING NEEDS IN THE KLONDIKE

The Klondike Gold Rush (1896–98) was the greatest gold rush in Canada's history. Almost overnight, Dawson City went from an unpopulated, mosquito-infested mud flat in the middle of the Yukon Territory to the largest city west of Winnipeg and north of Seattle. But those who struck gold found themselves in an odd position: there was nothing to buy, not even labour. At this time in the rest of North America the top wage for a working man was $1.50 a day. In Dawson, it was difficult to find someone who would work for 10 times that much.

But as economic needs became less important, other needs became more pronounced. Because of the isolation, aspects of life that would have had little or no value elsewhere commanded exorbitant prices. For example, "when one man drifted in with an ancient newspaper soaked in bacon grease, he was able to sell it for fifteen dollars"—equivalent to about $1000 today. With their economic needs satisfied, the needs of the grizzled miners changed dramatically. Because of their isolation, a need that became highly salient was for news of the outside world.

Source: Pierre Berton, *Klondike: The Last Great Gold Rush 1896–1899* (Toronto: Penguin Books, 1972), 373.

---

## The Two-Factor Theory of Motivation

**two-factor theory of motivation**
Argues that intrinsic factors influence work motivation, while extrinsic factors influence job satisfaction.

In an attempt to determine the most important factors causing job satisfaction or dissatisfaction, Frederick Herzberg asked a sample of employees to list factors that made them feel good about their jobs and then to list those that made them feel bad about their jobs. He was surprised to find that the factors mentioned in the two lists were completely different. He had expected many of the same items to appear on both lists, except reversed. For example, he expected high pay to make people feel good about their jobs and low pay to make people feel unhappy about their jobs.[42]

Instead, he found that while low pay did make people dissatisfied, high pay did not make them enthusiastic about their work. Factors that made them feel good about their work had more to do with *job content*—mastering a difficult task, learning a new skill, or completing a major job accomplishment. Factors that made them dissatisfied were low pay, a poor relationship with their supervisor or coworkers, and poor working conditions—factors dealing with the *job context*.

Subsequently, Herzberg realized that he was really dealing with two different concepts—job satisfaction and work motivation.[43] The factors that caused job dissatisfaction he labelled "hygienes," and the factors that made people feel good about their work he labelled "motivators." He concluded that job satisfaction was caused by extrinsic (hygiene) factors and motivation by intrinsic (motivator) factors. He suggested that to have both satisfied and motivated employees, an organization had to provide both extrinsic and intrinsic rewards (i.e., both hygienes and motivators). Hertzberg's theory fits well with Maslow's because the hygienes correspond to the lower-order needs and the motivators to the higher-order needs.

## Job Characteristics Theory of Motivation

Richard Hackman and Greg Oldham extended Herzberg's work by attempting to identify the specific job characteristics that cause intrinsic motivation and by developing a method for calculating the amount of intrinsic motivation in a particular job.[44] They identified what they called five *core job dimensions*—(1) task identity, (2) task significance, (3) skill variety, (4) job autonomy, and (5) job feedback—and suggested that jobs high in these dimensions are intrinsically motivating: people enjoy them for the satisfaction they derive from performing them rather than for the extrinsic rewards they receive from them.

**task identity** is defined as the extent to which a worker is able to perform a complete cycle of activities, from start to finish, rather than only one small part of the job cycle. **Task significance** is the perceived importance of the job in the general scheme of things. For example, the job of heart surgeon would carry more task significance than that of hot dog vendor. **Skill variety** is the extent to which a substantial number of skills are required for task completion. **Job autonomy** is the extent to which workers are able to decide for themselves how to perform their jobs. **Job feedback** refers to the level of feedback on work quantity and quality that an individual receives from the job itself. For example, a typist using a spell-check program gets feedback on the quality of work from the job itself. Bomb disposal experts do not need outside feedback to know whether they have been successful in their jobs!

Organizations that redesign their jobs to include higher amounts of the five core dimensions are said to be engaging in **job enrichment**. Many organizations, especially high-involvement firms, have job enrichment programs. As long as employees do not perceive the enrichment as simply an attempt to load more work onto them, most respond favourably to job enrichment. However, some organizations forget that if employees are expected to perform at a higher level, the compensation system should recognize this; otherwise, perceived inequity and reward dissatisfaction will result, undoing the otherwise favourable effects of job enrichment.

Although job characteristics theory is a separate theory, it fits well with the other content theories of motivation. As **Figure 3.6** illustrates, the intrinsic job characteristics identified by Hackman and Oldham correspond to the motivators identified by Herzberg and address the higher order needs delineated by Maslow. The same figure shows how these content theories relate to the three managerial strategies.

**task identity**
The extent to which a worker performs a complete cycle of job activities.

**task significance**
The perceived importance or social value of a given task.

**skill variety**
The variety of skills required for task completion.

**job autonomy**
The degree of freedom workers have in deciding how to perform their jobs.

**job feedback**
The extent to which the job itself provides feedback on worker performance.

**job enrichment**
The process of redesigning jobs to incorporate more of the five core dimensions of intrinsically satisfying work.

FIGURE 3.6

Content Theories of Motivation and Their Relationship to Managerial Strategy

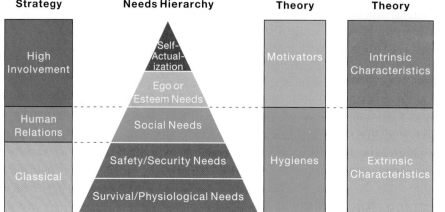

## PROCESS THEORIES OF MOTIVATION

Even when a multitude of people have the same need, different individuals will choose different paths or behaviours to satisfy that need. Process theories of motivation attempt to explain how individuals choose to pursue one path over another when attempting to satisfy a need.

### Reinforcement Theory of Motivation

The simplest process theory is **reinforcement theory**,[45] sometimes called behaviourism, operant conditioning, or behaviour modification. This theory's premise is that an individual will repeat behaviours that have led to need satisfaction in the past and will discontinue behaviours that do not contribute to need satisfaction. This theory is based on learning theory. All young children experiment with a variety of behaviours. They learn to repeat behaviours that have positive consequences and to discontinue behaviours that have negative ones.

For reinforcement theory to work, the individual must perceive a link between the behaviour and the consequence. For example, children who grow up in a household where rewards and punishments are provided in an unpredictable or arbitrary manner learn that there is little connection between behaviour and consequences. They also tend to develop a personality trait known as an "external locus of control"—as adults, they will tend to believe they have very little control over outcomes. In the work setting, these individuals tend to believe that the degree of job effort they exert has very little influence on the degree of performance they achieve or on the rewards they receive.

According to reinforcement theory, the key to predicting a person's future behaviour is to understand how that person and others around them were reinforced for various types of behaviour in the past. As an example, if someone grows up in an environment where most people are unemployed, and where those who are employed never earn more than

**reinforcement theory**
A theory that states a behaviour will be repeated if valued outcomes flow from that behaviour, or if performing the behaviour reduces undesirable outcomes.

minimum wage, that person may come to regard employment as a very unlikely way to satisfy the need for money. If the same person sees local drug dealers driving around in big cars and wearing fancy clothes, that person may perceive drug dealing as a much more viable way to satisfy the need for money.

Reinforcers can be of two types: positive and negative. With positive reinforcement, a reward follows a valued behaviour; with negative reinforcement, an undesirable consequence results whenever the valued behaviour does not occur. This undesirable consequence can be either the removal of something valued (such as docking a day's pay for an unauthorized absence) or the imposition of something not wanted (such as assigning an employee to the least desirable job in the plant on the day following an absence).

For those who are designing a reward system, the guidelines offered by reinforcement theory are quite clear. Desired behaviours for each employee need to be clearly specified. Then each time that behaviour occurs, it needs to be followed by a reward of significant value to the recipient. The closer in time the reward is to the behaviour, the better.

Clearly, reinforcement approaches can change behaviour, even when other methods have failed. For example, one problem afflicting many Canadians is obesity, and many diet plans have been developed to address this problem. Unfortunately, despite the large sums spent on these plans, Canadians are heavier than ever. Could we apply reinforcement theory to this problem? Compensation Today 3.8 describes what happened when researchers did so.

---

## COMPENSATION TODAY 3.8

### WANT TO HELP PEOPLE LOSE WEIGHT? PAY THEM TO TAKE POUNDS OFF!

Although earnings growth for most Canadians has stagnated, one area of growth for many Canadians is in their waistlines. Many remedies for this problem have been suggested, but most of these seem to be of little real help to those wishing to lose weight. Extra pounds may not only reduce quality of life but also pose a serious threat to our health.

Because existing methods are failing to solve the problem, doctors at the University of Pennsylvania decided to try a different approach. Knowing that financial incentives are effective for changing many types of human behaviour, they decided to conduct an experiment to see if they could be used to help people lose weight.

They selected 57 volunteers who wanted to lose weight. All participants were given the same overall goal—to lose 16 pounds (approximately 7 kilograms) in 16 weeks—and each was given one hour of counselling about the importance of diet and exercise in achieving this goal. The participants were then randomly assigned to one of three different experimental groups.

The first group was put under a lottery-based system, whereby they would receive money if they met monthly weight loss goals. The second group was put under a system where they put their own money into an account, which was matched by the researchers. If they met their monthly weight loss goals, they would receive the money for that month, but if they did not, they would lose the money. The third group received no financial incentives; they were just required to report in for monthly weigh-ins, like all the other participants.

What do you think happened? With your knowledge of compensation theory, are you ready to make a prediction? Remember that the only difference between the three groups was the financial incentive; all participants were equally interested in losing weight prior to being assigned to one of the three groups.

All participants had intrinsic motivation to lose weight, while participants in Groups 1 and 2 also had extrinsic motivation, in the form of the cash incentive. In fact, participants

(continued)

in Groups 1 or 2 were far more likely to meet the weight loss goal than those in Group 3. Some 52 percent of the lottery group met the 16-pound weight loss target, as did 47 percent of the deposit group, compared to just 10 percent of the group relying on intrinsic motivation alone. On average, participants in Groups 1 and 2 lost 13–14 pounds (some 6–6.5 kilograms) after 16 weeks, while those in Group 3 lost an average of just 4 pounds (about 2 kilograms) over the 16 weeks. Participants in the lottery group earned an average of $273 over the 16-week period, and those in the deposit group earned $378, while those in the third group ended up with no cash (none was offered to them) and very little weight loss.

Of course, many diets do result in weight loss; the trick is keeping the weight off. Participants who had been paid to lose weight did regain some of those pounds in the months following termination of the experiment; it is not clear how much of the weight loss will be permanent. But this experiment certainly confirms the effectiveness of financial incentives in causing at least short-term behaviour change. An intriguing sidelight to this experiment is that simply wanting to change wasn't sufficient to actually bring about change for most participants; it seems that many people need extrinsic motivation to help them do something they already want to do!

Further studies show that maybe financial incentives can support long-term changes. A study of college students found that those who were paid to go to the gym attended the gym more frequently, even when incentives were removed. Another study observing participants wishing to quit smoking found that those who were provided incentives had higher cessation rates 15 months after the incentives had ceased. Perhaps what is required to start a lifestyle change is a new habit formation. A primary monetary incentive can be the push someone needs in the change of his or her health behaviour.

Source: Kevin G. Volpp, Leslie K. John, Andrea B. Troxel, Laurie Norton, Jennifer Fassbender, and George Loewenstein, "Financial Incentive-based Approaches for Weight Loss: A Randomized Trial," *Journal of the American Medical Association* 300 (2008): 2631–37; Gary Charness, and Uri Gneezy, "Incentives to Exercise," *Econometrica* 77, no. 3 (2009): 909–31; Kevin G. Volpp, George Loewenstein, Andrea B. Troxel, Jalpa Doshi, Maureen Price, Mitchell Laskin, and Stephen E. Kimmel, "A Test of Financial Incentives to Improve Warfarin Adherence," *BMC Health Services Research* 8, no. 1 (2008): 272; Aditi P. Sen, David Huffman, George Loewenstein, David A. Asch, Jeffrey T. Kullgren, and Kevin G. Volpp, "Do Financial Incentives Reduce Intrinsic Motivation for Weight Loss? Evidence from Two Tests of Crowding Out," (2017). University of Pennsylvania ScholarlyCommons.

Behaviour modification theory also states that unrewarded behaviours eventually disappear, so this can be a way of dealing with undesirable behaviours. It is very important that undesirable behaviours not be inadvertently rewarded, as was the case in the opening vignette and other examples in the introduction of this chapter.

However, reinforcement theory can be difficult to apply. One problem is that it assumes that all desired behaviours are measurable and that it is practical to identify and respond to every instance of the behaviour. It neglects the cognitive variables and only focuses on that which is observable.[46] As we have seen, rewarding only some of the behaviours desired from an employee can cause serious problems.

A second problem is that reinforcement theory considers only those rewards that the organization can control. For example, an autoworker who welds pop bottles inside car rocker panels is not receiving any kind of company-based reward for doing so, but may be receiving psychological rewards for "outsmarting" the company. In other words, behaviourism is an extrinsically based theory: it does not recognize differences in how individuals value rewards or how they evaluate the costs of alternative behaviours. It also does not recognize intrinsic rewards or the possibility of altruism.

Third, there is the issue of what happens when rewards stop—does the desired behaviour cease? Reinforcement theory predicts that it eventually does, so behaviour needs to be continually rewarded under this system.

Some critics argue that behaviourism takes away employee responsibility for their actions, making them incapable of self-control,[47] and removes intrinsic motivation.[48] It can also make many employees feel manipulated, like powerless pawns; and it can cause resentment toward the punisher—even the rewarder in some cases. However, there is no doubt that reinforcement principles can change human behaviour.[49] Reinforcement theory appears to work best for simple behaviours and for short-term behavioural change.

## Expectancy Theory of Motivation

Although reinforcement theory is important, it does not help us understand the thought process that takes place when individuals choose to perform a particular behaviour from the virtually infinite possibilities. The main theory for explaining this process is known as the *expectancy theory of motivation*.[50] **Expectancy theory** suggests that the likelihood of performing one behaviour or another depends on three things: (1) the net value (valence) of the consequences of that behaviour, (2) the perceived likelihood that the behaviour will actually lead to those consequences (instrumentality), and (3) the perceived likelihood of actually being able to accomplish those behaviours (expectancy). As **Figure 3.7** indicates, valence, instrumentality, and expectancy must all be positive before a person exerts effort to perform a given behaviour. When there are various competing behaviours from which an individual must choose, they will pursue the behaviour with the highest net valence from among those with satisfactory instrumentality and expectancy.

In essence, individuals ask themselves three questions before acting:

1. Is the task worth doing—do the rewards exceed the costs? (Is net valence positive?)
2. Will I actually receive the rewards if I accomplish the task? (Is the instrumentality clear?)
3. Will I actually be able to accomplish the task if I exert the effort? (Is my expectancy strong?)

Only when the answers to all three questions are positive will the person attempt the task. Compensation Today 3.9 illustrates this process.

The implications of this theory for reward systems are quite clear. First, make sure that the net valence for performing a behaviour is positive *in the eyes of the person expected to perform the behaviour*. This involves maximizing the person's rewards while minimizing

**expectancy theory**
A theory stating that individuals are more likely to exert effort to perform a particular behaviour if they believe that behaviour will lead to valued consequences and if they expect they can perform the behaviour.

FIGURE 3.7

Expectancy Theory of Motivation

the costs of performing the behaviour. To accomplish this, you need to understand the needs and personal values of the people you are attempting to motivate. But motivating a group becomes much more complicated if the group members all vary in their needs and values. For this reason, many firms have an implicit preference for a homogeneous workforce and tend to hire "clones"—employees who are very similar to those they have now.

Second, make sure that instrumentality is strong. Employees must clearly understand that performance of the desired behaviours leads to the specified rewards. Trust and credibility may be an important issue here. Have you promised rewards in the past that failed to materialize?

And third, make sure that expectancy is strong—that employees have confidence in their ability to accomplish the desired behaviours. This may involve providing the physical and mental tools necessary to get the job done and creating a context that facilitates performance of the desired behaviours.

## Attribution Theory of Motivation

Expectancy theory does not distinguish between extrinsic and intrinsic rewards in determining the valence for a particular behaviour. It assumes that rewards simply add up: thus, people are more motivated to perform a behaviour that has both intrinsic and extrinsic rewards, all other factors being equal. This certainly is consistent with the findings of the weight loss experiment described in Compensation Today 3.8.

However, there is one theory that argues that extrinsic rewards may cancel out or actually destroy intrinsic rewards. This is known as **attribution theory.**[51] The premise of attribution theory (sometimes known as "cognitive evaluation theory") is that human beings are active creatures, continually engaging in a variety of activities without necessarily having a conscious understanding of their motives before performing them. But after performing an activity, people often feel compelled to try to understand why they did—"Now why did I do that?" In other words, people seek to attribute some motive to that activity. If there is an "obvious" reason for so doing, they will attribute their activity to that motive. The following story may help illustrate this concept.

> *An elderly man who lived next to a vacant lot had enjoyed his peace and quiet until the neighbourhood children selected the site for various noisy games every day after school. After vainly trying a number of approaches, such as admonishing them to be quiet or trying to convince them to play elsewhere, he tried a new approach. He gathered the children around him one day and announced that he had come to enjoy the sound of their play so much that he wanted to reward them. He told them that he would give each of them a dollar for each day they would come and play at the vacant lot.*
>
> *The children thought this was great, and the noise actually increased! However, after several days, the old man regretfully announced that because he was not a wealthy man, he would have to reduce their payment to 50 cents a day. Although the children grumbled, they accepted this. He subsequently lowered their pay to 25 cents and then to 10 cents, at which point the children announced that they would not be coming back to play anymore. It was simply not worth it for a dime a day!*

This story illustrates how the elderly man replaced intrinsic motivation with extrinsic motivation, which he then extinguished by removing the extrinsic rewards. Research studies in laboratory settings—usually with children or students as subjects—involving intrinsically interesting activities, such as doing a puzzle, have confirmed this result.[52] Some subjects are paid to make puzzles, while others are simply asked to make puzzles. Researchers find that once the pay ends, the paid group stops making puzzles, while the unpaid subjects elect to continue making puzzles. This is taken as evidence that the extrinsic reward has destroyed the intrinsic motivation for the paid group.

But what about situations where the extrinsic rewards are not removed, which is a more realistic scenario in actual workplaces? A study of software programmers found that various types of extrinsic motivation were correlated with intrinsic motivation, indicating that both intrinsic and extrinsic factors could motivate

**attribution theory**
Theory of motivation arguing that humans often act without understanding their motives for their behaviour and afterward attempt to attribute motives for their actions.

individuals in such positions. Extrinsic factors did not undermine intrinsic factors.[53] An analysis of 20 studies found that in work behaviour simulations in which extrinsic rewards are not removed, extrinsic rewards add to intrinsic rewards to create greater task behaviour. Additionally, in a recent study that used both field and laboratory research, findings were that among various occupations, an anticipated extrinsic reward for good performance had a relationship with performance pressure, self-determination, intrinsic job interest, and increased creativity.[54] Another study of actual companies also found that individual performance pay seemed to increase intrinsic motivation.[55]

What, then, are the implications of attribution theory for reward systems? E.L. Deci argues that pay should not be related to output and that intrinsic rewards should be used to motivate performance. Of course, this approach assumes that there is intrinsic motivation in the first place. If there is not, either intrinsic motivation must be generated by enriching jobs, or extrinsic means must be used.

Does this mean that you should never provide extrinsic rewards for good individual performance if it is already intrinsically motivated? Not necessarily. Some researchers argue that providing extrinsic rewards as recognition for accomplishment can actually increase feelings of equity and satisfaction without damaging intrinsic motivation, but only if rewards are not seen as driving, controlling, or evaluating behaviour.[56]

Consider the case of volunteers who work at a UNICEF gift shop. Suppose UNICEF decides it would like to recognize their services by providing $1 an hour for their work as a token of appreciation. Volunteers would fill in timecards which would be verified by a supervisor. Would this increase motivation? Likely not. We can predict that the volunteers will be insulted by the implication that they are involved with the organization to serve their own self-interest, that their time is worth just $1 an hour, and that they cannot be trusted. On the other hand, if dedicated service is recognized by paying a volunteer's expenses to a valued national convention, this will not likely decrease intrinsic motivation and may enhance overall commitment.

To explain this type of situation, some "rogue economists" have come up with the idea of "moral incentives" versus "economic incentives," analogous to our concepts of "intrinsic" versus "extrinsic" motivation.[57] In a variety of interesting experiments (such as the one described in Compensation Today 3.10), they found that adding economic incentives to moral incentives often seemed to destroy the power of the moral incentives, so that organizations actually ended up with less of the behaviour that they wanted. However, in almost all their experiments, the economic incentives were actually quite small. Larger economic incentives would no doubt have produced different results.

There are also different contexts in which intrinsic and extrinsic incentives are beneficial. For example, a 40-year meta-analysis on intrinsic and extrinsic incentives found that intrinsic rewards were a better predictor of work quality, while extrinsic rewards predicted higher quantity of work.[58] Also, employees in higher-level positions typically gained more satisfaction from intrinsic incentives, while employees in lower level positions gained more satisfaction from extrinsic rewards.[59] This is not to say that those in high positions do not expect high economic compensation. Rather, once a certain level of economic compensation has been achieved, such employees look for other incentives.

### FINING LATECOMERS INCREASES LATENESS!

A behaviour that many types of organizations would like to avoid is tardy arrivals, which can disrupt work flow. One organization that had this problem was not concerned about tardy employees, but tardy customers. Put yourself in the manager's shoes.

You are the manager of a day care facility for children. Parents are supposed to arrive at 4 p.m. sharp to pick up their children, but are often late, which upsets the children and requires a staff member to stay late until all the children are gone. You consult a friend, who happens to be a traditional economist, and the friend suggests fining all parents who are more than 10 minutes late. You set the fine at $3 per late appearance and wait for behaviour to change.

Well, behaviour does change all right—it gets worse! After the fine is instituted, the incidence of lateness more than doubles, much to the surprise of your economist friend! What happened?

Part of the explanation seems obvious. People didn't consider $3 to be enough of an incentive to reduce their lateness. But how does this explain the *increase* in lateness that took place? Rogue economist Steven Levitt (he is considered a "rogue" economist because he believes, unlike "traditional" economists, that economic factors are not the only factors that affect human behaviour) has come up with a theory that explains this result (which actually occurred at a real day care facility). His thesis is that in addition to economic incentives, people can also be motivated by moral and social incentives. "Moral incentives" centre around the desire of people to behave in ways that are consistent with (or at least not inconsistent with) personal values they hold dear. "Social incentives" centre around the desire of people to behave in ways that are consistent with (or at least not inconsistent with) the norms of their reference group or broader society.

Levitt explains what happened in this way. What the day care had done was to substitute an economic incentive for a moral incentive (the guilt parents were supposed to feel when they arrived late). For just a few dollars each time they were late, parents could "buy off" their guilt and end up with what amounted to cheap baby-sitting. Moreover, if the day care placed such a low value ($3) on lateness, then lateness must not be such a big problem, so why should I, as a parent, be overly concerned about it?

But this is still not the end of the story. After three months, the day care discontinued the fines. However, lateness didn't decline to its original level—it stayed at the new, higher level. Dropping the late fines apparently signalled that lateness was not a problem, and parents were now able to come late, feel no guilt, and pay no fine!

This argument still stands today. Samuel Bowles is an economist and author of the book, *The Moral Economy: Why Good Incentives Are No Substitute for Good Citizens*. He explains that self-interest can undermine our moral impulses. When this occurs, institutions suffer.

Bowles uses the example from the Boston Fire Department. The department had previously provided employees with unlimited sick days and found that firefighters were taking too many days off, especially calling in sick on Mondays and Fridays. The department implemented a new rule stating that employees were entitled to 15 sick days, and after that, their pay would be reduced. The next year, the number of sick days doubled, especially days around the holidays.

Bowles provides another example of "prisoner dilemma" experimental games. In this experiment, though money is involved, many participants acted in a way that benefitted others, thereby reducing their own monetary incentive. However, when experimenters add an economic reward for selflessness, participants showed less care for others and engaged in selfish behaviour.

It seems as if economic rewards impede on moral incentives mainly because of the symbolic meaning behind the reward.

Source: Stephen D. Levitt and Stephen J. Dubner, *Freakonomics: A Rogue Economist Explores the Hidden Side of Everything* (New York: William Morrow, 2005); Robert Armstrong, "'The Moral Economy: Why Good Incentives are No Substitutes' by Samuel Bowles," *Financial Times*, August 19, 2016.

## Economic Theory of Motivation

Although economic theory can be a useful predictor of some employees' behaviour, it reflects a much narrower view of human motivation than other theories. Economic theory assumes that people are motivated only by extrinsic (i.e., economic) rewards and that they always seek to maximize those rewards while minimizing their contributions to the organization. This

PA Images/Alamy Stock Photo

Some employees may be motivated by factors other than money.

**agency theory**
Agents (employees) will pursue their own self-interests rather than the interests of their principals (employers) unless they are closely monitored or their interests are aligned with the interests of their principals.

theory sees all work as inherently distasteful and assumes that people do as little of it as possible. You will recognize this as the theory on which classical organizations are based.

One of the most prominent economic theories is **agency theory**.[60] This theory makes a key distinction between principals (those who own the enterprise) and agents (those who work for them within the organization). Agency theory assumes that the interests of principals diverge from those of agents and that faced with a choice between advancing the principals' interests or advancing their own, agents will always seek to further their own. It follows that principals need procedures to monitor agent behaviour to minimize agent pursuit of their own interests at the expense of the principals. However, this monitoring is expensive, and principals seek to reduce these costs whenever possible. Therefore, principals tend to favour reward systems that closely tie individual rewards to specific behaviours desired by the principals, especially individual performance pay.

Economic theory represents a simplified view of employee behaviour. It assumes that all people are fixated at the lowest level of Maslow's needs hierarchy, that personal values such as honesty and a strong work ethic do not exist, and that intrinsic rewards have little or no relevance to behaviour. In general, economic theory is useful only if the employees of the organization actually match these assumptions. When they do, it can be a useful model of behaviour for designing reward systems. But when they do not, it can result in the development of reward systems that are suboptimal, ineffective, and counterproductive.

## MONEY AS A MOTIVATOR

So, how do we sum up the role of money as a motivator of performance? For Herzberg, money is not a true motivator; for Deci, it is actually a demotivator that extinguishes intrinsic motivation.

In answering this question, we first note that although human behaviour is driven by needs, money itself is not technically a need, but rather a generalized resource that can be exchanged for things that will satisfy needs. Thus, for those persons whose underlying needs are satisfied, money may not be much of a motivator, at least in its instrumental role as a vehicle for satisfying underlying needs.

In its role as a generalized resource, money gives recipients control over how their needs will be satisfied. For example, a hungry person might be given a sum of money sufficient to purchase an inexpensive meal or be given a voucher for a bowl of soup, redeemable only at a specified outlet. Both alternatives may satisfy the need for sustenance, but the money certainly gives the person more control over how to satisfy that need than does the voucher. This sense of control is in fact an important intrinsic human need.

Besides providing a sense of control, money also has a symbolic value: to many people, it represents status and accomplishment. In organizations, both the amount one is paid and *how* one is paid send important signals about how one is regarded by the employer. For example, a worker who receives a slightly smaller raise than a coworker, even if the raise itself is generous, may infer that the coworker is more highly regarded and has the inside track on the next promotion.

Money can also be a basis of social comparison; and again, it is the relative amount, not the absolute amount, that is important to people. For example, a study conducted at Harvard University found that when asked about whether they would prefer to earn $100 000 per year while all other employees earned $200 000, or to earn $50 000 when everyone else earned $25 000, the majority of participants (56 percent) chose the second option![61]

The multifaceted nature of money as a motivator adds complexity to the compensation process, as does the fact that people vary in their "money ethic"—that is, the inherent value they place on money.[62] But what about the argument that providing pay for performance does more harm than good, by destroying intrinsic motivation?[63]

Money can also satisfy social needs.

First, while there is evidence that pay based on individual performance can extinguish intrinsic motivation, this is only an issue where intrinsic motivation exists in the first place. Second, in most cases, motivation declines only when the extrinsic reward is subsequently removed. This emphasizes the importance of using economic rewards only in circumstances where they are likely to be sustained. Third, although money is a motivator for most people, there is no reason not to supplement it with nonmonetary rewards, including those that produce intrinsic motivation. Fourth, many of the concerns posited for individual performance pay plans do not apply to plans based on the performance of the group or the organization as a whole.

As a result of concerns about the possible drawbacks to monetary rewards, many firms have implemented **noncash employee recognition programs**.[64]

These programs provide nonmonetary rewards that "honour outstanding performance after the fact and are designed for awareness, role modelling, and retention of recipients."[65] The rewards may include social reinforcers, such as a mention in the company newsletter; plaques or letters of commendation; learning and development opportunities; merchandise or travel prizes; or extra time off. Overall, "recognition represents a reward experienced primarily at the symbolic level,"[66] and informational value (giving employees feedback on their performance)[67] although some of the rewards may embody practical or economic value (such as a restaurant voucher).

When offering nonmonetary rewards (and similar to monetary rewards), the rewards must be according to measurements of employee performance, contingent on performance, distributed in a timely fashion, and fair.[68]

Research shows that many Canadian firms are adopting noncash recognition programs; interestingly, however, they are not substituting them for cash-based recognition,[69] as critics of cash-based programs suggest. Instead, they are using noncash programs to supplement their cash recognition programs. There is some evidence to support this approach, as paying employees increasing amounts will not necessarily motivate them to increase their job-relevant knowledge or enhance aspects of their job (such as job autonomy or being a positive influence on others). However, nonmonetary rewards can help improve job conditions. As an example, providing training and development opportunities as a reward for good work can both motivate employees and increase their job-relevant knowledge.[70]

There is no question that money can be a highly effective motivator when the right performance pay plan is applied in the right context. That said, such programs face a number of

**noncash employee recognition programs**
A program that provides noncash rewards to employees in recognition of employee accomplishments or actions that are valued by the organization.

pitfalls, and they are complex both to design and to apply effectively (see later chapters). Pay based on individual performance is most problematic, and in many circumstances, development of intrinsic motivation (where feasible) may be preferable to individual performance pay.

# UNDERSTANDING ORGANIZATIONAL CITIZENSHIP BEHAVIOUR

Organizational citizenship behaviour is a relatively new concept. Basically, it describes voluntary or discretionary behaviours that go beyond task and membership behaviour. At a broad level, it is a "willingness to cooperate" in the pursuit of organizational goals. It is no coincidence that this concept has emerged simultaneously with the rise of high-involvement organizations. Because of the nature of their managerial strategy and the conditions of high uncertainty and dynamism in which they operate, high-involvement firms greatly value organizational citizenship behaviour, in contrast to human relations firms and especially classical firms.

The concept of citizenship behaviour continues to evolve from its original formulation,[71] and important conceptualization of citizenship behaviour suggests that it has five main dimensions.[72] *Altruism* is the willingness to offer help to a coworker, supervisor, or client without any expectation of personal reward for so doing, and without any repercussions if the help had been withheld. *General compliance* is the extent to which conscientiousness—in terms of attendance, use of work time, and adherence to policies—goes beyond the necessary minimum. *Courtesy* is the practice of "touching base" with people before taking actions that could affect their work. *Sportsmanship* is the ability to tolerate, with good grace, the minor nuisances and impositions that are a normal part of work life. *Civic virtue* is the extent to which individuals take an interest and participate in the broader governance and operation of the organization. Other researchers suggest that organizational citizenship behaviour can fit into one of two categories. The first category is behaviour directed towards the organization. The second category is behaviour that is directed towards individuals but has an indirect impact on the organization.[73]

## CAUSES OF CITIZENSHIP BEHAVIOUR

The principal source of citizenship behaviour is organizational identification. Two causes of organizational identification are (1) shared organizational goals and (2) feelings of membership (or belonging).

There are two ways in which shared organizational goals may affect organizational identification. In the first way, known as "organizational integration,"[74] the interests of the individual and the organization are congruent: "If the organization is successful, I will share in the rewards." An example would be a firm in which employees are also significant shareholders. The second way in which shared goals affect identification arises when the organization's goals match important values of the individual employee. Some researchers refer to this as "moral" or "normative" commitment. For example, people might join UNICEF because they want to help fight child poverty, or a person might choose to work in a hospital because of a desire to help heal the sick.

People with feelings of membership; that is, those who feel that they are valued and respected members of their organization, are much more likely to engage in citizenship behaviour. Their citizenship behaviour is also connected to perceptions of justice, fair treatment, and reciprocity: "The organization does whatever it can to look after my interests, and I will therefore do the same for the organization."

Employees with high organizational identification seek to further organizational goals in any way possible, ranging from increasing job effort to making innovative suggestions. Employees also promote a spirit of cooperation within the organization because this also furthers organizational goals. Other results of organizational identification are decreased turnover, absenteeism, grievances, and other negative behaviours.

A key value of organizational identification is that it acts as a counterweight to narrow self-interest. In the Green Giant case discussed in Chapter 1, employees pursued their own self-interest at the expense of the company's interests by "cheating" on the payment system. Had organizational identification been high, this result would have been much less likely.

## CREATING CITIZENSHIP BEHAVIOUR

So how can organizational identification be created, and what role can the reward system play in this process? Several preconditions are necessary for the development of citizenship behaviour. One of these is employment security. Employers cannot reasonably expect employees to be loyal to an organization that shows no loyalty to them. Trust is another key precondition—if employees do not trust management, little citizenship behaviour will take place.

Research also indicates that an organization that shows genuine concern for the needs of its employees—such as supporting employees' professional development and through benefits that help employees successfully mesh their work and family lives—offers more fertile ground for organizational citizenship.[75] Another precondition is a sense of distributive *and* procedural justice within the organization, and the sense that the organization is attempting—within the means available—to provide as fair a psychological contract and reward structure as possible. Distributive justice predicts conscientiousness and sportsmanship, both of which are dimensions of organizational citizenship behaviour.[76] In addition, both procedural justice[77] and supervisory fairness[78] have been shown to be key determinants of organizational citizenship.

One way of creating identification is by developing reward systems in which both the organization and its employees benefit when organizational goals are met. These may include employee stock plans as well as gain sharing, goal sharing, or profit sharing. Another way the reward system can foster shared goals and values is by attracting and retaining employees who already possess compatible values. The employer identifies the needs of people who already share organizational goals and values and then gears the reward system to those needs.

Participation in decision making, especially in goal setting, has also been shown to foster organizational identification. People with a role in setting organizational goals are much more likely to be committed to those goals. In addition, employee participation in developing the company reward system will likely produce reward systems that are consistent with employee needs and result in more trust in the system itself. But all types of participation in decision making have been shown to create greater commitment to the decisions that are made, besides providing a sense that employees are true "citizens" in the organization and that their views are valued and respected.

A good example of using employee participation to create organizational identification involves Byers Transport, a trucking company in western Canada that was purchased from its corporate owner by its employees.[79] With the change in ownership, management style became more open, with information sharing and participative management. In short, the firm moved from a classical to a high-involvement managerial style. After the employee purchase, many employee attitudes and behaviours changed almost overnight. Group norms, which had been somewhat poor under corporate ownership, improved dramatically.

Losses resulting from "shrinkage" (i.e., employee theft) declined dramatically, as did customer damage claims and employee turnover. Grievances disappeared. A new attitude of commitment and cooperation permeated the company. Truck drivers made great efforts to satisfy customers, and everyone, whatever their position, was always on the lookout for potential new customers. The result? A dramatic increase in profitability, which had been absent in the years prior to the employee purchase.

But that is not the end of the story. Because of the success of the firm under employee ownership coupled with high-involvement management, a corporate buyer extended a very lucrative buyout offer that the employee-owners found too good to refuse. After the buyout, though, management became more traditional, and many of the earlier improvements disappeared.

# BEHAVIOURAL IMPLICATIONS FOR DESIGNING REWARD SYSTEMS

So far in this chapter, we've discussed how to generate the types of employee behaviour that an organization needs. Now it is time to draw out the specific implications of this for designing reward systems that will produce the employee behaviours necessary for organizational success. As shown in Compensation Notebook 3.1, there are six main behavioural implications when designing effective reward systems.

---

**COMPENSATION NOTEBOOK 3.1**

### BEHAVIOURAL IMPLICATIONS FOR DESIGNING EFFECTIVE REWARD SYSTEMS

1. *Define* the employee behaviour that is really needed.
2. *Determine* the employee attributes and qualifications necessary to perform the needed behaviour.
3. *Identify* the needs that individuals possessing these qualifications are likely to find salient.

4. *Ensure* a positive valence for needed behaviour by providing rewards that address salient needs and by reducing the costs to the employee of performing the behaviour.
5. *Make it clear* that performance of the behaviour will lead to the promised rewards.
6. *Provide conditions* that make it likely that employee effort will actually lead to the desired behaviour.

---

## 1. DEFINE THE NECESSARY EMPLOYEE BEHAVIOUR

As discussed earlier in this chapter, the first step in designing a reward system that produces the desired employee behaviour is to clearly define the behaviours the firm really needs. Classical firms require task behaviour; human relations firms require task and membership behaviour; and high-involvement firms require task, membership, and organizational citizenship behaviour. But within these general types of behaviour, more specific behaviours can also be identified. For example, do we need our employees to be creative and innovative in coming up with ways to perform their job duties, or do we need them to be careful and consistent to ensure they are performing their job in the specified manner?

## 2. DETERMINE THE NECESSARY EMPLOYEE ATTRIBUTES

Once we understand the behaviour we expect from our employees, we can identify the necessary attributes and characteristics of the employees who would best be able to perform the required behaviour. Do we need highly educated employees with university degrees? Do we need technical school graduates? Do we need creative employees who will be innovative on the job? Do we need employees with advanced interpersonal and team skills? Do we need employees who are able to perform routine processes in a dependable and consistent manner without succumbing to boredom?

To identify the types of employees who will suit the needs of our firm, we need to examine their personal characteristics in relation to our behavioural expectations. Personal characteristics include the competencies, values, and personality of a given individual; thus, we need to identify the specific **personal competencies**, **personal values**, and **personality characteristics** that will fit best with the needs of our organization.

**personal competencies**
A person's physical, verbal, and mental skills.

**personal values**
A person's core beliefs about appropriate and inappropriate behaviour.

**personality characteristics**
A person's behavioural and emotional tendencies.

## 3. IDENTIFY SALIENT EMPLOYEE NEEDS

Once we have identified the desirable employee attributes, we can identify the needs our employees will find most important. As we discussed earlier, personal circumstances and personal characteristics influence the needs our employees will find salient.

Of particular importance are personal values and demographic characteristics. For example, employees who highly value learning may find opportunities for learning and growth most salient. For younger employees, needs for recreation and time off for travel may be more salient than for other employees. For older employees, needs for income security and supplementary health plans may be most salient. For employees with dependent children, financial needs may be the most salient—or, for those with younger children, child care needs.

One way of identifying the salient needs of our workforce is to analyze the personal values, **demographic characteristics**, and personal circumstances of our employees. Conducting surveys of our employees to identify their most salient needs can be a useful part of this process.

**demographic characteristics**
A person's age, gender, ethnicity, education, marital status, and similar characteristics.

## 4. ENSURE A POSITIVE REWARD VALENCE

According to the expectancy theory of motivation, the first question people ask when deciding whether to attempt any behaviour is, "Do the rewards flowing from performing this behaviour outweigh the costs of performing this behaviour?" In other words, is the net valence of this behaviour positive?

Reward systems that produce the highest net valence are more likely to lead employees to attempt to perform the desired behaviour. Knowing the salient needs of our employees allows us to develop rewards with a more positive valence.

However, besides increasing the positive valence of our rewards, we can also increase net valence by reducing the costs of performing the desired behaviour. There are four types of "costs" for a person in performing any behaviour—(1) tangible, (2) physical, (3) psychological, and (4) opportunity—and the more the employer can reduce these costs, the higher the net valence and the greater the likelihood of employees performing the desired behaviour.

Let us take a specific behaviour—accepting a job rather than continuing to remain unemployed. There are *tangible costs*, such as the cost of transportation and work clothes and *physical costs*, such as fatigue and possible health risks. *Psychological costs* may include stress and frustration, or having to violate one's personal values, as when a person strongly opposed to smoking is offered a job in a tobacco factory, or when an environmentalist is offered a job in a polluting industry. Finally, the *opportunity costs* of taking the job will reduce the opportunity to do other things, such as spending time with the family or engaging in leisure activities.

How might an employer reduce these costs? Transportation costs might be reduced by hiring employees who live nearby or by allowing work from home. Physical costs might be reduced by providing ergonomically designed equipment that minimizes the physical strain of the work. Psychological costs incurred by employees at the tobacco firm might be reduced by hiring only employees who are not opposed to smoking. Opportunity costs for employees with families might be reduced by having flexible work schedules or by developing work–life balance programs.

## 5. MAKE IT CLEAR THAT PERFORMANCE WILL LEAD TO REWARDS

If the balance of perceived benefits and costs nets out to a positive valence, the second question individuals will ask is, "What is the likelihood that the promised rewards will actually materialize?" If a person performs the desired behaviour (i.e., to accept and perform a particular job), will that person really receive the promised rewards? If workers perceive the likelihood—the instrumentality—of this to be low, then motivation will be low.

For example, a firm may promise starting pay of $18 an hour, with a raise to $25 after six months and to $32 after one year. It may also promise lucrative opportunities for overtime pay, as well as annual profit-sharing bonuses. This may all sound pretty good, but to be motivated by these promised rewards, an employee must believe that the employer will in fact follow through on its promises.

Therefore, a key issue is employer credibility: *Can the employer be trusted to carry through with their promised rewards?* A person's perception of the likelihood of promised rewards materializing is conditioned by her or his past work experiences and with this employer in particular. Does this employer have a history of promising rewards that never actually materialize?

For employers, if they promise certain rewards in return for certain employee behaviours, then they must provide those rewards when the behaviours are performed otherwise future promises will hold no credibility and no power to motivate. If an employer's credibility has been damaged, it can take a long period of consistently honouring promises before credibility and employee trust is restored. It is important that the employer makes only those reward promises that it is confident it will be able to keep.

## 6. PROVIDE CONDITIONS FOR EFFORT TO LEAD TO PERFORMANCE

If employees do believe that the promised rewards will materialize, the final question they will ask themselves is: *"What is the likelihood that I will actually be able to achieve the desired behaviour or result if I exert my best efforts?"* In other words, do employees expect that effort will lead to successful performance of the desired behaviour? For example, if the desired behavioural outcome is to double the sales in their sales territory, sales employees may believe that no amount of effort will achieve that result. If the expectancy of being able to perform a particular behaviour is low, then promising rewards for doing so will not motivate any extra employee effort.

So, how does an employer create a positive expectancy among employees for attempting to perform a particular behaviour? *First*, make sure that the desired behavioural outcome is realistic. *Second*, provide an organizational context that supports achievement of the desired behavioural outcome. Before making the effort, employees must perceive there is enough organizational support to make successful performance of the behaviour likely. Organizational support consists of the resources, training, and tools the organization needs in order for successful job performance to occur. *Third*, before they exert effort, employees must believe they possess the necessary personal competencies and abilities to achieve the desired performance—that their effort will lead to performance. It is an important part of the training process to create this expectancy, besides creating the actual skills and competencies.

## SUMMARY

This chapter has shown you how reward systems can affect behaviour in organizations. Reward systems may not only fail to produce the desired employee behaviour but actually create undesirable consequences, some of which could threaten the survival of the organization. There are potentially high costs of reward dissatisfaction such as unmotivated employees, low employee satisfaction, and high turnover. Reward dissatisfaction can cause violation of the psychological contract, perceived reward inequity, discrepancy between desired and actual reward levels, and a perceived lack of distributive and procedural justice.

The three types of desired employee behaviours (membership, task, and citizenship) are valued more by some firms than others. Task behaviour is the only one valued by classical firms, while human relations firms value task and membership behaviour, and high-involvement firms value all three. These behaviours can be encouraged by three key job attitudes—job satisfaction, work motivation, and organizational identification.

Your firm's managerial strategy will affect how you tailor the reward system. Classical organizations need to provide only enough rewards to create a tolerable psychological contract that results in the minimal degree of required membership behaviour. In contrast, human relations organizations rely on job satisfaction and positive group work norms. In a human relations firm, you must ensure that the reward systems are equitable and that they generate job satisfaction and a substantial degree of commitment. Because they typically require high-level behaviour, high-involvement organizations generally require the most complex reward systems. These reward systems must be seen as equitable and as adhering to principles of organizational justice. Of the three managerial strategies, reward dissatisfaction is most damaging to high-involvement firms, because this dissatisfaction undermines the foundation of trust needed for successful utilization of this strategy.

The chapter concludes with a discussion of six key implications (as summarized in Compensation Notebook 3.1) for effective reward system design that flow from the behavioural framework.

You should now have an understanding of how rewards link to behaviour, and how strategy links to rewards (covered in the previous chapter). The next step is understanding your available compensation options so that you can select the optimal combination for your organization's compensation strategy.

## KEY TERMS

affective commitment
agency theory
attribution theory
content theories of motivation
continuance commitment
demographic characteristics
distributive justice
equity sensitivity
equity theory
expectancy theory
job autonomy
job enrichment
job feedback
job satisfaction
Maslow's hierarchy of needs
membership behaviour
noncash employee recognition program

organizational citizenship behaviour
organizational commitment
organizational identification
personal competencies
personal values
personality characteristics
procedural justice
process theories of motivation
psychological contract
reinforcement theory
skill variety
task behaviour
task identity
task significance
two-factor theory of motivation
work motivation

## DISCUSSION QUESTIONS

1. Discuss the main types of reward problems. Have you ever encountered any of these problems?

2. Discuss how employee job attitudes and behaviours are linked with reward systems?

3. Discuss key aspects of reinforcement theory. What are the practical implications of this theory for managers?

4. Discuss the key aspects of expectancy theory. What are the practical implications of this theory for managers?

## EXERCISES

1. Go to http://queendom.com and browse through the free personality and values tests. Identify at least one test that would be relevant to employee motivation and take that test. Discuss what it tells you about your own motivation pattern, and how it might relate to the reward strategy that would best motivate you.

2. In a group of four to six people, discuss situations in which employees experienced reward dissatisfaction. What caused that dissatisfaction? How did people react to it? What were the consequences for the organization? Were they serious consequences? Why or why not?

3. This chapter contained two examples of auto companies—Toyota (Compensation Today 3.1) and CAMI (Compensation Today 3.2)—that wanted to adopt a high-involvement managerial strategy. Adopting a high-involvement management strategy was not successful at CAMI but was successful at Toyota. Are there any concepts from this chapter or previous chapters that could help explain this result? Assuming that management at CAMI really wanted to move away from the classical school, what should have been done differently?

4. Using a diagram, show the links (with arrows) between an organization's strategy, reward systems, employee attitudes and behaviours, and employee productivity.

1. Analyze *Case 1—Henderson Printing* in the Appendix. Why do you think there is a high turnover of new employees? Which concepts may help explain employee reactions to the compensation system? Do you think the compensation system is fair? Is it effective? What principles for effective reward systems does it violate? What changes should be made?

2. Read *Case 5—Plastco Packaging* in the Appendix. The Plastco machine operators appear to be suffering from low job satisfaction and motivation. Develop a plan for solving these problems by redesigning these jobs to add more intrinsic rewards. Besides these changes to job design, can you recommend any other changes to the various dimensions of organization structure (including the reward structure)?

## SIMULATION CROSS-REFERENCE

If you are using *Strategic Compensation: A Simulation* in conjunction with this text, you will find that the concepts in Chapter 3 are helpful in preparing the simulation.

# ENDNOTES

1. Steven Kerr, "On the Folly of Rewarding A, While Hoping for B," *Academy of Management Executive* 9, no. 1 (1995): 7–14. See also "More on the Folly," *Academy of Management Executive* 9, no. 1 (1995): 15–16; Robert A. Berenson and Thomas Rice, "Beyond Measurement and Reward: Methods of Motivating Quality Improvement and Accountability," *Health Services Research* 50 (2015): 2155–86; Anthony M. McDonnell, "Still Fighting the 'War for Talent'? Bridging the Science Versus Practice Gap," *Journal of Business Psychology* 26 (2011): 169–73.

2. James R. van Scotter, Stephan J. Motowidlo, and Thomas C. Cross, "Effects of Task Performance and Contextual Performance on Systemic Rewards," *Journal of Applied Psychology* 85, no. 4 (2000): 526–35. See also Ian R. Gellatly and P. Gregory Irving, "Personality, Autonomy, and Contextual Performance of Managers," *Human Performance* 14, no. 3 (2001): 229–43; Walter C. Borman and Stephan J. Motowidlo, *Organizational Citizenship Behaviour and Contextual Performance: A Special Issue of Human Performance*, vol. 10, (Psychology Press); J. Stacy Adams, "Inequity in Social Exchange," in *Advances in Experimental Social Psychology*, vol. 2, ed. L. Berkovitz (New York: Academic Press, 1965); Gaye Ozcelik and Cavide B.

Uyargil, "Performance Management Systems: Task-Contextual Dilemma Owing to the Involvement of the Psychological Contract and Organizational Citizenship Behaviour," *European Management Review* 16, no. 2 (2019): 347–62.

3. Denise M. Rousseau, *Psychological Contracts in Organizations: Understanding Written and Unwritten Agreements* (Thousand Oaks: Sage, 1995). See also Denise M. Rousseau and Violet T. Ho, "Psychological Contract Issues in Compensation," in *Compensation in Organizations: Current Research and Practice*, ed. Sara L. Rynes and Barry Gerhart (San Francisco: Jossey Bass, 2000); Waiganjo Esther Wangithi and Ng'ethe Jana Muceke, "Effect of Human Resource Management Practices on Psychological Contract in Organization," *International Business of Journal and Social Science* 3, no. 2 (2012): 117–22.

4. Elizabeth W. Morrison and Sandra L. Robinson, "When Employees Feel Betrayed: A Model of How Psychological Contract Violation Occurs," *Academy of Management Review* 22, no. 1 (1997): 228–56; Vincent Cassar, Sandra C. Buttigieg, and Rob B. Briner, "Causal Explanations of Psychological Contract Breach Characteristics," *The Psychologist-Manager Journal* 16, no. 2 (2013): 85–106.

5. Margaret A. Lucero and Robert E. Allen, "Employee Benefits: A Growing Source of Psychological Contract Violations," *Human Resource Management* 33, no. 3 (1994): 425–46; Charissa Freese, Marcel A. Croon, and Rene Schalk, "The Impact of Organizational Changes on Psychological Contracts: A Longitudinal Study," *Personnel Review* 40, no. 4 (2011): 404–22.

6. J. Stacy Adams, "Inequity in Social Exchange," in *Advances in Experimental Social Psychology*, vol. 2, ed. L. Berkovitz (New York: Academic Press, 1965); Elaine Hatfield, Jeanette Purvis, and Richard L. Rapson, "Equity Theory of Organizations," *Global Encyclopedia of Public Administration, Public Policy, and Governance* (2016): 1–11.

7. Andrew E. Clark and Andrew J. Oswald, "Satisfaction and Comparison Income," *Journal of Public Economics* 61 (1996): 359–81; Emily Breza, Supreet Kaur, and Yogita Shamdasani, "The Morale Effects of Pay Inequality," *The Quarterly Journal of Economics* 133, no. 2 (2017): 611–63.

8. Nancy C. Pratt, "CEOs Reap Unprecedented Riches While Employees' Pay Stagnates," *Compensation and Benefits Review* 28, no. 5 (1996): 20–24.

9. Franz Christian Ebert, Raymond Torres, and Konstantinos Papadakis, *Executive Compensation: Trends and Policy Issues* (Geneva: International Institute for Labour Studies, 2008).

10. Mark Friedman, "Wal-Mart CEO Doug McMillon Gets $25.6M Pay Package," *Arkansas Business*, April 23, 2014, http://www. arkansasbusiness.com/article/98329/wal-mart-ceo-dougmcmillon-earned-256-million-last-year, accessed August 20, 2019.

11. Crosby, "A Model of Egoistical Relative Deprivation," *Psychological Review* 83 (1976): 95–113.

12. Jerald Greenberg, "Organizational Justice: Yesterday, Today, and Tomorrow," *Journal of Management* 16, no. 2 (1990): 399–432

13. John Shields, Dow Scott, James W. Bishop, and Paulo Goelzer, "Pay Perceptions and Their Relationships with Cooperation, Commitment, and Intent to Quit," *Int. Studies of Mgt. & Org.* 42, no. 1 (2012): 68–86; Laetitia Hauret and Donald R. Williams, "Relative Income and Pay Satisfaction: Further Evidence on the Role of the Reference Group," *Journal of Happiness Studies* 20, no. 1 (2019): 307–29.

14. Jerald Greenberg, "Organizational Justice: Yesterday, Today, and Tomorrow," *Journal of Management* 16, no. 2 (1990): 399–432; Deborah E. Rupp, "An Employee-Centered Model of Organizational Justice and Social Responsibility," *Organizational Psychology Review* 1, no. 1 (2011): 72–94.

15. Michel Tremblay, Bruno Sire, and David Balkin, "The Role of Organizational Justice in Pay and Employee Benefit Satisfaction and Its Effects on Work Attitudes," *Group and Organization Management* 25, no. 3 (2000): 269–90; Charmi Patel, Pawan Budhwar, and Arup Varma, "Overall Justice Work

Group Identification and Work Outcomes: Test of Moderated Mediation Process," *Journal of World Business* 47, no 2. (2012): 213–22.

16. Robert Folger and Mary A. Konovsky, "Effects of Procedural and Distributive Justice on Reactions to Pay Raise Decisions," *Academy of Management Journal* 32, no. 1 (1989): 115–30; Nancy E. Day, "Perceived Pay Communication, Justice and Pay Satisfaction," *Employee Relations* 33, no. 5 (2011): 476–97.

17. Vida Scarpello and Foard F. Jones, "Why Justice Matters in Compensation Decision Making," *Journal of Organizational Behavior* 17 (1996): 285–99.

18. Michel Tremblay and Patrice Roussel, "Modelling the Role of Organizational Justice: Effects on Satisfaction and Unionization Propensity of Canadian Managers," *International Journal of Human Resource Management* 12, no. 5 (2001): 717–37.

19. Roland Theriault, *Mercer Compensation Manual* (Boucherville: G. Morin, 1992).

20. Richard S. Allen, Douglas E. Allen, Katherine Karl, and Charles S. White. "Are Millenials Really an Entitled Generation? An Investigation into Generational Equity Sensitivity Differences," *Journal of Business Diversity 15,* no. 2 (2015): 14–26.

21. R.C. Huseman, J.D. Hatfield, and E.W. Miles, "Test for Individual Perceptions of Job Equity: Some Preliminary Findings," *Perceptual and Motor Skills* 61 (1985): 1055–64.

22. Statistics Canada, "Labour Force Information," January 2020, https://www150.statcan.gc.ca/n1/pub/71-001-x/71-001-x2019012-eng.htm, accessed April 2020.

23. P.C. Smith, L. Kendall, and C. Hulin, *The Measurement of Satisfaction in Work and Retirement* (Chicago: Rand McNally, 1969); Mosammod Mahamuda Parvin and M.M. Nurul Kabir, "Factors Affecting Employee Job Satisfaction of Pharmaceutical Sector." *Australian Journal of Business and Management Research* 1, no. 9 (2011): 113–23

24. Susan J. Ashford, Cynthia Lee, and Philip Bobko, "Content, Causes, and Consequences of Job Insecurity: A Theory-based Measure and Substantive Test," *Academy of Management Journal* 32, no. 4 (1989): 803–29; Chris Dawson, Michail Veliziotis, and Benjamin Hopkins, "Temporary Employment, Job Satisfaction and Subjective Well-Being," *Economic and Industrial Democracy* 38, no. 1 (2017): 69–98.

25. Ian R. Gellatly, "Individual and Group Determinants of Employee Absenteeism: Test of a Causal Model," *Journal of Organizational Behavior* 16 (1995): 469–85; Chien-Hung Lin and Wen-Cheng Wang, "The Relationship Between Affective and Continuance Commitment," *Asian Economic and Social Society* 2, no. 5 (2012): 89–94.

26. Duncan Cramer, "Job Satisfaction and Organizational Continuance Commitment: A Two-Wave Panel Study," *Journal of Organizational Behaviour* 17 (1996): 389–400; Prachi Agarwal and S.M. Sajid, "A Study of Job Satisfaction,

Organizational Commitment and Turnover Intention among Public and Private Sector Employees," *Journal of Management Research* 17, no. 3 (2017): 123–36.

27. Robert P. Tett and John P. Meyer, "Job Satisfaction, Organizational Commitment, Turnover Intention, and Turnover: Path Analyses Based on Meta-Analytic Findings," *Personnel Psychology* 46, no. 2 (1993): 259–93; Esra Alniacik, Umit Alniacik, Serhat Erat, and Kultigin Akcin, "Does Person–Organization Fit Moderate the Effects of Affective Commitment and Job Satisfaction on Turnover Intentions?" *Procedia–Social and Behavioral Sciences* 99 (2013): 274–81.

28. Stephen J. Jaros, John M. Jermier, Jerry W. Koehler, and Terry Sincich, "Effects of Continuance, Affective, and Moral Commitment on the Withdrawal Process: An Evaluation of Eight Structural Equation Models," *Academy of Management Journal* 36, no. 5 (1993): 951–95.

29. Christian Vandenberghe, Alexandra Panaccio, and Ahmed Khalil Ben Ayed, "Continuance Commitment and Turnover: Examining the Moderating Role of Negative Affectivity and Risk Aversion," *Journal of Occupational and Organizational Psychology* 84, no. 2 (2011): 403–24.

30. Suzanne S. Masterson, Kyle Lewis, Barry M. Goldman, and M. Susan Taylor, "Integrating Justice and Social Exchange: The Differing Effects of Fair Procedures and Treatment on Work Relationships," *Academy of Management Journal* 43, no. 4 (2000): 738–39; Marc Ohana, Maryline Meyer, and Sophie Swaton, "Decision-Making in Social Enterprises: Exploring the Link Between Employee Participation and Organizational Commitment," *Nonprofit and Voluntary Sector Quarterly* 42, no. 6 (2012): 1092–110.

31. Joan E. Finegan, "The Impact of Personal and Organizational Values on Organizational Commitment," *Journal of Occupational and Organizational Psychology* 73 (2000): 149–69; Claartje L. ter Hoeven and Joost W.M. Verhoeven, "'Sharing is Caring' Corporate Social Responsibility Awareness Explaining the Relationship of Information Flow with Affective Commitment," *Corporate Communications: An International Journal* 18, no. 2 (2013): 264–79.

32. Caroline Gilbert, Sophie De Winne, and Luc Sels, "The Influence of Line Managers and HR Department on Employees' Affective Commitment," *The International Journal of Human Resources Management* 22, no. 8 (2011): 1618–37.

33. John E. Delery, N. Gupta, Jason D. Shaw, G. Douglas Jenkins, and Margot L. Ganster, "Unionization, Compensation, and Voice Effects on Quits and Retention," *Industrial Relations* 39, no. 4 (2000): 625–45; Matthew D. Hendricks, "Does it Pay to Pay Teachers More? Evidence from Texas," *Journal of Public Economics* 109 (2014): 50–63.

34. Phil C. Bryant and David G. Allen, "Compensation, Benefits and Employee Turnover: HR Strategies for Retaining Top Talent," *Compensation and Benefits Review* 45, no. 3 (2013): 171–75.

35. Irene Powell, Mark Montgomery, and James Cosgrove, "Compensation Structure and Establishment Quit and Fire Rates," *Industrial Relations* 33, no. 2 (1994): 229–48.

36. Phil C. Bryant and David G. Allen, "Compensation, Benefits and Employee Turnover: HR Strategies for Retaining Top Talent," *Compensation and Benefits Review* 45, no. 3 (2013): 171–75.

37. Vaibhav Dhawan and Zubin R. Mulla, "The role of pay and leadership in developing organizational commitment," *South Asian Journal of Management* 18, no. 2 (2011): 60–75; E.J. Lumley, Melinde Coetzee, R. Tladinyane, and Nadia Ferreira, "Exploring the Job Satisfaction and Organisational Commitment of Employees in the Information Technology Environment," *Southern African Business Review* 15, no. 1 (2011): 100–18.

38. Marcia P. Miceli and Paul W. Mulvey, "Consequences of Satisfaction with Pay Systems: Two Field Studies," *Industrial Relations* 39, no. 1 (2000): 62–87; E.J. Lumley, Melinde Coetzee, R. Tladinyane, and Nadia Ferreira, "Exploring the Job Satisfaction and Organisational Commitment of Employees in the Information Technology Environment," *Southern African Business Review* 15, no. 1 (2011): 100–18.

39. Phil C. Bryant and David G. Allen, "Compensation, Benefits and Employee Turnover: HR Strategies for Retaining Top Talent," *Compensation and Benefits Review* 45, no. 3 (2013): 171–75.

40. A.H. Maslow, *Motivation and Personality* (New York: Harper and Row, 1954).

41. C. Alderfer, *Existence, Relatedness, and Growth* (New York: The Free Press, 1972).

42. Frederick Herzberg, B. Mausner, and B.B. Snyderman, *The Motivation to Work* (New York: John Wiley, 1959).

43. Frederick Herzberg, *Work and the Nature of Man* (Cleveland: World, 1996).

44. J. Richard Hackman and Greg Oldham, *Work Redesign* (Reading: Addison-Wesley, 1980).

45. B.F. Skinner, *Science and Human Behavior* (New York: The Free Press, 1965).

46. T.J. Sharp, "Chronic Pain: A Reformulation of the Cognitive–Behavioural Model," *Behavior Research and Theory* 39, no. 7 (2001): 787–800.

47. A. Kohn, *Punished by Rewards* (Boston: Houghton Mifflin Company, 1993).

48. See E. Deci, *Intrinsic Motivation* (New York: Plenum Press, 1975); E. Deci and R. Ryan, *Intrinsic Motivation and Self-Determination in Human Behavior* (New York: Plenum Press, 1985).

49. K. O'Hara, C.M. Johnson, and T.A. Beehr, "Organizational Behavior Management in the Private Sector: A Review of Empirical Research and Recommendations for Further Investigation," *Academy of Management Review* 10 (1985): 848–64.

50. See Victor V. Vroom, *Work and Motivation* (New York: Wiley, 1964). Or see Edward E. Lawler, *Motivation in Work Organizations* (Monterey: Brooks/Cole, 1973).

51. See Deci, *Intrinsic Motivation*; see also Deci and Ryan, *Intrinsic Motivation*.

52. Ibid.; Martin S. Haggar and Nikos L.D. Chatzisarantis, "Causality Orientations Moderate the Undermining Effect of Awards of Intrinsic Motivation," *Journal of Experimental Social Psychology* 47 (2011): 485–89.

53. Sandeep Krishnamurthy, Shaoson Ou, and Arvind Tripathi, "Acceptance of Monetary Rewards in Open Source Software Development," *Research Policy* 43, no. 4 (2014): 632–44.

54. Uco J. Wiersma, "The Effects of Extrinsic Rewards in Intrinsic Motivation: A Meta-Analysis," *Journal of Occupational and Organizational Psychology* 65 (1992): 101–14. Robert Eisenberger and Justin Aselage, "Incremental Effects of Reward on Experienced Positive Outcomes for Intrinsic Interest and Creativity," *Journal of Organizational Behavior* (2009): 95–117.

55. Meiyu Fang and Barry Gerhart, "Does Pay for Performance Diminish Intrinsic Interest?" *International Journal of Human Resource Management* 23, no. 6 (2012): 1176–96.

56. J.M. Harackiewicz and J.R. Larson, "Managing Motivation: The Impact of Supervisor Feedback on Subordinate Task Interest," *Journal of Personality and Social Psychology* 51 (1986): 547–56; Christopher C. Cerasoli, Jessica M. Nicklin, and Michael T. Ford, "Intrinsic Motivation and Extrinsic Incentives Jointly Predict Performance: A 40-Year Meta-Analysis," *Psychological Bulletin* 140, no. 4 (2014): 1–29.

57. Stephen D. Levitt and Stephen J. Dubner, *Freakonomics: A Rogue Economist Explores the Hidden Side of Everything* (New York: William Morrow, 2005).

58. Christopher P. Cerasoli, Jessica M. Nicklin, and Michael T. Ford, "Intrinsic Motivation and Extrinsic Incentives Jointly Predict Performance: A 40-Year Meta-Analysis," *Psychological Bulletin* 140, no. 4 (2014): 1–29.

59. Muhammad Shahzad Latif, Mushtaq Ahmad, Muhammad Qasim, Momal Mushtaq, Amber Ferdoos, and Hummayoun Naeem, "Impact of Employee's Job Satisfaction on Organizational Performance," *European Journal of Business and Management* 5, no. 5 (2013): 166–71.

60. See also M. Jensen and W. Meckling, "Theory of the Firm: Managerial Behavior, Agency Costs, and Ownership Structure," *Journal of Financial Economics* 3 (1976): 305–60. See also Kathleen Eisenhardt, "Agency Theory: An Assessment and Review," *Academy of Management Review* 14, no. 1 (1989): 57–74.

61. Arthur C. Brooks, *Gross National Happiness* (New York: Basic Books, 2008).

62. Thomas L. Tang, Jwa K. Kim, and David S. Tang, "Does Attitude Toward Money Moderate the Relationship Between Intrinsic Job Satisfaction and Voluntary Turnover?" *Human Relations* 53, no. 2 (2000): 213–45; Roberto Luna-Arocas and Thomas Li-Ping Tang, "Are You Satisfied With Your Pay When You Compare? It Depends On Your Love of Money, Pay Comparison Standards, and Culture," *Journal of Business Ethics* 128, no. 2 (2015): 279–89.

63. Kohn, *Punished by Rewards*.

64. Richard J. Long and John L. Shields, "From Pay to Praise? Non-Cash Employee Recognition in Canadian and Australian Firms," *International Journal of Human Resource Management* 21, no. 8 (2010): 1145–72.

65. J.L. McAdams, "Nonmonetary Rewards: Cash Equivalents and Tangible Awards," in *The Compensation Handbook: A State of the Art Guide to Compensation Strategy and Design*, ed. L.A. Berger and D.R. Berger (New York: McGraw-Hill, 1999), 242.

66. J.-P. Brun and N. Dugas, "An Analysis of Employee Recognition: Perspectives on Human Resource Practices," *International Journal of Human Resource Management* 19, no. 4 (2008): 716–30.

67. Richard J. Long and John L. Shields, "From Pay to Praise? Non-Cash Employee Recognition in Canadian and Australian Firms," *International Journal of Human Resources Management* 21, no. 8 (2010): 1145–72.

68. Herman Aguinis, Harry Joo, and Ryan K. Gottfredson, "What Monetary Rewards Can and Cannot Do: How to Show Employees the Money," *Business Horizons* 56, no. 2 (2013): 241–49.

69. Richard J. Long and John L. Shields, "From Pay to Praise? Non-Cash Employee Recognition in Canadian and Australian Firms," *The International Journal of Human Resources Management* 21, no. 8 (2010): 1145–72.

70. Ibid.

71. T.S. Bateman and D.W. Organ, "Job Satisfaction and the Good Soldier: The Relationship Between Affect and Employee Citizenship," *Academy of Management Journal* 26 (1983): 587–95.

72. Dennis W. Organ, "The Motivational Basis of Organizational Citizenship Behavior," *Research in Organizational Behavior* 12 (1990): 43–72.

73. Jihad Mohammad, Farzana Quoquab, and Mohmad Adnan Alias, "Job Satisfaction and Organizational Citizenship Behaviour: An Empirical Study at Higher Learning Solutions," *Asian Academy of Management Journal* 16, no. 2 (2011): 149–64.

74. Chris Argyris, *Integrating the Individual and the Organization* (New York: Wiley, 1964); J. Henri Burgers, Justin J.P. Jansen, Frans A.J. Van den Bosch, and Henk W. Volberda, "Structural Differentiation and Corporate Venturing: The Moderating Role of Formal and Informal Integration Mechanisms," *Journal of Business Venturing* 24, no. 3 (2009): 206–20.

75. Susan J. Lambert, "Added Benefits: The Link Between Work–Life Benefits and Organizational Citizenship Behaviour," *Academy of Management Journal* 43, no. 5 (2000): 801–15;

Mercedes López-Domínguez, Mihaela Enache, Jose M. Sallan, and Pep Simo, "Transformational Leadership as an Antecedent of Change-Oriented Organizational Citizenship Behavior," *Journal of Business Research* 66, no. 10 (2013): 2147–52.

76. Lei Wang, Kim T. Hinrichs, Leonel Prieto, and Jon P. Howell, "Five Dimensions of Organizational Citizenship Behavior: Comparing Antecedents and Levels of Engagement in China and the U.S.," *Asia Pacific Journal of Management* 30, no. 1 (2013): 115–47.

77. Robert H. Moorman, "Relationship Between Organizational Justice and Organizational Citizenship Behaviors: Do Fairness Perceptions Influence Employee Citizenship?" *Journal of Applied Psychology* 76, no. 6 (1991): 845–55; Ung Hee Lee, Hye Kyuong Kim, and Young Hyung Kim, "Determinants of Organizational Citizenship Behavior and Its Outcomes," *Global Business and Management Research: An International Journal* 5, no. 1 (2013): 54–65.

78. Mary A. Konovsky and Dennis W. Organ, "Dispositional and Contextual Determinants of Organizational Citizenship Behaviour," *Journal of Organizational Behavior* 17 (1996): 253–66; Marius van Dijke, David De Cremer, David M. Mayer, and Niels Van Quaquebeke, "When Does Procedural Fairness Promote Organizational Citizenship Behavior? Integrating Empowering Leadership Types in Relational Justice Models," *Organizational Behavior and Human Decision Processes* 117, no. 2 (2012): 235–48.

79. Richard J. Long, "Employee Buyouts: The Canadian Experience," *Canadian Business Economics* 3, no. 4 (1995): 28–41.

# 4

# COMPONENTS OF COMPENSATION STRATEGY

## Learning Outcomes

### AFTER READING THIS CHAPTER, YOU SHOULD BE ABLE TO:

- Describe the role of base pay, performance pay, and indirect pay in the compensation mix, and discuss the advantages and disadvantages of each.
- Identify and differentiate between the three main methods for establishing base pay.
- Define market pricing and discuss its advantages, disadvantages, and applicability.
- Define job evaluation and discuss its advantages, disadvantages, and applicability.
- Define the pay-for-knowledge system and discuss its advantages, disadvantages, and applicability.

Pay systems have been evolving in Canada, the United States, and globally over the past three decades. Here are a few key changes to employee pay systems over this period.

1. There is an increasing use of market data, especially in the United States. In Canada, organizations also depend heavily on market data; however, job evaluations continue to be extensively used because of pay equity requirements and concerns about internal equity.

2. Strategic rewards designs have ebbed and flowed, at times overcoming the inertia of the field's perpetual instinct to copy the practices of others. Businesses are challenging compensation professionals to align pay systems with business strategy to create a unique competitive advantage.

3. Merit budgets are not significantly different year over year. In 2019, employers increased their merit budgets to 2.6 percent, a .01 percent increase from the year before. Given that unemployment rates dropped to 5.4 percent in 2019—the lowest it has been in 43 years—and employers have increasing problems with attraction and retention, this finding is surprising.

4. Base pay increases have stagnated, with annual increases dropping to 1–3 percent today; employee wages have barely kept up with inflation in the past 35 years.

5. While base pay has stagnated, benefits costs have increased steadily, especially in the United States where benefits represent approximately 30 percent of total rewards. In Canada, the figure is lower (about 20 percent), largely because of health care benefits provided by the government. Defined contribution pension plans are increasing in both countries. Work–life benefits are popular currently.

6. While skills, knowledge, and competencies are being rewarded by many organizations, typically relatively few people are paid using formal skill-, knowledge-, or competency-based pay systems.

7. Incentive pay has surged in a variety of forms but is still used far more heavily with executives and managers than with other employees. There are many forms of incentive plans rewarding individual performance (e.g., individual bonus, spot awards), group or unit performance (e.g., gain sharing, project or team bonus), or corporate performance (e.g., profit sharing, stock options, employee share ownership plan).

8. In Canada, 86 percent of organizations use individual performance to determine base salary adjustments year over year, and 49 percent use a five-level rating system (from lowest performance to highest performance) to determine merit increases. High performers received 1.88 times the salary of an average performer in 2018.

Sources: Gerald E. Ledford Jr., "The Changing Landscape of Employee Rewards: Observations and Prescriptions," *Organizational Dynamics* 43 (2014): 168–79; Gerald E. Ledford Jr., "Overview of the Commentaries on the Changing Landscape of Employee Rewards: Observations and Prescriptions," Compensation *and Benefits Review* 46, no. 5–6 (2014): 254–61; Canadian Inflation Rate Trends; Mercer Press Release, "Salary Budgets Indicative of a 'New Normal' as Employers Remain Cautious of Slow Moving Economy," September 9, 2016; Mercer Press Release, "Empower Your Workforce for the Future: 2018/2019 Key Findings from Canada's Compensation Planning Survey," September 18, 2018; Mercer Press Release, "Salary Increase Budgets to Increase 2.6% in 2019 and 2020," August 22, 2019; Pete Evans, "Canada's Jobless Rate Drops to 5.4%, Lowest Level in 43 Years," *CBC News*, June 7, 2019.

# INTRODUCTION TO COMPENSATION MIX CHOICES

Why does the person who works as a secretary at your college or university get paid per hour, while the person who cuts your hair get paid per head? In fact, why use time-based pay at all? Some compensation systems do not. For example, realtors get paid only when they sell a house, auto salespeople are paid only when they sell a car, and stockbrokers are paid only when they make a trade. Carpet installers are paid for each square metre of carpet laid, long-haul truck drivers are paid per kilometre driven, and dentists are paid for each tooth drilled. Why not pay everybody this way?

That's a good question—and one that will be addressed in this chapter. This chapter is the first of three (Chapters 4–6) that together constitute what you need to know to be able to formulate reward and compensation strategy. Chapters 4–6 provide the tools you need to formulate reward and compensation strategy, while Chapters 7–13 provide the more technical knowledge that you will need in order to transform your compensation strategy into a functioning compensation system.

In designing any compensation strategy, we must address two key questions:

- What role (if any) should each of the three compensation components (base pay, performance pay, indirect pay) play in the compensation mix, and how should each component be structured?
- What total level of compensation should be provided?

This chapter and Chapter 5 address the first question by examining the choices that need to be made regarding each of the three compensation components. We will defer the second question until Chapter 6.

**Figure 4.1** represents the "menu" of choices for a firm's compensation mix. We will start the discussion on performance pay *in general* and then discuss specific performance pay choices in Chapter 6.

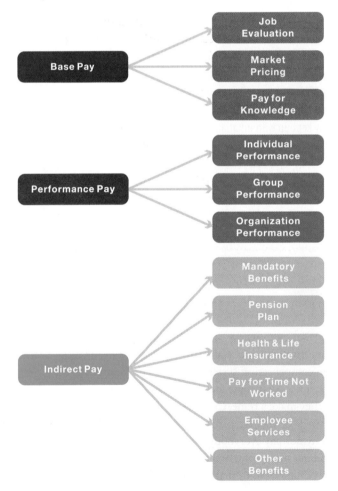

**FIGURE 4.1**

**Compensation Mix Choices**

As Figure 4.1 shows, the first strategic decision to be made is about the relative proportions of base pay, performance pay, and indirect pay to include in the compensation mix. Within this, there are three key decisions: (1) what method(s) should be used for establishing base pay, (2) what type(s) of performance pay (if any) should be provided, and (3) which elements of indirect pay should be included. This chapter provides the basis for making decisions about the proportions of base pay, performance pay, and indirect pay to include in your compensation strategy, and for deciding which of the three methods for determining base pay will be used.

## COMPONENTS OF THE COMPENSATION MIX

In designing a compensation system, firms must choose which of the three fundamental components to include in the compensation mix, and how much of total compensation each of these components will account for. A compensation system can include one, two, or all three of these fundamental components of the compensation mix. To complicate things further, it usually makes sense for different choices to be made for different employee groups within the firm.

### BASE PAY

Base pay is the portion of an individual's compensation that is based on time worked, not on output produced or results achieved. For a majority of employees in Canada, base pay serves as the largest component of their compensation package. According to research conducted by one of the authors, base pay accounts for about 75–80 percent of the compensation for a typical employee, performance pay for 5–10 percent, and indirect pay for about 15 percent of total compensation.

However, these proportions vary across firms (and across occupational groups), with some firms providing virtually 100 percent of their compensation in the form of base pay (as in the case of firms that rely mainly on hourly paid part-time workers), while others provide virtually 100 percent in the form of performance pay (as in the case of salespeople working on straight commission). Until recently, there had been trends toward increased performance pay (especially that geared to group or organizational performance) and increased indirect pay (particularly health benefits), but these trends appear to have levelled off in recent years, perhaps due to the difficult economic circumstances that have characterized a large part of the first decade of the 21st century.

Base pay is "guaranteed" by the employer: if a person works for a certain amount of time, he or she is paid a prespecified amount of money. In some cases, this amount is calculated on an hourly basis (e.g., $15 per hour); in others, daily (e.g., $300 per day); in others, weekly (e.g., $1500 per week), monthly (e.g., $6000 per month), or annually (e.g., $72 000 per year). When calculated on an hourly basis, base pay is known as a **wage**; when calculated on a weekly, monthly, or annual basis, it is known as a **salary**.

**wage**
Pay based on an hourly time period.

**salary**
Pay based on a weekly, monthly, or annual time period.

### Why Use Base Pay?

Wouldn't it be more efficient just to use output-related pay? Why not eliminate base pay, as some employers have done? The answer is that output-related pay cannot always be used, which forces the use of base pay. In addition, base pay is sometimes preferable to output-related pay, even where output-related pay is feasible.

For some organizations, output-related pay is impractical. Substitution of output-related pay for time-based pay is feasible only for jobs in which the output is:

**a.** easy to measure,

**b.** easy to price in terms of its value to the employer,

**c.** easy to attribute to individual employees,

**d.** controllable by the individual employee, and

**e.** relatively stable.

Obviously, most jobs do not meet all these criteria, and attempts to use output-related pay in such jobs can cause serious problems.

In some organizations, output-related pay is possible but not desirable because of the unintended consequences. For example, some mines do not use output-related compensation because of a concern that this might lead to a strong push for production at the expense of safety. In the retail sector, salespeople may become too aggressive or may resort to unethical sales practices in order to maximize their commission income. Jobs that combine some measurable outputs with immeasurable outputs are also not good candidates for a pay system based only on output because employees tend to focus on the measured behaviours and neglect other behaviours.

In some organizations, output-related pay may be practical and desirable from the employer's point of view, but not from the employee's viewpoint. In general, people prefer certainty in their rewards and thus prefer a large component of base pay in their compensation mix. Trade unions have worked for many years to make wages more certain and have generally pushed for more base pay and less performance pay. (Note, however, that unions may have lost the will or ability to oppose performance pay; recent research suggests that unionized employers in Canada no longer differ from non-union employers in their proportions of base and performance pay.[1])

❚ Commission pay is used in many auto dealerships.

The general preference among employees is for base pay so it may be necessary to offer higher total pay in order to induce employees to accept jobs in which all pay is performance-contingent. This may actually result in higher total compensation costs as employees demand a premium for the additional risk.[2] If the performance-contingent pay plan does not boost output sufficiently to cover the additional pay costs, then a firm is better off with a time-based pay system.

So far, base pay has been portrayed as something to be used because no other alternative is viable, and this is the principal motivation for using it. But base pay can also be used for more positive reasons.

1. Flexibility. With time-based pay, the employer is essentially buying time from the employee. Within certain limits, this time may be directed in many ways and redirected as need arises. Base pay doesn't confine employees' attention to only one or two behaviours, as output-based pay tends to do.

2. Base pay allows the employer to recognize and encourage important job behaviours that don't directly produce output, such as skill development.

3. Base pay can signal the relative importance of jobs within the organization. Generally, jobs of greater importance to the organization carry higher pay rates.

4. Base pay demonstrates a commitment on the part of the employer to the employee, creating a greater likelihood of employee commitment to the employer.

5. Depending on the method used to establish it, base pay can support a particular managerial strategy. For example, a pay-for-knowledge base pay strategy supports a high-involvement managerial strategy.

6. Finally, one very important reason for the use of base pay is simplicity—it is usually much simpler to implement and administer than an output-related system.

## Disadvantages of Base Pay

Base pay also carries some disadvantages.

1. Base pay represents more of a fixed employer commitment than performance pay, especially if salaries are used. It is not linked to variability in an employer's ability to pay in the way that performance pay can be.

2. While base pay does contribute to membership behaviour, it does not directly motivate task behaviour, nor does it signal key task behaviours.

3. Because base pay does not relate organizational success directly to individual success, it does not directly contribute to citizenship behaviour.

4. Base pay is not self-correcting. In an output-related system, employees who do not perform up to standard tend to voluntarily remove themselves from the organization because they are unable to earn enough money. Time-based pay provides no such mechanism.

Time-based pay and output/performance-related pay are not mutually exclusive and can be combined. Managers can then capture the advantages of both while minimizing the disadvantages. In recent years, there has been a trend away from compensation systems that rely solely on either base pay or performance pay. Many firms that have traditionally relied only on base pay are starting to add performance-contingent elements to their pay systems; others that have traditionally relied only on performance pay (such as stock brokerage firms) are starting to add base pay to their compensation systems.

# PERFORMANCE PAY

Performance pay can be defined as any type of financial reward provided only when certain specified performance results occur. It is sometimes known as "performance-contingent pay," "variable pay," or "at-risk pay." Pay-for-performance plans can be classified into three main categories, depending on whether the performance relates to the individual employee, the group or work team, or the entire organization. *Individual performance pay plans* include piece rates, commissions, merit pay, and targeted incentives. *Group performance pay plans* include productivity gain-sharing plans, goal-sharing plans, and other types of team-based pay. *Organizational performance pay plans* include employee profit-sharing plans, employee stock plans, and other organizational pay plans.

## Why Use Performance Pay?

Paying employees only when the desired performance takes place sounds like a wonderful idea—if you are an employer. The latter part of the 20th century did see a dramatic growth in performance pay, particularly group and organizational performance pay. Yet many employers still choose not to use performance pay at all, and among those that do, it usually constitutes a relatively small proportion of total compensation. So, why should organizations consider using performance pay?

Performance pay plans have several advantages.

1. Properly designed, they can signal key employee behaviours and motivate employees to achieve them.
2. They can reduce the need for other types of mechanisms for controlling employee behaviour. When employees know that their pay is dependent on performing particular behaviours, they won't need a supervisor watching them to make sure they are working.
3. Such plans can raise employee interest in performance and provide employees with information about their current performance levels.
4. Different types of performance pay can be used to support specific managerial strategies. For example, individual performance pay can support a classical managerial strategy. Group- or organization-based performance pay can support a high-involvement managerial strategy.
5. Finally, performance pay plans make pay more variable and thus can help link compensation levels to the firm's ability to pay. This linkage helps stabilize an organization's employment levels,[3] lessening the need to lay off employees in difficult times only to rehire them when business improves. This employment stability has advantages for both employers and employees because employers risk losing employees whenever they are forced to lay them off, and employees often prefer reduced-pay employment to layoffs.

## Disadvantages of Performance Pay

It is difficult to generalize about the disadvantages of performance pay plans because the types of performance pay plans differ radically and each has its own specific advantages, disadvantages, and limitations. (The specific advantages and drawbacks for each type of performance pay plan will be covered in Chapter 5.) That said, one general drawback is that employees generally prefer predictable and certain rewards to unpredictable and uncertain rewards. Of course, employees usually do not object to performance pay if it is clearly an add-on, to top off base pay and indirect pay. But employees will generally resist *substitution* of performance pay for base pay or indirect pay.

To induce employees to accept this substitution, it may be necessary to offer higher total compensation than would otherwise be necessary. Some organizations that rely heavily on performance pay appear to pay a very steep price for so doing.

For example, *The Atlantic* reported that a Wall Street Trader complained that his $3.6 million bonus should have been $8 million based on his performance.[4] *The Globe and Mail* reported that some stock traders received as much as $800 000 in gross pay several years ago. Is it really necessary to pay this much? Is it really *efficient* to pay this much?

Moreover, pay for performance systems do not work when the company does not have enough money to reward all high performers at a level that would be considered meaningful. Possessing the funds would require having enough money to continuously provide meaningful rewards, administer the necessary resources and training opportunities to attain performance goals, and offer instruction for those manage the pay for performance system.[5]

Sometimes the higher total compensation may not even retain the high-priced employees. At Canaccord Genuity Group Inc., Canada's largest independent brokerage, between 30 and 40 senior investment bankers, traders, and analysts at the director and managing director level received compensation exceeding $500 000 a year. After losing some of its biggest producers, Canaccord started to request its senior employees to commit to staying with the company for the next year in order to receive their fiscal year-end bonuses.[6] However, due to the backlash that the brokerage firm received, Canaccord later offered an alternative bonus scheme that allowed senior capital market employees to be paid a smaller bonus in cash, with the remaining amount paid in stock that was to vest over a set amount of years.[7]

In addition, as discussed in previous chapters, performance pay may cause employees to focus only on aspects of behaviour that are being measured, ignoring other unmeasured but still important behaviours. If poorly designed, performance pay can have unanticipated negative consequences.[8] Negative consequences can include focusing on the short term and neglecting long-term implications, supporting only average performance by placing caps on expectations, decreasing creativity and risk taking thereby creating obedience, encouraging a focus on self rather than the interests of others, discouraging teamwork, and fostering an environment that is win–lose for earning the allotted money.[9] Getting performance pay to work right is usually no easy matter; base pay is often much simpler and more flexible.

## INDIRECT PAY

At Alberta-based Imperial Oil, employees have company matching saving plans, extended health and dental plans, short- and long-term disability benefits, and company-paid and optional life insurance plans. The company also offers flexible company-paid pension plan options, scheduled and floating earned days off, statutory and floating holidays, competitive vacation entitlement, company-paid educational assistance, discounts on Esso gasoline and home heating oil, and relocation assistance and support.[10]

These features cost Imperial a lot of money. So why provide them? Many companies don't. Why not keep things simple and just use direct pay?

In Canada, indirect pay is a major expenditure for many firms. In the past, indirect pay was known as "fringe benefits," but as the extent and costs of these benefits increased, they became known simply as "benefits." In this book, "indirect pay" is preferred, because this term acknowledges that benefits are in fact integral to total compensation for many firms and should be considered a component of employee pay just like base pay and performance pay. Often, employees and even employers underestimate the impact of indirect pay on the total pay package. This needs to change, given the cost of benefits and the strategic role they can play in the compensation system.

Among Canadian companies, 52 percent have noted increases in benefit costs at around 6.2 percent between 2013 and 2014. Among the benefits offered, over 90 percent of employers provide full-time employees with vision care coverage, private or semi-private hospital accommodation, out-of-country medical coverage, paramedical services, chiropractic coverage, physiotherapy, major restorative dental services, accidental death and dismemberment and long-term disability. Most organizations do not have a determined annual maximum for prescription coverage, but typically reimbursement is up to 89 percent of the claim. Furthermore, there has been an increase in the number of employers who provide full-time employees with optional critical illness insurance.

Although cost-containment attempts have been made, spending on benefits programs continues to pose as a large expenditure for employers and the costs continue to grow. For employers in Canada, the average yearly spending is $8330 per employee. The cause of the increases can be associated with the pervasiveness of chronic diseases and mental health issues.[11]

One study has suggested that indirect pay in Canada averaged 15 percent of total compensation in medium to large private-sector firms; this ranged from 17 percent in the manufacturing sector down to 10 percent in the accommodation/food industry, where many employers don't provide any benefits beyond the statutory minimum. Other research puts this cost between 10–20 percent of total compensation, depending on the type of employers surveyed.[12] Besides including larger employers, which pay more benefits, this sample included public sector organizations. Indirect pay can vary across sectors and company size. Public sector firms traditionally have provided more benefits, on average, than private sector firms. As an example, 81.9 percent of government workers in Ontario have a registered pension plan as part of their benefits plan, while only 25 percent of private-sector workers possess such a plan. From those who are covered under a registered pension plan, 94.7 percent of government workers have a defined benefit pension plan as compared to 41.5 percent of private sector workers.[13]

So, what do employers hope to gain from these expenditures? Why do some employers invest heavily in indirect pay, while others provide only the minimum required by law? Why bother to provide indirect pay at all? Is indirect pay a costly frill, or can it play a significant role in furthering key compensation objectives? This section of the chapter provides the foundation for addressing these questions.

Indirect pay can be anything that costs the employer money, addresses some type of employee need (thus conferring some type of "benefit" on the employee), and is not included as part of base or performance pay. There are six main types or categories of indirect pay, as shown in Compensation Notebook 4.1.

These pay systems vary in other ways. One key variation is choice—that is, whether employees can choose what benefits they receive (a flexible benefits system) or whether they cannot (a fixed benefits system). Another variation is responsibility for the costs—whether the employer covers all costs, or whether employees are required to share in the costs. Yet another important difference is whether coverage varies for different employee groups. All these issues will be discussed in more detail in Chapter 12.

## Why Use Indirect Pay?

Why do firms provide indirect pay? There are eight main motives.

1. Competitive pressure. If competitors are offering benefits that are important to the people the firm wants to hire, then an employer may need to offer similar benefits to attract those employees. For example, some employees would never dream of working for an employer that did not provide an adequate pension plan.

   To satisfy the security needs of their members, unions have always bargained strongly for comprehensive employee benefits, and unionized firms have had to respond to these pressures. To remove one possible incentive for unionization, non-union firms may match the packages won by unions at other firms (although they do not always do so). On average, employees in unionized firms can receive about 45 percent higher benefits than comparable non-union Canadian employees. However, research suggests that the union's comparatively better benefits may be at the expense of unionized employees' base pay. In addition, unions used to be vehemently opposed to individual performance pay, but this is no longer the case. Therefore, some of the union's security measures for employees have been reduced.[14] Certain types of indirect pay receive more favourable income tax treatment than direct pay (see Chapter 12). In these cases, a firm may use indirect pay to provide a higher total amount of after-tax compensation to employees than it would if the firm had paid out the same number of dollars in the form of direct pay.

2. Many benefits items, such as extended medical or dental coverage, can be purchased more cheaply by the employer than by the employee, due to group discounts from economies of scale in purchasing these items. (Indeed, some employees, such as those

with serious health problems, might not even be able to acquire such insurance on their own.) Again, this provides a higher level of reward to employees for the same amount of company money.

3. Benefits can protect the financial security and peace of mind of employees, thereby helping maintain good employee performance. Employees who have concerns about their ability to deal with health expenses, or what would happen should they become disabled, or who have personal problems, may have difficulty focusing on their work.

4. Many employers feel a genuine sense of responsibility for the welfare of their employees and want to help protect them from adversity. Others may not have the same concern but still do not want to appear hardhearted when employees encounter financial or health problems. The benefits system provides a systematic way for dealing with these types of problems.

5. Benefits can reinforce a particular managerial strategy. For example, the human relations strategy relies on a stable workforce. Because benefits for employees usually increase as their tenure increases, benefits can encourage membership behaviour. They can also create a sense of gratitude and obligation on the part of employees toward their employer—a key feature of the human relations strategy. It is no coincidence that the boom in benefits plans started during the 1950s and 1960s, when human relations firms were becoming preeminent. But indirect pay can be used to reinforce other managerial strategies as well. For example, because high-involvement companies focus on employee learning and development, they generally provide generous tuition reimbursement and educational leave plans. These two benefits can help provide the intrinsic rewards on which these organizations rely for employee retention and motivation.

6. Specific benefits can be used to promote consequences that benefit the organization. For example, subsidizing fitness classes or providing supplemental medical coverage may result in healthier employees who miss less work due to sickness. In addition, employee assistance programs may help employees resolve personal problems that could have a negative impact on work performance. Provision of company cars may reinforce a particular image for the sales force. Purchase discounts on company products may prevent the potential embarrassment of company employees purchasing products from a competitor and also help give employees direct knowledge of the company's products. Compensation Today 4.1 gives more examples of companies providing their own products as part of the employee benefits package.

## COMPENSATION TODAY 4.1

### PICK YOUR PERK: FREE PORK, BEER, BUCKS, OR PROZAC?

Would you rather have free beer, free pork, free bucks, or free Prozac? Is that choice too tranquil? Then how about free Viagra?

As part of their indirect pay packages, employees at Labatt Brewing Companies can get two free cases of beer a month,

employees at Big Sky Farms of Saskatchewan receive two sides of pork every year, and employees at Birchwood Automotive Group can earn "Birchwood Bucks" when they hit financial targets. This can be used towards live auction bids on items such as iPads and big screen TVs. Eli Lilly Corporation employees receive free Prozac (and any other drug the company manufactures). Employees at Pfizer Corporation receive free Viagra (which retails at $15 a pill!) along with other drugs it manufactures, and employees of auto manufacturers receive purchase discounts on new vehicles. Imperial Oil Canada offers employees discounts on Esso gasoline and home heating oil. In the travel business, employees are eligible for free or low-cost flights and package tours, as long as they select them from unsold inventory. Many retail stores offer employees discounts on the products they sell.

In addition to providing a valued benefit to employees and helping employees become familiar with company products, most of these benefits carry no tax liability to the employee because companies are generally allowed to provide their own products to employees without having to declare them as taxable benefits.

Sources: Doug Murray, "The Best Benefits Companies Can Offer," *Slice*, August 18, 2017; "15 Companies with Amazing Employee Perks," *Workopolis*, April 2, 2014.

Many employers provide non-traditional benefits.

## Disadvantages of Indirect Pay

If indirect pay has all these advantages, why doesn't every firm use it? Indirect pay also has numerous disadvantages.

1. The cost of indirect pay can be substantial.
2. Indirect pay is generally a rigid, fixed cost. Once a firm commits itself to providing certain benefits (such as a pension plan), it is liable for the costs of maintaining these benefits, even if the firm is not performing well.
3. Once a benefit is provided, it becomes very difficult (and sometimes even illegal) to eliminate it. Even if the benefit is not highly valued by employees, simply eliminating it (without replacing it with something else) is likely to cause a negative reaction among employees. Moreover, where benefits are part of the terms and conditions of employment, as they are in union contracts, to unilaterally discontinue them may be illegal.
4. It is often difficult to develop a benefits package that meets the true needs of employees and that does not waste money on benefits that are not valued highly by employees.

5. Administration and communication of a benefits program can be much more costly than simply providing higher direct pay, particularly for smaller firms, which do not enjoy economies of scale when purchasing and administering benefits.

6. There is almost no direct link between indirect pay and specific employee task behaviour. Because most or all employees in a firm are typically covered by benefits, regardless of employee performance, and because the amount of the benefits received does not vary with performance, indirect pay is the opposite of performance pay and is not a good motivator for task behaviour.

7. A benefits program may succeed too well at creating employee stability, when unhappy employees remain with the firm simply because they do not want to forgo the generous benefits package.

8. Certain specific benefits, or the means of administering them, may actually promote undesirable behaviour. For example, an excessively generous or poorly designed sick leave policy may encourage absences by increasing the attractiveness of not coming to work and may also indirectly penalize those who do come to work by requiring them to do the work of the absentees.

9. Despite the large amount of money expended on benefits, not a lot is known about the impact of indirect pay on employee and company performance. Over two decades ago, experts complained that "the state of knowledge about the influence of benefits on employee attitudes and behaviours is dismal."[15] Since then, with the specific exception of pensions, not much has improved.

While we know that satisfaction with benefits is an important component of overall reward satisfaction,[16] there has been no research that might tell us whether eliminating the benefits system and adding the equivalent amount to salaries would contribute more to reward satisfaction. In theory, a properly designed benefits system that provides valued benefits to employees *should* deliver more reward satisfaction than simply adding extra pay, due to the tax advantages of benefits plans and to the economies of scale when benefits are purchased. However, this proposition has never been effectively tested.

But even if it is true that benefits are preferable to extra direct pay, there must be a point beyond which the value of additional indirect pay declines below the value of additional direct pay. Many employers believe that this point has now been reached. After a steady upward trend beginning in the 1960s,[17] benefits costs peaked in 1995 at 21.4 percent of total compensation.[18] After that, they edged down every year until 2000, when they settled at 19.7 percent of total compensation in large firms[19] and lower than that in smaller firms. In the 2000s, benefits costs began edging up again due to the increased costs of health benefits, particularly prescription drug plans.[20] Also, due to poor investment returns realized by pension funds caused by the 2008–09 financial meltdown, coupled with increased employee longevity, some types of pension plans (particularly those known as "defined benefit" plans) have become much more costly for employers. Recent research suggests that these costs have stabilized between 10–20 percent.[21]

In general, indirect pay is not a good investment for classical firms because it provides no task motivation. Perhaps the only circumstance in which it may be a good investment for such firms is in situations involving high training costs. Because a classical firm is usually not a very satisfying organization to work for, the company needs some means of retaining its investment in trained employees; thus, using indirect pay to tie the employee to the firm may be a good strategy for protecting this investment. Of course, this commitment will likely be of a grudging, continuance type.

This is why classical organizations normally minimize the use of indirect pay, except as a means to retain key employees. But ironically, much to the dismay of classical managers, many classical firms have ended up with very extensive benefits programs as a result of unions and the collective bargaining process. Most of these firms are probably aware that they receive very little value from these programs, and some have likely attempted to use flexible benefits as a ploy to cut costs.

If a classical organization must provide benefits, either as a result of the collective bargaining process or in an effort to match the benefits of competitors, a traditional fixed benefits system will probably fit best, with employees sharing the costs of the benefits payouts (such as paying a proportion of every dental claim) to discourage frivolous use of the system. In situations where pay is tied to seniority and where employee productivity drops with age, generous pension plans may be desirable to encourage highly paid employees to retire.

In contrast, for human relations firms, indirect pay is a cornerstone of the managerial strategy, which is designed to show high concern for employees and to encourage high membership behaviour. As discussed earlier, human relations strategies appear to be losing popularity due to changes in the work environment. But in firms where human relations is still an effective managerial strategy, indirect pay remains a key part of the compensation strategy, although efforts are made to contain the costs of benefits. While these benefits systems may include some flexible elements, a fully flexible benefits system does not fit well with this approach.

The high-involvement firms face a dilemma regarding indirect pay. In some ways, indirect pay does not fit with the high-involvement concept because it does not relate to company performance. However, the key asset of any high-involvement firm is its employees, so it needs to be sure that the absence of a benefits system doesn't cause them to leave. Such a firm also needs to offer sufficient benefits that employees' lower-order needs for security are satisfied so that they can be motivated by their higher-order needs.

A high-involvement organization requires a high level of commitment from its employees, so its benefits system needs to recognize and facilitate that commitment. For example, family-friendly benefits, such as child care, elder care, and flexible work schedules, help employees. High-involvement firms also have a genuine concern for the well-being of their employees and strive to help them deal with unforeseen problems.

In general, high-involvement organizations tend to structure benefits to reinforce the employer–employee partnership. Thus, a flexible benefits system with cost sharing on the individual benefits is a good fit. But fixed benefits that encourage highly desired behaviours, such as tuition reimbursement and educational leave plans, also have a role. A key point is that benefits programs in high-involvement companies are not focused on continuance commitment. A high-involvement organization does not want to "trap" people who don't fit the organization.

Compensation Notebook 4.2 summarizes the advantages and disadvantages of the three fundamental compensation mix components.

## ADVANTAGES AND DISADVANTAGES OF THE COMPENSATION MIX COMPONENTS

| Component | Advantages | Disadvantages |
| --- | --- | --- |
| Base pay | • Flexibility<br>• Can cover all valued job behaviours<br>• Can signal relative importance of jobs<br>• Demonstrates commitment to employee<br>• Can support managerial strategy<br>• Simplicity | • Fixed pay commitment<br>• Does not motivate task behaviour<br>• Does not encourage citizenship behaviour<br>• Not self-correcting |
| Performance pay | • Signals key behaviours and motivates action<br>• Reduces need for control mechanisms<br>• Creates employee interest in performance<br>• Can support managerial strategy<br>• Relates pay to firm's ability to pay | • Employees prefer predictable rewards<br>• May require higher compensation<br>• May cause focus only on rewarded behaviours<br>• May cause unanticipated consequences<br>• Usually more complex than base pay |
| Indirect pay | • Can help attract employees<br>• Matches unionized firms<br>• Favourable tax treatment<br>• Economies of scale in purchasing<br>• Can provide valued rewards for no cash<br>• Provide employee peace of mind<br>• Helps employer deal humanely with problems<br>• Can help promote company products<br>• Can support managerial strategy | • Cost can be substantial<br>• Rigidity<br>• Difficult to develop efficient benefits package<br>• Administration and communication costly<br>• Does not motivate task behaviour<br>• May cause excessive employee stability<br>• May encourage undesirable behaviour |

**market pricing**
Establishing base pay by determining the average amount of pay other employers are offering for a given job.

**job evaluation**
Establishing base pay by ranking all jobs in the firm according to their value to that firm.

**pay-for-knowledge system (PKS)**
Establishing base pay according to the total value of the skills and competencies an employee has acquired.

# BASE PAY METHODS: MARKET PRICING

Suppose, like most employers, you have decided to include base pay in your compensation system. How do you determine the value of each job to the organization so that it can be compensated accordingly? There are three main methods. The first—market pricing—is to simply offer the average of what other employers in the region are paying for a particular job. The second—job evaluation—is to systematically rank all jobs in the organization in terms of their value to the employer and then calibrate this system to the labour market. The third is to develop a system based on the total value of the skills and competencies that each employee has acquired, known as a pay-for-knowledge system (PKS).

In the remainder of this chapter, we will discuss each of these three methods, focusing on the major considerations in deciding which method(s) will best fit your organization.

However, except for the pay-for-knowledge system, where an understanding of the design issues is relevant in deciding whether to make it a part of your compensation strategy, we will defer discussion of the technical aspects of these methods to Chapters 7, 8, and 9. Right now, we want to focus on factors that influence your decisions regarding which methods fit best with your compensation strategy, as a foundation for learning how to use the compensation strategy formulation process in Chapter 6.

Each of the three methods for determining base pay has advantages and disadvantages, and it is essential to understand these when deciding which of these methods is best suited for your firm's compensation strategy. Compensation Notebook 4.3 summarizes these advantages and disadvantages. We now discuss them for each method in turn.

Market pricing is the simplest of the three methods and is the most common method used in small firms. The method is straightforward: if you need a secretary or a machinist, you observe what other firms are paying for these jobs and then make similar offers. If you need exceptional performance from your employees and you can afford it, you may pay somewhat above the "going rate" in order to attract the most qualified individuals. But if you don't need exceptional performance and are prepared to put up with higher turnover, you may decide to pay somewhat less than the going rate.

## COMPENSATION NOTEBOOK 4.3

### ADVANTAGES AND DISADVANTAGES OF THE METHODS FOR BASE PAY

| Method | Advantages | Disadvantages |
|---|---|---|
| Market pricing | • Simplicity and cost<br>• Keeps jobs aligned with market conditions | • "Going rate" not always easy to identify<br>• Job definitions may vary from the market data<br>• Does not address internal equity<br>• Lack of control of compensation strategy<br>• May violate pay equity legislation |
| Job evaluation | • Centralized control of compensation costs<br>• Signals importance of different jobs<br>• Promotes internal equity<br>• Makes calibration to the market easier<br>• Systematic way to determine pay for new jobs<br>• Availability of packaged plans from consultants<br>• Fits well with classical and human relations<br>• Low discontinuation rate | • May impede high involvement<br>• More costly to develop than market pricing<br>• Need for job descriptions<br>• May become an adversarial process<br>• Costly to maintain<br>• Can inhibit flexibility and skill development |

*(continued)*

| Method | Advantages | Disadvantages |
|---|---|---|
| **Pay for knowledge** | • Incentive for employee skill development<br>• No disincentive to movement<br>• High workforce flexibility<br>• Does not require job descriptions<br>• Jobs are broader, with more intrinsic rewards<br>• May improve customer service<br>• Supports high-involvement management | • May raise labour costs<br>• "Topping out" problem<br>• Resistance by senior employees to rotation<br>• Higher training costs<br>• Complex to develop and administer<br>• May also need to maintain job-based system<br>• May be difficult to calibrate system to market<br>• Not all employees may have desire or capability<br>• Unions may resist because not based on seniority<br>• High discontinuation rate |

As the labour market changes, the employer adjusts the pay levels of current employees and the starting pay levels for new employees in accordance with these changes. To simplify the process of determining the "market rates" for each job, some companies use compensation consulting firms that specialize in collecting these data and making them available to clients on a commercial basis. Data are also available through government agencies (such as Statistics Canada), industry associations, organizations such as the Conference Board of Canada, and websites.

## ADVANTAGES OF MARKET PRICING

Market pricing has two key advantages.

1. Relative simplicity and cost. Other methods are much more complicated to design and apply, and all other pay systems must ultimately include references to the market to calibrate their systems. As an example of complexity, the job evaluation method depends on formalized, detailed, and up-to-date job descriptions. But many firms do not have such job descriptions and do not want to develop them. Descriptions are not needed in pay-for-knowledge systems, but those systems are difficult to develop and administer. Thus, market pricing is usually a much cheaper system than either of the alternatives.

2. Keeps all jobs in the organization aligned with market conditions. This prevents turnover caused by uncompetitive wages and makes recruiting easier. For the other two base pay methods, not all jobs are necessarily aligned with the market.

# DISADVANTAGES OF MARKET PRICING

Market pricing has numerous drawbacks.

1. It is not as simple as it sounds. One difficulty (among many) is that identifying one specific going rate for a given job can be elusive. Different wage surveys turn up different results because they make different judgments about which jobs to survey and how to define different labour markets. Labour markets can be defined in several ways—in terms of industry type, occupational group, geographic area, and firm size. As a result, market pricing often does not result in standardized, usable information.

2. Different employers define jobs differently. For example, a "secretary" in some firms serves mainly as a typist or receptionist, while in other firms, "secretaries" serve more as executive assistants or even as office managers. Thus, one firm may report that it is paying its "secretaries" $25 000 per annum, while another pays $45 000. For this reason, a wage survey that indicates an "average" pay of $35 000 for "secretaries" may be seriously misleading.

3. Getting a definitive market price for a given job may not be possible. There is strong evidence that there is no such thing as a standard "market wage" for a given job.[22] Studies have found that even in a single geographic area, wage rates for the same job titles vary dramatically.[23] For many job titles, some employers have been known to pay two to three times what other employers do. Of course, some of this discrepancy may be due to inconsistencies in job definitions or to differences between industries. However, research shows that there are often wide discrepancies in pay for identical jobs in a single industry and geographic area.[24]

4. Although this result is often mystifying for economists, it should not be for human resources specialists. We know that membership behaviour is motivated by the total mix of rewards from a job, not from pay alone, and these "identical" jobs likely vary considerably in the total package of rewards. Compensation surveys often do not adequately account for performance pay, such as profit sharing, and usually do not take indirect pay into account at all. Moreover, surveys take no account of the other extrinsic rewards (such as job security or opportunities for promotion) and intrinsic rewards (such as job autonomy or skill variety) that some jobs may offer. Given that the total spectrum of rewards varies widely across firms, it would be extraordinary if there were *not* wide differences in cash compensation across firms. All of this illustrates the problems inherent in comparing compensation statistics across firms.

5. It does not address internal equity. When market-pricing jobs, organizations make little or no attempt to weight the value of each job *to their own organizations*. Thus, jobs that are vital to the organization's success may pay less than jobs of lesser importance, simply because of data from the labour market. Furthermore, if a firm is geographically dispersed, market conditions may vary in different parts of the country, causing the same job to be paid differently in other parts of the company. These differences can cause employee resentment.

6. It results in a lack of control. A firm that uses only market pricing is allowing competitors to set its compensation policy. Because it does not tailor compensation to suit its own strategy and needs, it forgoes the opportunity to use compensation as a source of competitive advantage. By using only market pricing, an organization may be allowing the market to drive its strategy.

7. The market does not necessarily produce pay systems that are equitable from a societal point of view. Critics point to a "pay gap" between jobs that have traditionally been performed by women and those that have been performed by men. They argue that the market has systematically undervalued work performed by women and that when a firm adopts market-based pay, it perpetuates these inequities. In response, many Canadian jurisdictions have passed pay equity legislation (discussed more fully in later chapters), which requires that jobs of equal value be compensated equally, whatever the market may suggest. Firms in these jurisdictions must include some type of job evaluation in their compensation systems, whether they want to or not.

## BASE PAY METHODS: JOB EVALUATION

Job evaluation systems involve analyzing job descriptions and then comparing all jobs in the organization in a systematic manner. The most common approach is to identify several key compensable factors and then evaluate each job according to how much of each factor is present. This creates a ranking of all jobs, known as a "hierarchy of jobs." Exact pay levels for each job are determined by relating certain key jobs or benchmark jobs to the external market and then interpolating the rest.

Job evaluation first gained popularity in the 1920s and 1930s as large classical organizations began to dominate industry. For them, job evaluation provided a method for centralizing and controlling compensation costs. Before this time, compensation was handled in a haphazard, often chaotic manner, with individual supervisors and managers having the authority to pay employees as they saw fit. Lack of control over such a key cost element was a major frustration to top management in classical firms, and job evaluation was seen as a way of both gaining control and ensuring that compensation costs would be no higher than they had to be. Job evaluation also fit perfectly with the narrowly structured jobs that these types of organizations tend to have.

In the 1940s and 1950s, human relations firms regarded it as an important tool for fostering a sense of fairness among employees, thereby keeping them loyal and satisfied and preventing unionization. While it was a means of controlling costs, its ability to foster a sense of reward equity was seen by human relations firms as its most valuable feature.

### ADVANTAGES OF JOB EVALUATION

Job evaluation has several major advantages.

1. It enables centralized control of compensation costs and prevents jobs from being overpaid relative to their value to the firm.

2. Because job evaluation links pay level to the importance or value of the job to the organization, it signals the importance of jobs to employees and motivates people to seek promotions.

3. It is a systematic way to promote equitable pay within the organization and to reduce the impact of factors such as favouritism and nepotism. When used effectively, job evaluation should also eliminate gender-based pay inequities.

4. Its system of standardized jobs makes it easier to determine market values for jobs after they have been subjected to job evaluation.

5. Because job evaluation is based on job descriptions, it encourages the development of those descriptions, which can bring significant broader advantages. When accurate and up-to-date, job descriptions inform employees about their roles in the organization, guide recruiters in hiring new employees, and provide some assurance that all important tasks are being done. They also allow for tight control of employees, if that is part of the firm's managerial strategy.

6. Job evaluation provides a systematic way to determine pay for new jobs.

7. Over time, a number of consulting firms that specialize in job evaluation have emerged, with well-established technologies for conducting job evaluations that organizations can use when implementing job evaluation programs.

8. Job evaluation fits with and reinforces both the classical and human relations managerial strategies particularly well but can also be used in high-involvement organizations to ensure fairness of pay.

## DISADVANTAGES OF JOB EVALUATION

Job evaluation has numerous disadvantages, some related to the process itself and others related to the organizational rigidity it can create.

1. Job evaluation programs require the use of comprehensive job descriptions, which many organizations may not have. Developing and continuously updating of job descriptions is an onerous process. Job descriptions are costly to develop and maintain and involve continual updating as jobs change. For organizations operating in dynamic environments, this can be a significant problem.

2. Applying job evaluations can become an adversarial process as it is in the financial interests of employees to inflate their jobs whenever possible. If job inflation occurs, it not only inflates the costs of the pay system, but also causes inequity between inflated jobs and jobs more honestly evaluated.

3. Although it is presented as a fair and scientific way of achieving equitable pay, most employees realize that there is still substantial subjectivity in the process. Job evaluation systems, along with market pricing systems, have been accused of perpetuating rather than combating gender-based pay inequity.[25] However, this is not a problem inherent in job evaluation; rather, it's the result of the way job evaluation has been used.

4. The compensable factors outlined in job evaluations are often abstract and ambiguous. The factors listed also demand comparisons of very different jobs. For instance, if a Human Resources professional (who does not have firsthand knowledge of either job) is asked to evaluate the accountability of both a marketing professional and a technical systems analyst, this would be hard to substantiate.[26]

5. The most important criticism of job evaluation systems is that they inhibit change, flexibility, and skill development.[27] Job descriptions tend to create a "not my job" syndrome, as some employees use their job descriptions to avoid taking on extra duties. When circumstances change, job descriptions can slow organizational adaptation, because employees remain unwilling to change until their current job description changes. Professor Edward Lawler, one of the foremost proponents of high-involvement management, argues that job evaluation impedes the transformation of classical and human relations organizations into high-involvement organizations.[28] He advocates the use of pay-for-knowledge systems instead. It should be noted, however, that while we

consider job descriptions a disadvantage because it can decrease organizational flexibility, these descriptions are very important for organizations. They help organizations in effective management.

Critics of job evaluation contend that there is no incentive for employees to learn jobs that are not in the direct line of advancement. If advancement to better jobs is not possible, there is no extrinsic incentive to learn additional skills.

6. Finally, developing and maintaining a job evaluation system can be costly, especially compared to the market pricing method. And, of course, job evaluation does not entirely eliminate the need for references to the market, which still must be done for a number of benchmark jobs in order to align the job evaluation system with the market.

Some companies, such as General Electric, have replaced job evaluation programs with "broad banding"—the practice of reducing the dozens of pay grades used by some large firms to as few as six large job bands.[29] Some supporters of job evaluation argue that broad banding can solve the rigidity problems it causes,[30] but others point out that it is illogical to go to all the trouble of making fine distinctions between jobs and then throw jobs together into large bands.[31] For these reasons, some firms that adopt broad banding simply eliminate job evaluation altogether. However, it appears that most firms that say they use broad banding are keeping job evaluation and are simply pruning down the number of pay grades they use to some extent—but rarely to as few as six pay grades.

Despite its disadvantages, research shows that the great majority of medium to large Canadian firms (75–80 percent) use job evaluation, and use of job evaluation actually appears to be growing. Some of this increase may be due to pay equity legislation (enacted in a number of jurisdictions, including Ontario and Quebec), which requires the use of a systematic method to compare job values within organizations.

Research also shows that about one-third of medium to large Canadian firms use broad banding and that most of these firms (about 80 percent) also use job evaluation. Interestingly, while broad banding has enjoyed a relatively high adoption rate, it also has a relatively high discontinuation rate, so the net effect has been very little change in overall incidence over the past few years.

Overall, these results suggest that most medium to large Canadian firms believe that the advantages of job evaluation outweigh its disadvantages. Clearly, job evaluation poses more problems when the organization is faced with rapid change, so it seems most viable for firms using classical or human relations managerial strategies. Interestingly, however, research suggests that high-involvement firms are actually *more likely* than other firms to use job evaluation. This finding is quite surprising and may indicate that job evaluation is really not incompatible with high-involvement management. It is possible that high-involvement firms see job evaluation as a way to maintain equitable pay relationships, which are essential for these firms.

## BASE PAY METHODS: PAY FOR KNOWLEDGE

The third method for determining base pay is radically different from job evaluation. It involves basing pay on the capabilities of individuals rather than on the characteristics of jobs. It is often called *person-based pay*, as opposed to *job-based pay*. There are various labels for this method, including pay for knowledge, skill-based pay, and competency-based pay, and these terms are often used interchangeably.

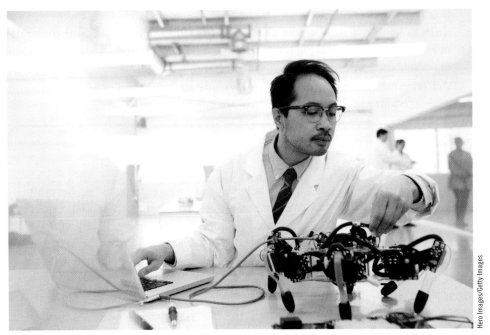

Some jobs are paid through skill-based pay systems.

However, competency-based pay, usually applied at the managerial and professional level, is distinct from skill-based pay (SBP), usually applied at the operational level. The term *pay for knowledge* includes both competency- and skill-based pay, but most of the research has focused on skill-based pay. Under the right conditions, with the right plan design, it is clear that skill-based pay can be successful and add value to an organization.[32] By contrast, research on the effectiveness of competency-based pay is scant. Most of the discussion here will therefore focus on skill-based pay, but we will touch briefly on competency-based pay at the end of this section.

## ADVANTAGES OF SKILL-BASED PAY

The premise of skill-based pay (SBP) systems is that employees are paid according to their skills, knowledge, and competencies, regardless of the job they happen to be doing at the time. Using an SBP system for base pay has several advantages.

1. It provides a major incentive for employees to learn a variety of skills, which then makes it easier to shift employees from one job to another as needed. Recent research shows that SBP promotes workforce flexibility, which often increases workplace productivity.[33]

2. SBP avoids the disincentive to movement caused by traditional job evaluation systems, which result in strictly defined jobs that are "owned" by the people currently doing them. Under traditional pay systems, if a nut on a machine needs tightening, someone must call a mechanic, because maintenance is not part of the machine operator's job description. However, under SBP, an operator simply grabs a wrench and tightens the nut.

   This flexibility is especially beneficial for organizations for which production and service processes peak and ebb unpredictably. For example, a company may have a big customer order that needs expediting or is experiencing a parts shortage in a particular production process; in both situations, SBP allows employees to move from idle

**competency-based pay**
Pay that is based on the characteristics, rather than the performance, of individual employees; usually applied to managerial or professional employees.

**skill-based pay (SBP)**
Pay that is based on the specific skills and capabilities of individual employees, rather than on the specific tasks they are carrying out; usually applied to operational-level employees.

functions to active functions. Of course, SBP also makes it easier to cover employee absences and vacations. Because the system relies on flexible skills, SBP companies must use job rotation, and job rotation itself has been shown to be beneficial for some organizations.[34]

Compensation Today 4.2 illustrates how SBP can facilitate flexibility and change, whereas traditional methods for base pay can inhibit change.[35]

---

**COMPENSATION TODAY 4.2**

### HEADACHES AT TYLENOL

As a result of the 1982 Tylenol poisoning tragedy (where persons unknown tampered with bottles of Tylenol tablets, resulting in numerous deaths), Johnson & Johnson decided to completely redo its Tylenol packaging to add greater security.

At the time, it had two packaging plants: one skill-based, the other job-based. The skill-based plant quickly installed the new technology and got back into production. Not so with the traditional job-based, seniority-driven plant. Seniority rights and traditional pay grades reduced employee flexibility in adapting to the new technology. In addition, unlike the skill-based plant, the traditional plant did not have a history of providing training, valuing personal growth, and encouraging employees to do new things. The transition to new packaging equipment was a major challenge at this plant.

---

1. A major advantage over job evaluation is that it does not need job descriptions and thereby avoids many of the problems of job descriptions. This is a significant advantage for organizations facing rapid change.

2. Jobs in SBP companies are broader and provide more intrinsic rewards. This advantage comes with related advantages. For example, knowledgeable employees performing broader jobs may be more effective at customer service because they understand more of the business. According to two prominent experts: "Skill-based pay prepares employees to handle a wider range of customer issues without switching the customer from place to place. This is more efficient for the organization and for the customer."[36]

3. Because SBP allows individuals and teams to be more self-managing, and because it uses the workforce more efficiently, a firm using SBP should be able to operate with a smaller labour force. This staffing reduction results from a reduced need for managerial, supervisory, and inspection positions, as well as specialty positions, such as maintenance mechanics and electricians.

4. A key advantage is that it supports behaviours needed by high-involvement firms. When employees are knowledgeable about their organization, they can make more effective decisions, exercise good judgment, and take quick action when necessary. For example, when Shell Canada wanted to build a new, high-involvement chemical plant, the company saw that this would be difficult if not impossible using traditional pay methods, and made skill-based pay a central part of this process, as Compensation Today 4.3 describes.

5. SBP not only fits with a high-involvement management strategy, but also helps promote change to high-involvement practices. As one expert puts it:

   *[Skill-based pay] can be a powerful force in helping an organization live up to a commitment to become a high-involvement organization. This is because employees, acting in their own self-interest, begin to exert pressure for greater training, information, and control over job rotation and other key decisions. In short, they begin to demand that the organization behave more like a high-involvement organization.*[37]

## SKILL-BASED PAY FINDS GOOD CHEMISTRY AT SHELL SARNIA

One of the first organizations in Canada to implement skill-based pay was the Shell Chemical plant in Sarnia, Ontario, which opened in 1978. The plant produces polypropylene and isopropyl alcohol in a 24-hour continuous process operation. The plant produces 75 grades of state-of-the-art plastics in pea-sized pellets. It then sells these versatile polymers worldwide for use in products such as car door panels, carpets, toys, and pop bottles. Consistently high product quality is essential. However, the production process is very complicated, and many things can go wrong during the multi-staged production process.

Quick and accurate reactions to production problems are essential at a major production plant, but in the past, traditional plant design had made problem solving very difficult. Production processes were usually divided into distinct departments, within which each employee had a narrowly specified job. Few employees understood the entire production process and the complex interrelations among the various production phases.

Shell had noticed numerous problems in its traditional plants, including slow responses to production problems, underuse of employees, high boredom levels, employee dissatisfaction, and employee turnover. To prevent these problems in the new plant, Shell decided to base its new plant on the high-involvement model. At the same time, the company also wanted to develop a collaborative relationship with the union (the Communications, Energy, and Paperworkers Union) by involving it in the plant design process as well as in the continuing operation of the plant.

The new design eliminated department separations and created 20-person "shift teams" to operate the plant during each shift. These shift teams were supported by a craft team of electricians, pipefitters, and other specialized personnel, who were present only during the day shift or during emergency situations. Each member of the shift team was expected to learn to perform all necessary tasks in the production process.

The company recognized at the outset that the traditional approach to compensating operators, which defined jobs narrowly and had a different pay grade for each job, would not be compatible with this new system. Therefore, job categories on each shift team were reduced to one: shift team member. To foster employee multiskilling and flexibility, a pay-for-knowledge system was developed for all hourly employees.

Today, the system is still in place. When new employees start at the plant, they receive the training needed to perform a basic set of shift functions and are paid a base rate. To increase their pay rate, workers need to demonstrate competence in one additional job knowledge cluster and in four modules of a "specialty skill." (For the purposes of training and compensation, the "operations" area of the complex is divided into 10 job-knowledge clusters.) Employees are able to learn all skills if they are interested in doing so. Each specialty skill (e.g., instrumentation, electrical, pipefitting) is further divided into 40 skill modules, and every worker is expected to select one specialty skill. Thus, there are 12 job phases and 10 levels in the pay progression system, and workers make the top pay when they have mastered all 10 job-knowledge clusters and all 40 modules of their specialty skill. On average, this takes about six to seven years. Coworkers and managers test the employee's ability by signing check sheets that confirm the employee's competence in a skill. Once an employee has mastered all phases, he or she will reach the top pay rate. If a skill is no longer used, the employee must learn a new skill but will never be penalized.

How well does the system work? When interviewed in 2001, company officials indicated that the original skill-based pay system, implemented more than 20 years previously, had shown such success that it had been carried forward with very few changes. Managers believe that this system has helped in the reduction of downtime and production disruptions. However, Shell Sarnia is now looking to sell its operations, stating that this plant no longer fits with Shell's "evolving portfolio."

Sources: Norm Halpern, "Sociotechnical Systems Design: The Shell Sarnia Experience," in *Quality of Working Life: Contemporary Cases*, ed. J.B. Cunningham and T.H. White (Ottawa: Labour Canada, 1984), 31–75; HRDC, "Moving Parts and Moving People: Sociotechnical Design of a New Plant," in *Labour Management Innovations in Canada* (Ottawa: Human Resources Development Canada, 1994), 72–76; Personal communications with company officials; Joseph H. Boyett and Jimmie T. Boyett, *The Skill-Based Pay Design Manual*. iUniverse, 2004; "Shell Looks to Sell Its Sarnia Operations," *CBC News*, January 10, 2019.

# DISADVANTAGES OF SKILL-BASED PAY

Skill-based pay also has several drawbacks.

1. Employees may be "overpaid" relative to competitor companies, especially if SBP has been in place for some time and has resulted in most employees earning the top pay level ("topping out"). In general, employees operating under SBP earn considerably more than employees not working under this system. However, SBP companies feel that the flexibility gained outweighs the cost disadvantage.

2. When workers top out, or are earning the top pay level in the skill grid, what is the incentive to continue learning and updating skills? Skills can also become out of date, so there needs to be a system for requiring topped-out employees to reskill.

3. If employees are not rotated through jobs regularly, then their skills atrophy. However, senior employees may resent spending time doing the less-advanced jobs in order for less-senior employees to perform the more advanced jobs. As one pair of experts put it: "At some point, having all chefs and no dishwashers (and having to pay chef wages to those who are assigned to scrub pots and pans) is uncompetitive. And probably dissatisfying to certified chefs with dishpan hands."[38]

4. Skill-based pay systems lead to increased training costs, both in terms of the cost of providing the training and in terms of lost work time, if employees need to be taken off the job for training.

5. These systems are more complex to administer than job-based pay systems, due to the need for certification procedures to determine whether an employee is entitled to be paid for a new skill.

6. Aligning skill-based pay systems to the market may also be more difficult than for a job evaluation system if there are no other firms with skill-based pay systems to use as a comparison. Moreover, for most firms, applying SBP to all jobs is not feasible, and this creates a need to maintain dual skill- and job-based systems.

7. Not all employees may have the ability or desire to learn multiple jobs. A firm wishing to use SBP must be sure it has a workforce that is willing and able to continually learn new skills.

8. Unions may resist SBP because wages are based on skill levels instead of seniority. But note that many SBP systems are found in unionized firms.

9. Skill-based pay systems may appear to violate some pay equity laws, which generally stipulate that employees should be paid for what they actually do rather than for their capabilities.[39] Thus, a woman performing a bagging operation in a dog food plant who receives lower pay than a man doing the same job may appear to be unfairly treated. However, most pay equity laws do make exceptions for factors such as skill levels and relevant experience, as long as these are applied consistently to male *and* female employees.

10. SBP has a relatively high failure rate. Research by one of the authors suggests that as many as 75 percent of SBP plans are discontinued within four years.

This last disadvantage—that skill-based pay plans have a high discontinuation rate—should not be that surprising. Given all the complexities and potential drawbacks of skill-based pay, it is likely to benefit only a limited number of companies—in particular, those that need a highly flexible workforce. These would primarily be firms with complex technologies or unpredictable production or service demands. Moreover, investing in more knowledgeable employees pays off only if the organization is structured in such a way as to use this knowledge. Classical and human relations organizations would not receive much value from a skill-based pay system. For all these reasons, the proportion of firms using skill-based pay has not grown significantly in recent years.[40]

Research indicates that, as expected, high-involvement firms are most likely to use skill-based pay. Other Canadian research shows that firms with a participative culture are more likely to adopt SBP.[41] Moreover, a study of 15 American firms that implemented skill-based pay systems found that high-involvement management was a key success factor for SBP compensation systems:

> It is important to note that skill-based pay is not so much a compensation system as it is a radical departure from traditional organizational design. It works best in work systems where there is a high level of employee involvement, where work has been organized in self-managed teams ... and where there is a commitment to high levels of investment in human capital.[42]

Some research has found that traditional, unionized organizations can benefit from SBP, but only if both management and the union are willing to adopt collaborative roles.[43] Overall, the keys to success appear to be implementation in the right circumstances, along with effective plan design and effective implementation. However, in spite of the fact that SBP has a longstanding history and high visibility, enthusiasm, and use have dwindled over time.[44] When deciding whether SBP may fit, it is important to understand the key issues involved in developing a skill-based pay system.

## ISSUES IN DEVELOPING A SKILL-BASED PAY SYSTEM

There are five key issues in developing a skill-based pay system: (1) deciding which employee groups to include, (2) designing the skill blocks, (3) linking these skill blocks to pay, (4) providing learning opportunities, and (5) certifying skill achievement.

### To Whom Should Skill-based Pay Apply?

The most active early adopters of skill-based pay systems were continuous process operations, with products ranging from chemicals to steel to dog food. Because of their high task interdependence, high capital intensity, and overriding need to keep production running, these operations are ideal sites for skill-based pay. Increasingly, though, SBP has also been applied to other types of manufacturing firms and to the service sector.

Whenever the organization needs high-level and diverse employee skills and could benefit from high employee flexibility, SBP may pay off. In their study of firms using skill-based pay in the United States, Jenkins and his colleagues found examples of successful SBP plans in a wide range of manufacturing industries, as well as in many service industries, including financial services, computer services, utilities, health services, and retailing.[45] Probably the most important factor in all of this is whether SBP will be part of a high-involvement managerial strategy at the adopting firm.

### Designing Skill Blocks

After deciding where to implement SBP, the next step is to identify the job skills that are required for effective performance of the work system and then to "bundle" them into appropriate "skill blocks." Skills can typically be differentiated along two dimensions—horizontal and vertical. The horizontal dimension covers different *types* of skills, while the vertical dimension covers the *depth* of each skill.

Generally, skill blocks are set out in a grid, defined by these two dimensions. **Table 4.1** provides an example for a chemical plant. As the table shows, there are five horizontal skill types and four vertical skill levels, with a total of 18 skill blocks. As employees complete each skill block, they receive an increase in pay, as indicated by the dollar values shown in each block. (Although employees are usually expected to complete the horizontal row of skills before moving vertically to the next higher row of skills, there may be some circumstances where it makes sense to allow some vertical skill development before the entire row is completed.) In this illustration, a fully skilled chemical plant operator will be earning $17 000 more per year than an entry-level operator just starting out with the firm.

There are many possible ways to arrange a skill-based system. The Shell Sarnia chemical plant (described in Compensation Today 4.3) has 10 "job-knowledge clusters" for the basic operation of the plant. In addition, it has three specialty skills (instrumentation, electrical, and pipefitting), from which all shift team members must select one. To be fully qualified in a specialty skill, team members must complete 40 training modules.

At Shell Sarnia, a shift team member receives a pay increase when he or she completes one job knowledge cluster and four modules of a specialty skill. Thus, 10 pay raises are possible beyond the entry-level base pay that each employee receives on joining the company. The amounts of these raises are determined by collective bargaining. Employees can complete the job-knowledge clusters in any order, but specialty modules normally have a specified progression. Typically, it takes six or seven years for a shift team member to reach the top rate.

## TABLE 4.1

### EXAMPLE OF SKILL GRID FOR CHEMICAL PLANT

| | Operations | Packaging | Testing | Maintenance | Coordination/ Administration |
|---|---|---|---|---|---|
| **Level IV** | | Able to operate all production equipment for all products $1400 | Able to conduct all lab, chemical, and statistical tests $1400 | Able to diagnose and conduct major repairs on all plant equipment $1400 | Able to do all production and team coordination $1400 |
| **Level III** | Able to operate all production equipment for liquid products $1000 | Able to carry out all packaging processes $1000 | Able to conduct advanced testing and statistical analysis $1000 | Able to diagnose and repair the most common major malfunctions $1000 | Able to develop production and labour schedules $1000 |
| **Level II** | Able to operate all production equipment for dry products $800 | Able to package liquid products $800 | Able to analyze routine samples and do advanced quality control $800 | Able to deal with minor breakdowns and conduct routine maintenance $800 | Able to complete basic production and labour reports $800 |
| **Level I** | Able to operate basic production equipment $600 | Able to package dry products $600 | Able to collect routine samples and monitor product quality $600 | Able to make routine adjustments to all equipment $600 | |

A system of skill blocks can range from simple to complex. A simple system was used by General Mills at a plant producing fruit drinks.[46] There were four main steps in the production process, and each step became a skill block. Within each skill block, there were three skill levels, with a raise for completion of each. Employees could start in any skill block, complete all skill levels within that block, or move to another skill block after accomplishing two levels within that block.

At an information technology firm, the company wanted to design a skill-based pay system for technical support engineers, but there was no established set of procedures from which to form the skill blocks.[47] Instead, managers were asked to identify the key dimensions of this work. They came up with seven dimensions: hardware, software, customer database, documentation, network interface, written communication, and interpersonal interaction. For each dimension, they identified and ranked the specific skills needed, from simplest to most complex. They arranged these into four vertical skill blocks, with the first block including the simplest skills for each of the seven dimensions, with the second block including somewhat more complex skills for each dimension, and so on. Engineers received a pay increase on completion of each skill block.

In designing skill blocks, you need to deal with numerous issues. One issue is how many skill blocks to have. There is no clear answer, and it probably varies from case to case; research has found, however, that more successful plans have a slightly higher number of skill blocks (an average of 11) than less successful ones (an average of nine).[48] Generally, the more complex and diverse the array of skills in a system, the more skill blocks are needed.

How long should it take to master a skill block? There is no hard and fast rule on this, but one study found the average was 20 weeks.[49] This finding suggests that the average plan requires about four to five years for a worker to reach the top skill levels. Of course, the more complex the set of skills required, the longer it will take. The general consensus on this matter is that for most skill-based pay plans, an employee should be able to progress through the system in no more than six to seven years.

## Pricing the Skill Blocks

Once the skill blocks are established, they need to be priced—that is, the amount of money a worker will receive from mastering that block needs to be established. The *relative amount* of increase for each skill block should depend on how difficult the skill block is and/or how long it usually takes for an employee to master that skill block, and on the value of that skill block to the company. But how is the *absolute amount* of the pay for each skill block determined? The most common method for determining this is the **high–low method**.

Let us use the system depicted in Table 4.1 to illustrate this method. First, the firm would determine the market pay rates for an entry-level chemical plant operator and for a job that contains all the skills in Level IV. Suppose these annual rates are $40 000 and $50 833. The firm then adjusts these amounts for its pay-level strategy—for example, to pay 10 percent above the market at entry level and 20 percent above the market at top level. Thus, the entry-level pay would be $44 000, and the top-level pay would be $61 000, creating a difference of $17 000. This $17 000 would then be allocated across the skill blocks according to their relative importance or the amount of time required to master them.

This process may be complicated by the fact that it is often difficult to find market data for jobs that precisely match the entry-level and top-level skill sets used under the SBP.

**high–low method**
Determines entry-level and skill-block pay amounts by pricing comparable entry-level and top-level jobs in the market and allocating the difference to the various skill blocks.

Another issue is whether to lead, lag, or match the market, and whether the same policy should apply at the entry and the top levels. In general, entry-level pay has to at least match the market in order to attract employees with the learning abilities needed to progress through the system, but it will probably be advisable to lead the market to some degree to be sure to attract employees with high learning potential. Typically, as the individual progresses through the system, pay levels should lead the market more as the value of the employee increases.[50]

One final question is whether SBP employees should also be paid on other individual bases, such as seniority or individual merit. For seniority, the answer should almost always be "no," because progression by seniority is the antithesis to knowledge-based progression. In most cases, the answer for individual merit pay should also be "no," because it is at odds with the team approach that is usually essential for SBP to pay off. The exception to this rule may be where each employee works separately and independently of other employees.

This is not to say that performance appraisal (beyond the skill certification process) should not be used, but simply that it should generally not be linked to individual raises. In fact, performance appraisal may be useful and even essential to make sure that skill levels are being maintained and to identify and correct substandard performance. One major study found that 45 percent of organizations with skill-based pay conducted regular performance appraisals.[51]

However, while seniority or individual merit pay does not fit well with skill-based pay, group- and organization-based performance pay fits very well.[52] Gain sharing or goal sharing can provide SBP employees with a financial reward for the increased productivity they are expected to generate, and profit sharing and stock ownership can help reinforce the citizenship behaviour that is so critical to the success of skill-based pay systems.

## Providing Learning/Training Opportunities

Providing opportunities for employees to learn the requisite skills is essential in skill-based pay systems. One expert argues that this is the single most difficult issue with pay-for-knowledge plans.[53] Because pay is tied to skill development, employees will want training opportunities. However, training can be very expensive, both in terms of the direct training costs and in terms of time away from the job. This often conflicts with the productivity of the unit and even with other reward systems.

For example, at an information technology firm, the company discovered that managers were not using the employee training funds they had been allocated.[54] Why? Time devoted to training reduced the efficiency measures for their departments, so those managers who encouraged the most training for their personnel received the *lowest* performance ratings! The problem was solved by revising the appraisal system so that the amount of training undertaken by subordinates became a positive managerial performance indicator.

Companies using SBP have an array of training techniques to choose from. Training techniques may include classroom training, interactive computer-based training, and on-the-job peer training. On-the-job training is generally the largest component in most plans, especially at the lower skill levels. But a problem that often arises is "bottlenecking" because some skills take longer to learn than others, and for some skills, there are fewer opportunities to learn them.

Training and certification are essential for successful skill-based pay systems.

For example, there may be a need for only two workers to perform the product-testing function at a given time, with one of them being a skilled employee to teach the unskilled employee, and it may take six months to learn this skill. This may result in a whole queue of employees waiting for an opportunity to learn this particular job before they can complete their current skill level. This happened at General Mills: although it was expected that employees could reach the top rate in two to three years, the reality was four to five years, which created employee frustration.[55]

How much paid time off should be provided for off-the-job training? And should employees use some of their own time for training? In general, both are required; but if a high level of job performance and involvement is expected as part of the system, it would be unfair to consume a major portion of an employee's nonwork time for training. Often, the tradeoff made is that work time is provided for training at the lower skill levels but not at the top skill levels, where classroom training often plays a major role. Out-of-pocket costs, such as tuition fees, are almost always covered, however.

## Certifying Skill/Knowledge Block Achievement

A key concern for any firm using skill-based pay is to have a valid system for determining when an employee has mastered a particular skill block (a process known as **skill certification**) that is both valid and accepted as fair by employees. In some cases, an employee must spend a minimum period of time working at a particular skill before certification is granted. The purpose of this rule is to ensure proficiency in the skill and to provide enough reinforcement in that skill that it will be retained.

**skill certification**
The testing process that determines whether an individual has mastered a given skill block and should be granted the pay raise associated with that skill block.

Skill certification systems vary in their complexity and processes. Shell Sarnia has a relatively straightforward three-step process. All employees are provided with self-training materials indicating the certification requirements for each skill block. When employees are ready to be tested, they must ask a coworker (already certified for that skill) to confirm that they are ready. If the shift team coordinator agrees, the final checkoff is done by staff experts who specialize in the certification process.

At General Mills, the system was almost completely peer-based. Peer trainers used detailed checklists to certify employees. Although there was a concern that employees may "go easy" on one another to avoid conflict, the company did not believe this was a major problem due to the safeguards built into the system. First, all team members must ratify the certification. Second, employees must requalify whenever they rotate back into the skill again. Third, if an employee is found to be unable to perform skills for which she or he is certified, the employee *and* the certifier forgo their next pay increase. And fourth, the plant manager has final authority for approving certifications, although few certifications have been refused by the plant manager.

A recent case study on skill-based pay system was recently discussed at a conference. The company is located north of Montreal, Quebec, and is a leader in the design and manufacturing of plastic cartons for specialty eggs. All employees are hired at the basic entry-level skill block and remain in this block for two to three weeks, contingent on how quickly they master the necessary skills. A trainer works with them to support them in their training. After their first three months, both their supervisors and their trainers use an assessment form to determine whether they have mastered the necessary skills. If the assessment validates that they have, the employee receives their first-level certification and the subsequent wage increase. The trainer monitors each employee's progress, trains them, and acts as a resource for those employees. To be promoted to the next level, a second assessment is executed during their second year. This assessment is performed using both written tests and trainers' observations of the employees on the factory floor.[56]

## Other Skill-based Pay Issues

Two other issues are important to the success of skill-based pay plans. First, almost all such plans require considerable refinement after initial implementation, so it is important to monitor them on an ongoing basis. Many firms have found that the ideal vehicle is a joint employee–management committee.

Second, many human resource and management practices must be adjusted to fit with the skill-based pay system if it is to pay off for the organization. The IT company example illustrates how changes in one aspect of the system (adding SBP) can be hindered by failure to change other parts (the managers' performance appraisal criteria). Another example is hiring practices, where the ability to perform the entry-level job (based on previous experience at other firms) should not be the sole criterion for selection. Instead, the key recruitment needs are for employees with the ability to master *all* the necessary skills, a willingness to learn, the ability to help and teach others, and a disposition to work cooperatively in a group setting. For this reason, many SBP firms give the group or team a major role in the hiring process. In general, a whole range of human resource practices characterized by the high-involvement managerial strategy need to be in place for SBP to realize its full potential.

# COMPETENCY-BASED PAY SYSTEMS

As mentioned earlier, a considerable number of firms are now attempting to apply the concept of pay for knowledge to their professional and managerial personnel through the use of competency-based pay systems. These can vary greatly in format. For example, a defence electronics firm has a master list of more than 30 competencies that apply to professional and managerial staff, and each department selects those most relevant to its operations.[57] Pay raises are tied to achievement of each competency. In another case, a manufacturing firm pays managers for their degree of progress in mastering four managerial competencies deemed applicable to all managerial jobs. In a third case, professional and managerial employees negotiate "learning contracts" with their supervisor, and pay increases are based on accomplishment of these objectives.

In general, competency-based systems are much more problematic than skill-based systems. First of all, little is known about their effectiveness. This lack of research is partly due to the lack of precision and confusion regarding just what constitutes a "competency-based system." Some systems appear to be little more than a trait-rating appraisal system under a new guise. For example, a list of possible "competencies" might include personality traits such as "self-confidence" and "assertiveness" as well as "flexibility" and "initiative."[58] Although personality traits can be assessed with established psychometric measures, these measures work better as part of the selection process than as part of an ongoing competency-based pay program.

Thus, part of the problem of researching competency-based systems is the wide variation in definitions of "competencies." The following definition is adopted here: "competencies are demonstrable characteristics of the person, including knowledge, skills, and behaviours, that enable performance."[59] Why not just pay people for their performance, rather than factors at least one step removed from performance? An answer is that individual performance can be difficult or even counterproductive to measure. Another answer is that identifying valid competencies can serve as the basis for an effective training and development program. When specific competencies have a dollar value, both administrative and employee attention is focused on exactly what needs to be learned, and this attention can increase the rate of skill development.

In developing any competency-based pay system, there are four main issues:

1. identifying competencies that demonstrably affect performance,

2. devising methods to measure achievement of each competency,

3. compensating each competency, and

4. providing learning opportunities.

Unfortunately, many "competency-based" systems fail on all four counts.

Many consulting companies sell "competency-based" systems that are simply menus of any kind of trait imaginable. Firms are expected to select "appropriate" competencies whether or not they are valid for that employer. A better process is to develop a list of competencies that distinguish high performers from other employees in a particular occupational group, then test all employees in that group on the presence of these competencies, and then statistically identify the competencies that differentiate the top performers from the other employees. Of course, to do this, you must already have valid performance measures for each employee. Another potential problem with this approach is that it is valid only as long as the factors that differentiated performance in the past continue to be valid.

The second issue is measurement. For some competencies, it may be difficult to develop reliable and valid measures that will be perceived as fair by employees.

Third, effectively linking achievement of competencies to pay is not a straightforward task; there is no generally accepted method for so doing, unlike for skill-based pay. If a statistical process has been used to identify the key competencies, these data can be used to determine the relative weighting of each competency relative to performance. However, deciding the absolute dollar value for each competency is highly subjective, because there is no external test equivalent to the high–low method used for skill-based pay. Whether to reward achievement of competencies with raises to base pay or with one-shot bonuses is another question. If a competency is likely to be enduring, then an increase to base pay seems in order; if not, a one-shot bonus is appropriate. A simple way of linking competencies to pay is to factor achievement of competencies into an existing merit raise system.[60]

The fourth issue, providing learning opportunities, is not necessarily straightforward either, because some competencies are more inherent than learnable. But as with skill-based pay, providing opportunities to develop key competencies is essential to the success of the system.

Finally, not all organizations need all employees to have the full range of competencies possessed by top performers. Thus, an overambitious competency-based pay system may cause a firm to pay for capabilities it cannot use, leading to employee frustration and higher costs to the employer.

# SUMMARY

This chapter provided you with a menu of compensation options so that you can select the most appropriate mix to include when designing a compensation strategy. You learned the roles of base pay, performance pay, and indirect pay within a compensation system, along with motives for their use and their advantages and disadvantages.

Although base pay remains the largest component in most pay systems, there has been a trend toward supplementing it with performance pay. At the same time, some firms that traditionally have not used base pay are adding it to their compensation mix.

You also now understand the advantages and disadvantages of indirect pay and know why a properly designed indirect pay component can play a significant role in meeting compensation objectives. However, the role depends on the characteristics of the firm, most notably its managerial strategy.

The three methods for establishing base pay (market pricing, job evaluation, and pay for knowledge) and the advantages and disadvantages were also discussed. You learned that some of these fit different managerial strategies (and different employee groups) better than others. All this information should help you decide which base pay method (or combination of base pay methods) will provide the best foundation for compensation for your organization and for the different employee groups within your organization.

## KEY TERMS

competency-based pay
high–low method
job evaluation
market pricing
pay-for-knowledge system (PKS)

salary
skill-based pay (SBP)
skill block
skill certification
wage

## DISCUSSION QUESTIONS

1. Discuss why it is not always desirable, or even possible, to use output-based pay.

2. Discuss why organizations might prefer job evaluation to market pricing.

3. Discuss the key steps in designing a skill-based pay system.

4. What are the key criticisms of competency-based pay systems?

## EXERCISES

1. Using Salary Wizard (https://www.monster.ca/salary/), identify four different types of jobs in which you have some interest. Choose jobs that are as different from one another as possible. For each job, record the "median base salary." Then click on the "Bonuses" tab and record the "median total cash compensation." ("Total cash compensation" represents base pay plus performance pay, but does not include indirect pay, which is not considered "cash compensation.")

   a. For each job, subtract the "median base salary" from the "median total cash compensation" and then divide this difference by the "median total cash compensation" to derive the proportion of cash compensation that is in the form of performance pay. You will likely see considerable variation in the proportion of performance pay across the four jobs. Would this information affect your decision whether to accept a particular job? What kinds of jobs seem to have more performance pay, and what kinds of jobs seem to have less?

2. Form small groups of four to six people. Each group member should describe the compensation mix for her or his most recent employer, focusing on the extent to which base pay, performance pay, and indirect pay are used by each employer. What types of employers seem to use more or less of a particular component? Do the different pay systems seem to fit with the firm's managerial strategy, as far as you can determine?

3. In a small group, discuss how important benefits will be to you in choosing your next job. Then have each member identify the three benefits that are most important to him or her. Do these vary across individuals in your group? If so, discuss why.

4. Three firms are briefly described below. For each firm, identify the role (if any) that you believe indirect pay should play in the compensation system, and give examples of specific benefits to offer. Explain your choices.

   a. A chicken processing firm in British Columbia hires some employees to "de-gut" chickens. The jobs do not require complex skills and turnover is almost 100 percent.

   b. A retail clothing chain offers personalized service and caters to upscale customers. It is located in major cities across Canada and employs approximately 600 sales staff.

   c. A computer software firm develops customized software for specialized applications for individual clients. Located near Ottawa, it employs about 1000 people.

1. Analyze *Case 2—The Fit Stop* in the Appendix and determine whether base pay should be an important component of compensation for the sales staff. If so, identify the most appropriate method for determining base pay for the sales staff. What factors did you consider in making these decisions?

2. Analyze *Case 3—Multi-Products Corporation* in the Appendix and determine what would be the most appropriate method for determining base pay. What factors led you to the choice you made?

## SIMULATION CROSS-REFERENCE

If you are using *Strategic Compensation: A Simulation* in conjunction with this text, you will find that the concepts in Chapter 4 are helpful in preparing the simulation.

# ENDNOTES

1. Richard J. Long and John L. Shields, "Do Unions Affect Pay Methods of Canadian Firms? A Longitudinal Study," *Relations industrielles/Industrial Relations* 64, no. 3 (2009): 442–65.

2. Daniel J.B. Mitchell, David Lewin, and Edward E. Lawler, "Alternative Pay Systems, Firm Performance, and Productivity," in *Paying for Productivity: A Look at the Evidence*, ed. Alan S. Blinder (Washington, DC: Brookings Institution, 1990), 15–87; Thomas Lemieux, W. Bentley MacLeod, and Daniel Parent, "Performance pay and wage inequality," *The Quarterly Journal of Economics* 124, no. 1 (2009): 1–49.

3. Barry Gerhart and Charlie O. Trevor, "Employment Variability Under Different Managerial Compensation Systems," *Academy of Management Journal* 39, no. 6 (1996): 1692–712; Frank Giancola, "Earnings-At-Risk Pay Plans: Use Only as Directed," *WorldatWork Journal* First Quarter (2012); Christine Bevilaqua and Parbudyal Singh, "Pay for Performance: Panacea or Pandora's Box? Revisiting an Old Debate in the Current Economic Environment," *Compensation and Benefits Review* 41, no. 5 (2009): 20–26.

4. Gillian B. White, "A Former Wall Street Trader on Why He Left Banking," *The Atlantic*, July 20, 2016, https://www.theatlantic.com/business/archive/2016/07/sam-polk-wall-street/492101/, accessed September 22, 2019.

5. Myron Glassman, Aaron Glassman, Paul J. Champagne, and Michael T. Zugelder. "Evaluating Pay-for-Performance Systems: Critical Issues for Implementation," *Compensation & Benefits Review* 42, no. 4 (2010): 231–38.

6. Miall McGee, "Bonus Policy Sparks Discord," *The Globe and Mail*, 20 May 2016, B1.

7. "Canaccord Backtracks on Bonus Policy," *The Globe and Mail*, May 16, 2018, https://www.theglobeandmail.com/newsletters/streetwise-and-rob-insight-newsletter/canaccord-backtracks-on-bonus-policy/article30224486/, accessed September 22, 2019.

8. Al-Karim Samnani and Parbudyal Singh, "Performance Enhancing Compensation Practices and Employee Productivity: The Role of Workplace Bullying," *Human Resource Management Review* 24, no. 1 (2014); 5–16.

9. James S. Bowman, "The Success of Failure: The Paradox of Performance Pay," *Review of Public Personnel Administration* 30, no.1 (2010): 70–88.

10. Imperial Oil Canada website: http://www.imperialoil.ca/Canada-English/workingwithus.aspx, accessed July 23, 2016.

11. "Employee Benefits Still Significant Cost for Employers," *HR Reporter*, November 9, 2015, https://www.hrreporter.com/article/25878-employee-benefits-still-significant-cost-for-employers/, accessed September 22, 2019.

12. Carolyn Baarda, *Compensation Planning Outlook 2001* (Ottawa: Conference Board of Canada, 2000); Karla Thorpe, "Employee Benefits—The Dragon Will Soon Awake," *Conference Board of Canada*, http://www.conferenceboard.ca/topics/humanresource/commentaries/12-11-02/employee_benefits%E2%80%94the_dragon_will_soon_awake.aspx, accessed September 23, 2016.

13. "Comparing Government and Private Sector Compensation in Ontario, 2018," *Fraser Institute*, October 24, 2018, https://www.fraserinstitute.org/studies/comparing-government-and-private-sector-compensation-in-ontario-2018, accessed September 22, 2019.

14. Stephane Renaud, "Unions, Wages, and Total Compensation in Canada," *Relations industrielles/Industrial Relations* 53, no. 4 (1998): 710–29; Richard J. Long, and John L Shields, "Do Unions Affect Pay Methods of Canadian Firms? A Longitudinal Study," *Relations Industrielles/Industrial Relations* 64, no. 3 (2009): 442–65.

15. Barry Gerhart and George T. Milkovich, "Employee Compensation: Research and Practice," in *Handbook of Industrial and Organizational Psychology*, ed. M.D. Dunnette and L.M. Hough (Palo Alto: Consulting Psychologists Press, 1992), 484–569.

16. Timothy A. Judge, "Validity of the Dimensions of the Pay Satisfaction Questionnaire: Evidence of Differential Prediction," *Personnel Psychology* 46 (1993): 331–55; Frank Giancola, "How important are benefit plans to your employees and how satisfied are they with your offerings?" *Employee Benefit Plan Review* 68, no. 1 (2013): 27–30.

17. Robert J. McKay, *Canadian Handbook of Flexible Benefits* (New York: Wiley, 1996).

18. Nathalie B. Carlyle, *Compensation Planning Outlook 1997* (Ottawa: Conference Board of Canada, 1996).

19. Baarda, *Compensation Planning Outlook 2001.*

20. David Brown, "Benefits Providers Strive to Meet Clients' Wellness Needs," *Canadian HR Reporter* 18, no. 6 (2005): 6–7.

21. Thorpe, "Employee Benefits—The Dragon Will Soon Awake."

22. Sara L. Rynes and George T. Milkovich, "Wage Surveys: Dispelling Some Myths about the Market Wage," *Personnel Psychology* 39, no. 1 (1986): 71–90.

23. Luis Gomez-Mejia and David Balkin, *Compensation, Organizational Strategy, and Firm Performance* (Cincinnati: South-Western, 1992); Nina Gupta, Samantha A. Conroy, and John E. Delery, "The Many Faces of Pay Variation," *Human Resource Management Review* 22, no. 2 (2012): 100–15.

24. K.E. Foster, "An Anatomy of Company Pay Policies," *Personnel*, September 1995, 66–72; Francesca Franco, "Compensation and Organisational Performance: Theory, Research and Practice," *European Accounting Review* 21, no. 1 (2012): 183–86.

25. Nan J. Weiner, "Job Evaluation Systems: A Critique," *Human Resource Management Review* 1, no. 2 (1991): 119–32; Howard Risher, "The Search for Pay Equity is Now 50 Years Old," *Compensation and Benefits Review* 45, no. 4 (2013): 187–90.

26. Ibid.

27. Nina Gupta and G. Douglas Jenkins, "Practical Problems in Using Job Evaluation Systems to Determine Compensation," *Human Resource Management Review* 1, no. 2 (1991): 133–44; Amah, Edwinah, C. Nwuche, and N. Chukwuigwe, "Effective reward and incentive scheme for effective organizations," *Research Journal of Finance and Accounting* 4, no. 13 (2013): 73–79.

28. Edward E. Lawler, Susan A. Mohrman, and Gerald E. Ledford, *Creating High Performance Organizations* (San Francisco: Jossey-Bass, 1995).

29. Gerald E. Ledford, "Designing Nimble Reward Systems," *Compensation and Benefits Review* 27, no. 4 (1995): 46–54; Cortney Whalen, and Mary E. Guy, "Broadbanding trends in the states," *Review of Public Personnel Administration* 28, no. 4 (2008): 349–66.

30. Jared J. Llorens, and R. Paul Battaglio Jr., "Human Resources Management in a Changing World: Reassessing Public Human Resources Management Education," *Review of Public Personnel Administration* 30, no. 1 (2010): 112–32.

31. Gerald E. Ledford, "Designing Nimble Reward Systems," *Compensation and Benefits Review* 27, no. 4 (1995): 46–54.

32. Frank Giancola, "Skill-based Pay: Fad or Classic?" *Compensation and Benefits Review* 43, no. 4 (2011): 220–26.

33. Atul Mitra, Nina Gupta, and Jason D. Shaw, "A Comparative Examination of Traditional and Skill-based Pay Plans," *Journal of Managerial Psychology* 26, no. 4 (2011): 278–96.

34. Lisa Cheraskin and Michael A. Campion, "Study Clarifies Job-Rotation Benefits," *Personnel Journal* 75, no. 11 (1996): 31–38; Casad, Scott, "Implications of job rotation literature for performance improvement practitioners," *Performance Improvement Quarterly* 25, no. 2 (2012): 27–41.

35. Edward E. Lawler, *Strategic Pay: Aligning Organizational Strategies and Pay Systems* (San Francisco: Jossey-Bass, 1990), 161; Amah Edwinah, C. Nwuche, and N. Chukwuigwe, "Effective reward and incentive scheme for effective organizations," *Research Journal of Finance and Accounting* 4, no. 13 (2013): 73–79.

36. Jay R. Schuster and Patricia K. Zingheim, *The New Pay: Linking Employee and Organizational Performance* (New York: Lexington Books, 1992), 108.

37. Gerald Ledford, "The Design of Skill-based Pay Plans," in *The Compensation Handbook*, ed. Milton L. Rock and Lance A. Berger (New York: McGraw-Hill, 1991), 199–217.

38. Milkovich and Newman, *Compensation*, 193.

39. Gerald Barrett, "Comparison of Skill-based Pay with Traditional Job Evaluation Techniques," *Human Resource Management Review* 1, no. 2 (1991): 97–105.

40. Frank R. Giancola, "Skill-based Pay: Fad or Classic?" *Compensation and Benefits Review* 43, no. 4 (2011): 220–26.

41. Sylvie St-Onge, Victor Y. Haines, and Alain Klarsfeld, "Skill-based Pay: Antecedents and Outcomes," *Relations industrielles/Industrial Relations* 59, no. 4 (2004): 651–80.

42. Marc J. Wallace, "Sustaining Success with Alternative Rewards," in *The Compensation Handbook*, ed. Milton L. Rock and Lance A. Berger (New York: McGraw-Hill, 1991), 147–57.

43. Kenneth Mericle and Dong-One Kim, "From Job-based Pay to Skill-based Pay in Unionized Establishments: A Three Plant Comparative Analysis," *Relations industrielles/Industrial Relations* 54, no. 3 (1999): 549–80; Kathryn M. Bartol and Laura L. Hagmann, "Team-based pay plans: A key to effective teamwork," *Compensation & Benefits Review* 24, no. 6 (1992): 24–29.

44. Frank L. Giancola, "Skill-based pay: Fad or classic?" *Compensation & Benefits Review* 43, no. 4 (2011): 220–26.

45. G. Douglas Jenkins, Gerald E. Ledford, Nina Gupta, and D. Harold Doty, *Skill-based Pay: Practices, Payoffs, Pitfalls, and Prescriptions* (Scottsdale: American Compensation Association, 1992).

46. Gerald E. Ledford and Gary Bergel, "Skill-based Pay Case Number 1: General Mills," *Compensation and Benefits Review* 23, no. 2 (1991): 24–38.

47. Peter V. LeBlanc, "Skill-based Pay Case Number 2: Northern Telecom," *Compensation and Benefits Review* 23, no. 2 (1991): 39–56.

48. Jenkins et al., *Skill-based Pay*.

49. John Shields, and Catherine Dolle-Samuel, "9 Developing person-based base pay systems," *Managing Employee Performance and Reward: Concepts, Practices, Strategies* (2015): 202.

50. Ibid.

51. Ibid.

52. Ann Armstrong, "The Design and Implementation of Skill-Based Systems," *Proceedings of the Administrative Sciences Association of Canada, Personnel and Human Resources Division* 12, no. 8 (1991): 21–31; Elizabeth M. Doherty, and Jerry L. McAdams, "Micro and Macro Perspectives on Gain Sharing," *Handbook of Organizational Consultation*, Second Edition (2019): 351.

53. LeBlanc, "Skill-based Pay Case Number 2"; Alexandre Léné, "Skill-based pay in practice," *European Journal of Training and Development* 38, no. 7 (2014): 628–41.

54. Ibid.

55. Ledford and Gary Bergel, "Skill-based Pay Case Number 1."

56. Daniel Beaupre, "Compensation-based skills development applied to manufacturing employees: A case study in Quebec," *In 6th Annual Conference of the EuroMed Academy of Business* (2013).

57. Gerald E. Ledford and Robert L. Heneman, "Pay for Skills, Knowledge, and Competencies," in *The Compensation Handbook*, ed. Lance A. Berger and Dorothy R. Berger (New York: McGraw-Hill, 2000), 143–56.

58. Richard S. Williams, *Performance Management* (London: International Thompson Business Press, 1998).

59. Ledford and Heneman, "Pay for Skills, Knowledge, and Competencies."

60. Duncan Brown, "Relating Competencies to Pay," in *The Compensation Handbook*, ed. Lance A. Berger and Dorothy R. Berger (New York: McGraw-Hill, 2000), 157–71.

CHAPTER

5

# PERFORMANCE PAY CHOICES

## Learning Outcomes

AFTER READING THIS CHAPTER, YOU SHOULD BE ABLE TO:

- Define and discuss the applicability of the main types of individual performance pay.

- Define and discuss the applicability of the main types of group performance pay.

- Define and discuss the applicability of the three main types of organization performance pay.

A major soft drink maker has a prominent booth at the Canadian National Exhibition in Toronto each summer. The company employs students at minimum wage to serve soft drinks to customers. There are no benefits, and the only opportunity for advancement is to become a shift supervisor, which pays only slightly more money. Shift supervisors are also temporary employees. The jobs are dull and repetitive—simply serving soft drinks all day. A manager with an enclosed office at the back of the booth is in charge but is frequently not around because the booth operates 12 hours a day, every day. Turnover is high on this job, with most employees not lasting the whole summer.

Management does not trust these employees and makes this clear in many ways. For example, to discourage employees from "pocketing" any receipts, they have sewn the pockets shut on all employee uniforms. As further insurance against employee dishonesty, a count is kept of all the paper cups used in a day, and this is balanced against actual cash on hand.

Although employees are supposed to be friendly and courteous to customers, they frequently are not. Furthermore, when the manager is not around, horseplay is frequent. The supervisors, who are usually the same age as the servers, either tolerate or join in the horseplay. In some cases, it gets so bad that customers are discouraged from approaching the booth.

Many employees have found a way to augment the meagre extrinsic rewards of the job by simply retrieving used cups from the trash and reusing them. In this way, the employees augment their income, while the official count of cups and the receipts still balance.

Not all employees participate in the horseplay or the cup fraud. This behaviour would violate their values, such as a strong work ethic or a strong sense of honesty—or simply because they are afraid of being caught. Denying themselves access to the extrinsic rewards received by the other employees, these employees often quit, leaving only dishonest and/or irresponsible employees. These are the only employees for whom the ratio of rewards to contributions is balanced—and the only employees likely to come back next summer! Thus, the reward system used by this company ends up creating a workforce of dishonest, irresponsible employees.

# INTRODUCTION TO PERFORMANCE PAY CHOICES

Clearly, the reward system at the soft drink booth at the Canadian National Exhibition is dysfunctional, especially when combined with an incomplete attempt at classical management. Here's the question: How would you improve things?

Most of the behaviour problems occur when there is no supervision—as would be expected under a classical management system. One obvious approach is to hire more supervisors. However, hiring additional supervisors would add to costs, and it still would not solve the problem of inadequate rewards and the inability to attract or retain conscientious employees.

Could we address this problem by changing the reward system? You will have no doubt noticed that the rewards are not currently linked to good employee performance; in fact, quite the opposite—those employees behaving in the worst manner receive the highest rewards, in terms of both fun (the horseplay) and money (the cup scams). Is there some way we could address the problems at the soft drink booth by using performance pay?

**Figure 5.1** shows the "menu" of performance pay choices that might be included in a compensation strategy. Could any of these choices help produce the employee behaviour we want; that is, conscientious task behaviour and enough membership behaviour that most employees will at least last out the summer?

The objective of this chapter is to provide you with enough knowledge of the various choices you have for performance pay to be able to answer questions like this, and to decide which types of performance pay (if any) will be useful components of your compensation strategy. The advantages and disadvantages of the various types of performance pay plans will be discussed, along with the factors to consider when deciding whether a specific type of performance pay will suit your organization. We will focus on what you need to know when formulating a compensation strategy. Specific design issues for performance plans will be covered later in the book. In this chapter we will discuss the advantages and challenges of profit sharing, an organizational level performance pay choice, and under what conditions profit sharing works best. However, in Chapter 11, we focus on design and implementation issues, such as deciding on the formula for the profit-sharing bonus and who would be eligible. Therefore, while the topics are similar, the focus is different. It is also important to point out that the material in this chapter applies mainly to the private sector, as pay-for-performance is very limited in the public sector, where it is mainly used at the individual level as merit pay and bonuses. We will return to this issue in the next section when we discuss individual performance pay.

We will start with pay plans that are geared to individual employee performance. After that, we will examine pay plans geared to group or team performance, and then conclude with pay plans geared to the performance of the organization as a whole.

**FIGURE 5.1**

Performance Pay Choices

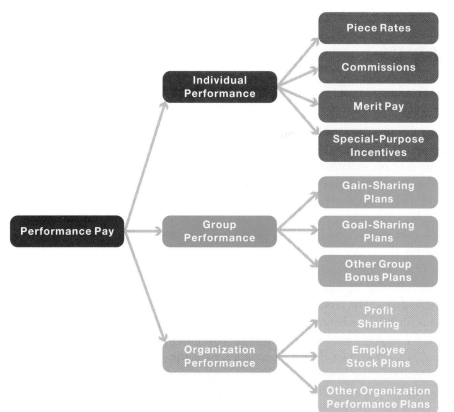

# INDIVIDUAL PERFORMANCE PAY

There are four main types of individual performance pay, two of which may substitute for time-based pay, and two of which are always used in conjunction with base pay.

Instead of being paid by the amount of time worked, individual employees may be paid according to the amount of output they produce. There are two approaches to output-related pay: *piece rates* and *sales commissions*. Piece rates and commissions need not supplant base pay entirely; they can be used in combination with base pay, which is the most common arrangement. The other two types of individual incentives—*merit pay* and *special-purpose incentives*—are always used in conjunction with base pay. Merit pay can be further differentiated into *merit raises* (which increase base pay) and *merit bonuses* (which do not increase base pay). Although not strictly a form of merit pay, *promotions* (which typically increase base pay) can serve the same purposes as merit raises, so they will also be discussed in this section.

In Canada, merit raises are by far the most common form of performance pay (used by about 80 percent of medium to large Canadian firms), followed by sales commissions and merit bonuses (both used by about 35 percent of firms). Special-purpose incentives are used by about one-fifth of Canadian firms, while piece rates are used by only about 10 percent of firms. Sales commissions have become more popular over time, special-purpose incentives have become less popular, and other plans have stayed about the same. It is interesting that piece rates, merit bonuses, and special-purpose incentives show high discontinuation rates: about half the firms that had adopted these plans no longer had them four years later.

## PIECE RATES

Under piece rates, an employee receives a specified sum of money for each unit of output produced or processed. The objective of piece rates is to maximize individual productivity by linking output to reward. Piece rates are commonly associated with the manufacturing sector, but they are also used in the service sector. Barbers are paid per head, tree planters are paid per tree, freelance journalists are paid per column inch in print media, and physicians are paid per procedure. In the service sector, market pricing is generally used to set the piece rate, although there are exceptions. For example, medical doctors negotiate with provincial governments and provincial colleges of physicians and surgeons to set their fee schedules.

In the manufacturing sector, where piece rates were "invented" by Frederick Winslow Taylor at the beginning of the 20th century, the process is more complicated. First, a job analyst or methods engineer times how long a particular task or job typically takes to perform, allowing for factors such as operator fatigue, rest breaks, worker ability, and unavoidable delays. The result is a *production standard*—that is, the number of units that could be produced in an hour by a typical worker.

Next, the employer establishes the average amount of money that a worker with the skills and ability to perform these tasks should earn hourly. This amount is typically based on the prevailing wage in the industry for this type of worker, although it may also be based on negotiated union rates. This hourly amount is then divided by the production standard. The result is the *piece rate*—the monetary payment per piece produced, in dollars and cents. This type of piece rate is the simplest and is known as a straight piece rate.

**piece rates**
A pay system under which individuals receive a specified sum of money for each unit of output they produce or process.

**straight piece rate**
The same specified sum of money is paid for each piece produced or processed, regardless of how many pieces are produced or processed.

Barbers and hairdressers usually charge fees per head.

A more complicated type of piece rate is the **differential piece rate**, under which an employee receives a lower rate if the production standard is not met and then a higher rate (for all pieces) once the production standard is met. The idea is to encourage all workers to meet the production standard.

**differential piece rate**
A lower sum of money per piece is paid if employee production does not meet the production standard, and then a higher sum per piece is paid once the production standard is met.

## Advantages of Piece Rates

Piece rate systems have several advantages.

1. If designed correctly and used in the right circumstances, they are highly motivational in producing task behaviour. Because they tie valued rewards (money) to clearly specified performance outcomes (pieces produced), piece rates are in line with two of the key conditions for motivation identified by expectancy theory—valence and instrumentality—and have been generally found to increase worker productivity.[1]

2. They reduce the need for external control of employees through supervision.

3. They link compensation to output, thereby linking compensation to employer ability to pay, which reduces employer risk.

4. They provide specific information about the "standard" level of output expected, so that both supervisors and workers know what is expected from a "day's work."

## Disadvantages of Piece Rates

However, piece rates have many disadvantages.

1. They can be applied in only a limited number of circumstances. Jobs with a high degree of interdependence are not good candidates for piece rates because an individual cannot control the rate of production, nor can responsibility for productivity be attributed to a specific individual. In jobs with diverse activities and tasks, keeping track of progress

in the various task areas would be very difficult. Jobs for which only some tasks can be measured are not good candidates, nor are jobs where quality cannot be monitored.

2. Jobs for which tasks are continually changing, or for which tools, materials, and technologies are rapidly changing, are not amenable to piece rates. Piece rates need to be recalculated each time a major change occurs. However, the biggest problem with change is that each change provides an opportunity for friction between employees and management. For example, if a better machine is purchased and a worker can now produce twice as much, it makes sense to cut the piece rate in half. Although workers may understand this rationale, they may not be pleased if their piece rate is cut. Moreover, if there is little trust between management and workers, workers may suspect that management is using new technology as an excuse to cut the piece rate.

3. Setting the piece rate is not as "scientific" a process as it seems. For example, timing jobs depends on worker participation. When jobs are first timed, employees will probably not perform the work in the shortest possible time, for fear that doing so will only help establish a high or "tight" rate. Experienced industrial engineers compensate for these tendencies by guessing how much the workers are slowing their normal speed. Thus, the "scientific process" has already deteriorated into a guessing game—and pits workers against management. In addition, the allowances made for factors such as faulty materials and machine breakdowns are often arbitrary. Thus, standards may only be very rough estimates, with some jobs ending up with "tight" rates and others having "loose" ones.

4. Despite the motivational potential of piece rate systems, they often do not motivate maximum effort because of social forces within the work group. Because production is an important part of the activity of the work group, it is likely that group norms will define acceptable rates of production. While a few members of the work group may be able to produce far above standard, most will not, and they will exert pressure on the high producers to moderate their production levels. High producers are known as "rate busters" because other workers fear that management will note their high performance and cut the piece rate. If management has a history of cutting piece rates, workers will not be motivated to increase productivity.

5. If management has laid off workers whenever productivity has increased, workers will not favour high production because they do not want to work themselves out of a job.

6. Piece rate systems can create conflict among workers. Workers may all compete for the "loose" jobs and attempt to avoid the "tight" ones. In addition, there is little incentive to advise or help new workers, or to do any job that does not relate directly to production, such as maintaining equipment or keeping the work area clean.

7. Issues related to product or service quality may arise. Because the emphasis is on quantity, workers may be tempted to cut corners on quality, which requires increased inspection and monitoring. In addition, even with inspection or monitoring, quality is not likely to be much above minimum acceptable levels. Of course, inspection/monitoring and record keeping can increase overall production costs considerably.

8. Problems may develop with equipment and material use. For example, workers may find that they can reach the production standard on a drilling job more easily if they replace their drill bits more frequently or run their machines at high speed. However, drill bits are expensive and machines burn out more quickly at higher speed. Unless these costs are incorporated into the pay system, the worker is unlikely to be concerned about these issues. Incorporating these extra costs increases the complexity of the system.

**9.** Piece rates may cause workers to be more concerned about production than safety. For example, on-time delivery incentives for pizza delivery drivers have been found to be related to reckless driving. In addition, many mines do not use piece rates for fear that miners will sacrifice safety for production in order to maximize their earnings. Research shows that workers paid by piece rates do experience more health and safety issues than other employees.[2]

In order for piece work to succeed in a manufacturing setting, there must be trust between management and workers. This trust facilitates both rate setting and rate changes and assures workers that management will not cut rates arbitrarily. Piece rate systems also require job security so that workers can be sure that increased productivity will not put them out of a job. The irony is that the firms most likely to want to use piece rates—classical firms—are the firms least likely to provide these conditions. It should not be surprising that most manufacturing firms have abandoned piece rates over the years.[3] However, Compensation Today 5.1 provides an interesting exception to this trend and shows how piece rates can work well when used in a high-trust workplace in which management understands what it takes for piece rates to succeed.

---

**COMPENSATION TODAY 5.1**

### PIECE RATES SPARK PRODUCTIVITY AT LINCOLN ELECTRIC

Lincoln Electric, based in Ohio, is a Fortune 1000 company that is a global producer of arc welders. While it is an acknowledged industry leader in its field, the company often attracts more attention for its reward system. The company provides no base pay and very little indirect pay to its production workers; instead, all are paid on an intricate piece rate system. Employees are even timed with a stopwatch. The firm offers no paid sick days and only the minimum paid holidays allowed by law. Lincoln employees have to pay their own health insurance and have no choice about accepting overtime work and unexpected job assignments. If older workers decrease in productivity, they earn less. Management also does not take seniority into account for promotions. The firm has no union to protect the interests of the company's 3400 employees.

This sounds like a classical manager's dream. But what worker would want a job at a sweatshop like this if he or she could find something better? Think of the employee turnover there must be! Imagine all the problems there must be with conflict over piece rates and adversarial relations between workers and management.

But in fact, productivity is very high at this company, and hardly anyone ever quits. Workers and management have an excellent relationship. Whenever jobs become available, there are hundreds of applicants. Over the past 50 years, the company has never lost money. What is going on? Doesn't this example contradict research into the problems with piece rates?

In fact, this case actually reinforces the key points about piece rates. In reality, Lincoln is not a classical organization, nor is it a human relations organization. Consider some of the other policies of the firm. First, job security. The company makes it a policy never to lay off employees. According to a company spokesperson, "We don't lay off anyone unless he steals, lies, fights, or has a record of very low productivity." This policy has yet to be broken since it was first enacted around 1948. The firm guarantees workers at least 30 hours of work a week, even in lean times, which means that workers don't have to worry about working themselves out of a job. Even during the economic recession, amid many workers losing their jobs elsewhere, employees at Lincoln Electric knew that they would be protected. Though their hours were reduced to a 32-hour work week, they still felt content in knowing that they had a pay cheque to bring home.

Employees don't have to worry about cuts to the piece rate either. If workers think up a way to improve productivity, the company never cuts piece rates.

*(continued)*

But doesn't this system cause employees to think only about themselves, rather than the best interests of the firm? To avoid self-centred motivation, the firm also provides profit sharing to all employees, which is distributed according to employee merit. In some years, this bonus can approach 100 percent of regular earnings. In 2012, the company spent US$99.3 million in pre-tax profits to provide bonuses for workers. The average bonus was therefore about US$34 000 per employee. Another feature is an employee stock purchase plan under which employees own a large chunk of the company's shares. Profit sharing and employee stock ownership balance the self-centred perspective caused by the piece rates and encourage citizenship behaviour, with job security as the foundation. One production employee expressed, "It's a competitive environment, definitely, where the more you make, the more money's in your pocket. But each guy knows that the other guys depend on him to make good-quality products, so when challenges come up, they know they need to work in a team environment. There is a natural incentive."

Extrinsically, the result is production workers who are among the highest paid in the United States. Lincoln employees earn approximately 20 percent more than their peers. Intrinsically, the result is employees who are highly committed to their employer. Because of the self-control these features generate, the company has very few supervisors. As opposed to competitors in the sector that would have one supervisor for approximately 10 employees, Lincoln has one supervisor for every 60–70 employees.

Trust between management and employees is the foundation of this system, accompanied by a system of open communication. For this reason, the company has an elected advisory board of employees that meets with top management twice a month. (There is no union, although this type of manufacturing is normally unionized.) Mutual trust also allows adjustments to the piece rates to be made in a non-adversarial way without the conflict that normally accompanies this process.

One reason for the good employee–management relationship is the pay system for managers. Managers are not treated much differently from workers. They, too, depend heavily on profit sharing for their income. They receive no executive "perks"—no cars, no executive dining room, no club memberships, and no reserved parking. The company understands that during hard economic times, abatement must not only come from the bottom. During the recession, the CEO at the time, John Stropki, reduced executive salaries in a cost-cutting effort and accepted a 55 percent reduction in his bonus in 2009, as compared to the previous year. This tactic helped the company encourage its employees to work through difficult times collaboratively. When new MBAs join the firm, they must spend eight weeks on the welding line so that they truly come to understand and appreciate Lincoln's unique shop-floor culture. Recruitment of both managers and workers is a lengthy process, the key criterion being their "fit" with the high-involvement managerial strategy.

Shareholders may feel apprehension toward such an extreme commitment to providing its employees with security. However, share prices have increased by 15 percent annually. Furthermore, average revenue growth stands at about five percent annually. This long-held model has enjoyed continued success generation over generation.

Sources: Kenneth W. Chilton, "Lincoln Electric's Incentive System: A Reservoir of Trust," *Compensation and Benefits Review* 26, no. 6 (1994): 29–34; Gary Johns, *Organizational Behaviour: Understanding and Managing Life at Work* (New York: HarperCollins, 1996); David Kerly and Felicia Biberica, "At Lincoln Electric, A Leading Maker of Welding Machines, Jobs are Guaranteed," *ABC News*, July 17, 2010; Dan Caplinger, "What Makes Lincoln Electric One of America's Best Companies," *The Motley Fool*, February 27, 2013; "Why Lincoln Electric May be the Model for Saving America's Manufacturing Sector: A Review of Frank Koller's Book, *Spark*," *Changing Winds*, June 24, 2015.

## Applicability of Piece Rates

When are piece rates a viable option? Suitable options are those where individual workers control their own production, interdependence between workers is low, each unit of production can be easily measured and priced, individuals perform a limited number of tasks (all of which can be compensated with piece rates), tasks do not change frequently, increased productivity will not cause layoffs, and quality standards can be monitored efficiently and effectively. Ironically, these conditions are more likely to prevail in the service sector, rather than in the manufacturing sector, which is where piece rates originated.

# SALES COMMISSIONS

**Sales commissions** are used to compensate sales personnel in many organizations, from auto dealerships to real estate firms to stock brokerages. Typically, salespeople receive a certain percentage of their gross sales, with the commission rate often varying with the products or services sold. In contrast to piece rates, commissions have remained a popular payment system, although they are more popular as a complement to base pay than as a complete substitute. When there is no base pay and the sales worker's pay flows only from commissions, this is known as **straight commission**.

**sales commissions**
Pay that is geared to the dollar volume of sales or transactions conducted.

**straight commission**
Pay that is geared only to the volume of sales or transactions, with no base pay component.

## Advantages of Commissions

There are many reasons commissions are popular.

1. Commission rates are relatively easy to set and measure.
2. There is usually less interdependence among sales employees than among production workers, which means that their work output is more distinct.
3. In theory, an almost unlimited number of sales can be made without creating a need to reduce the sales force, so sales personnel don't have to worry about working themselves out of a job.
4. Commissions reduce the need for other control mechanisms, such as supervision or internalized commitment. In many businesses where selling takes place away from the business premises, direct supervision is difficult; output-based control may be a good option for these firms, especially if the sales force does not have an internalized commitment to the company.
5. Commissions can serve as a source of feedback and as a self-correcting mechanism. In other words, sales personnel can easily see whether their performance is adequate, and they tend to leave the organization if they are unsuccessful because their earnings will be unsatisfactory.
6. Commissions reduce employer risk because worker pay is linked directly to sales revenue.
7. Finally, and most important, sales commissions increase sales. From a motivational perspective, it is easy to see why. The necessary behaviour (making sales) is clearly defined. The valence of successful behaviour (earning more money) is very positive compared to the valence of unsuccessful behaviour (earning less money). In addition, instrumentality is high (successful behaviour leads to rewards). Therefore, commissions fit well with motivation theory.

## Disadvantages of Commissions

However, we should recognize some possible drawbacks to using commissions.

1. Income to the salesperson may be highly variable, making personal financial planning difficult. Because most people prefer more predictable pay, it may be difficult to attract high-calibre applicants. In addition, sole reliance on commissions may cause high turnover. Some of these problems are illustrated by the following quote, from a sales representative who works on straight commission for a firm that sells consumer telecommunications equipment: "If I go on vacation, I lose money. If I'm sick, I lose money. If I am not willing to drop everything on a moment's notice to close with a customer, I lose money. I can't see how anyone could stay in this job for long. It's like a trapeze act

and I'm working without a net!"[4] In this person's organization, half of all sales reps quit within six months. However, because the costs of recruitment and training are quite low, the company is willing to accept this turnover because those who quit tend to be low performers.

2. To attract and retain top performers, firms that use individual commissions often end up providing a higher total pay than would be necessary if a different compensation mix were used.

3. During recessionary times, commission income may drop sharply through no fault of the salesperson. This may compel good salespeople to leave the firm.

4. During the period when they are learning the business and developing customer contacts, new salespeople receive little income, which may cause them to leave.

5. A salesperson may resist doing work that does not directly contribute to new sales, such as training new salespeople, keeping up records, and servicing clients.

6. Straight commission may encourage salespeople to be overly aggressive, to make misleading claims about the product to encourage sales, or to attempt to sell more units or more expensive units than the customer needs.

7. Commission systems often produce intense competition among salespeople, resulting in conflict and a lack of cooperation.

8. Apportioning responsibility for making sales can be a major problem. Customers may be "sold" by one salesperson, but after taking a few days to think it over, they may place the order with any salesperson who happens to be available, who then gets the credit for the sale. This can cause resentment and conflict among salespeople. To avoid this problem, companies often devise systems for apportioning customers or establishing sales territories. However, fair systems for apportioning customers and setting up sales territories may be difficult to devise and use of fixed territories creates difficulties if sales conditions change.

A variety of other issues can arise when using commissions, especially straight commissions. For example, because the sales rep—not the firm—is absorbing the risk of poor performance, the employer may be less careful in recruitment and selection. When certain salespeople are not performing well, instead of helping them improve (possibly through training and coaching), management may be tempted to just let them "sink or swim" and simply hire other salespeople to replace them when they sink.

Although this approach may seem viable, these practices may have hidden costs. First, although the firm is not paying the sales rep when he or she makes no sales, the firm is also not receiving any sales revenue. Second, these practices may encourage high turnover, such that recruiting and training new salespeople does become a significant cost. Third, customers may be disconcerted by a continuing turnover of salespeople, and they may tire of always having to deal with someone new.

Furthermore, employers should not be surprised when salespeople work the system to maximize their own income rather than the company's welfare. Under straight commission, the employer is showing very little commitment to the salesperson and is implicitly saying that the only attachment between the firm and the salesperson is a financial one. In addition, salespeople will be resistant to changes in the system because they then need to learn all over again how to maximize their income from it.

When the compensation system needs to be changed, salespeople may be suspicious of management's motives and see the changes as a disguised attempt to reduce their earnings. The following incident illustrates the lengths to which one company went to try to deal with this problem.

*In one case . . . the vice president of sales for a multi-media communications company hired a professional wrestler to pose as a salesperson at the company's annual sales meeting. When the sales VP announced the change in the compensation plan and started to go through the details, the wrestler-cum-salesperson charged to the front of the room, lifted the sales VP off the ground, held him over his head, and threatened to toss him to the back of the room if he didn't leave the compensation plan well enough alone. At this point, the company's regional sales managers rushed up to the front of the room to calm the "angry" salesperson by explaining the virtues of the new plan.[5]*

Interestingly, although this ruse did forestall questions and angry debate from the sales reps, it did not eliminate the grumbling about the new plan.

A final problem is that commissions on sales volume focus attention on gross revenue generation, not profitability of sales. Sales personnel may be tempted to focus on selling low-margin, fast-moving items or to cut prices excessively. To avoid these problems, some companies base their commissions on different indicators. For example, IBM shifted to a system whereby commissions were no longer based on sales revenues,[6] but rather on profitability of sales (60 percent) and customer satisfaction (40 percent). IBM recognized that for this system to work, it would have to provide information on profit margins to each sales rep—information that had long been a closely guarded secret.

To deal with income fluctuations, a company can provide a base salary with commissions on top. This dual system also "pays" the individual for work not directly related to sales. A variation of this is the "draw" system, whereby an employee receives regular advances against future commissions to smooth out income fluctuations. Managers can also vary commission rates to reflect the profitability or the selling ease of particular products. They can also reduce excessive competition among sales personnel by apportioning potential customers on a systematic basis, such as by geographic district or customer type. The most important way of avoiding problems is not to use commissions in circumstances where they are not appropriate.

## Applicability of Commissions

In what circumstances are commissions appropriate? Coletti and Chicelli have suggested three key dimensions: (1) degree of independence, (2) degree of persuasive skills required, and (3) length of sales cycle (the time between meeting a new customer and closing the deal).[7] The more that each salesperson works independently of others, the higher the degree of persuasive skills required. The shorter the length of the sales cycle, the greater should be the proportion of commission to base pay.

Coletti and Chicelli also distinguish four types of selling, based on whether the product and customer are new or established. **Maintenance selling** is selling established products to existing customers; **conversion selling** is selling established products to new customers; **leverage selling** is selling new products to existing customers; and **new market selling** is selling new products to new customers. Coletti and Chicelli suggest that because new market selling requires the most initiative on the part of the sales rep, it should have a high

**maintenance selling**
Selling established products to existing customers.

**conversion selling**
Selling established products to new customers.

**leverage selling**
Selling new products to existing customers.

**new market selling**
Selling new products to new customers.

incentive opportunity (high ratio of commission to base pay), whereas conversion selling and leverage selling should have a moderate incentive opportunity, and maintenance selling should have a low incentive opportunity.

The managerial strategy of the firm is another important criterion in selecting commission systems. For example, the self-control that high-involvement firms generate may make extrinsic output-based controls like commissions unnecessary; therefore, commission programs are unlikely to be beneficial. In contrast, classical firms need output-based control wherever direct control is not feasible so they tend to use straight commissions. Similarly, human relations firms must show that they value employee loyalty by providing base pay, but they can also provide some commissions to supplement behaviour control in circumstances where there is no cohesive group to exert social control—for example, when sales reps work alone.

One Canadian study of commission sales systems found they are seldom used for (1) sales jobs that are highly programmable (i.e., behaviours can easily be observed but individual sales cannot easily be measured); (2) jobs that involve working inside the office; (3) jobs that include important nonselling tasks or that require cooperation in closing sales; and (4) jobs in large organizations. The researchers also found that organizations that use a higher proportion of base pay have lower employee turnover than those that rely more heavily on commissions. A more recent study of sales professionals that compared quota-bonus compensation plans to quota-commission sales plans found that commission plans improved sales productivity by an average of 24 percent after considering industry, territory, and period effects. However, the change in productivity was statistically more significant for those with lower ability levels as compared to those with higher ability levels. Also, a sales group that either reached their quota or were far from achieving their quota decreased their efforts and held off pursuing further sales until the next period. However, groups that were close to reaching their quota but had not yet reached the quota were more likely to seek sales that would have taken place in future periods. Lastly, the bonus plan much better promoted activities that were not directly related to the incentive pay as compared to the commission plan.[8]

## MERIT PAY

The objective of merit pay is to recognize and encourage continuing good performance by individual employees. Merit pay includes merit raises, merit bonuses, and promotions—all of which are always used in combination with base pay. What differentiates merit pay from other types of performance pay is that merit pay is generally based on appraisals of overall employee performance, not just on specific aspects of it.

As mentioned in the introduction, the material in this chapter (and Chapter 11) applies mainly to the private sector; however, the applicability and use of performance pay in the public sector, mainly in the form of merit pay, has generated both academic and practitioner interest, so a quick discussion is useful here. There is a strong belief in some quarters that the public and nonprofit sectors can operate in a more business-like manner so as to enjoy some of the efficiencies of the private sector. This has led to some reform in public sector management and the use of new performance management and incentive systems.[9] Some authors note that employees in the public sector and nonprofits tend to be motivated by different factors,[10] thus leading to variations in the effectiveness of pay for performance pay systems. There are additional contextual factors that may cause variations in outcomes across sectors, such as the role of unions and limited funding in the public sector. The public and press are also more vigilant and critical when taxpayers' money is used to reward public servants. However, while the context is different, the advantages and disadvantages discussed below are still relevant.

## Merit Raises

Merit raises represent a permanent increase to base pay. Thus, merit raises are extremely expensive for the employer, especially when given to young employees who may benefit from the same raise for 30 years or more. This expense is increased even more if indirect pay—such as pension benefits—is geared to direct pay levels, which is the usual practice. Merit raises are normally based on employee performance during the previous year, but managers hope the increased performance level will be permanent so that the permanent cost increase is justified. This is, of course, difficult to predict, and most organizations simply grant the increase and hope for the best.

Merit raises offer one way for employees to advance their pay within their pay ranges. Other ways that employees can advance through the pay range include raises based on seniority or skill improvements. Surveys have found that North Americans believe that being paid according to merit is a good idea, as long as performance standards are fair and objective and as long as performance appraisals help improve job performance.[11] While most organizations say they use merit pay, research points to a high degree of skepticism among both managers and employees regarding the extent to which pay is truly related to meritorious performance.[12] However, a review of 42 empirical studies found that despite this skepticism, there is a significant positive relationship between performance appraisals and prior employee performance.[13] Furthermore, an additional study found that, of all the pay for performance plans, merit pay had the strongest relationship to increased performance.[14]

Because merit raises are generally based on appraised performance, they can consider overall employee performance, rather than just a slice of it, as piece rates, commissions, and special incentives tend to do. They can also provide feedback to employees on how they can improve their performance to warrant a merit raise in the future and can help retain high-calibre employees.

There are many issues related to merit raises.

- *Performance measurement.* As will be discussed in Chapter 10, performance appraisal is not an exact science. Studies have found that both managers and employees often have little confidence in the results of performance appraisals.[15] This may explain why many managers are reluctant to differentiate among employees in terms of pay: they have doubts about the validity of the data on which these differentiations are to be based. They may also be concerned about antagonizing subordinates.

- *Pay raises for above-average performers are similar to those given to average performers.* To be motivating, the difference in pay increase between high level and average level performers must be perceived as significant. Yet exactly how much this difference should be is not always clear.

- *Once an employee rises to the top of his or her pay range, there are no more merit raises.* An organization cannot afford to provide merit pay raises indefinitely: it can only pay so much to a bookkeeper or a junior supervisor, no matter how meritorious the individual. At that point, what is the motivation to continue to improve performance or even to maintain the high performance level that has earned the merit raises?

merit raise
An increase to an employee's base pay in recognition of good job performance.

Traditionally, the answer is the carrot and the stick—the carrot of promotion to a higher-paying job and the stick of dismissal. However, it is legally difficult to dismiss someone who is performing at an acceptable level, even if that person is being paid to perform at a superior level. Even if it were possible, such action would tend to destroy the system's motivational value, for merit raises would be perceived as increasing vulnerability to dismissal.

Organizations are also becoming flatter and with many firms experiencing slow or even negative growth, promotion opportunities are becoming increasingly rare. And even for organizations that do offer opportunities for promotion, rewarding outstanding performance in a lower-level position with promotion to the next higher position is not necessarily a wise policy, as will be discussed later in the chapter.

If merit raises are the only element of performance pay, an organization could rely on intrinsic motivation and organizational identification to maintain performance (in a high-involvement organization), or possibly on social norms (in a human relations organization), but classical organizations would not be able to do so. One solution may be merit bonuses (discussed in the following section).

- Merit raises are usually based on a judgment by a superior and could cause antagonism between the superior and the other employees. Merit raises can also cause divisiveness and resentment when only a few of its members are singled out for merit raises.

- Rewarding only one or two employees when effective performance depends on cooperation among all employees can lead to conflict and reduced cooperation. This problem is severe when the amount of money for merit raises is fixed for a given department or when the supervisor is allowed to provide merit raises to only a fixed proportion of the subordinates. This creates a zero-sum game—if you get more, I get less or none at all. This system does not encourage cooperation among employees!

Although merit raises are appealing, the disadvantages pose significant challenges. For firms in which close collaboration among employees is necessary and separating out individual performance is not feasible, it is best to substitute other methods of reward for individual merit pay as you have learned. A debate has also been raging in Canada and the United States about the need for merit pay for teachers (see Compensation Today 5.2).

## Merit Bonuses

Merit raises have many problems, including the topping-out problem and the risk of providing a long-term future reward for short-term past performance. A **merit bonus** avoids these problems because they are granted only for the period in which good performance occurs, and good performance must be repeated each year in order for employees to continue to receive them. Merit bonuses can also be used in conjunction with a merit raise system. For example, for those employees no longer eligible for further merit raises, an opportunity to obtain an annual merit bonus may keep them focused on performance.

Merit bonuses also have the advantage of not being a fixed amount; they can be varied from year to year depending on the employer's financial circumstances. They can also be paid out in lump sums, either quarterly or annually, and they may have more visibility as a result. Some firms like to prepare completely separate cheques to reinforce this visibility.

### GRADE THE TEACHERS?

Performance pay for teachers comes up every few decades when politicians become worried about school performance. It has been a bigger issue in the United States, where teachers are paid less than their Canadian counterparts. Former President Barack Obama's education reforms include US$4 billion for states that make their schools more accountable and specifically link standardized tests to teacher performance. Its purpose was to significantly improve the country's poorest performing schools in terms of graduation rates and math and reading test scores. One of the calls for linking teachers' pay to performance in Canada comes from the private sector. A report by the Canadian Council of Chief Executives says that the current teacher compensation model, which is based on education level and seniority, is ineffective. While the report dismisses merit pay, it advocates linking teacher evaluation to the speed of progressing through the pay grids and implementing levels with greater responsibilities and higher pay at each level.

While the proponents cited improved teaching quality and increased professional status as the benefits of performance pay for teachers, the idea received widespread opposition from teachers and unions, which cited a long list of disadvantages of performance pay. First and foremost, opponents say that teachers enter the profession not for money but for the satisfaction of making a difference in students' learning. Wayne Phillips, a 25-year veteran teacher in Alberta and the recipient of a teaching excellence award from the prime minister, said that continuously looking for innovative ways to teach was a fact of life for the profession. Second, teachers worry that the focus on standardized tests will distort curriculum and classroom time by taking time away from subjects like drama and music, and the emphasis on individual financial awards will discourage teamwork and sharing of good ideas among teachers. Third, subjective evaluation such as the principal's assessment and student feedback may contain bias, and more sophisticated and objective evaluation may prove to be too expensive to implement. Fourth, the results of the experiments in the United States are mixed, with some reporting success while others reporting no obvious student progress. The opponents suggest that rather than fiddling with the pay system, providing better professional development and developing stronger practice standards will improve teaching quality and produce better student outcomes.

The proponents of performance pay claim that the system rewards those who perform better and puts pressure on those who do not, and cite successful examples of performance pay. Some schools in the United States awarded performance pay to the entire school, which promotes schools paying close attention to their weakest students and encourages shared responsibility for those students. In a rare Canadian instance of merit pay, the extra money was used for professional development. At the Calgary Girls School, a privately run but publicly funded school in Alberta, teachers can receive $1000 to cover the costs of attending workshops and taking university courses.

Programs around the world have used a performance rating for teachers and have found great success. Chile, for example, has an incentive pay system for teachers. This system has presented higher student standardized scores in language and math. Chile attributes its highest scores, as compared to any other Latin American country, in part due to this program. Further success of performance-based pay for teachers has been proven successful in England, India, and Israel. Some states remain in favour of teacher evaluations. The National Council on Teacher Quality, a research and policy group, located in Washington, DC, thinks that reverting to a system that did not provide the feedback required for teachers to improve their lessons and for policymakers to make informed personnel decisions is a mistake.

However, most states in the United States have not found this program to be very successful. The states that agreed to use this performance rating system grappled with how to measure teacher performance. Because most teachers did not have standardized tests related to their grade and subject, several new tests were created, or teachers were forced to create their own. Complaints were made regarding such testing. On other occasions, such as the situation for half of New York City teachers, teachers were appraised based on subjects they did not teach. Teachers complained that they were being held responsible for the material in which they were inexperienced without being given the training necessary to excel. Other complaints were regarding the apparent objectivity of the measures of student growth.

*(continued)*

Because of the mainly poor results, fewer states are using test scores to evaluate teachers. A report by the National Council on Teacher Quality stated that 34 states now require scores to be used in teacher evaluations. Only four years ago, 43 states were doing so. Also, according to recent findings, Obama's reform failed to generate meaningful results. Test scores, graduation rates, and rates of college enrolment were no better in schools that were part of the grant program than those that were not. In fact, of students who attended the participating schools, one-third either displayed no improvement or had worse results.

Amidst the American findings, the Canadian view of performance pay for teachers continues to be mixed. The Fraser Institute in Canada, a Canadian public policy organization, believes that the current education is out-dated and that "excellence goes unrewarded [while] mediocrity goes unaddressed." A study by the Fraser Institute contended that, when properly designed, such a program has the potential to support varying student populations using a cost-effective method. However, the Ontario Teachers' Foundation argues that this study is based on case studies from "obscure" places. The Foundation contends that education should not be considered a business. It believes that this is a simplistic solution that discounts major concerns in the classroom, such as poverty, mental illness, and parental engagement. Furthermore, the Foundation argues that this system would push teachers to "teach the test," fixing lesson plans to be based on standardized test scores as opposed to essential learning.

Sources: Caroline Alphonso, "Teachers' Pay Should Be Based on Performance, Not Years Worked: Report," *The Globe and Mail*, January 23, 2014; Ben Levin, Canada Research Chair in Education Leadership and Policy, University of Toronto, "Want Better Teachers? Merit Pay Isn't the Answer," *The Blog*, January 23, 2013; Erin Andersen, "Should Canada Offer Merit Pay to Teachers?" *The Globe and Mail*, February 5, 2010; Emma Brown, "Obama Administration Spent Billions to Fix Failing Schools, And It Didn't Work," *Washington Post*, January 19, 2017; Matt Barnum, "No Thanks, Obama: 9 States No Longer Require Test Scores Be Used to Judge Teachers," *Chalkbeat*, October 8, 2019; Angela MacLeod, "Provinces Should Introduce Incentive Pay for Teachers," *Fraser Institute*, December 18, 2018; Aedan Helmer, "Union Dismisses Study Touting Teacher Pay Based on Student Performance," *Toronto Sun*, September 9, 2014.

However, merit bonuses still have many of the disadvantages of merit raises. They depend on reliable and accepted performance appraisal measures, managers and employees may have little faith in the available measures, or they can cause poor relations between supervisors and their subordinates and between employees and their coworkers, especially if the bonus pool is limited. Merit bonuses are also not suited for work that depends on collaboration and cooperation. Because bonuses apply only for one year, they can be perceived as less valuable than merit raises and will need to be much higher in dollar value to attract an equivalent amount of attention from employees.

One key issue is how to set the amount of the total available bonus pool. If it is simply an arbitrary decision by top management, this may cause dissatisfaction, especially if the decision results in low bonuses or limited numbers of bonuses. Some firms are now tying the bonus pool to some measure of organizational performance, such as profitability, and then allocating this amount to employees based on individual merit.

Basing the bonus pool on organizational performance does help gear employee compensation to a firm's ability to pay. The problem with this approach is that it weakens the instrumentality of the merit system (i.e., the likelihood of good performance leading to a reward), thus making it less motivational than it would otherwise be. Furthermore, if the company is not making profits, there will be no merit bonuses, which will make the merit system completely irrelevant.

## Promotions as Rewards

Another way of recognizing individual performance is through promotions—when this is a viable strategy, as not all organizations have scope for promotions. When used, these can be highly valued rewards and powerful incentives because they normally carry both extrinsic and intrinsic rewards: extrinsic because they normally bring both recognition and a pay raise, and intrinsic because higher-level jobs typically contain more of the elements of intrinsically motivating work, such as more variety or more autonomy.

Because promotions bring many rewards, many organizations rely on them as their major reward for superior individual performance. They expect a promotion-from-within policy to be a key factor in motivating good employee performance. The great majority of employees believe that promotion-from-within policies are an important means to recognize the contributions that existing employees have made to the firm. To refuse employees fair consideration for promotional opportunities is very demotivating to a workforce. This can be a problem in family-owned firms, where promotions may be limited to family members.

Even when promotions are not restricted, depending on promotions as the main source of rewards for good employee performance can cause problems. First, heavy reliance on promotions in lieu of other rewards can result in a meaningless reward system if the organization has few upper-level vacancies. This is a problem for firms that are expanding slowly or not at all or that are reducing their hierarchy in order to cut costs or to move toward a high-involvement managerial strategy. Even in expanding firms, only rarely do firms have sufficient upper-level vacancies to reward all deserving candidates. In addition, for high-involvement firms, tying rewards mainly to movement up the hierarchy is inconsistent with their managerial philosophy and sends the wrong message to employees.

In organizations where promotions are an important part of the reward strategy, the psychological consequences for those not promoted can be detrimental to their future motivation. Suppose a company has one vacancy and three deserving candidates. No matter how good they are, two will be turned down. What message do the rejected individuals take from this? Probably that the firm does not value their contributions as highly as they thought. It may also shake their confidence in the fairness of the reward system. As discussed in Chapter 3, perceptions of unfairness can cause performance to decline or even departure from the firm.

Some employees may not see a promotion as a reward worth seeking. Promotions typically don't bring only pluses; they also bring negatives, such as longer hours or more stressful work. In some cases, they may require the employee to relocate. For many employees, the net valence of a promotion is not positive. Therefore, it is not seen as a reward, and so it does not serve as an incentive.

From the organization's point of view, promoting an outstanding performer to a higher level position (usually a managerial one) can lead to serious problems if the attributes required for success in the higher position are different from those of the lower position. For example, an outstanding salesperson might become a very poor sales manager. The skills and abilities that make for a successful salesperson, such as independence, competitiveness, and aggressiveness, may be undesirable in a sales manager, whose success depends on effectiveness at recruiting, training, coordinating, and supporting the sales staff. In addition, the sales manager loses the satisfaction of dealing directly with customers and personally closing sales, which may have been a strong motivating force as a salesperson.

In circumstances such as these, promotions based on outstanding performance in a qualitatively different job from the new job can have negative consequences for both the employer and the employee. In addition, as an employee progresses up the hierarchy, the jobs become systematically more different from those below them.

Lawrence J. Peter has summarized the results of a strict promote-from-within policy in what he has modestly dubbed the "Peter principle": "In a hierarchy, every employee tends to rise to his [or her] level of incompetence."[16] What he means is that individuals will be promoted only if they are performing competently in their present job. If they are not performing well, they will stay where they are. Thus, "in time, every post tends to be occupied by an employee who is incompetent to carry out his or her duties." Although exaggerated, the Peter principle does contain an element of truth.

For these reasons, it seems clear that promotions should not be used as the sole component of a system for rewarding superior performance. It may be preferable to base promotions on factors other than current performance, assuming that the candidate is at least competent in her or his current duties. However, this can create other difficulties, such as the perception that the organization does not care about outstanding performance.

Outstanding performers must be considered for available promotions if they wish to be considered for one. It may be possible to prepare such individuals through training and development programs. Failing this, management must provide the candidate with an explanation of why she or he is unsuitable for the promotion. Ideally, unsuitable candidates will reach this conclusion on their own after discussions with management.

In some instances, it may be desirable to place an individual in the higher position on a trial basis. If so, that person should be given every possible opportunity to succeed in order to prevent perceptions of injustice. But for this approach to succeed, a graceful way to return to the former job must be available. One way of doing this is to provide a title such as "acting department manager."

In order to avoid the problem of forcing employees to move up the managerial hierarchy because it is the only way to advance their pay levels, some companies have created dual-track programs for advancement, with a technical track (sometimes known as a "technical ladder") and a managerial track. The technical track provides a series of steps through which employees can increase their contribution and value to the organization (and their pay) without becoming managers. Similarly, pay-for-knowledge systems provide an avenue for advancing pay levels without requiring promotion to management positions.

## Applicability of Merit Pay

Although most companies claim to use merit pay, it rarely applies to all employees. Nor should it. Applying merit pay to employee groups for whom it is unsuited is a recipe for frustration and failure. How do you decide which employee groups (if any) are suitable for the application of merit pay? Eight questions can help guide this decision. In general, all these questions should be answered "yes" before individual merit pay is included in the compensation structure for a given employee group.

### Is Individual Performance Variable?

In many jobs, performance variation may not be possible, as in the case of many routine, lower-level jobs in traditional classical organizations. If performance is not variable, why waste time and effort attempting to measure variations?

### Is Performance Controllable by the Individual?

If circumstances affecting employee performance are beyond the employee's control, then gearing pay to individual performance makes no sense.

## Can Individual Performance be Separated Out?

If the performance of individuals cannot be separated out from the performance of others with whom they work, then an individually based merit system cannot be used. However, some type of team-based performance pay might work.

## Can an Accurate Performance Appraisal System be Developed?

Do jobs change so quickly that it is virtually impossible to come up with valid, up-to-date performance measures and standards? Does the organization have the resources to develop a reliable and valid system and to train raters in its use?

## Will Pay Actually be Linked to Performance Appraisals?

Is the organization prepared to set aside sufficient funds to justify the merit process and allocate the money to create meaningful pay differences between meritorious employees and other employees? If not, nobody will take the process seriously.

## Will the Merit System Serve a Purpose that Cannot be Served in Some Other Way?

There are three main purposes for merit pay: to motivate employee performance, to maintain equity by making rewards commensurate with contributions, and for salary progression—to raise the pay of high performers so that they will not be lured away by other firms. Can these purposes be served in other ways? As was noted in Chapter 3, intrinsic rewards are generally more effective than extrinsic rewards for motivating task behaviour. If intrinsic motivation already exists, then merit pay may not add much motivation and could even detract from motivation, especially if the merit pay system is not seen as fair.

If merit pay is intended to demonstrate equity, then the system needs to be monitored carefully to ensure that it actually does so from the employees' perspective. If persons perceived as undeserving receive merit increases, or those deserving do not, a merit system may cause perceptions of inequity. An alternative method for recognizing differences in employee value to the organization is through pay for knowledge.

As for retaining key employees, a variety of means (other than merit pay) are available to foster membership behaviour, as discussed in earlier chapters. If pay ranges are used, experience, seniority, and/or skill levels can be used as vehicles for movement through the range, rather than merit raises.

## Are Any Undesirable Side Effects Readily Manageable?

One possible undesirable side effect occurs when employees concentrate only on aspects of the job most visible in the performance appraisal process. For many organizations, organizational citizenship behaviour may be far more valuable than simple task behaviour; yet most performance appraisal systems focus mainly on task behaviour. In fact, there is some evidence that appraisals focusing on specific goals and performance improvements actually decrease citizenship behaviour.[17] Another side effect may be conflict or lack of cooperation among employees as they jockey for scarce merit increases.

## Will the Merit System Fit with the Firm's Culture and Strategy?

In classical organizations, merit pay for rank-and-file employees is often prohibited by union contracts because employees in these organizations are usually skeptical about the organization's ability to fairly administer merit systems. Most classical organizations have found direct control of behaviour and job simplification to be the most effective means of controlling and motivating behaviour. Many classical organizations have adopted computer monitoring of employee behaviour in preference to traditional appraisal systems.

Individual merit pay does not fit with human relations organizations either, because supervisors are concerned about social unity within the organization. Although many human relations firms use some form of merit pay, the reality is that either most individuals receive high ratings and receive the same merit pay, or that there is very little distinction in merit raises between those employees receiving higher ratings and those receiving lower ratings. Interestingly, these practices are not necessarily dysfunctional for human relations organizations. They recognize that their main control mechanism—cohesive groups and positive work norms—could easily be subverted by an individual merit pay system.

At first glance, individual merit pay might appear to fit well with high-involvement organizations because of their need for high-level employee performance. But a closer look reveals that most high-involvement organizations have fluid jobs, team-based processes, interdependence among employees, and flat structures—none of which fit well with traditional individual performance appraisal. Ability and willingness to perform as needed, along with citizenship behaviour, are the keys to effective performance in these organizations. Motivation for task behaviour is best provided by intrinsic sources and internalized commitment to the organization.

All these issues may shed light on why merit pay systems based on performance appraisal are often unsatisfactory. Optimal conditions for individual merit pay are rare, and they may become increasingly rare as concepts like flex time and flexplace become more common. However, this does not necessarily suggest that performance appraisal should be dropped (see Chapter 10). All organizations need some system for providing feedback to individuals and groups on their performance; if done correctly, performance appraisal may be a satisfactory means of providing this feedback. Of course, as discussed in Chapter 3, the best feedback occurs when jobs themselves are designed to provide feedback directly.

## SPECIAL-PURPOSE INCENTIVES

special-purpose incentive
An incentive designed to motivate a specific type of employee behaviour.

In order to foster certain behaviours that are of special importance to an organization, or to counteract behaviours that are causing problems, some firms have developed **special-purpose incentive** programs (sometimes known as "targeted incentive programs"). For example, bonuses can be provided for finding insects during vegetable processing, as seen in Chapter 1. Employees can be given bonuses for minimizing waste or for high customer satisfaction ratings. Book sales reps can be given bonuses for bringing in new authors. Baseball players can be given bonuses for scoring home runs. The possibilities are virtually endless.

Although the advantages and disadvantages of special-purpose incentives vary with the specific nature of the plan, their overall advantage is that they focus employee attention on a behaviour of key importance to the firm. The disadvantage is they may focus employee attention *only* on the specific behaviour being sought, potentially causing employee neglect of other important behaviours. Poorly designed targeted incentives can have a variety of unanticipated consequences, as was the case at Green Giant, where employees "gamed the system" to maximize their bonuses—but the company did not get cleaner product. As discussed in Chapter 3, getting people to do something they would not otherwise do only using financial incentives is a process fraught with peril.

Two of the most common special-purpose incentives are suggestion programs (to encourage creativity) and attendance programs (to discourage absenteeism).

## Incentives for Creativity

Suggestion systems are intended to promote and reward innovative thinking by employees. In general, if an employee has a suggestion that may improve organizational effectiveness, she or he submits it through the suggestion system. It is then evaluated by a committee, and if it is implemented, the employee receives a percentage (usually between 10–20 percent) of the projected cost savings during the first year. When the savings from the suggestion are difficult to compute, a standard lump sum is awarded. Thus, suggestion systems have three components: (1) a system through which suggestions are channelled, (2) a systematic process for evaluating them, and (3) an incentive for submitting usable ideas.

suggestion system
An incentive plan through which employees receive cash bonuses for submitting money-saving suggestions.

Suggestions resulting in improvements in product/service quality or lower product/service costs can result in increased organizational effectiveness.[18] Acting on employee suggestions can lead to perceptions among employees that management is responsive and may have positive impacts on increased employee participation and organizational culture.

While they can be effective, suggestion systems face several problems. First, although the ideas may seem like good ones to the employee, most are not adopted due to practicality or cost. Unless the reasons for rejecting a suggestion are explained to and accepted by the submitter, there may be resentment and a reluctance to contribute further suggestions. Second, if a suggestion is adopted, it is often difficult to arrive at a fair reward and employees may feel that the reward amount is not equitable. Third, supervisors or staff specialists may resent employees who make suggestions, feeling that this reflects negatively on their own performance. Fourth, coworkers may resent the individual making the suggestion if implementing the suggestion disrupts existing work practices. Fifth, there may be the issue of who receives the credit for the idea because it may have been developed by several individuals. In some cases, employees (including supervisors) have been accused by other employees of "stealing" their ideas.

These systems assume that people have useful suggestions but are not motivated to submit them without the carrot of an incentive. This assumption applies mainly to classical and, to some extent, to human relations organizations. Ironically, the problems associated with suggestion systems are most likely to occur in classical organizations, which may explain why many classical organizations do not bother with these systems and do not find them useful if they adopt them.

In a high-involvement organization, employees are likely willing to submit suggestions regardless of whether there are bonuses because of their internalized commitment. Therefore, a suggestion system is likely most useful to human relations organizations, particularly if it's group-based, where everyone in the group shares in the rewards from adopted suggestions.

Group-based suggestion systems avoid many of the problems discussed earlier and have been found to be more effective than individual-based suggestion systems.[19] Group-based suggestion systems could suit high-involvement organizations. Indeed, many group-based performance pay plans include mechanisms for employee suggestions. These will be discussed in the next section of this chapter.

## Incentives for Attendance

Because of a concern with employee absenteeism, some organizations have started providing incentives for regular attendance.[20] For example, a collective agreement between La-Z-Boy Canada (named for the recliners the company produces, not its employees!) and its union included a new clause providing for an attendance bonus. Employees who do not have absences in a calendar year receive eight hours of their base rate deposited into their RRSP account.

While attendance plans vary, one approach is to provide a bonus or prize to employees who have a perfect attendance record in a given time period. One interesting system was used by a manufacturing plant.[21] Each day that an employee came to work on time, he or she was allowed to draw one card from a deck of playing cards. At the end of the week, the employee with the best five-card poker hand in each department received a cash prize. This plan reduced absenteeism by about 18 percent.

Other plans pay employees for any unused "sick" or "personal" leave days to which they might otherwise be entitled. Typically, employees receive a proportion of their daily pay, although sometimes a fixed amount is used. Overall, the purpose of an attendance incentive plan is not to encourage sick employees to come to work, but to discourage discretionary absences (where people skip work because they want to, not because they have to) by putting a price on these absences.

Therefore, the two main advantages to attendance incentive plans are that they discourage discretionary absences and they recognize employees who don't miss work. Many employees feel that this is inequitable, and an attendance program can at least partly rectify this inequity.

One of the drawbacks of attendance plans include the cost of the bonus and the extra paperwork involved. Another drawback is once an individual becomes ineligible for the bonus (by exceeding the number of allowable absences), they no longer have any incentive to limit absences during the review period. There is also the issue of whether "legitimate" absences should detract from the record, and if so, how they should be defined and verified is a drawback. Some employers may have a philosophical objection to paying extra for something (attendance) that should be taken as a given. However, perhaps the greatest drawback is that the incentive plan may treat only the symptoms, without getting at the true source of the problem.

If absenteeism is a problem, a first step is to try to understand the cause. Attendance incentive programs assume that absenteeism is caused by a lack of employee will to attend. That may be partly true, but there are other possible reasons for absenteeism. Are there more appropriate solutions? For example, we know that reward and job dissatisfaction affect absenteeism, and high absenteeism may just be the tip of the iceberg of underlying and more serious problems facing the organization.[22]

One possibility is that the workplace itself may be responsible for an excessive number of accidents or injuries, or it may provide conditions that promote illness. For example, the work may be highly stressful or employees may not want to face another day of boring, tedious, or repetitive work. Factors such as these, as well as factors like dissatisfaction with the boss or dissatisfaction with rewards, have been shown to lead to negative group norms regarding attendance, which influence individual attendance behaviour.[23]

## Applicability of Special-Purpose Incentives

Special-purpose incentives may be useful in changing employee behaviour, but as discussed in Chapter 3, they need to be carefully thought out. A potential problem is that where intrinsic motivation already exists, financial incentives may serve to replace this with extrinsic motivation. Where intrinsic motivation does not exist, employees may attempt to "game the system" by behaving in ways that maximize their incentive payouts while their performance suffers in other ways. Special-purpose incentives are therefore most appropriate in circumstances where intrinsic motivation does not already exist, where both intended and unintended behaviours are easy to observe, and where no other alternatives for inducing the desired behaviour are feasible. In general, they don't fit with high-involvement organizations, but may fit with classical and human relations firms under some circumstances.

Compensation Notebook 5.1 summarizes the advantages and disadvantages of the major individual performance pay plans.

---

### COMPENSATION NOTEBOOK 5.1

#### ADVANTAGES AND DISADVANTAGES OF INDIVIDUAL PERFORMANCE PAY PLANS

| PLAN | ADVANTAGES | DISADVANTAGES |
|---|---|---|
| Piece rates | • Can be highly motivational<br>• May reduce the need for external control of employees<br>• Reduces employer risk by relating pay to output<br>• Can make expected levels of performance clear | • Are applicable only in limited circumstances<br>• May not be as "scientific" as they appear<br>• May pit workers against management<br>• Social forces may constrain employee effort<br>• Product/service quality may suffer<br>• May cause conflict among employees<br>• May cause abuse of equipment or tools<br>• May cause accidents |
| Sales commissions | • Relatively easy to set and measure<br>• Unlimited opportunity for sales<br>• Reduces the need for employee control<br>• Can serve as source of feedback<br>• Reduces employer risk by linking pay to sales<br>• Highly motivational to increase sales | • Uncertain employee income may cause turnover<br>• Pay may be higher due to employee risk<br>• Low earnings for new sales workers<br>• Workers may avoid tasks unrelated to sales<br>• May encourage overly aggressive sales staff<br>• May cause conflict among sales workers<br>• May cause neglect of good HR practices<br>• May focus attention on sales volume, not profitability |

*(continued)*

| PLAN | ADVANTAGES | DISADVANTAGES |
|------|-----------|---------------|
| **Merit raises** | • Focuses attention on overall performance<br>• Provides feedback to employees<br>• A means for advancement through the pay range<br>• Helps retain outstanding employees<br>• Can foster perceptions of equity | • Very expensive because they are permanent raises<br>• Requires an effective employee appraisal system<br>• Need to ensure a noticeable difference in pay<br>• Employees will eventually "top out"<br>• May cause antagonism toward supervisor<br>• May inhibit collaborative behaviour<br>• Not suitable where work is highly interdependent |
| **Merit bonuses** | • More flexible because they are not permanent<br>• Can be related to the financial conditions of firm<br>• Can serve as solution to "topping out" problem | • Need valid performance measures<br>• Not suitable where work is highly interdependent<br>• Bonus amount may need to be higher |
| **Special-purpose incentives** | • Focuses attention on key employee behaviours<br>• Depends on the specific nature of plan | • Employees may focus only on rewarded behaviours<br>• Depends on the specific nature of plan |

## GROUP PERFORMANCE PAY

In this section, we will first examine the oldest and best-known group performance pay plan—productivity gain sharing—followed by goal-sharing plans, and then other group/team pay plans. Group/team performance pay plans are less common than individual performance pay and appear to have declined in popularity in recent years. This decline follows a period of rapid expansion in the latter part of the 20th century.

## GAIN-SHARING PLANS

**gain-sharing plan**
Group performance pay plan that shares cost savings or productivity gains generated by a work group with all members of that group.

In **gain-sharing plans**, whenever employees in a work group are able to improve productivity or reduce costs, the resulting savings are split between the company and the work group; then the employee portion is systematically shared among group members. While gain sharing can cause employees to work harder, most of the productivity gains come from working smarter and more cooperatively. Key to most gain-sharing plans is a mechanism (typically an employee–management committee) for encouraging employee participation and productivity-enhancing or cost-saving suggestions. Gain-sharing programs depend on a historical base line of cost per unit produced or processed to determine whether productivity has increased, and if so, by how much.

Proponents argue that besides stimulating valuable suggestions, gain sharing contributes to productivity in a variety of ways.[24] One source of this improved productivity is the direct incentive: people work more productively because they expect to receive a share of the financial benefit. But as critics point out, this source of motivation is weak because the extent to which an individual's increased effort will be reflected in their overall income is small.

Gain sharing can help generate group norms that are favourable to productivity. These positive group norms develop because gain sharing promotes the internalization of company objectives and, it follows, self-control. Positive group norms can enhance productivity by stimulating work effort, promoting cooperation among employees and with management, fostering increased employee acceptance of change, and reducing the need for supervisory control. Those employees who are not capable of self-control can still be controlled by group norms (under behavioural theory) or mutual monitoring (under agency theory), where employees monitor one another's performance.

In support of this argument, a study of Canadian manufacturing firms found that those that used gain sharing or profit sharing had significantly less formal hierarchy—and about 31 percent fewer managers—than firms that did not.[25] Because external management controls are costly, reducing them should produce significant savings for the firm, whether or not other productivity improvements occur.

Read Compensation Today 5.3 for an example of a successful gain-sharing plan at a Parisian restaurant.

## COMPENSATION TODAY 5.3

In 2007, Bouillon Chartier, a famous restaurant in Paris, France, with the help of a management consultant, set out to create a team-based bonus plan. The restaurant was a historical monument that served affordable French food delicious enough to be included in earlier French songs and poetry. In 2007, the restaurant served 800 international customers a day, for 365 days of the year.

To understand the goal of the bonus plan, one must understand the business strategy. Bouillon prided itself on its affordable prices and did not have the intention of changing this model. Therefore, the growth needed to be from elsewhere. The target was to increase the customer base. To increase customers, the restaurant had to enhance staff performance both in the dining room and in the kitchen. To achieve the restaurant's strategic goals, the restaurant set out to implement a Voluntary Gain-Sharing program (VGS).

The goal of the VGS was to allow employees to share in the success of the restaurant. The other goal was to give management a new performance measurement tool to help reach yearly targets. The performance metrics for serving staff included seating turnover, customer satisfaction, and selling of the higher priced products and drinks. The performance metrics for kitchen staff included productivity and control of food costs, food safety and cleanliness, and customer satisfaction.

With the plan to add a VGS, the restaurant wanted to ensure that the plan was both motivating and transparent enough for employees to see their potential earnings and thus motivate their behaviour. They wanted to ensure that the goals were set at the team level, rather than company-wide, so that there was a more precise line of sight. The consultant advocated for a bonus of four percent of an employee's annual wage when the team and company achieve its target. If the team and company exceed the target, the payout will increase to 12 percent of an employee's annual wage. If the team and company were below 80 percent of the target, the payout could decrease to zero percent. The factors of the plan would be carefully explained to encourage employee comprehension.

*(continued)*

In order to implement the VGS plan, employee agreement was required. However, employees rejected the original plan and opted for a permanent salary increase. The restaurant did not give up. They continuously communicated the team's quarterly performance throughout the year to explain what the employees' earnings would have been had they accepted the VGS plan. By the end of the year, and after a slight change to the set-up, 90 percent of employees were in favour of the VGS plan and the plan was implemented. Ten years later, after a successful implementation of the gain-sharing plan, the restaurant serves approximately 1600 customers a day—double what it had served before the gain-sharing plan. Furthermore, the restaurant saw an increase of 60 percent of average meals per day and 70 percent of revenue. The targets of seating turnover and kitchen productivity have increased every year as well. The return on investments for the plan was the best part. The payout of VGS amounts for just one percent of the company's yearly revenue, while the increase of annual gross margin is equivalent to 20 years of bonuses. All this has been at no cost to customer satisfaction.

Source: Philippe Wallerich, "An Example of Successful Gain-Sharing Plan in a Most Popular Parisian Restaurant," *LinkedIn*, April 5, 2017.

## Advantages of Gain-Sharing Plans

Gain-sharing plans offer firms many advantages.

1. From an employer's point of view, the most attractive feature is that they are self-funding. The plans themselves produce the funds from which the gain-sharing bonuses are paid.

2. Gain-sharing plans can generate productivity-enhancing or money-saving suggestions.

3. Gain sharing can help create positive work group norms, leading to more worker effort, cooperation, and receptivity to change.

4. Gain sharing can lead to internalized worker commitment, which can lead to self-control and reduced costs of external management control. Increased employee commitment also reduces costs by reducing turnover and absenteeism.

5. Gain sharing can lead to increased employee awareness of the business and improved communication between management and employees.

6. Unlike organizational performance pay, gain sharing can also be applied to not-for-profit and government organizations.

## Disadvantages of Gain-Sharing Plans

However, gain sharing has these potential disadvantages.

1. There are the costs of establishing and administering the program and the costs of the managerial and employee time devoted to the program (including time spent in gain-sharing committee meetings, preparing for meetings, evaluating suggestions, and communicating about the program), and often, for gain sharing to work well, the cost of additional employee training.

2. Gain sharing is not very open to rapidly changing circumstances because it relies on a historical base line to measure productivity changes. When products or technologies change frequently, it is very difficult to determine whether productivity gains (or losses) are due to increased worker input or to other factors. Management will not want to pay out productivity bonuses if causes and effects cannot be defined clearly.

3. Workers may focus only on what they can do to maximize their bonuses, even if their actions have negative consequences for the organization as a whole. For example, a shipping team at a trucking firm may load shipments very quickly, thus increasing their productivity but in such a way that more breakage occurs once the truck is moving; or a customer service team may handle more customer calls by reducing the quality of the team's assistance.

4. Labour–management conflict may increase because it provides additional matters to argue about. When poorly implemented, gain sharing can become a dissatisfier and a demotivator rather than a motivator. Even in firms where there is trust between management and workers, this trust can be tested by all the changes necessary to get a gain-sharing system working properly.

5. Collective reward systems such as gain sharing can open the door to "free riding"— that is, individual employees may shirk or otherwise restrict their work effort, thus becoming "free riders."[26] Any additional effort expended by an individual employee will have only a negligible effect on the reward he or she receives, yet because that employee still shares in the benefits of the cumulative efforts of other employees, there is little cost to that individual in minimizing his or her work effort. If this can't be controlled by group norms, the firm may need to incur the expense of additional supervision.

6. Getting gain-sharing plans to work effectively is difficult, as indicated by their high discontinuation rates. Research by one of the authors found that 78 percent of firms that had gain sharing no longer had it four years later. It appears that many of the firms that adopted gain sharing may not have been suited for it.

## Applicability of Gain Sharing

The evidence is clear that gain sharing can have positive results, but not always.[27] So where is gain sharing likely to succeed? Unions have started to adopt gain-sharing plans more frequently. Unions prefer using gain-sharing plans rather than profit-sharing plans. A major reason for union preference is because workers have a greater ability to control the costs in the bonus formula and the subsequent pay when productivity increases as compared to profit-sharing plans. Profit sharing is viewed as being too strongly at the mercy of the manager's manipulation.[28]

Classical firms generally do not look favourably on gain sharing because it doesn't allow individual accountability and because it permits free riding. However, human relations organizations may find gain sharing attractive because it aligns with their concept of group cooperation. At human relations firms, some of the foundations for effective gain sharing are likely already in place, such as trust between managers and employees. Also, strong and favourable social norms may be able to prevent free-riding, and job security may calm fears of layoffs arising from productivity increases.

But it is in high-involvement organizations that the payoff for gain sharing is potentially greatest because almost all the conditions for its success are already in place, including trust, communications, training, a participative culture, broad-based jobs, and reasonable job security. Also, these organizations are likely to be favourably disposed toward gain sharing because it aligns with their managerial philosophy of encouraging teamwork, participation, innovation, and problem solving. Gain sharing also supports the use of work teams, which are often a prominent feature of high-involvement firms.

▌ Some groups get paid based on work done as a team.

However, high-involvement firms are often operating in a dynamic environment where rapid change is a defining feature. This makes it difficult to establish the historical base lines on which gain sharing depends. An analysis of data from the Workplace and Employee Survey (WES) found that group pay (unfortunately, the WES does not distinguish between the various forms of group pay) was related to profitability in firms not pursuing an innovator business strategy, but not in firms that were.

## GOAL-SHARING PLANS

**goal-sharing plan**
A group performance pay plan in which a work group receives a bonus when it meets prespecified performance goals.

In **goal-sharing plans**, management sets goals for one or more performance indicators for a work group or team, to be met within a specified time period; if the goals are met, all team members receive a bonus.[29] Goal-sharing plans are quite different from gain-sharing plans. In gain sharing, cost savings are quantified and then shared between the company and the employee group; also, unlike in goal sharing, there are no set goals other than to improve as much as possible relative to the historical base line. Thus, goal sharing is much more of an "all or nothing" type of plan than gain sharing. Under gain sharing, the employees receive a portion of any productivity gain, whereas under goal sharing, employees receive nothing if the group goal is not met, even though the employee group may have made significant progress toward meeting the goal.

Like gain sharing, goal sharing grew rapidly in the last two decades of the 20th century but may now be waning in popularity. It is likely that 10–12 percent of medium to large firms now have goal-sharing plans, which still makes it the most common type of group pay plan.

### Advantages of Goal Sharing

Goal-sharing plans have some of the same advantages as gain-sharing plans, as well as several advantages *over* gain-sharing plans.

1. Goal-sharing plans are more flexible and are simpler to develop than gain-sharing plans. They can therefore be applied in a much broader set of circumstances. They can also be tied to specific objectives that support the company's strategy, besides increased productivity or cost savings.

2. Because they are less complex, goal-sharing systems are less costly to operate than gain-sharing systems. Also, because meaningful performance increases must take place before any bonus is paid out, the company retains 100 percent of the gains below the bonus target.

3. Goals and goal-sharing bonuses can be adjusted as circumstances require.

4. Goal setting is a powerful motivational tool for stimulating the performance of employee groups as well as individual employees.[30]

5. Goal sharing, like gain sharing, can help generate positive group norms relating to employee performance, cooperation with management, and receptivity to change; it can also result in less need for supervision. Furthermore, it motivates group members to help new employees learn their jobs quickly and effectively. A collaborative attitude results, and workers who develop better ways of performing their jobs are more likely to share their knowledge than otherwise.

## Disadvantages of Goal Sharing

Goal-sharing plans also have many disadvantages.

1. While flexible, these plans can be much more arbitrary than gain-sharing plans. The goal levels necessary to qualify for a bonus and the sizes of bonuses are often the result of arbitrary management decisions rather than a clearly spelled-out formula. In addition, goal-sharing plans may be modified or dropped at any time. These characteristics do not enhance motivation. For example, if employees perceive goals to be unrealistic (low expectancy), or the bonus sufficiently attractive relative to the effort required (low valence), they will not exert extra effort to meet them. In addition, if employees believe the program can be modified or ended at any time, they will be skeptical whether the promised rewards will actually materialize or continue once goals are met (low instrumentality).

2. Goal-sharing systems often have no established basis for judging the value of meeting a particular goal, as well as no fixed, mutually agreed-upon formula for apportioning gains between the company and employees. Employees may doubt whether they are being fairly compensated for meeting goals and may feel that the company is trying to "rip them off" by providing token rewards for major gains in productivity; this can lead to reward dissatisfaction.

3. Setting goals appropriately can be very difficult. If goals are seen to be too difficult, they will be ignored by employees. If goals are too easy, the firm will pay out money unnecessarily, and these easy goals will set a de facto limit on performance. Going beyond the specified goal brings no additional pay and may cause management to increase goals in future years, so why make the extra effort?

4. Many situational factors can affect goal achievement, so using identical goals for different work groups may be unfair. However, attempts to correct this unfairness by developing "easier" goals for some work groups simply builds resentment elsewhere.

5. Employee dissatisfaction may develop if everyone worked hard to reach the goal but didn't quite succeed and therefore received no reward. Managers may be tempted to redress this resentment by lowering the goal and providing the reward anyway, but this could teach employees that they need not attain the goal in order to receive their bonuses.

6. **Goal sharing can produce conflict.** A work team may become frustrated if one or two workers who are unwilling or unable to perform at the necessary level prevent the group from attaining the goal. On the other hand, conflict may occur if the group believes that some members are pushing "too hard" to achieve or surpass goals.

7. **Goal-sharing plans have a high discontinuation rate.**

Many of the issues with goal sharing can be overcome. Extensive employee participation in the development of these plans can help create realistic goals and increase employee motivation for goal achievement. Multitiered goals can be used to recognize different goal achievement levels; this can reduce frustration if a team can't meet a top goal. Also, management can quantify the value of the specified goals in order to give some assurance of equity when determining reward size.

### Applicability of Goal Sharing

Most experts suggest that to work well, group goal-sharing plans must be designed with input from employees, should clearly communicate factors affecting goal achievement and ways that employees can influence these factors, and should communicate progress toward meeting goals on an ongoing basis. Management must comprehend the characteristics and personalities of their employees as goal acceptance, and goal commitment is dependant on individual attributes such as self-efficacy and self-esteem.[31] The key factor for success is a high level of trust between management and employees. Thus, goal sharing is likely to be most effective in high-involvement organizations, somewhat effective in human relations organizations, and ineffective in classical organizations. A caveat to this is that goal-sharing plans may not work well in highly dynamic firms (which high-involvement firms tend to be), as this makes it difficult or impossible to set realistic goals.[32]

## OTHER TYPES OF GROUP PERFORMANCE PAY PLANS

Besides gain sharing and goal sharing, there are many other types of group bonus plans. These can be placed in two main categories: *competitive bonus plans* and *pooled performance plans*.

A **competitive bonus plan** rewards work groups or teams for outperforming other work groups or teams. For example, many real estate firms with multi-office operations encourage competition among sales offices by providing a bonus to all sales personnel in the highest-producing office each month. In retail chains, all employees in a particular store may receive a bonus if their store has the highest customer satisfaction ratings in the chain in a given time period.

Competitive bonus plans are most suited to circumstances in which the groups do not need to work closely with one another. In general, competitive bonus systems that pit one group against another should be used only when the groups are truly independent and never need to cooperate with one another. These plans do not fit well with human relations organizations or high-involvement firms.

The other type of team-based reward system is **pooled performance pay**. One example of pooled performance pay is **group commissions**, where the pay for a group of sales reps is based on the total sales the group generates, with each member receiving an equal share of the resulting commissions. Another example is **group piece rates**, in which group members are paid based on the number of completed products or components produced by the group. For example, tree planters might be paid according to the total number of trees planted by a team of planters, with the money then shared equally among members of the planting team.

**competitive bonus plan**
A group pay plan that rewards work groups for outperforming other work groups.

**pooled performance pay**
A pay plan in which the performance results of a group are pooled and group members share equally in the performance bonus.

**group commissions**
A performance pay plan in which the commissions of a group of sales workers are pooled and then shared equally among members of the group.

**group piece rates**
A performance pay plan in which group members get paid based on the number of completed products produced by the group.

The value of these plans is that each group member wants the other group members to succeed, and each shares tips and techniques for better performance. In other words, this type of plan encourages teamwork. The danger with these plans is that they may encourage free riding. However, this may not be a problem if the groups are kept relatively small and if members understand that their well-being is maximized when all perform to the best of their abilities.

Compensation Notebook 5.2 summarizes the advantages and disadvantages of group performance pay plans.

## COMPENSATION NOTEBOOK 5.2

### ADVANTAGES AND DISADVANTAGES OF GROUP PERFORMANCE PAY PLANS

| PLAN | ADVANTAGES | DISADVANTAGES |
|---|---|---|
| **Gain sharing** | • Self-funding if designed properly<br>• Can stimulate higher productivity<br>• May enhance labour–management cooperation<br>• May create positive group norms<br>• May improve employee cooperation<br>• May reduce need for external control<br>• May increase employee commitment<br>• May generate cost-saving suggestions<br>• Can increase employee knowledge of the business | • Costs of establishing and administering plan<br>• Costs of employee and managerial time<br>• Not amenable to changing circumstances<br>• May focus attention on group's interests only<br>• May create "free riders"<br>• May create more opportunities for conflict<br>• May become a dissatisfier<br>• High discontinuation rate |
| **Goal sharing** | • Simple to develop<br>• More flexible than gain sharing<br>• Only rewards major productivity gains<br>• May create positive group norms<br>• May encourage cooperation<br>• May reduce need for external control | • Can be arbitrary in goal levels and bonus amounts<br>• Less continuity than gain sharing<br>• Difficulty in establishing realistic and equitable goals<br>• May not meet criteria for good employee motivation<br>• May cause frustration if some do not contribute<br>• May cause frustration if efforts fall slightly short<br>• No incentive to surpass goal<br>• High discontinuation rate |
| **Other group plans** | • Competition between groups can be motivational<br>• May encourage group members to assist others<br>• Depends on specific nature of plan | • Can cause conflict between work groups<br>• May encourage free riders<br>• High discontinuation rate<br>• Depends on specific nature of plan |

# ORGANIZATION PERFORMANCE PAY PLANS

Organization performance pay plans include *profit-sharing plans*, *employee stock plans* (sometimes called "employee share plans"), and other plans, often known as *long-term incentives*. Profit-sharing and employee stock plans experienced growing popularity in the latter decades of the 20th century; however, research by one of the authors suggests that their popularity may have levelled out in the past few years. Among medium to large Canadian firms, profit-sharing and employee stock plans are about equal in popularity: nearly 25 percent of firms report profit-sharing plans and about the same proportion report having at least one employee stock plan.

Bloomberg/Getty Images

▌ Canadian Tire was an early adopter of profit sharing.

## PROFIT SHARING

**employee profit-sharing plan**
A formal pay program in which a firm provides bonus payments to employees based on the profitability of the firm.

**current distribution profit-sharing plan**
A profit-sharing plan that distributes the profit-sharing bonus to employees in the form of cash or shares, at least annually.

To be recognized as having an **employee profit-sharing plan**, a firm must have a formal program in which payments are made to a broad cross-section of employees on at least an annual basis, based on a formula that relates the size of the bonus pool to the profitability of the business. While it is not necessary that all employees or groups be included, plans that restrict profit sharing only to managers are generally not considered "true" employee profit-sharing plans.

Profit-sharing plans may take one of three forms. The **current distribution profit-sharing plan** (also called a "cash plan") pays a portion of company profits to employees in cash or occasionally in company shares. (When shares are used, it is also considered a type of employee stock plan.) In most firms, the distribution is annual, but it can be more frequent, depending on the availability of profit data.

In a **deferred profit-sharing plan (DPSP)**, an employee's share of the profit bonus pool is placed in a trust fund to be distributed at a future date, usually on the employee's retirement or on termination of employment. This type of plan is often used as a type of retirement savings plan. A **combination profit-sharing plan** provides both cash (or shares) and a deferred component. A combination plan gives the employee the opportunity to take advantage of the provisions for tax deferral in federal tax legislation to help build some retirement income; it also provides a more visible incentive to employees through the cash portion.

**deferred profit-sharing plan (DPSP)**
A profit-sharing plan in which the profit-sharing bonuses are allocated to employee accounts but not actually paid out until a later date, usually on termination or retirement.

**combination profit-sharing plan**
A plan that combines the current distribution and deferred profit-sharing plans by paying some of the profit-sharing bonus on a current (cash) basis and deferring the remainder.

## Advantages of Profit-Sharing Plans

As part of a study about profit sharing, researchers asked a business owner whether his firm had employee profit sharing.[33] His reply: "Give away my profits to employees? Why would I want to do *that?*" Why would employers want to share their profits with their employees?

1. When the interests of employees are aligned with those of the employer, employees may be more motivated to improve company performance. Profit sharing can contribute to the development of favourable group norms, improved cooperation among employees and between employees and management, improved labour–management relations, and greater organizational identification, which may strengthen organizational citizenship behaviour. Profit sharing allows for greater enticement for effort, cooperation, information sharing, and innovation. Such an effort can enhance workplace performance and productivity. Besides, profit sharing can establish a more collaborative workplace with increased corporate transparency.[34]

2. Improved norms can reduce the need for supervision, thereby reducing costs. Profit sharing also aligns with and supports a move toward high-involvement management for firms moving in that direction.

3. Profit sharing is a reward related to company ability to pay. By adding profit sharing to its compensation mix, an employer can offer a more lucrative compensation package when conditions permit, but is not locked into higher fixed pay because it doesn't have to continue profit-sharing payments when business conditions are unfavourable and the firm makes no profits. In the same vein, profit sharing is the only way that some organizations can afford to offer a retirement plan because it means they have no obligation to contribute to the pension plan when they cannot afford to do so.

4. Recent Canadian research shows that, on average, employees in firms with profit sharing have higher total earnings than those in firms that do not provide profit sharing.[35] This helps the firm attract and retain employees.

5. Profit sharing may reduce the need for layoffs in poor economic circumstances because labour costs are automatically adjusted downward. This reduces the risk of losing good employees because of layoffs; it also provides employees with greater job security.

6. If profit sharing helps create a more cooperative workplace, employees may gain greater job satisfaction from working in a harmonious environment.

7. Finally, profit sharing is far simpler to set up and administer than plans such as gain sharing. Profit measures are readily available in virtually all firms. There is no need to compute base lines or to try to quantify the value of cost savings. In addition, administration is relatively simple, and the plan and its results are relatively easy to communicate to employees.

## Disadvantages of Profit Sharing

As with all performance pay plans, profit sharing also has its disadvantages.

1. It may not pay off for the employer. The costs of the profit-sharing bonus and for administering the profit-sharing system may exceed the benefits.

2. As a collective reward system, profit sharing may actually reduce employee performance by causing free riding, just as in group-based pay systems. Because the connection between individual performance and the expected reward for that performance is more fragile, profit sharing has a weaker "line of sight" between individual employee performance and the bonus amount than group pay and so may have little direct impact on employee performance. So many factors intervene between worker performance and company profitability that worker performance can improve dramatically while profits actually go down or even disappear—owing, for example, to market conditions or poor management decisions.

3. Unions may oppose profit sharing because its results are subject to management manipulation, or because employers will be tempted to substitute uncertain rewards from profit for certain rewards from base pay.

4. Profit sharing requires employers to share financial information about the company. This is a concern mainly for classical employers, who do not feel that employees can be trusted with financial information.

## Applicability of Profit Sharing

In a major study, the CEOs of Canadian firms that had adopted profit sharing said that they saw profit sharing as a way either to increase company performance (by improving employee motivation, promoting teamwork, or helping employees understand the business) or to provide better rewards to employees, thereby improving employee commitment and loyalty. Most CEOs said they believed profit sharing had helped their companies achieve these goals.[36]

These results fit well with an American study as described in Compensation Today 5.4, which found that companies that made extensive use of organization-based performance rewards—such as profit-sharing and employee stock plans—showed a much higher five-year survival rate than firms that did not use organization-based performance pay—a finding that would come as a surprise to stock analysts and investors! Studies have also shown that profit sharing improves employment stability.[37] However, while the research is clear that profit sharing can help company performance, it also suggests that profit sharing is ineffective in between one-quarter and one-third of the firms in which it has been implemented.[38]

---

**COMPENSATION TODAY 5.4**

### HOW MANY STOCK ANALYSTS DOES IT TAKE TO CHANGE A LIGHT BULB?

How many stock market analysts does it take to change a light bulb? The answer: None. If the bulb really needed changing, the market would have already changed it.

The humour in this joke relies on stock market analysts' belief in the "infallibility of the market"—the notion that the stock market considers all information about a company and accurately incorporates it into the valuation of the company's shares. Yet the "infallibility of the market" is, in fact, a fiction. Through their own individual actions, stock analysts continually pass collective judgment on the decisions of company management and influence changes in the firm's share price. Investors *are* the market!

Management decisions in publicly traded corporations are evaluated in terms of whether they "add value" to a company—whether they cause a company's share price to go up or down. Therefore, researchers have started to examine the quality of management decisions in terms of the market's reaction to them. But is the market always right? Or does the market sometimes act on erroneous assumptions?

An interesting study by Theresa Welbourne and Alice Andrews examined the five-year survival rate of firms that were first listed on a stock exchange in 1988. The study then related this rate to the extent to which these firms had organization-based performance rewards, such as profit-sharing and employee stock plans. Their results were impressive. They found that the use of organization-based performance rewards significantly increased the likelihood of company survival.

This is an interesting finding in its own right, but the researchers made another interesting discovery. They examined whether the stock market had valued the shares of companies with organizational rewards more highly than those of firms without organizational rewards at the time of the initial public offering. It should have, as these firms ended up with a higher survival rate.

But it did not. In fact, firms with organizational rewards were valued significantly *lower* than firms without these rewards. The researchers concluded that "investors seem to respond negatively to a factor that actually has a positive impact on survival chances." They also found that despite believing that organizational rewards had played some role in their company's success, the top executives of survivor companies substantially undervalued the role that organizational rewards had actually played in company survival. This suggests that business culture itself may have a tradition of discounting the impact of organizational rewards.

Further research on employee ownership and company survival that used data from U.S. public companies found that companies with employee ownership of five percent or more were 76 percent as likely as other companies to survive within 13 years. The increased survival rate can be attributed to increased employment stability. The promise of employment security supports a more collaborative culture, thereby enhancing employee commitment and readiness to be more flexible when economic hardships do occur.

Sources: Theresa M. Welbourne and Alice N. Andrews, "Predicting the Performance of Initial Public Offerings: Should Human Resource Management Be in the Equation?" *Academy of Management Journal* 39, no. 4 (1996): 891–919; Rhokeun Park, Douglas Kruse, and James Sesil, "Does Employee Ownership Enhance Firm Survival?" in *Employee Participation, Firm Performance and Survival* (Bingley, UK: Emerald Group Publishing, 2004), 3–33.

There is also research that finds that there are conditions that must be met for the plan to succeed. Two contingencies exist that ensure improved organizational performance. The first contingency is organizational and management characteristics. This first contingency suggests that profit sharing works best in smaller firms, or at minimum, divided into smaller units so employees can see the connection between their behaviour and the overall consequences. Profit sharing is also most successful in the hierarchically flat and highly participative workplace. As well, profit sharing is more successful in a goal-setting workplace that offers unification between individual and organizational goals, where goals are created together by managers and employees and offer manager and stakeholder performance evaluations. In addition, employees must have proper support to achieve the goals that would allow them to receive the profit.

The second contingency is plan characteristics that are necessary for the profit-sharing plan's success. Factors include larger payouts that are contingent on performance to support those that are the highest performers. There must be a straightforward formula that shows a clear line between actions and payout. Pay must be frequent enough to show that employees will be rewarded for their actions. Lastly, profit-sharing plans are most successful when offered strictly to managers, professionals, and those that have the potential to affect profit.[39]

Research also shows that the most important single factor in the success or failure of profit sharing is practice of a high-involvement managerial strategy.[40] Given this, it is not surprising that high-involvement firms are the ones most likely to implement profit sharing.[41] Overall, profit sharing seems particularly important in companies where a high level of cooperation is needed across company units, between management and employees, and among employees, and where much or most of the work is performed in teams. Profit sharing helps promote the internalization of company goals and provides a mechanism for keeping employees informed about the financial state of the business. A recent Canadian study suggests that profit sharing can foster a positive organizational culture that promotes teamwork and increased employee participation.[42]

Profit sharing may also be useful in human relations organizations to the extent that it serves as an additional means of cementing loyalty to the firm and fostering positive work norms. However, the impact of profit sharing is not likely to be dramatic because the participative culture that is necessary to maximize the contribution of profit sharing is not generally in place at human relations firms.

For classical firms, profit sharing yields few benefits. It is not compatible with the classical managerial philosophy, which views workers and management as adversaries and which requires that individuals be accountable for their own performance. In situations of low trust, profit sharing becomes another source of conflict: employees believe that management is trying to use profit sharing to reduce other compensation or to weaken union allegiance, and that management will find ways to manipulate the system to cheat them out of their rightful share of the profits. In addition, management's reluctance to release financial information fosters mistrust and makes it difficult for employees to understand how they could contribute to profitability. In addition, a major potential benefit of profit sharing—the ability to operate with less hierarchy and fewer supervisors—is not viable in classical firms.

For profit sharing to succeed, there must be some expectation of profits in at least the first one or two years of the plan. The profitability level should be sufficient to afford a noticeable annual payout amount—at least three to five percent of total compensation for each employee. Firms with highly unstable profits and a weak "line of sight" between employee performance and profitability are not ideal candidates. Finally, there must be reasonably good relations between management and employees, and management must be willing to share financial information and value employee input.

Economists contend that profit sharing would have more impact if it substituted for base pay; however, consultants and practitioners universally oppose this practice,[43] arguing instead that competitive base pay and an equitable compensation system are preconditions for successful profit sharing. Interestingly, research based on Canadian WES data found that firms that pay above the average for their industry are more likely to adopt profit sharing than other firms.[44] The same study found that firms pursuing a low-cost strategy were more likely to adopt profit sharing, consistent with the notion that profit sharing fits better with firms that have less volatile profits, as innovator firms tend to have. Other research based on the same data set found that growth in total employee earnings in the five years after a firm had adopted employee profit sharing was significantly higher than that of firms that had not adopted profit sharing, indicating that profit sharing does, on average, increase total employee earnings.[45]

# EMPLOYEE STOCK PLANS

An **employee stock plan** is any type of plan through which employees acquire shares in the firm that employs them. There are three main types of employee stock plans: *employee stock bonus plans*, *employee share purchase plans*, and *employee stock option plans*.

An **employee stock bonus plan** is very simple in concept: an employer provides company shares to employees at no cost to the employee, either by outright grant or in conjunction with some other performance pay plan, such as profit sharing. In an **employee share purchase plan**, employees provide some kind of direct payment in return for company shares, but they usually do not have to pay full market price for these shares. (Compensation Today 5.5 describes two typical employee share purchase plans—one in a private corporation and one in a public corporation.) In an **employee stock option plan**, employees are provided with options to purchase company shares at some future time at a set price, which they will exercise if the market price rises to exceed this price.

Employee stock plans enjoyed rapid growth during the latter part of the 20th century, but their popularity appears to have levelled out during the last decade. This is not surprising in light of the down-market conditions that have prevailed in the new millennium. In addition, there has been controversy regarding whether employee stock plans (particularly executive stock plans) actually serve the interests of shareholders. Of the three main types of employee stock plans, employee share purchase plans are the most common (used by about 20 percent of medium to large Canadian firms), followed by employee stock option plans (used by about 10 percent of firms), and employee stock bonus plans (used by about two percent of firms).

**employee stock plan**
Any type of plan through which employees acquire shares in the firm that employs them.

**employee stock bonus plan**
A plan through which employees receive shares in their employer firm at no cost to the employee.

**employee share purchase plan**
A plan through which employees may purchase shares in their employer firm.

**employee stock option plan**
A plan through which employees are provided with options to purchase shares in their employer at a fixed price within a limited time period.

---

## COMPENSATION TODAY 5.5

### A Special Blend for Starbucks Employees

Executives at Starbucks were likely fuelled by caffeine when they created the compensation and benefits package for their employees (whom they refer to as "partners"). Starbucks offers extended health coverage, employee assistance programs such as referrals for child and elder care, health care, or emotional concerns; tuition reimbursement; and many other perks. And there's more!

The "Bean Stock" provides eligible partners with restricted stock units. Upon completion of the vesting period, Starbucks employees are entitled to a specified number of shares dependent on the company's success and profitability, the employee's position, the employee's annual salary, and the fair market value of the company's stock on the date of the grant. Starbucks also offers a Stock Investment Plan (SIP), in which employees are eligible to purchase stock at a five percent discount. Employees can contribute 1–10 percent of their earnings.

Starbucks has an RRSP plan. If an employee chooses to contribute to the plan, Starbucks will match the contributions up to a maximum of two percent of the employee's salary directly into a Deferred Profit-Sharing Plan.

A long-time employee's experience at Starbucks can explain the benefits of such a program. She started working part-time at Starbucks while attending university in 1992. Just a year earlier, Starbucks had started to offer stock compensation to its employees. Once the employee had worked 360 hours, she became eligible for shares. This employee continues to work for Starbucks as a diversity consultant in the Human Resources department. The stock has had a return of about 13 000 percent throughout her employment. Through this, the employee was able to pay $2500 in student loans, put $60 000 on a down payment on her first house, travel abroad to Thailand and Bali, and soon sell her shares to pay for her wedding.

Sources: Samantha Sharf, "Why Starbucks Pays Its Baristas With Stock: A Beginners' Guide to Company Stock," *Forbes*, March 18, 2015; "Starbucks Coffee Canada," https://globalassets.starbucks.com/assets/d7ea56b34e27429e8171d7c4e8d65fc7.pdf, accessed November 17, 2019.

## Advantages of Employee Stock Plans

Employee stock plans can bring several advantages to firms.

1. By aligning the goals of employees with those of the owners, share ownership may cause employees "to think like owners" and internalize company goals. This can lead to enhanced citizenship and membership behaviours.

2. Employee share ownership can create a stronger understanding of and concern for overall company performance and promote cooperation among employees and between employees and management.

3. Especially if accompanied by employee participation, share ownership can provide employees with a say in the enterprise and a sense of control over their own destiny.

4. Employee stock plans can improve the compensation package, making it easier to attract and retain employees. The financial gains to employees can be enormous—the employee share plan at Microsoft has created thousands of employee millionaires. A stock plan can also serve as a retirement plan, which is especially valuable in firms that do not want to commit to formal pension plans.

5. Companies with a significant amount of employee ownership have been found to provide better job security to their employees.[46]

6. Employee stock plans may lead to improved management, because share-owning employees may hold managers to a higher performance standard than they otherwise would.

7. Unlike most forms of performance pay, employee stock plans do not require the company to lay out cash. Thus, for companies that are cash-poor and that cannot afford pay raises, shares may be one way to reward employees.

8. Large-scale employee ownership plans, in which employees acquire a significant portion of the ownership, can serve as the catalyst for a more flexible and entrepreneurial high-involvement type of organization.

## Disadvantages of Employee Share Plans

Employee stock plans have some general disadvantages and some specific disadvantages pertaining to each type of plan.

1. Establishing and administering these plans carries a cost. In addition, providing a large number of shares to employees at a below-market price can dilute the holdings of other shareholders. This is particularly true for stock bonus or stock option plans.

2. If the share price declines, employees may become demoralized or disgruntled, especially when the decline in share prices is due to poor management performance rather than general market conditions.

3. If employees want to participate in decision making to improve company performance but management does not provide them with opportunities to do so, then employee backlash may occur.

4. For share purchase plans, a problem may be that employees do not have the money to invest in these plans, even if the shares are offered to them at a significantly discounted price.

5. For employees, investing in their employer may be risky because they risk losing not only their jobs if the firm performs poorly, but also their savings. (Of course, this is a

concern only for share purchase plans, not stock bonus or stock option plans.) Risks of share ownership are particularly high for employee–owners in privately held corporations, where no outside market exists for their shares.

6. For privately held corporations, using share plans is more complicated than for publicly traded corporations, because many necessary mechanisms are not in place and have to be created. Procedures for issuing, pricing, selling, and trading shares need to be developed, as well as procedures for shareholder voting and communication of financial information. In addition, many owners of privately held corporations do not want to give up any control of their companies.

## Applicability of Employee Stock Plans

Employee stock plans are used by firms in a wide variety of industries and in both publicly traded and privately held firms. Various studies have found that the effects of employee stock plans on company performance range from moderately positive to neutral.[47] However, when combined with employee participation, employee share ownership can have dramatic results. For example, one American study found that firms that introduced employee ownership and that practised employee participation in decision making grew 11–17 percent faster than their competitors, whereas firms that simply introduced employee ownership showed no difference from their competitors. A British study found that firms that possess stock plans require alternate forms of employee involvement and say in decision making in order to have an impact on company performance when only a portion of employees participated in the stock ownership plan.[48]

Many other studies have consistently found that combining an employee stock plan with employee participation greatly increases the performance effects of employee ownership.[49] Moreover, firms that combine ownership with employee participation have been found to provide a significantly greater financial return (including both employment earnings and share earnings) to their employees than comparable conventional firms.[50]

What about the results of employee stock options? A major study conducted at Rutgers University, using a matched-sample longitudinal design, found that firms that adopted broad-based stock option programs were more productive—by about 6.3 percent—than comparable firms even *before* they adopted the programs. Then, after adopting stock option programs, these companies more than doubled their productivity advantage (to 14 percent) over their competitors. In a more recent study of U.S. Panel data that analyzed both executive and broad-based stock option adoption, a positive impact on productivity was found for both stock option plans. However, over five years after adoption, though the executive plan continued to show increased productivity, productivity levels for the broad-based plans declined. Nevertheless, the authors continued to see merit in this plan, at least for purposes of incentive and employee attraction and retention.[51]

As with profit-sharing plans, employee stock plans fit best with high-involvement organizations. In fact, the idea of ownership fits even better with high-involvement organizations than profit sharing does, because it connotes a greater degree of unity of purpose between employees and the other owners. It also carries expectations about information and control rights. Overall, employee ownership on its own has the potential to deliver to employees three of the four elements that Edward Lawler, a leading compensation scholar, deems essential for high-involvement organizations: power, information, and rewards (the other key element is knowledge); thus, it can help organizations move toward high involvement.[52]

For human relations organizations, employee stock plans may hold some benefits, especially if employees regard these plans as an attractive part of the compensation system. They may help retain employees and foster positive group norms. However, because these organizations are not likely to provide opportunities for participation, nor the information and training needed for effective participation, the positive consequences are likely to be limited. There is also the risk of damage to morale if share prices drop.

In classical organizations, given the adversarial nature of employee–management relations, employee share ownership is not likely to be offered, nor is it likely to be greeted with much enthusiasm by employees, especially if they are required to give up something in exchange. Unless the share plan is very generous, there is not likely to be much interest among employees. If stock bonuses or stock options are granted outright, employees in a classical firm are likely to sell their shares at the first possible opportunity.

Employees in classical firms who do retain their shares and who attempt to improve company performance are likely to experience hostility from their peers because coworkers are likely to be concerned that productivity increases may lead to negative consequences such as layoffs. Attempts to increase employee involvement in decision making will likely be met with indifference or resistance from classical managers because these managers are unlikely to believe that the workers are capable of making useful suggestions or participating responsibly in decision making. These attitudes are likely to lead to frustration on the part of employee–owners.

## OTHER ORGANIZATION PERFORMANCE PAY PLANS

In the latter part of the 20th century, it became evident that the organization performance pay plans in place did not do enough to encourage a long-term perspective on organization performance. Noting that many company initiatives may take years to succeed, they asked themselves whether incentives could be developed that would look at performance from a longer perspective. The most prominent of these are now known as **long-term incentives (LTIs)**. In essence, these plans are set up so that a payout is contingent on the achievement of three- to five-year performance goals.[53]

Long-term compensation has traditionally involved stock options and stock grants. However, LTIs may use performance units rather than shares. A **performance unit plan** grants an organization member (usually an executive) a number of performance units, each of which carries a monetary value to be realized if certain performance targets are met. There are two ways to establish a value for these units. One way is to issue units where the value of each unit is constant but the number of units actually payable depends on the degree of attainment of targeted goals. The second way is to vary the value of each unit based on the degree of goal attainment.

A **performance share plan** uses company shares instead of units. Depending on the degree of goal attainment, the individual receives a certain number of company shares at the end of the performance period. This plan has a double-barrelled incentive: to meet targeted goals and to increase company share value.

As with stock options, LTIs were originally granted only to the three or four top executives (as will be discussed in Chapter 6, where we devote a special section ["Executives"] to executive compensation). But in 1996, a major departure from this practice occurred when apparel giant Levi Strauss announced a six-year, long-term incentive plan that included *all* employees.[54] Unfortunately, by 1999, the company was so far from meeting its LTI goals

**long-term incentives (LTIs)**
A type of performance pay in which the incentives are tied to an organization performance horizon that ranges beyond one year, often three to five years.

**performance unit plan**
A long-term incentive in which the bonus amounts are expressed in units for which the monetary value will fluctuate, depending on degree of goal accomplishment.

**performance share plan**
A long-term incentive in which the bonus amounts are expressed in company shares.

that the program was cancelled.[55] Nonetheless, it appears that the Levi Strauss example may have caused some firms to follow suit. According to research conducted by one of the authors, about five percent of Canadian firms had adopted broad-based LTIs (those that include nonmanagerial employees) by 2000. However, growth in these plans subsequently appeared to level off and may have since declined.

Because the use of LTIs as broad-based employee performance pay plans is relatively new, almost nothing is known about their effects on corporate performance. One challenge for researchers is to separate the impact of LTIs from that of the many other factors that affect firm performance over a three- to five-year period.

Most of the advantages and disadvantages of goal sharing can be expected to apply to broad-based LTIs, with a particular disadvantage being the difficulty of estimating realistic goals for the three- to five-year period that LTIs cover. Realistic goals are hard enough to estimate for the one-year period that goal-sharing programs typically cover, let alone a longer period. In addition, many employees may leave the firm during the performance period and may not expect to see any benefit from the plan. Overall, such plans are useful only for firms with a very stable workforce in a very stable industry, where events are predictable over the longer term. Given the economic volatility of the past few years, such circumstances would seem rare, so such plans may be of little value to most firms.

Compensation Notebook 5.3 summarizes the advantages and disadvantages of the main types of organization performance pay plans.

---

### COMPENSATION NOTEBOOK 5.3

#### ADVANTAGES AND DISADVANTAGES OF ORGANIZATION PERFORMANCE PAY PLANS

| PLAN | ADVANTAGES | DISADVANTAGES |
|---|---|---|
| Profit-sharing plans | • May contribute to higher employee productivity<br>• May foster increased cooperation<br>• May improve labour–management relations<br>• May increase organizational identification<br>• Can reduce need for employee supervision<br>• May help employees understand the business<br>• May result in more attractive compensation package<br>• Ties compensation to ability to pay<br>• May help employment stability<br>• May be used as a retirement plan<br>• Relatively simple to set up and administer<br>• Relatively low discontinuation rate | • May not pay off<br>• May not motivate due to weak "line of sight"<br>• Subject to the "free-rider" problem<br>• Employees like predictable reward<br>• May be opposed by unions<br>• Administrative costs |

*(continued)*

| PLAN | ADVANTAGES | DISADVANTAGES |
|------|-----------|---------------|
| Employee stock plans | • Aligns interests of employers and employees<br>• May stimulate improved management<br>• May increase employee–management cooperation<br>• Fosters employee interest in firm performance<br>• Can improve perceptions of equity in firm<br>• Can be used as retirement fund<br>• Can increase employee job security<br>• Does not require firm to lay out cash | • Possible dilution of shareholder equity<br>• Cost of establishing and managing plan<br>• Employee dissatisfaction if share prices decline<br>• More difficult to establish in private corporations<br>• Employees may not have funds to purchase shares<br>• Employees have "all their eggs in one basket" |
| Long-term incentives | • Encourages a long-term focus<br>• Can encourage better understanding of business | • Difficulty in establishing realistic long-term goals<br>• "Line of sight" may be weak |

# SUMMARY

This chapter completes our discussion of the compensation "menu" by discussing the performance pay choices available within each of the three main categories of performance pay (individual, group, and organization).

You learned the four types of pay geared to individual performance (piece rates, sales commissions, merit pay, and special-purpose incentives), three main types of pay geared to group performance (gain-sharing plans, goal-sharing plans, and other group performance pay plans), and three main types of pay geared to organization performance (profit sharing, employee stock plans, and long-term incentives).

Individual performance pay plans generally promote task behaviour. Each type of individual performance pay can be effective when properly designed and applied in the right circumstances. Whenever possible, intrinsic motivation to motivate task behaviour is superior to extrinsic motivation. Because many individual performance plans tend to foster an adversarial employee–management relationship, classical firms that use these plans need to watch for loopholes and develop ways to close them.

Group performance pay promotes task behaviour, positive social behaviour within groups/teams, and favourable group norms. Group performance rewards are appropriate where good individual performance is not possible without effective cooperation from other members of the work group or team, and where it is difficult or impractical to measure individual performance. It fits well with high-involvement firms and can likely be used effectively by most human relations firms. Group performance pay does not fit classical organizations well.

Organization performance pay is intended to promote organizational citizenship and membership behaviour, as well as positive group norms. It fits well with high-involvement management, but may also benefit human relations firms, depending on the type and the design of the plan selected. Organization performance pay does not suit classical organizations.

The key for compensation strategy is to select those pay plans that fit your organization best and apply them only to those employees for whom they are a good fit.

## KEY TERMS

combination profit-sharing plan
competitive bonus plan
conversion selling
current distribution profit-sharing plan
deferred profit-sharing plan (DPSP)
differential piece rate
employee profit-sharing plan
employee share purchase plan
employee stock bonus plan
employee stock option plan
employee stock plan
gain-sharing plan
goal-sharing plan
group commissions
group piece rates

leverage selling
long-term incentives (LTIs)
maintenance selling
merit bonus
merit raise
new market selling
performance share plan
performance unit plan
piece rates
pooled performance pay
sales commissions
special-purpose incentive
straight commission
straight piece rate
suggestion system

## DISCUSSION QUESTIONS

1. Discuss the key advantages and disadvantages of piece rates?

2. What are the key advantages and disadvantages of gain-sharing and goal-sharing plans?

3. Discuss the considerations you would use in deciding whether to apply profit sharing or employee share ownership to a given organization.

4. Of the pay plans discussed in this chapter, which one would best apply to essential workers during a crisis such as the COVID-19 pandemic? Why?

## EXERCISES

1. Implemented for the right reasons, an employee share plan can be an effective organizational pay plan. Using the ESOP Association of Canada website (https://www.esopcanada.ca/faq), explain the motives for implementing employee share ownership plans in Canada.

2. Form small groups of four to six people. Try to design a merit pay system for college and university professors. Share the results with the class.

3. Form small groups of four to six people. Each group member will contact one local retailer and find out about its pay system for its sales staff. Compare the systems and discuss whether any of these systems are linked to the type of product sold and the type of sales activity. Do they fit with the advice offered in this chapter? Do they fit with the firm's managerial strategy, as far as you can determine? Get together with other groups and share your conclusions.

4. Form groups of six to eight people. Divide each group in half. With one group proposing and one group opposing, debate this topic: "University professors should be paid only through merit pay."

1. Read *Case 6—Alliston Instruments* in the Appendix and then analyze the pay system. Why is the new pay system apparently not working? Do you think that the individual production bonus system could work if some changes were made? What changes? Is individual performance pay suitable for this company? If management insists on some type of individual performance pay system, what type would you recommend?

2. Suppose that management at Alliston Instruments (*Case 6*, Appendix) has decided to scrap the current individual performance pay system. However, the company has not decided what, if anything, will replace this system and have called you in to advise them. They want you to examine the group and organization performance plans available and recommend the one that fits best with the company and the problems it faces. In preparing your report, be sure to include the pros and cons of each approach and reasons that your recommended approach is the best.

3. Do you think that The Fit Stop Ltd. (*Case 2,* Appendix) would be a suitable organization in which to implement an organization performance pay plan? Explain why or why not. If The Fit Stop is suitable, what type of organization performance plan would be most appropriate? Describe the key elements of this plan as applied to The Fit Stop.

## SIMULATION CROSS-REFERENCE

If you are using *Strategic Compensation: A Simulation* in conjunction with this text, you will find that the concepts in Chapter 5 are helpful in preparing the simulation.

# ENDNOTES

1. Bo Johansson, Kjell Rask, and Magnus Stenberg, "Piece Rates and Their Effects on Health and Safety—A Literature Review," *Applied Ergonomics* 41 (2010): 607–14.

2. John S. Heywood, Xiangdong Wei, and Guangliang Ye, "Piece Rates for Professors," *Economics Letters* 113 (2011): 285–87.

3. Susan Helper, Morris M. Kleiner, and Yingchun Wang, "Analyzing Compensation Methods in Manufacturing: Piece Rates, Time Rates, or Gain Sharing?" National Bureau of Economic Research, Working Paper #16540 (2010).

4. David A. Harrison, Meghna Virick, and Sonja William, "Working Without a Net: Time, Performance, and Turnover Under Maximally Contingent Rewards," *Journal of Applied Psychology* 81, no. 4 (1996): 331–45.

5. William Keenan, "Beyond the Basics," in *Commissions, Bonuses, and Beyond,* ed. William Keenan (Chicago: Irwin, 1994), xv–xviii.

6. Ira Sagar, "IBM Leans on Its Sales Force," *Business Week*, February 7, 1994, 110; Pankaj M. Madhani, "Compensation, Ethical Sales Behavior and Customer Lifetime Value," *Compensation & Benefits Review* 46, no. 4 (2014): 204–18.

7. Jerome A. Coletti and David J. Chicelli, "Increasing Sales Force Effectiveness Through the Compensation Plan," in *The Compensation Handbook*, ed. Milton L. Rock and Lance A. Berger (New York: McGraw-Hill, 1991), 290–306.

8. Michel Tremblay, Jerome Cote, and David Balkin, "Explaining Sales Compensation Strategy Using Agency, Transaction Cost

Analysis, and Institutional Theories," paper presented at the Academy of Management Annual Meetings, Boston, 1997; Sunil Kishore, Raghunath Singh Rao, Om Narasimhan, and George John, "Bonuses Versus Commissions: A Field Study," *Journal of Marketing Research* 50, no. 3 (2013): 317–33.

9. Antoinette Weibel, Katja Rost, and Margit Osterloh, "Pay for Performance in the Public Sector: Benefits and (Hidden) Costs," *Journal of Public Administration—Research and Theory* 20, no. 2 (2010): 387–412.

10. Parbudyal Singh and Natasha Loncar, "Antecedents of Pay Satisfaction in a Unionized Environment," *Relations Industrielles/Industrial Relations* 65, no. 3, (2010), 470–90; Michael Atkinson, Murray Fulton, and Boa Kim, "Why Do Governments Use Pay for Performance? Contrasting Theories and Interview Evidence," *Canadian Public Administration* 57, no. 3 (2014): 436–58.

11. Robert L. Heneman, "Merit Pay Research," *Research in Personnel and Human Resources Management* 8 (1990): 203–63; James S Bowman, "The Success of Failure: the Paradox of Performance Pay," *Review of Public Personnel Administration* 30, no. 1 (2010): 70–88.

12. Steven Kerr, "On the Folly of Rewarding A, While Hoping for B," *Academy of Management Executives* 9, no. 1 (1995): 7–14; Stephen Miller, "Employers Seek Better Approaches to Pay for Performance: Merit Pay Raises and Annual Bonuses Failing to Drive Employee Performance," *HRNews* (2016).

13. Robert L. Heneman and Jon M. Werner, *Merit Pay: Linking Pay to Performance in a Changing World* (Reading: Addison-Wesley, 2005).

14. Sanghee Park and Michael C. Sturman, "How and What You Pay Matters: The Relative Effectiveness of Merit Pay, Bonuses and Long-Term Incentives on Future Job Performance," *Compensation & Benefits Review* 44, no. 2 (2012): 80–85.

15. Edward E. Lawler, *Rewarding Excellence: Pay Strategies for the New Economy* (San Francisco: Jossey-Bass, 2000); Shahina Javad and S. D. Sumod, "It's Time to Bring Performance Appraisal into the Twenty-First Century," *Human Resource Management International Digest* 23, no. 7 (2015): 23–26.

16. Lawrence J. Peter and Raymond Hull, *The Peter Principle* (New York: William Morrow, 1969).

17. Henry M. Findley, William F. Giles, and Kevin W. Mossholder, "Performance Appraisal Process and System Facets: Relationships with Contextual Performance," *Journal of Applied Psychology* 85, no. 4 (2000): 634–40; R.R. Reilly and Z.H. Aronson, "Managing Contextual Performance," in Smither, J.W. and London, M. (eds), *Performance Management: Putting Research into Practice* (San Francisco, CA: Jossey-Bass, 2009).

18. Richard J. Long, "Group-Based Pay, Participatory Practices, and Workplace Performance." Paper presented at the Conference on the Evolving Workplace, Ottawa, September 28–29, 2005.

19. See ibid; see also Jerry L. McAdams, "Employee Involvement and Performance Reward Plans," *Compensation and Benefits Review* 27, no. 2 (1995): 45–55.

20. Patricia L. Booth, *Employee Absenteeism: Strategies for Promoting an Attendance-Oriented Corporate Culture* (Ottawa: Conference Board of Canada, 1993); Cecilia Rapp, and Jörgen Eklund, "Sustainable Development of a Suggestion System: Factors Influencing Improvement Activities in a Confectionary Csompany," *Human Factors and Ergonomics in Manufacturing & Service Industries* 17, no. 1 (2007): 79–94.

21. See Edward E. Lawler, "Reward Systems," in *Improving Life at Work: Behavioral Sciences Approaches to Organizational Change*, ed. J. Richard Hackman and J. Lloyd Suttle (Santa Monica: Goodyear, 1977). For a more recent example of an attendance lottery that also showed positive results, see Wolter H.J. Hassink and Pierre Koning, "Do Financial Bonuses Reduce Employee Absenteeism? Evidence from a Lottery," *Industrial and Labor Relations Review* 62, no. 3 (2009): 327–42.

22. Paul S. Goodman and Robert S. Atkin, *Absenteeism: New Approaches to Understanding, Measuring, and Managing Employee Absence* (San Francisco: Jossey-Bass, 1984); Jan F. Ybema, Peter GW Smulders, and Paulien M. Bongers, "Antecedents and Consequences of Employee Absenteeism: A Longitudinal Perspective on the Role of Job Satisfaction and Burnout," *European Journal of Work and Organizational Psychology* 19, no. 1 (2010): 102–24.

23. Ian R. Gellatly and Andrew A. Luchak, "Personal and Organizational Determinants of Perceived Absence Norms," *Human Relations* 51, no. 8 (1998): 1085–102; Sascha Alexander Ruhle, and Stefan Süß, "Presenteeism and Absenteeism at Work—An Analysis of Archetypes of Sickness Attendance Cultures," *Journal of Business and Psychology* (2019): 1–15.

24. Brian Graham-Moore and Timothy L. Ross, *Gainsharing and Employee Involvement* (Washington, DC: BNA Books, 1995); Elizabeth M. Doherty and Jerry L. McAdams, "Micro and Macro Perspectives on Gain Sharing," *Handbook of Organizational Consultation*, Second Edition (New York: Routledge, 2019), 351.

25. Richard J. Long, "Gain Sharing, Hierarchy, and Managers: Are They Substitutes?" in *Proceedings of the Administrative Sciences Association of Canada, Organization Theory Division*, 15, no. 12 (1994): 51–60.

26. See M. Olson, *The Logic of Collective Action* (Cambridge, MA: Harvard University Press, 1971); see also M. Jensen and W. Meckling, "Theory of the Firm: Managerial Behavior, Agency Costs, and Ownership Structure," *Financial Economics* 3 (1973): 305–60.

27. See Denis Collins, *Gain Sharing and Power: Lessons from Six Scanlon Plans* (Ithaca: Cornell University Press, 1998); see also Susan W. Bowie-McCoy, Ann C. Wendt, and Roger Chope, "Gain Sharing in Public Accounting: Working

Smarter and Harder," *Industrial Relations* 32, no. 3 (1993): 432–45; M. Wallace, *Rewards and Renewal: America's Search for Competitive Advantage Through Alternative Pay Strategies* (Scottsdale: American Compensation Association, 1990); Richard B. Freeman, Joseph R. Blasi, and Douglas L. Kruse, "Introduction to 'Shared Capitalism at Work: Employee Ownership, Profit and Gain Sharing, and Broad-based Stock Options'," in *Shared Capitalism at Work: Employee Ownership, Profit and Gain Sharing, and Broad-based Stock Options* (Chicago: University of Chicago Press, 2010), 1–37.

28. See Dong-One Kim, "Determinants of the Survival of Gainsharing Programs," *Industrial and Labor Relations Review* 53, no. 1 (1999): 21–42; Dong-One Kim, "Factors Influencing Organizational Performance in Gainsharing Programs," *Industrial Relations* 35, no. 2 (1996): 227–44; William N. Cooke, "Employee Participation Programs, Group-Based Incentives, and Company Performance: A Union-Non-Union Comparison," *Industrial and Labor Relations Review* 47, no. 3 (1994): 594–609; John E. McCarthy, Paula B. Voos, Adrienne E. Eaton, Douglas L. Kruse, and Joseph R. Blasi, "Solidarity and Sharing: Unions and Shared Capitalism," *Employee Ownership* (2011): 27.

29. John G. Belcher, *How to Design and Implement a Results-Oriented Variable Pay System* (New York: American Management Association, 1996).

30. Kathryn M. Bartol and Edwin A. Locke, "Incentives and Motivation," in *Compensation in Organizations: Current Research and Practice*, ed. Sara L. Rynes and Barry Gerhart (San Francisco: Jossey-Bass, 2000), 104–50; Bobby Medlin and Kenneth W. Green Jr., "Enhancing Performance Through Goal Setting, Engagement, and Optimism," *Industrial Management & Data Systems* 109, no. 7 (2009): 943–56.

31. John G. Belcher, *How to Design and Implement a Results-Oriented Variable Pay System* (New York: American Management Association, 1996); Sreenivasan Ramasamy, "Goal Setting—Individual, Group and Organizational Level," *International Journal of Global Management* 1, no. 1 (2010): 51.

32. Michael Beer and Mark D. Cannon, "Promise and Peril in Implementing Pay-for-Performance," *Human Resource Management* 43, no. 1 (2004): 3–48.

33. Richard J. Long, "The Incidence and Nature of Employee Profit Sharing and Share Ownership in Canada," *Relations industrielles/Industrial Relations* 47, no. 3 (1992): 463–88.

34. David E. Tyson, *Profit Sharing in Canada: The Complete Guide to Designing and Implementing Plans That Really Work* (Toronto: Wiley, 1996); Joseph Blasi, Douglas Kruse, and Richard B. Freeman, "Broad-Based Employee Stock Ownership and Profit Sharing: History, Evidence, and Policy Implications," *Journal of Participation and Employee Ownership* 1, no. 1 (2018): 38–60.

35. Richard J. Long and Tony Fang, "Do Employees Profit from Profit Sharing? Evidence from Canadian Panel Data," *Industrial and Labour Relations Review* 65, no. 4 (2012): 899–927.

36. Richard J. Long, "Motives for Profit Sharing: A Study of Canadian Chief Executive Officers," *Relations industrielles/Industrial Relations* 52, no. 4 (1997): 712–33.

37. See James Chelius and Robert S. Smith, "Profit Sharing and Employment Stability," *Industrial and Labor Relations Review* 43, no. 3 (1990): 256–74; see also Barry Gerhart and Charlie O. Trevor, "Employment Variability Under Different Managerial Compensation Systems," *Academy of Management Journal* 39, no. 6 (1996): 1692–712; Lutz Bellmann and Iris Möller. "Profit Sharing and Employment Stability," *Schmalenbach Business Review* 62, no. 1 (2010): 73–92.

38. See Michel Magnan and Sylvie St-Onge, "The Impact of Profit Sharing on the Performance of Financial Services Firms," *Journal of Management Studies* 42, no. 4 (2005): 761–91; C. Doucouliagos, "Worker Participation and Productivity in Labour-Managed and Participatory Capitalist Firms: A Meta-Analysis," *Industrial and Labor Relations Review* 49, no. 1 (1995): 58–77; Douglas L. Kruse, *Profit Sharing: Does It Make a Difference?* (Kalamazoo: W.E. Upjohn Institute, 1993); Maya K. Kroumova and Mila B. Lazarova, "Broad-Based Incentive Plans, HR Practices and Company Performance," *Human Resource Management Journal* 19, no. 4 (2009): 355–74.

39. Kym Hambly, Rinu Vimal Kumar, Mark Harcourt, Helen Lam, and Geoffrey Wood, "Profit-Sharing as an Incentive," *The International Journal of Human Resource Management* (2017): 1–21.

40. Richard J. Long, "Employee Profit Sharing: Consequences and Moderators," *Relations Industrielles/Industrial Relations* 55, no. 3 (2000): 477–504; see also Seongsu Kim, "Does Profit Sharing Increase Firms' Profits?" *Journal of Labor Research* 19, no. 2 (1998): 351–70; Richard J. Long and Tony Fang, "Do Employees Profit from Profit Sharing? Evidence from Canadian Panel Data," *ILR Review* 65, no. 4 (2012): 899–927.

41. See also Richard J. Long, "Performance Pay in Canada," in *Paying for Performance: An International Comparison*, ed. Michelle Brown and John S. Heywood (Armonk: M.E. Sharpe, 2002); Richard J. Long, "Motives for Profit Sharing: A Study of Canadian Chief Executive Officers," *Relations industrielles/Industrial Relations* 52, no. 4 (1997): 712–33; Terry H. Wagar and Richard J. Long, "Profit Sharing in Canada: Incidence and Predictors," *Proceedings of the Administrative Sciences Association of Canada (Human Resources Division)* 16, no. 9 (1995): 97–105.

42. Jennifer Harrison, Parbudyal Singh, and Shayna Frawley, "What does employee ownership effectiveness look like? The case of a Canadian-based firm," *Canadian Journal of Administrative Sciences* 35, no. 1 (2018): 5–19.

43. Tyson, *Profit Sharing in Canada*; Noélie Delahaie and Richard Duhautois, "Profit-Sharing and Wages: An Empirical Analysis Using French Data between 2000 and 2007," *British Journal of Industrial Relations* 57, no. 1 (2019): 107–42.

44. Richard J. Long and Tony Fang, "Is Compensation Actually Strategic? The Case of Employee Profit Sharing," *Proceedings of the Administrative Sciences Association of Canada (Human Resources Division)* 28, no. 9 (2007).

45. Long and Fang, "Do Employees Profit from Profit Sharing?"

46. Douglas L. Kruse, Richard B. Freeman, and Joseph R. Blasi, "Do Workers Gain by Sharing? Employee Outcomes Under Employee Ownership, Profit Sharing, and Broad-based Stock Options," in *Shared Capitalism at Work: Employee Ownership, Profit and Gain Sharing, and Broad-Based Stock Options*, ed. Kruse, Freeman, and Blasi (Chicago: University of Chicago Press, 2010), 257–91.

47. See Joseph Blasi and Douglas Kruse, "Economic Performance and Employee Ownership, Profit Sharing, and Stock Options: The NBER Study," *Journal of Employee Ownership Law and Finance* 20, no. 4 (2008): 31–40; Andrew M. Robinson and Nicholas Wilson, "Employee Financial Participation and Productivity: An Empirical Reappraisal," *British Journal of Industrial Relations* 44, no. 1 (2006): 31–50; C. Doucouliagos, "Worker Participation and Productivity."

48. Corey Rosen and Michael Quarrey, "How Well Is Employee Ownership Working?" *Harvard Business Review* 65 (1987): 126–30; Andrew Pendleton and Andrew Robinson, "Employee Stock Ownership, Involvement, and Productivity: An Interaction-Based Approach," *ILR Review* 64, no. 1 (2010): 3–29.

49. See Joseph Blasi and Douglas Kruse, "Economic Performance and Employee Ownership, Profit Sharing, and Stock Options: The NBER Study," *Journal of Employee Ownership Law and Finance* 20, no. 4 (2008): 31–40; Robinson and Wilson, "Employee Financial Participation and Productivity," *BJIR* 44, no. 1 (2006): 31–50; see also P.A. Kardas, K. Gale, R. Marens, P. Sommers, and G. Winther, "Employment and Sales Growth in Washington State Employee Ownership Companies: A Comparative Analysis," *Journal of Employee Ownership Law and Finance* 6, no. 2 (1994): 83–131.

50. P.A. Kardas, A.L. Scharf, and J. Keogh, "Wealth and Income Consequences of Employee Ownership: A Comparative Study from Washington State," *Journal of Employee Ownership Law and Finance* 10, no. 4 (1998): 3–52; Douglas L. Kruse, Richard B. Freeman, and Joseph R. Blasi, eds. *Shared Capitalism at Work: Employee Ownership, Profit and Gain Sharing, and Broad-Based Stock Options* (Chicago: University of Chicago Press, 2010).

51. Joseph Blasi, Douglas Kruse, James Sesil, and Maya Kroumova, "Broad-based Stock Options and Company Performance," *Journal of Employee Ownership Law and Finance* 12, no. 3 (2000): 69–102; James C. Sesil and Yu Peng Lin, "The Impact of Employee Stock Option Adoption and Incidence on Productivity: Evidence from U.S. Panel Data," *Industrial Relations: A Journal of Economy and Society* 50, no. 3 (2011): 514–34.

52. Edward E. Lawler, *The Ultimate Advantage: Creating the High Involvement Organization* (San Francisco: Jossey-Bass, 1992).

53. Charles Peck, *Long-Term Unit/Share Programs* (New York: Conference Board, 1995).

54. "Keep Your Pants On! Levi Offers Huge Employee Bonus," *StarPhoenix* [Saskatoon], June 13, 1996, C11.

55. Karl Schoenberger, "Levi Strauss Stitches Together Turnaround Plan," *The Globe and Mail*, July 4, 2000, B11.

# 6

# FORMULATING THE REWARD AND COMPENSATION STRATEGY

- Describe the constraints that limit the design of a compensation strategy.
- Explain the compensation strategy formulation process and describe each step.
- Discuss the considerations in deciding whether to adopt a lead, lag, or match compensation-level policy.
- Describe utility analysis and explain how it can be used.
- Apply the compensation strategy formulation process to specific organizations.
- Explain how to evaluate a compensation strategy prior to implementation.
- Discuss the special issues involved in compensating contingent workers, executives, and international employees.

Many people have probably watched on YouTube the hilarious safety demonstration by a WestJet flight attendant. How did WestJet create such a fun work culture? How did the culture contribute to business success?

WestJet was founded by Clive Beddoe and a group of entrepreneurs who understood customers' needs for low-cost, frequent-flight travel—Clive was a customer himself. The airline industry is a tough business because of deregulation, fluctuating fuel costs, and a challenging labour relations climate. From the very beginning WestJet created an "Owners Care" brand and used human resources practices to foster a unique culture that bolstered its competitive advantage. Their motto is: "We take care of our people. Our people take care of our guests. Our guests take care of our business." Their four-pillar business strategy consists of people and culture, guest experience and performance, revenue and growth, and cost and margins.

People and culture were front and centre in WestJet's business strategy. The company's compensation program was built on offering a competitive compensation package oriented toward developing a culture of ownership. Employees—whether full-time, part-time, or casual—became owners through a generous share purchase plan; they also shared company profits. The Employee Share Purchase Plan (ESPP) let employees purchase company shares starting from $25 per pay up to 20 percent of their salary. The company matched the employees' contribution dollar-for-dollar. WestJet also shared 10–20 percent of its profit with the employees, which was paid out twice a year with big celebrations.

WestJet's other people practices, such as recruiting, training and development, and talent management, all reflected and reinforced the "Owners Care" culture. One particular practice is worth mentioning. The employees were given a voice in company decisions through the internal association called PACT (Pro-Active Communication Team). The board of directors included an employee representative.

The focus on people and culture brought WestJet strong results in guest experience and performance, revenue and growth, and cost and margins. In 2015, WestJet flew more than 20 million guests and serviced more than 100 destinations. Waterstone Human Capital named WestJet one of Canada's 10 most-admired corporate cultures for a record sixth time in 2015. In 2018, WestJet launched Swoop, a low-cost carrier, along with premium seats.

In this high-involvement firm, employees participated in many aspects of the business, including compensation decisions. Employees were committed to company goals; they understood the company's context and the kind of behaviour that was required.

However, in the past few years, WestJet has faced significant challenges. WestJet's net earnings decreased significantly from $137 million net in 2010 to $91 million in 2018. Furthermore, WestJet pilots unionized in 2017, and flight attendants unionized in 2018. In 2018, 91 percent of WestJet's pilots voted in agreement to strike. Unionization may indicate that the caring and cohesive culture is dissipating. What is going on with WestJet? Compensation may be a part of the answer.

Changes in the compensation plan can inadvertently be damaging to the company's culture. WestJet plans to pay commission to flight attendants on Swoop airlines for in-flight purchased food and drinks. This issue can be explained with attribution theory. Attribution theory posits that if rewards are viewed as directly manipulating behaviour, extrinsic rewards may cripple intrinsic motivation. Flight attendants once enjoyed the banter with customers, but contingent monetary rewards could make the banter less enjoyable.

WestJet's volatile economic conditions could also be affecting the culture. During financial crises, high-involvement management strategies are impaired by cost-cutting measures, which reduces job satisfaction and employee well-being. Reduced job satisfaction and employee well-being decrease positive performance effects. Organizational performance pay during dire economic times also produces the same impact on employees.

The culture is likely to drastically change over the next few years. WestJet has been acquired by Onex Corp., a private equity investor. In a conference call leading up to the purchase to address employee concerns, the

*(continued)*

share-purchase plan featured prominently. If the company is to be moved to private, there are no shares to invest. Thus far, WestJet has no pension plan. Onex explained the employees could cash their shares or reinvest in the airline when it becomes a private entity. Employees will no longer be "owners."

Sources: Parbudyal Singh, *Case—WestJet Airlines: Clear Skies or Turbulence Ahead?* (2012); WestJet 2015 Annual Report; WestJet 2016 Management Information Circular; Marty Parker, "Employee Compensation Is an Integral Part of Corporate Culture," *Financial Post*, March 19, 2012; Ben Nelms, "WestJet Seeks to Allay Employee Concerns Over Share Purchase Plan, Job Security Following Onex Takeover," *The Globe and Mail*, May 14, 2019; "2019 First Quarter Report," *WestJet*, May 6, 2019; Kaylen Small, "WestJet Flight Attendants Set to Unionize," *Global News*, July 9, 2018; Ross Marowits, "WestJet Pilots Vow Not to Disrupt Long Weekend as a Goodwill Gesture," *CTV News*, May 10, 2018; Saul Estrin, Paul Geroski, and Geoff Stewart, "Employee Share Ownership, Profit-Sharing and Participation," *International Journal of Industrial Organization* 6, no. 1: 1–6; Kyle Bakx, "WestJet and Air Canada: How Little Separates the Airlines Anymore," *CBC*, May 12, 2018; Stephen Wood and Chidiebere Ogbonnaya, "High-Involvement Management, Economic Recession, Well-Being, and Organizational Performance," *Journal of Management* 44, no. 8: 3070–95.

# INTRODUCTION TO COMPENSATION STRATEGY

There are many approaches to compensation strategy development. WestJet's route involves employee participation. An equally viable alternative is for the CEO, with a small team, to analyze the firm's financial situation and other aspects of its context and decide what the compensation strategy will be for the coming year or years. Whoever develops the compensation strategy must understand the organization, its employees, its context and constraints, and the compensation options available.

Recall from Chapter 1 that the *reward strategy* is the plan for the mix of rewards that the organization intends to provide its members—and for how those rewards will be provided—in order to elicit the behaviours necessary for success. The *compensation strategy* is one part of the reward strategy and has two main aspects: the *mix* of base pay, performance pay, and indirect pay to be used, and the *total amount or level* of compensation to be provided to employees. Thus, the two key questions for compensation strategy are "*How* is compensation to be paid?" and "How *much* compensation is to be paid?"

Answering these questions effectively is not a simple matter, and the purpose of this chapter is to provide an approach to doing so—a compensation strategy formulation process. However, to apply this process effectively, you need a foundation of four basic understandings: (1) an understanding of your organization and its context, (2) an understanding of your workforce, (3) an understanding of your compensation options, and (4) an understanding of your compensation constraints. Chapters 1 through 5 focused on the first three understandings, and the fourth—compensation constraints—will be discussed next. We will then introduce the compensation strategy formulation process and discuss the special issues involved in developing compensation for three unique groups—contingent employees, executives, and international employees. The chapter concludes with an extended example to show how to apply the compensation strategy formulation process to a specific organization.

## CONSTRAINTS ON COMPENSATION STRATEGY

The owners of the Screaming Tale Restaurants (Compensation Today 6.1) claimed the restaurants had no employees, just "volunteer workers" or "commission agents" working only for the tips that customers provided, thus relieving the firm of the need to pay even

### IS THIS LEGAL?

A while back, management at the Screaming Tale Restaurants in Port Hope and Belleville, Ontario, cooked up a great recipe for cutting labour costs: Don't pay your staff! They eliminated payroll for serving staff by using "volunteer" staff who worked solely for the tips they received. Aside from the obvious advantage—it saved the wages that would otherwise have been paid to servers—this arrangement eliminated the mandatory benefits and payroll taxes that would have to be paid to the government (which can add nearly 20 percent to compensation costs), as well as the administrative work of calculating pay and preparing paycheques. Quite a competitive advantage!

However, after two "volunteers" complained, the Ontario Ministry of Labour launched an investigation to determine whether this arrangement violated provincial employment standards legislation which requires that a minimum wage be paid to all persons considered to be employees. Under the law, money received as tips does not count toward this minimum wage.

One of the restaurant chain's owners, Aldo Mauro, said that the restaurants had come under attack because they had learned to operate more efficiently by reducing labour costs. In an interview with *The Globe and Mail*, Mauro said that his company specialized in rescuing distressed restaurants and turning them into profitable ones and that it had used "volunteer" workers in the past throughout southeastern Ontario.

Brent Bowser, a manager of the chain's restaurant in Port Hope, said that the restaurant provided a location where workers could act as service agents and do their business. The complaints, Bowser said, had come from employees who didn't hustle.

Was this practice legal? Take a "guess" before reading the text below.

Source: "'Volunteer' Staff: One Way to Cut Costs," Human Resources Management in Canada, *Report Bulletin* 161 (1996): 3.

minimum wages or any mandatory benefits. It turned out, however, that this arrangement was illegal, and the restaurants closed just as they were being investigated for violations of the Ontario Employment Standards Act. This case illustrates that employers cannot do whatever they want in regard to compensation, even if they can find employees willing to accept the compensation arrangements. There are a number of constraints that establish the boundaries within which the compensation system must be designed. There are four types of constraints: (1) legislated (as in the Screaming Tale case), (2) labour market, (3) product/service market, and (4) financial. Before formulating your compensation strategy, it is essential that you have an understanding of these constraints.

## LEGISLATED CONSTRAINTS

In Canada, jurisdiction over labour markets is split between the federal government and the provincial/territorial governments. The federal government has the power to pass labour legislation covering all federal employees (including those in federal Crown corporations) as well as workers in a number of specified industries, including transportation, communications, defence, uranium mining, and firms engaged in interprovincial or international trade. In addition to employees of the federal government and its agencies, federal labour law covers about 10 percent of private sector employees. All other employees are covered under provincial and territorial legislation.

Four types of legislation affect compensation systems. First, every province has an employment standards act, which sets minimum standards for wages; hours of work; termination benefits; and vacation, statutory holiday, and leave entitlements; and the minimum age for employment. (The equivalent federal legislation is known as the Canada Labour Code.)

Second, all jurisdictions have human rights acts, which prohibit employment discrimination based on factors such as gender, ethnicity, and age. Some jurisdictions also have specific pay equity legislation, which is aimed at redressing past pay inequities experienced by female employees.

Third, all jurisdictions have legislation relating to unions and collective bargaining. This legislation affects compensation in unionized firms by requiring that all compensation arrangements be approved by the union. It also has an indirect impact on compensation, in that some non-union firms match the settlements negotiated by unionized competitors to reduce the incentive for unionization. Finally, all jurisdictions have income and corporate tax laws, which can have a strong influence on the type of compensation offered.

While we will focus on legislation, it is important to note that pay decisions may also be influenced by common-law constraints through the courts and/or quasi-judicial bodies such as labour relations boards and pay equity tribunals. While the various legislatures across Canada craft labour and employment law, it is sometimes up to the courts and other bodies vested with similar powers to interpret these laws when there are challenges. The decisions coming out of these institutions are binding on the parties and establish precedence for similar cases. Over time, a large body of common law related to compensation (and other fields) has developed. We will not deal with the common law in detail in this text; however, you will see examples of court decisions in this chapter (see, for example, Compensation Today 6.1, Compensation Today 6.2, and Compensation Today 6.3) and pay equity in Chapter 7. If this material sparks an interest for you, then a program or course in labour and employment law—or even a law degree—may be a career path!

## Employment Standards Legislation

**employment standards legislation**
Legislation that sets minimum standards for pay and other conditions of employment.

**Employment standards legislation** stipulates the minimum standards for pay and other conditions of employment by which every employer must abide. These standards relate to paid time off, maximum hours of work before overtime pay provisions take effect, minimum levels of overtime pay, and the minimum wage. Currently, the provincial minimum hourly rates range from $11.15 in Newfoundland and Labrador to $15 in Alberta. In the territories, the minimum hourly wage ranges from $12.71 in Yukon to $13 in Nunavut.[1]

Although minimum wage legislation applies to most workers, there are some exceptions. Some jurisdictions exclude domestic servants, in-home caregivers, some types of farm labourers, and students in training programs. Also, in some jurisdictions, minimum wage rates are lower for certain classes of workers (e.g., Ontario students under 18 years who work fewer than 28 hours a week) and higher for others (e.g., Ontario employees who work from their homes). Employers do not have to pay minimum wages (or other mandatory benefits) to persons who are classified as contractors or agents because they are exempted from employment standards legislation.

What is the legal difference between an employee and a contractor? According to the Canada Revenue Agency (for whom the employee/

Many fast-food workers earn minimum wages.

contractor difference is important for tax purposes), a contractor need not work at the payer's premises; can accept or refuse work from the payer; can choose the time and manner in which the work will be completed; the working relationship does not appear to have a component of continuity, integration, loyalty, nor subordination; and the worker has the ability to hire another person to complete the work. By contrast, a person is deemed an employee if the payer directs how and where the work is performed, controls the worker's absences, establishes the work schedule and the worker's rules of conduct, can impose disciplinary actions on the worker, the work environment between the worker and payer is that of subordination, or the worker requires permission to work for other employers while working for this payer.[2]

By this standard, the "volunteer workers" at the Screaming Tale Restaurant clearly should have been classified as employees rather than as self-employed "commission agents." Moreover, although restaurant employees must declare gratuities for income tax purposes, gratuities do not count toward employee earnings to help satisfy minimum wage requirements. Thus, employers must always pay employees the minimum wage, regardless of any gratuities that employees may receive.

So where does this leave employees who are paid only commissions or piece rates? For example, what happens if sales personnel who are compensated only by commission—such as automobile salespeople—achieve very few or no sales in a given period? The procedure for checking whether the minimum wage is being paid is to take the total amount earned by an employee during a workweek, then divide that by the number of hours worked. If that amount comes out to less than the minimum wage, the employer is required to pay the difference to the employee.

Another important issue covered by employment standards laws is overtime pay. Rather than hiring new employees, many firms use overtime when additional production is needed. This avoids the cost of hiring new employees, as well as the problem of layoffs if the amount of available work declines. However, employees cannot be forced to work overtime, nor can any employee who is covered by the Employment Standards Act voluntarily waive the right to overtime pay.

Employment standards laws normally require higher rates of pay (usually 1.5 times normal earnings) for hours worked in excess of stipulated limits—generally eight hours per day and 40–48 hours per week, depending on the jurisdiction. However, many workers are exempted from this part of employment standards laws, including professionals, teachers, supervisors, managers, residential care workers, students, certain agricultural workers, and commission sales workers when they work away from the employer's place of business. (But note that other commission sales workers as well as piece rate workers are covered.) Employees covered under employment standards laws are not allowed to waive their rights under the legislation (with one exception—unionized employees in British Columbia).[3]

Although many employers believe that salaried workers are exempt from overtime, this is not necessarily the case. Moreover, simply calling an employee a manager or a professional does not necessarily end the obligation to pay overtime. The key criterion is the nature of the work performed and the amount of independent control the worker has over it. For example, employees who are deemed "accountants" do not have to be paid overtime; but a 2008 class action suit against KPMG found that accounting technicians *do* have to be paid overtime, and KPMG agreed to pay a $10 million settlement. For many other employers—such as the Canadian Imperial Bank of Commerce (see Compensation Today 6.2)—overtime has been a controversial issue, to be decided by long and drawn-out court battles.

### THINK YOUR EMPLOYER OWES YOU OVERTIME BUT WON'T PAY? SUE THE BOSS!

After 10 years of employment as a teller at the Canadian Imperial Bank of Commerce (CIBC), Dara Fresco calculated that her employer owed her about $50 000 for overtime that she was discouraged from recording. So, in June 2007, she did something that few employees would dare—she launched a class action suit from her vantage point as head teller at a Toronto branch of the CIBC—a position she continues to hold as the lawsuit wends its way through the courts.

Fresco contends that she and many other employees at the CIBC are assigned heavy workloads that cannot be completed during standard business hours and must work several extra hours every week to keep up. However, she alleges that her managers at the branch discourage her from reporting these hours as overtime.

The CIBC's response to this allegation is that discouraging the reporting of overtime is not a policy of the CIBC, and that all employees are properly paid for any overtime hours they work. The bank has committed itself to fighting this suit—in which the plaintiffs are claiming $500 million—for as long as it takes, which may be a long time indeed. For example, it wasn't until June 2012 that the Ontario Court of Appeal ruled that the lawsuit could go forward as a class action. This decision did not reflect any judgment on the merits of the case; it just meant that the suit could proceed to the next stage, which is putting the arguments of the plaintiffs and defendant before the courts.

As of the time of writing the text, this case had not concluded. However, an Ontario judge claimed that he will issue a ruling for this case likely in 2020. The judge also claimed that if he discovers that the bank's practices and policies violated the Canada Labour Code, the court would determine a way in which to pay out individual or aggregate compensation.

Another class action lawsuit by Scotiabank employee Cindy Fulawka was settled in 2016 for $40 million, where current and former employees who were similarly affected can submit claims for any unpaid overtime that was required or permitted by Scotiabank, regardless of whether it was pre-approved at the time by their manager. And the claims period goes back to 2000.

Sources: Laura Fric and Adam Hirsh, "Settlement Approved in Overtime Class Action," *Class Action Settlement*, August 12, 2014; Roy O'Connor LLP website, http://royoconnor.ca/cases/unpaid-overtime-class-action-cibc-canadian-imperial-bank-commerce, accessed September 26, 2016; Michael Lewis, "Ruling Expected in New Year In Largest-Ever Unpaid Overtime Lawsuit," *The Star*, December 12, 2019.

There are many other employment standards that affect pay, such as the requirement to pay a certain minimum amount of "call-out" pay whenever an employee is called out to work (although this does not apply to all employee groups). Also included in employment standards or equivalent laws are employee layoff and severance provisions (discussed in more detail in Chapter 12).

### Human Rights Legislation

**human rights legislation**
Legislation that prohibits discrimination in hiring or employment on the basis of race, ethnic origin, religion, gender, marital status, age, or sexual orientation.

Even when employers comply with employment standards laws, they are still not free to pay employees whatever they want. Every Canadian jurisdiction has **human rights legislation** that prohibits discrimination in hiring and employment on the basis of race, ethnic origin, religion, gender, marital status, or age (within specified age ranges—normally 18–65). Some jurisdictions have placed sexual orientation in this list as well.

To prove compliance with human rights laws, employers must be able to demonstrate that differences in pay among employees are related solely to factors such as job duties, experience, qualifications, seniority, or performance. For example, if a member of one ethnic group is paid significantly less than a member of another ethnic group with similar job duties, the employer must be able to prove that this difference is due to one or more of the factors just noted.

All Canadian jurisdictions have some form of equal pay legislation aimed at addressing wage inequality between male and female employees. These laws prohibit employers from paying male and female employees differently if they do "identical, similar, or substantially similar work." The original federal legislation—the Canadian Human Rights Act—was enacted in 1976 and went one step further, stipulating that male and female employees must receive equal pay for work of *equal value*, even if the work is not substantially similar.

More recently, the Canadian Human Rights Act has been superseded in the area of pay equity by the Public Service Equitable Compensation Act, which is an act that was passed to ensure equal pay for work of fair value in the federal public sector. The act holds employers responsible for ensuring that pay is equitable, either by equitable compensation plans for those who are not unionized, or, for those who are unionized, a fair collective bargaining compensation process. For those who are unionized, employers and bargaining agents are jointly responsible for ensuring fair pay through established wage-setting practices during the wage setting process, rather than through a separate pay equity process or through complaint-based litigation that occurs as an adjustment after the fact (a process that sometimes takes years or even decades).[4] Reactions to this new law have been mixed, however, with many legal scholars arguing that it will not effectively promote pay equity in the federal public sector.[5]

Many provinces and territories have enacted pay equity laws whose specific intent is to redress gender pay inequities, although in some of these jurisdictions (Manitoba, New Brunswick, Nova Scotia, and Prince Edward Island), the law applies only to governmental bodies and agencies. Quebec and Ontario have enacted pay equity legislation that applies to all employers (in Quebec) or all employers with at least 10 employees (in Ontario). Pay equity schemes require the employer to divide the workforce into job classes designated either as male or female. (A job class is designated male or female if at least 60 or 70 percent [varying by jurisdiction] of the occupants of that job class are male or female.) After that, a gender-neutral job evaluation system is applied to each job class.

If a female-dominated job class that is evaluated as equal to a male-dominated job class is less well compensated than the male class, the imbalance must be redressed. Although it is theoretically possible to redress this imbalance by reducing wages in the male-dominated class, this practice is prohibited. As Compensation Today 6.3 indicates, employers face heavy restrictions regarding how they are permitted to deal with the imbalance once it has been formally identified. (How to comply with pay equity laws will be covered in more depth in Chapter 7.)

## COMPENSATION TODAY 6.3

### DON'T CROSS THESE WORKERS!

In 1994, the Nova Scotia Pay Equity Commission awarded a substantial wage increase, to be phased in over a four-year period, to female crossing guards employed by the City of Dartmouth. The commission concluded that these workers were being paid significantly less than male employees of the City who were doing work of equal value.

In response, the City of Dartmouth decided to lay off all the crossing guards and contract the work to a private company that paid lower rates and was not covered by the Pay Equity Commission ruling. However, the Nova Scotia Court of Appeal disallowed this course of action on the grounds that once the award was issued, the City was prohibited from entering into contracts for reasons intended to "defeat the purpose of the Pay Equity Act."

## Trade Union Legislation

**trade union legislation**
Legislation that defines the rights of parties involved in a collective bargaining relationship.

When a group of employees is represented by a union, according to **trade union legislation**, any changes to pay, hours of work, and working conditions must be negotiated with the union. Employers cannot change these things unless the union agrees. Also, employers cannot make separate compensation arrangements with individual members of the bargaining unit. A unionized firm that wants to change its compensation system must first convince the union to accept these changes. This can be a long process and, in many cases, it rules out certain types of pay practices—such as individual performance pay and profit sharing—that unions have traditionally opposed. Such opposition stems, in part, from unions not wanting employers to have absolute power over pay decisions for employees, as performance is usually decided upon by management.

Unions once had a strong impact on the structure and level of employee and even executive compensation.[6] Unionized employees still tend to receive more extensive employee benefits than non-union employees and also in the past enjoyed a wage premium, with wages averaging about 10 percent higher than those of comparable non-union employees, although this varies greatly across industries.[7] However, the union wage premium appears to have been declining in recent years[8] and may have disappeared entirely in some industries.

Unionized employees have been more likely to work under a seniority-based system rather than a performance-based pay system because unions believe that seniority-based systems are fairer to members and are easier to monitor than performance-based ones. However, this too appears to be changing; research shows that unionized firms do not differ significantly from other firms in the proportions of base pay, individual performance pay, group performance pay, and organizational performance pay, although unionized firms continue to provide a significantly higher proportion of indirect pay than do non-union employers.[9] Unions also continue to allow employees, through the unions, to have a say in the employment relationship.

## Tax Legislation

The final way that legislation can influence the pay system is through income and corporate tax laws, which encourage certain pay approaches and discourage others. For example, tax laws have played a significant role in the movement away from direct pay (which is fully taxed) and toward indirect pay (which often is not). However, this role may have diminished in recent years, now that employee benefits are increasingly becoming subject to income tax. At the same time, changes to tax laws enacted in 2000 are encouraging the use of stock options (see Chapter 11).

As a final note, changing a worker's status from "employee" to "independent contractor" ("self-employed" is the term used in the Income Tax Act) can have significant income tax benefits for workers. An employee can apply very few tax deductions against income; an independent contractor enjoys many more potential deductions. For example, if an employee uses a portion of his or her home for an office, there is no tax deduction, but an independent contractor who does the same can deduct all costs related to that space. Employees cannot deduct the cost of transportation to and from work, but independent contractors can do so for any work-related travel. Thus, independent contractor status may be attractive to some employees.

# LABOUR MARKET CONSTRAINTS

Another key constraint on compensation decisions is the labour market. The **labour market** is the available pool of labour from which employers choose their employees. Labour markets are normally segmented by occupational type and geographical area. In a given geographical area, both supply of and demand for a particular type of labour may be high or low. Each combination of supply-demand factors creates a unique situation for employers. For example, when demand is high but supply is low, the labour market is considered *tight*, which means it is difficult to attract qualified employees without raising compensation levels. Conversely, when demand is low and supply is high, the labour market is considered *loose*, which makes it much easier to attract employees at compensation levels favourable to the employer.

Labour markets vary by region; thus, firms that operate on a national level must decide whether to adjust compensation based on the local labour market or to keep standard compensation levels across the country. For example, a bank may determine the pay for customer service representatives based on the market rate for these employees in Toronto, where the firm's head office is located. But in many local labour markets, such as a small town in Nova Scotia, attracting the necessary employees may be possible for much less than is being offered to Toronto employees. Should the bank therefore pay lower rates to its Nova Scotia employees than to its Ontario employees? Is this fair? Is it worth the trouble? Questions like these need to be resolved when setting compensation levels.

As discussed in Chapter 4, identifying market pay is more complex than it sounds. The specifics of a given labour market pose a real constraint for firms because a compensation system that is too far below market will not attract the necessary employees, and one that is too far above market will unduly increase costs. Paying above market is especially a problem when product/service markets are highly competitive. (We will discuss issues involved in evaluating the labour market in Chapter 9.)

**labour market**
Constraints on compensation strategy flowing from the relative levels of demand and supply for particular occupational groups.

# PRODUCT/SERVICE MARKET CONSTRAINTS

Another key constraint is the market for an organization's products or services. When demand is low and/or supply is high, the result is a highly competitive business environment, and firms that pay more for their labour than competitors may be at a serious disadvantage unless they are more productive.

**Product/service market constraints** are especially severe in industries that are highly labour-intensive because labour costs constitute a higher proportion of total costs in these firms. These constraints are even more severe if competitors are able to move their production to labour markets where the cost of labour is much lower, or where legislated constraints (such as minimum wage laws and mandatory benefits) are less onerous. In contrast, firms in markets where demand for their product is high, supply is low, and competitors are few have much more latitude when designing their compensation systems.

Another product/service factor that affects compensation is volatility. Firms that experience severe swings in demand for their products/services need to be able to adjust. Some firms use a high proportion of contingent workers, who are subject to different compensation constraints than core employees; other firms include more variable pay in their compensation systems.

**product/service market constraints**
Constraints on compensation strategy caused by the nature of the product or service market in which the firm operates.

## FINANCIAL CONSTRAINTS OF THE ORGANIZATION

Many organizations face financial constraints that affect the compensation system they use. In the private sector, the financial performance of the organization is a constraint: unprofitable firms are much more limited in their compensation options than profitable ones. The company's stage of growth (for example, new or fast-growing firms are often short of cash) is another constraint.

For public sector organizations, financial constraints are usually the result of the funding limitations placed on them by those providing the funds. Many public sector organizations, such as hospitals, post-secondary institutions, and the Canadian military, face funding restrictions that severely limit the compensation they can offer.

Rather than accepting these financial constraints, organizations try to change them. Private sector firms may relocate to areas where labour is more plentiful or where employment standards are less costly. Some firms may resort to tactics of debatable ethicality by, for example, classifying employees as independent contractors to escape having to pay mandatory benefits. Finally, some firms attempt to escape union constraints by weakening the union or by contracting work to non-union enterprises. Public institutions may seek additional sources of funding.

## FORMULATING THE COMPENSATION STRATEGY

Now that you understand your organization, people, compensation choices, and compensation constraints, you are finally in a position to formulate your compensation strategy. This section discusses the process of formulating compensation strategy by taking you through the five steps depicted in **Figure 6.1**.

**FIGURE 6.1**

The Compensation Strategy Formulation Process

Define the Required Behaviour

Define the Role of Compensation

Determine the Compensation Mix

Determine the Compensation Level

Evaluate the Proposed Strategy

First, we need to define the employee behaviours necessary for organizational success and identify the characteristics and qualifications of the people who will be able to perform those behaviours. Second, within the system the firm develops, we need to define the specific roles to be played by the reward system and compensation system. Third, we need to determine the most appropriate mix of the three compensation components. Fourth, we need to develop policies for establishing the total amount of compensation that employees will receive. Fifth, we need to conduct a pre-implementation evaluation of the proposed strategy to verify that it meets our criteria for success.

## DEFINE THE REQUIRED BEHAVIOUR

The first step is to define the behaviour your organization needs. Recall from Chapter 3 that organizations need three main types of behaviour: *membership behaviour*, *task behaviour*, and *citizenship behaviour*. The importance of these behaviours varies across different organizations.

- *Membership behaviour:* What are the costs of turnover? Is affective commitment necessary, or is continuance commitment sufficient?
- *Task behaviour:* Are tasks simple or complex? Do employees work under supervision? Are high performance levels required?
- *Citizenship behaviour:* How important is cooperation for each company unit and the individuals in it? To what extent can extra employee initiative or ideas make a difference to organizational performance?

For some firms, high levels of membership, task, or citizenship behaviour may be nice but not worth the cost; for others, high levels of one or more of these are essential. To understand the relative importance of the three types of behaviour, you need to understand the organization's context, the most important aspect of which is the managerial strategy. As discussed in Chapter 2, classical organizations need only minimal membership behaviour, only adequate task behaviour, and no citizenship behaviour; human relations organizations need high membership behaviour, adequate task behaviour, and some citizenship behaviour; and high-involvement organizations require high levels of all three.

While every organization needs its employees to perform task behaviours, the nature of these behaviours can vary enormously. Obviously, gutting a chicken is different from designing a computer program, piloting an airplane, writing a newspaper editorial, or performing surgery. Tasks vary in terms of complexity, skill, performance level, material (i.e., things or people), and consequences of errors. Packing a chicken wing in a box of chicken legs is an error, as is removing a patient's healthy kidney instead of the diseased kidney (as actually happened at an American hospital in 2008), but the consequences of these two errors differ dramatically.

In addition, the task behaviours required have implications for the organizational and reward systems needed to produce those behaviours. **Compensation Notebook 6.1** lists 16 dimensions of task behaviour. In general, the first choice in each of these dimensions (e.g., tasks that are simple, procedural, low-skilled, narrow, and have low interdependence and individual output) is suited for a reward system consistent with the classical school of thought, whereas tasks characterized by the second choice in each dimension (e.g., tasks that are complex, creative, highly skilled, broad, and have high interdependence and team-based output) are suited to reward systems associated with the high-involvement management strategy.

Employers often do not understand their real behavioural needs and have established recruiting systems that work at cross-purposes to those needs. For example, many university graduates have been told by recruiters that the firm is seeking creative, innovative, free-thinking employees, only to discover that what the organization really wants are people who will do what they are told in a reliable manner. These recruiters might believe that statements about creativity and innovation are an effective way to attract high-quality recruits. If that is the case, they are failing to consider the costs of disillusioned employees who might quit when they discover the discrepancy between their expectations and those of their bosses. (Or worse, those bosses might be stuck with disgruntled employees who do not quit.)

Once the required behaviours have been defined, you need to identify the education, skills, and other characteristics these employees will need if they are to perform those behaviours. Those are the people the organization must attract, retain, and motivate, so it is important to understand their needs. Without that understanding, the organization may end up providing rewards these people do not value highly, a result that is both ineffective and costly.

In the past, firms have relied on promises of rapid advancement in order to attract and retain employees. But with many firms becoming flatter and experiencing slower growth, they have needed to develop other types of rewards (including compensation) to make up for the loss of advancement opportunities. As discussed in earlier chapters, some firms have turned to pay-for-knowledge systems, while others have developed **technical ladders**—that is, defined progressions of skills development and workplace movement intended to keep work interesting (and provide higher compensation) by allowing the employee to master new jobs and work activities.

**technical ladder**
Defined progression of skills development to keep work interesting and provide opportunities for higher compensation.

## DEFINE THE ROLE OF COMPENSATION

All organizations must have some system for generating the behaviour they require. As discussed in Chapter 2, there are three organizational systems (managerial strategies) that can be used to generate the required behaviour, and the reward system plays a different role within each. *Classical organizations* tend to focus on economic needs as the main motivator of behaviour; *human relations organizations*, on social needs; and *high-involvement organizations*, on employee needs for participation, growth, and development.

In defining the role that compensation will serve in our reward strategy, we need to consider to what extent intrinsic versus extrinsic rewards can be used to motivate behaviour. What intrinsic rewards does the organization offer? These may be extensive or nonexistent. (Of course, where intrinsic rewards are nonexistent, it may be possible to create them through employee participation in decision making or work redesign, as was discussed in Chapter 3.) Where intrinsic rewards are not as available, the compensation system needs to be relied on more heavily to motivate behaviour.

Tradeoffs are possible between compensation and other rewards. For example, some firms want to hire employees who are equipped with the skills and experience to perform the needed behaviours immediately upon joining the firm. Other firms are willing to hire employees who possess the ability to develop the necessary skills and then train them to perform the needed behaviours. Potential employees may see this training as an intrinsic reward (an opportunity for learning and growth) or as an extrinsic one (because it will likely lead to a better-paying position) or as both. Training programs make it possible to attract employees for less compensation than would otherwise be necessary. In contrast, hiring fully skilled and experienced employees requires much higher compensation, although this may be offset by lower training costs and more immediate productivity.

**Table 6.1** provides six examples of how the role of compensation can vary across organizational settings.

## Role of Compensation for the UNICEF Store

The first example in Table 6.1, a gift shop operated by UNICEF to generate funds to help children around the globe provides no role for compensation. Membership and task behaviour are motivated by intrinsic rewards, including the knowledge that volunteers are helping save young lives; in addition, there is a high degree of congruence between organizational goals and personal goals, which also stimulates organizational citizenship behaviour. This type of organization suits the high-involvement managerial strategy.

The task behaviour (serving customers, ringing up sales) does not necessarily contain many intrinsic rewards (although volunteers are given considerable autonomy in how they perform their roles), so the direct motivation from the task itself is moderate. But this task behaviour is motivated by the knowledge that performing these mundane tasks is helping save the lives of children globally. Membership behaviour may also be motivated by the extrinsic social rewards (from mingling with like-minded volunteers, for example) that result from membership in this organization. Of course, the success of this reward strategy depends on the availability of people who have time to contribute, whose goals and needs match those of the organization, and whose economic needs have already been met by other means. In fact, this group has been shrinking as busy dual-income families have become the norm.

## Role of Compensation for the Chicken-Processing Plant

This example is similar to the one described in Compensation Today 2.4. At this organization, there are no intrinsic or extrinsic rewards for production-line workers other than compensation, so the only way to motivate membership behaviour is through pay. However, because the costs of turnover are so low, there is no need to offer compensation beyond the minimum level necessary to attract a sufficient stream of applicants who are able to

TABLE 6.1

Role of Compensation and Intrinsic/Extrinsic Rewards in Producing Behaviour for Different Organizations

| Required Behaviour | Role of Intrinsic Rewards | Role of Extrinsic Rewards Other than Compensation | Role of Compensation |
|---|---|---|---|
| **UNICEF STORE (CASHIERS/CLERKS)** | | | |
| Membership behaviour | High role | Moderate role | No role |
| Task behaviour | Moderate role | No role | No role |
| Citizenship behaviour | High role | No role | No role |
| **CHICKEN-PROCESSING PLANT (PRODUCTION-LINE WORKERS)** | | | |
| Membership behaviour | No role | No role | High role |
| Task behaviour | No role | No role | No role |
| Citizenship behaviour | No role | No role | No role |
| **TREE-PLANTING FIRM (TREE PLANTERS)** | | | |
| Membership behaviour | Low to moderate role | Low to moderate role | High role |
| Task behaviour | Low to moderate role | No role | High role |
| Citizenship behaviour | No role | No role | No role |
| **VACATION RESORT (SERVICE WORKERS)** | | | |
| Membership behaviour | Moderate role | High role | Moderate role |
| Task behaviour | Low role | No role | Moderate role |
| Citizenship behaviour | No role | No role | No role |
| **HOSPITAL (NURSING STAFF)** | | | |
| Membership behaviour | High role | Moderate role | Moderate role |
| Task behaviour | Moderate role | No role | No role |
| Citizenship behaviour | High role | No role | No role |
| **HIGH-TECH ELECTRONICS FIRM (DESIGN ENGINEERS)** | | | |
| Membership behaviour | Moderate role | Moderate role | Moderate role |
| Task behaviour | High role | Moderate role | Low role |
| Citizenship behaviour | Moderate role | Moderate role | High role |

perform the necessary task behaviours. The compensation system is not used to stimulate task behaviour; that is done directly by the technology and the supervisor. Compensation-based behaviour control (such as piece rates) is not really viable due to the interdependent nature of the work. This classical firm is not concerned about citizenship behaviour, so it does not waste money promoting it.

## Role of Compensation for the Tree-Planting Firm

The tree-planting firm has contracts with major forestry firms to undertake reforestation work. While there may be some intrinsic motivation for individual tree planters who see reforestation work as socially valuable and enjoy the autonomy and task identity, this alone would never motivate the necessary membership and task behaviour. Because tree planters work and live together in camps in remote areas, some may perceive some extrinsic social rewards. On the other hand, because of the remote locations, many tree planters experience negative social rewards due to isolation from friends and family.

Clearly, the key motivator is money. Pay can be used both to foster the necessary membership behaviour and to direct task behaviour. This can be accomplished through piece rates, where tree planters are paid according to number of trees planted. Their output is identifiable, and the tasks are not interdependent. This approach fits with a classical managerial strategy.

## Role of Compensation for the Vacation Resort

The fourth example is a vacation resort that employs seasonal service workers. The work itself does not provide many intrinsic rewards, although there may be some satisfaction in helping guests enjoy their stay. But there are high extrinsic rewards, because the resort locale has many attractions and the resort allows free use of its recreational facilities for off-duty employees. The resort also encourages friendly social relations among staff. The role of pay in attracting employees is moderate. Pay also plays a moderate role in motivating task behaviour, through the tips that workers receive from guests and the small bonuses that the firm provides to employees who receive outstanding service ratings from guests. The firm does not expect or require much citizenship behaviour from employees. This firm practises a human relations strategy.

Tips supplement the pay for some employees.

## Role of Compensation for the Hospital

Nursing staff receive many intrinsic rewards from the role they play in their organization, because of the work they do and the congruence between their goals and those of the organization. However, there are few extrinsic rewards and many undesirable features, such as shift work. Along with intrinsic rewards, compensation is used to elicit membership behaviour, but it is not used to direct task behaviour or to foster citizenship behaviour; intrinsic rewards serve this purpose. This approach fits best with a high-involvement strategy.

## Role of Compensation for the High-Tech Electronics Firm

The high-tech electronics firm practises a high-involvement strategy because the success of any new product depends on creativity, innovation, and cooperation among all parts of the organization. For design engineers, there is considerable intrinsic satisfaction in designing a successful product, and they derive some extrinsic rewards from advancing their own expertise and knowledge through the extensive training the firm provides. The firm also provides a substantial degree of job security. The primary purpose of compensation is to motivate membership and to foster citizenship behaviour through profit-sharing and employee stock ownership programs.

## Behavioural Objectives for Compensation

Once the role of compensation has been defined, organizations can develop specific behavioural objectives. These objectives flow from the analysis just completed and may be rudimentary or comprehensive. For example, the chicken-processing firm may be perfectly happy if the compensation system generates a minimum level of membership behaviour, as task behaviour will be shaped by other means. The tree-planting firm goes a step further, relying on its compensation system not only to attract employees but also to direct and control employee task behaviour.

In contrast, the electronics firm views its compensation system as an important part of the rewards it offers to attract high-calibre, committed employees. The firm also views it as a major part of its rewards strategy to foster high organizational citizenship and team-oriented behaviours. The firm may also use compensation to promote learning and development (through a pay-for-knowledge system or payment of tuition fees) and to promote risk-taking behaviour. But unlike the tree-planting firm, it will not depend on its compensation system to promote specific task behaviours. As discussed in Chapter 3, using the compensation system to promote specific task behaviours is a risky process and is suitable in only a very limited number of circumstances.

Table 6.2 illustrates the behavioural objectives that each of these organizations might set for its compensation system, along with some indicators of goal achievement.

**TABLE 6.2**

## Sample Behavioural Objectives for Compensation Systems

| COMPENSATION OBJECTIVE | INDICATOR |
| --- | --- |
| **UNICEF STORE (CASHIERS/CLERKS)** | |
| • None (no compensation system) | • None |
| **CHICKEN-PROCESSING PLANT (PRODUCTION WORKERS)** | |
| • Attract job applicants able to perform basic tasks | • Flow of willing applicants exceeds terminations by 10 percent |
| **TREE-PLANTING FIRM (TREE PLANTERS)** | |
| • Attract applicants to staff initial needs and replace turnover | • Number of applicants exceeds requirements by 100 percent |
| • Maintain high retention | • Turnover during planting season less than 10 percent |
| • Motivate tree-planting behaviour | • Average production exceeds 200 trees per hour |
| **VACATION RESORT (SERVICE WORKERS)** | |
| • Attract applicants to staff initial needs | • Number of applicants exceeds requirements by 100 percent |
| • Maintain reasonable retention | • Turnover during season less than 20 percent |
| • Promote friendly guest service | • Customer surveys |
| | • Less than two percent of customers make complaints |
| **HOSPITAL (NURSING STAFF)** | |
| • Attract applicants to exceed turnover and maintain quality | • Number of applicants exceeds vacancies by 200 percent |
| • Maintain moderate to high retention | • Annual turnover less than 12 percent |
| **HIGH-TECH ELECTRONICS (DESIGN ENGINEERS)** | |
| • Attract top-quality applicants well in excess of needs | • Number of applicants exceeds vacancies by 300 percent |
| • Maintain very high retention | • 75 percent acceptance rate of job offers |
| • Promote creativity and risk taking | • Turnover less than five percent |
| • Promote high citizenship behaviour | • Number of new projects proposed per engineer |
| • Promote learning and development | • Number of suggestions pertaining to department |
| | • Employee surveys |
| | • Number of suggestions extending beyond department |
| | • Improvement in employee qualifications |

## DETERMINE THE COMPENSATION MIX

Once an organization has identified the required behaviours and defined the role the compensation system will play in generating those behaviours, the next step is to identify the mix of compensation components that will elicit that behaviour in the most effective and efficient way. (Figure 4.1 and Figure 5.1 summarize the available choices.)

Several questions must be addressed. What role will be played by base pay, performance pay, and indirect pay? How will each component be structured? For example, will the foundation for base pay be job evaluation, market pricing, or pay for knowledge? Will performance pay be linked to individual, group, or organizational performance? What specific benefits or services will be included in indirect pay, which benefits will be shared-cost, and what degree of choice will employees have in the benefits they receive?

The answers depend on the behaviours the firm requires, the organizational context (especially managerial strategy), the needs of the employees being sought, and the constraints facing the organization. Unfortunately, there is no simple formula for finding these answers: management must rely on a high degree of informed judgment at this point. A further complication is that the mix of principal compensation components also needs to be considered in the context of the total level of compensation to be provided. For example, the greater the variable portion of the compensation, the greater the total compensation generally necessary to compensate employees for the resulting uncertainty and risk.

## DETERMINE THE COMPENSATION LEVEL

How much compensation should be offered? Within the constraints discussed earlier, policies need to be established for determining the total amount of compensation that individuals or groups of employees will receive. In general, the question to be asked is: *Will we lag, lead, or match our relevant labour market in terms of total compensation levels?* This question is complicated by the fact that an employer may not have the same lead, lag, or match strategy for all employee groups.

### Lagging the Market

When considering whether to use a **lag compensation-level strategy**, the first question is: Do we have a choice? In some cases, the organization's financial circumstances are such that there is no choice but to lag the market. A key question is whether the organization can offer noncash rewards (perhaps including some indirect pay items) to make up for this lag. For example, the organization may sweeten its total package by offering items that cost the firm little or no cash, such as purchase discounts on company products. Or these firms may offer flexible schedules or useful training to employees. When cash is short, providing extrinsic rewards other than money, along with intrinsic rewards, becomes even more important.

It is common for small, rapidly growing firms to have cash shortages. To entice crucial employees, these firms often offer company stock, which has no current cash cost. They may also offer other types of performance pay payable only when and if the company can afford to pay. To make this worthwhile in the eyes of employees, the future payout typically needs to be set quite high to compensate employees for the risk of not receiving anything at all. Another potentially valuable reward that this type of firm can offer is advancement opportunities, in addition to intrinsic rewards such as task variety or participation in decision making.

**lag compensation-level strategy**
A compensation-level strategy based on paying below the average compensation level in a given labour market.

Research consistently shows that smaller firms pay less than large firms do. For example, a study of law firms in the province of Ontario found that large firms provide more extrinsic rewards for lawyers than that of small firms (salary, benefits, and believed potential for promotion) and a Statistics Canada study revealed that in the manufacturing sector, small firms paid 24 percent less than the average pay in their sector.[10] Differences may be due to a higher unionization rate in large firms (which can force wages up), tighter cost controls in small firms, or lower ability to pay in small firms. In fact, while their savings in labour costs might appear to be a competitive advantage, small firms appear to pay a steep price for their compensation savings.

Statistics Canada also found that productivity in small firms was 32 percent lower than industrial averages. A study of Italian manufacturing firms found that productivity in small firms is lower. The authors contribute this difference to efficiency producing endeavours, such as the application of information and communications technology, labour skills and training opportunities, the amount of financing into research and design, and the establishment of innovations.[11] Other research indicate that small firms have higher turnover rates and less-qualified employees than larger firms, which helps explain their lower productivity.

But what about firms that do have a choice in pay level? Many firms that could pay more make a conscious decision to pay below market. The motive for doing so is obvious—to save on compensation costs. But there are costs to this strategy. On average, firms that pay below market have a lower quality of applicants and higher turnover than other firms do. Not surprisingly, employees also experience more reward dissatisfaction than employees at other firms do. Unless a firm has carefully analyzed these costs, it may find that the costs of this strategy exceed the benefits. Firms that find lag strategies cost-effective are firms where the costs of both turnover and recruitment are low, where labour constitutes a high percentage of total costs, and where it is possible to contain the negative consequences of reward dissatisfaction.

Other firms that find below-market pay policies viable are those that offer other types of rewards that are highly valued by employees. With these alternative rewards, these firms may avoid the problems of poor-quality applicants, high turnover, and reward dissatisfaction.

## Leading the Market

**lead compensation policy**
A compensation level strategy based on paying above the average compensation level in a given labour market.

Why would an organization ever choose a **lead compensation policy**? There are actually many reasons. An organization may need to lead the market if it offers poor noncompensation rewards, if there are negative aspects associated with employment by this firm, or if the firm needs very high-quality applicants. Firms where recruiting costs, turnover costs, and consequences of reward dissatisfaction are all high may find this approach cost-effective. Firms that value employee stability or whose customer service needs employee stability may also favour this strategy. In addition, firms in which labour costs are low as a proportion of total costs find this strategy less costly than firms that are labour-intensive.

High compensation may be necessary to the organization's goals or to its total reward strategy. Firms seeking employees who have abilities beyond those required for their entry-level jobs or who require heavy training investments may wish to secure their work force with high compensation. For example, firms using a pay-for-knowledge system consistently pay above market. Some firms with performance pay plans, such as profit sharing, may also end up paying above the market. Many firms gear base and indirect pay to the market and then add profit sharing, which causes total pay to exceed the market in profitable years.

In some cases, firms do not intend to lead the market in total compensation but end up doing so nonetheless. This can occur if the compensation structure results in increases beyond market increases, if there is no systematic assessment of market trends, or if there is a strong union. Firms can also end up paying over market if they have poorly designed compensation systems—ones that include rewards that do not add value for the employee or the employer but that still cost money.

By maintaining the same pay scales across Canada, large firms that are geographically dispersed can end up leading the market in parts of the country, even if they are only matching the market in other parts of the country. But from their point of view, the cost of determining a market-matching wage for every branch of the organization is not worth the effort. Furthermore, inconsistent wages for similar jobs may create perceptions of inequity and make it difficult to transfer employees to branches in lower-wage areas.

## Matching the Market

Many firms settle on a "match the market" compensation level policy as a way of "playing it safe." A **match compensation policy** avoids the possible disadvantages of paying below market while enabling them to remain cost-competitive by not offering excessively high wages. They are not sure whether a lag or a lead policy will pay off, so they stick to the middle. In some cases, of course, this is the optimal solution, but this cannot be confirmed without systematic analysis.

**match compensation policy**
A compensation-level strategy based on paying at average compensation levels in a given labour market.

## Utility Analysis

To help managers determine which compensation-level strategy is most appropriate—which can be a complicated process—computer-based utility analysis models have been developed.[12] **Utility analysis** is an approach to analyzing whether a lead, lag, or match strategy would be most efficient for a given organization. In summary, you would have to consider a few factors and how these affects the costs and benefits of the strategy. For instance, you would need to calculate the impact of the change in policy on turnover rates and the costs for turnover, the quality of the employees and the effects on productivity, the change in the number of employees on the need for office space and equipment, and so on.

**utility analysis**
A method used to analyze whether a lead, lag, or match compensation-level strategy is most efficient for a given organization.

A major advantage of utility analysis is the ability to answer "what if" questions. Normally, the analysis is run for a whole range of estimates, including worst-case and best-case projections. Analysis also helps identify the minimum conditions necessary for a change in policy to pay off. For example, we might determine that we need a productivity gain of at least a certain percent to move to a lead policy. We can then ask: How likely is that?

But before making the final decision, we must come back to a basic point: that the pay level strategy chosen must also support the corporate and managerial strategies and must fit the organizational context. If we are practising a high-involvement management strategy, a lag strategy may destroy the close, carefully nurtured relationship between the organization and the employees. However, firms using a classical strategy may have no such concern and have much less to lose by choosing a lag strategy. The organization's business strategy could also be relevant: Is the firm's strategy based on friendly, knowledgeable tellers or on low-cost service?

Given the complexity and uncertainty of this analytical process, is it any wonder that many firms throw up their hands and just stick with their current policy unless they are forced to change?

## Hybrid Compensation Policies

**hybrid compensation policy**
A compensation-level strategy that varies across employee groups or compensation components.

Instead of choosing a straight lead, lag, or match strategy, firms may choose a hybrid compensation policy. For example, a firm could choose to lag for entry-level positions, especially if applicants are plentiful, but to lead in higher-level positions in order to avoid turnover of highly trained personnel. Or, a firm may have different policies for different compensation components—for example, to lag in base pay, to lead in performance pay, and to match in indirect pay. The firm may also choose to have different pay level policies for different employee groups.

Read the following scenario to test your understanding of the close links between method of pay and amount of pay.

Imagine that you are the owner of a medium-sized firm in the service sector and that you have hired two different compensation consultants to devise a compensation strategy for you. Each has come up with a separate plan (we will call them Plan A and Plan B) in which employees will receive an average $4000 per month in total compensation, but there are some differences between the plans. You now submit each plan to a different independent expert for evaluation.

One expert, reviewing Plan A, reports that you are very lucky you consulted her, because $4000 per month is too high a pay level! But the other expert, reviewing Plan B, reports that a $4000 pay level is just fine! In confusion, you submit their reports to your next-door neighbour, who happens to be the compensation manager for a prominent local firm. He tells you that both independent experts are right! What is going on here?

Plan A calls for the $4000 to be distributed as 67 percent to base pay and 33 percent to indirect pay. In Plan B, the distribution is 50 percent base pay, 25 percent performance pay, and 25 percent indirect pay. Plan B is projected to produce value for the organization in excess of $4000 per employee (because of its performance pay component), whereas Plan A is projected to produce value of less than $4000 per employee. Thus, the *nature* of the compensation mix affects the *amount* of compensation you can afford to pay.

## EVALUATE THE PROPOSED COMPENSATION STRATEGY

Compensation Notebook 1.1 in Chapter 1 listed eight goals for a compensation system. At this point, before implementation, it is important to review the proposed strategy against these criteria.

### Three Basic Screens

Three of these criteria—*affordability*, *legality*, and *employee attraction*—can be considered screens through which the strategy must pass. If it can't pass all these criteria, the strategy is a nonstarter.

Clearly, if a compensation strategy results in costs beyond the financial means of the organization, it can go no further. To determine whether the compensation strategy passes this screen, management needs to project the cost of the system and then compare it to what the organization can afford. However, this is often not a clear-cut process because both the costs of the system and the funds available are often difficult to determine in advance. In many cases, the success of the compensation strategy itself plays a major role in determining whether the funds are available to meet the payroll. In a business organization, future revenues and profitability can be difficult to predict, especially for firms in turbulent environments. And although public sector organizations may be able to predict their budgets more accurately, many of them are prone to sudden budget cuts, which have a direct impact on what they can afford.

Before making the final decision, you need to derive a cost estimate of the new compensation system. This requires knowledge of the number and types of employees who will be employed over the next year. To make these estimates, you need to project the volume of business or service to be provided over the coming year. Once you have done this, multiply the projected total compensation for each employee by the number of employees. The resulting number should indicate whether the program is affordable.

Although there can be areas of ambiguity, legality is more straightforward to determine than affordability. Does your plan meet the minimum standards under the employment standards legislation in your jurisdiction? If piece rates or commissions are used, do they meet the standards for minimum pay and overtime under the relevant employment standards legislation? Does your plan comply with human rights legislation and pay equity legislation? If your firm intends to use independent contractors, do they meet the necessary criteria to be so classified? If there is any uncertainty at all, many experts recommend getting an advance ruling from the appropriate federal or provincial/territorial government body.

Regarding the third important criterion, when coupled with the other rewards the organization will offer, will the reward and compensation system really be able to attract employees with the necessary qualifications? There are many ways of testing the labour market to assess this (see Chapter 9).

## Other Evaluation Criteria

After passing through these basic screens, you need to review the other criteria. Will the resulting behaviour contribute toward the achievement of organizational goals? Could the system end up promoting behaviour that is detrimental to goal achievement? Might the system promote some behaviours at the expense of other important behaviours? Does the compensation system match your managerial strategy and organizational structure?

Another issue is equity. Will the system be seen as equitable by those in it? Of course, no system will be considered completely equitable by all employees. But to what degree will it be perceived as equitable, and by how many employees? A major issue to consider is the value of an equitable system to the organization. As discussed earlier, some organizations can tolerate perceived inequities in their compensation systems, but others cannot. For those organizations that cannot, equity is another screen through which the strategy must pass before final approval. One way of checking for equity is to present the proposed plan to focus groups of employees.

Finally, even if the compensation strategy meets all the criteria, one question remains: Is it the most cost-effective strategy for meeting all of them? The only way to answer this is by identifying all the viable alternative compensation strategies and evaluating them against these same criteria. But given the complexity of this process, few firms have the resources or energy to do so. This is why many of them rely on compensation consultants; however, there is no guarantee that consultants will come up with the optimal plan either.

Once the strategy has been implemented, it will need ongoing evaluation to determine whether it is performing as planned and whether adjustments need to be made. It is a rare compensation system that doesn't have some wrinkles to be ironed out. As discussed earlier, even a strategy that was optimal when implemented can become ineffective if circumstances change. The evaluation and adaptation of compensation systems is discussed in Chapter 13.

## WHO DEVELOPS THE COMPENSATION STRATEGY?

If compensation is to serve as a strategic tool, it needs to support the organization's corporate and managerial strategy. For this to happen, those developing the optimal compensation strategy must have an understanding of the organization, its people, its compensation options, and its compensation constraints.

This suggests that the body charged with developing the overall compensation strategy should be the same one responsible for the other strategic decisions in the organization. In many organizations, this means the CEO. The key contribution that top management brings to the compensation strategy process is an understanding of the strategic context for compensation. But, normally, top management does not have expert knowledge in the other three necessary understandings; therefore, human resources and compensation specialists must bring this knowledge to the process. Compensation specialists must carry out the detailed design of the compensation system within the parameters set by the compensation strategy. These specialists may be in-house or outside consultants; however, if outside consultants are used, it is crucial that the process be actively managed by the firm itself.

Another important issue is the stage at which broad employee representation is included in the design process. If the organization is unionized, the compensation system must be acceptable to the union members. But organizations vary greatly in the degree of employee involvement they provide prior to adopting a proposed compensation system. In traditional classical organizations, there is usually no such involvement.

Because an understanding of both employee needs and acceptance by employees is necessary for the compensation system to achieve maximum success, many compensation experts recommend extensive employee involvement right from the early stages. But this is possible only in high-involvement organizations. There are many different stages at which employees can be involved, and it is rare for them to be involved in the initial formation of the compensation strategy.

It is more common for employees to be involved in the design of the specific elements of the compensation system. For example, employees are often involved in developing and managing employee benefits or designing and managing a profit-sharing plan, often through joint employee–management committees. In general, the more employee involvement in the development process, the more likely the plan will address important employee needs and the more likely it will be seen as equitable.

Not all organizations are able to generate effective employee involvement. Three critical conditions are employee commitment to organizational goals, trust between management and employees, and open and effective communication and information sharing. In general, high-involvement organizations are able to work with the most employee involvement, classical organizations with the least, and human relations organizations somewhere in between.

## COMPENSATION STRATEGY FOR SPECIAL EMPLOYEE GROUPS

Should the compensation strategy be different for different employee groups? Traditionally, this has been the case for most organizations. Employees are usually categorized into several groups, usually known as *job families*, and a separate compensation system is used for each group. There are six generic groups: hourly paid employees, clerical employees, sales employees, professional employees, managerial employees, and executives. Most firms also differentiate between permanent full-time employees and contingent workers—that is, workers who are part-time or temporary. Some even have separate systems for new hires and existing employees.

Traditional hierarchical organizations (which include both classical and human relations organizations) have always based compensation on hierarchical level, on the assumption that jobs (and employees) higher in the organization are more valuable and thus should be compensated at a higher level. Classical organizations typically pay their lowest-level employees based on individual performance (piece work or commission) if they can, or on the number of hours worked. Employees higher in the hierarchy are provided with salaries and limited indirect pay. Top management is provided base pay, indirect pay, and a large component of organizational performance pay. The logic behind providing organizational performance pay to only top management is that—in classical organizations—only they are in a position to significantly affect the organization's success.

The compensation system in human relations firms is not much different, except that there is a greater tendency to put all employees on salary. Also, indirect pay is typically more generous than in classical firms. But organizational performance pay is still confined to senior management.

Over the years, two major trends have emerged: a greater tendency to extend group and organizational performance pay throughout the organization, and a trend toward greater similarity of treatment for employees within the compensation system. Sales employees often have base pay included in their compensation plans, while other employees have an element of performance pay added to their compensation. Stock options used to be provided only to senior management; today, many firms provide them to all employees. Perks that were once restricted to top management are now either being offered widely or are being eliminated. Some firms are moving away from hourly pay toward "all salary" systems to reduce distinctions among employee groups. In many cases, these changes are being made to create a greater sense of cohesion and unity among the workforce, particularly in firms that adopt the high-involvement model.

According to the framework developed in this book, the compensation system for a given employee group should differ from that of other employee groups if the behaviour required of it differs significantly from that of others or if the needs of the employees in the various employee groups are significantly different. If the required behaviour is similar, then the compensation system should reflect that similarity. Aside from sales employees (discussed in Chapter 4), there are three main groups for whom the compensation system often differs dramatically from the compensation norm—*contingent workers*, *executives*, and *international employees* (expatriate and foreign employees).

## CONTINGENT WORKERS

One trend is the increasing use of **contingent workers**—that is, workers who are not employed on a full-time permanent basis. According to the International Monetary Fund (IMF), "the rise of part-time employment and temporary contracts challenges the current structure of social-insurance systems." The transformation to such a workforce is occurring at a fast rate in Canada. According to Randstad Canada, if taking into account the various types of contingent workers, freelancers, independent contractors, and consultants, 20–30 percent of Canadians are already "non traditional" workers.[13] In a census by Statistics

**contingent workers**
Workers not employed on a permanent full-time basis.

Canada, it was discovered that 1.8 million Canadians, or one in eight paid workers, held some type of temporary employment, and 52 percent of such workers were those in contract positions held by professionals. In 1996, around 19 percent of Canadian employees were part-time workers, an increase of nearly 50 percent since 1976.[14] Other types of contingent workers—temporary full-time employees, independent contractors, and persons hired from temporary help agencies—also made up an increasing proportion of the workforce.[15]

Some observers have even wondered whether this trend heralded the end of the full-time permanent job as the standard model of employment.[16] There seems to be a new trend toward what some refer to as "precarious work," a concept that captures a broader spectrum of work that's not standard—such as part-time employment, self-employment, contract work, and temporary work—where the work is not generally well paid, is insecure, and not is well protected by the law.[17] In some sectors, such as the knowledge and creative sectors, there are some estimates that precarious work accounts for as much as 40 percent of all workers.[18]

However, the trend toward contingent workers (sometimes known as "nonstandard workers") appears to have increased at lower rates recently than in the past, at least with respect to some types of contingent workers. For example, the proportion of part-time employees grew marginally between 1996 and 2015, holding steady at about 19–20 percent of the employed workforce.[19]

Why do firms employ contingent workers? In some cases, contingent workers are hired to handle highly skilled work for which the skills do not exist within the organization—such as designing a new computer system or planning a plant expansion—because the organization cannot afford to maintain or use their skills on an ongoing basis. In other cases, contingent workers are hired to help regular employees handle overflow work and temporary peaks in workflow. Contingent workers are also hired as temporary replacements to handle vacations, parental leaves, and other forms of leave. The key difference from regular, permanent employees is that contingent workers are employed only when needed and are released when they are not.

However, sometimes contingent workers are hired to do the regular work of the organization on an ongoing basis. For example, retailers may hire a few full-time cashiers but have most of this work done by part-time workers. Using part-timers helps deal with a workload that fluctuates with time of day, day of the week, and even day of the month. Often these employees are not really temporary, nor are they peripheral to the main operations of the business; they are employed only at the will of the organization. However, some firms differentiate between casual part-time and permanent part-time employees. Members of the latter group are not really contingent workers because the firm makes a commitment to provide a certain minimal level of employment on a continuing basis.

Use of contingent workers generally frees employers from many of the legal constraints that apply to permanent employees. For example, contingent workers are typically exempt from severance pay provisions, as well as from employee benefits. Contract employees (although not part-time employees) are exempt from employment standards provisions and mandatory benefits. No cause is needed for dropping a contingent worker from the workforce, so this makes it easy to correct selection errors. Some employers, especially those from the classical school, may believe that contingent workers are easier to manage because the employer can hold the threat of dismissal over their heads.

Some firms see contingent workers as a way to reduce the cost of labour, and attempt to substitute contingent workers for regular employees whenever possible. For other firms, the motives are more complicated. These firms see their labour force as consisting of two groups of employees. One group consists of core employees, who are committed, loyal, and highly knowledgeable, with skills and training that have taken years to acquire. They are compensated accordingly. But it is too expensive to use these core employees for routine, repetitive, low-skilled work, so contingent workers (the second group) are used for this type of work. Using contingent workers to do a portion of the organization's regular work also protects core employees if product/service demand drops. Research in the United States showed that firms offering the most costly benefits to permanent employees used significantly more contingent workers than employers offering more modest benefits.[20]

The key issue is how to pay these employees. If the work they are doing is the same as that of permanent employees and the current compensation system is effective, management will want to use the same compensation system for both groups of employees. But if management believes that the compensation system has become too generous or expensive, particularly for some types of work, they may deal with this problem by using a different compensation system for contingent workers. Of course, if the behaviour expected of contingent workers is significantly different from that of regular employees, then a different compensation system may well be justified.

In organizations where contingent workers perform regular, important functions, such as in banking, the same compensation system is often extended to all employees. For example, the Royal Bank introduced a "one employee" policy where all employees participate in the same compensation system. But this is not the norm. In a Conference Board study, only 20 percent of respondents indicated that their firms offered the same benefits to contingent workers who worked side by side with regular employees. Other research has shown that contingent workers are often paid less than regular workers and receive fewer benefits.[21]

Some contingent workers enjoy full benefits.

According to equity theory, this discrepancy in pay should lead to perceptions of inequity among contingent workers, from which negative consequences might arise. Interestingly, while a recent analysis of 62 studies found that workers employed by temporary help agencies did have lower job satisfaction than permanent employees, the job satisfaction of temporary workers hired as contractors did not differ from that of permanent employees.[22] Another study found that hiring contingent workers to reduce labour costs actually caused higher quit rates among permanent employees (who may see this practice as a signal that their work is not highly valued by their employers), but lower quit rates when contingent workers were hired for the purpose of providing more employment stability to permanent workers.[23]

Unfortunately, there has been little direct research into this issue, although studies have found that turnover is much higher among part-time workers than among full-time workers.[24] Also, contingent workers were found in some studies to have lower performance. For example, in a survey of 229 British firms that used high-performance work systems, the use of contingent labour reduced the productivity payoff that is typically related to high-performance work systems.[25]

Contingent workers do not necessarily have decreased job satisfaction. Only part-time workers who were in search of a full-time job had decreased job satisfaction.[26] Some individuals are involuntarily working as part-time workers due to business conditions, or the inability to find full-time work.[27] One factor that may influence employee reactions is whether the employees are doing contingent work voluntarily or involuntarily. Research indicates that the majority (approximately 80 percent) of part-time employees in Canada are engaged in part-time employment because they prefer it or because their circumstances prevent them from accepting full-time employment.[28] One can expect that involuntary part-time employees will be less satisfied with part-time work and exhibit higher turnover than employees who prefer part-time employment. But while some studies have borne out this expectation, such as studies of Canadian nurses[29] and temporary help employees,[30] others have not.[31]

## EXECUTIVES

Another issue that has been attracting a lot of attention recently is executive pay. This is partly because executive pay has been escalating while the pay of rank-and-file employees has been stagnating, partly because disclosure laws have made executive pay more visible, and partly because some top executives have profited handsomely while managing their companies right into bankruptcy. Compensation Today 6.4 describes one particularly egregious example.

Until the financial meltdown of 2008–09, the most striking case of executive mismanagement was Enron Corporation, where mismanagement and fraudulent accounting practices caused the collapse of the firm in 2002, along with the collapse of its auditing firm, Arthur Andersen. Just before thousands of Enron employees lost their jobs, life savings, and pensions, corporate executives were receiving bonuses and cashing in stock options worth millions of dollars.

In the wake of the Enron collapse, some changes were made to financial accounting standards in the hope of preventing a replay of this collapse. However, what legislators did not realize at the time—although some insightful observers did—was that the root of the problem is the *system* for executive pay (which has been very resistant to change), under which executives have huge incentives to take risky, dubious, or even fraudulent actions.

The problem is not so much that executives make "too much money," but that the huge amounts of money at stake magnify the detrimental effects of poorly designed compensation systems.

In the United States, which leads the world in executive pay, executive compensation jumped from an average of 43 times the pay of the average worker in 1960 to more than 100 times by 1990.[32] Executive pay also soared in Canada, resulting in a doubling of the gap between workers and top corporate executives between 1970 and 1990.[33] Coming at a time when many employers were downsizing and evidence that executive pay often bears little relationship to company performance, this awareness of executive salaries caused a major outcry.

In 1992, the U.S. Securities and Exchange Commission (SEC) toughened its already stringent requirements for disclosure of top executive salaries in publicly traded corporations. Then in 1994, the SEC took this a step further by limiting the tax deductibility (for corporate taxes) of nonperformance-related executive compensation to $1 million per year. In 1993, the Ontario government passed similar legislation, which resulted in the Ontario Securities Commission establishing the first disclosure requirements ever imposed on top executive salaries in Canada.

The outcome of all this? By 2002, the average compensation of CEOs in publicly traded U.S. corporations was more than 500 times the pay of the average worker,[34] and by 2007, it was 521 times higher.[35] All during a period when compensation for most workers had shown no real gain. This figure has fallen in recent years to 335 times higher in 2015[36] and 278 times higher in 2018.[37]

In 2018, Canada's 100 highest paid CEOs made 227 times more than the average worker made,[38] up from 197 in 2017.[39] A major reason for CEO pay increase in Canada was a surge in the use of executive stock options following a legislative change in 2000 that made those options much more tax-favourable and that brought Canadian tax treatment of options in line with U.S. tax treatment.

What message does this send to employees? How do you think they will react to exhortations from their CEO that "we all need to pull together" to ensure the success of "our company"? Sure, workers are likely to be disgruntled, but at least managers will side with the executives because they understand how important the work of executives is.

Or will they? Listen to a manager at United Technologies, which had downsized by 30 000 employees over the past six years. A 20-year veteran of the firm, with good performance reviews, he was doing slightly better than his industry's average, with increases of about four percent a year over the previous three years. At the same time, though, the pay of the company's CEO had increased dramatically:

*I used to go to work enthusiastically. Now, I just go in to do what I have to do. I feel overloaded to the point of burnout. Most of my colleagues are actively looking for other jobs or are just resigned to doing the minimum. At the same time, the CEO is paid millions, and his salary is going up faster than anyone else's. It makes me angry and resentful.*[40]

In Canada in the 1990s, the wage gap between top executives and their employees was not as large as in the United States. In 2000, Canadian executives earned about half what CEOs in comparable U.S. firms received.[41] However, the pay of the top 50 Canadian executives went from 85 times the pay of the average Canadian worker in 1995 to 398 times in 2007,[42] and by 2009, the pay of executives in Canada had risen to the same heights as that of U.S. executives.[43] A major reason for this was a surge in the use of executive stock options in Canada following a legislative change in 2000 that made those options much more tax-favourable and that brought Canadian tax treatment of options in line with U.S. tax treatment.

One thing to note is that the salary levels of Canadian and U.S. corporate executives are not the same as top executives of all organizations. Take Mark Carney, a former Governor of the Bank of Canada from 2008 to 2013. Carney had 13 years' experience in senior positions with private financial firms as well as a doctorate in economics from Oxford University. His actions could make or break the Canadian economy and could affect the lives of millions of Canadians and their families, as well as the success of tens of thousands of businesses. Yet his salary range was $425 300 to $500 300—a major drop from his previous private sector pay. Nonetheless, he was one of the most highly paid executives in the federal government, earning more than his boss, the Minister of Finance ($233 247)—more, even, than the prime minister ($315 462).

Carney's pay may sound pretty good to the average Canadian wage earner, who received about $43 680 in 2011. But compare Carney's compensation with that of William Downe, CEO of the Toronto-Dominion Bank, who earned $11 420 242 in 2011, and Carney's salary doesn't seem quite so high.

## Why Do Corporate Executives Make So Much?

Why do corporate executives make so much? Much of the answer has to do with bonuses and incentives. Let us look at the most recently available (2018) data on the compensation of 10 of Canada's highest-paid executives (see **Table 6.3**). Their base pay, while substantial, amounted to a very small portion of their total compensation.

So, what constitutes the majority of compensation that is *not* base salary? While Table 6.3 doesn't break this out, data published by *The Globe and Mail* indicate that the largest chunk of this was earnings from stock grants and stock options, followed by annual cash bonuses. See Compensation Today 6.5 for an example of controversial bonuses. Executive pensions and "other compensation" (which includes the value of benefits received by the executives, such as car and housing allowances, interest-free loans, and insurance premiums) accounted for the remainder. Overall, the proportion of pay accounted for by stock grants and stock options has actually declined over the past few years, mainly due to poor stock market performance.

TABLE 6.3

## Compensation of Canada's 10 Highest-Paid Executives in 2018

| RANK | NAME OF CEO | COMPANY | BASE SALARY | TOTAL COMPENSATION |
|------|-------------|---------|-------------|--------------------|
| 1. | Donald Walker | Magna International Inc. | $421 899 | $26 427 738 |
| 2. | Keith Creel | Canadian Pacific Railway | $1 436 594 | $20 105 600 |
| 3. | James Smith | Thomson Reuters Corp. | $2 077 040 | $18 783 773 |
| 4. | Linda Hasenfratz | Linamar Corp. | $630 315 | $16 470 653 |
| 5. | Al Monaco | Enbridge Inc. | $1 514 574 | $16 261 802 |
| 6. | Doug Suttles | Encana Corp. | $1 427 965 | $15 823 403 |
| 7. | Mark Barrenechea | Open Text Corp. | $1 251 928 | $15 816 593 |
| 8. | Steven Williams | Suncor Energy Inc. | $1 415 769 | $14 820 002 |
| 9. | Alain Bellemare | Bombardier Inc. | $1 445 360 | $13 800 503 |
| 10. | David McKay | Royal Bank of Canada | $1 500 000 | $13 360 877 |

Source: Global Governance Advisors: "How much are Canada's top CEOs paid? Here's the Full Breakdown," *The Globe and Mail*, June 20, 2018, accessed February 2020.

---

## COMPENSATION TODAY 6.5

### EXECUTIVE BONUSES—PLAYING GAMES WITH THE NUMBERS?

The 2015 Pan American Games involved 6132 athletes representing 41 National Olympic Committees (NOCs) in the Americas, making it the largest multi-sport event hosted in Canada, in terms of athletes competing. Yet controversy over executive bonuses also caught public attention. The province, the opposition parties, and the auditor general debated the need to pay $5.7 million in bonus pay to 53 senior executives. Pan Am senior managers were paid a base salary, and a bonus—that in some instances equalled the base pay—if the games were on schedule and on budget, and if the executives stayed with the Games until they were completed.

While the opposition and the auditor general believed that the Games went over budget, the province insisted that the Games stayed within budget. The opposition parties criticized the practice of paying bonuses by stating that bonuses are not available for many ordinary Ontarians. The province pointed to practices of other sporting events around the world and advice from a human resources consulting firm to "attract the unique skills and experience" required to do the job and ensure "certain targets and certain achievements will be accomplished." Despite the debate, the auditor general said that Ontarians can take pride in the Games as they were on time, with no major incidents and with Canada earning its best-ever medal count.

Sources: "Ontario Auditor General Finds Pan Am Games $342M over Budget, But Bonuses Still Paid," *The Canadian Press*, June 8, 2016; Adrian Morrow, "Wynne under Fire over Bonuses to Pan Am Executives," *The Globe and Mail*, September 16, 2015; Paul Bliss and Kendra Mangione, "Pan Am Games Exec Had $239K Salary Before Bonus: Documents," *CTV Toronto*, September 25, 2015; Pan American Games, *Wikipedia*, https://en.wikipedia.org/wiki/2015_Pan_American_Games, accessed July 29, 2016.

---

What factors determine how much executives receive? As already discussed, the sector in which they work makes an enormous difference, with executives in the private sector receiving much more than executives in the public sector. What else? Some observers argue that executive pay should be tied to the financial performance of the corporation, but research in both the United States[44] and Canada[45] shows little or no relationship between executive compensation and company performance once stock options are excluded. When these are *included*, there is a significant relationship between the stock value and executive compensation, although it is more likely that stock value is affecting the value of executive compensation than the other way around.[46]

Rather than ability, the most important factor affecting executive compensation is firm size: CEOs of large firms make more than CEOs of small firms.[47] Another important factor is whether the firm is controlled by management or the owners. In many large firms with widely dispersed ownership (known as "management-controlled firms"), there is no single owner with the power to significantly affect management decisions. In general, all other things being equal, executives in management-controlled firms earn significantly more than executives in owner-controlled firms.[48] In other words, firms in which top executives determine their own salaries set those salaries higher than firms where top executive salaries are set by owners.

Studies in the United States suggest two other important factors.[49] Firms with fewer hierarchical levels (after controlling for size) pay their top executives less than firms with more hierarchical levels, and firms that are more diversified pay their CEOs more than firms that are less diversified.[50] The first factor makes sense when you consider that hierarchical organizations must increase pay at each hierarchical level in order to provide an incentive for employees to move up the hierarchy;[51] the second makes sense because more diversified organizations are more complex to manage than less diversified ones.

But these factors still do not explain all the variations in executive pay nor all the escalation that has taken place.[52] One way of examining this is to understand how large corporations set executive pay. The board of directors sets up a compensation committee consisting of several directors. The committee then hires a compensation firm to provide data on how "comparable" CEOs are being compensated and uses these data as a basis for their decisions. This sounds like a rational and reasonable process.

However, the process may not always be as "rational" as it sounds. First of all, the compensation consultants hired are often recommended by the CEO, and it is in consultants' best interests to keep the CEO happy if they want to do other business with the firm. So, when looking for appropriate comparators, the consultant will certainly not be interested in erring on the low side. Furthermore, many boards (especially in management-controlled firms) are populated by directors recommended by top management, and these directors will not wish to incur ill will by being stingy with executive pay. One prominent observer[53]—a former compensation consultant now highly critical of executive compensation practices—also points out that no board of directors wishes to believe that it has an average or below-average CEO, and that most firms attempt to pay above the median market value. If the majority of firms do this, then a continually rising "market" for executive compensation is inevitable.[54] Compensation consulting firms then use this rising "market" to justify more increases to executives, and so it goes.

Moreover, many corporate directors are often themselves CEOs and can be expected to be highly sympathetic to other CEOs. And of course, high executive salaries can be used as evidence favouring higher compensation when it is *their* turn to be compensated as CEOs. All told, unless someone on the compensation committee is representing the owners' interests, there is little incentive to hold executive pay down.

Perhaps this will change as shareholders become more militant and as institutional investors, such as pension funds, take a more active role in corporate affairs to push for better corporate governance, as the Ontario Teachers' Pension Fund[55] and the Canada Pension Plan Investment Review Board[56] (Canada's largest institutional investor) are already attempting to do. Another possibility is to give shareholders the opportunity at the company's annual meeting to have a "say on pay"—that is, the opportunity to vote on and possibly reject the proposed executive compensation. In response to share-holder pressure, many Canadian companies have voluntarily adopted a nonbinding version of this policy,[57] and proponents are arguing for laws that would require such a vote, similar to the one passed in the United States in the wake of the 2008–09 financial meltdown.

## Executive Pay and Performance

It was noted earlier that CEO compensation does not necessarily bear any relationship to company financial performance. But should it? The obvious answer would seem to be "yes," but is this really correct? The research suggests mixed evidence: in some instances, the relationship is positive, some neutral, and some negative. One prominent commentator in this area argues that "contrary to much of what one reads in the academic and practitioner press, there is no sound theoretical basis to expect a strong relationship between executive pay and firm performance."[58]

To what extent can a top executive actually influence organizational performance? In the short run, not much, especially in large organizations. In most organizations, financial performance is a function of many factors, many of which are beyond the control of the CEO, especially in the short run. But research does show that CEOs have an increasing impact over longer time periods.[59] This is not surprising. In general, the role of a top executive is to formulate the strategy that will best achieve the organization's goals and then create an organizational system for carrying out that strategy. Especially in large organizations, this process may take years to pay off.

The current conditions facing the firm are another important consideration. A CEO who takes over an organization in a tailspin may be considered a great success if he or she can slow the descent in the first year and start to turn things around in the following two or three years. Does this CEO really deserve less than a CEO who takes over a prosperous firm operating in a highly favourable competitive environment?

Moreover, it may not be in the best interests of the organization or the shareholders to tie executive pay too closely to current or short-term performance. There are all kinds of tricks and manoeuvres to make short-run performance look good that could ruin the firm in the longer run. For example, a CEO could cut research and development expenditures, saving money now but causing a shortage of new products when the old ones become obsolete. A CEO could also cut employee compensation, causing the most talented employees to gradually leave, which will affect long-term productivity. In addition, a CEO could forgo long-term capital investments that might be very beneficial to the firm but that would take years to pay off.

## Problems with Executive Stock Options

To encourage a long-term perspective, many firms incorporated extensive stock options into their executive pay. Contributing to their popularity was that stock options were seen as an almost costless way of compensating executives. But as shareholders came to realize that stock options had a very real cost in terms of dilution of equity,[60] stock options increasingly came under critical scrutiny. Also, in a declining stock market, executives may be penalized despite good performance, while in a rising stock market, they may reap windfall gains unrelated to their personal performance. Moreover, in recent years some executives have turned to "zero cost collars"—hedges that tend to decouple performance of the company shares from financial returns, effectively reducing risk.[61] Because hedges do not have to be publicly reported, other shareholders may not know that the CEO is decoupling his or her financial returns from those of the company. As Lavelle puts it: "An executive who hedges is a little bit like the captain of a ship who sees an iceberg up ahead and heads for his lifeboat without waking the sleeping passengers."[62]

However, the biggest problem with large-scale executive stock options is not their cost, and it is not the negative impact they may have on employee morale; rather, it has to do with their hidden incentives for mismanagement. As the final report of the court-appointed examiner for the Enron inquiry stated:

> The evidence suggests that the compensation system provided what proved to be an overpowering motivation for implementing [accounting] transactions that distorted Enron's reported financial results. Evidence further shows that flawed or aggressive accounting . . . enabled the Enron officers to obtain greatly inflated bonuses and to realize substantial proceeds from the sale of Enron stock they received as part of their compensation packages. In fact, during a three-year period from 1998 through 2000, a group of twenty-one officers received in excess of $1 billion in the form of salary, bonus, and gross proceeds from the sale of Enron stock.[63]

As a result of problems such as this, there has been some investor backlash against executive stock options. For example, the Ontario Teachers' Pension Fund, the second largest institutional investor in Canada, has been pressing for changes so that the basis for CEO compensation depends on factors such as short-term growth incentives, achievement of return on equity or return on capital employed targets, replacing relative total shareholder return with absolute total shareholder return for longer term targets, among other factors, rather than simply on whether the stock price goes up.[64] And the Canada Pension Plan Investment Board (the largest institutional investor in Canada) has urged that stock option plans be discontinued entirely. Stock options are problematic in many areas, including their effectiveness in aligning management interests with those of the shareholders, the potential dilutive impact on existing shareholdings, their tendency to focus management on short-term performance, their use as a cash incentive rather than an ownership incentive, and intractable accounting issues."[65] After extensive study, Canada's Institute for Governance of Private and Public Organizations also recommended, in a 2012 policy paper, that executive stock options be phased out.[66] While both prominent academics[67] and corporate executives, such as Bill Gates of Microsoft,[68] also now support the elimination of executive stock options, some experts go even further than this. Roger Martin, former Dean of the Rotman School of Management at the University of Toronto, has urged that the use of all stock-based compensation for executives be discontinued entirely.[69] His argument is that any type of stock-based compensation for executives is flawed, because these systems create incentives for executives to manipulate stock prices, which is relatively easy for them to do even without resorting to overtly fraudulent practices. As Martin explains: "Stock-based compensation creates the direct and clear incentive to raise expectations of future earnings and then sell the stock before expectations fall—and then do it all over again."[70] Not all executives succumb to this temptation, but why structure executive compensation in

Some executives enjoy company perks.

such a way that dishonest executives are rewarded for their misdeeds, while honest managers are penalized for their honesty? Martin suggests that executives of publicly traded firms be compensated for real, long-term earnings growth, in the same way that executives of corporations that are not publicly traded are often rewarded.

Interestingly, empirical evidence to back up Martin's perspective on executive stock options is now available. Researchers in the United States have found that the likelihood of a firm using questionable accounting practices is directly related to the amount of stock options that executives have been granted.[71] Other researchers have found that stock options are in fact a very expensive way to motivate executives, and that restricted stock is much superior.[72]

Restricted stock is an alternative to stock options. The essence of restricted stock is that executives are granted shares of company stock but are not allowed to actually receive them unless certain conditions are met. Sometimes the condition is a holding period—say, of three years—during which the stock is forfeited if the CEO leaves the firm. In other cases, the executive will not receive the shares unless certain performance targets are reached.

In addition, as a result of the problems inherent in stock options, long-term unit/share plans have become increasingly popular (see Chapter 5). If structured properly, long-term unit/share plans can provide a longer-term perspective (three to five years) to counterbalance the short-term perspective that other types of incentives promote.[73]

Of course, a more fundamental question can also be asked: Why should it be necessary to provide incentives to individuals who are already being compensated handsomely for doing their jobs? Is there a concern that without multimillion-dollar stock packages, executives will simply goof off? The response to this question usually focuses on attraction and retention, for which there is rationale if considering the external market. But even here, there is room for debate. American researchers found that a CEO's total compensation relative to that of others in the industry had no effect on CEO retention, suggesting that when CEOs leave a company, they do so for reasons other than compensation. Research has found that CEOs leave their firm because their connections with other executives help them discover better opportunities in other firms.[74]

## Other Executive Perks

Indirect pay can be another important component of executive pay, especially for executives who are not in the top pay echelon. Many executives receive a number of perks of considerable value, the most common of which are company cars, country club memberships, access to the company plane, free travel for family members, payment of financial planning fees, and supplemental executive retirement plans. In Canada, one significant form of indirect pay for some executives (mainly those who are lured from the United States) is the equalization of personal income taxation rates with those in the United States, so that these executives end up receiving the same amount of after-tax income as they would have if they were living in the United States. This is achieved by simply reimbursing executives for the difference between income taxes in Canada and the United States.

One controversial item of indirect pay for executives is known as the "golden parachute." Golden parachutes may be structured in many ways, but the essence is that an executive who is dismissed for any reason within a certain time frame (for example, five years) is guaranteed a large severance payment, usually amounting to three to five years' pay. Sometimes there is no time limit on these payments, and they kick in whenever the CEO is dismissed.

Many observers argue that such "parachutes" take away the incentive for good performance because the executive will be paid very nicely regardless of performance. Opposing observers argue that these parachutes encourage executives not to fight takeover bids that may be beneficial to shareholders but that would cause the CEO to lose his or her job. In addition, they argue that it would be difficult to lure good executives away from highly paid jobs with other firms without some financial guarantees to protect them if things do not work out. But opponents ask: Why would you want to hire an executive who has so little faith that an ironclad guarantee is required?

## Decision Issues for CEO Pay

So how should a CEO be paid? There are six main issues to decide:

1. the amount of performance pay relative to base pay and indirect pay,
2. the amount of short-term (annual) performance pay versus longer-term performance pay,
3. the nature of the performance pay itself,
4. the specific performance indicators used as criteria for the performance pay,
5. the stringency of the performance criteria,
6. the time period to be used as the performance period for the incentive.

How do you decide the best way to handle each of these decision issues? As with all types of compensation, the first question is, What do we want the executive compensation system to accomplish? Besides attraction and retention, there are two main aspects to consider: a behavioural one and a symbolic one.

The behavioural aspect addresses the kind of executive behaviour the company wants. Research has shown that executives, like most people, tend to pursue actions that maximize their compensation. Therefore, the compensation system should promote executive behaviour that fosters the achievement of organizational goals and that serves the organization's long-term interests.

Moreover, the way top executives are compensated influences the rest of the firm's compensation system. An executive tends to design the firm's compensation system to foster employee behaviour that in turn helps the executive achieve his or her compensation rewards. This is known as a "cascading effect." Of course, a cascading effect in a compensation system is fine as long as both executive and employee behaviours are in line with the objectives and strategy the organization is pursuing.

The executive compensation system also has very important symbolic value. Because of its visibility, executive pay is seen as a signal of the kinds of behaviours the organization values. The behaviours for which top executives are rewarded tend to be emulated by subordinates. Another symbolic aspect is an equity or fairness dimension. If executive pay is structured very differently from the pay of other employees, this may cause serious motivational problems and other negative consequences that result from reward dissatisfaction. Recall the manager at United Technologies (see "Executives" in the chapter) who had reduced his commitment to the organization because of his dissatisfaction with top executive pay levels. Other employees at the same firm were actively seeking other jobs or were reducing their effort to the minimum for the same reason.

The need for perceived equity is a much bigger problem in some types of organizations than in others. In classical organizations, perceived inequity is a minimal problem: as long as the cost of turnover is low, extra job effort and citizenship behaviour are not really needed, and controls constrain dysfunctional behaviour. In human relations firms, perceived equity may not be a big problem either, as long as the firm has traditionally demonstrated high concern for employees and has paid relatively well.

But excessive CEO compensation can be a big problem for high-involvement organizations, where a sense of equity is essential for generating the cooperative and citizenship behaviour that is crucial for success. As Lawler puts it: "High involvement management requires that senior managers ... give up some of the special perquisites and financial rewards they receive."[75] This is because extreme divergence between executive pay and that of other employees makes it almost impossible for a commonality of interests to emerge.

Some experts are now calling for executive pay to be geared to subjective indicators (such as employee morale and organizational culture) as well as financial performance indicators. The Institute for Governance of Private and Public Organizations is a leading proponent of this approach and has presented a variety of thoughtful recommendations for executive pay in its 2012 policy paper.[76]

## EXPATRIATE AND FOREIGN EMPLOYEES

As Canadian companies respond to globalization, an increasing number have established operations outside Canada. Of course, employees of these foreign operations must be paid, but compensation practices that are suitable in Canada may not be appropriate in other countries. Labour market conditions, product market conditions, and legal and cultural conditions vary dramatically between countries.

A key question is whether the employees are foreign nationals or expatriate Canadians sent to play a role in operating foreign subsidiaries. The compensation policy issues are very different for each of these groups. For firms creating compensation packages for home-country expatriates (those who are sent to foreign countries from Canada), the key question is how to create a compensation package that ensures that expatriates do not lose financially compared to their home-country peers but is still cost-effective for the company. There are four main approaches to expatriate compensation: (1) balance sheet, (2) negotiation, (3) localization, and (4) lump sum.

## 1. Balance Sheet Approach

**balance sheet approach to expatriate pay**
Approach to designing expatriate compensation that attempts to provide a standard of living comparable with the home country.

The most common approach has been the balance sheet approach. The objective of the balance sheet approach is to create a compensation system that enables expatriates to maintain a standard of living comparable with what they would enjoy in their home country, regardless of the host country they are sent to. Expatriate expenses are broken down into four main categories: (1) income taxes, (2) housing, (3) goods and services, and (4) a "reserve" or "discretionary" component. Costs of comparable income taxes, housing, and goods and services in the host country are calculated and then converted into Canadian dollars, and the "reserve" amount is added. This total amount (paid in Canadian dollars) is the base pay for the expatriate. The reserve amount is calculated by determining how much a comparable Canada-based employee would have left as discretionary income. In some cases, an additional amount may be added to base pay as a "hardship allowance" to compensate expatriates who are sent to locations that have health and safety risks or other undesirable aspects.

There are several potential problems with this procedure, including changes in the currency exchange rates in the period after conversion to Canadian dollars, as well as changes in tax rates, housing costs, or other living costs. To deal with these problems, management can take an *equalization approach*. For example, for income taxes, the company can deduct the cost of Canadian income taxes from the expatriate's pay and then pay the expatriate's actual income taxes in the host country, which could be more or less than the Canadian amount. This creates a tax-neutral treatment from the expatriate's point of view.

An equalization approach for housing expenses is similar. Reasonable Canadian costs are calculated, and this amount is deducted from the expatriate's income. The company then pays whatever it actually takes to provide comparable housing in the host country, either directly to the foreign property owner or through payment to the employee in the local currency. The same basic procedure can be followed for other living expenses. The key advantage of this approach is that expatriate employees are treated equally regardless of the host country, and that compensation does not need to change as exchange rates or local circumstances change. Employees can also be transferred from one host country to another without changing the way they are compensated.

## 2. Negotiation Approach

**negotiation approach to expatriate pay**
Approach to designing expatriate compensation that entails negotiation between employer and employee to create a mutually acceptable compensation package.

Besides the balance sheet approach, several other approaches to expatriate pay have been developed. Negotiation is a process in which the employer and employee negotiate a mutually acceptable package. However, there are numerous problems with this approach. First, the employee may not be very knowledgeable about conditions in the host country and thus may find it difficult to judge whether a package is reasonable or not. Second, there is the potential for inequity if different packages are negotiated for different employees, especially if the differences are based only on the negotiating skills of the employees. Third, the packages often have no systematic procedure for changing them in response to changes in host-country conditions.

## 3. Localization Approach

Localization is the practice of paying expatriate employees the same compensation as local nationals in equivalent positions. This method fits best with assignments that will be long term, with companies that have extensive operations (and well-developed compensation systems) in the host country and in host countries that have higher compensation levels than Canada, as is generally the case with Canadian employees assigned to the United States. Localization to home-country (i.e., Canadian) rates is also often done for foreign nationals who have been assigned work in Canada on other than a temporary basis.

## 4. Lump-Sum Approach

Another approach to expatriate compensation is the **lump-sum approach**. This method differs from the balance sheet approach in that the various allowance amounts (such as for housing) are paid directly in home-country (i.e., Canadian) dollars to the employee, who may then decide to live in a lower standard of housing than the norm and pocket the remainder of that allowance. Problems with this approach include changes in foreign exchange or local conditions, and possible losses of some tax advantages. For example, in some countries, housing allowances are not taxed as income to the employee, although salary paid directly to the employee is.

## Other Issues in Expatriate Pay

One issue common to all approaches is the amount of premium to pay for foreign assignments. These premiums are paid over and above the standard compensation that preserves the employee's standard of living, and they vary considerably for different countries. There is no system for determining the amounts of these premiums, and the only method may be to assess employees' degree of aversion to each country. Of course, what may be paradise to one employee may be purgatory to another, so this is a subjective process.

The usual method for paying foreign premiums is to prorate them and add the prorated amount to the monthly paycheque. However, this method artificially inflates monthly pay and may make employees reluctant to transfer from a high-premium country to a lower-premium country or to repatriate to Canada. To deal with this problem, some firms use "mobility bonuses"—employees are paid the premium as an up-front bonus, thus removing disincentives for transfer.

Besides financial considerations, it is important to consider a variety of other factors that may affect whether an employee will find a foreign posting attractive and rewarding. For example, to what extent will the posting contribute to career development and opportunities for advancement? To what extent will such a posting be intrinsically rewarding, through the experience of a different cultural environment? Recent research has shown that those firms adopting a "total rewards" approach to compensating expatriate employees generate much higher affective commitment to the firm than those firms relying solely on financial considerations.[77]

"Third-country nationals"—employees of the firm not based in the home country who are assigned to a third country—are treated differently from expatriates. For example, suppose that a Canadian firm assigns a Spanish employee from its Spanish subsidiary to its operation in Chile. Should the employee be compensated in Spanish currency using a balance sheet approach, or should the employee be localized? While the same decision rules could be used as for Canadian expatriates, this does get very complicated, especially if the balance sheet approach is used. Another problem occurs when employees from two or more foreign countries are assigned to the same third country. For one, the balance sheet approach may be most appropriate, while for another, the localization approach is best. However, unless localization is used for both employees, they will have very different compensation levels, even if they perform the same work. To avoid this problem, some companies use the same rates as would apply to Canadian expatriates in Chile, but this may not be fair to third-country nationals from high-wage countries such as the United States. Unfortunately, there are no simple solutions.

A final issue is compensation of local nationals in foreign countries. The home-country (Canadian) compensation system would probably be inappropriate, but this is not to say that the most appropriate compensation strategy is to simply copy local competitors. The same understandings discussed earlier in the chapter—understanding your context, people, compensation options, and compensation constraints—need to be applied to the foreign subsidiary, along with the five steps in the compensation strategy formulation process. The resulting compensation system could be different from that used in the home country and from that used by local competitors.

Note that because of the complexity of international compensation, the objective of this section has been to acquaint the reader with some of the key issues; more detailed information is available elsewhere.[78]

## COMPENSATION STRATEGY FORMULATION: AN EXAMPLE

Congratulations! You've now toiled through six chapters of heavy compensation knowledge, and you now know everything you need to know to develop a compensation strategy. But can you actually do it? If you are like most people, everything still feels pretty abstract. In this last section it is time to see if you have what it takes to be a compensation strategist. So, let us put you in the hot seat. But be forewarned: not everyone will be up to this challenge!

### YOUR CHALLENGE

You are president and CEO of Canada Chemicals Corporation, a firm that produces industrial chemicals. Although the firm is profitable, profits have been slipping in recent years, and you see some other disturbing signs. While there could be many causes for these problems, at least part of your problem may be your compensation strategy. But be wary: things are seldom as simple as they seem! Formulating a new compensation strategy (and deciding whether to actually go ahead with it) is a complex task requiring concentration, so be prepared for a whopping headache before you are done! You may even find it useful to input the data into a computer spreadsheet for easier manipulation.

### YOUR COMPANY

Canada Chemicals Corporation produces two main categories of industrial chemicals. Some of the chemicals are off-the-shelf (OTS) products, while others are custom- developed in conjunction with purchasers. Custom-developed chemicals take much longer to sell, because their specifications have to be worked out between the purchaser and your company.

## The Sales Process

The chemical sales engineer's job is to interface with customers, assess their needs, and determine whether an off-the-shelf product would suit their needs. If not, she or he must identify the technical requirements for the product and then develop preliminary chemical specifications for a product that meets these requirements. In some cases, a minor modification of an OTS product does the trick. In others, modification of a previous custom product works. In still other cases, a new custom product needs to be developed from scratch.

This custom-product information is then sent to the Chemistry Department, which further refines the product formulation, examines whether there is a cheaper way of producing the product (e.g., modifying a custom product that the sales engineer wasn't aware of), verifies that it will meet customer needs, and then develops the production specifications. These specifications are then sent to the Production Department, which develops a cost estimate for the product, plus a preliminary estimate of how long it will take to produce the product. These estimates go to the Vice President of Sales, who develops a price and delivery date based on these estimates and relays this information to the district sales manager. All this information then goes back to the sales engineer, who prepares a detailed proposal for the customer.

But there may be other steps. Often this proposal is reviewed by the customer's chemists, who may suggest changes to the product formulation. If they do, the whole process needs to be repeated. Sometimes the customer balks at the price or delivery date, and it is up to the sales engineer to discuss this with the district sales manager to see whether any break on price or change in delivery date can be negotiated. If the sales manager recommends a new price, the revised proposal goes back to the Vice President of Sales for approval. If it is a timing problem, the sales manager takes it up with Production, which can either refuse or agree to changes in the delivery date but may impose extra costs for doing so. This all then goes back to the sales engineer, who then goes back to the customer.

Despite the complexity of the custom product process, the company actually makes a much higher margin of profit on custom products than on off-the-shelf products because there has been increasing competition in OTS products, which has caused prices to be cut to the bone. For OTS products, production costs (including labour and materials) account for 55 percent of the final selling price, resulting in a gross margin of 45 percent. For custom products, production costs amount to 35 percent, leaving a gross margin of 65 percent.

## The Production Process

Production for both OTS and custom products is complex, for it uses an array of complex mixing and refracting equipment, much of it computer-controlled. Products are made in batches of varying sizes, ranging from 10 litres to 50 000 litres. In addition, a wide array of production processes are used. Production employees require a considerable amount of skill and experience, and many of them have certificates from technical schools.

The production employees unionized about two years ago and are paid an hourly wage which matches the wage levels at other unionized plants but is about 10 percent higher than at two non-union chemical plants that have recently opened. The company has a modest pension plan and some health and life insurance benefits, but total indirect pay is relatively modest for the industry, amounting to about 15 percent of total compensation. Tasks have been subdivided into many different jobs and pay rates for each job are set by job evaluation. Jobs are defined narrowly and are considered boring by most production workers. Turnover among production workers is about 20 percent per year, somewhat high for the industry.

## Company Size

Overall, the company has about 360 employees, and total compensation runs at about $27 million per year. There are 100 sales engineers, 160 production employees, 25 chemists and lab technicians, 40 managers and supervisors, and about 15 other administrative staff. Administrative and technical staff are paid a salary that is based on job evaluation and that is intended to match the market. Turnover among these employees is about 15 percent per year.

The company does about $60 million of business a year and earned a before-tax profit of about $7.5 million last year. The company is capitalized at $45 million and is listed on the Toronto Stock Exchange.

## The Problems

Although the company's financial performance was good in the past, you see several disturbing signs. Total sales revenue has stagnated over the past three or four years, and profits have been declining steadily. (They peaked at $12 million three years ago.)

The reduced profits are occurring for two reasons. First, additional competitors have entered the field for OTS products, driving prices down. Second, the proportion of custom product sales has declined from about 40 percent to about 25 percent over the past three years. Customers are complaining about slow service and misformulated products. They can now go to alternative suppliers, whereas several years ago there were virtually no other suppliers. (A product's failure to meet customer requirements is very costly for Canada Chemicals, because the entire purchase price must then be refunded and sometimes damages must be paid. Almost always, the firm loses the customer.)

## Problems in Attracting and Retaining Sales Engineers

You believe that some of these problems may have to do with your sales engineers. Sales engineers have a bachelor's degree in chemical engineering. When they join the firm, they are given a two-month intensive course on company products, ways to assess customer needs, and related skills. They are then assigned a territory, under the supervision and guidance of a senior sales engineer in a nearby territory. Canada is divided into five sales regions, with a regional sales manager for each region.

Currently, each sales engineer averages about $75 000 in total compensation, approximately 40 percent of which is base pay, 40 percent is commission based on volume of sales, and 20 percent is indirect pay. (Most sales engineers consider the free use of a company car as their most important benefit.) Base pay is $30 000, indirect pay is $15 000, and commissions are five percent on gross sales (the average annual sales per sales engineer is $600 000), which results in an average of $30 000 in performance pay per sales engineer (which of course varies for each sales engineer, depending on their sales). This system matches industry standards.

However, you perceive problems with the current sales compensation system. First, it is becoming difficult to attract sales engineers, who are usually hired right from university. Last year, there were only 160 applicants for the 30 vacancies, and three out of every four job offers the company made were rejected.

Many of those who refused job offers cited the compensation system as a deterrent. They indicated that while the average direct compensation of $60 000 plus car sounded okay, and while they were impressed that some sales engineers earned as much as $90 000 in direct pay (the company has about 10 sales engineers in this league), most were concerned about the uncertainty of their pay, given that they had high student loans to pay off. They were concerned that pay might be low in the first couple of years (direct pay in the first two years averaged $45 000 per year) and therefore, most new graduates turned down the firm's offers.

You are concerned about the high turnover rate of new sales engineers—many are leaving in their first year. In fact, of the 30 you hire each year to fill vacancies, only 10 remain after the first year. The company also loses about 10 experienced sales engineers each year. Job stress is often cited as a reason for leaving.

## Other Concerns with Sales Engineers

Besides the problems attracting and retaining sales engineers, there are a number of other concerns regarding the sales engineers. New sales engineers report that senior sales engineers show very little interest in helping them do their jobs, even though advice and tips from them would be very valuable. When questioned about this problem by their district managers, the experienced sales engineers defend themselves vigorously, arguing that the only way they can make enough money is to spend all their time selling and that they have little time to help anyone else.

Another concern is that most sales engineers seem to be focusing on the OTS products, even though the custom-designed products carry a much higher profit margin for the company. Sales engineers report that selling custom products is just too time consuming and frustrating, citing lack of cooperation from the other departments. As one sales engineer put it, "With friends like those [in the Chemistry and Production Departments], who needs enemies? They don't seem to understand what it takes to sell a product and seem to work against me more than with me. Besides, with prices dropping on the OTS products, I've got to pay most of my attention to moving these products if I want to make a living."

Finally, high animosity and conflict among the chemists, the production personnel, and the sales engineers has you very concerned. Production accuses the sales engineers of always trying to cut prices on their products to stimulate sales and accuses the chemists of coming up with production specifications that are overly complex and that do not meet customer requirements, resulting in wasted product. The chemists accuse the sales engineers of not taking the time to really find out customers' needs and turning in poorly defined customer requests, which often result in the wrong type of product. They view the Production Department as technically incompetent, fouling up the final product.

The sales engineers accuse the chemists of being too fussy in what they want, too slow to formulate the product, and too likely to misformulate products. They accuse Production of overpricing products, being too slow in delivery, and producing poor-quality products. Also, the sales engineers deeply resent top management for leaning on them to sell more custom products, although there is little money in it for them, and for making them scapegoats for the company's drop in profitability.

# FORMULATING THE NEW COMPENSATION STRATEGY AT CANADA CHEMICALS

You believe that most of the problems the firm is facing are due to the poor performance of the sales engineers. But when you call in the VP of Sales and ask him to explain this poor performance, he repeats the party line that the problems are not of his making. Rather, they are caused by the other departments and by the poor quality of sales engineers that the Human Resources Department is recruiting.

You then march into the Human Resources Department and demand to know why it is failing to do its job effectively. "If we are matching the market in total compensation, why can't we find decent sales engineers? Maybe something is wrong with our recruitment and selection procedures or with our recruiters. Maybe we even need a new head of Human Resources!" But like everybody else, HR claims that it is not its fault! So, you reply that if it is not HR's fault, whose fault is it?

After some hesitation, the Human Resources personnel begin to reply. You know what they are going to say: "We need to pay our sales engineers more money." More money! Always more money! Don't they know our profits are going down? But they reply that there is more to it than that. It is the whole managerial system. "Aha," you reply, "so now it's all *my* fault!"

But after calming down, you start to realize they are making sense. They talk about how the organization seemed to function fine when the environment was stable and there were few competitors. But with the increasingly competitive environment, the classical structure just doesn't seem to be performing well.

## Defining the Required Behaviour

The Human Resources manager explains: "We have a small-batch, intensive technology. We want our competitive strategy to be more like a prospector than a defender. Most of the task behaviour that we need requires creativity, high interdependence, and high skill. We require well-educated, highly skilled people who need to collaborate across departments. High membership, task, and organizational citizenship behaviour are needed. We are a relatively small organization, so do we really need all the hierarchy and centralized decision making? Shouldn't we be moving toward a more high-involvement, flexible, collaborative managerial strategy?"

When they put it that way, you can't help but agree. So how do you get there? There are many things that need to be changed, but none of them will work unless you also change your compensation system. To do that, you put together an executive task force, consisting of you, the manager of Human Resources (just now promoted to VP of Human Resources, reporting directly to you rather than to the VP of Finance and Administration), and the VPs of Sales, Chemistry, Production, and Finance and Administration.

First, the task force examines the whole array of rewards—both intrinsic and extrinsic—that the organization provides. They are depressed by what they find. At the moment, the only reward perceived by employees as having any value is compensation, and almost nobody is satisfied with that either. The jobs are seen as boring, promotions are rare and based mainly on whether top management likes a person, and training is infrequent. The VP of Human Resources suggests that by moving to a high-involvement strategy, the firm could offer many new intrinsic and extrinsic rewards. But it is also clear that the compensation strategy itself must also change.

## Determining the Compensation Mix

To redesign the sales compensation system, you create a design task force, which includes you, the VPs of Human Resources and Sales, several regional sales managers, and several sales engineers, especially several younger ones. Its first decision is to create teams of five to eight sales engineers who will be responsible for sales in a given geographic area. Although each engineer will have her or his own territory, all will also be expected to help cover the territories of other team members when they are away or need help.

Using the template illustrated in **Figure 6.2**, the task force formulates the following sales compensation strategy. To improve income stability, the new strategy will redistribute pay between base pay and performance pay, by increasing base pay to 50 percent of compensation (from 40 percent) and reducing performance pay to 30 percent

---

FIGURE 6.2

## Compensation Strategy Template

**JOB FAMILY:** _Sales Engineer_

**TOTAL COMPENSATION LEVEL: MATCH?** ____     **LEAD?** _20%_     **LAG?** ____

|  | Proportion of Total Pay |
|---|---|
| 1. **Base Pay** | 50% |
|    a. Job evaluation | ~ |
|    b. Market pricing | 50% |
|    c. Pay for knowledge | ~ |
| 2. **Performance Pay** | 30% |
|    a. **Individual performance pay** | |
|      i. Piece rate | ~ |
|      ii. Commissions | 10% |
|      iii. Merit bonuses | ~ |
|      iv. Special incentives _____ | ~ |
|    b. **Group performance pay** | |
|      i. Gain sharing | ~ |
|      ii. Goal sharing | ~ |
|      iii. Other group pay _Group Commissions_ | 10% |
|    c. **Organization performance pay** | |
|      i. Profit sharing | 5% |
|      ii. Stock plan | 5% |
|      iii. Other organization pay | ~ |
| 3. **Indirect Pay** | 20% |
|    a. Mandatory benefits | 8% |
|    b. Pension plan | 4% |
|    c. Health & life insurance | 3% |
|    d. Paid time off | ~ |
|    e. Employee services | ~ |
|    f. Other benefits _Automobile_ | 5% |

(from 40 percent). There will also be a major redistribution *within* performance pay, aimed at improving teamwork. Only 10 percent will now be allocated to individual commissions, and a group commission plan targeted to comprise about 10 percent of compensation will be introduced. Under the group commission plan, all members of a sales team will share equally in commissions based on the total sales of that team.

To encourage more sales of custom products, commissions will now be based half on total sales volume and half on gross margin. The actual commission rates will be as follows: individual commissions—0.75 percent of individual volume, 1.45 percent of individual gross margin; group commissions—0.75 percent of sales team volume, 1.45 percent of sales team gross margin. Thus, total commissions for each sales engineer will be 1.5 percent of volume and 2.9 percent of gross margin, compared to the previous five percent of total volume.

After considering the options, the task force decides to recommend profit sharing for all employees; this will increase employee interest in the bottom line and create greater cohesion and cooperation within the firm. The task force also proposes a company stock plan to reinforce this interest. The hope is that these organizational performance pay plans will create a commonality of goals with the organization and serve as a source of retirement savings because most employees regard the current pension plan as inadequate.

The design task force then sets up an employee task force to help design the specific features of the profit-sharing and stock plans. The union is cautious about participating in this process but finally agrees to allow two union officials to sit in on these meetings as "observers." However, they make it clear that this does not necessarily mean they will sign on to any plan that is developed, especially if they have to give up any direct wages. They also make it clear that their preference would be to improve the regular, defined benefit pension plan.

The proposed stock plan will allow employees to invest up to five percent of their total compensation in company shares, and the company will match each share one-for-one. If employees take full advantage of this plan, it will amount to a five percent increase in their total compensation. There will be a minimum one-year holding period for the shares, and employees will be able to place these shares in an RRSP. This will allow them to deduct their contributions from income tax; it will also serve as a vehicle for retirement savings.

The profit-sharing plan will pay out in cash every quarter and will be designed to amount to at least five percent of pay in a typical year. (One purpose of this plan is to provide a source of funds to invest in company shares because many employees have indicated that it would be very difficult for them to do so out of their current earnings.) Based on projected profits for the coming year, the rate needs to be set at 14 percent of pre-tax profits in order to amount to five percent of total compensation. You worry about this, especially when you realize that the stock plan could cost an equivalent amount if all employees participate, but you agree that there is no point in doing any of this if it does not make a noticeable difference to employees.

## Determining the Compensation Level

To improve its ability to attract and retain top-calibre sales engineers, the company decides to substantially lead the market in total compensation for sales engineers by 20 percent. However, 10 percent will be provided by the new profit-sharing and stock plans, so half of the 20 percent lead is certainly not guaranteed and will be paid out only if the company succeeds. This reduces the risk to the company of such a high lead policy.

## Evaluating the Proposed Compensation Strategy

The following table shows what the typical sales engineer is projected to earn under the proposed new compensation system, compared to the average under the current system.

|  | CURRENT SYSTEM | NEW SYSTEM |
|---|---|---|
| Base pay | $30 000 | $45 000 |
| Individual commissions | 30 000 | 9000 |
| Group commissions | – | 9000 |
| Profit sharing | – | 4500 |
| Share plan | – | 4500 |
| Indirect pay | 15 000 | 18 000 |
| Total | $75 000 | $90 000 |

The firm now must assess the impact of the new plan on the company. It will cost at least $1.5 million more in sales compensation annually. Will it be worth it?

Answering that question is not easy and we have to make many assumptions. **Table 6.4** illustrates an attempt to generate some projections. The second column represents the current system as a basis for comparison, while the next two columns provide "best-guess" projections of what might happen in years 1 and 2 under the new sales compensation plan. The same table has columns showing what might happen under pessimistic expectations. (Of course, we have no guarantee that the past year's results will be repeated this coming year if we don't change anything, but we will leave that issue aside for now.)

## Projections for Year 1

Our first assumption is that total sales volume in year 1 under the new system will remain constant. This will be the result of two opposing forces. On the one side is improved employee relations: more cooperation among sales engineers; more training by senior engineers; better cooperation among sales engineers, chemists, and production; a higher calibre of sales engineers hired; and lower turnover of new sales engineers—all which should work to increase sales. But against that, we expect sales engineers to devote more time to selling custom products, which is more time consuming. In addition, the sales levels of senior sales engineers may drop somewhat as they spend more time helping junior sales engineers. And, of course, the new compensation system may result in the loss of some senior sales engineers, also reducing sales.

These factors will certainly reduce sales of OTS products—but by how much? We are estimating that the new system should boost the mix of custom products sold in the first year by 33 percent, from $15 000 000 to $19 950 000, and that sales of OTS product will drop to $40 050 000, resulting in no net change in sales volume.

These projections will depend on our turnover assumptions. We are assuming that the new pay system will cut the annual turnover of first-year sales engineers from 20 engineers to 10, and of middle-level sales engineers from 10 to five. But what about senior sales engineers? Under the proposed new plan, their compensation will actually drop because their earnings are currently based mainly on high-volume, low-margin OTS products. Furthermore, part of their commissions will now be based on the average in their sales team (which is the effect of the group commissions), which will also bring down their pay.

**TABLE 6.4**

Canada Chemicals Corporation—Projected Results of New Sales Compensation System

| | CURRENT SYSTEM | PROPOSED SYSTEM, PROJECTED RESULTS | | PROPOSED SYSTEM, PESSIMISTIC EXPECTATIONS | |
|---|---|---|---|---|---|
| | | YEAR 1 | YEAR 2 | YEAR 1 | YEAR 2 |
| Sales volume | $60 000 000 | $60 000 000 | $63 000 000 | $55 140 000 | $60 000 000 |
| Proportion of custom products | 25% | 33% | 40% | 36% | 33% |
| **Gross margin** | $30 000 000 | $30 990 000 | $33 390 000 | $28 762 500 | $30 990 000 |
| Sales engineer compensation | $7 500 000 | $9 000 000 | $9 261 368 | $8 688 000 | $9 000 000 |
| Sales engineer turnover | 30/100 | 25/100 | 15/100 | 25/100 | 15/100 |
| Sales training costs | $225 000 | $300 000 | $180 000 | $300 000 | $180 000 |
| Additional training costs | — | $150 000 | $150 000 | $150 000 | $150 000 |
| Recruitment costs | $180 000 | $150 000 | $90 000 | $150 000 | $90 000 |
| **Gross margin** (after subtracting direct sales costs) | $22 095 000 | $21 390 000 | $23 708 633 | $19 474 500 | $21 570 000 |
| Add production cost savings | — | $580 200 | $1 184 400 | $262 875 | $580 200 |
| **Net margin** | $22 095 000 | $22 119 000 | $24 893 033 | $19 737 375 | $22 150 200 |
| Subtract administrative overhead | $14 595 000 | $13 865 250 | $14 252 018 | $14 157 150 | $13 865 250 |
| Add additional production cost savings | — | $1 450 500 | $2 072 700 | $788 625 | $1 450 500 |
| **Gross profit before taxes** | $7 500 000 | $9 554 250 | $12 712 500 | $6 368 850 | $9 735 450 |
| Subtract additional profit-sharing costs | — | $966 041 | $1 281 420 | $641 979 | $981 333 |
| Subtract additional shares plan costs | — | $966 041* | $966 041* | $966 041* | $966 041* |
| **Net profit before taxes** | $7 500 000 | $7 622 169 | $10 465 040 | $4 760 831 | $7 788 077 |

*Note: This assumes that all employees will purchase their full allotment of shares, which is unlikely. This also assumes that the shares contributed by the company are purchased on the market. However, if the company wished to conserve cash, it could issue treasury shares. This would, of course, dilute shareholder equity.

For example, consider a sales engineer who is currently selling $1 050 000 worth of OTS product and $150 000 worth of custom product, thereby earning direct compensation of $90 000 (i.e., five percent of $1 200 000 plus $30 000 base pay). Even if that engineer maintains these sales volumes, his or her direct pay will drop to $86 582 under the new plan. But these sales volumes are unlikely to be maintained because senior engineers will be expected to shift their focus to custom products and to spend more time training new sales engineers. As a result, their income will likely drop more than this.

How will they react to this? Assume the worst—that we lose all 10 of our top-producing sales engineers. This will increase turnover to 25 sales engineers in the first year of the new plan and exert a downward push on total sales at least in year 1, until they are replaced by new sales engineers.

What about other costs? Currently, sales training costs about $7500 per new engineer, most of which is the cost of base pay and benefits during the two-month training period. However, this cost will actually go up in year 1 under the new plan, even though we need to train only 25 engineers, rather than 30. This is because base pay and indirect pay will be higher under the new plan. We may save a little on recruiting costs, which have been running at $6000 per recruit, but in order to get the new system working, it will need to be explained to all sales engineers, who will need training for their new roles. Allocate a week to that—the cost of which will be at least $150 000, probably more.

On the positive side of the ledger, the profitability of sales is expected to go up as more custom product is sold. If we reach our 33 percent increase target for custom products in year 1 and have no loss in total volume, gross margin will increase from $30 000 000 to $30 990 000. But after direct sales costs are included, gross margin will actually decrease from $22 095 000 to $21 390 000. Thus, if all the assumptions work out the way we expect them to, the new compensation system will decrease profits by about $705 000 in year 1 compared to what they would have been with no change in the compensation system—not a very promising result.

But wait one minute! We haven't considered that the new sales compensation may produce improvements in other areas, such as production costs. Currently, the chemists and production staff are wasting considerable time and effort because the sales engineers are bringing in sloppy custom orders that have not carefully assessed customer requirements. In some cases, the result has been unacceptable product, which is also costly.

You believe that production costs can be cut by at least two percent in year 1 as a result of higher-calibre sales engineers, lower turnover, and more motivation to sell custom products. This would increase the net margin to $21 969 000. That means the firm would almost break even in year 1 of the new compensation system—not bad when you consider that most organizational changes result in an initial dip in productivity because of the costs and turmoil involved in getting the new system up and running.

But the sales compensation system is not the only aspect of compensation being changed. We are also extending profit sharing and stock ownership to everybody (assuming the union signs on). Beyond the projected cost of the new sales compensation system (which includes the costs of profit-sharing and stock plans), these two plans will cost an additional $1 932 081 to extend to the other 260 employees. Can we afford this?

Well, we may be able to if we assume that profit sharing and stock ownership will together reduce turnover, improve cooperation among departments, and improve productivity among the production and administrative employees (we have already included the projected impact of these plans on the sales engineers). We estimate that this should result in a five percent reduction in production costs as well as a five percent reduction in administrative costs in year 1. This slightly outweighs the costs of these two programs, so the net effect of all this will be virtually no change in profitability in year 1.

But what if we are being too optimistic? Can we really shift attention toward custom products, with all the extra work that entails, and lose some of our top-producing sales engineers, and still expect to maintain total sales volume? And what if the productivity increases and cost savings don't materialize the way we expect them to? Are we risking the company?

Let us see what happens when we change some key assumptions to be more pessimistic. This is what column 4 in Table 6.4 does. We are still assuming that the volume of custom products will increase to $19 995 000; but we are now assuming that total sales volume will drop by $4 995 000 to $55 050 000. Instead of a two percent drop in production costs due to better work by the sales engineers, we will project a one percent reduction. Changing these two assumptions drops sales compensation to $8 688 000 (compared with $9 million in the first projection) but also drops net margin to $19 737 735—a drop of over $2.25 million compared with what it would be if we carried on with the current system.

But that's not all! Let us tone down the productivity and administrative cost savings for the nonsales employees to three from five percent. All this results in a reduction of projected profit from $7.5 million under the current system to just over $4.5 million under the proposed new system. It won't put us out of business, but shareholders won't be happy.

But what if no cost savings at all materialize? We will still make a profit of more than $3 million. It doesn't look as if we are risking the company, even if everything goes wrong. Of course, if everything does go wrong, you will likely be looking for another job, unless you own enough shares to control the board of directors!

To sum up the results of all these projections: if all goes well, we gain nothing; if all goes badly, we suffer reduced profits of nearly $4.5 million. Would you take that deal? Not likely! So far, it doesn't seem as if the new compensation strategy would be worth all the trouble and turmoil it would likely cause. But we were not expecting it to pay off in year 1 anyway. Changes in behaviour take time, and getting everyone up to speed on the new system won't happen overnight. Let us do some projections for a two-year period. (Luckily, you have this all loaded on a computer spreadsheet!)

## Projections for Year 2

Column 3 in Table 6.4 provides projections for year 2 of the new system. It assumes that turnover of sales engineers will drop to half the original level, that sales engineers will work together to help one another, and that working with the other departments will become significantly easier. Total sales are assumed to increase by five percent to $63 million, and 40 percent of that is assumed to be custom products. Although sales compensation by these calculations exceeds $9 million, gross margin after sales costs rises to $23 708 633. In addition, we expect more experienced sales engineers to be able to provide better custom proposals and to reduce production costs by four percent compared to the current system. All this results in a net margin of $24 893 033—a gain of $2.81 million from what would have happened without the new system.

For the rest of the picture, we expect administrative and overhead costs to rise by five percent to accommodate the higher sales volume, but then to be reduced by seven percent as the impact of reduced turnover and more committed and cooperative employees becomes significant. For the same reasons, we expect a seven percent drop in production costs from pre-implementation levels. The net effect is profitability almost $3 million higher than it would have been without the new system. This should make shareholders happy, as well as employees (who will also be shareholders). What's more, we will have a more flexible, cooperative company that is better suited for the contextual variables it faces.

But let us be pessimistic again. What happens in year 2 under pessimistic assumptions? That's what column 5 in Table 6.4 shows. We are assuming that after the disastrous first year (shown in column 4), sales volume recovers to the original levels but that custom work stays steady at $19 950 000. Assuming that the improved performance of sales engineers reduces production costs by two percent, the net margin is $22 150 200—virtually identical to what it would have been with no changes in compensation. Assuming other cost savings of five percent, total profit for year 2 amounts to just over $7.5 million, similar to what it would have been without the new system. Of course, because of the nearly $3 million profit shortfall in year 1 (under the pessimistic projections), we are behind about $3 million over the two years.

## Making the Decision

Do we go ahead with the new compensation system? If our expected projections represent reality, then of course, the answer is "yes." But there are so many assumptions that could be wrong. How much confidence do we have in our "best-guess" projections? What if the pessimistic estimates are closer to the truth? Why not just play it safe and stick with the current system? What would you do?

There is one key assumption we have not examined. For comparison purposes, we have assumed that if we do nothing, things will stay the same, including our $7.5 million profit. But is that really a good assumption? Consider that profitability has been dropping by a million dollars per year for the past three years. Consider all the problems that are emerging. Consider the fact that application of the strategic framework (described in Chapter 2) predicts that the performance decline will continue because of a mismatch between the contextual variables and the classical school of management the organization has been practising.

If this is true, then even with the pessimistic projections, the new system looks good. Overall, it appears that the risks of not doing anything are greater than the risks of going ahead. If you fail to act because you are not completely sure about the consequences of your actions, then you will never act. In short, whatever your decision, you will lose some sleep over it. But making decisions like this is the reason you are paid the big bucks!

There are still a few things that you need to do before going ahead. One is to develop goals and indicators for evaluating your strategy, as will be discussed next. Another is to check the legality of the new plan, even if there seem to be no obvious legal problems with it. If the position of sales engineer is a primarily male job class, and if you are in a jurisdiction with pay equity laws, you may have to modify pay levels of some of your female job classes (although this won't affect many employees in this particular company) because pay is going up for your male group. However, this adjustment may not be possible until the system has been in place for a year because you don't know whether the pay of sales engineers will actually go up, or by how much.

## Setting Goals for the New Strategy

You've decided to go ahead, but you are still aware that this is not a sure thing. You need to design a process for evaluating the success of the new compensation system once it has been implemented. To do this, you need to develop the specific goals you hope the plan will achieve, along with performance indicators for evaluating whether these goals are being achieved. This should enable you to evaluate whether modifications to the compensation plan are needed and identify what those modifications should be. Examples of possible compensation goals and performance indicators are shown in **Table 6.5**.

## Canada Chemicals Corporation—Goals for New Sales Compensation System

| Goal | Indicator |
| --- | --- |
| **MEMBERSHIP BEHAVIOUR** | |
| 1. Increase attraction of new sales engineers | • Increase qualified applicants from 160 to 400<br>• Increase offer acceptance rate from 25 to 50 percent |
| 2. Increase retention of new sales engineers | • Reduce turnover of first-year engineers from 67 to 33 percent |
| 3. Increase retention of other sales engineers | • Reduce turnover from 14 to 7 percent |
| **TASK BEHAVIOUR** | |
| 4. Increase sales of custom product | • Increase from 25 percent of sales to 33 percent in year 1<br>• Increase to 40 percent of sales in year 2 |
| 5. Maintain/increase total sales volume | • Maintain total sales volume in year 1<br>• Increase total sales volume by 5 percent in year 2 |
| 6. Improve cooperation with other sales engineers | • Sales employee surveys |
| 7. Improve quality of custom proposals | • Reduction in rejected product due to sales errors<br>• Reduction in hours by chemists processing proposals |
| **CITIZENSHIP BEHAVIOUR** | |
| 8. Increase cooperation with other departments | • Surveys of other departments |
| 9. Increase flow of suggestions for improvement | • Number of suggestions submitted |
| **FINANCIAL GOALS (OVERALL COMPENSATION SYSTEM)** | |
| 10. Production costs | • Reduce by 7 percent in year 1<br>• Reduce by 11 percent in year 2 |
| 11. Net profit | • Exceed $7.5 million in year 1<br>• Exceed $10.5 million in year 2 |

## Remaining Tasks

Before the new sales compensation plan is implemented, you need to identify the other variables in the managerial strategy that must change to make the compensation system work. You may also need to modify the compensation strategy for other employee groups in the firm. Afterwards, the most important tasks will be to develop the implementation plan, create the necessary infrastructure for operating the new compensation system, and then manage it on an ongoing basis. Even a sound compensation strategy can be torpedoed by poor implementation and weak ongoing management. These issues are covered in depth in Chapter 13.

# SUMMARY

Chapter 6 tackles the problem of how to design the compensation strategy that will best fit a given firm. Four key understandings form the necessary foundation of knowledge for compensation strategy formulation—(1) understanding your organization and its context, (2) understanding your work force, (3) understanding your compensation options, and (4) understanding your compensation constraints. The first five chapters of this book covered the first three understandings, while this chapter identified four types of constraints that set the parameters for compensation strategy—legislative, labour market, product/service market, and financial constraints—and illustrated how understanding them is essential for formulating the compensation strategy.

Next, you learned the five main steps in formulating the compensation strategy: (1) defining the required behaviour, (2) defining the role of compensation, (3) determining the compensation mix, (4) determining the compensation level, and (5) evaluating the proposed strategy.

The question of who should be involved in compensation strategy formulation was addressed, followed by an examination of the issues related to developing compensation strategy for contingent workers, executives, and international employees.

Finally, you learned how to apply the five steps of the compensation strategy formulation process by appointing yourself CEO of Canada Chemicals Corporation and working your way through to a decision on a compensation strategy for the firm.

The remaining three parts of this book focus on how to convert the compensation strategy from a blueprint into an operational compensation system. Part Three covers the technical processes for evaluating jobs, evaluating the market, and evaluating individuals. Part Four discusses the key issues in designing effective performance pay plans and indirect pay plans. Part Five covers the processes for implementation, ongoing management, evaluation, and adaptation of the compensation system.

# KEY TERMS

balance sheet approach to expatriate pay
contingent workers
employment standards legislation
human rights legislation
hybrid compensation policy
labour market
lag compensation-level strategy
lead compensation policy

localization approach to expatriate pay
lump-sum approach to expatriate pay
match compensation policy
negotiation approach to expatriate pay
product/service market constraints
technical ladder
trade union legislation
utility analysis

# DISCUSSION QUESTIONS

1. Managers need to possess four key understandings in order to formulate an effective compensation strategy. Discuss how each understanding contributes to effective compensation strategy formulation.

2. Discuss the legislated constraints that set the parameters for the compensation strategy.

3. Discuss and explain the five main steps in the compensation strategy formulation process (Figure 6.1). Which do you think is the most difficult step?

4. Discuss specific considerations in deciding whether to adopt a lead, lag, or match compensation level policy.

5. What are the key factors influencing executive compensation in Canada? Can executive pay be justified?

6. What are the key problems with executive stock options?

# EXERCISES

1. How do the employment standards in your province vary from those in other provinces? Go to the Employment and Social Development Canada (ESDC) website (http://srv116.services.gc.ca/dimt-wid/sm-mw/rpt1.aspx?lang=eng#ftb2-ref) and compare the minimum wages aspect of employment standards in your province with those of your neighbouring provinces.

2. In your role as CEO of Canada Chemicals Corporation (described earlier in the chapter), you have just finished formulating a new compensation strategy for sales engineers. It occurs to you that given your movement toward high-involvement management, your firm may also need a new compensation strategy for production workers, administrative staff, and technical staff. Using a strategic compensation template similar to that used in Figure 6.2, formulate a compensation strategy for each of these employee groups.

3. You are a prominent compensation consultant and you have been hired by the board of directors of Canada Chemicals Corporation to recommend a compensation strategy for the firm's top executives. In your report, be sure to provide the reasoning for each of your recommendations, along with the advantages and disadvantages of each recommended compensation element.

4. Canada Chemicals Corporation has decided to move to a high-involvement managerial strategy and has hired you as a consultant to implement that process. Aside from the compensation strategy, what other changes need to be made if this conversion is to succeed? Is there any way to increase the intrinsic and extrinsic rewards (besides through compensation) provided by the firm? How could this be done?

5. Form groups of four to six and debate the topic "Canadian CEOs deserve their pay." Groups are to be assigned to oppose or defend this proposition. Each group should come up with about four to six key points to support their position.

## CASE QUESTIONS

1. Read *Case 2—The Fit Stop* in the Appendix. The CEO Susan Superfit has hired you to formulate a compensation strategy for her firm. Using the five-step compensation strategy formulation process (Figure 6.1), formulate such a strategy, and summarize it using a strategic template similar to that shown in Figure 6.2. Give your rationale for each element of the strategy.

2. Using the five-step compensation strategy formulation process (Figure 6.1), formulate a compensation strategy for production workers in *Case 3—Multi-Products Corporation* in the Appendix and summarize it using a strategic template similar to that shown in Figure 6.2. Justify your recommendations.

## SIMULATION CROSS-REFERENCE

If you are using *Strategic Compensation: A Simulation* in conjunction with this text, you will find that the concepts in Chapter 6 are helpful in preparing the simulation.

# ENDNOTES

1. For the latest information on employment standards, including minimum wages, go to Employment and Social Development Canada (ESDC), *Current and Forthcoming Minimum Hourly Wage Rates for Experienced Adult Workers in Canada*, at http://srv116.services.gc.ca/dimt-wid/sm-mw/rpt1.aspx, accessed January 18, 2020.

2. For more details on the distinction between employees and contractors, go to https://www.canada.ca/en/revenue-agency/services/forms-publications/publications/rc4110/employee-self-employed.html#determining_employment_status, accessed January 18, 2020.

3. David B. Fairey, "Exclusion of Unionized Workers from Employment Standards Law," *Relations Industrielles/Industrial Relations* 64, no. 1 (2009): 112–33.

4. Government of Canada, at https://www.canada.ca/en/treasury-board-secretariat/services/innovation/equitable-compensation/fact-sheet-public-sector-equitable-compensation-act.html, accessed January 18, 2020.

5. See http://ir.lib.uwo.ca/cgi/viewcontent.cgi?article=1119&context=uwojls, accessed October 19, 2016.

6. Parbudyal Singh and Naresh Agarwal, "Union Presence and Executive Compensation," *Journal of Labor Research* 23, no. 4 (2002): 631–46; Rafeal Gomez and Konstantinos Tzioumis, "What Do Unions Do to CEO Compensation," *CEP Discussion Paper* no. 720 (2006): 1–31.

7. Stephane Renaud, "Unions, Wages, and Total Compensation in Canada," *Relations Industrielles/Industrial Relations* 53, no. 4 (1998): 710–29.

8. Anil Verma and Tony Fang, "Union Wage Premium," *Perspectives on Labour and Income* 14, no. 4 (2002): 17–23. See also Scott Walsworth and Richard J. Long, "Is the Union Employment Suppression Effect Diminishing? Further Evidence from Canada," *Relations industrielles/Industrial Relations* 67, no. 4 (2012): 654–80.

9. Richard J. Long and John L. Shields, "Do Unions Affect Pay Methods of Canadian Firms? A Longitudinal Study," *Relations industrielles/Industrial Relations* 64, no. 3 (2009): 442–65.

10. See "Wages, Productivity Fall at Small Firms," *StarPhoenix* [Saskatoon], October 4, 1996, D9; David S. Evans and Linda S. Leighton, "Why Do Smaller Firms Pay Less?" *Journal of Human Resources* 24, no. 2 (1989): 299–318; Jean A. Wallace and Fiona M. Kay, "Are Small Firms More Beautiful or Is Bigger Better? A Study of Compensation Differentials and Law Firm Internal Labour Markets," *The Sociological Quarterly*, 50, (2009): 474–96.

11. Cristiano Antonelli, Francesco Crespi, and Giuseppe Scellato, "Productivity Growth Persistence: Firm Strategies, Size and System Properties," *Small Business Economics* 45, no. 1 (2015): 129–47.

12. Brian S. Klaas and John A. McClendon, "To Lead, Lag, or Match: Estimating the Financial Impact of Pay Level Strategies," *Personnel Psychology* 49, no. 1 (1996): 121–41.

13. See https://www.theglobeandmail.com/report-on-business/rob-commentary/the-gig-economy-is-here-and-we-arent-ready/article36678505/, accessed January 18, 2020.

14. Isik Zeytinoglu, "Flexible Work Arrangements: An Overview of Developments in Canada," in *Changing Work Relationships in Industrialized Countries*, ed. Isik Zeytinoglu (Amsterdam: John Benjamins, 1999), 41–58; Diane Galarneau, "Temporary employment in the downturn," Statistics Canada, November 2010, https://www150.statcan.gc.ca/n1/en/pub/75-001-x/2010111/pdf/11371-eng.pdf?st=gYfiiME2.

15. Sharon Lebrun, "Growing Contract Workforce Hindered by Lack of Rules," *Canadian HR Reporter*, May 19, 1997, 1–2.

16. Zeytinoglu, "Flexible Work Arrangements."

17. Cynthia Cranford, Leah Vosko, and Nancy Zukewich, "Precarious Employment in the Canadian Labour Market," *Just Labour* 3 (2003): 6–23; Joan Benach, Alejandra Vives, Marcelo Amable, Christophe Vanroelen, Gemma Tarafa, and Carles Muntaner, "Precarious Employment: Understanding an Emerging Social Determinant of Health," *Annual Review of Public Health* 35, (2014): 229–53.

18. Aleksandra Sagan, "Precarious Work in Canada Now a White-Collar Problem," *Huffington Post*, March 28, 2016, at http://www.huffingtonpost.ca/2016/03/28/librarians-fight-precarious-work-s-creep-into-white-collar-jobs_n_9553272.html, accessed September 26, 2016.

19. Statistics Canada, "Full-Time and Part-time Employment," at http://www.statcan.gc.ca/tables-tableaux/sum-som/l01/cst01/labor12-eng.htm, accessed July 31, 2016; Human Resources and Skills Development, at http://www4.hrsdc.gc.ca/.3ndic.1t.4r@-eng.jsp?iid=13. For earlier data, see Statistics Canada, *Labour Force Survey Statistics, 1996–2000* (Ottawa: 2001).

20. Susan N. Houseman, "New Institute Survey on Flexible Staffing," *Employment Research* 4, no. 1 (1997): 1–4; Chung-An Chen and Jeffrey L. Brudney, "A cross-sector comparison of using nonstandard workers: Explaining use and impacts on the employment relationship," *Administration & Society* 41, no. 3 (2009): 313–39.

21. Isik U. Zeytinolgu and Gordon B. Cooke, "Non-Standard Work and Benefits: Has Anything Changed Since the Wallace Report?" *Relations industrielles/Industrial Relations* 60, no. 1 (2005): 29–60; Christa L. Wilkin, "I Can't Get No Job Satisfaction: Meta-Analysis Comparing Permanent and Contingent Workers," *Journal of Organizational Behavior* 34, no. 1 (2013): 47–64.

22. Christa L. Wilkin, "'I Can't Get No Job Satisfaction': Meta-Analysis Comparing Permanent and Contingent Workers," *Journal of Organizational Behavior* 34, no.1 (2013): 47–64.

23. Sean A. Way, David P. Lepak, Charles H. Fay, and James W. Thacker, "Contingent Workers' Impact on Standard Employee Withdrawal Behaviors: Does What You Use Them For Matter?" *Human Resource Management* 49, no. 1 (2010): 109–38.

24. Chris Tilly, "Dualism in Part-Time Employment," *Relations industrielles/Industrial Relations* 31, no. 2 (1992): 330–47; Stanley W. Siebert and Nikolay Zubanov, "Searching for the Optimal Level of Employee Turnover: A Study of a Large UK Retail Organization," *Academy of Management Journal* 52, no. 2 (2009): 294–313.

25. Anne Bourhis, "Attitudinal and Behavioural Reactions of Permanent and Contingent Employees," *Proceedings of the Administrative Sciences Association of Canada, Human Resources Division* 17, no. 9 (1996): 23–33; Luigi Stirpe, Jaime Bonache, and Antonio Revilla, "Differentiating the Workforce: The Performance Effects of Using Contingent Labor in a Context of High-Performance Work Systems," *Journal of Business Research* 67, no. 7 (2014): 1334–41.

26. Bourhis, "Attitudinal and Behavioural Reactions."; Giovanni Russo, "Job and Life Satisfaction Among Part-Time and Full-Time Workers: The 'Identity' Approach," *Review of Social Economy* 70, no. 3 (2012): 315–43.

27. Statistics Canada, https://www150.statcan.gc.ca/t1/tbl1/en/tv.action?pid=1410002901, accessed January 18, 2020.

28. Ibid.

29. M. Armstrong-Stassen, M.E. Horsburgh, and S.J. Cameron, "The Reactions of Full-Time and Part-Time Nurses to Restructuring in the Canadian Health Care System," in *Academy of Management Best Paper Proceedings*, ed. D.P. Moore (Dallas, 1994), 96–100.

30. Moshe Krausz, "Effects of Short- and Long-Term Preference for Temporary Work upon Psychological Outcomes," *International Journal of Manpower* 21, no. 8 (2000): 635–47.

31. Bourhis, "Attitudinal and Behavioural Reactions."

32. Derek Bok, *The Cost of Talent* (New York: The Free Press, 1993).

33. S. Lohr, "Executive Pay Becomes a 'Hot-Button' Issue," *The Globe and Mail*, January 22, 1992, B1.

34. Christopher Farrell, "Stock Options for All!" *Business Week Online*, September 20, 2002.

35. Franz Christian Ebert, Raymond Torres, and Konstantinos Papadakis, *Executive Compensation: Trends and Policy Issues* (Geneva: International Institute for Labour Studies, 2008).

36. AFL-CIO, "CEO Paywatch," at http://www.aflcio.org/Corporate-Watch/Paywatch-2016, accessed July 31, 2016.

37. Dominic Rushe, "Top U.S. bosses earn 278 times more than their employees," *The Guardian*, August 14, 2019 at https://www.theguardian.com/us-news/2019/aug/14/ceo-worker-pay-gap, accessed April 17, 2020.

38. Canadian Centre for Policy Alternatives, "High CEO pay shatters previous records, now 227 times more than average worker pay," January 2, 2020 at https://www.policyalternatives.ca/newsroom/news-releases/high-ceo-pay-shatters-previous-records-now-227-times-more-average-worker-pay.

39. Canadian Centre for Policy Alternatives, "The Pay Clock: CEO vs Average Pay in Canada, at https://www.policyalternatives.ca/ceo, accessed September 26, 2016.

40. John A. Byrne, "How High Can CEO Pay Go: Special Report," *Business Week*, April 22, 1996.

41. "50 Best Paid Executives," *Report on Business Magazine*, July 2000, 135–36.

42. Hugh Mackenzie, *Banner Year for Canada's CEOs: Record High Pay Increase* (Toronto: Canadian Centre for Policy Alternatives, 2009).

43. Yvan Allaire, *Pay for Value: Cutting the Gordian Knot of Executive Compensation* (Montreal: Institute for Governance of Public and Private Organizations, 2012).

44. Luis R. Gomez-Mejia and David Balkin, *Compensation, Organizational Strategy, and Firm Performance* (Cincinnati: South-Western, 1992); Catherine T. Jeppson, Wayne W. Smith, and Ronald S. Stone, "CEO Compensation and Firm Performance: Is There Any Relationship," *Journal of Business and Economics Research* 7, no. 11 (2009): 81–93.

45. See Parbudyal Singh and Naresh Agarwal, "Executive Compensation: Examining an Old Issue from New Perspectives," *Compensation and Benefits Review*, March/April, 2003, 48–54; Parbudyal Singh and Naresh Agarwal, "The Effects of Firm Strategy on Executive Compensation, *Canadian Journal of Administrative Sciences* 19, no. 1 (2002): 42–56; Michel L. Magnan, Sylvie St-Onge, and Linda Thorne, "A Comparative Analysis of the Determinants of Executive Compensation Between Canadian and U.S. Firms," *Relations industrielles/Industrial Relations* 50, no. 2 (1995): 297–319. See also Zhou Xianming, "CEO Pay, Firm Size, and Corporate Performance: Evidence from Canada," *Canadian Journal of Economics* 33, no. 1 (2000): 213–51; Barbara Shecter, "Say on Pay Movement Gains Traction in Canada; Shareholders are Becoming Increasingly Aggressive on Executive Compensation," *National Post*, May 2, 2015; Imad Kutum, "Is there a Relation between CEO Remuneration and Banks' Size and Performance?" *International Journal of Accounting and Financial Reporting* 5, no. 1 (2015): 272–85.

46. Caroline Yang, Parbudyal Singh, and Jing Wang, "The effects of firm size and firm performance on CEO pay in Canada: A Re-Examination and Extension," *Canadian Journal of Administrative Studies*, August (2019), https://doi.org/10.1002/cjas.1542; Zhou, "CEO Pay"; Suman Basuroy, Kimberly C. Gleason, and Yezen H. Kannan, "CEO Compensation, Customer Satisfaction, and Firm Value," *Review of Accounting & Finance* 13, no. 4 (2014): 326–52; Arron Scott Fleming and Ludwig Christian Schaupp, "Factor Analysis of Executive Compensation Determinants: Survey Evidence from Executives and Non-Executive Investors," *Corporate Governance* 12, no. 1 (2004): 16–41.

47. See Gordon Wang and Parbudyal Singh, "The Evolution of CEO Compensation over the Organizational Life Cycle: A

Contingency Explanation," *Human Resource Management Review* 24, no. 2, (2014): 144–59; Marko Tevio, "The Difference That CEOs Make: An Assignment Model," *American Economic Review* 98, no. 3 (2008): 642–68. See also Magnan et al., "A Comparative Analysis"; Zhou, "CEO Pay."

48. Magnan et al., "A Comparative Analysis"; Stephen G. Sapp, "The Impact of Corporate Governance on Executive Compensation," *European Financial Management* 14, no. 4 (2008): 710–46.

49. Gomez-Mejia and Balkin, *Compensation*.

50. Kevin J. Sigler, "CEO Compensation and Company Performance," *Business and Economics Journal* 31, no. 1 (2011): 1–8.

51. Mariassunta Giannetti, "Serial CEO Incentives and the Structure of Managerial Contracts," *Journal of Financial Intermediation* 20, no. 4 (2011): 633–62.

52. Lucian Bebchuk and Yaniv Grinstein, *The Growth of Executive Pay*, Discussion Paper #510 (Cambridge, MA: Harvard Law School, 2005).

53. Graef S. Crystal, *In Search of Excess: The Overcompensation of American Executives* (New York: W.W. Norton, 1991).

54. John C. Bogle, "Reflections on CEO Compensation," *Academy of Management Perspectives* 22, no. 2 (2008): 21–25.

55. Katherine Macklem, "Teachers' Pet Peeves," *Maclean's*, April 30, 2001, 32–33; Hanne S. Birkmose and Konstantinos Sergakis, "Enforcing Shareholder Duties," *European Company Law* 15, no. 6 (2018): 192–93.

56. Canada Pension Plan Investment Board (CPPIB), *Proxy Voting Principles and Guidelines*, http://www.cppib.com/documents/1969/CPPIB_Proxy_Voting_Principles_and_Guidelines_EN_2019.pdf, (Toronto: 2018).

57. Janet McFarland, "Executive Compensation: Shareholders Have Their Say," *Globe and Mail*, June 11, 2012.

58. Luis R. Gomez-Mejia, "Executive Compensation: A Reassessment and a Future Research Agenda," *Research in Personnel and Human Resources Management* 12 (1994): 161–222; Rob Davies, "'Negligible' Link Between Executive Pay and Firm's Performance, Says Study," *The Guardian*, https://www.theguardian.com/business/2016/dec/27/negligible-link-between-executive-pay-and-firms-performance-says-study, accessed January 21, 2020; Caroline Yang, Parbudyal Singh, and Jing Wang, "The effects of firm size and firm performance on CEO pay in Canada: A Re-Examination and Extension," *Canadian Journal of Administrative Studies*, August (2019), https://doi.org/10.1002/cjas.1542.

59. Gomez-Mejia and Balkin, *Compensation*; Alison Mackey, "The Effect of CEOs on Firm Performance," *Strategic Management Journal* 29, no. 12 (2008): 1357–67.

60. Jennifer Reingold, "Executive Pay: Special Report," *Business Week*, April 21, 1997.

61. Louis Lavelle, "Executive Pay," *Business Week*, April 16, 2001, 76–80; Lee M. Dunham and Ken Washer, "The Ethics of Hedging by Executives," *Journal of Business Ethics* 111, no. 2 (2012): 157–64.

62. Louis Lavelle, "Undermining Pay for Performance," *Business Week*, January 15, 2001, 70–71.

63. Neal Batson, *Final Report of Neal Batson, Court-Appointed Examiner* (New York: U.S. Bankruptcy Court of New York, 2003), 91.

64. Macklem, "Teachers' Pet Peeves"; "Is Management Compensation Rewarding the Right Behavior?" *Ontario Teachers' Pension Plan*, March 2018, http://files.constantcontact.com/ddc1ccd2301/6b2b0665-ad1e-4c2c-80b4-ce9b26cff5c2.pdf.

65. CPPIB, *Proxy Voting Principles and Guidelines*, 9.

66. Allaire, *Pay for Value*.

67. Recently, Michael C. Jensen, a professor at the Harvard Business School who is regarded as the "father" of executive stock option plans, has recanted, believing them to damage corporate performance and shareholder interests. See Claudia C. Deutsch, "An Early Advocate of Stock Options Debunks Himself," *New York Times Online*, April 3, 2005.

68. "Gates Regrets Paying with Stock Options," *CNN Money Online*, May 3, 2005.

69. Roger L. Martin, "Taking Stock: If You Want Managers to Act in Their Shareholders' Best Interests, Take Away Their Company Stock," *Harvard Business Review* 81, no. 1 (2003): 1–19; "Roger Martin on Executive Compensation," *Canadian Business*, https://www.canadianbusiness.com/blogs-and-comment/roger-martin-on-executive-compensation/, June 16, 2011.

70. Roger L. Martin, "The Fundamental Problem with Stock-based Compensation," *Rotman Management*, 2003, 7–9.

71. Jared Harris and Philip Bromiley, "Incentives to Cheat: The Influence of Executive Compensation and Firm Performance on Financial Misrepresentation," *Organization Science* 18, no. 3 (2007): 350–67.

72. Brian J. Hall and Kevin J. Murphy, *Stock Options for Undiversified Executives* (National Bureau of Economic Research, 2000); Zhiyong Dong, Cong Wang, and Fei Xie, "Do Executive Stock Options Induce Excessive Risk Taking?" *Journal of Banking & Finance* 34, no. 10 (2010): 2518–29.

73. Bogle, "Reflections."

74. Maria Hassenhuttl and J. Richard Harrison, "Exit or Loyalty: The Effects of Compensation on CEO Turnover," paper presented at the Academy of Management Conference, Toronto, 2000; Yun Liu, "Outside Options and CEO Turnover: The Network Effect," *Journal of Corporate Finance*, 28 (2014): 201–17.

75. Edward E. Lawler, *The Ultimate Advantage: Creating the High-Involvement Organization* (San Francisco: Jossey-Bass, 1992), 329.

76. Allaire, *Pay for Value*.

77. Christelle Tornikoski, "Fostering Expatriate Affective Commitment: A Total Reward Perspective," *Cross Cultural Management: An International Journal* 18, no. 2 (2011): 214–35.

78. See Peter J. Dowling, Marion Festing, Allen D. Engle, and Stefan Groschl, *International Human Resource Management: A Canadian Perspective* (Toronto: Nelson Education, 2009); David E. Tyson, ed., *Carswell's Compensation Guide* (Toronto: Thomson Carswell, 2008).

# 7

# EVALUATING JOBS: THE JOB EVALUATION PROCESS

At a secondary school, how valuable is a school secretary relative to an audiovisual technician? What about a law clerk and an investigator at a law firm? How about an HR manager and a service manager at a baked goods manufacturer? How about a health technician compared to a transportation worker at a hospital? Given that the jobs in each of these pairs differ considerably in the nature of their duties and necessary skills, are we not trying to compare apples and oranges when we compare the value of each job to the other?

In fact, that is precisely the kind of task that job evaluation is designed to accomplish. In Ontario, application of a gender-neutral job evaluation system, in conformance with the procedures applied under pay equity legislation in Ontario, determined that the jobs in each pair are similar in value, despite their other differences and despite the fact that they had previously been paid significantly differently. As a result of this process, the first job in each pair (which was held primarily by females) received substantial raises to bring it in line with the pay of the second job in each pair (which was held primarily by males). The secretaries received a raise of $7680 per annum, the law clerks received a raise of $4.28 an hour, the HR managers received an increase of $4.65 an hour, and the health technicians received a raise of $2.79 an hour.

# INTRODUCTION TO EFFECTIVE JOB EVALUATION

By now, you have formulated a compensation strategy for each of your major employee groups. This is a milestone on your road to effective compensation. But you don't yet have a compensation *system*. Chapters 1 to 6 provided the foundation and conceptual toolkit for developing a compensation strategy while Chapters 7 to 13 focus on how to transform your compensation *strategy* into a successful compensation *system*.

Chapters 7 to 10 (Part Three) describe the technical processes necessary to measure the value of each job to your organization and, within each job, to measure the contribution made by each employee. Determining what each employee should be paid is a function of three key factors: the relative importance of the employee's job to the organization, the value placed on that job by the labour market, and the performance of the employee doing that job.

This chapter and Chapter 8 focus on how to establish the relative value of different jobs to the organization—the job evaluation process—as well as how to apply dollar values to your job evaluation system. Chapter 9 describes how to collect and interpret relevant labour market data to determine how the market values the jobs that your organization has. Chapter 10 describes how to evaluate individual employee performance to produce a solid foundation for a merit pay system.

Chapters 11 and 12 (Part Four) discuss how to design effective performance pay and indirect pay plans, and Chapter 13 (Part Five) discusses how to successfully implement your compensation system.

Let us now turn to our first order of business—job evaluation. In conducting job evaluation, key objectives are to ensure that all jobs in the organization are compensated equitably and are *perceived* by organizational members as being compensated equitably. Effective job evaluation should ensure that jobs are not underpaid—which would make it difficult to attract qualified employees—and not overpaid—which is important from a cost and competitive viewpoint. The output of the job evaluation process is a hierarchy of jobs, where all jobs of a similar *value* to the organization, however different they may be from one another, are located at the same level on the jobs hierarchy. This jobs hierarchy provides the foundation for the development of pay grades and pay ranges.

This chapter covers job analysis, the foundation for all job evaluation systems, and the different job evaluation methods. The processes and issues involved with conducting and managing job evaluation, and the necessary steps for conforming to Canadian pay equity legislation, using the Ontario Pay Equity Act as a model, will also be examined. Chapter 8 focuses on how to design and apply the most commonly used job evaluation system—the point method—and how to convert the results of job evaluation into a base pay structure.

## JOB ANALYSIS

**job analysis**
The process of collecting information on which job descriptions are based.

**job description**
A summary of the duties, responsibilities, and reporting relationships pertaining to a particular job.

**job specifications**
The employee qualifications deemed necessary to successfully perform the duties for a given job.

A precondition for job evaluation is accurate information about the jobs to be evaluated. The purpose of job analysis is to obtain this job information, which is usually summarized in the form of a job description. A job description is a summary of the duties, responsibilities, and reporting relationships that pertain to a particular job. Derived from the job analysis and description are the job specifications, which are the employee qualifications deemed necessary to successfully perform the duties the job involves. The qualifications required for a job are sometimes summarized by the acronym KSAOs, which stands for "knowledge," "skills," "abilities," and "other" characteristics necessary for job performance.

Beyond establishing compensation, job descriptions can serve a wide variety of organizational purposes. These include attracting and selecting employees, developing training programs, providing guidance to employees and supervisors, developing employee performance standards, and helping ensure that all necessary organizational activities are being undertaken and that no important activities are falling between the cracks. As was discussed in Chapter 4, job descriptions are time consuming to prepare and maintain, especially in dynamic firms where jobs and task demands change frequently, and they can cause rigidity if they are defined too narrowly or interpreted too literally.

## NATURE OF REQUIRED INFORMATION

What information is needed for effective job evaluation? If job descriptions are accurate and up to date, they may provide all the necessary information for evaluating jobs. However, experience suggests that this is rare, even though many organizations expend considerable effort on developing job descriptions. As one compensation practitioner puts it:

> More time, money, and patience are wasted on job or class descriptions than on any other aspect of personnel administration. [Yet] in almost twenty-five years of consulting, my firm has never had a client lay claim to an up-to-date and complete set of job descriptions. [Moreover,] job descriptions never contain all the information required to evaluate jobs for compensation.[1]

Just why is using job descriptions for job evaluation so problematic? First, some firms are not willing to put in the effort to develop and update job descriptions. But a bigger problem is that in many organizations, especially those in more dynamic environments, job duties are changing all the time—something that often escapes the notice of the Human Resources Department. Moreover, as this chapter will show, conducting an effective job analysis is an onerous task because there are many obstacles to the collection of valid data. Sometimes, considerable effort is expended yet the resulting job descriptions omit certain pieces of information that are essential for effective job evaluation.

Compensation Notebook 7.1 lists the key elements of a useful job description; Compensation Notebook 7.2 lists some important considerations when developing job descriptions; and **Figure 7.1** shows a detailed example of a job description.

---

## COMPENSATION NOTEBOOK 7.1

### BASIC ELEMENTS OF A USEFUL JOB DESCRIPTION

1. Job title, department or location, reporting relationships, and date when job analysis was originally completed or updated.

2. A brief statement of job purpose or objectives.

3. A list of the major duties of the job, in order of priority or importance. Some indication of the proportion of time spent on each duty may be useful, although this may not be feasible for some jobs. In describing these duties, be sure to include the tools, equipment, or work aids that are used in performing these duties.

4. An indication of responsibilities for people, results, and organizational assets, including cash, tools, equipment, and facilities, along with the spending or budget authorities attached to the job. The consequences of error or poor performance could also be explained. Included here is the nature and extent of supervision given and received.

5. The mental and physical effort demanded by the job.

6. The conditions under which the work is performed, including the quality of the work environment and any hazards or dangers that may be involved in job performance.

7. A specification of the qualifications needed to perform the job, including skills, training, education, and abilities, as well as any certificates or licences required.

---

## COMPENSATION NOTEBOOK 7.2

### IMPORTANT POINTS TO REMEMBER ABOUT JOB DESCRIPTIONS

1. Describe all ongoing aspects of the job. Also include duties or responsibilities that you are expected to carry out, even if on an infrequent basis. For example, you prepare a report once every two months; this report is usually 20 pages or longer, requires statistical research and analysis, and takes four to six days to prepare.

2. List each job duty and its related tasks, starting with the duties that take the largest portion of time. A duty is a distinct area of responsibility; a task is a particular work action performed to accomplish the duty.

3. Include enough detail about the job. Be clear and concise. For example, "handles mail" could mean any or all of the following: receiving, logging, reading, and distributing mail, and locating background material related to the correspondence and attaching it for the reader's information.

4. Show how often, how much, or how long a task or a responsibility takes to perform.

5. Indicate the approximate amount of working time spent on each major duty, using percentages, number of hours per day, frequency (daily, weekly, monthly).

6. Explain technical terms, describing processes and equipment in easy-to-understand language. Be specific about the degree of responsibility involved and the equipment, processes, and work aids used.

*(continued)*

7. Ask yourself "how" and "why." This may help you more accurately describe aspects of the job. Use an alternative task statement format where there is too much information in a single sentence.

8. Define abilities that had not been previously rated or that are now being realigned due to changes in the job environment or requirements.

9. Focus on the facts. Do not overstate or understate duties, knowledge, skills, abilities, and other characteristics.

10. Avoid general references to personality, interest, intelligence, or judgment.

11. Avoid use of ambiguous or qualitative words, such as "assist" or "complex" without providing clarifying examples.

12. Begin each task statement with an action verb in the first-person, present tense (e.g., write, calibrate, analyze). Use the *Glossary of Active Verbs* (http://www.payequity.gov.on.ca/en/tools/Pages/glossary_verbs.aspx*)* to help clarify actions and tasks.

13. Exclude duties and responsibilities no longer performed, or any future requirements, in the description.

14. Exclude skills, education, or experience a staff member has or may acquire that are not required by the current position.

15. The supervisor may develop a composite position description representative of a group when two or more individuals hold the same type of position (e.g., customer service clerks).

16. Employees should not assume responsibilities and authority that is not theirs. However, supervisors should make clear those responsibilities that are required.

Source: (c) Queen's Printer for Ontario, 2020. Reproduced with permission. This information is subject to change without notice. The most current version can be found at http://www.payequity.gov.on.ca/en/tools/Pages/guide_info.aspx and http://www.payequity.gov.on.ca/en/tools/Pages/glossary_verbs.aspx.

## METHODS OF JOB ANALYSIS

If the necessary information to conduct job evaluation does not already exist, how can it be obtained? This is where job analysis comes in. There are four principal methods of job analysis: observation, interviews, questionnaires, and functional job analysis. However, the first three can be conducted only in organizations that already have examples of the jobs that need to be evaluated. Organizations that are just being created or that are introducing new jobs must depend on the fourth method, functional job analysis.

The job analysis process can be conducted by HR personnel from the Human Resources Department or by outside consultants. Often, managers and supervisors (as well as the job incumbents) may do most of the actual work in collecting the job information, but there always needs to be a central body to ensure consistency of results.

### Observation

Observation involves watching the employee as the job is performed and noting the kinds of activities performed, with whom they are performed, and with what tools or equipment. The extreme version of this process is the time-and-motion study (see the discussion of piece rates in Chapter 5). Observation is mainly useful for jobs in which the activities can be easily observed and for which the work cycle is short (i.e., all the important activities of the job can be seen in a short period of observation). For most jobs, observation is useful only as a supplement to other methods.

### Interviews

Interviews can be conducted with a sample of employees, or their supervisors, or both. Interviewing only one or the other of these groups has drawbacks. Interviews with employees can generate valid information, but the employee perspective on the importance of various job

FIGURE 7.1

Example of a Detailed Job Description

## Space Toy Corporation

**Job Title:** ADMINISTRATIVE SECRETARY I

**Departments:** All

**Reports to:** Department Head or Division Manager

**Updated:** January 30, 2020

### Summary Statement

Under the supervision of a Manager, the incumbent performs a variety of administrative support and office clerical functions for a Department Head and/or Division Manager.

These duties include taking and preparing minutes, composing and typing administrative/confidential/legal documents, arranging of appointments and travel plans, and performing the general duties of a private secretary. Responsibilities may include supervising a small clerical staff.

**How long have the duties and the distribution of time been substantially as below?**

3 years

### Major Duties and Responsibilities

1. Liaises with other departments, divisions, outside agencies, committees, or boards regarding office administrative matters pertaining to the immediate supervisor.
2. Prepares, maintains, and provides letters, memoranda, reports, forms, and other materials from rough draft, final working draft notes, and dictation notes for supervisor's review and signature, in accordance with department or division policy.
3. Composes and prepares correspondence of a simple and straightforward nature for the division or department.
4. Performs other secretarial and clerical functions such as assembling, taking and preparing minutes, agendas, or other reports for division or department committees.
5. Answers telephones and personal inquiries. Provides information and referrals to employees and the general public, as required.
6. Develops and maintains efficient and up-to-date filing system.
7. Arranges meetings and schedules out-of-town travel for departmental or division personnel.
8. Ensures that adequate operating levels of office supplies, equipment, and furniture are maintained by preparing and processing requisitions and verifying completed purchase orders. Also prepares vouchers and billings for division services, travel requests, other reports related to revenues collected and financial or budget statements. May be required to administer and disburse petty cash.
9. Maintains accurate records of hours worked by division or department employees. Includes securing timesheets, calculating overtime and benefits accrued, and preparing related payroll reports. Prepares various personnel action forms and coordinates with the Office of Employee Services to assure compliance with policies and procedures.
10. May be required to supervise clerical staff or to be lead person for secretarial staff. Assigns tasks and reviews work of subordinates.
11. Coordinates all details related to special projects and events, that is the annual sales conference and the quarterly division general meetings.
12. Performs other related duties as assigned.

### Minimum Qualifications and Skills

1. Graduation from high school or the equivalent, and four years' work experience in an office performing secretarial or office clerical duties. Office administration training may be substituted for one year's experience if the course work is sufficient to be the equivalent.

*(continued)*

**FIGURE 7.1**

## Example of a Detailed Job Description (*Continued*)

2. Demonstrated proficiency in the use of personal computers, with a working knowledge of computer software for filing, word processing, spreadsheets, database management, and emailing. Ability to type 60 wpm net. Ability to record minutes of meetings in an accurate, efficient, and timely manner. Shorthand and speedwriting skills would be an asset.
3. A working knowledge of various standard office equipment and other specified technical equipment such as a business calculator, copying machine, fax machine, etc.
4. A working knowledge of modern office policies and procedures in a computerized and local network environment.
5. Ability to schedule appointments, develop and maintain complex filing systems, and keep orderly records.
6. Ability to relate well with co-workers, supervisors, other employees, client groups, and the general public, and provide leadership and work direction to subordinates.
7. Possession of a valid driver's licence.

### Mental Effort

- Mental and visual concentration during computer work four or five hours daily for accuracy in data entry and editing.
- Listening and mental attentiveness in dealing with customer or public queries and manager's requirements.
- Mental effort required in multi-tasking and handling interruptions that require constant refocusing.

### Physical Effort

- Performs multiple, repeated, and sustained hand–eye movements on computer keyboard and screen up to four to five hours daily.
- Lifts and shelves office supplies (up to 30 pounds) daily.
- Sits for extended periods of up to five hours daily, operating computer and other office equipment.

### Working Conditions

- Works in confined space of four-feet high, minimum-grade baffled privacy station.
- Governed by concurrent and dynamic deadlines, despite conflicting priorities and frequent interruptions.
- Intermittent exposure to co-workers/clients; occasional handling of queries and calls from upset or irate people.
- Frequent exposure to glare from computer screen, printer toners, or chemicals.
- Lifting of boxes that can result in injury to back, feet, or hands.

### Type of Supervision Received

- Reports to a department head or division manager. Works under general instructions to prioritize and complete assigned tasks. Assignments are periodically checked for progress by the immediate supervisor.

### Type of Supervision and/or Assistance Given

- May be required to supervise clerical staff or to be lead person for secretarial staff.
- Assigns, prioritizes tasks, and reviews work of subordinate staff.

Source: © Queen's Printer for Ontario, 2020. Reproduced with permission. This information is subject to change without notice. Found at http://www.payequity.gov.on.ca/en/DocsEN/spacetoy.pdf#search=space%20toy

Interviews can be used for job data.

duties may be different from that of the supervisor. Moreover, if employees know that the job analysis is being conducted for the purpose of job evaluation, it is in their interest to portray the job in a way that maximizes its value. Interviewing supervisors may produce more objective information, but supervisors may not be as aware of the realities of the job as the employees.

In the interests of accuracy, interviewing both the supervisor and a representative sample of employees for each job being analyzed is best. (Of course, it may turn out that employees who were seemingly doing the same jobs are actually doing different jobs, and it is important for the job analysis to be able to pick up this difference so that the jobs can be formally differentiated.) The main drawback to interviewing so many people is the cost of the time involved, both for the job analyst and for the interviewees. A structured interview format reduces the time requirement and provides more consistent information.

## Questionnaires

Questionnaires vary on two dimensions. They may be open-ended or closed-ended, and they may be firm-specific or proprietary. An open-ended questionnaire asks the respondent (either the supervisor or the job incumbent) a series of questions, such as the purpose and main duties of the job. A closed-ended questionnaire asks the respondent to select from a list the phrases that best describe the job. To cover the variety of jobs in an organization, the questionnaire must contain a wide variety of possible duties and activities. Care must be taken to ensure that the questionnaire is both reliable (i.e., that two independent observers would answer it in the same way) and valid (i.e., that the information collected accurately reflects reality.)

Because the development of reliable and valid questionnaires is a complex process, many organizations use proprietary questionnaires developed by outside specialists. Perhaps the best known is the *Position Analysis Questionnaire* (PAQ) developed more than 30 years ago by industrial psychologist Ernest J. McCormick.[2] The PAQ focuses on the behaviours that make up a job and uses 187 items (called "job elements") to describe work activities.

There are other standardized instruments. For example, the *Management Position Description Questionnaire* (MPDQ) focuses on the task-centred characteristics of managerial jobs.[3] The *Executive Position Description Questionnaire* (EPDQ) focuses on the behaviours of senior managers.[4] Many consulting firms have developed their own versions of standardized instruments. Some consulting firms are willing to customize their basic instruments when individual employers have special needs.

### Functional Job Analysis

Functional job analysis (FJA) is an attempt to develop generic descriptions of jobs using a common set of job functions. FJA was pioneered in the United States in the 1930s when the federal government created the *Dictionary of Occupational Titles*, which has now been replaced by a system known as *O\*Net* (with the "O" standing for occupation). A version of this system was used by the Canadian federal government to create the *National Occupational Classification*, which includes more than 30 000 descriptions of jobs in 520 occupational groups.

FJA has been refined over the years. The current system uses a series of task statements that contain four elements for each job: (1) who performs what; (2) to whom or what; (3) with what tools, equipment, or processes; (4) to achieve what purpose or outcome. The following is an example for the job of "residential counsellor" in a group home for "wayward youth": "The Counsellor (1) records behaviour (2) of group home residents (3) using standardized record sheets (4) to determine the cause of undesirable behaviours."[5] FJA produces a series of statements like this one that, taken together, describe the job.

Managers can then analyze these statements to draw conclusions about the nature of the job, as well as the skills, effort, responsibility, and working conditions associated with it. However, depending on the job, it may be difficult to draw conclusions about all these factors, such as working conditions or responsibility. Organizations will have to modify the standard job descriptions to suit their specific circumstances and the specific responsibilities they plan to attach to each job.

## IDENTIFYING JOB FAMILIES

For administrative purposes (such as recruitment, selection, and training, as well as compensation), it is often convenient to identify jobs that are related to one another and then to cluster them in "job families." The key thing relating jobs in a job family is that the level and type of skill and/or knowledge required for the jobs in that family is quite similar. For example, a chemical plant may have the following job families for nonmanagerial staff: clerical (clerks, receptionists, secretaries), trades (plumbers, electricians, welders), technical (lab technicians, instrumentation technicians), operators (production control workers), professionals (chemists, plant engineers), and maintenance (janitors, cleaners). However, regardless of the number of job families an organization has, it is important that as many job families as possible be included under the same job evaluation system. As you will see from the opening vignette in the next chapter, using different job evaluation systems for different job families is a recipe for inequity.

Unless there is a compelling need to compensate different job families in different ways—for example, when sales personnel work on commission—jobs should be grouped in such a way as to minimize, as much as possible, the number of job families. Differentiation of employee groups for compensation purposes should be based on strategic or behavioural considerations, as discussed in Chapter 6, not simply on job differences. Many organizations will find that all their jobs can actually be slotted into eight job families or less: (1) executives, (2) managers, (3) professionals, (4) technical staff, (5) sales staff, (6) production/operations workers, (7) trades, and (8) support staff. "Executives" includes senior managers; "managers" includes the remaining managerial staff and supervisors; "professionals" includes employees with professional designations, such as accountants, engineers, IT specialists, and human resources professionals; "technical staff" includes lab technicians, control room operators, and engineering assistants; "sales staff" includes sales representatives and sales engineers; "productions/operations workers" includes production workers, labourers, and delivery truck drivers; "trades" includes electricians, plumbers, and mechanics; and "support staff" includes secretaries, clerks, and janitorial staff.

## PITFALLS IN JOB ANALYSIS

There are several possible pitfalls in the job analysis process. The first is the risk of analyzing the jobholder instead of the job. For example, the jobholder being interviewed may go above and beyond the call of duty, doing much more than the job calls for. Conversely, some jobholders may perform only a portion of the intended job duties. But the analysis of the job should not be unduly influenced by either case.

Another problem is that job descriptions have been subject to gender bias. For example, Kelly claims that "it has been well-documented that job analysts are particularly prone to allow gender bias to influence their analysis of jobs unless trained to do otherwise." Though more current laws surrounding pay equity have created substantial improvements to the job evaluation process in both Canada and the United States, the language used in job descriptions still poses an issue.[6] Traditionally, different language has been applied to duties performed by men and women even though the actual duties may be virtually identical. For example, when men direct the work of employees, they "manage" these employees; when women do so, they "supervise" employees. These types of language differences must be avoided. Also, jobs traditionally held by males are often described in technical terms that sound impressive, while female jobs are often described in simpler, less impressive language, even though the importance and difficulty of the duties are similar.

Regardless of possible gender bias, technical jargon is an impediment to effective understanding of jobs and needs to be translated into everyday language for the job description. For example, instead of "calibrates the FP25 flow meter and adjusts circulant flow commensurate with these calibrations," try "performs simple tests of the measuring accuracy of the water meters and adjusts the water flow accordingly."

But while simplifying the language as much as possible, avoid oversimplifying job duties. For example, "performs general office duties" would be more informative expressed as follows: "answers incoming telephone calls from clients and redirects to the appropriate information officer, operates word processing equipment to prepare letters and reports, uses spreadsheet programs to prepare drafts of department budget," and so on. In the process, it is essential to ensure that both women's and men's jobs are described accurately, using simple, straightforward, precise, and bias-free language. There should also be a check on job titles to make sure they are gender-neutral.

Another issue has to do with jobs that are dynamic. Job analysis and the information it produces is useful only as long as the job stays constant.[7] When the job changes, this information may become not only obsolete but also misleading, causing a variety of inappropriate decisions in areas such as recruitment and selection, training, and compensation. This problem is most likely to occur in high-involvement organizations because they tend to operate in the most dynamic environments. To avoid this problem, the updating of job descriptions needs to be an ongoing process, and supervisors and workers need to be reminded to report significant changes in job duties as they occur. However, they may fail to do this or duties may change gradually and thus go undetected.

## JOB EVALUATION METHODS

Over time, five methods for job evaluation have evolved: (1) ranking, (2) classification or grading, (3) factor comparison, (4) statistical/policy capturing, and (5) the point method. Compensation consulting firms have also developed numerous proprietary systems which use some variation of the five basic methods. For example, the Hay Plan (or Profile Method), developed many years ago by Hay Associates, combines features of the factor comparison and point methods and is intended mainly for management and executive jobs. Kelly provides a thorough description of the Hay Plan, as well as 10 other proprietary plans offered by consulting firms operating in Canada.[8] However, this chapter focuses on the five most used generic methods.

These five basic job evaluation plans can be divided into two main categories: (1) "whole job" methods, in which human judgment is the main determinant of the job hierarchy, and (2) methods that use quantitative factors to establish the job hierarchy. Ranking and classification/grading are whole job methods, the factor comparison, statistical/policy capturing, and point methods are quantitative methods.

### RANKING/PAIRED COMPARISON

**ranking method**
The relative values of different jobs are determined by knowledgeable individuals.

**paired comparison method**
Every job is compared with every other job, providing a basis for a ranking of jobs.

Simple ranking is the least complicated system for deriving an ordering of jobs. The **ranking method** involves asking a group of "judges" (e.g., managers, human resource specialists) to examine a set of job descriptions and to rank jobs according to their overall worth to the organization. The specific criteria are left up to each judge, and often these criteria are not formally identified. Using a group of judges is believed to cancel out individual biases in ranking.

One variant of this approach is the **paired comparison method**, in which each job is compared with every other job, one pair at a time. The number of times each job is ranked above another job is recorded, and these pair rankings are used as the basis for ranking the entire set of jobs. This method is more systematic than simple ranking; one drawback to it is the very large number of comparisons that must be made if a large number of jobs are being evaluated.

Once a hierarchy of jobs has been created, new jobs can be added using a method known as "slotting." New jobs are compared with the hierarchy of existing jobs and "slotted" into the most appropriate level.

Although less complex than many other systems, ranking and paired comparison methods have a number of drawbacks. First, it may be difficult to get the group of judges to agree on rankings because the relative importance of each job factor may be weighted differently by each judge. Second, this method does not establish the *relative* intervals between jobs. For example, the ninth-, tenth-, and eleventh-ranked jobs may be quite close in terms of importance, while the eighth-ranked job may be much more important than the ninth. This method would not recognize that difference.

Perhaps most important, this method provides no explicit basis for explaining why jobs are ranked as they are, which leaves the results of the plan open to charges of inequity. Indeed, because of its subjectivity, the ranking/paired comparison method is not deemed an acceptable method for job evaluation for organizations in jurisdictions covered by pay equity legislation. Under pay equity legislation, four categories of factors must be taken into account when evaluating jobs—skill required, effort, responsibility, and working conditions—and whole job ranking does not take these factors separately into account.

This problem could be rectified by comparing each job to the others using each of the four factor categories separately, providing a separate ranking on each factor category. The factors could then be weighted in terms of importance, and then a composite score could be developed for each job. However, although this would satisfy pay equity provisions, it would not be useful for firms with large numbers of jobs or where jobs change quickly because a change in any job would require a new ranking for each factor category for every job in the system (although an adapted version may be acceptable, as will be discussed later in the chapter).

## CLASSIFICATION/GRADING

The **classification/grading method** establishes and defines general classes of jobs (e.g., managerial, professional, technical, clerical) and then creates a series of grade descriptions for each class. Different grades possess different levels of knowledge and skills, complexity of duties, supervision, and other key characteristics. Organizations compare jobs using these grade descriptions within the appropriate job class and then select the pay grade that best matches them. Jobs in the same grade within a given class receive the same remuneration.

**Figure 7.2** illustrates a hypothetical classification guide for employees in the "nonprofessional" job class at an electrical utility. There are five pay grades, each of which would carry a different pay range. Let us assume that we wish to determine the appropriate salary for the job of computer operator. The job description indicates that some training and skill are necessary, but tasks are simple, errors are easily detected, and operators work under direct supervision of the senior computer operator. Which grade would you place this job in?

Did you pick NP-2? This job description appears to match that grade most closely. Pay ranges (in terms of dollar values) for each pay grade are usually set by identifying the market rates for typical or "benchmark" jobs in each pay grade. Where employees are unionized, pay ranges are set through collective bargaining.

The number of job classes used depends largely on the nature of the organization and on the variety of jobs found. Many organizations that use this system have separate classes for managerial, professional, clerical, and blue-collar jobs. The number of pay grades usually depends on the skill range and the number of jobs in each job class.

This method has the advantage of being straightforward and inexpensive, besides being flexible enough to encompass a large number of jobs. Because the basis for a particular job rating is spelled out, the results are easier to defend than those derived by simple ranking. However, descriptions of pay grades must be general in order to encompass several types of jobs, so there still may be disagreement about the exact grade placement for each job. As well, because this method considers the job only as a whole, no weighting is applied to different job factors, some of which may be more important than others.

**classification/grading method**
The use of generic grade descriptions for various classes of jobs to assign pay grades to specific jobs.

FIGURE 7.2

Sample Guide for Job Classification Method

| | Rocky Mountain Hydro Corporation |
|---|---|

Job Classification Guide
(Nonprofessional Job Class)

Instructions: Match the job description with one of the following categories in order to establish the appropriate pay grade.

| Pay Grade | Characteristics of Typical Job |
|---|---|
| NP-1 | Works under direct supervision. Tasks are simple, repetitive, and require little initiative. When made, mistakes or errors are easily detected and are not costly. Minimal level of education and training required. Examples: janitor, file clerk, general labourer. |
| NP-2 | Works under direct supervision. Tasks are generally simple and repetitive, although some training is required. Little initiative is necessary. Although easily detected, some mistakes or errors can be costly. Examples: switchboard operator/receptionist, accounting clerk, trenching machine operator. |
| NP-3 | Generally, but not always, works under direct supervision. Although most tasks are routine, some require use of discretion. Mistakes or errors may not be easily detected and can be costly. Minimum of high school education and/or substantial training required. May have direct customer contact. Examples: customer service representative, senior accounting clerk, control room monitor. |
| NP-4 | Frequently does not work under direct supervision. Some tasks are complicated and require considerable education or training. Considerable use of independent judgment may be required. Consequences of error may be severe and/or costly. May use costly equipment and/or materials in executing job. May involve supervision of others. Examples: accountant, senior control room monitor, electrical repair crew member, safety inspector, executive secretary. |
| NP-5 | Does not work under direct supervision, but has responsibility for the supervision of others. Tasks are varied and require independent judgment. Substantial education, training, or experience required. Responsible for detecting errors of subordinates. Errors by subordinates not detected by incumbent may be difficult to detect and/or extremely serious. Examples: electrical repair crew leader, senior safety inspector, shift supervisor (plant), trenching and cable crew leader. |

Depending on the grade descriptions (i.e., on whether they contain the four essential factor categories required for pay equity) and the breadth of the job classes (the broader, the better), this method of job evaluation may or may not be acceptable for pay equity purposes. However, this system has historically been very popular with government civil service organizations.

## FACTOR COMPARISON METHOD

Because of its complexity, the factor comparison method is used less often than the other methods. This method identifies several major factors against which all jobs in a job class can be assessed and then rates the extent to which each factor is present in each of a large set of "key jobs" thought to be properly compensated at the present time.

Organizations use statistical analysis (multiple regression) to determine the dollar value of varying degrees of each factor. Then they rate the remaining jobs for each factor and determine compensation by applying the dollar values derived by the multiple regression analysis. The use of these factors is what distinguishes this method from the previous two methods (which are "whole job methods" in that they attempt to compare one whole job against other whole jobs). Depending on whether the factors conform to the four required factor categories, this method may be acceptable under pay equity legal requirements.

> **factor comparison method**
> Assigns pay levels to jobs based on the extent to which they embody various job factors.

## STATISTICAL/POLICY CAPTURING METHOD

The statistical/policy capturing method is perhaps the most complicated method of job evaluation. This method uses questionnaires to gather information about the task elements of each job to be evaluated, as well as the typical time spent on each task and the relative importance of each task. Information is also collected regarding the level of skill or education required for each job, and possibly data on the quantity and quality of output expected for each job. Market data for certain jobs that match well (in terms of job characteristics) with jobs in the external market are incorporated, and multiple regression analysis is applied to derive a formula for the value of the different job characteristics. This formula can then be used to evaluate the jobs that do not have good market matches.

This approach can also be used in conjunction with internal data based on current pay rates to identify and rectify inequities within current pay structures. Used properly, this method is acceptable under pay equity legislation, as confirmed by a ruling by the Ontario Pay Equity Hearings Tribunal.[9]

> **statistical/policy capturing method**
> Combines use of statistical methods and job questionnaires to derive job values based on prevailing external or internal pay rates.

## THE POINT METHOD

The point method of job evaluation (sometimes known as the "point-factor method") is the most widely used system of job evaluation. This method identifies key job characteristics (known as "compensable factors") that differentiate the value of various jobs, weights these factors, and then determines how much of each factor is present in a given job by assigning a certain number of points to each job for that factor. The point totals are used to create a hierarchy of jobs. As discussed in the next chapter, this hierarchy of jobs is then transformed into a set of pay grades and pay ranges, based on the market rates of certain key or benchmark jobs. Because the point method is by far the most commonly used job evaluation system in Canada and is generally the most appropriate job evaluation method for most organizations, Chapter 8 is devoted to this method of job evaluation.

> **point method**
> Establishes job values by the application of points to each job, based on compensable factors.

# CONDUCTING AND MANAGING THE JOB EVALUATION PROCESS

There are three main purposes for conducting job evaluation: to control wage costs, to create an equitable pay structure, and to create perceptions of equitable pay among those covered by the system. Whether all three of these objectives are achieved depends on the processes used to conduct job evaluations and to manage them on an ongoing basis. Organizations need to answer five main questions before setting up a job evaluation process: (1) Who conducts the job evaluations? (2) How should the process be communicated? (3) How should the job evaluation results be applied? (4) What appeal/review mechanisms have been (or need to be) established? and (5) How should job evaluations be updated?

## WHO CONDUCTS THE JOB EVALUATIONS?

Most organizations create a job evaluation committee to oversee the job evaluation process, although some firms assign the task exclusively to their compensation manager, while others use outside consultants. When a committee is used, it typically consists of experts in job evaluation (from either inside or outside the company), the compensation manager, and a representative sample of supervisors from the departments where jobs are being evaluated. In some cases, rank-and-file employees are included.

In unionized firms, there is usually a joint union–management job evaluation committee, although some unions may prefer not to participate in the process. However, at the least, there should be continuing two-way communication with the union to try to prevent misunderstandings.

Employee participation in developing the job evaluation method and carrying out the process usually leads to greater employee satisfaction with the results. However, this participation may not be helpful in classical organizations, which often have an adversarial culture and lack common goals. Also, employee participation will not be effective unless the committee members receive training in job evaluation and understand its goals.

Several conditions are necessary for a job evaluation committee to succeed. First, the parameters and terms of reference for the committee, including its authority, must be spelled out. This is often vague because top management is unsure how much authority they should delegate to the committee. This authority question is a common problem for both classical and human relations firms. Second, technical and clerical support resources need to be made available to the committee. Third, the committee needs training in job evaluation, as well as in effective group functioning, including areas such as open communication and active involvement.

## COMMUNICATING THE JOB EVALUATION PROCESS

A key issue in conducting job evaluation is communicating the process. To foster perceptions of equity, communication is essential. In general, employees must have an opportunity to understand the job evaluation process and its scope and parameters, including the type of results that will likely occur. But just as important, the committee members need to know what will *not* happen. For example, job evaluation will not be used as a ploy to cut jobs or to ferret out individual employees with performance deficiencies.

A variety of methods can be used to ensure adequate communication. Of course, if employees sit on the job evaluation committee, they can serve as a conduit for information to the rest of the staff. In addition, small group meetings led by a member of the job evaluation committee can help communicate to staff; so can formal written reports and policy documents. Overall, it is important to establish two-way communications so that employee concerns and questions can be received and addressed.

A concern for many employers is whether they should reveal the detailed results of job evaluation to employees or simply present the outcome in terms of which pay grade their job has been placed in. The answer depends on the nature of the organization as well as on the purposes of the job evaluation. If the organization is a classical one and the main objective is to develop an internal pay structure that controls labour costs, management will conduct the job evaluations and not release the detailed results. For these organizations, this is probably best approach because the lack of trust and poor relations that often exist would likely lead to this information being misinterpreted or used in unproductive ways.

But if perceptions of compensation equity are important, as they are in human relations and high-involvement organizations, then more open transmission of information is desirable. Employees will doubt that the system is fair unless they understand how it works.

## APPLYING JOB EVALUATION RESULTS

After the new base pay structure has been completed, the pay for some jobs will likely increase, while the pay for others will likely decrease. How to handle employees whose current pay is out of line with the new pay ranges for their jobs is an important issue for the future success and perceived fairness of the new pay structure.

### Employees Below the Range

Employees who are currently paid below the new pay ranges for their jobs are referred to as "green-circled employees," and they should be moved up to at least the minimum of the pay range for their jobs as soon as possible. (If these employees are experienced and performing well, they should be moved up well past the minimum because new employees will be coming in at that level.) This move would normally be the first priority with the compensation funds that are available. It would be very inequitable for experienced employees to be left below new employees coming in at the bottom of the new pay range.

### Employees Above the Range

A trickier problem is what to do with individuals who are currently being paid above the maximum of the new pay range for their jobs. The most direct way to address this inequity would be to reduce their pay to the maximum of the job's pay range. However, this approach can cause serious morale problems because most people regard pay reduction to be unfair if it doesn't apply to everyone or if it doesn't seem necessary from an economic point of view. In this case, opposition to the new pay structure could result.

Moreover, unilateral reduction of employee pay is illegal for unionized employees and for employees with specific written contracts. And unilateral reduction of pay for other employees could expose the employer to accusations of "constructive dismissal." According to this legal concept, an employer who unilaterally worsens an employee's terms and conditions of employment is really dismissing that employee. An employee who finds the new terms of employment unacceptable and terminates his or her employment has grounds for an unjust dismissal suit against the employer. Depending on the employee's seniority, the nature of the job, and other factors, court-imposed settlements can be quite costly.

An employer can avoid this by offering severance pay, but this can also be costly (see Chapter 12). The only situations where an employer can avoid paying severance are at the end of fixed-term contracts or in cases of just-cause dismissal. No severance payment at all is required if it can be established that the employer had just cause for dismissing an employee. However, after reviewing recent court cases, some legal experts have concluded that proving "just cause" is so difficult that an employer will generally be better off just to "pay severance and get it over with."[10]

Pay cuts are also not illegal if they are voluntarily accepted by the affected individuals. However, there can be no duress—such as threatening to fire or demote the employee if he or she doesn't take a pay cut—or constructive dismissal may be charged. When the employee agrees to a pay cut, this is known as "mutual rescission"—that is, both employer and employee have agreed to end the current employment agreement and negotiate a new one.

Because of these legal issues, a common approach is to "red-circle" individuals who are being paid above their pay range and freeze their pay at current levels until salary scales catch up (due to adjustments for inflation). While this works quite well in times of high inflation, it doesn't work well in times of low inflation or when pay levels are static. It is particularly unsatisfactory when there are many red-circled employees and when the firm's financial viability is at stake. However, there may be no good alternatives. To avoid this problem and maintain flexibility, some employers are now attempting to free themselves from the constraints of constructive dismissal law by putting all employees on revolving fixed-term contracts.

Although employers may feel that they are being more than generous by red-circling rather than reducing pay, this practice can still cause serious motivational problems for the affected employees. Nobody looks forward to a static income (or a declining one, when inflation is considered). In addition, there is no potential for financial reward for good performance during the period it takes for the pay scale to catch up and possibly not even afterward because most systems do not allow raises for employees who have reached the maximum of their pay range.

A compromise solution is to continue to grant raises based on performance, but not to adjust the base pay rate for inflation. Of course, this lengthens the period of adjustment, increases compensation costs, and prolongs inequity. Other employees may start to ask why they should receive less money than somebody else who is doing the same work. So a better approach might be to treat red-circled individuals as if they are at the maximum of their pay range and therefore ineligible for merit raises (or scale increases) but still eligible for merit bonuses.

Other solutions may be available, depending on circumstances. For example, if some red-circled employees are close to retirement, the problem for them will be resolved when they retire. It may be desirable to hasten this process by offering early retirement incentives, thus allowing the firm to bring in a new person at the bottom of the pay range. In other cases, it may be possible to promote the red-circled employee into a job in the next-higher pay grade or to add temporary duties to their jobs that would justify their current pay level.

Another approach is to examine employee performance levels. Perhaps red-circled employees who are performing very well can be allowed to maintain their current pay level until inflation solves the problem, or until they can be promoted to a job in a higher pay grade. Other employees might be offered a buyout severance package; however, deciding who should be offered buyout packages requires careful consideration of the costs of the buyout. Chapter 12 provides some examples of what these costs might be.

## DEVELOPING APPEAL/REVIEW MECHANISMS

One key element of procedural justice is the opportunity for an individual or group to appeal decisions they believe to be unfair. The logical body to approach first is the job evaluation committee, which can review its decisions in light of the concerns expressed and any new information the complainant provides. Sometimes the problem is not due to the final decision itself but rather to misunderstandings about the process used to make the decision. At this point, effective communication may solve the problem. Of course, it may be that the complainant is actually correct, and the decision should be changed.

If the complainant does not receive satisfaction at this level, at least one other avenue of appeal should be available. For unionized employees, the typical recourse is to initiate a grievance. In a non-union firm, it may be appropriate to designate a senior company official (often the head of Human Resources) to review the matter and make a final decision. However, overruling the job evaluation committee is not something to be taken lightly, because committee members may interpret such decisions as undermining their authority or showing a lack of confidence in their decisions. When the committee is often overruled, committee members will grow increasingly cynical about the role they are playing, and it may become difficult to find good members willing to serve.

## UPDATING JOB EVALUATIONS

At least four events can trigger a need to re-evaluate jobs.

1. The job itself has changed significantly. It is important to have some procedure for identifying jobs that have changed because this information may not always reach those who are tasked with maintaining the job evaluation system.

2. The organization's strategy has changed, such that certain behaviours have become valued more or less highly than in the past.

3. There are signs that the job evaluation system is no longer working effectively. These signs could include a high level of appeals, or an inability to fill certain jobs with competent individuals.

4. Legislative conditions require it, such as when new pay equity legislation is introduced in a given jurisdiction.

Failure to update job evaluations is most likely to occur in organizations that have depended on outside consultants to develop and implement their job evaluation systems. Once the consultants leave, the tendency is to just forget about the system, especially if the consultants have not provided internal employees with the expertise to maintain the job evaluation system. As a part of any consulting contract, the organization should ensure that the consultant trains internal staff so that they have a full understanding of the job evaluation system and are able to maintain it. Otherwise, provisions will have to be made to retain the consultant on a continuing basis.

The gender pay gap persists in Canada.

# CONFORMING TO PAY EQUITY REQUIREMENTS

Up until now, we have described generic job evaluation procedures. Using them effectively *should* ensure gender equity. However, given concerns about gender bias in pay in Canada,[11] many Canadian jurisdictions do not want to leave this to chance and have imposed specific procedures on employers for ensuring pay equity.[12] In this final section, we address the complexities of conforming to specific pay equity requirements—a subject that is not well understood by the general public.[13] Although some experts remain to be convinced that gender bias is a problem, or that pay equity laws are an appropriate solution, many studies have found that gender bias exists.[14] Compensation Today 7.1 provides an example of a unique approach to researching this issue.

---

## COMPENSATION TODAY 7.1

### WOULD I BE TREATED THIS WAY IF I WERE A MAN?

Many female employees have asked themselves this question. In the past, studies purporting to find gender bias in pay have been criticized on the grounds that any differences found between pay for males and pay for females doing work of a different nature but of "equal value" have not been able to use proper experimental designs. The best experimental design is where the key variable of interest (in this case, gender) is changed for some members of the experimental group but not for others, and the before and after results are compared for each group of subjects. Obviously, this experimental design is not feasible here.

Or is it? Two researchers have come up with a unique solution to this problem of experimental design. Their subjects consist of people residing in the United States who did change genders, about half from male to female, and half from female to male. What they found was that the average earnings of female to male subjects increased slightly, while the pay of male to female subjects dropped by about one-third. While women who became men didn't gain much, at least in terms of pay, men who became women lost a lot.

In a follow-up study at the University of Amsterdam in the Department of Economics, the authors explored the earnings of transsexuals. The authors found that men who were to transition to women earned the same as other men before their transition, and women who were to transition to men earned the same as other men before their transition. When the men transitioned to women, they received 20–25 percent less when they became female. However, this was not the case for women who transitioned to men. Though this study was from a different continent and seven years later, the findings remains similar.

Source: Kristen Schilt and Matthew Wiswall, "Before and After: Gender Transitions, Human Capital, and Workplace Experiences," *The B.E. Journal of Economic Analysis and Policy* 8, no. 1 (2008): Article 39 (online); Lydia Geijtenbeek and Erik Plug, "Is There a Penalty for Becoming a Woman? Is There a Premium for Becoming a Man? Evidence From a Sample of Transsexual Workers," *IZA Discussion Paper No. 9077* (2015).

We focus on compliance with the Ontario Pay Equity Act (OPEA) to illustrate the process because Ontario is the largest jurisdiction, because the original Quebec legislation is patterned after Ontario's (Quebec recently made changes to the legislation that are different from Ontario's approach, including child care policies), and because the OPEA has broad application (i.e., it covers all employers with 10 employees or more). In contrast, most of the other jurisdictions that have pay equity legislation (Manitoba, New Brunswick, Nova Scotia, Prince Edward Island, Yukon, and the federal jurisdiction) cover only public sector employees. (The exception is the Northwest Territories, where the legislation applies only to private sector workers.) The Pay Equity Task Force, commissioned by the federal government, concluded in 2004 that the Ontario model should be applied to all employers under federal jurisdiction;[15] however, this change has not occurred as yet even though the current federal government has recently revisited the issue. Recent research has shown that the OPEA has succeeded in reducing (but not eliminating) the gender wage gap in Ontario.[16]

Listed below are the main steps in the Ontario process. Each will be discussed in turn. (Detailed information is available on the Ontario Pay Equity Commission website.)

1. Determine what rules apply.
2. Identify female and male job classes.
3. Establish a body for conducting the pay equity process
4. Select a gender-neutral job comparison system.
5. Collect job information.
6. Compare jobs.
7. Check for permissible differences.
8. Adjust compensation.
9. Communicate the results.
10. Maintain pay equity.

## THE GENDER PAY GAP IN CANADA—IT MATTERS WHERE YOU LIVE!

According to a study by Catalyst Canada, a Toronto-based research organization, Canadian working women are making about $8000 less a year than men doing equivalent job. This makes the gender pay gap in Canada twice the global average pay gap, which is around $4000.

A study by Glassdoor in 2019 included over half a million salaries reported by employers over three years. Researchers found, among countries considered in their study, which included the United States, United Kingdom, France, Germany, Australia, the Netherlands, and Singapore, that Canada sat in the middle in terms of the pay gaps. Germany had the widest gap, while France had the smallest. Women in Canada earned 84 cents for every $1 made by men, which is a 16.1 percent male pay advantage. However, the study went further and calculated an "adjusted pay gap," where they considered aspects such as education, years on the job, occupation, and title. The difference between men and women decreased, where women then earned 96 cents for every $1, which is a four percent male pay advantage. When considering the adjusted pay gap, Canada had the second smallest pay gap and tied with France. The Netherlands had the most substantial adjusted difference.

Though a better outcome for Canada, this four percent difference is still an issue. When researchers calculated the implications of the adjusted difference, they used the United States as an example. The United States had a 4.9 percent adjusted difference. Considering the 4.9 percent with the average American annual salary reported as $55 450, women lose $81 000 over a 30-year working life.

Researchers from Statistics Canada have noted, "Given that women in Canada have surpassed men in educational attainment, diversified their fields of study at post-secondary institutions, and increased their representation in higher-status occupations, the persistence of gender-based wage inequality warranted continued attention."[17] Women's decisions to take time off to have children or choose jobs that do not lead to advancement are often blamed for the gap. Alex Johnston, Executive Director of Catalyst Canada, says that the gap exists even when these factors are removed. Citing a recent study that tracked MBA graduates since 2008, Johnston says that the differences can be seen in the different opportunities that men and women are offered early in their careers. As a result, even though women comprise nearly half of the Canadian labour force, they made up just 5.3 percent of Canadian CEOs and held just 15.9 percent of board seats in S&P/TSX 60 companies. Even when they do possess C-suite positions, the pay difference is the widest at this level.

Another research project by Canadian Centre for Policy Alternatives shows a ranking of Canadian cities by the gender wage gap. Victoria takes overall top spot in the survey in terms of success in addressing this issue—it is the only major Canadian city where there are more women than men on municipal council. Gatineau comes in a close second and, while it has the lowest gender wage gap in the country, women can still expect to make only 87 percent of what men make. Oshawa can be proud of its efforts in getting women into executive seats—44 percent of senior managers are women. On the other side of the ranking, women in Kitchener-Waterloo face the biggest gender pay gap in the country—earning just 66 percent of what men do.

Yet another and a more recent study of the gender pay gap across cities in Canada had slightly different findings. The top three cities where the gender pay gap was relatively small included Kingston, Ontario, St. John's, Newfoundland, and Victoria, British Columbia. However, the difference between first-place Kingston and last-place Barrie was 7.1 percentage points, which means that the difference between the best and worst is very large. However, the most substantial gaps between the "best" and "worst" cities were factors such as gender and leadership, the education domain (wherein the "worst" cities women representation in a STEM field was low), and economic opportunity (including factors such as level of employment, employment income, and poverty relative to men).

Sources: Mary Beach, "Gender Pay Gap More Than Twice Global Average." *The Globe and Mail*, May 5, 2015; Nicola Middlemiss, "Kitchener-Waterloo Worst for Women," *HRM Canada*, July 20, 2015; Erica Alini, "Women in Canada Earn Less Than Men- Even for the Same Job: Glassdoor," *Global News*, March 26, 2019; Armina Ligaya, "Canada's Gender Wage Gap Narrows: Women Earn $4.13 Less Than Men Per Hour," *Global News*, October 7, 2019; Katherine Scott, "The Best and Worst Places to be a Woman in Canada 2019," *Canadian Centre for Policy Alternatives*, March 2019.

# DETERMINE WHAT RULES APPLY

If your organization employs fewer than 10 people in Ontario (including part-time employees), Ontario pay equity laws do not apply. They also do not apply if your organization is in the federal jurisdiction. Slightly different procedures apply to private sector employers with 10–99 employees than to employers with 100 or more. The differences relate to the requirement that the pay equity plan be "posted." All public sector employers and all private sector employers with 100 or more employees must formalize their pay equity plan in a format outlined by the OPEA and post it where all employees have easy access to it. Smaller private sector employers have the option of posting a plan or not posting. Those that do not post it are required to inform any requesting employee of the process that was conducted to achieve pay equity and the results of this process.

These differences aside, the general process for pay equity is the same for all employers covered by the Act. First, the number of pay equity plans needs to be determined. If the organization is unionized, it needs one pay equity plan for each bargaining unit in an establishment, and one for all non-union employees within the same establishment. If the firm is not unionized, there will generally be only one pay equity plan. A single employer may differentiate employees by geographical region and thus may have two or more "establishments" within the province. This would entitle the employer to have different pay equity plans for each establishment.

# IDENTIFY FEMALE AND MALE JOB CLASSES

The second step in the pay equity process is to determine whether your organization has any female job classes within each pay equity plan. A job class is a group of jobs that have similar duties, require similar qualifications, are filled by similar recruitment procedures, and have the same compensation schedule. Female job classes are those in which (1) at least 60 percent of employees holding them are women, (2) females have traditionally dominated this job class, or (3) most people commonly associate the job with female employees.

Thus, you may have no job classes that are 60 percent female, but if you have jobs that are covered under points (2) or (3), then you still have a female job class. For example, if your company has two secretaries, one of whom is male, you still must consider "secretary" a female job class. Even if your organization employs just one nurse, who happens to be male, the "nurse" job class must be considered a female job class.

If your organization has no female job classes, then there is no need to go any further in the pay equity process. But if it does, the next step is to determine whether there are any male job classes in the same pay equity plan. Male job classes are defined by the same criteria as above, except that 70 percent is the minimum proportion of male jobholders necessary for a job class to be considered a male job class. If there are no male job classes in that pay equity plan, then the pay equity process does not apply unless the firm has two or more pay equity plans and one of those has a male job class, or unless the firm is in the public sector and is allowed to use the "proxy approach" to job comparison (see later in this chapter). Of course, if the firm later creates any male job classes, pay equity will then apply.

# ESTABLISH A BODY FOR CONDUCTING THE PAY EQUITY PROCESS

If pay equity laws do apply, the next step is to carry out the pay equity process. If there is a bargaining agent, the Act requires that that agent be fully involved in all aspects of the pay equity process. This is usually done through a joint union–management pay equity committee. Although not required for non-union employers, it is strongly recommended that employers also establish a joint employee–management pay equity committee.

The benefits of such a committee were discussed earlier in this chapter in the section on job evaluation committees. However, it is probably even more important to establish such a committee for the pay equity process. The diverse viewpoints likely to be found among committee members will help ensure that potential pay inequities are identified. This body can also serve as a communications mechanism and create more employee confidence in the process and its results.

This committee should have a mix of employees who hold various jobs throughout the organization and should include both female and male members if possible. Training in the pay equity process is essential for members. Moreover, it is useful to establish some ground rules for committee operation, covering issues such as confidentiality, decision-making processes, and the role of the committee and its members.

## SELECT A GENDER-NEUTRAL JOB COMPARISON SYSTEM

The committee needs to identify and develop a gender-neutral job evaluation system that allows comparison of job classes in terms of the four required factor groups: skill, effort, responsibility, and working conditions. The most commonly used system for pay equity is the point method. While the ranking and classification methods can be adapted to meet the requirements of pay equity laws, these are probably worthwhile only if the organization already uses them and is happy with them.

## COLLECT JOB INFORMATION

The next step is to gather information for evaluating the jobs. This is the process of job analysis described earlier in the chapter. Key here is avoiding gender biases as well as the pitfalls in the job analysis process that were described earlier.

## COMPARE JOBS

After the information has been collected, the committee applies the job evaluation system to each job class and develops a job hierarchy (one for each pay equity plan). There are three main approaches to comparing female and male job classes: job to job, proportional value, or proxy (only for public sector employers).

## JOB-TO-JOB METHOD

**job-to-job method**
Establishes pay equity by comparing a female job class to a male class that is comparable in terms of job evaluation criteria.

In the **job-to-job method**, a male job class "comparator" is sought for each female job class. This comparator male class needs to be similar to the female class by having an equal or comparable number of points as the female job class, not by job similarities. For example, if the "electrician" job class has a similar point total to the "nurse" job class, then the "electrician" class can serve as the comparator job class for the nurse class. If there are two or more male comparator classes similar in point totals to one female class, the appropriate one is the lower paid. (Incidentally, neither the OPEA nor the Pay Equity Commission provides any guidance on exactly how similar the point totals have to be before the female and male job classes are considered "equal or comparable.")

The committee then compares total compensation (including benefits) for the two jobs. If the male job class (electrician) is receiving higher pay than the female job class (nurse), then pay inequity *may* exist and, if so, will need to be corrected.

What if there is no male job class at the same level in the job hierarchy to use as a comparator? In this case, if the organization has other pay equity plans at other establishments, the other pay plan(s) should be checked to see if an equivalent male comparator job class can be found there. If not, an attempt should be made to identify male job classes that are of lower value (according to job evaluation) but that are being paid more than the female job class. If several male job classes match this criterion, the appropriate comparator is the one with the *highest* pay rate. But what if a suitable comparator still cannot be found?

## Proportional Value Method

The next course of action is the **proportional value method**, which was introduced in mid-1993 to deal with the problem of lack of a male comparator, which can occur in the job-to-job method. The proportional value method requires the employer to calculate what a male job class at the same point in the job hierarchy where the female job is placed would *theoretically* pay, based on data only from the other male job classes.

Let us use a simple example. Suppose that an organization has one female job class (label it "F1") and two male job classes ("M1" and "M2"). The job evaluation points and hourly pay rates (including benefits) for these jobs are as follows:

- M2: 800 points ($24 per hour)
- F1: 600 points ($15 per hour)
- M1: 400 points ($12 an hour)

As can be seen, there is no equivalent male comparator for the female job class, so the job-to-job method cannot be used. There is a gap in the male job hierarchy at 600 points, but we can use proportional value to fill this gap by examining classes M1 and M2 to see what a male class evaluated at 600 points would theoretically pay. Job classes M1 and M2 would be plotted on a graph, a straight line would be drawn that fits these points (very simple in this example, with just two points), and then 600 points would be read from the graph, which would be $18 per hour. (In fact, in this example, no complicated calculations are really necessary to show that a male job midway between 400 and 800 points would pay $18 an hour.)

*What we have apparently found is pay inequity because class F1 is receiving only $15 an hour. This $3 inequity must be corrected, unless it is found to stem from what are known as "permissible differences." If the entire difference does result from permissible differences, it is not considered to be a pay inequity, and no pay adjustments are required.*

## Proxy Comparison Method

What if the proportional value approach doesn't work either, because there are no male job classes (or only one)? For most organizations, this brings the pay equity process to a halt. But in what is known as the "broader public sector" (which includes municipal governments, colleges, hospitals, and the like), the **proxy comparison method** must then be used. In this method, the employer must select another public sector employer that has completed pay equity procedures and collect information on the female job classes in that "proxy" organization. This information is then subjected to job evaluation, and the proportional value method is used to calibrate the employer's female job classes. The key issue in this process is, of course, selection of the proxy employer.

## CHECK FOR PERMISSIBLE DIFFERENCES

Pay differences are not considered pay inequities if they are due to "permissible differences." So, what are these permissible differences? In the words of the Ontario Pay Equity Commission, **permissible differences** are allowed "where the employer is able to show that the difference is the result of the following: a formal seniority system, a temporary training or developmental assignment, a merit compensation plan, red-circling, or a temporary skills shortage."[18] (The "merit compensation plan" must be based on formal criteria and be communicated to all employees in order to be eligible as a permissible difference.)

Note, however, that the use of a permissible difference does not necessarily exclude a male job class from being used as a comparator. In some cases, permissible differences will account for the entire gap between a female job class and a male one; in other cases, however, they will account for only a portion of the difference. In such cases, the remaining portion must be addressed.

Besides those reasons cited above, there are two other allowable reasons for a difference between female and male pay. One is bargaining strength. Under the Act, after "pay equity has been achieved in an establishment, differences in compensation between a female job class and male job class are permissible if the employer is able to show that the difference is the result of differences in bargaining strength."[19] But just how does an employer show that? Neither the OPEA nor the guidelines provided by the Pay Equity Commission offer any guidance on that question, although both emphasize that the onus is on the employer to prove that an exception based on bargaining strength meets the requirements of the Act. It appears that this section of the Act has never been used successfully. Compensation Today 7.3 discusses an interesting case involving unions.

The other allowable reason is very rarely encountered. Where an arbitrator or other tribunal *not* related to interest arbitration (interest arbitration is used to determine pay and benefits when the union and management reach an impasse in the bargaining process) raises the pay of a male comparator job class, the employer may select a different male comparator job class and, if one cannot be found, may use the proportional value method instead. This provision can be used only after pay equity has been achieved in the first instance, and it may serve to limit the requirement to maintain pay equity over time.

There is one other possible exception in the pay equity process. An employer (in conjunction with the bargaining agent, if any) may designate certain jobs as "casual." Casual jobs do not fall under the purview of pay equity legislation. However, there are strict limitations on using this designation. A job *cannot* be designated as casual when:

**a.** the work is performed for at least one-third of the normal work period that applies to similar full-time work; or

**b.** the work is performed on a seasonal basis in the same position for the same employer; or

**c.** the work is performed on a regular and continuing basis, although for less than one-third of the normal work period that applies to similar full-time work.

Given these constraints, very few jobs can be classified as "casual."[20]

permissible differences
Pay differences between female and male job classes that are not considered inequitable because they stem from certain specified allowable circumstances, such as seniority.

## NEGOTIATING PAY EQUITY AGREEMENTS WITH BARGAINING AGENTS

Following a pay equity complaint in 2002, Ottawa Public Library (OPL) reached an agreement with Ottawa–Carleton Public Employees' Union (CUPE) Local 503 in January 2006 to implement a pay equity plan. The parties agreed that the City of Ottawa would be the establishment for the purposes of pay equity, and male comparators were chosen from the City of Ottawa (the City), who were also represented by CUPE Local 503. The pay equity plan gave retroactive increases to applicable employees, set a 2.25 percent and 2.75 percent increase for 2005 and 2006, respectively, and set out a salary adjustments formula with respect to the years 2005 and 2006. At the time the agreement was negotiated, the parties were aware that an interest arbitration was going to determine wage increases for the Inside/Outside Unit male comparators. In March 2006, the interest arbitration awarded the Inside/Outside unit a three percent wage increase in each of 2005 and 2006. A second interim award released in December 2006 resulted in a further three percent wage increase for 2007, and the final award, issued in December 2007, awarded a 3.25 percent wage increase for 2008. The collective bargaining process involving the CUPE Local 503 and the OPL resulted in lower negotiated wage increases for the years 2005, 2006, and 2008 than were achieved for the Inside/Outside unit through interest arbitration. Consequently, a pay equity gap was created between the OPL's female job classes and the City of Ottawa's male job class comparators.

The Review Officer's Order (the directive from the officer assigned by the Pay Equity Commission) determined that the pay equity agreement reached in January 2006 achieved pay equity, and therefore the OPL was not required to eliminate the gap created by the 2005 and 2006 wage adjustments awarded to the City of Ottawa's Inside/Outside unit. The union made an application to dispute that part of the Order. The Review Officer also found that the Library Board failed to maintain pay equity with respect to matching economic increases awarded to male comparators since 2008 in the Inside/Outside unit with the rates of compensation of female job classes in the OPL's bargaining unit. The employer took issue with that conclusion in its application, and the matter was decided by the Pay Equity Tribunal. The key rulings were:

**a.** The Tribunal found that the wording of the agreement of the parties was not clear and after hearing evidence of the negotiations, determined that there was no agreement that pay equity was achieved. Because not all the adjustments contemplated under the pay equity plan had been implemented, under the PEA, pay equity is not achieved until all adjustments owing are paid out. Therefore, the Tribunal found pay equity was not achieved. Accordingly, the Tribunal found the agreement was intended to provide a point-in-time comparator to allow the parties to immediately implement retroactive payments and left open the possibility of subsequent maintenance adjustments if the Inside/Outside plan pay rates were subsequently altered.

**b.** With regard to bargaining strength (a defence brought up by OPL and a "permissible difference" that may be allowed under the Act), because the Tribunal had determined that pay equity had not been achieved, the OPL arguably could not rely on this defence [section 8(2)]. The Tribunal did assess the issue and found that even if the defence was available, the OPL had not met the burden to demonstrate on a balance of probabilities that the differences in wages achieved by the union in 2005, 2006, and 2008 for the Inside/Outside unit as compared to the OPL unit over the same period were due to a differences in bargaining strength. The OPL argued the Inside/Outside unit is bigger (in the sense that it contains far more employees), more diverse in jobs and services, and has a greater impact on the health and safety of the citizens of and visitors to the City of Ottawa; the collective agreement covering the Inside/Outside unit has an interest arbitration clause whereas the collective agreement applicable to the OPL unit does not.

What are the take-aways from this story? When negotiating pay equity agreements, be clear as to the intentions of the parties. In the absence of an agreement, the provisions of the PEA will apply. Pay, equity once achieved, must be maintained with rare exceptions as the exemptions under bargaining strength [s. 8 (2)] will rarely be successful.

Sources: *Ottawa Public Library Board v Ottawa-Carleton Public Employees Union*, 2015 CanLII 6950 (ON PEHT); *Ottawa Citizen*, "Ottawa Library Faces $2.3 Million Pay Equity Tab," February 11, 2015.

While pay equity must be applied to all except designated "casual" employees, it does not have to be applied to all independent contractors. However, the conditions for this exclusion are stringent. For example, individuals who provided day care for children in their own homes were deemed to be employees of an Ontario county (and thus subject to pay equity provisions); they were not deemed to be independent contractors, as the county had maintained. The day care providers filed their income tax returns as self-employed persons, held their own general liability insurance, and purchased most of their own equipment. However, because the county had a rigorous selection process for providers, often had a lengthy relationship with them, exercised control through its placement procedures, held regular mandatory orientation and training sessions, made regular inspection visits, and had established discipline and termination procedures, the Pay Equity Tribunal deemed them to be employees, not independent contractors. In a recent case illustrating the challenges in determining wo are independent contractors, drivers working for Uber Technologies Inc. sought $200 million in damages for anyone who worked for Uber in Ontario since 2012. While the drivers argued that they should be considered employees, the company claimed that the drivers were independent contractors due to the flexible nature of the job, the ability of drivers to set their schedule, and the control that comes with being their own boss. However, the Ontario courts debated just how much control the drivers really had and deemed the drivers as employees. They stated several examples, such as the drivers being forced to partake in inspections, the drivers being required to use the Uber phone application, and the fact that Uber paid the drivers at set intervals.[21]

## ADJUST COMPENSATION

The Ontario pay equity legislation does not necessarily require employers to correct the full extent of pay inequities immediately (although the employer may well decide to do so, if this is within its financial means), as long as the employer has "posted" its pay equity plan. Essentially, this means that all employees have been provided access to the process that was conducted in determining pay equity and have received their own personal copy if they have requested it. (New employers coming under the purview of the Act are expected to correct pay inequities immediately, regardless of whether they post a pay equity plan.)

If an employer has posted a pay equity plan, it must devote at least one percent of the previous year's payroll toward correcting pay inequities. This must then be done every year until all inequities are corrected. If the one percent is not sufficient to correct the inequities, the OPEA specifies how the available money will be distributed:

- The [inequitable female] job class or classes with the lowest job rate in the plan must receive a greater adjustment than other [inequitable female] job classes in the same plan until pay equity is achieved.
- Each female job class must receive an adjustment each year until pay equity is achieved.
- All positions in a job class will receive the same adjustments in dollar terms.[22]

Finally, with regard to employers who are tempted to avoid higher compensation costs, the Act specifically prohibits the achievement of pay equity through the lowering of pay levels for male comparator jobs.

## COMMUNICATE THE RESULTS

Once the pay equity plan has been developed, it should be communicated to employees so that they understand both the process and the results. The only organizations *required* to post their pay equity plans are public sector employers and private sector employers with 100 or more employees. However, an employer that does not post its plan is obligated under the Act to disclose both the process undertaken to ensure pay equity and the results of that process to any employee who asks.

Monkey Business Images/Shutterstock.com

In some jurisdictions, there is legislation on equal pay for work of equal value.

## MAINTAIN PAY EQUITY

Even organizations that have achieved pay equity are not free of their OPEA obligations. Employers are responsible for actively ensuring that pay equity is maintained over time. Many changes can occur in an organization that can affect pay equity. These include:

- restructuring within the organization
- certification of a bargaining agent after a deemed-approved plan changes in the gender of a job class,
- new or vanishing job classes,
- a new male comparator job class for a female job class,
- a change in the value of work performed in a job class,
- a change in compensation system or compensation levels.[23]

Let us now examine each of these briefly.

## Structural or Bargaining Agent Change

Various types of organizational restructuring may trigger a review of pay equity. For example, when one firm takes over or merges with another, the pay system must be reviewed for equity, looking at all jobs under the new structure. When a new bargaining agent is certified, or an old bargaining agent is *de*certified, it will be necessary either to create another pay equity plan or to merge the previous pay equity plans.

## Gender Changes in a Job Class

If the workforce changes such that the percentage of males and females in a particular job class changes, then this class may change from male to female, from female to male, from one of these to gender-neutral, or from gender-neutral to one of these. However, a change in the percentage of males and females does not automatically change the gender status of the job class. For example, if the percentage of secretaries who are female changes from 95 percent to 50 percent, this does not mean that the secretary job class will be reclassified as gender-neutral. In this case, "secretary" would stay a female job class because historically this has been a female job and because of the existence of a stereotype that this is a female job.

## New Job Classes

Sometimes an employer creates a new job class, which then must be assessed for gender. If it turns out to be a female job class, then the process described earlier applies, where the job-to-job or proportional value approach must be used to check for inequity. If a new male job class is created, two questions need to be asked: Should this job be used as a comparator to a female job class (if the job-to-job method is used)? And does this job affect the value for jobs established through a proportional value system?

## Vanishing Job Classes

Sometimes a job class will vanish. Reasons may include technological change, company restructuring, or the sale or closure of a business or unit. If a female job class vanishes or its gender changes, "its incumbents must be paid the full amount of their pay equity adjustments owing up until the date on which the job class disappears."[24]

If a male job class vanishes, the implications depend on whether the job-to-job or proportional value method has been used. If the job-to-job method has been used and the vanished male job class had been used as a comparator, a new comparator must be found. But if the new comparator is paid less than the female class, compensation for the female class cannot be lowered. If the proportional value method has been used, the usual procedure is to remove that class from the male job pay line (as discussed earlier in conjunction with the "proportional value method") and then to reassess female jobs against the new male pay line. But if the results indicate a lower pay level for the female job class(es), their pay cannot be reduced from their original pay equity entitlement.

## Job Value Changes

Sometimes a male or female job class changes in value, especially if duties or job requirements change. If the change is significant enough to warrant a change in position in the job hierarchy (the employer determines this repositioning through its gender-neutral job evaluation process), the pay level needs to be reassessed in the manner described earlier. Then, depending on whether it is a female or male job, the procedures described above apply.

## Compensation Changes

Various changes in the compensation system or compensation levels may have implications for pay equity. For example, if a male job class comparator receives a compensation increase greater than that received by the female job class, pay equity is threatened. Even when the female job class and its comparator receive equal percentage increases, if these percentages apply before the female job has achieved full pay equity, the pay increase actually widens the pay gap between the male and female jobs. In both these cases, money must be found to reclose these gaps, and this money cannot be deducted from the one percent minimum of annual payroll already dedicated to eliminating pay equity gaps.

## Communication about Pay Equity Plan Changes

If any of these changes occur and have pay equity implications, the employer (or, if there is a bargaining agent, the employer and the bargaining agent) must revise the pay equity plan accordingly and repost it. The only employers not required to repost changes to their pay equity plan are those employing fewer than 100 employees and those that did not post a plan originally.

## Pay Equity in the Federal Jurisdiction

In 2018, Canada introduced historic proactive pay equity legislation for those working under the federal jurisdiction. The legislation was enacted to establish a fair compensation process and ensure equal pay for work of equal value. The act pertains to federally regulated employers with 10 or more employees, including parliamentary workplaces, the Prime Minister's and Ministers' offices, banks, airports, airlines, and telecommunications companies.

On the day of the act's passing, the Minister of Status of Women, Maryam Monsef, stated, "Today's introduction of proactive pay equity legislation is a historic step to advance gender equality and help eliminate the gender wage gap. Women have waited too long to receive equal pay for work of equal value. Proactive pay equity for federally regulated employees, along with investments our government has made in quality childcare, affordable housing and poverty reduction, as well as measures we have brought in to create more flexible work arrangements, promote more women in STEM fields, the trades, and entrepreneurship, and ensure zero tolerance for workplace harassment and violence, will increase women's financial security, grow the middle class, and strengthen our economy so that all Canadians benefit."[25]

The legislation places the onus on employers in federally regulated workplaces to scrutinize their compensation practices. Before this act was in place, Ontario and Quebec were the only two jurisdictions in Canada with a proactive approach to pay equity in both the public and private sectors. The federal government previously had pay equity under a complaint-based system. Thus, employers were not required to actively analyze their compensation practices and employees were held responsible for making a formal complaint.[26]

The new legislation requires employers to institute a pay equity plan within three years of being subjected to the act. The program must outline the number of employees and job classes in their workplace and the gender makeup within the job classes. Then the employer would appraise the value of work performed by each job, determine the compensation related to each job class, and compare the compensation between female-predominant (60 percent or more) and male-predominant job classes of similar value. The employer would outline the results and adjust the compensation for female-predominant jobs that are underpaid, and supply details of the dispute resolution procedures. Pay equity plans must then be reviewed and amended every five years. Furthermore, in unionized settings, or non-unionized employers with 100 or more employees, a pay equity committee must be established to develop or update the pay equity plan. Lastly, employees must be provided with the chance to comment on the proposed plan before it is completed and implemented.[27]

In addition to the required steps for employers, Canada introduced the first-ever Pay Equity Commissioner in September 2019.[28] The Pay Equity Commissioner was appointed to play roles in both education and enforcement of the legislation. The Commission, alongside subject-matter experts, will help individuals understand their rights under the act, and facilitate dispute resolution of pay equity. The Commissioner has the power to enact enforcement, using audits, investigations, and the ability to issue orders and monetary penalties.[29]

Employers with 10–99 employees who are found in violation of the act could face penalties of up to $30 000 per day, while those with 100 or more employees are up to $50 000 per day. The bill establishes remuneration for various forms of payment, including salaries, commissions, vacation pay, bonuses, employer contributions to pension plans, and health insurance plans.[30]

. . . . . . . . . . . . . . . . . . . . . . . . . . . . . . . . . . . . . . . . . . . . . . . . . . . . . . . . . . . . . . . . . . . . . . . . . . . . . . . . . . . . . . . . . . . . .

# SUMMARY

The purpose of this chapter has been to start developing your understanding of the key technical processes necessary to transform the compensation strategy into an operating compensation system, beginning with the process for evaluating jobs. Not all organizations will decide to use job evaluation. But for those that do, this chapter has provided the fundamentals of how to develop an effective job evaluation system. It has explained the process of job analysis, which provides the information (known as a "job description") that is the foundation for any effective job evaluation system. It has described various job analysis methods, and it has outlined some possible pitfalls in the process.

The five main methods for job evaluation (ranking/paired comparison, classification/grading, factor comparison, statistical/policy capturing, and the point method) were discussed. Chapter 8 will be devoted to the most common method: the point method.

For job evaluation to be both equitable and seen to be equitable, a process for conducting and managing job evaluation is crucial. Organizations need to work out procedures for who will conduct the job evaluation, how it will be communicated, how results will be applied, how procedural justice can be established, and how job evaluations will be updated.

Finally, many jurisdictions have pay equity legislation which mandate specific procedures for identifying jobs for which there is gender inequity in pay and for correcting any inequities thereby detected. Although these laws vary somewhat across jurisdictions, most of them are modelled on Ontario's pay equity legislation. Because of this, and because Ontario is the largest single jurisdiction, this chapter has presented you with an overview of the process for achieving and maintaining pay equity in Ontario.

## KEY TERMS

classification/grading method
factor comparison method
job analysis
job description
job specifications
job-to-job method
paired comparison method

permissible differences
point method
proportional value method
proxy comparison method
ranking method
statistical/policy capturing method

## DISCUSSION QUESTIONS

1. Discuss the purpose of job evaluation and the main steps in conducting job evaluation.

2. Discuss the advantages and potential pitfalls of job analysis.

3. Discuss the key aspects of ranking/paired comparisons and classification/grading methods of doing job evaluations.

4. Discuss the issue of red-circled employees and the way they should be handled. Assume that your current or most recent employer has developed a new pay structure and that 20 percent of current employees are above their new maximum pay ranges. How should you deal with this problem?

5. Discuss the general process for conforming to pay equity legislation. Does legislating pay equity seem like a good idea to you?

6. What is the gender pay gap in Canada? Can pay equity legislation close this gap? Why? Why not?

## EXERCISES

1. To trace the steps required to create a gender-neutral job evaluation system that complies with Ontario Pay Equity legislation, go to http://www.payequity.gov.on.ca/en/tools/Pages/space_toy_co.aspx.

2. Complete the position analysis questionnaire for your most recent job found at https://www.asu.edu/hr/documents/PAQuestionnaire.pdf). Bring the results to class. In small groups, share your position analysis information and develop a job description for each job from that information.

3. In your class, do a quick anonymous survey of the pay of students (in their current or last job). Ask each student to write only his/her gender and pay on a piece of paper without personal identifiers. Is there a gender pay gap? Discuss your results. If there is a gap, what could be some of the reasons for it?

4. Examine the job description presented below. Using the information in Compensation Notebook 7.1, assess whether this is a good job description and what improvements could be made to it.

---

**Beaver Manufacturing Corporation**

**Job Title: Drafter 1**                    **Department: Engineering (Drafting Section)**
**Reports to: Head of Drafting**                              **Updated: January 15, 2016**

**Job Purpose**

This employee uses computer-aided design (CAD) techniques to produce and update drawings of plant facilities, based on rough sketches, diagrams, notes, and verbal instructions provided by design engineers.

---

**Main Job Duties** (listed duties are illustrative, not restrictive)

1. Prepare finished CAD drawings from sketches, diagrams, notes, and verbal instructions.
2. Search computer databases for existing information on which to base drawings.
3. Meet with engineers to clarify drawing requirements and to discuss revisions to drawings.
4. Assist with site verifications of existing facilities.
5. Share in filing of facilities records.
6. Assist other staff in locating facilities records information.

**Other Job Information**

Works under the supervision of senior drafters, who check product before sending it to engineers for final approval. Engineers provide final check on output. If undetected, errors can cause serious facilities damage. Basic keyboarding skills and ability to use computer-assisted design equipment are required. Considerable concentration is required to transform input materials into finished product. Work is mainly performed in a quiet office environment. Some exterior facilities inspection required.

**Job Specifications**

High school graduation plus a two-year diploma in computer-assisted design from a recognized technical institute. Ability to communicate effectively in verbal and nonverbal modes.

## CASE QUESTION

1. Read *Case 7—Eastern Provincial University* in the Appendix. Examine the job descriptions that are used at the university. What are their strengths and weaknesses? What would you change about them?

## SIMULATION CROSS-REFERENCE

If you are using *Strategic Compensation: A Simulation* in conjunction with this text, you will find that the concepts in Chapter 7 are helpful in preparing the simulation.

# ENDNOTES

1. Ian King, Compensation Administration and Equitable Pay Programs—A Practical Guide (Toronto: CCH Canadian, 1992), 4.

2. S.M. McPhail, P.R. Jeanneret, E.J. McCormick, and R.C. Mecham, *Position Analysis Questionnaire: Job Analysis Manual* (Palo Alto: Consulting Psychologists Press, 1991).

3. W.W. Tornow and P.R. Pinto, "The Development of a Managerial Job Taxonomy: A System for Describing, Classifying, and Evaluating Executive Positions," *Journal of Applied Psychology* 61 (1976): 410–18.

4. J.K. Hemphill, "Job Descriptions for the Executive," *Harvard Business Review* 37 (1954): 55–69.

5. Sidney A. Fine, A.M. Holt, and M.F. Hutchinson, "Functional Job Analysis: How to Standardize Task Statements," *Methods for Manpower Analysis* (Kalamazoo: W.E. Upjohn Institute for Employment Research, 1974).

6. John G. Kelly, *Pay Equity Management* (Toronto: CCH Canadian, 1994), 23; see also Nan Weiner, "Effective Redress of Pay Inequities," *Canadian Public Policy* 28 (2002): S101–S115 for a discussion on how job descriptions can be biased; Brian Beal, "Vive La Difference—But Not in Pay," *Human Resources Management International Digest* 25, no. 2 (2017): 16–18.

7. Parbudyal Singh, "Job Analysis for a Changing Workplace," *Human Resource Management Review* 18, no. 2 (2008): 87–99.

8. Kelly, *Pay Equity Management.*

9. "Policy-Capturing Job Evaluation Methodology Considered," *Focus on Canadian Employment and Equality Rights* 5, no. 28 (2000): 222–23.

10. Howard Levitt, "Pay Severance and Get It Over With!" *Financial Post Online*, April 25, 2007 (online).

11. Pay Equity Task Force, *Pay Equity: A New Approach to a Fundamental Right* (Ottawa: Department of Justice, 2004).

12. Tammy Schirle, "The Gender Pay Gap in the Canadian Provinces, 1997–2014," *Canadian Public Policy* 41, no 4 (2015): 309–19.

13. Anne Forrest, "Pay Equity: The State of the Debate," in *Industrial Relations in the New Millennium: Selected Papers from the XXXVIIth Annual CIRA Conference,* ed. Y. Reshef, C. Bernier, D. Harrisson, and T.H. Wagar, (2001): 65–78; Ontario Nonprofit Network, *Decent Work For Women*, March, 2018, https://theonn.ca/wp-content/uploads/2018/04/Decent-work-for-Women-Literature-Review-March-2018.pdf, accessed January 25, 2020.

14. Kristen Schilt and Matthew Wiswall, "Before and After: Gender Transitions, Human Capital, and Workplace Experiences," *B.E. Journal of Economic Analysis and Policy* 8, no. 1 (2008): Article 39 (online).

15. Pay Equity Task Force, *Pay Equity.*

16. Parbudyal Singh and Ping Peng, "Canada's Bold Experiment with Pay Equity," *Gender in Management: An International Journal* 25, no. 7 (2010): 570–85.

17. Armina Ligaya, "Canada's Gender Wage Gap Narrows: Women Earn $4.13 Less Than Men Per Hour," *Global News*, October 7, 2019, https://globalnews.ca/news/6001276/gender-wage-gap-women-canada/.

18. Pay Equity Commission, *Maintaining Pay Equity: Using the Job-to-Job and Proportional Value Comparison Methods* (Toronto: Ontario Pay Equity Commission, 1995), 32; Pay Equity Commission, *A Guide to Interpreting Ontario's Pay Equity Act,* (Toronto: Ontario Pay Equity Commission, 2019).

19. Ibid.

20. Ibid.

21. "Home Care Providers Entitled to Pay Equity," *Ontario Pay and Employment Equity Guide,* February 2000, 3; Kristine Owram, "Uber Drivers are Employees, Not Contractors, Canadian Lawsuit Argues," *Financial Post,* January 23, 2017, https://business.financialpost.com/transportation/uber-drivers-are-employees-not-contractors-canadian-lawsuit-argues, accessed January 25, 2020.

22. Pay Equity Commission, *Step by Step to Pay Equity: A Guide for Small Business* (Toronto: Ontario Pay Equity Commission, 2011).

23. Ibid.

24. Ibid.

25. Government of Canada, *Government of Canada Introduces Historic Proactive Pay Equity Legislation* (Ottawa: Employment and Social Development Canada, 2018).

26. Ibid.

27. Government of Canada, *Backgrounder: Proactive Pay Equity* (Employment and Social Development, 2018).

28. Canadian Human Rights Commission, *News Release—Canadian Human Rights Commission Welcomes Canada's First Pay Equity Commissioner* (Ottawa: Canadian Human Rights Commission, 2019).

29. Government of Canada, *Government of Canada Introduces Historic Proactive Pay Equity Legislation* (Ottawa: Employment and Social Development Canada, 2018).

30. Jessica Bungay and Chris Pelkey, "Breaking Glass Ceilings," *HR Reporter,* October 30, 2019, https://www.hrreporter.com/employment-law/news/breaking-glass-ceilings/322313, accessed February 1, 2020.

# EVALUATING JOBS:
# THE POINT METHOD
# OF JOB EVALUATION

## Learning Outcomes

AFTER READING THIS CHAPTER, YOU
SHOULD BE ABLE TO:

- Describe the steps in designing a point system of job evaluation.

- Identify the possible pitfalls in designing a point system of job evaluation.

- Design a base pay structure, including pay grades and pay ranges.

## NURSES OR PAINTERS: WHO IS MORE VALUABLE TO A HOSPITAL?

Who performs work that is more valuable to a hospital—nurses or painters? Intuitively, we might think nurses. But that is not what the job evaluation system at a U.S. hospital concluded, and certainly not what their pay scales indicated, as painters were paid considerably more than nurses at that hospital.

Is this really fair? How could we objectively determine which job is more valuable to a hospital? Let us compare the jobs systematically, using the four basic categories of compensable factors required under pay equity legislation.

- Skill: To perform a nurse's job requires medical skills (including a licence and postsecondary training), interpersonal skills, and communication skills. A painter's job requires manual dexterity and the ability to mix paint.

- Effort: A nurse's job requires some physical effort, such as helping to lift patients and standing or walking for extended periods of time. Painters are required to be on their feet constantly, to climb ladders, and to exercise continuous repetitive movement over the entire duration of their shift. However, painters do not need to expend much mental effort, while nurses must continually be alert in order to monitor patients' health and provide correct dosages of medication.

- Responsibility: Nurses are responsible for the health and welfare of human beings. Painters are responsible for neatly painted walls and ceilings.

- Working conditions: Working conditions for painters are often smelly, unpleasant, or dangerous, especially when working at heights, such as when painting ceilings. Working conditions for nurses may also be smelly, unpleasant, or dangerous, as when they need to empty bedpans, clean or bathe patients, clean up pus and vomit, and suffer the risk of contracting communicable diseases from patients. Other unpleasant working conditions of the nurse's job include dealing with patients in severe pain and their distraught family members, in addition to discovering dead patients.

This analysis suggests that a nurse's job should be evaluated more highly than a painter's job on all factors except physical effort, and therefore should be paid more, not less. Why didn't the hospital's job evaluation system pick this up? Because two separate job evaluation systems were used—one for nursing staff and one for maintenance staff.

Which job is more valuable to the organization?

Source: Nan J. Weiner and Morley Gunderson, *Pay Equity: Issues, Options, and Experiences* (Toronto: Butterworths, 1990).

# USING THE POINT METHOD TO DESIGN A JOB EVALUATION SYSTEM

With a properly designed job evaluation (JE) system and base pay structure, inequities such as those found at this hospital should not occur. This chapter first describes how to design a job evaluation system using the point method of job evaluation, then it identifies the pitfalls in so doing, and finally it shows how to develop a base pay structure.

The point method of job evaluation has many advantages, including its high degree of precision in measuring jobs. This method can be applied with a high degree of consistency thereby removing one possible source of employee–management conflict. As well, this system provides not only an ordering of jobs but also the relative value of each job. This information allows jobs to be clustered in pay grades more easily (discussed later in the chapter). It also helps to establish internal equity through a systematic process of evaluating and ranking jobs in terms of their value to the organization.

Another potential advantage of the point method is that a large body of knowledge has been built up about it. Many "ready-made" plans are offered by compensation consulting firms, although using these can be costly and there is no guarantee that the consultant's system will be the best fit with the organization. For firms that cannot afford these services, some good guidebooks are available, as well as web-based materials.[1]

There are five main steps in developing a job evaluation system using the point method:

1. Identify key job characteristics (known as "compensable factors") that differentiate the value of various jobs.

2. Develop a measuring scale for each factor (a process known as "scaling the factors") so that the extent to which each factor is present in a job can be quantified.

3. Weight each factor according to its importance to the firm. This produces a system that can be used to provide a point total for each factor for each job.

4. Apply the job evaluation system to every job included under the JE system. This generates a point total for each job, which then forms the basis for a ranked list of all jobs (the "hierarchy of jobs") included in the JE system.

5. Test the resulting jobs hierarchy for reliability, validity, and market fit, and make any necessary revisions to the JE system. (Revisions are almost always necessary!)

Once the job evaluation system has been finalized, all jobs are scored on the JE system to derive a final hierarchy of jobs, which then serves as the foundation for the base pay structure (see later in the chapter). We now discuss each of the job evaluation steps in turn.

## IDENTIFYING COMPENSABLE FACTORS

**compensable factors**
Characteristics of jobs that are valued by the organization and differentiate jobs from one another.

Compensable factors can be defined as "those characteristics in the work that the organization values, that help it pursue its strategy and achieve its objectives."[2] Compensable factors are based on the work performed, support the strategy and values of the organization, distinguish between jobs, and are acknowledged as significant by employees. These factors typically include job inputs (such as education, training, or experience), job requirements (e.g., mental effort, physical effort, decision making), job outputs (e.g., accuracy of output, consequences of mistakes), and job conditions (e.g., nature of work environment, hazards that may be encountered). The compensable factors are grounded in job analysis, job descriptions, and the job specifications discussed in the previous chapter. In developing a list of potential compensable factors, it is important to examine the job descriptions for job factors that are common across jobs (e.g., education, decision making, physical effort). These factors can then be put into categories. The job specifications would help to determine the range in these factors required to perform these jobs (e.g., minimum of a high school diploma and a maximum of a doctoral degree), discussed in more detail below.

The variety of factors that can be used by different organizations is almost limitless, but four main categories of factors are more or less universal: skill, effort, responsibility, and working conditions. Every point method system of job evaluation should include representation from each of these factor categories. Under pay equity legislation, organizations are required to use these four categories in evaluating work.

For example, "skill" might be represented by the factors of "education" and "experience." "Effort" could be represented by "mental effort" and "physical effort." "Responsibility" might be represented by "consequences of errors" and "value of assets used." Working conditions might be represented by "unpleasantness of work environment" and "hazards to physical safety."

Compensation Notebook 8.1 lists some of the specific factors that can be used by organizations, clustered according to the four factor categories. As the table illustrates, the four categories can include just about any characteristic that an organization might want to measure. Many factors are generic, while others may be more specific to the firm. A customer-oriented firm might include "amount of customer contact" as a compensable factor, thus implying that jobs with more customer contact are more important than those with less. A firm in which innovation and the development of new products and services are important might include a factor titled "amount of innovative behaviour." A firm concerned with costs might have a factor titled "responsibility for cost containment."

How many factors should be used? There is no simple answer to this question. There must be enough that they capture all the key aspects of work that are important to the organization, but not so many that they start to overlap or add very little additional value to the system. In general, the broader the group of jobs to be covered with a single job evaluation system, the greater the number of factors that will be needed. In recent years, there has been a trend toward broadening the inclusiveness of job evaluation systems in order to ensure fairness for all employee groups and also in response to pay equity laws. For example, Ontario's legislation requires single plans for each union bargaining unit, regardless of whether both blue-collar and white-collar jobs are included in the unit; if the organization is not unionized, the law requires that the same job evaluation system cover all jobs at a given establishment.

Overall, it is difficult to see how a valid point system could operate with less than about eight factors (with at least one from each factor category); however, systems that include more than a dozen factors may be including marginal factors that add very little to the ability to differentiate job values.

After the factors have been selected, it is essential to develop a clear definition of each that clearly conveys the meaning of the factor and differentiates it from other factors. If this cannot be done for a given factor, then that factor should be dropped from the system.

One trend has been for some firms to purposely omit certain traditional factors. For example, many firms have the factor "number of subordinates," but some firms have started to drop that factor, for several reasons. One is that an assembly-line supervisor may have 30 subordinates, but these employees are effectively supervised by the technology, whereas the director of a research project may have four subordinates doing highly complex work for which constant supervision, coordination, and interaction are essential. Moreover, this factor implies that managers who expand their staffs will be rewarded, while those who improve efficiency and cut back their staffs will be penalized. Many firms no longer want to send that message.

## EXAMPLES OF COMMONLY USED COMPENSABLE FACTORS

| Skill | Responsibility | Effort | Working Conditions |
|---|---|---|---|
| Ability to do detailed or routine work | Accountability | Mental effort: Attention demand | Bodily fluids |
| Accuracy | Accuracy | Mental effort: Concentration using the five senses | Cleaning up after others |
| Analytical ability | Budget responsibility | Mental effort: Effects from dealing with people | Danger |
| Communicating in a second language | Cash (responsibility for) | Mental effort: Handling complaints or emergencies | Dirtiness |
| Communication skills: Verbal/written | Confidentiality | Mental effort: Listening | Disagreeableness |
| Contacts with public/clients/staff | Contact with the public and/or customers/clients, etc. | Mental effort: Mental strain (intensity, frequency, duration) | Exposure to accident hazard |
| Counselling, advising, or negotiating | Coordination of workflow/tasks | Mental effort: Reading instruments | Exposure to health hazard, eyestrain |
| Creativity | Consequence and/or cost of errors | Mental effort: Verifying columns of numbers | Exposure to toxic chemicals, toners, inks |
| Decision-making | Details | Mental effort: Visual | Infectious diseases, airborne viruses |
| Dexterity | Determining company policy | Mental effort: Watching a computer screen | Injuries: Exposure to machinery, tools, or equipment |
| Education | Effects of volume of work | Physical effort: Assembly | Open office, crowded conditions |
| Experience, on-the-job or off-the-job | Effects on other operations | Physical effort: Bending | Monotony |
| Independence of action | Equipment, machinery | Physical effort: Keyboarding | Physical environment and surroundings |
| Interpersonal skills | Financial decisions | Physical effort: Lifting (children or adults) | Physical or verbal abuse from clients or patients |
| Interpretation or explaining (complexity) | Goodwill and public relations | Physical effort: Lifting (inanimate objects) | Stress of multiple demands |

| Skill | Responsibility | Effort | Working Conditions |
|---|---|---|---|
| Judgment | Information, including confidential | Physical effort: Manual effort | Temperature hot or cold |
| Knowledge: Theoretical and/or technical | Initiative required | Physical effort: Packing | Time pressure |
| Knowledge of machinery | Materials, supplies | Physical effort: Physical strain (intensity, frequency, duration) | Travel, in or out of town, trouble spots |
| Knowledge of materials and processes | Methods | Physical effort: Pushing or pulling | Violence (including the threat of) |
| Licenses or certificates | Payroll | Physical effort: Sitting for long periods of time | |
| Managerial techniques | Personnel | Physical effort: Speed | |
| Manual quickness | Physical property | Physical effort: Standing | |
| Manual or motor skills | Plant and services | | |
| Physical skill (coordination) | Products | | |
| Problem solving | Property | | |
| Resourcefulness | Quality of work | | |
| Social skills | Records | | |
| Training programs or additional self-study | Resources | | |
| Versatility | Safekeeping | | |
| | Safety and health of others | | |
| | Spoilage of materials | | |
| | Storage, usage, maintenance, repair of resources | | |
| | Supervision of others | | |
| | Training, orienting, motivating, evaluating staff | | |
| | Volume of work | | |

Source: © Queen's Printer for Ontario, 2009. Reproduced with permission. This information is subject to change without notice. The most current version can be found at http://www.payequity.gov.on.ca/en/DocsEN/Minikit_EN.pdf

# SCALING THE FACTORS

After the compensable factors have been selected and defined, a number of "degrees" (sometimes called "levels") are established, resulting in a measurement scale for each factor. These degrees represent gradations in the extent to which a certain factor is present in a particular job being rated. For example, it may be decided that there should be five possible "degrees" or levels for the factor of "consequences of error." Each degree needs to be carefully defined and arranged so that degree 2 always contains more of that factor than degree 1, and so on. **Table 8.1** provides examples of factors with their degree definitions.

How many degrees should be used? The number of degrees for a particular factor depends on the range of that factor. There is no reason for all factors in a job evaluation system to have the same number of degrees. For example, if relevant education ranges from elementary school to a university doctorate, then seven or eight degrees might be used. Where the range is from elementary school to completion of high school, only three or four degrees might be used. But at the same time, "working conditions" might be assigned

**TABLE 8.1**

## Sample Compensable Factors Illustrating Degrees

### Factor: Formal Education
This factor deals with the level of formal education required to perform the job.

| | |
|---|---|
| Degree 1: | Completion of Grade 9 |
| Degree 2: | Completion of high school |
| Degree 3: | One year of postsecondary education |
| Degree 4: | Two years of postsecondary education |
| Degree 5: | University bachelor's degree or major professional designation |
| Degree 6: | University master's degree or bachelor's degree plus professional designation |
| Degree 7: | University/medical school doctorate |
| Degree 8: | Medical doctorate plus additional medical specialization |

### Factor: Ingenuity
This factor deals with the need for ingenuity in dealing with problems arising from normal work assignments in this job. It includes the frequency, extent, and importance of ingenuity for successful job performance. It is limited by the amount of guidance/supervision that is available.

| | |
|---|---|
| Degree 1: | Work procedures and problems are standard; very little ingenuity required. |
| Degree 2: | Work procedures and problems are mainly standard; occasional ingenuity required. |
| Degree 3: | Work procedures and problems are often nonstandard; some ingenuity required. |
| Degree 4: | Work procedures are mainly nonstandard; considerable ingenuity required, but considerable guidance available. |
| Degree 5: | Work procedures are mainly nonstandard; considerable ingenuity required and little guidance available; consequences of poor choices of solution are not serious. |
| Degree 6: | Work procedures are mainly nonstandard; high ingenuity required and little guidance available; consequences of poor choices of solution are moderate. |
| Degree 7: | Work procedures are mainly nonstandard; high ingenuity required; little guidance; consequences of poor choices are very serious. |

### Factor: Responsibility for Personnel, Policies and Practices

This factor measures the extent to which key activities and responsibilities are achieved through the direction, management, education, training, evaluation, motivation, and control of the work and of others. It does not measure the interpersonal skills required in other types of contacts. Policies can be health and safety rules or special programs.

| | |
|---|---|
| **Degree 1:** | Provides informal training or instruction to coworkers. |
| **Degree 2:** | Provides functional or technical guidance and/or informal training or instruction to coworkers. Occasionally coordinates work of others. |
| **Degree 3:** | Coordinates the work of others including the assignment of tasks to junior staff. |
| **Degree 4:** | Supervises work within a work unit of subordinates. Determines the training and education needs of subordinates. |
| **Degree 5:** | Supervises work of subordinates. Coordinates the work of others including the assignment of tasks. Responsible for hiring and performance management. |
| **Degree 6:** | Direct and indirect supervision and responsibility for human resources in several work units of subordinates. Consults with subordinates who supervise others about hiring and performance management. |

### Factor: Interpersonal Skills/Contacts

This subfactor measures the job requirement to deal effectively with people both within and outside the organization. This subfactor considers the type, importance, and purpose of contacts and the degree of interpersonal skills required.

| | |
|---|---|
| **Degree 1:** | Contacts are primarily within the organization to exchange straightforward information. |
| **Degree 2:** | Contacts may be both within and outside the organization frequently to exchange information and/or answer routine, straightforward questions. |
| **Degree 3:** | Contacts may be both within and outside the organization frequently to deal with unclear or imprecise requests for information; to provide explanations and instructions on complex issues. |
| **Degree 4:** | Contacts may be both within and outside the organization frequently to deal with unclear or imprecise requests for information; to provide explanations that may be disliked … persuading, influencing, counselling and/or negotiating in work with others. |
| **Degree 5:** | Contacts may be both within and outside the organization frequently to deal with unclear or imprecise requests for information; to provide explanations and leadership on issues. |

Source: © Queen's Printer for Ontario, 2016. Modified and reproduced with permission. This information is subject to change without notice. The most current version can be found at http://www.payequity.gov.on.ca/en/tools/Pages/je12.aspx.

five degrees, and "experience" might be assigned seven degrees, depending on the variation in working conditions in the organization and the variation in experience required by different jobs in the organization.

# WEIGHTING THE FACTORS

The compensable factors that have been selected are not likely to be equal in importance to the firm. To recognize this variation in importance, each factor needs to be weighted according to its relative importance. For example, in one firm, "education" may be viewed as the most important factor, followed by "experience," then "customer contact" and "mental complexity," with "physical environment" considered the least important factor. If the maximum number of points that any job may receive is arbitrarily set at 1000, then the maximum points for education might be set at 350 points, experience at 250 points, customer contact at 200 points, mental complexity at 150 points, and physical environment 50 points.

These points are then distributed across the degrees that were defined in the previous step. For example, if "education" has seven degrees, then degree 1 might be assigned 50 points, degree 2 might be assigned 100 points, and so on, all the way to degree 7, which would be assigned 350 points. However, there is no reason why the point intervals between degrees should be identical, and it may be appropriate in many instances to vary the point intervals between degrees.

How are the factor weights derived? There are two methods—statistical analysis and expert judgment (sometimes known as the "a priori" method). Statistical analysis uses a sample of existing jobs that have already been rated and that are thought to be paid correctly. The existing pay rate for each of these jobs (or the market rate for each job can be used, if it is different from company pay rates) is also fed into the equation. Multiple regression analysis is used to determine the role that each factor plays in influencing the pay rate in this sample of jobs. These weights are then applied to all jobs covered by the job evaluation system.

There are, however, several drawbacks to this approach. One drawback is that it is complex and not easily understood. Another is that it assumes the current pay structure (or the market pay structure, if used) for the sample of benchmark or criterion jobs is appropriate and that all other jobs should be aligned with this pay structure. Thus, this approach perpetuates existing pay practices and may therefore be unacceptable for pay equity purposes.

The other alternative—expert judgment—requires forming a panel or committee of knowledgeable individuals within the organization. These individuals must have a good understanding of the organization, its strategy, and its needs, as well as an accurate understanding of the meanings of each factor. Each individual independently derives a set of factor weightings and brings this set to the committee. If there are major discrepancies, the reasons need to be identified. For example, one or more of the factor definitions may be unclear, or different individuals may have different understandings of the types of behaviour required. The committee members then rework their weightings and repeat this process until the factor weightings converge.

Once the factors and degrees have been defined and weighted, the committee develops a summary rating chart, on which they will record the points allocated for each factor for a given job. At the end of the job evaluation process, there will be a filled-in copy of this summary chart for every job.

**Figure 8.1** provides an example of a summary rating chart based on one used by a Canadian hospital. This rating chart uses 10 factors: three from the "skill" category (education, experience, mental skill), two from the "effort" category (mental effort, physical effort), three from the "responsibility" category (importance of accuracy, patient contact, supervisory responsibilities), and two from "working conditions" (job hazards, job/work environment). Eight degrees have been established for education, seven for experience, and five for each of the remaining factors. The maximum total number of points that a job can receive is 1000, and the minimum a job can receive is 90 points. The factor weights (as indicated by the maximum points available for a given factor) range from 210 points (education) to 55 (job/work environment). (Although this example has a round number of points (1000) as its maximum, there is no inherent advantage to this. A maximum could just as easily be 1140 points, and that wouldn't affect the quality of the job evaluation system.)

**FIGURE 8.1**

Sample Summary Rating Chart for Point Method of job Evaluation

| Job title: —————— | Degree Rating | | | | | | | | Points Allocated |
|---|---|---|---|---|---|---|---|---|---|
| Factor | 1 | 2 | 3 | 4 | 5 | 6 | 7 | 8 | |
| a)  Education | 10 | 25 | 45 | 70 | 100 | 135 | 185 | 210 | |
| b)  Experience | 0 | 15 | 35 | 60 | 90 | 120 | 150 | — | |
| c)  Mental skill | 15 | 35 | 65 | 100 | 125 | — | — | — | |
| d)  Mental effort | 15 | 35 | 60 | 80 | 100 | — | — | — | |
| e)  Physical effort | 15 | 30 | 40 | 50 | 65 | — | — | — | |
| f)  Importance of accuracy | 15 | 30 | 45 | 65 | 80 | — | — | — | |
| g)  Patient contact | 10 | 30 | 45 | 60 | 75 | — | — | — | |
| h)  Supervisory responsibility | 0 | 20 | 35 | 50 | 75 | — | — | — | |
| i)  Job hazards | 0 | 15 | 30 | 45 | 65 | — | — | — | |
| j)  Job/work environment | 10 | 20 | 30 | 40 | 55 | — | — | — | |
| Total Points for This Job | | | | | | | | | |

## APPLYING THE JOB EVALUATION SYSTEM

After the job evaluation system has been established, it is applied to all the jobs covered by that system. Then a "hierarchy of jobs" is generated. A good way to summarize the results of the job evaluation, and the resulting hierarchy of jobs, is by developing a table similar to **Table 8.2**. This table incorporates the results for a hypothetical set of hospital jobs, based on the job evaluation results taken from the summary rating charts shown in Figure 8.1. Of course, in rating these jobs, evaluators are working with the actual factor and degree definitions, which are not shown in Figure 8.1, and applying them to each job description. However, as an example, for the factor of education, the factor and degree definitions shown in Table 8.1 were used.

What does the hierarchy of jobs in Table 8.2 tell us? First, among this sample of hospital jobs (normally all hospital jobs would be included rather than just some of them), the most valuable job to the organization is head of surgery, while the least valuable job is grounds worker. According to the job evaluation system, the job of head of surgery is about 5.5 times more valuable to the hospital than the job of grounds worker. (This is determined by dividing the point total for the job of head of surgery by the point total for the job of grounds worker.) This also implies that the head of surgery job should be paid about 5.5 times as much as the grounds worker job.

You will also notice that the job of ward nurse is worth more than twice as much (2.5 times) to the hospital than the job of painter, which answers our question in the opening vignette. In fact, in this sample of hospital jobs, only the grounds worker job is less valuable to the hospital than the painter job.

Are there any pay relationships that surprise you? Some may be surprised that the janitor/cleaner job is actually more valuable to the hospital than many other jobs, such as pharmacist's assistant or accounting clerk. We can examine this unusual result by looking at

## TABLE 8.2

Results of Job Evaluation Applied to Jobs at a Canadian Hospital

| Job Title | (a) Educa- tion | (b) Experi- ence | (c) Mental Skill | (d) Mental Effort | (e) Physical Effort | (f) Accu- racy | (g) Contact | (h) Sup. Resp. | (i) Job Haz- ards | (j) Job/ Work Environ. | Total Points |
|---|---|---|---|---|---|---|---|---|---|---|---|
| Head of surgery | 210 | 150 | 125 | 100 | 40 | 80 | 60 | 75 | 30 | 30 | 900 |
| Thoracic surgeon | 210 | 90 | 125 | 100 | 50 | 80 | 75 | 20 | 30 | 30 | 810 |
| Director of nursing | 135 | 150 | 125 | 100 | 30 | 80 | 60 | 75 | 15 | 30 | 800 |
| Staff physician | 185 | 60 | 125 | 100 | 50 | 80 | 75 | 0 | 30 | 30 | 735 |
| Head ward nurse | 135 | 60 | 100 | 80 | 50 | 80 | 75 | 35 | 30 | 30 | 675 |
| Chief pharmacist | 135 | 90 | 100 | 80 | 15 | 80 | 10 | 75 | 15 | 20 | 620 |
| Registered nurse | 135 | 35 | 65 | 60 | 40 | 65 | 75 | 0 | 30 | 30 | 535 |
| Ward nurse | 100 | 15 | 65 | 60 | 40 | 65 | 75 | 0 | 30 | 30 | 480 |
| Pharmacist | 100 | 15 | 65 | 60 | 15 | 80 | 30 | 0 | 15 | 20 | 400 |
| Accountant | 135 | 35 | 65 | 60 | 15 | 45 | 10 | 0 | 0 | 10 | 375 |
| Medical lab tech. | 70 | 15 | 35 | 35 | 30 | 80 | 30 | 0 | 45 | 30 | 370 |
| Nurse's aide | 45 | 0 | 35 | 35 | 50 | 45 | 60 | 0 | 30 | 30 | 330 |
| Janitor/cleaner | 25 | 15 | 35 | 15 | 50 | 30 | 10 | 0 | 45 | 40 | 265 |
| Pharmacist's asst. | 45 | 0 | 35 | 35 | 15 | 80 | 10 | 0 | 15 | 10 | 245 |
| Orderly | 25 | 0 | 35 | 15 | 50 | 30 | 30 | 0 | 30 | 30 | 245 |
| Admitting clerk | 25 | 15 | 35 | 35 | 15 | 45 | 45 | 0 | 15 | 0 | 230 |
| Food prep. worker | 25 | 0 | 35 | 15 | 40 | 45 | 10 | 0 | 15 | 20 | 215 |
| Accounting clerk | 45 | 15 | 35 | 35 | 15 | 45 | 10 | 0 | 0 | 10 | 210 |
| Painter | 10 | 15 | 15 | 15 | 50 | 30 | 10 | 0 | 30 | 20 | 195 |
| Grounds worker | 10 | 0 | 15 | 15 | 65 | 15 | 10 | 0 | 15 | 20 | 165 |

COMPENSABLE FACTORS

the factor scores. A relatively low level of education is required for the janitor/cleaner job, yet it scores high on the factors of physical effort, job hazards, and job/work environment (meaning it has an undesirable work environment). Besides being exposed to infectious patients, cleaners must deal with and properly dispose of many dangerous substances, such as highly infectious body fluids, pus, blood, and vomit, and they must be meticulous in their cleaning to render all surfaces sterile and germ-free. How well they succeed can directly affect the health of patients and other staff. As a result, we would expect the job of janitor/cleaner to be valued more by a hospital than by a corporate office.

## TESTING THE JOB EVALUATION SYSTEM

We should not yet assume that the relationships presented in Table 8.2, or that the underlying job evaluation system on which they are based, are valid. A long process must be completed before we have reasonable assurance that the job evaluation system has **validity**.

### Testing for Reliability

How do we know that the job evaluation system we have developed is actually a true measure of relative job values? The first test of the system is its **reliability**. Reliability is the extent to which a measuring instrument consistently produces the same results when repeatedly applied to the same circumstances, whether by the same or different persons. In other words, does the job evaluation system produce the same point scores for each factor for a given job, for every evaluator who applies the system?

For example, if one person applies the job evaluation system to a nurse's job and gets point scores of 125 for mental skill, 80 for mental effort, and 40 for physical effort, while a different person who independently applies the job evaluation to the nurse's job gets point scores of 65, 100, and 50 for the same factors, then the system may not be reliable. Using an unreliable job evaluation system is the same as using an elastic tape measure to measure distance. This problem must be identified and fixed before proceeding any further.

Thus, the first step in testing is for the job evaluation system to be applied independently by a variety of raters to the same set of jobs and then to compare the results. (Incidentally, the best way of applying the system is for each rater to evaluate all jobs on the first factor, then all on the second factor, and so on; this encourages consistent treatment of each factor.) If discrepancies across raters are discovered, the precise nature of the problem needs to be identified. The problem could lie in the factor definitions, which may not be sufficiently clear, or in the degree definitions, or in the job information (i.e., the job descriptions) on which the evaluators are basing their ratings, which may not contain sufficient information for accurate rating.

By comparing the results of the different evaluators on the different factors, it is possible to identify whether certain factors are problematic. For example, if the evaluators seem to agree fairly closely on how most factors should be rated for most jobs but there is a lot of discrepancy for, say, "mental effort," then there may be a problem with this factor. If there seem to be one or two jobs where the evaluators are diverging on most factors, then there could be a problem with the job descriptions for these jobs. Other potential pitfalls in designing and applying a point method job evaluation system are discussed in more detail later in the chapter.

Once the problems have been identified and corrected, the system should be applied again by a different set of independent raters. If discrepancies remain, they must be dealt with, and the process must be repeated until consistency is achieved. There is absolutely no point in going further in testing the system if reliability has not first been achieved.

## Testing for Market Fit

Once reliability has been achieved, it is necessary to calibrate the system to the market, so that JE points can be related to dollars. Calibrating to the market provides yet another test of the system. The organization selects a number of "key" or "benchmark" jobs, each of which has a good match ("market comparator job") in a set of valid market data. These benchmark jobs should be selected so that there is a spread across the range of job evaluation points. That is, some jobs with a high point total should be selected, some with a low point total, and some that fall in between. Including at least some jobs that are strongly related to the nature of the business and that represent sizable numbers of employees is also desirable. The normal practice is to use about 10–15 percent of the total number of jobs to be evaluated.

In the case of the hospital example in Table 8.2, a reasonable choice of benchmark jobs might be head of surgery, director of nursing, registered nurse, medical lab technician, janitor/cleaner, admitting clerk, and grounds worker. However, the choice of benchmark jobs also must be made in the context of the availability of good market data for the jobs chosen. Now we need a set of compensation survey data that will include as many of our jobs as possible. (Chapter 9 discusses how to find such a database; for now, we will assume we have one.)

When using compensation survey data, job evaluators need to specify the geographic location to which these data refer. In our case, let us assume that the hospital is in Toronto. We therefore select the Toronto area as our geographic area for the compensation data. After examining our database, we discover that there are suitable matches for the head of surgery, director of nursing, and grounds worker jobs, based on comparing the job descriptions of our benchmark jobs to the market comparator jobs. We still need a high-point-total and a low-point-total job. For the high-point job, "cardiologist" is available in the data set and for the low-point job, "painter" has a good match. Let us assume that "cardiologist" is a reasonable comparator for our "thoracic surgeon" job, and to have a more representation from the high-point jobs, we add "staff physician," assuming that "family practitioner" is a good match. To balance that, we add "nurse's aide," for which the "nurse assistant" seems a good match.

We now go into the database and identify the average total compensation for our market comparator jobs. **Table 8.3** summarizes the results of this process.

We now plot each benchmark job on a graph, with its job evaluation point score on the horizontal axis and the compensation value (in dollars) for its market comparator job on the vertical axis. A spreadsheet program (such as Microsoft Excel) is then used to calculate and produce a straight regression line that best "fits" the pattern of plots on the graph. **Figure 8.2** shows the resulting market line, including the plots for our nine benchmark jobs. If we are planning to either lead or lag the market, we need to adjust the market line upward or downward by the percentage lead or lag to create our pay policy line, which serves as the foundation of our base pay structure. If

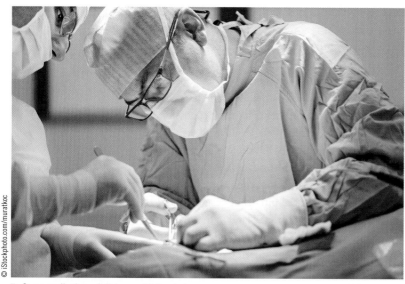

© iStockphoto.com/muratkoc

Some medical specialists earn high salaries.

we are planning to match the market, then our market line simply becomes our pay policy line. In this example, assume that we are planning to match the market, so Figure 8.2 also becomes our pay policy line.

TABLE 8.3

Benchmark Jobs and Market Comparator Jobs for a Canadian Hospital

| BENCHMARK JOB | JOB EVALUATION POINTS | MARKET COMPARATOR JOB | AVERAGE TOTAL COMPENSATION |
|---|---|---|---|
| Thoracic surgeon | 810 | Cardiologist | $191 346 |
| Staff physician | 735 | Family practitioner | 125 407 |
| Head ward nurse | 675 | Nurse supervisor | 69 043 |
| Registered nurse | 535 | Registered nurse | 56 056 |
| Medical lab tech. | 370 | Medical lab tech. | 49 692 |
| Nurse's aide | 330 | Nurse assistant | 33 722 |
| Janitor/cleaner | 265 | Hospital cleaner | 27 267 |
| Admitting clerk | 230 | Admitting clerk | 36 078 |

FIGURE 8.2

Sample Market Line for a Canadian Hospital

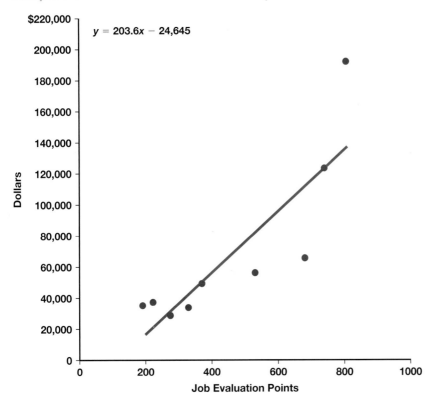

$y = 203.6x - 24,645$

Note that a "match the market" strategy does not imply that every one of our jobs will actually match the market. Some jobs may be above the market and some may be below, but the average results overall will approximately match the market. To determine what the average annual compensation would be for any job under the new job evaluation system, draw a vertical line up from the horizontal axis (at the JE point score for the job you are pricing) until it intersects the pay policy line. Draw a horizontal line from there to the vertical axis, and the amount indicated is the pay for the job.

A more precise way to calculate proposed pay for a given job is to use the equation for the regression (market/pay policy) line that is generated by the computer, which is in the $y = mx + b$ format, where "$y$" is the dollar value of the job, "$m$" is the slope of the market/pay policy line, "$x$" is the JE points total for that job, and "$b$" is a constant (the constant "$b$" could be a minus or a plus, depending on where the regression line intercepts the vertical axis). For the hospital example, the equation is $y = 203.6 \times x - 24\,645$. Therefore, the annual pay of a job with 810 points (the thoracic surgeon) would be $203.6 \times 810 - 24\,645$, which equals \$140 271.

As it calculates the regression (market) line, the spreadsheet program also calculates a **correlation coefficient** (sometimes called a "regression coefficient") that summarizes the extent to which the plots on the graph approach a straight line. A correlation coefficient can range from +1 to −1. Either +1 or −1 occur when all the plots happen to fall in a perfectly straight line (this virtually never happens); +1 indicates a positive relationship between job evaluation points and pay rates, and −1 indicates a negative or inverse relationship between job evaluation points and pay rates. An inverse relationship would mean that pay is lower for jobs with higher job evaluation points. Needless to say, you should never have a minus sign in front of your coefficient!

The coefficient indicates the "goodness of fit" between the point values established by job evaluation and the pay rates ascertained from the market. Obviously, a coefficient that approaches zero is bad, because this says that there is little or no relationship between the value of jobs as determined by job evaluation and the value of jobs as determined by the market. If you were to stick with your job evaluation system with a low coefficient, you would find that you were paying far more than you need to for some jobs and not enough to attract employees to others.

So then, the closer the coefficient is to 1, the better? Not necessarily. Some differences from the market line may well be justifiable if a job is more (or less) important to your organization than it is to the typical organization, or if you are using a different compensation strategy from your comparator firms. There is no hard and fast rule about exactly what the coefficient should be. But it certainly should be closer to 1 than to 0, and anything less than 0.80 needs to be carefully examined.

Another aspect to examine is the slope of your regression line. If it is too steep then you may end up compensating jobs at the top end of your system too much and jobs at the bottom end too little. A steep slope often means there is not enough spread in job evaluation point scores between the lower value jobs and the higher value jobs. On the other hand, if the slope is too flat, you may be compensating jobs at the bottom too much and jobs at the top too little. One final aspect is the average height of the pay policy line on the vertical (dollar) axis. If it is too high, you may end up paying all jobs too much; if it is too low, you may end up paying all jobs too little.

## Exploring Solutions to Job Evaluation Problems

How do you decide what needs to be modified in your system if you have a coefficient problem, a slope problem, or a height problem? The first thing to do is check that your benchmark jobs are equivalent to the market comparator jobs in the market you have matched them with. (For example, the thoracic surgeon/cardiologist match may be questionable for our hospital sample, as might the staff physician/family practitioner match.) Compare the job descriptions carefully. You should also re-examine your market sample: Are the other organizations in your market sample really appropriate comparators? (This topic is discussed further in the next chapter.)

If you are satisfied with these comparisons, then you could examine the "outlier jobs"—those that have the farthest vertical distance from the market line—to determine why they are discrepant. Have they been badly evaluated (e.g., their point total is incorrect, because the job evaluation system was applied poorly to that job), or are there problems with the job evaluation system itself (e.g., some factors have been weighted too heavily or too lightly)? Have the wrong factors been included in the job evaluation system, or has a key factor been omitted? There is no formula to find the right answer—it requires judgment based on studying the pattern of results. However, you must avoid the temptation to simply adjust the JE points of the outlier jobs so that the correlation coefficient looks better. This will not solve underlying problems in your JE system, and will cause more problems later on.

In our hospital example, the correlation coefficient is .87, which is acceptable. Now let us examine the outliers. You can tell which job each plot represents by looking at the JE point totals. For example, working from the left, the first plot is the "painter" job (it has the lowest JE point total of the benchmark jobs, 195 points), the second is the "admitting clerk" job, and so on. The extent to which a job is an outlier is indicated by the vertical distance that its plot is from the regression line, either above or below the line. As you can see, the greatest outlier is the "thoracic surgeon," which has a difference of about $51 000 ($191 346 – $140 271). What this result means is that while the market is paying a thoracic surgeon an average annual total compensation of about $191 000 (assuming the "cardiologist" job is actually a good match for "thoracic surgeon"), we are proposing to pay thoracic surgeons about $140 000. Given that difference, will we be able to attract the thoracic surgeons we need?

The next largest outlier is the "head ward nurse" job, which we are proposing to pay nearly $44 000 above the market (the difference between $112 785 and $69 043). While we won't have any trouble attracting and retaining head nurses, can we really afford to pay so much above the market for this job? Similarly, we would pay registered nurses about $28 000 above the market, and $8800 above the market for nurse's aides. The proposed pay for the staff physician, medical lab tech, and janitor/cleaner jobs appear to be pretty close to the market, but we are proposing to pay the admitting clerk nearly $14 000 below the market, and the painter about $18 000 below the market, a level that might not even meet minimum wage standards. Although we didn't include the grounds worker job as one of the benchmarks, given that the grounds worker job has fewer JE points than the painter, we would almost certainly be in violation of minimum wage laws for the grounds worker job.

These results suggest that we need to re-examine our job evaluation system. First, we need to check the basics—that we have a valid market sample of comparator firms, that we have made a good choice of benchmark jobs, and that we have valid market comparator jobs for each benchmark job. For the market sample, the Salary Expert website unfortunately does not provide any information about the nature of its sample, nor does it allow us to structure the market sample by including only appropriate market comparator firms. But let us assume that the market sample is fine, as well as the benchmark job matches.

At this point, our main concern is the outliers. If we proceed from here, some jobs will be paid much less than the market while some will be paid much more than the market. If our objective is to be in line with the market, then we don't need to create a job evaluation system—we could have just used a market pricing system.

The relevant question is whether these discrepancies are too large. It would seem that they are, so we need to examine our job evaluation system to see what is causing this problem. Because our system does seem to pay staff physicians at the market but thoracic surgeons significantly less than the market, it appears that a specialization within medicine makes a big difference in pay. Maybe we need to increase the point difference between degrees 7 and 8 on our education factor. Or maybe we need another factor that differentiates better between the two jobs.

As for the "overpayment" of nursing staff, it may be that certain factors that they score high on are too heavily weighted, or maybe we need more degrees on these factors. As for "underpayment" of admitting clerks and painters, what factors are pulling them down? Are these factors weighted too heavily? Are the factors pulling them up not weighted heavily enough, or do we need to include an additional factor that captures the nature of the work better? Or has the market simply been overcompensating these jobs relative to the value of the work? Unfortunately, there is no formula to use in answering all these questions; it is a matter of judgment and trial and error. This helps explain why job evaluation systems that are designed from the ground up can take years to develop.

Finally, any changes we make to the job evaluation system create a need to re-evaluate all jobs in the JE system, not just those jobs appearing to cause problems for us.

## Testing for Total Compensation Costs

Testing for what total compensation costs would be under the proposed compensation system is also useful. Pay policy graphs can be used to estimate the total compensation of the proposed system. For example, the rate for each job, as established by the pay policy line, can be multiplied by the number of people holding that job; we can then derive an estimate of the total compensation that would be payable under the proposed job evaluation. For an ongoing organization, this can then be compared with the current compensation cost.

It can then be determined whether the organization can afford this amount. If not, changes must be made to the pay level strategy, the job evaluation system, or other aspects of the pay structure. For example, if the JE system results in most jobs receiving high point totals, perhaps the system may not be differentiating adequately between jobs of lower and higher value.

Job evaluations help to establish internal equity among different jobs.

It is also conceivable that the new plan will result in a reduction in the current payroll costs. While this may seem desirable to the employer, too large a reduction can cause perceptions of inequity among employees, which may create a higher turnover rate, particularly among the most marketable employees. Moreover, a job evaluation system that reduces the pay of most employees is not likely to be well accepted, especially the next time around. There may be many appeals of the results, and many employees may devote great effort to getting their jobs re-evaluated. Chapter 13 discusses all these issues in more detail.

## POSSIBLE PITFALLS OF THE POINT METHOD OF JOB EVALUATION

Although point method plans have many advantages, there are also drawbacks. Besides the complexity of developing them, perhaps the biggest drawback is that although point method plans may appear scientific, the process of selecting relevant factors and applying particular weights is still subjective. There are many opportunities for errors to enter the system, perhaps even destroying its validity, despite the efforts that are devoted to developing and maintaining the system.

Four main categories of pitfalls need to be avoided in developing a point method job evaluation plan: (1) inconsistent construct formation, (2) factor overlaps, (3) hierarchical grounding, and (4) gender bias.[3] Each of these will now be examined, along with some additional pitfalls that fall outside these categories. A thorough understanding of these pitfalls is the best defence against them.

### INCONSISTENT CONSTRUCT FORMATION

In a point system of job evaluation, carefully established compensable factors are the key to success. Each factor must be based on a separate and well-defined construct. Factors may fail to meet this test in three areas: (1) the factor itself may be ambiguously defined, so that it is not clear to the evaluator what the factor is meant to pick up; (2) the degree or level definitions may not be consistent with the factor definition; and (3) the definitions for each degree or level may not all be degrees of the same construct.

#### Ambiguous Factor Definitions

Some factors may be designed in such a way that they are actually tapping multiple constructs. For example, consider the following definition of "complexity of duties":

> *Complexity of Duties: This factor measures the complexity of duties involved, the degree of independent action, the extent to which the duties are circumscribed by standard practice, the exercise of judgment and the type of decisions made, the amount of resourcefulness and planning the job requires, the creative effort in devising new methods, policies, procedures or products, scientific discoveries, and original application.*[4]

Notice how this example contains numerous factors. If they are all important, they need to be turned into separate factors. (And, if some of these are not important, they should be dropped.) At least four separate factors could be extracted from this factor definition: independent action/circumscribed duties, resourcefulness, planning, and creative effort.

## Inconsistent Factor and Degree Definitions

In some cases, the statements defining the different degrees of a given factor are actually measuring something other than the factor to which they ostensibly apply. Consider the following example for the factor of "analytical ability":

*Analytical Ability: This factor measures the extent to which analytical ability is required to perform job duties. Analytical ability is the ability to examine information and data, to detect patterns, explanations, and causes of various phenomena, using a variety of analytical tools and procedures.*

*Degree 1: Little necessity for creativity in performance of job duties.*

*Degree 2: New ideas and approaches to job duties occasionally needed.*

*Degree 3: Frequent need to develop new approaches to job duties.*

*Degree 4: Continually must use creativity in performing job duties.*

Notice how these degree statements focus on creativity and innovation in performing job duties, which is not necessarily the same as analytical ability. For example, accountants may analyze financial statements to identify potential company problems, but this does not necessarily call for creative ability. On the other hand, a graphic artist in charge of developing new company logos may need considerable creativity but does not really use analytical tools and procedures in performing this job.

## Inconsistent Degree Statements

In a variation of the above problem, sometimes different degree statements are actually measuring different constructs, and only some of the statements are actually focusing on the factor they are supposed to measure. Consider the following example for the factor of "supervisory responsibility":

*Supervisory Responsibility: This factor deals with the extent of responsibility for managing employees and overseeing their day-to-day work.*

*Degree 1: No supervisory responsibilities.*

*Degree 2: Responsible for supervision of one to three subordinates.*

*Degree 3: Responsible for supervision of four to nine subordinates.*

*Degree 4: Responsible for supervision of 10 or more subordinates.*

*Degree 5: Responsible for development of all department policies.*

Which one of these is not like the others? Clearly, the statement for degree 5 is focusing on a different construct than the other degrees. For example, it may be possible to be responsible for development of department policy with very few or even no employees.

## FACTOR OVERLAPS

One problem that often occurs in point systems is overlapping factors. If this does occur, then some factors are counted twice and thus are being too heavily weighted. This sometimes occurs because factor titles sound different even though their descriptions are actually very similar. For example, consider the factors of "judgment" and "freedom to act":

*Judgment: This factor deals with the extent to which the exercise of independent judgment is required in the performance of job duties.*

*Degree 1: Prescribed directions and rules limit the scope for independent judgment.*

*Degree 2: Standardized work routines limit the scope for independent judgment.*

*Degree 3: Similar procedures and methods limit the scope for independent judgment.*

*Freedom to Act: This factor deals with the extent to which incumbents of this job are free to act as they see fit in performing their job duties.*

*Degree 1: Duties are routine and specifically delineated; work is closely controlled.*

*Degree 2: Duties are somewhat routine and clearly delineated; work is closely controlled.*

*Degree 3: Characteristics of the position are such that activities and methods are clearly defined, and/or work is frequently reviewed.[5]*

Note how these factors are virtually indistinguishable.

## HIERARCHICAL GROUNDING

The purpose of the point method of job evaluation is to derive a hierarchy of jobs by examining the individual components ("factors") in those jobs. However, some factors in some systems "appear to confuse the outcome with the process. That is, they say if this job is at a high level in the [organization] hierarchy, then it should be highly rated. This is circular reasoning."[6] For example, take the factor of "responsibility for action":

*Responsibility for Action: This factor deals with the extent to which the jobholder is expected to take independent action in addressing and solving managerial problems, and the importance of taking this action.*

*Degree 1: Reports to the section supervisor.*

*Degree 2: Reports to the department manager.*

*Degree 3: Reports to the division manager.*

*Degree 4: Reports to the vice president.*

*Degree 5: Reports to the president.*

Notice how the degree definitions copy the existing organization hierarchy, by assuming that the higher the job is in the hierarchy, the more responsibility for action it has. Thus, the job evaluation system is not actually deriving an independent hierarchy of jobs, which is the real goal of job evaluation. There is a strong tendency for jobs higher in the organizational hierarchy to pay more, and this example illustrates how inequity can arise as a result. What these degree statements are really saying is that no one who reports to a section supervisor has any responsibility to take action, when this may not be true at all for many jobs.

## GENDER BIAS

Gender bias occurs when a job receives a higher or lower evaluation than it should because the job incumbents are predominantly from one gender. A job evaluation system that is thought to have gender bias can be very costly for a company, as Bell Canada and Qualcomm Technologies found out; see Compensation Today 8.1.

So, what should you watch out for? There are at least six ways in which gender bias can arise in job evaluation:

- Separate job families have been delineated.[7]
- A factor is valued when it is found in "male jobs" but not when it is found in "female jobs."[8]
- Job content is confused with stereotypes of inherent female attributes.[9]

- Factors found in female jobs are ignored.[10]
- There is an insufficient range of degree statements.[11]
- The job descriptions are biased.[12]

Some researchers have found that insufficient training of raters can introduce unreliability and bias into the job evaluation process if raters fall back on unconscious stereotypes that have contributed to gender-based inequities in the past.[13] Let us examine each of these problems.

## Separate Job Evaluation Systems for Different Job Families

In the past, each job family in an organization was evaluated under a different job evaluation system. This can defeat the purpose of job evaluation, which is to generate a hierarchy of jobs within the organization using a common measure of job value. It can also cause gender bias. Even when jobs are evaluated fairly within job families or classes, they may not be evaluated fairly between job classes if separate job families are used for male and female jobs. The opening vignette described how nurses were shortchanged by this practice. This is why the same system of job evaluation should cover all job families that are subject to job evaluation. In many Canadian jurisdictions, this is required by law.

## Differential Valuation of Factors

One example of how factors can be valued differently is "visibility of dirt." Jobs carried out under dirty working conditions, such as mechanic or garbage collector, have typically been rated more highly on working conditions (i.e., they are deemed to have worse working conditions) than jobs performed in seemingly "clean" working conditions, such as in hospitals or hotels. However, working conditions in hospitals and hotels may not be as "clean" as they appear, especially from the perspective of those employees, such as nurses or maids, whose job it is to create and maintain those "clean" working conditions. Conditions may be clean by the time nurses or maids complete their shift, but that is because of the dirt and mess they handled during their shift!

Another example of this type of inequity comes from a municipality in the United States, where the hazards of entering people's homes (e.g., being bitten by a dog, or being assaulted by a resident) were factored into job evaluations for meter readers (who were male) but not for public health nurses (who were female). Yet both had to enter people's homes as a part of their responsibilities.[14]

## Confusing Job Content with Stereotypes

Certain jobs traditionally held by women are often viewed as "low-skill" jobs because the ability to do these jobs is considered "inherent to women." For example, in the U.S. Department of Labor's Directory of Occupational Titles, "dog pound attendant" was once ranked higher than "child care worker." When this inequity was questioned, the response given was that dog pound attendants were more highly rated because dog care skills were more difficult to acquire than child care skills.[15] The argument was that any skills needed to work with young children were inherent in women and therefore did not deserve to be highly rated. Of course, anybody who has actually worked with small children knows that considerable skill is necessary to be effective and that both females and males vary greatly in these skills.

## Ignoring Factors Found in Jobs Traditionally Performed by Women

In a major study of job evaluation instruments, researchers found that many factors relevant to jobs traditionally performed by women had been omitted. For example, under "effort," there were rarely factors for "involuntary interruptions" (as many secretaries must cope with) or for "dealing with upset people" (as complaints clerks at department stores and nurses at hospitals must do).[16]

Some researchers have noted that the whole area of "emotional labour" has seldom been adequately incorporated into job evaluation plans.[17] One aspect of emotional labour is dealing with people and groups who are angry, distrustful, upset, unreasonable, psychologically impaired, or under the influence of drugs or alcohol—conditions that nurses and social workers must contend with every day. Another aspect of emotional labour is the need to stay cheerful, courteous, friendly, and helpful, even in adverse circumstances, as is the case in many service-oriented jobs. Compensation Notebook 8.2 lists a whole range of frequently omitted factors in jobs typically held by women.

---

### COMPENSATION NOTEBOOK 8.2

#### EXAMPLES OF FREQUENTLY OVERLOOKED CONTENT IN JOBS TRADITIONALLY PERFORMED BY WOMEN

**SKILLS**

- Scheduling appointments
- Writing correspondence and standard letters, taking minutes, proofreading, and editing
- Operating and maintaining office machines
- Hand-eye coordination and fine motor skills such as rapid finger dexterity (e.g., typing, giving injections)
- Establishing and maintaining filing and scheduling systems and data retrieval
- Training and orienting new staff

**EFFORT**

- Balancing multiple demands
- Calming upset, ill, or dissatisfied people and gathering information from them
- Eyestrain from reading handwritten material or from time spent at the computer
- Providing care and emotional support
- Frequent bending or lifting
- Prolonged concentration

**RESPONSIBILITY**

- Responsibility for damage to equipment
- Acting on behalf of absent supervisors
- Representing the employer through communications with the public
- Developing and coordinating work schedules and planning meetings

---

## Insufficient Range of Degrees

Once a job evaluation system has all the factors necessary to accurately assess the full range of jobs, the final concern is to ensure that there is sufficient range among the degrees to make appropriate distinctions between jobs. Weiner[18] cites the following example for "working conditions":

*Working Conditions: This factor deals with the physical conditions under which the job is normally performed.*

*Degree 1: Standard office conditions.*

*Degree 2: Inside work with possible exposure to dirt, oil, noise.*

*Degree 3: Some exposure to disagreeable conditions, such as fumes, cold, dust.*

*Degree 4: Constant exposure to disagreeable conditions. Continuous outside work.*

This example illustrates several problems. For example, "standard office conditions" does not distinguish between spacious private offices and offices that may be crowded, noisy, and hot, with frequent interruptions and distractions. Also, outside work (traditionally male) is assumed to be the most onerous. Is this always true? In some occupations, workers (e.g., gardeners, painters) are outside only during relatively pleasant conditions. Should outside work always be considered more onerous than working in a crowded, hot, noisy office, with constant interruptions?

## Biased Job Descriptions

Finally, even when the job evaluation system itself is fair and free of bias, one possible source of bias remains—the information on which the job evaluation is based. As discussed in Chapter 7, there is evidence that descriptions of jobs traditionally performed by women have been subject to bias during job analysis. A dramatic case of this occurred in 2012, when the federal government agreed to a $150 million settlement with public health nurses following an investigation by the Canadian Human Rights Tribunal.[19] Here, the job descriptions had resulted in nurses being classified as "administrative and clerical staff" rather than as "health professionals."

## Other Pitfalls of Job Evaluation

Chapter 4 discussed the pros and cons of job evaluation systems in some depth. Job evaluation is subject to a few other pitfalls besides the ones described there. As with job analysis, there is a tendency to evaluate the jobholder rather than the job itself.[20] For example, evaluators might think to themselves: "This is Joe's job. Joe really doesn't seem to work very hard anymore. Therefore, his job does not deserve a high rating." Joe's performance is irrelevant when a job evaluation is being conducted; it is the importance of his job that we are evaluating, but it is easy to lose sight of that distinction.

Another pitfall develops when job evaluation becomes an adversarial process and a source of conflict between employees and management. But the biggest pitfall is that job evaluations may fall out of date quickly, so that continually updating them requires a commitment of time and effort. Yet if they are not updated, they can become a source of inequity rather than a source of employee satisfaction.

When a job does change substantially in duties, and when the revised point total for the job warrants it, there should be a prompt reclassification from one grade to the next. But even here, it is possible for inequity to creep in. For example, a manager may inflate a job description to reclassify a job to a higher grade for the purposes of rewarding a specific individual. A U.S. study found that more powerful departments in an organization were more likely to have their requests for reclassifications approved than were less powerful departments.[21] Obviously, such tendencies must be avoided if the system is to be fair. See Compensation Today 8.2 for an example of challenges that can face job evaluation systems.

## COMPENSATION TODAY 8.2

### STRIKE TWO FOR JOB EVALUATIONS

The city of Cambridge faced a turbulent month in February 2017. The discord started with the city's newly proposed job evaluation system for city workers. The workers and their union were in complete opposition to the proposal and were quick to act.

The city's outdoor workers were the first to strike. Because Cambridge outdoor workers were the third-lowest paid of any municipality in Ontario, the union did not see the use in a job evaluation system. The union feared that the city would try to prove that workers have different responsibilities from that of other city's workers. One individual complained, "How many different ways do you flood the ice in an arena? How many different ways do you bury a body in the cemetery? How many different ways do you plow a road or fix a water main? You know what? We all do it the same frikin' way." On the opposing side, the city felt that the job evaluation system would allow for equal representation from both parties. The city complained that the union's process for determining salaries was arbitrary, and there were no evidence-based means to support their decisions.

Though the outdoor worker strike ended in 180 workers receiving hourly increases and a two percent annual increase in each of the four years of the contract, the fight was not over. The next to strike that month were the indoor city workers.

The city of Cambridge attempted to use a job-evaluation process on administrative and professional staff, including customer service staff, building inspectors, bylaw officers, and technical services. The job evaluation system was used to justify moving such positions to a lower pay level. The proposal was that employees would keep their wages from that which they received when they were hired, but new hires would receive a lower pay. The union complained that the city was breaking a promise from a grandfathered system. However, the city alleged that 1882 workers were overpaid, which amounted to $325 000 in overpayments annually.

After much deliberation, an agreement was reached. Those with grandparented wages were frozen, and they would also receive a one percent lump sum amount in their annual payments over three years based on the maximum salary for their position grade. Workers whose wages were not frozen benefited from a two percent cost of living increase each year during the contract and a 1.7 percent retroactive wage increase from the previous year.

The purpose of the job evaluation system is to create a fair and equitable process; however, it seems that in this case, workers felt it was imposed to do the opposite.

Sources: Jeff Hicks, "City of Cambridge Outside Workers Begin Strike," *The Record*, February 2, 2017; Richard Vivian, "Job Evaluation Pay at Heart of City Inside Workers' Strike," *Cambridge Times*, February 16, 2017; Record Staff, "Settlement Reached in Cambridge Inside Workers Strike," *The Record*, February 24, 2017.

# DETERMINING THE BASE PAY STRUCTURE

Whichever method of job evaluation has been used, by now the organization has created a hierarchy of jobs. But there is still no pay structure. A **base pay structure** normally consists of pay grades and pay ranges, along with the criteria for salary movement within the pay range. A **pay grade** is a grouping of jobs of similar value (although not necessarily of a similar nature) to the organization, based on similar point totals. A pay grade is always defined in terms of points (e.g., Pay Grade 1 consists of all jobs that have point totals from 100–200 points, Pay Grade 2 consists of all jobs that have point totals from 201–300 points, and so on). A **pay range** provides the actual minimum and maximum pay rate, in dollar terms, for all the jobs that fall into a particular pay grade. The pay rates are influenced by market pay, which we will further review in Chapter 9.

## ESTABLISHING PAY GRADES

In establishing a base pay structure, a fundamental question is whether to use pay grades. If the answer is "yes," as it is for most firms, the number of pay grades must be decided, as well as the size of the pay grades.

### Why Use Pay Grades?

Why have pay grades at all? Why not pay each job a different rate, based on what the pay policy graph indicates? There are five main reasons for clustering jobs into pay grades. First, the use of grades recognizes that job evaluation is essentially a subjective process, no matter which method is used, and that it makes little sense to try to make very fine distinctions between jobs. Second, pay grades make it easier to justify and explain pay rates to employees. If employees notice someone earning more money in a job that resembles their own, they may perceive inequity.

Third, pay grades simplify the administration of the pay system by eliminating the need for separate rates and pay ranges for every job. Fourth, having jobs clustered within pay grades makes it easier for employees to move across jobs in the same pay grade. Fifth, pay grades create more stability for the pay system. For example, if a job changes, but not substantially, there is likely no need to re-evaluate, unless the job is right at the boundary between two pay grades.

On the downside, pay grades do create problems relating to jobs on the margins of each grade. Employees with jobs on the borderline between two grades will naturally push to have their jobs placed in the higher grade. But if this is done, then the next-lower job becomes the marginal job. No one wants his or her job to be the first one not included in the higher grade.

### How Many Pay Grades?

How many pay grades should there be? One consideration is the total range of pay of the jobs covered by the particular job evaluation system. If the jobs in the same pay structure range from $20 000 to $300 000 per year, there is much greater scope for pay grades than if the jobs range from $25 000 to $75 000. Another consideration is the width of the pay ranges to be used. If pay ranges are narrow, then the only way for an employee to significantly increase his or her pay is through promotion to a job in the next-higher pay grade. To provide opportunities for promotion to jobs in higher pay grades, it may be desirable to have many pay grades. Of course, the number of pay grades will be in inverse proportion to the size of the pay grades—the more pay grades, the smaller the size of the pay grades.

**base pay structure**
The structure of pay grades and pay ranges, along with the criteria for movement within pay ranges, that applies to base pay.

**pay grade**
A grouping of jobs of similar value to the organization, typically grouped by point totals.

**pay range**
The minimum and maximum pay rates (in dollars) for jobs in a particular pay grade.

## Establishing Pay Grade Sizes

**equal interval approach**
Method to establish pay grade widths, in which the point spreads are equal for all pay grades.

**equal increase approach**
Method to establish pay grade sizes, in which each pay grade increases in width by a constant number of points from the preceding pay grade.

**equal percentage approach**
Method to establish pay grade sizes, in which each pay grade increases in width by an equal percentage from the preceding pay grade.

A key question is how to establish the pay grade widths and boundaries. In some cases, these are arbitrary. For example, suppose that job evaluation points in a particular pay structure can be as low as 100 points or as high as 1000 points and that the organization has decided to have nine pay grades. Dividing the possible range of points (which is 900) by nine yields pay grades of 100 points in width. Thus, Pay Grade 1 is 100–200 points, Pay Grade 2 is 201–300 points, and so on. This is known as the **equal interval approach**.

A major problem with the equal interval approach is that it tends to bunch too many jobs together in the lower pay grades that should not necessarily be in the same pay grade; yet at the same time, it has too many relatively small pay grades at the top of the pay system. Two methods for addressing this issue are the **equal increase approach** and the **equal percentage approach**. Based on the notion that jobs in higher pay grades are more complex, the width of each pay grade increases by either a constant number of points from the previous grade or a constant percentage from the previous grade. Compensation Notebook 8.3 gives examples of how to calculate each of these approaches.

---

### COMPENSATION NOTEBOOK 8.3

#### CALCULATING PAY GRADE WIDTHS USING THE EQUAL INCREASE AND EQUAL PERCENTAGE APPROACHES

As an example of how you would calculate pay grade widths using the equal increase approach, assume that you have decided to use nine pay grades (as in the text example) and that the minimum points possible in your job evaluation system is 100 and the maximum possible is 1000. To apply the equal increase approach, you need to first arbitrarily set the width of your first pay grade. To give an indication of what this should be, first divide the total range of points in your system (900) by nine, which equals 100 points. (This, of course, is the size of the pay grades under an equal interval approach.) Because you want the pay grades to be narrower at the bottom of your system, and wider at the top of your system, the width of your first pay grade must obviously be less than 100 points; let us say 50 points. We then must determine what increase in each grade width would result in our system finishing at 1000 points, while producing nine pay grades. Although there are mathematical formulas that could be used for working this out, trial and error also works fine.

We first try increasing each pay grade width by 10 points (i.e., the width of Grade 2 becomes 60 points, the width of Grade 3 becomes 70 points, the width of Grade 4 becomes 80 points, etc.), but this results in our ninth pay grade not reaching the 1000 point maximum of our system. To reach this, our pay grade widths need to add up to 900 points or so, and right now they add up to 810 points. We have two choices now: we can either increase our first pay grade size and reapply the grade increases; or we can make the grade increases larger. Bumping up the grade increases to 12 points raises our total to 882 points—still not quite enough—but bumping up the grade increases to 13 points raises our total to 918 points—too much. However, if we reduce our starting grade width to 48 points, and stick to the 13-point increase, this gives us our 900 points total that we were looking for. (Note that because each pay grade actually starts one point higher than the end of the previous pay grade, this has the effect of adding one point to Pay Grades 2–9. You can simply lop these eight points off the maximum of Pay Grade 9 to keep it to the 1000-point maximum.)

The equal percentage increase approach can be simpler to calculate. The first part of the process is the same as the first paragraph of this Notebook. So, let us select 50 points as our starting grade width. We then need to select a constant percentage by which each grade width will increase from the previous grade width—a percentage that will results in grades that add up to about 900 points. The easiest way to do this is with an "annuity calculator" (which calculates the impact of increasing a value by particular percentage) that you can easily find online. For our example, we will use http://www.1728.org/annuity.htm. (You can still use trial and error in coming up with the best combination of starting grade width and percentage increases—it is just a bit more tedious to calculate.)

First, click on "rate," because the percentage rate is what we are trying to find out. Next, in the "total row," put "850" (this is derived by taking the 900 point total grade width that we are seeking, and subtracting the grade width of the first grade, which is 50 points, leaving us with 850 points we want to determine). After that, put "50" in the "annual amount" row, because each pay grade will equal 50 points plus the percentage increase applied to that pay grade. Finally, enter "8" in the "years" row, which reflects the number of pay grades we wish to have, after subtracting the first pay grade, which will stay at 50 points.

Now, click "calculate" and the "rate" 16.6336 appears. That is the percentage by which each pay grade width will increase from the previous pay grade width. For example, the width of Pay Grade 2 will be 50 times 1.166336, which equals 58.3—round to 58 points. So, Pay Grade 1 will be 50 points wide (with a minimum of 100 points and maximum of 150 points). Pay Grade 2 will be 58 points wide (with a minimum of 151 and a maximum of 209). To calculate Pay Grade 3, multiply 58 times 1.166336, which equals 67.6 points—round to 68 points. Therefore, Pay Grade 3 will have a minimum of 210 points (one point above where Pay Grade 3 left off) and a maximum of 278 points. Repeat this process for all nine pay grades. (Note: Because of rounding, you will find that the maximum of Pay Grade 9 comes a little short of 1000 points—simply round up the maximum of Pay Grade 9 to 1000 points.)

Another approach is to consider the possibility of error in the system. For example, what would be the point difference for a job if it were consistently evaluated one degree higher or one degree lower than it should be? Assume that this would result in a 200-point overevaluation or underevaluation. Then 200 points could be used as the width of the pay grades, the logic being that no job would then be more than one pay grade higher or lower than it should be. However, one expert recommends dividing this maximum error by three, on the assumption that, in reality, two-thirds of the degree errors would cancel out.[22]

During the 1990s, many companies reduced the number of pay grades in their compensation systems, thereby creating large or "fat" grades. This process, known as broad banding, enjoyed some popularity because of the flexibility it provided. However, the fewer the pay grades (sometimes known as "bands" under this system), the less meaning job evaluation results have, for jobs with very different point totals may end up in the same band and thus receive similar pay. Moreover, broad pay grades open the door to inconsistency across departments and to the possibility of pay being determined by factors such as favouritism. And, broad bands also create a bigger distinction between the pay rate of a job that just makes it into a particular pay band, and a job that just falls short, ending up in the next-lower pay band. As these problems have become more apparent, the popularity of broad banding has faded.

Finally, a thorny issue is what to do with jobs that end up near but just below grade boundaries. One solution is to do nothing and just leave jobs where they fall. But this solution invites feelings of inequity as well as attempts by these jobholders to get their jobs re-evaluated. Some firms attempt to deal with this problem by keeping job evaluation points secret, which can lead to other problems such as distrust of the evaluation system. As mentioned earlier, another method is not to use arbitrary point cutoffs but rather to look for "natural breaks" in the job hierarchy. There is no ideal solution to this problem, which is inherent in the use of pay grades.

**broad banding**
The practice of reducing the number of pay grades by creating large or "fat" grades, sometimes known as "bands."

# ESTABLISHING PAY RANGES

Once the pay grades have been established, the next task is to decide on the pay range for each grade in actual dollar terms. It is possible to establish a pay range of "zero"—that is, to pay all jobs in a pay grade the same flat rate. But this does not allow any room to recognize the differential qualifications of employees as they enter a pay grade, nor does it allow for raises based on seniority or performance. To provide latitude for this, most organizations do use pay ranges.

There are four main questions about pay ranges. First, how are the midpoints of the ranges (in dollar terms) determined? Second, how should the range spreads be determined (i.e., the minimum and the maximum pay rates for each pay grade)? Third, should range overlaps be permitted? And fourth, how should movement through the range take place?

## Establishing the Range Midpoints

As an example of how to establish the midpoint of the pay range, let us start with the graph shown in **Figure 8.3**, which shows a sample market line. This market line needs to be converted to a pay policy line. If the compensation strategy for the employees in the job evaluation system is to pay 10 percent above market, then a new line will be drawn 10 percent above the market line. This will become the pay policy line. (If the pay strategy is to match the market, then the market line becomes the pay policy line.)

After the pay policy line has been drawn, the pay grades are marked off on the graph using vertical lines. Next, a horizontal line is drawn where the midpoint of each pay grade intersects the pay policy line. This is illustrated by the broken lines in **Figure 8.4**. The horizontal line for Pay Grade 1 (which has a grade midpoint of 190 points) intersects the pay policy line at about $32 500—which is then taken as the midpoint in the pay range for this pay grade. Similarly, the horizontal line for Pay Grade 2 (which has a grade midpoint of 335.5 points) intersects the pay policy line at about $36 900, so this is taken as the midpoint of the pay range for Pay Grade 2.

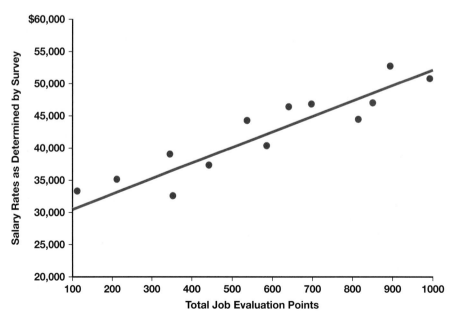

**FIGURE 8.3**

SAMPLE MARKET LINE

FIGURE 8.4
## ILLUSTRATION OF A BASE PAY STRUCTURE

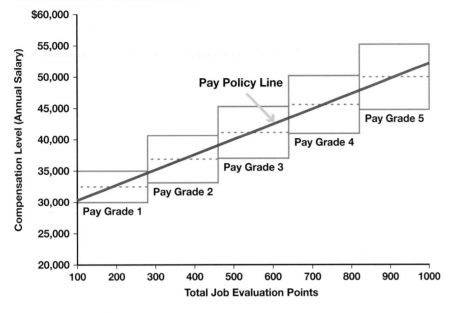

The differentials in range midpoints between the grades are known as the intergrade differentials. Intergrade differentials may be expressed in dollars or in percentages. In dollar terms, they may be constant or they may increase as one rises up through the hierarchy of jobs. The purpose of increasing intergrade differentials is to maintain the attractiveness of promotions. In the pay structure illustrated in Figure 8.4, the intergrade differentials stay constant at $4400 throughout the structure, although the intergrade differential percentages actually decline. For example, the intergrade differential percentage between Pay Grade 1 and Pay Grade 2 is about 13.5 percent, but it is only about 11.9 percent between Pay Grades 2 and 3. Between Grades 3 and 4, the intergrade differential percentage is 10.7 percent, and between Grades 4 and 5, 9.6 percent. This means that, as a proportion of pay, promotions in the higher grades are becoming relatively less attractive than promotions in the lower grades. One way to increase this percentage would be to widen the pay grades as the system goes up.

### Establishing the Range Spreads

Now that we have the range midpoints, we need to decide on the range spreads—that is, the dollar value of the difference between the maximum and the minimum of the pay range for each pay grade. To maintain the integrity of the system, the dollar value differences between the range midpoint and the range minimum, and the range midpoint and the range maximum, need to be equal. Otherwise, you are arbitrarily moving the range midpoint, after all the work you have just devoted to establishing it!

There are no hard and fast rules for establishing range spreads, but there are several considerations. The first is the extent to which the organization wants to use compensation to recognize differences between employees performing the same jobs. How important is experience? And how much can performance vary across individuals in the same job? If the organization places no value on experience, and performance does not really vary across employees, the answer is simple—no spread! Instead, the midpoint becomes the flat pay rate for the job, so that all jobs in Pay Grade 1 pay $32 500.

**intergrade differentials**
The differences between the range midpoints of adjacent pay grades in a pay structure, expressed in dollars.

**intergrade differential percentage**
Calculated by dividing the intergrade differential (expressed in dollars) of each pay grade by the midpoint (in dollars) of the previous pay grade.

**range spread**
The difference between the maximum and the minimum pay level, in dollars, for a given pay range.

Thus, the pay range should reflect the range of performance or experience within jobs. But how do you determine this? The time it takes to become proficient at that job might be a good indicator. For example, if a job requires a person to work for four years to become fully proficient, then that job needs a much greater spread in pay range than a job that requires six months for proficiency. And even after four years, when that person reaches proficiency, there may still be variations in performance that the organization wants to recognize.

Another consideration is opportunities for promotion. If the organization is growing slowly or not at all, there may be few promotional opportunities to use as a means to increase employee pay. Or it may not be desirable to promote valued employees to management jobs just to get them a pay raise. In these circumstances, a wider pay range can be used to accommodate and retain high-performing employees.

Yet another consideration is how many steps or increments the organization intends to have in the range. The more increments it wants to use, the greater the range spread needs to be. In general, the range spread is wider for higher pay grades, the assumption being that experience makes more of a difference to performance in those grades and that there is more scope for performance variation in jobs in higher pay grades. Another common reason for an increasing range spread is that pay grades tend to get larger for jobs higher in the job hierarchy.

Another way to set the minimum and maximum for each pay range is by referring to the labour market. Labour market data normally provide not only the midpoints or averages for each job, but also the ranges and quartiles. Quartiles indicate the pay for the lowest quarter of employees, then the second quarter, and so on. One way of setting the range minimum would be to use the top of the bottom quartile for a typical job in that pay grade as the range minimum, and the top of the third quartile as the range maximum.

**range spread percentage**
A percentage calculated by dividing the range spread for a given pay range by the minimum for that pay range.

Overall, the following **range spread percentages** seem typical in Canada—10–20 percent for production and clerical jobs, 20–30 percent for professional jobs, and 25–50 percent for managerial jobs. In general, the range spreads increase for pay grades higher up the job hierarchy to recognize the greater complexity of these jobs. Also, the fewer the pay grades, the larger the pay ranges; the more the pay grades, the smaller the pay ranges.

In our example, Figure 8.4 shows the minimum and maximum of the pay range for each pay grade. The lower line in Pay Grade 1 represents the range minimum for that pay grade (which is $30 000), while the upper line represents the range maximum (which is $35 000). Overall, the graph shows that the pay ranges for the five pay grades are as follows:

|  | Points Range for Pay Grade | Pay Range Minimum | Pay Range Maximum | Pay Range Midpoint |
|---|---|---|---|---|
| Pay Grade 1 | 100–280 | $30 000 | $35 000 | $32 500 |
| Pay Grade 2 | 281–460 | $33 650 | $40 150 | $36 900 |
| Pay Grade 3 | 461–640 | $37 000 | $45 600 | $41 300 |
| Pay Grade 4 | 641–820 | $41 100 | $50 400 | $45 700 |
| Pay Grade 5 | 821–1000 | $44 600 | $55 600 | $50 100 |

As we develop a base pay structure, it is always useful to step back and take a hard look at what we have done so far. How well does the pay structure depicted in Figure 8.4 work? It has five pay grades, covering 180 job evaluation points each. The minimum pay for any job is $30 000, while the maximum is $55 600. The range spread for Pay Grade 1 is $5000, and the range spread percentage is about 17 percent, calculated by dividing the range spread by the range minimum ($30 000) for that pay grade. The range spread for Pay Grade 5 is $11 000, or 25 percent. The intergrade differential percentages vary from 13.5 percent between Pay Grade 1 and Pay Grade 2 to 9.6 percent between Pay Grade 4 and Pay Grade 5, although they stay constant in dollar terms at $4400. (In fact, when we use equal point spreads to delineate pay grades, as we have in this example, the range midpoint for each grade will always be the same dollar amount higher than the range midpoint of the previous grade.)

Given that the total pay range of jobs in this pay structure is so narrow (from $30 000 to $55 000), five pay grades may be appropriate. However, if we were developing a base pay structure for the hospital example discussed earlier, this number of pay grades would be much too low, given the very large dispersion in pay and jobs at the hospital. At the hospital, 10–15 pay grades would likely be necessary to adequately reflect the dispersion across jobs, depending on the method used for establishing pay grade sizes. For example, increasing the size of the pay grades as jobs increase in value would allow use of fewer pay grades at the hospital (possibly 10–12 grades), but using equal-sized grades would probably require at least 15 grades.

The intergrade differential percentages actually decline, so this may reduce the incentive for promotion to a job in a higher pay grade or reduce perceptions of equity among those getting promotions. The final potential problem is the overlaps between pay ranges.

## Overlaps Between Pay Ranges

In Figure 8.4, the pay range for each pay grade overlaps with the previous one. When there is an overlap, an employee in a lower pay grade can actually earn more than an employee in a higher pay grade. This may be seen as a threat to the integrity of the job evaluation system. So why have overlaps?

Overlaps occur because of pay ranges. If there were very small spreads in each pay range, there would be little or no overlap. As range spreads increase, so does overlap. One purpose that overlap serves is to reduce the differences in pay between adjacent pay grades, thus reducing the difference in pay between jobs that fall on either side of the pay grade boundary. Overlaps also allow the pay of top performers in a lower grade to increase without having to promote them to a job in a higher pay grade. Finally, many people believe it would not be fair for an inexperienced employee coming into a new job to earn more than a seasoned, experienced, high-performing employee in a job in the next lower pay grade.

When should overlap be a concern? One possible rule is that it should not be possible for a person in Pay Grade 1 to be making as much as a person in Pay Grade 3. That is, when overlap starts to cover two pay grades, it tends to negate the job values established by the job evaluation system and to reduce the incentive for promotion. In addition, it can also create problems after promotion occurs. Normally, a person who has been promoted expects a raise as she or he assumes the new job. However, if that person is already earning more than the midpoint of the next higher pay grade, then she or he has to enter that pay grade above the midpoint. This severely limits the room for pay increases as the promoted individual gains increased experience and improves performance. As Figure 8.4 shows, if someone at the top of the pay range for a job in Pay Grade 4 were promoted to a job in Pay Grade 5, that employee would receive no increase unless she or he came in above the midpoint of the new pay range.

One way to avoid the problem of excessive overlap is to make sure that the top of the previous pay range is always lower than the midpoint of the next one, perhaps halfway between the midpoint and the minimum. Certainly, the top of a pay range should always be lower than the bottom of the range two grades up. Note that the pay structure in Figure 8.4 meets these criteria for the lower pay grades, but not for the higher grades.

### Gaps Between Pay Ranges

One final issue is the opposite problem of too much overlap—when there are gaps between the pay ranges. In this case, not only are there no overlaps, but the ranges do not connect up. For example, consider the following pay ranges:

| | |
|---|---|
| Pay Grade 1 | $20 000–$24 000 |
| Pay Grade 2 | $28 000–$34 000 |
| Pay Grade 3 | $36 000–$44 000 |

As you can see, the maximum of the pay range for Pay Grade 1 is $24 000, but the minimum of the range for Pay Grade 2 is $28 000. Thus there is a $4000 gap between the pay ranges for Pay Grades 1 and 2. We can also see a $2000 gap between Pay Grades 2 and 3. The problem with gaps is that they do the opposite of overlaps—they exaggerate the pay differences between jobs in one pay grade and jobs in the next pay grade. In general, there should be no such gaps.

If gaps do exist, this could be a sign of either an insufficient number of pay grades in the pay system or pay ranges that are too small. Often, this problem arises when the "equal interval" approach to setting pay grade widths is used, and it can sometimes be solved by switching to the "equal increase" or "equal percentage" approach to establishing pay grades. Sometimes all three of the above might be needed to produce the best solution to this problem.

## MOVEMENT THROUGH THE PAY RANGE

Once the pay range is defined for each pay grade, criteria must be established to determine how placement and movement within the range will occur. The three most common criteria are experience, seniority, and performance. In some cases, all three are used. For example, a person's initial placement in the pay range may be determined by previous experience. Seniority (in terms of years in the job) or performance—or both—can then be used to determine future increases within the pay range.

As one example of how to combine seniority and performance, some firms allow employees to reach the midpoint of their pay range using annual seniority increases, but to pass that point requires meritorious performance. This is known as a split pay range, with the midpoint serving as a "control point" to prevent pay increases unless they are based on performance. But this is just one possibility of many.

How many steps or increments should there be within a pay range? And what should be the size of each increment be? Although a pay range may have as few as three or as many as fifteen increments, most have six or seven for non-management positions, and four or five for management positions.[23] To be effective, a pay raise should constitute a "**just noticeable difference (JND)**." If it doesn't reach that level, it may have little motivational or reward value.

**just noticeable difference (JND)**
The amount of pay increase necessary to be considered significant by employees receiving the increase.

In times of low inflation, a JND may be four percent. Look back at Pay Grade 1 in Figure 8.4. The minimum is $30 000 and the maximum is $35 000. A four percent pay raise from the minimum would be $1200. Because the range is $5000, divide it by $1200, which equals about four. Four increments would allow four raises of about four percent each, so this might be a reasonable number of steps for Pay Grade 1.

What about for the other pay grades? Let us try another—say, Pay Grade 5. For Pay Grade 5, four percent of the minimum is $1784. The range is $11 000, so dividing by $1784 equals just over six. Therefore, six increments might be used for this pay grade.

Some organizations do not use fixed steps or increments. Instead, they view the minimum as the entry-level pay for an employee with no experience, and the midpoint as the normal pay that a typical employee receives. Pay raises above the midpoint are awarded only if performance is above average and pay reaches the maximum for the range at the discretion of the supervisor, who may vary both the timing and the amount of the raises. However, this procedure does not fit well with motivation theory, which suggests that motivation is maximized when the link between future performance and future pay increases is very clear. Moreover, the flexibility of this method opens the door to inconsistency and favouritism.

## OTHER POSSIBLE ELEMENTS OF BASE PAY STRUCTURE

Base pay structure can include several other elements. For example, for jobs with hourly pay, overtime premiums are typically required by law when workers exceed a certain number of daily or weekly hours. However, many employers go beyond the statutory minimum, especially unionized employers. In other cases, the organization may offer shift differentials, where pay for an undesirable work shift (usually the night shift) is higher than for other shifts. Some employers may offer isolation premiums to boost the compensation of employees who work in remote areas. These are just some of the possibilities that may be incorporated into a base pay structure.

## LIVING WAGE

The implementation of living wages in some jurisdictions will have additional implications for job evaluations. A living wage is different from the minimum wage and can be described as the minimum income necessary for a worker to meet the needs of his family in a particular community; that is, it takes into account the basic needs of a worker to help provide for a decent standard of living. The Canadian Living Wage Framework lists five key principles of the initiative. The living wage is meant to: (1) allow working families to escape poverty; (2) create healthy childhood development; (3) encourage gender equality; (4) lessen severe financial stress and allow for a minimum level of economic security; and (5) enable all individuals to partake in the social, cultural, and civic life of the community.[24]

The concept of living wages has been attracting recent attention in Canada with dozens of communities and employers moving forward with living wage initiatives, including the City of Cambridge, Ontario; the public-school board in Hamilton; and Vancity, a credit union in British Columbia. In British Columbia alone, 150 employers have chosen to adopt the living wage policy, including private companies, nonprofits, co-operatives, and other local governments.[25] These organizations pay wages that are higher than the legislated minimum wages in their jurisdictions. However, it is worth noting that most employers that have embraced the living wage policies employ high-skilled workers and had already previously paid wages higher than that of minimum wage.[26]

**living wage**
the minimum income necessary to help a worker enjoy a decent standard of living.

The living wage varies greatly for different regions in the same province. For example, although the minimum wage in Ontario is $14, as of November 2019, the living wage in Toronto is $22.08. However, a smaller and less expensive region such as London, Ontario has a living wage of $16.20 per hour.[27] The living wage is calculated as the hourly rate which a household with two adults working full-time with two children can meet its basic needs after government transfers are added, and deductions are subtracted (such as income tax and the Employment Insurance premium).[28] It takes into consideration regional costs for factors such as childcare, housing, transportation, food, clothing, hydro, medical, phone, education, Internet access, and other expenses such as recreation, modest vacations, and household items. However, the living wage does not consider factors such as money for debt repayment nor savings for retirement.[29]

The concept of a living wage is still relatively new in Canada, and most of the current research surrounding living wage policy is based on theory rather than sound evidence. When looking at similar policies implemented in the United States, only some research exists in this area, and the findings from these studies are either inconclusive or have not found to show any improvement in poverty reduction. A need exists for more evidence-based Canadian research.[30] Compensation Today 8.3 highlights a potential problem that has to be resolved to ensure internal equity.

## COMPENSATION TODAY 8.3

### THE DEBATE ON A LIVING WAGE

While the living wage movement in Canada is in its infancy, it has been attracting considerable attention, especially among poverty activists. Outside Canada, the debate has been intense, including the United Kingdom where the Living Wage campaign has gained some momentum. In 2005, the Greater London Authority established the Living Wage Unit to calculate the London Living Wage and the issue soon generated interest throughout the United Kingdom. Employers started to voluntarily implement the Living Wage. In April 2016, the UK government introduced a compulsory National Living Wage for workers over age of 25. In April 2020, the national living wage in the United Kingdom is set to rise by 6.2 percent in what the government refers to as "the biggest cash increase ever." This rise is over four times the rate of inflation and would move hourly pay for workers over 25 from £8.21 to £8.72 an hour.

The concept of a living wage is very appealing. It means a wage that a person working 40 hours a week, with no additional income, will be able to provide the basics for quality of life, such as food, shelter, utilities, transport, health care, minimal recreation, one course a year to upgrade his or her education, and child care. Advocates say that it will reduce poverty and help businesses improve productivity. The implementation can be very complicated. Criticism of a living wage can be summarized into four points.

- If all workers' wages are increased to the new living wage, what about people who have longer service and better skills at the same job? For instance, if all new hires are paid at the living wage (e.g., $18/hour), what about a five-year service employee who is paid at $17/hour? Should this worker also expect an increase? Should the increase be the absolute amount of $1 or should it be proportional to the increase in the starting pay? This is an issue that job evaluations can help to address.

- If all workers get a subsequent increase, would the employer's cost be transferred to the customers for private employers or the public for public employers? For example, 2400 employees of Welsh National Health Service each received an initial increase up to £470 in 2014 as a result of implementing a living wage. That is an extra £1 million of payroll cost that the public will have to bear.

- Not all workers support a family and the family sizes vary. As a result, living wages may benefit workers who may not be the original intended beneficiary; for example, a young worker who recently entered the workforce and has no dependants to support.

- The current minimum wage and wage differential encourage employers to hire less experienced workers who are paid less while learning the job. A living wage will reduce employers' incentive to hire novice workers and provide on-job training, which may lead to more youth unemployment.

An independent report published in 2019 found that there is no evidence of job loss due to the rising wages. However, this policy has not helped to decrease the growing number of families in poverty in the United Kingdom. Plus, in 2019, the average worker's pay (when taking inflation into account) still bought less than what it had 11 years ago. Some critics say that the benefits of the living wage are lost due to larger issues that must be tackled. They claim that rather than putting a band-aid on the situation, the government must focus on reducing housing costs, ensuring social security adequately supports people, and spending government money on investing in skilled jobs in each region of the United Kingdom.

The UK government has now declared that by 2024 the age for the national living wage will be lowered to 21 and the living wage will be increased to £10.50 an hour. Some contend that this plan is a step in the right direction for the country, but much more is needed to be done to truly tackle pay inequity.

Sources: "UK 'Jobs-Rich, Pay-Poor' Economy to Continue," *WorldatWork*, May 17, 2016; E. James Brennan, "Living Wage Versus Minimum Wage," *Compensation Café*, August 26, 2013; Living Wage Foundation website, http://www.livingwage.org.uk/what-living-wage, accessed August 1, 2016; Michael Babad, "The Quest for a 'Living Wage' Gathers Steam," *The Globe and Mail*, October 3, 2014; Tom Cooper and Trish Hennessey, "The Promise of the Living Wage Movement," *Toronto Star*, May 27, 2016; Andy Verity, "National Living Wage to Increase by 6.2% in April," *BBC News*, December 31, 2019; Joanna Partridge, "Aldi to Become UK's 'Best-Paying Supermarket' With Wage Rise," *The Guardian*, January 21, 2020; Jess Sheldon, "Minimum Wage and Living Wage: Millions to Get Pay Rise in 2020—Will you Get £930 Extra?" *Express*, December 31, 2019.

## SUMMARY

This chapter has shown you how to develop a point system of job evaluation and a base pay structure. You have learned the five main steps in developing this method (identifying compensable factors, scaling the factors, weighting the factors, applying the system, and testing the system), as well as the possible pitfalls in using this method.

Although the point method appears to be objective and scientific, it is still subjective and susceptible to problems that could compromise its reliability and validity. You can avoid these pitfalls if you understand them well. The four main types of pitfalls are inconsistency within the factors, overlaps between factors, hierarchical grounding, and gender bias. All these have commonly afflicted job evaluation systems (and those who are subject to these systems) in the past.

You have also learned that after establishing a hierarchy of jobs by job evaluation, you must create a base pay structure. This includes developing pay grades and pay ranges, along with the criteria for movement through the range.

## KEY TERMS

base pay structure
benchmark job
broad banding
compensable factors
correlation coefficient
equal increase approach
equal interval approach
equal percentage approach
intergrade differential percentage
intergrade differentials
just noticeable difference (JND)

living wage
market comparator job
market line
pay grade
pay policy line
pay range
range spread
range spread percentage
reliability
validity

# DISCUSSION QUESTIONS

1. Discuss the issue of gender bias in compensation and the ways it can affect the development of a base pay structure. In your employment experience, have you noticed possible examples of gender bias in compensation?

2. Discuss the hierarchy of jobs for a Canadian hospital shown in Table 8.2. Does everything about this ranking of job values make sense to you? Are there specific jobs that seem out of order to you? If so, which ones? Why do you think so?

3. Apart from gender bias, what are the key pitfalls of job evaluations? How can you minimize their potential problems?

4. Discuss how pay grades and pay ranges help organizations manage compensation.

5. What are the pros and cons of governments instituting a living wage?

# EXERCISES

1. In a small group or on your own, select benchmark jobs for the Canadian hospital in Table 8.2. Then use Monster's Salary Wizard (https://www.monster.ca/salary/) as your market database to find appropriate market comparator jobs and price them. For the purposes of the market survey data, assume that the hospital is in the city in which you reside. Display this information in a table similar to Table 8.3. Compare your table to Table 8.3 and discuss why they differ.

2. After completing Question 1, use Microsoft Excel to prepare a market line based on data from your benchmark jobs and market comparator jobs. Examine the resulting line and discuss all the possible issues surrounding its validity, including the correlation coefficient, the outliers, and the slope and height of the line.

3. Rank the hospital jobs shown in Table 8.2 according to your own impressions of how valuable each job is to the hospital, disregarding the hypothetical job evaluation results. Share your rankings with other classmates and discuss any differences in your rankings. Also discuss any differences from the rankings shown in Table 8.2.

4. In a small group or on your own, use Figure 8.2 to develop a base pay structure for a Canadian hospital, including pay grades and ranges, and criteria for salary movement within the range.

# CASE QUESTIONS

1. Using the point method and the four basic factor categories, develop a job evaluation system for the university in *Case 7—Eastern Provincial University* in the Appendix. Then apply your system to the different jobs to derive a single hierarchy of jobs. Summarize this information in a table similar to Table 8.2.

2. After completing Question 1, apply the procedures required under the Ontario Pay Equity Act to determine whether pay equity exists for the female job classes at Eastern Provincial University. The following are the annual salaries in the four job classes (as of 2012):

- Clerk Steno I: $36 341; II: $47 379; III: $69 057 (Job class 95 percent female)
- Draftsperson I: $41 179; II: $47 379; III: $58 522 (Job class 80 percent male)
- Grounds Worker I: $29 721; II: $36 341; III: $41 178 (Job class 85 percent male)
- Medical Laboratory Technologist I: $47 379; II: $58 522 (Job class 90 percent female)

## SIMULATION CROSS-REFERENCE

If you are using Strategic Compensation: A Simulation in conjunction with this text, you will find that the concepts in Chapter 8 are helpful in preparing the simulation.

# ENDNOTES

1. A useful guidebook has been produced by the Ontario Pay Equity Commission that includes the steps in the job evaluation process; see Step by Step to Pay Equity, at http://www.payequity.gov.on.ca/en/DocsEN/minikit.pdf, accessed August 8, 2016.

2. George T. Milkovich and Jerry M. Newman, *Compensation* (Chicago: Irwin, 1996), 37.

3. Nan J. Weiner, "Job Evaluation Systems: A Critique," *Human Resource Management Review* 1, no. 2 (1991): 119–32.

4. Weiner, "Job Evaluation Systems," 124.

5. Based on ibid., 126.

6. Ibid., 127.

7. Susan Corby, "Equality in the Public Sector: The Sky Darkens," in *Working for the State*, pp. 108–25. Palgrave Macmillan, London, 2011.

8. The terms "male jobs" and "female jobs" are used to denote jobs that have traditionally been occupied mainly by males or females. These terms are used as a shorthand in pay equity literature and carry no implications about the specific nature of these jobs, nor whether males or females are more suited to these jobs. See Monica Biernat, M.J. Tocci, and Joan C. Williams, "The Language of Performance Evaluations: Gender-Based Shifts in Content and Consistency of Judgment," *Social Psychological and Personality Science* 3, no. 2 (2012): 186–92.

9. Ibid.; Anne-Francoise Bender and Frederique Pigeyre, "Job Evaluation and Gender Pay Equity: A French Example," *Equality, Diversity and Inclusion: An International Journal* 35, no. 4 (2016): 267–79.

10. Anne-Francoise Bender and Frederique Pigeyre, "Job Evaluation and Gender Pay Equity: A French Example," *Equality, Diversity and Inclusion: An International Journal* 35, no. 4 (2016): 267–79

11. John Shields and Catherine Dolle-Samuel, "8 Developing Position-Based Base Pay Systems," *Managing Employee Performance & Reward: Concepts, Practices, Strategies* (2015): 180.

12. Weiner, "Job Evaluation Systems"; Danielle Gaucher, Justin Friesen, and Aaron C. Kay, "Evidence that Gendered Wording in Job Advertisements Exists and Sustains Gender Inequality," *Journal of Personality and Social Psychology* 101, no. 1 (2011): 109.

13. John Kervin and Marika Elek, "Where's the Bias? Sources and Types of Gender Bias in Job Evaluation," in *Industrial Relations in the New Millennium: Selected Papers from the XXXVIIth Annual CIRA Conference*, ed. Y. Reshef, C. Bernier, D. Harrisson, and T.H. Wagar (2001), 79–90; Amanda J. Koch, Susan D. D'Mello, and Paul R. Sackett, "A Meta-Analysis of Gender Stereotypes and Bias in Experimental Simulations of Employment Decision Making," *Journal of Applied Psychology* 100, no. 1 (2015): 128.

14. Weiner, "Job Evaluation Systems."

15. Ibid.

16. R. Steinberg and L. Haignere, *Equitable Compensation: Methodological Criteria for Comparable Worth, Working Paper #16* (Albany: Center for Women in Government, SUNY, 1985).

17. Ronnie J. Steinberg, "Emotional Labour in Job Evaluation: Redesigning Compensation Practices," *Annals of the American Academy of Political and Social Science* 561 (1999): 143–57; Kay Gilbert, "Promises and Practices: Job Evaluation and Equal Pay Forty Years On!" *Industrial Relations Journal* 43, no. 2 (2012): 137–51.

18. Weiner, "Job Evaluation Systems," 130.

19. *CBC News Online*, "Gender Equality Case Nets Nurses $150M," July 3, 2012.

20. Nan J. Weiner and Morley Gunderson, *Pay Equity: Issues, Options, and Experiences* (Toronto: Butterworths, 1990); Isaac Chaneta, "Effects of Job Evaluation on Decisions Involving Pay Equity," *Asian Social Science* 10, no. 4 (2014): 145.

21. Theresa Welbourne and Charlie O. Trevor, "The Roles of Departmental and Position Power in Job Evaluation," *Academy*

*of Management Journal* 43, no. 4 (2000): 761–71; Vicki Fairbanks Taylor, "Gaining Experience Using the Classification Method: A Job Evaluation Exercise," *Journal of Human Resources Education* 8, no. 2/3 (2014): 32–45.

22. Roland Theriault, *Mercer Compensation Manual* (Boucherville: G. Morin, 1992).

23. Conny Herbert Antoni, Xavier Baeten, Ben J.M. Emans, and Mari Kira, eds, *Shaping Pay in Europe: A Stakeholder Approach.* Vol. 53. Peter Lang, 2007.

24. Christine Saulnier, *A Living Wage for St. John's, Newfoundland and Labrador* (Canadian Centre for Policy Alternatives, 2019).

25. Renee Bernard and Lisa Steacy, "Five More B.C. Cities Commit to Paying Employees Living Wage: Advocate," *City News*, January 2, 2020, https://www.citynews1130.com/2020/01/02/five-more-b-c-cities-commit-to-paying-employees-living-wage-advocate/, accessed February 22, 2020.

26. Emily P. Boyle, Bethany F. Daigle, and Sarah B. McRae. *Will a Higher Minimum Wage Decrease Poverty in New Brunswick? A Review of the Evidence on Minimum Wages and Other Policy Alternatives* (New Brunswick Institute for Research, Data and Training, 2018).

27. Kate Dubinski, "How Much Do You Have to Make to Live with 'Economic Security'?" *CBC*, November 4, 2019, https://www.cbc.ca/news/canada/london/london-ontario-living-wage-2019-1.5346550, accessed February 22, 2020.

28. Christine Saulnier, *A Living Wage for St. John's, Newfoundland and Labrador* (Canadian Centre for Policy Alternatives, 2019).

29. Ibid.

30. Emily P. Boyle, Bethany F. Daigle, and Sarah B. McRae, *Will a Higher Minimum Wage Decrease Poverty in New Brunswick? A Review of the Evidence on Minimum Wages and Other Policy Alternatives* (New Brunswick Institute for Research, Data and Training, 2018).

# EVALUATING

# THE MARKET

AFTER READING THIS CHAPTER, YOU
SHOULD BE ABLE TO:

- Discuss the key considerations in understanding labour markets.

- Identify possible sources of compensation data.

- Describe the steps for conducting compensation surveys.

- Analyze, interpret, and apply compensation survey data.

## WHERE WOULD YOU CHOOSE TO WORK?

If you had to choose an industry based strictly on how much it pays its employees, which would you pick? The following are the average weekly earnings for different Canadian industries for the most recent available data (November 2019):

| | Average Weekly Earnings ($) |
|---|---|
| Mining, quarrying, and oil and gas extraction | 2254.16 |
| Utilities | 1937.46 |
| Management of companies and enterprises | 1629.46 |
| Information and cultural industries | 1342.56 |
| Professional, scientific, and technical services | 1472.37 |
| Finance and insurance | 1347.83 |
| Public administration | 1350.92 |
| Goods-producing industries | 1303.71 |
| Construction | 1270.96 |
| Forestry, logging, and support | 1179.64 |
| Manufacturing | 1157.93 |
| Educational services | 1085.41 |
| Transportation and warehousing | 1101.90 |
| Real estate and rental and leasing | 976.63 |
| Service-producing industries | 985.14 |
| Health care and social assistance | 947.39 |
| Administrative and support, waste management and remediation services | 854.62 |
| Other services (except public administration) | 857.73 |
| Trade | 814.90 |
| Arts, entertainment, and recreation | 626.15 |
| Accommodation and food services | 428.96 |

[Note: This table does not take into account the different jobs in the industry, as the weekly earnings are averages. Mining, Oil, and Gas may have more incumbents, for instance, holding highly paid jobs such as engineers and geoscientists and their large number drives the high average industry number. Accommodation and Food Services may have more incumbents holding lower-paid jobs such as waiters and chambermaids and their number drives the low average industry number.]

Source: Statistics Canada, Employment and average weekly earnings (including overtime) for all employees by province and territory, monthly, seasonally adjusted, (2020), at http://www.statcan.gc.ca/tables-tableaux/sum-som/l01/cst01/labor93a-eng.htm, accessed February 25, 2020.

Of course, all these seem pretty miserly when you compare them with the average pay for players in the National Hockey League (NHL), which is about $100 000 a week (assuming they work 40 weeks a year). This is nice for hockey players, but is one week of an average hockey player's work really worth more than the combined weekly work of 106 Canadian health and social service workers, or 233 accommodation and food services workers? What scale would you use for judging? By the way, average pay is even higher for players in the National Basketball Association and Major League Baseball than the NHL!

# INTRODUCTION TO WHAT IS APPROPRIATE COMPENSATION

In 2012–13, National Hockey League (NHL) employers decided they were overpaying their players and locked them out for half the season to cut their pay. This was after a season-long lockout by the owners in 2004–05 during which the average NHL player salary was cut by about 20 percent. No employer, not even an NHL owner, can afford to ignore product/service market and financial constraints when setting pay, as this could result in a compensation system set at a level that puts the employer out of business. After the 2004–05 lockout, average hockey salaries rose again until they exceeded pre-lockout levels by 2007–08, and then rose again by about 30 percent over the three seasons after that, motivating the owners to impose the 2012–13 lockout in another attempt to cut player salaries. Up to today, the NHL and employers try to restrain salaries through methods such as collective bargaining and salary caps.

Understanding the market is not only advisable for professional sports, but every other sector. In 2018, the Royal Mounted Canadian Police (RCMP) won the right to unionize. For the first time in their existence, the RCMP had a bargaining agent, the National Police Federation. One of the primary reasons for the decision to unionize was due to RCMP compensation. In 2009, the federal government established a law to limit significant increases in salaries for government workers.[1] Because of this legislation, RCMP officers were ranked 72nd out of 80th place for Canadian police forces base salaries according to a 2016 survey. Whereas RCMP constables earn between $53 000 and $86 110,[2] the salary of a police officer in Toronto starts at $70 000 and within four years a police officer will earn around $100 000.[3]

By March 2020, the union is expected to return with newly proposed compensation ranges for the RCMP. These changes will mean significant increases in costs for the federal, provincial, and municipal governments. Municipalities that use RCMP officers pay

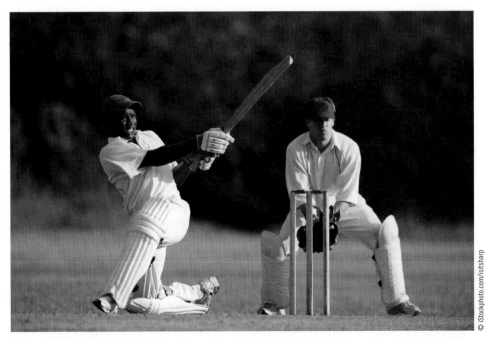

Is pay fair for professional sports players?

a portion of the RCMP salaries. Areas with 5000–14 999 residents pay 70 percent of the cost for RCMP officers. Regions with populations of 15 000 pay 90 percent of the cost for RCMP officers. With some municipalities rapidly increasing in population, the costs for these regions will be particularly burdensome.

Not all municipalities who use RCMP officers see this change as a drawback. Maja Tait is the mayor of Sooke, British Columbia, a municipality that uses RCMP officers and is nearing 15 000 people. Tait exclaimed, "Salaries are a part of providing a more equitable, safe working environment. Municipalities like ours have seen a lot of turnover in their RCMP force as officers leave to work in (higher paying) municipal forces. That is obviously not a good situation as we lose the relationships and community memory of those officers when they leave."[4]

How do you determine the appropriate amount to pay your employees? Clearly, a key factor is understanding the labour market and how it works. However, as discussed in Chapter 4, identifying the "going market rate" for individual jobs can be a complex and elusive process because there may be no single market rate for many jobs. After a brief discussion of labour markets, this chapter identifies sources of compensation data, including third-party and in-house surveys. Following that, it describes how to conduct a compensation survey. The chapter concludes with an illustration of how to analyze and interpret compensation survey data.

## UNDERSTANDING LABOUR MARKETS

Why do people get paid what they do? Surely it is based on the value or importance of the job they do. Well, consider this. The Prime Minister of Canada earns $357 800[5] per year. The lowest-paid hockey player with the Toronto Maple Leafs receives US$700 000 per year. Is being a benchwarmer on a professional hockey team a more important job than being Prime Minister of Canada? What's going on here?

In general, the price (wage) for a particular type of labour depends on the demand for that labour relative to its supply, constrained by the ability of employers to pay. In theory, whenever there is a surplus of a particular type of labour, the price for that labour falls. In reality, wages seldom decline in ongoing firms unless the employer is experiencing financial difficulties and wage cutting is seen as a necessity. This is because wage cuts often have negative consequences for the employer, such as increased turnover and reduced employee performance (see Chapter 3). However, new firms may take advantage of a labour surplus by hiring employees at a lower rate than existing employers are paying.

In theory, when faced with a labour scarcity, firms in the private sector are willing to increase the price for labour (in terms of total compensation) until the price matches the value (in terms of net revenue generated) that the firm receives from that labour. However, in reality, how much an employer is willing to pay for a particular type of labour is a function of a variety of factors, including the employer's ability to pay. Key factors include company profitability, the importance of that labour to the organization, and the proportion of labour costs to total costs. For example, if labour is only a small portion of a firm's total costs (as in the resources industry), that firm can afford to pay much more for its labour than firms in which labour is a high proportion of total costs (as in the retail sector).

Labour scarcity helps explain why soccer player David Beckham commanded the kinds of fees he did for endorsing various products and services (see Compensation Today 9.1). There is only one David Beckham! Of course, you could rightfully say there is only one of you, but nobody offers you anything to endorse their products!

### EARN IT LIKE BECKHAM! LOSE IT LIKE TIGER!

Soccer player and celebrity husband David Beckham may not be the soccer player he once was, but he still raked in the cash while playing towards the end of his career. In 2007, it was reported that he had signed a five-year deal with the Los Angeles Galaxy of U.S. Major League Soccer (MLS) that could be worth as much as $250 million to him in salary and endorsements. Of this sum, $32.5 million would be his pay as a player for the Galaxy (for which the Galaxy had to get an exemption from the league's maximum salary of $2.4 million per year), $20 million would come from wearing the "Herbalife" logo on his shirt, and the rest would come from other endorsements and a share of the profits from the merchandising of items like Beckham soccer shirts.

What made Beckham worth so much? At that stage in his soccer career (he announced his retirement as a professional player in 2013), it was not his soccer skills—there are many players who were good as or better than Beckham at that time. Instead, what the Galaxy and the other sponsors were paying for was his very famous name and his ability to attract notice from the press and the public. If Beckham could raise soccer anywhere close to the popularity of the other major American sports, then the value of every MLS franchise would skyrocket, especially that of the Galaxy. Herbalife was gambling that its association with Beckham would raise its net revenues by more than $20 million over the next five years.

Of course, whether these gambles would pay off for the Galaxy or for Beckham's other sponsors was never certain. Indeed, in 2008 Beckham's endorsement earnings ranked far behind those of golfer Tiger Woods, who was dubbed the "most impactful endorser in the history of marketing" by some experts at that time. In 2008 alone, Woods earned $23 million in winnings and $105 million in endorsements and was credited with catapulting Nike to the fourth-largest golf retailer and with tripling the sales of sports video game producers Electronic Arts.

But Woods turned out to be a bad bet for his sponsors after news of his various marital infidelities came out in late 2009 and his subsequent golf performance plummeted. He was dropped by several key sponsors, although enough of them stuck with him (most notably Nike) that he was still able to earn $55 million in endorsements in 2012, exceeding Beckham's $37 million that same year. As time passes, and if Tiger returns to his winning ways, his economic value to sponsors will no doubt rise, although it remains to be seen whether he will ever be able to regain his "most impactful endorser" status.

For public sector organizations such as school boards, hospitals, and government departments, the ability of employees to generate revenue is obviously not a factor. Instead, the key issue is the employer's ability to pay. If taxpayers (through their elected representatives on the school board) set the school district budget at $50 million, then only this amount is available for all purposes, including teacher salaries. In Canada, public sector employees are highly unionized, so most public sector pay is determined through collective bargaining. If the union has the right to strike, as most do, then key factors are how essential the service is, how willing public officials (and the general public) are to endure a strike, how much budget is available for pay increases, and how easy it is to obtain a budget increase. Higher pay levels can be granted without a budget increase, but the money must come from somewhere, usually through a reduction in the number of persons employed by the organization.

In general, the public sector has been experiencing wage compression. Public sector employees at the lower end of the job hierarchy usually earn more than comparable employees in the private sector, while public sector employees at the top of the job hierarchy usually earn less than they would in the private sector.[6] This differential at the lower end is explained by the relative power of public sector unions due to their ability to disrupt important public services. Pay equity programs, which have been in place much longer in public sector organizations, may also have helped increase the pay of lower-level public sector workers.[7]

By contrast, pay for top-level government officials is constrained by the visibility of their salaries as well as by a reluctance among taxpayers to pay public employees a lot more than they themselves are earning. There are no such constraints on private sector employers regarding their top-level employees, so the wage gap between the public and private sectors is wide in this top employment bracket.

Several general patterns in compensation levels can be identified. Historically, unionized employees have received considerably more compensation than comparable non-union employees, although the so-called union wage premium has declined greatly in Canada in recent years and may even have disappeared in some sectors.[8] Male employees earn more than female employees on average (although this gap has been gradually decreasing;[9] employees in large firms earn more than those in small firms; employees in Alberta, Ontario, Saskatchewan, and Newfoundland earn more than those in other provinces; and, as the opening vignette showed, employees in the resource sector earn more than those in the service sector.

Aside from the relative scarcity of labour and its perceived value to the employer, pay is affected by what are known as **compensating differentials**. For example, many of the high-paying jobs in the resource sector are cyclical—in other words, workers in that sector often must endure periods of unemployment. Their higher wage levels serve in effect as compensation for this employment volatility. Similarly, the cost of living in Alberta and Ontario is higher than in most other provinces, and the higher wage rates help compensate for this reality.

Compensating differentials can also be triggered by negative employment features such as poor working conditions and jobs for which failure rates are high. For example, many people who try selling life insurance fail, but those who succeed can earn very high compensation. Another example of a negative feature is a poor industry reputation—for example, forestry is widely perceived as environmentally unfriendly, and the tobacco industry is in social disfavour.

However, does this theory really work? Are salaries, say, for sanitation workers a result of undesirable work conditions? See Compensation Today 9.2 for an explanation.

**compensating differential**
A higher compensation level offered by an employer because of undesirable aspects of the employment.

Salaries for some jobs vary with cost of living.

### The Dirt on Compensation

In Chapter 3, we discussed how employees take a variety of costs and benefits into account when deciding where to seek and accept employment. When considering a job as a sanitation worker, it is easy to list the costs. Garbage is smelly, dirty, and rodent-infested. One sanitation worker claimed they saw a human leg in the dumpster. There is heavy lifting involved and long hours. Workers must weave through traffic and be mindful of safety concerns. Worst of all, there is a stigma attached to the title. Many of us have been told by teachers, "If you don't study, you will end up as a garbage man." Little did we know as children that some sanitation workers earn more than teachers.

The economic theory of compensating differentials explains that individuals may be offered an additional amount of income due to the undesirable nature of the job. Because of the less favourable conditions and the negative view of the industry, salaries must be higher to entice people to pursue that line of work.

In an article published by CNN, two sanitation workers in New York City were interviewed. One of the workers was earning $112 000, and the other was earning $110 000. Their salaries increased in the last eight out of nine years of work. One of the sanitation workers dropped out of high school in Grade 10 and has worked in the industry for 10 years. His salary started at $80 000. This man supported eight out of nine of his children. The second sanitation worker also dropped out of school before moving to the United States from Guyana. He was looking to buy a house right outside of New York City.

Considering the job does not require any education nor trained skill, the sanitation workers' compensation allows for quite a comfortable lifestyle. The average high school dropout in the United States earns $24 000 annually. Not only are sanitation workers earning more than most high school dropouts, but some are earning more than many university graduates. By comparison, the median salary for teachers in New York City is just under $62 000. Sanitation workers' compensation has also seen a steady increase year over year. Since the recession ended in 2009, worker salaries have increased, on average, by 14 percent. Sanitation workers' wages have increased by 18 percent. Though the job may possess a negative stigma, we wouldn't say that it is trash after all!

Source: Patrick Gillespie, "The $100 000 Job, Garbage Workers," *CNN*, February 25, 2016.

# DEFINING THE RELEVANT LABOUR MARKET

Labour markets are complex. Luckily, an employer does not need to understand the labour market as a whole, but only that segment that pertains to the specific jobs the employer needs to fill. Essentially, an employer needs to know what its competitors are paying their employees.

Two kinds of competitors are relevant: competitors in the same labour market, and competitors in the same product/service market. Sometimes firms in different industries compete for the same labour—for example, insurance companies, chemical manufacturers, and airlines all need accounting clerks. But in other cases, labour is so specialized that certain jobs are found only within the same industry. For example, if you are a chemical manufacturer and need chemical process control engineers, you don't have to compete with an insurance company or an airline to hire them.

Labour markets and product/service markets serve as constraints to employers. If an employer is paying less than its competitors in the labour market, it will not be able to attract and retain good employees. If an employer is paying more than its competitors in the same product/service market, it may have difficulty offering its product or service at a competitive price.

There are two other important dimensions of the labour market: occupational grouping and the geographic scope—local, regional, national, or international. These two dimensions overlap depending on how specialized and industry-specific the occupational grouping is.

For example, if you are looking for a secretary, the market is usually local. Almost every organization of any size employs one or more secretaries so they can be found in almost all labour markets. But at the same time, not every organization employs a chemical process engineer, and these employees may be very scarce in some local labour markets. In general, the more specialized the occupation, the wider the geographic scope of the market for that occupation. For example, it may be possible to hire production and office staff locally but necessary to seek technical staff across a larger region, senior managerial staff on a national basis, and specialized professional staff nationally or internationally.

Thus, before setting out to collect data, the employer needs to identify the occupational groups, the geographic boundaries for that group, and the industry boundaries for the information. As discussed later in this chapter, the employer must also identify the specific compensation data it needs to make informed decisions.

Compensation data sources sometimes allow firms to customize information on the organizations they are comparing themselves with. The selected comparator organizations are known as **market comparator firms**. In putting together this sample of market comparator firms, the trick is to maintain a broad enough sample to be representative while focusing on firms as similar as possible to the target firm. Relevant characteristics in selecting this sample include the type of product or service the firm provides, the geographic area over which it operates, the size of the firm, and whether the firm is union or non-union. However, depending on the industry, even a non-union firm should include some unionized firms in its market sample to ensure wage competitiveness. Overall, there is no precise formula for selecting a market sample. Instead, it is a balancing act informed by judgment and knowledge of your human resource needs.

# SOURCES OF COMPENSATION DATA

Once an organization has identified the type of labour market information it needs, it must then acquire that information. All market information is based on compensation surveys but organizations do not all need to conduct their own surveys. There are three main "third party" sources of compensation data: government agencies, industry groups, and compensation consulting firms. Many of these organizations have websites that offer compensation data (see Compensation Notebook 9.1), although there may be a fee for accessing this information.

## THIRD-PARTY SURVEYS

### Government Agencies

A variety of government agencies survey employers to collect labour market information. At the federal level, these include Statistics Canada;[10] Employment and Social Development Canada, which maintains information on collective agreements as well as other pay information; and the Government of Canada Labour Market Information website. Most provincial labour departments also publish some data on compensation levels. So do some municipal governments.

## Industry Groups

Most industries have industry associations, many of which collect data on pay rates within their industries. Many professional associations also collect data on their own occupational groups. Additionally, some organizations share collective bargaining agreements that contain compensation data.

## Compensation Consultants

There are many firms for which collecting labour market information is an important business. These include large international firms such as Aon Hewitt Associates, Hay Group Towers Watson, and Mercer, as well as many smaller firms that operate on a local or regional basis. One concern is that these data may come mostly from their client firms and thus do not necessarily comprise a representative sample.

## Free Compensation Data Websites

Free websites providing compensation data have come online in recent years; the most notable of these are Salary Wizard and PayScale. There are concerns about the validity of the data from these websites, as Compensation Today 9.3 explains.

## Advantages and Disadvantages of Third-Party Surveys

Using compensation data acquired from third-party sources has both advantages and disadvantages. The two most obvious advantages are ease and cost. Normally, when firms are asked to participate in compensation surveys, they are promised the results, so the only cost is the cost of the time spent responding to the survey. And it is much easier to use third-party data than to design and conduct an in-house survey.

However, there are several disadvantages. Third-party surveys may not cover the desired jobs, compensation characteristics, or employers. In addition, aggregate data are often provided, rather than company-by-company data, so that it is not possible to separate out those employers who are the most appropriate comparators for your organization.

## TRADITIONAL AND NEW SALARY SURVEYS

Most compensation professionals are pretty clear about the salary survey process when working with compensation data providers. They select surveys that cover their industry and geography/locations, review the participants list to determine that they are proper comparators with whom they may compete for talent, match their benchmark jobs to the survey benchmark jobs, submit their data, receive the report from the provider, and analyze the data. The confidence in the survey data comes from, among other factors, knowing that the job matches are completed by trained compensation professionals and managers, who know the jobs from both job-specific information and the talent management big picture perspective. They know that the focus is on the job, not the person doing the job.

Now, with advances in technology, some compensation data providers are changing this process. Take PayScale, for example. The company has revolutionized salary surveys.

Instead of doing job matches, individuals and companies can type in a job title; answer a few questions about the skills, experience, and education required for the job, and a few questions on the scope of the job, such as budget and numbers of people reporting to the role in the case of management positions; then type in the salary of the job; and get a report of the job profile and how much the job is paid on the market with average, median, and percentiles. PayScale states that the profiles are reviewed using advanced proprietary algorithms to check for outliers or illogical data sequences and compare more than 250 compensable factors to find the ideal match for the job. PayScale claims that it will turn compensation into a true science, rather than an art. While innovation in compensation technology helps to move the profession forward, the verdict is still pending on this methodology. One concern is the self-reported data. Would the average worker have the skills to put in the correct data for his or her job? How about the human nature that makes us all think highly of our own jobs and ourselves? Take a look at the PayScale website. What are your thoughts?

Salary surveys can be done through telephone interviews.

**COMPARING TRADITIONAL SALARY SURVEY AND PAYSCALE**

|  | Traditional Salary Survey | Payscale |
|---|---|---|
| Who provides data | Employer | Employee |
| Job match | Done by compensation professionals and manager | Done by algorithms |
| Skills required to generate report | High | Low |
| Skills required to analyze result | High | High |
| Up-front cost | High | Low |
| Suitable for | Medium to large organizations with jobs that have multiple incumbents | Smaller organizations and individuals who want to price one job at a time |

Sources: http://www.payscale.com; http://www.wynfordgroup.com/.

## IN-HOUSE SURVEYS

A final option is to carry out your own compensation survey. This can be done informally or formally.

### Informal Surveys

Informal approaches range from a quick review of "help wanted" ads to a question posed to a group of colleagues at an industry function to a few telephone calls to other firms. Informal surveys are usually simple and quick but may have poor reliability and validity.

### Formal Surveys

Formal surveys can be undertaken by internal staff or can be contracted to compensation firms. The main advantage of in-house surveys is that the employer controls the entire process, thereby ensuring the quality and appropriateness of the data. Another advantage is that the employer avoids paying the consulting fees, which can be high, depending on the amount of customization required. However, there are many disadvantages to conducting your own survey. First, if the survey is to be done by internal staff, then someone with the required expertise must be available. In addition, many employers surveyed may be reluctant to reveal their compensation practices to their competitors in the absence of any intermediary organization. For these reasons, most firms prefer to contract out the survey to professionals in the field.

## CONDUCTING COMPENSATION SURVEYS

In conducting a compensation survey, there are four main steps: (1) identify the jobs that are to be surveyed, (2) determine the information to be collected about each job, (3) identify which employers are to be surveyed, and (4) determine the method of data collection.

# IDENTIFY THE JOBS TO BE SURVEYED

Most organizations do not collect market data about every job they have for several reasons. First, it would be very costly to do so. Second, the organization often has unique jobs for which it is hard to find matches. Third, a full-scale survey is not necessary. The usual rule of thumb is that surveying about 10–15 percent of jobs should be sufficient to calibrate the system. Moreover, it is not necessary to survey these key or benchmark jobs every year. Instead, data can be obtained on the annual increases in pay rates, and the job rates updated on this basis.[11]

**key job matching**
Including jobs on a compensation survey that are well understood and numerous in the labour market and asking respondents to supply compensation information for those jobs.

Essential to any compensation survey is an effective method for matching an organization's jobs to those being surveyed. The most common approach is known as key job matching, which involves selecting certain jobs that are well understood and numerous in the job market and asking employers to compare their jobs with these jobs. Typically, a job title and a brief job summary are provided. Employers are then asked whether they have any of these jobs, and if so, to provide their compensation data. When selecting these jobs, it is important to represent a variety of job families and to provide examples within each family at both the entry level and the top level.

# DETERMINE WHAT INFORMATION TO COLLECT

Simply collecting information about wage and salary levels does not generally provide an adequate basis for comparison. Information about the base pay, performance pay, and indirect pay, as well as the weekly hours of work, must be collected for each job in the survey. In addition to the formal pay ranges for each job, knowing where most employees actually are in the pay range is also useful. You can determine this by asking how many employees are in each quartile of the pay range. Compensation Notebook 9.2 provides a list of typical questions to ask when conducting a compensation survey. **Figure 9.1** provides an actual survey form used by one human resources consulting firm.

---

## COMPENSATION NOTEBOOK 9.2

### TYPICAL COMPENSATION SURVEY QUESTIONS

#### A. GENERAL QUESTIONS

1. Name of employer
2. Number of employees
3. Location of employees
4. Main products or services produced

#### B. QUESTIONS FOR EACH JOB

1. Do you have any employees performing the job described below? [The description for the specific job being surveyed appears here.]
2. How many?
3. Are the employees in this job union members?
4. What was the average base pay, performance pay, and indirect pay (estimate a dollar value for the benefits provided) received by employees in this job over the last year?
5. What is the minimum, maximum, and midpoint of the pay range for this job?
6. How many employees are in each quartile of the pay range?
7. On what basis do employees move through the pay range? (e.g., seniority, merit, training)
8. How long does it take a typical employee to move from the bottom to the top of the pay range?
9. What is the standard workweek for this job, in terms of hours?
10. Are these employees eligible for overtime? At what pay rate?

---

**FIGURE 9.1**

Sample Compensation Survey Form

**Salary and Benefits Survey**

**SALARY INFORMATION**

| Benchmark Job Title | Your Job Title | Number of Incumbents | Quality of Job Match (Please Check One) | | | Average Annual Base Salary | Check If Job Is Bonus Eligible | Average Bonus Paid | Minimum of Salary Range | Maximum of Salary Range |
|---|---|---|---|---|---|---|---|---|---|---|
| | | | Poor (0–60%) | Good (60–80%) | Excellent (80–100%) | | | | | |
| | | | | | | | | | | |
| | | | | | | | | | | |
| | | | | | | | | | | |
| | | | | | | | | | | |
| | | | | | | | | | | |
| | | | | | | | | | | |
| | | | | | | | | | | |
| | | | | | | | | | | |

1. What are wage increases based on? _____ Cost of Living _____ Performance _____ Seniority _____ Skills/Competencies _____ Market Information _____
   Other (please describe) _____

**HOURS OF WORK AND SCHEDULING**

1. What are your regular weekly business hours (e.g., 36 hours/week, 37.5 hours/week, 40 hours/week, etc.)? _____
2. Do you provide one or more alternative workweek schedules to your employees (e.g., 4.5 day week, one day off every other week or every third week, etc.) ___ Yes ___ No
   If yes, what is your arrangement? _____
3. What is the annual vacation allowance for employees? (e.g. **1–5** years service earn **3** weeks per year, etc.)
   ___–___ years service earn ___ weeks per year
   ___–___ years service earn ___ weeks per year
4. Do you have an allowance for paid absences due to illness and/or pressing necessity? ___ Yes ___ No
   If yes, what is your annual sick leave allowance? _____ How is this earned? _____
5. In addition to legislated statutory holidays, do you provide any other days as paid days off (e.g., Boxing Day)? ___ Yes ___ No If yes, how many? _____

Source: Salary and Benefits Survey, Koenig and Associates. Reprinted with permission.

**FIGURE 9.1**

Sample Compensation Survey Form (*Continued*)

6. Overtime is paid after _____ hours are worked in a week. At what rate is overtime paid? _____

   a. What groups of employees are eligible for overtime pay? (check as many as apply) \_\_\_\_ All \_\_\_\_ Admin \_\_\_\_ Technical \_\_\_\_ Professional

      \_\_\_\_ Management \_\_\_\_ Other _____

   b. Are employees allowed to take time off in lieu of overtime pay? \_\_\_\_ Yes \_\_\_\_ No  If yes, please briefly describe policy. _____

**BENEFITS**

1. Please indicate (✓) which of the following benefits are provided. Detail how the cost is shared between the employer and employee (e.g., 50/50, 25/75), for each benefit listed.

2. Please indicate which of the following programs/benefits are provided. Please provide any relevant details about the design of the program in the Comments section.

| BENEFIT | ✓ | Employer % | Employee % |
|---|---|---|---|
| Group Life Insurance | | | |
| Accidental Death & Dismemberment | | | |
| Short-Term Disability | | | |
| Long-Term Disability | | | |
| Supplementary Health Care | | | |
| Dental Plan | | | |

| BENEFIT | ✓ | Employer % | Employee % |
|---|---|---|---|
| Vision Care Plan | | | |
| Employee Assistance Plan | | | |
| Fitness Plan (e.g., club membership) | | | |
| Pension Plan | | | |
| Group RRSP | | | |
| Other (please list) | | | |

| Program/Benefit Offered | Available to: | | | | | | Max Value | Comments/Details (please add additional pages as necessary) |
|---|---|---|---|---|---|---|---|---|
| | All | Admin | Technical | Professional | Mgmt | Other | | |
| Incentive Pay Program (e.g., share ownership, commissions, etc.) | | | | | | | | |
| Personal Vehicle Allowance ($x/month) | | | | | | | | |
| Company Vehicle Is Personal Use Allowed? | | | | | | | | |
| Payment of Professional Dues | | | | | | | | |
| Payment of Association/Society Memberships | | | | | | | | |
| Other Bonus Payments (e.g., Christmas bonus, etc.) | | | | | | | | |

3. Do you provide an Education/Training Allowance to employees? \_\_\_\_ Yes \_\_\_\_ No

Source: *Salary and Benefits Survey*, Koenig and Associates. Reprinted with permission.

# DETERMINE WHOM TO SURVEY

Determining which employers to survey is not a simple matter. In general, firms like to survey other employers that they perceive as similar to themselves in industry type, geographic location, and size. But the sample generally varies, depending on whether the jobs being surveyed are filled by the local, regional, national, or international labour markets.

# DETERMINE HOW TO COLLECT THE DATA

There are four ways to collect the information: (1) personal interviews, (2) questionnaires, (3) telephone interviews, and (4) the Internet.

## Personal Interviews

In general, the personal interview is thought to provide the best-quality information. In an interview, you can ensure that the jobs being surveyed are actually similar to the job data reported and that the questions are being interpreted properly. However, this method is very costly to use on any significant scale.

## Questionnaires

By far the cheapest method of data collection is the mail survey or questionnaire. However, it is also the least reliable method because there is no control over who is filling out the survey and no way of knowing whether it is being done correctly. Chores such as filling out a questionnaire are often delegated to the most junior member of the HR department.

## Telephone Interviews

A compromise method is the telephone interview. It is much cheaper than the personal interview, yet it produces a higher quality of information than the questionnaire approach because there is an opportunity to confirm job matches and to clarify survey questions. This method also provides some control over who the respondent is.

## Internet Surveys

Internet surveys can be faster than mail surveys and can facilitate the tabulation of data. Moreover, using the Internet allows for easier contact with respondents throughout the survey process. Research indicates that compared to mail surveys, Internet surveys generate quicker responses and higher response rates; they also cost less and yield data of no less quality than that produced by mail surveys.[12] Compared to face-to-face interviews, response rates are lower; however, for sensitive data where there is a social desirability aspect, Internet surveys produce more valid results, and at a fraction of the cost.[13] Internet surveys can sometimes produce more accurate information because the time pressure of face-to-face and telephone interviews may cause respondents to respond with guesses about data instead of taking the time to look up the information.[14] In sum, there seems to be very little downside to online surveys.

# ANALYZING AND INTERPRETING SURVEY DATA

After you have conducted a compensation survey, you have a set of raw data—a list of employers surveyed and what they are paying for different jobs. It is hoped for each job you have the minimum, maximum, and midpoints of the pay ranges, and the mean base pay, performance pay, indirect pay, and total compensation. Now what?

# ANALYTICAL PROCEDURES

The first steps in analyzing the survey data involve assessing the central tendency of pay and the variation across employers. There are two ways to assess central tendency. Using a **mean average** (sometimes known as a **simple average**), you add up the midpoints of the pay range for a given job at each company and divide the sum by the total number of companies. Of course, this weights all employers equally, regardless of whether they employ one or one thousand of the employees performing the target job. Therefore, some firms compute a **weighted mean** (sometimes known as a **weighted average**) by weighting each employer according to how many employees that employer has performing the target job. You can also calculate a simple average or weighted average of the mean base pay, performance pay, and indirect pay across the sample of firms. A simple average mean pay gives an indication of pay policies used by a typical firm for a given job, while a weighted average mean pay gives a better indication of what the typical employee in a given job is earning.

One problem with a mean is that it can be distorted by extreme values. One way of avoiding extreme values when measuring central tendency is to use the **median**, which is the middle value in a ranking of pay levels, below which half of employers are paying less and above which half are paying more.

Dispersion of pay across employers can be assessed in several ways. One way is to look at the mean total compensation for the lowest-paying employer and then determine what percentage more the highest-paying employer is paying. For example, if the lowest-paying employer pays its secretaries a mean total compensation of $30 000, and the highest-paying employer pays its secretaries a mean total compensation of $45 000, then the dispersion in secretarial compensation across firms is 50 percent.

Another way of examining dispersion across employers is to look at **quartiles** or **deciles**. For example, the mean total compensation levels at each firm for a given job are arranged from lowest to highest, and then the list is divided into either four groups (quartiles) or 10 groups (deciles). The mean total compensation within each quartile or decile is then computed. This method allows an assessment of detailed pay statistics, such as what the top 25 percent of firms (using quartiles) are paying on average.

Percentiles, which indicate the amount below which a certain percentage of employers would fall, can also be used. For example, if $60 000 is at the 90th percentile of total compensation for a given job, that means that 90 percent of firms pay less than that and 10 percent pay more. The **interquartile range** is the difference between the 25th and 75th percentile values, divided by the 25th percentile value. If this quotient is very large, it may indicate problems with the job matching, where some of the jobs in the sample are not equivalent.[15]

A major issue in analyzing compensation data is determining whether to focus on range midpoints or actual mean compensation levels. Range midpoints and pay ranges do not actually describe what the typical employee in the job earns; and pay ranges deal only with base pay, so a lot of the compensation picture could be missing. For example, most employees in the survey could be at the top of the pay range or the bottom. One way of assessing where employees are actually being paid in the pay range is to ask respondents to report the number of employees in each quartile of the pay range for each job.

A useful statistic in assessing the distribution of employees within their pay range is known as the **compa-ratio**. The compa-ratio is calculated by taking the mean base pay of all employees holding a particular job and then dividing this amount by the midpoint of the pay range for that job. A compa-ratio of greater than one means that, on average, employees

---

**mean or simple average**
A measure of central tendency of a set of values derived by summing the values and dividing by the number of values.

**weighted mean or weighted average**
A measure of central tendency of a set of values that adjusts the average based on the number of cases to which each value pertains.

**median**
The middle value in an ordered list of values.

**quartiles or deciles**
Division of an ordered list of values into either four groups (quartiles) or 10 groups (deciles).

**interquartile range**
A measure of pay dispersion across employers, calculated by dividing the difference between the 25th and 75th percentile values by the value of the 25th percentile.

**compa-ratio**
A measure of distribution of employees within their pay range calculated by dividing the mean base pay by the midpoint of the pay range.

are being paid above the midpoint at that firm; a compa-ratio of less than one means that, on average, employees are being paid below the midpoint.

The same procedure can be applied to the compa-ratio of an individual employee; that is, his/her base pay divided by the mid-point of the pay range.

Besides analyzing the level of compensation, analyzing survey data may also indicate the typical structure of compensation (or pay mix) across employers. To start, you could calculate the proportion of base pay, performance pay, and indirect pay (as a percentage of total compensation) for a given job at each firm and then average these values (either a simple average, or a weighted average, or both). In this way, you might discover that firms in the sample pay 70 percent of their secretaries' total compensation in base pay, 10 percent in performance pay, and 20 percent in indirect pay, on average. You can also look at the percentages for each firm to examine particular compensation issues, such as variation in the use of performance pay.

# INTERPRETING SURVEY DATA

The best way to illustrate the issues involved in interpreting survey data is to work through a detailed example. **Table 9.1** provides an example of compensation survey results for the job of "accounting clerk."

In this example, we have surveyed 10 companies and have data regarding the number of accounting clerks that each firm employs; the minimum, maximum, and midpoints of the base pay ranges; the mean amounts of base pay, performance pay, indirect pay, and total compensation paid to accounting clerks at each firm; and the distribution of accounting clerks across the pay range in each firm by quartile.

The job summary used on the survey was based on the Government of Canada National Occupational Classification for "Accounting and Related Clerks":

> This unit group includes clerks who calculate, prepare and process bills, invoices, accounts payable and receivable, budgets and other routine financial records according to established procedures. They are employed throughout the private and public sectors. Examples of related titles include costing clerk, ledger clerk, audit clerk, finance clerk, budget clerk, billing clerk, tax return preparer, accounts payable clerk, accounts receivable clerk, invoice clerk, deposit clerk, tax clerk, and freight-rate clerk.

## Inspecting the Data

What can we observe from Table 9.1? Base pay range midpoints range from $24 000 (Company J) to $32 000 (Company A). The average base pay range midpoint is $28 050, and the weighted average midpoint is $26 936. This suggests that firms that employ more accounting clerks have a lower pay range than firms that employ fewer. The median range midpoint is $28 500. (When there is an even number of cases, the median is the average of the middle two cases.)

As Table 9.1 shows, mean base pay is lowest at Company J ($24 600) and highest at Company A ($33 400). Interestingly, however, when total compensation is considered, Company I pays the least ($31 375) due to poor indirect pay and no performance pay, and Company B pays the most ($46 340). There is quite a high dispersion (48 percent) between the lowest- and highest-paying firms, which may suggest that the job duties of accounting clerks may be different at these firms.

## TABLE 9.1

### Results of Compensation Survey: Accounting Clerk

| Company | Total Employment | Number of Accounting Clerks Employed | Base Pay Range Minimum | Base Pay Range Midpoint | Base Pay Range Maximum | Mean Base Pay | Mean Performance Pay | Mean Indirect Pay | Mean Total Compensation | Compa-Ratio | Base Pay Quartile 1 | 2 | 3 | 4 |
|---|---|---|---|---|---|---|---|---|---|---|---|---|---|---|
| A | 700 | 5 | $29 000 | $32 000 | $35 000 | $33 400 | $3340 | $6680 | $43 420 | 1.04 | 1 (20%) | 0 (—) | 1 (20%) | 3 (60%) |
| B | 1700 | 20 | 28 000 | 31 000 | 34 000 | 33 100 | 4965 | 8275 | 46 340 | 1.07 | 2 (10%) | 1 (5%) | 1 (5%) | 16 (80%) |
| C | 800 | 6 | 29 000 | 30 000 | 31 000 | 30 667 | 6133 | 9200 | 46 000 | 1.02 | 1 (17%) | 0 (—) | 0 (—) | 5 (83%) |
| D | 2000 | 25 | 28 000 | 30 000 | 32 000 | 31 560 | 1578 | 12 624 | 45 762 | 1.05 | 2 (8%) | 1 (4%) | 1 (4%) | 21 (84%) |
| E | 700 | 9 | 6000 | 30 000 | 34 000 | 31 333 | 3133 | 9400 | 43 866 | 1.04 | 2 (22%) | 1 (11%) | 1 (11%) | 5 (56%) |
| F | 4000 | 45 | 25 000 | 27 000 | 29 000 | 27 544 | 1377 | 9640 | 38 561 | 1.02 | 11 (24%) | 6 (13%) | 8 (18%) | 20 (44%) |
| G | 5000 | 65 | 23 500 | 26 500 | 29 500 | 25 923 | — | 7777 | 33 700 | 0.98 | 20 (31%) | 15 (23%) | 10 (15%) | 20 (31%) |
| H | 7000 | 80 | 22 000 | 25 000 | 28 000 | 25 050 | — | 8768 | 33 818 | 1.00 | 24 (30%) | 18 (23%) | 10 (13%) | 28 (35%) |
| I | 1000 | 10 | 21 000 | 25 000 | 29 000 | 25 100 | — | 6275 | 31 375 | 1.00 | 0 (—) | 7 (70%) | 2 (20%) | 1 (10%) |
| J | 1000 | 10 | 21 000 | 24 000 | 27 000 | 24 600 | 3690 | 6150 | 34 440 | 1.03 | 0 (—) | 4 (40%) | 4 (40%) | 2 (20%) |
| Simple Average | | | 25 250 | 28 050 | 30 850 | 28 827 | 2422 | 8479 | 39 728 | | | | | |
| Weighted Average | | | 24 165 | 26 936 | 29 707 | 27 307 | 1161 | 8797 | 37 266 | | | | | |

Let us examine performance pay and indirect pay. As Table 9.1 shows, performance pay ranges from $1377 (Company F) to $6133 (Company C), while three companies (G, H, I) do not offer any performance pay. Indirect pay ranges from $6150 (Company J) to $12 624 (Company D). Using the data in Table 9.1, we have calculated below the percentage of total compensation for each pay component in the compensation mix:

| | Base Pay (%) | Performance Pay (%) | Indirect Pay (%) |
|---|---|---|---|
| Company A | 77 | 8 | 15 |
| Company B | 71 | 11 | 18 |
| Company C | 67 | 13 | 20 |
| Company D | 69 | 3 | 28 |
| Company E | 71 | 7 | 21 |
| Company F | 71 | 4 | 25 |
| Company G | 77 | — | 23 |
| Company H | 74 | — | 26 |
| Company I | 80 | — | 20 |
| Company J | 71 | 11 | 18 |
| Average | 73 | 6 | 21 |

As this table shows, the companies vary considerably in their compensation mixes and compensation levels. Base pay constitutes as much as 80 percent of total compensation in Company I, or as little as 67 percent in Company C. Performance pay ranges from as much as 13 percent of total compensation to none being offered, and indirect pay ranges from 28 percent down to 15 percent.

## Drawing Inferences from the Data

What can we make of these substantial differences in pay policies for the same job? We can infer from its low starting pay ($21 000) that Company I may be willing to accept inexperienced and/or untrained employees and then provide them with on-the-job training. With its wide pay range, the company can reward increased experience over time. Even so, total compensation is constrained by low indirect pay and zero performance pay. So how will Company I keep its accounting clerks once they are trained?

Company I might promote these individuals rapidly to higher-level jobs, such as senior accounting clerk, which may carry a considerably higher pay scale. Perhaps the jobs at Company I have some intrinsic or extrinsic rewards that other firms do not offer, such as high job security. Or perhaps Company I cannot afford to pay any more than what it pays and has to put up with hiring inexperienced employees who quit to take better-paying jobs once they are trained.

What about the width of the pay ranges? They vary from $2000 in Company C to $8000 in Company I. The mean width of the base pay range is $5600. Beyond these facts, careful examination suggests that there may be some patterns. For example, Company C, with a pay range of only $2000, offers a high starting base pay ($29 000).

Company C also has high performance pay, which may be used to differentiate employees, as there is very little progression through the pay range.

Perhaps Company C hires only highly experienced and well-trained accounting clerks. It employs only six of them, yet it expects these six to handle all the clerical accounting duties for a company of 800 employees. In comparison, Company E has nine accounting clerks for 700 employees. Many factors could explain this difference in staffing, and it may not mean that the accounting clerks at Company C do more work than those at Company E.

Company I (along with Company E) has the widest pay range—$8000. However, because the firm's starting pay is so low ($21 000), it needs a wide range to keep good employees as they become more experienced. In contrast to Company C, Company I is likely using pay range to differentiate employees because it has no performance pay.

This raises a question. What is the value of performance pay to employees? In our example, we have factored it into total compensation as if it is of equivalent value to base pay (dollar for dollar). But is a dollar of performance pay really worth a dollar of base pay? Most financial experts would say no, because performance pay is uncertain. If the performance pay is based on individual performance and is allocated in a zero-sum way, there may be a strong possibility that an individual will not receive any performance pay in a given year. If the performance pay is based on company performance, such as a profit-sharing plan, there is no guarantee that the necessary threshold level will be reached next year, even if it was reached this year.

What about indirect pay? Because of the tax advantages of many types of indirect pay, some might argue that a dollar of indirect pay is worth more than a dollar of base pay. But that depends on the structure of the indirect pay and on the needs of the employee. Some employees may place very little value on benefits, because they don't use most of them. In fact, they may not even be aware of many of the benefits for which they are eligible.

In short, some firms may be spending a lot of money on benefits that employees don't care about. (This is one of the problems that flexible benefits are intended to solve, by allowing employees to maximize their own cash value of benefits.) Thus, one dollar of benefits may be worth more than one dollar of pay to some employees and less than one dollar to others.

Let's examine the data from another angle. In this survey, indirect pay averages about 21 percent of total compensation. But it is higher in larger companies than in smaller companies, which is typical. For example, indirect pay averaged 26 percent of total compensation in companies with 2000 or more employees, and 19 percent in companies with fewer than 2000 employees. On the other hand, smaller firms used performance pay more heavily: performance pay constituted eight percent of total compensation in firms with fewer than 2000 employees, and only two percent in firms with 2000 or more employees. Overall, large firms paid somewhat less ($37 960) than smaller firms ($40 906). But the compensation in the larger firms was less risky because they had higher indirect pay and lower performance pay than smaller firms.

## Examining Pay Range Distribution

Finally, we need to examine the distribution of employees within their pay ranges. The last five columns in Table 9.1 present this information. They show that the distribution across the quartiles of top-paying firms is very different from that of the lower-paying firms, with the majority of their employees in the top (fourth) quartile.

This distribution difference is not surprising. Examine Company D, which has 84 percent of its accounting clerks in the top quartile. Although Company D does not pay the highest maximum base pay, it does provide some performance pay, along with the best benefits (indirect pay). Why would anyone ever quit? No one does, so eventually most employees end up in the top pay quartile. In contrast, Companies F to J have only a minority of their employees in the top bracket. This suggests higher turnover. In addition, let's examine Company H, where just 35 percent of the clerks are in the top bracket. As Table 9.1 shows, 30 percent are also in the bottom quartile. One can infer that this firm has high turnover and is continually hiring new clerks. As these employees gain experience, they are likely able to get jobs with better paying firms, so they quit. The table also shows a sharp drop between quartiles 1 and 2, and between quartiles 2 and 3.

In addition, Companies I and J probably cannot find acceptable employees at the low end of their pay ranges and are bringing new clerks in at the second quartile. The bottom end of their pay ranges is really irrelevant. Because of low indirect pay at Company I, there is nothing to retain their employees as they gain experience, so they appear to quit at their first opportunity.

The compa-ratios also indicate actual base pay relative to the pay range midpoints and show that most firms are currently paying their employees in the top half of the pay range, with the exception of companies G, H, and I, which are paying slightly below or at the midpoints.

## Applying Survey Data

This example shows that interpreting survey data is a complex process. But once interpreted, how do you apply your results? If you are using a job evaluation system, you will use the survey data from key (benchmark) jobs to develop a market line and to calibrate the job evaluation system against that, as described in the previous chapter. If you are using a skill-based pay system, you will need information from jobs that match the bottom of the skill grid and the top of the skill grid, as described in Chapter 4.

If you are using market pricing, you simply apply the market rates to your jobs, after adjusting for compensation mix strategy and compensation level strategy. You do not need to survey each job every year; if you survey one-fifth of the jobs each year, you can update the others based on estimates of annual increases. With this method, you will end up market-testing every job every five years. Of course, surveys may be done more frequently for a particular job if there are indications, such as difficulty in recruiting or excessively high turnover, that the pay level is inappropriate.

But before applying the data, you need to complete one more step. Because compensation surveys deal with historical data, they are always somewhat out of date. Furthermore, the pay system being planned must apply to the upcoming year, so there needs to be some consideration of the amount the market will increase in a year. You need to adjust the survey data through a process known as **aging the data**.

**aging the data**
The process of adjusting compensation data to bring it up to date with the time period in which the new compensation will take effect.

The application of market data can raise some thorny issues. For example, what happens when the pay rate indicated by job evaluation differs from that indicated by market data? Although there is not much research evidence on that question, one experimental study of U.S. compensation managers[16] found that market data tended to outweigh job evaluation data. That is, managers' inclination was to abandon internal equity if it conflicted with market data. This is one reason that some argue that pay equity legislation is essential because this inclination tends to replicate market practices even if they are not equitable.

# LIMITATIONS OF COMPENSATION SURVEYS

Compensation surveys have many limitations. First, they may vary dramatically in quality of job matches and methodology. Second, they may omit important information. For example, for most firms, adequately quantifying performance pay and indirect pay is not a simple process, and some surveys may omit important elements. Third, unless compensation survey data are available for individual employers in the market sample (as was the case in Table 9.1 but is rare in compensation survey data), we cannot surmise anything about the compensation strategies practised by other firms. Fourth, compensation data may not fit all the jobs an organization has, especially if these jobs are organized differently from the norm.

Furthermore, compensation surveys were developed when compensation systems were much simpler than they are today. Thus, recent extensive use of indirect pay and performance pay has complicated data gathering enormously. For example, the value of stock options is very difficult to estimate, as is that of long-term incentives. In addition, some firms may provide other important benefits that are difficult to price out in monetary terms, such as purchase discounts or the use of company recreational facilities. To make matters still more complicated, some firms include these items when reporting indirect pay, while others do not. So, overall, surveys cannot capture the entire range of rewards—both extrinsic and intrinsic—offered by organizations.

Another issue is that there may be bias in the sample of firms responding to compensation surveys. Traditional firms with simple pay systems find it much easier to reply to compensation surveys than nontraditional firms that have nonstandard jobs and complex pay systems. Thus, compensation surveys may misrepresent actual pay trends.

Finally, while compensation surveys attempt to reflect the value placed on jobs by the labour market, the use of these surveys assumes that the market values jobs fairly. As discussed in previous chapters, the market may underprice certain jobs, including those dominated by women. Underpricing puts employers in a quandary. If they wish to be fair, they may need to pay certain jobs (such as those traditionally held by women) more than the market would dictate. However, this practice may put them at a competitive disadvantage, especially if their competitors do not adjust their pay rates at the same time. For this reason, many critics of market compensation have little faith in voluntary measures to correct historic inequities and argue that pay equity legislation is essential to create a level playing field for all employers. Compensation Today 9.4 discusses a case where there were pay equity issues with market data.

---

## COMPENSATION TODAY 9.4

### NURSING HOMES NEED MORE THAN MARKET

On April 30, 2019, the Ontario Divisional Court released a significant decision after a 13-year battle for nursing home workers. The Court favored the stance of the Union, the Service Employees' International Union, Local 1 (SEIU1) that female-dominated workplaces must achieve and continue to determine pay equity for their workers by using the proxy method of comparison. The proxy method of comparison is a way for women in female-dominated, public-sector organizations to attain pay equity when there is a lack of a male comparator in the workplace. Employers must collect information regarding job value and pay rates from another public-sector organization that has already achieved pay equity.

In 1995, the SEIU1 and the employers, the Participating Nursing Homes had used the proxy method to strive to achieve pay equity by comparing to male proxy comparators from the Municipal Homes for the Aged. However, since this endeavour, PNH used compensation data from comparative female job classes, and the pay equity gap resurfaced. SEIU1 argued that by using market information that focused only on directly relevant female-dominated jobs, that the system further perpetuated systemic discrimination and gender-based wage inequity. Using this method, underpriced female jobs continued to be underpaid. They argued that by looking to the market and comparing to other female dominated jobs, the system would preserve historical disadvantage and stereotyping.

The Court favoured the Union's stance and requested that the parties negotiate a Gender Neutral Comparison System to decide whether there was a need for compensation adjustments. The Court maintained that female-dominated workplaces have a right to ensure pay equity relative to male comparators under the proxy method.

Sources: John Dujay, "Unions Celebrate 'Tremendously Significant' Pay Equity Victory in Ontario," *HR Reporter*, June 27, 2019; Seiu Healthcare, "Ontario Nurses' Association and SEIU Local 1 v Participating Nursing Homes," 2019 ONSC 2168 (Divisional Court File No 362/16 and 364/16); "Participating Nursing Homes v Ontario Nurses' Association and SEIU Local 1 (Divisional Court File No. 444/16 and 445/16)"; Pay Equity Hearings Tribunal, "Ontario Nurses' Association, Applicant v Participating Nursing Homes, Respondent v Ministry of the Attorney General, Intervenor," January 21, 2016.

## SUMMARY

This chapter has explained how to evaluate the "market rate" for a given set of jobs. Different industries vary widely in how much they pay their employees, thus raising the question "Why do people get paid what they do?" After a discussion of the factors affecting pay rates, the chapter turned to the question of how to define the relevant labour market. From there, it presented you with the various sources of compensation data, and the steps for conducting a compensation survey. The chapter concluded with a discussion of how to analyze and interpret survey data.

Chapter 10 completes our discussion of how compensation values are determined by describing the processes for evaluating individual employees, known as performance appraisal.

## KEY TERMS

aging the data
compa-ratio
compensating differential
interquartile range
key job matching

market comparator firms
mean or simple average
median
quartiles or deciles
weighted mean or weighted average

## DISCUSSION QUESTIONS

1. Examine the list of industries and pay rates in the opening vignette. Discuss possible reasons each industry has the relative pay level that it does.

2. Based on the concept of "compensating differentials," develop a list of job/organizational characteristics that would make you willing to work for less money. Then develop a list of job/organizational characteristics that would cause you to want more money to accept a given job. Rank each list in order of the importance to you of each characteristic. In a small group, compare your lists and discuss possible reasons for any differences.

3. What are some of the procedures used to analyze market data? How useful are these?

4. What are the key limitations of market surveys?

# EXERCISES

1. Take four jobs that are of interest to you and that are included in both the PayScale (http://www.payscale.com/research/CA/Country=Canada/Salary) and Salary Wizard databases (http://monsterca.salary.com/Canada-SalaryWizard). Using your own geographic area as the basis for your search, identify what compensation each of these websites indicates for each of the four jobs. How close are the two websites? What are some possible reasons for the differences?

2. How fair is the pay of NHL hockey players relative to their performance? Use the Canadian Business website (http://www.canadianbusiness.com/lists-and-rankings/puck-money) for your information source on what the market is paying NHL hockey players relative to their performances. Do you have any suggestions for developing a fairer pay system that pegs player pay to player performance?

3. **Table 9.2** provides data from a compensation survey for the job of industrial engineer, collected from the same employers as the compensation survey for accounting clerks discussed earlier in the chapter. The following job summary used in the survey was based on the National Occupational Classification for "Industrial and Manufacturing Engineers":

Industrial and Manufacturing Engineers conduct studies and develop and supervise programs to achieve efficient industrial production and efficient utilization of industrial human resources, machinery, and materials. Industrial and Manufacturing Engineers are employed in consulting firms, manufacturing and processing companies, and in government, financial, health care and other institutions. Example titles include cost engineer, computer integrated manufacturing engineer, fire prevention engineer, plant engineer, work measurement engineers, methods engineer, industrial engineer, manufacturing engineer, quality control engineer, safety engineer, production engineer, time-study engineer.

a. Assume you are managing a high-involvement firm that employs about 800 people and you employ 10 industrial engineers. Develop a compensation structure for this job, indicating the amount of base pay the job will provide (including the pay ranges) and the amount and type of performance pay and indirect pay. Assume the survey data are eight months out of date, and your new compensation structure will take effect in four months and apply to the following 12-month period.

b. After completing part a, develop a compensation structure for the same firm; but this time, assume it uses the human relations managerial strategy. Then do the same for the classical managerial strategy. How do these three compensation structures differ?

4. In a large group, survey the hourly pay levels for all those group members who are currently employed or were recently employed in common jobs such as salesclerk, cashier, or fast-food worker. If there are differences in pay within the same job type, discuss why these may exist.

## CASE QUESTION

1. You are the head of human resources at Alliston Instruments (refer to *Case 6* in the Appendix). You would like to do a compensation survey to determine whether your pay rates are in line with those in the industry. Using the steps described in this chapter, design the process for doing so.

## SIMULATION CROSS-REFERENCE

If you are using Strategic Compensation: A Simulation in conjunction with this text, you will find that the concepts in Chapter 9 are helpful in preparing the simulation.

TABLE 9.2

## Results of Compensation Survey: Industrial Engineer

| COMPANY | TOTAL EMPLOYMENT | NUMBER OF INDUSTRIAL ENGINEERS EMPLOYED | BASE PAY RANGE MINIMUM | BASE PAY RANGE MIDPOINT | BASE PAY RANGE MAXIMUM | MEAN BASE PAY | MEAN PERFOR- MANCE PAY | MEAN INDIRECT PAY | MEAN TOTAL COMPENSATION | BASE PAY QUARTILE 1 | 2 | 3 | 4 |
|---|---|---|---|---|---|---|---|---|---|---|---|---|---|
| A | 700 | 2 | $50 000 | $55 000 | $60 000 | $56 000 | $6720 | $11 200 | $73 920 | 1 | — | — | 1 |
| B | 1700 | 5 | 48 000 | 52 000 | 56 000 | 54 000 | 9720 | 13 500 | 77 220 | 1 | — | 1 | 3 |
| C | 800 | 1 | 54 000 | 60 000 | 66 000 | 66 000 | 13 200 | 29 800 | 99 000 | — | — | — | 1 |
| D | 2000 | 12 | 44 000 | 50 000 | 56 000 | 54 666 | 5467 | 21 866 | 81 999 | — | 1 | 2 | 9 |
| E | 700 | 4 | 50 000 | 58 000 | 66 000 | 62 250 | 9338 | 18 675 | 90 263 | — | 1 | 2 | 3 |
| F | 4000 | 17 | 45 000 | 51 000 | 57 000 | 52 205 | 5221 | 18 272 | 75 698 | 5 | 2 | 1 | 9 |
| G | 5000 | 21 | 43 000 | 48 000 | 53 000 | 48 095 | — | 14 429 | 65 524 | 8 | 3 | 2 | 8 |
| H | 7000 | 40 | 42 000 | 50 000 | 58 000 | 50 100 | 5010 | 17 535 | 72 645 | 12 | 6 | 3 | 18 |
| I | 1000 | 4 | 46 000 | 54 000 | 60 000 | 55 250 | — | 13 813 | 69 063 | 1 | — | 1 | 2 |
| J | 1000 | 3 | 47 000 | 52 000 | 57 000 | 54 667 | 8200 | 13 667 | 76 534 | — | 1 | — | 2 |
| Simple Average | | | 46 900 | 53 000 | 58 900 | 55 323 | 6288 | 16 276 | 78 187 | | | | |
| Weighted Average | | | 43 991 | 50 541 | 57 018 | 51 738 | 4513 | 17 046 | 73 298 | | | | |

# ENDNOTES

1. Tim Collins, "Unionized RCMP Spells Increased Costs for Municipalities," *Victoria News*, September 5, 2019, https://www.vicnews.com/news/unionized-rcmp-spells-increased-costs-for-municipalities/, accessed February 26, 2020.

2. Catharine Tunney, "New RCMP Union Hopes to Start Salary Bargaining by Mid-March," *CBC*, January 7, 2020, https://www.cbc.ca/news/politics/rcmp-union-bargaining-march-1.5416128, accessed February 29, 2020.

3. Jennifer Pagliaro and Wendy Gillis, "Toronto Police Officers are Being Offered a Farther Bigger Raise Than Other City Workers," *The Start*, February 27, 2019, https://www.thestar.com/news/city_hall/2019/02/27/toronto-police-are-being-offered-a-far-bigger-raise-than-other-city-workers.html, accessed February 29, 2020.

4. Tim Collins, "Unionized RCMP Spells Increased Costs for Municipalities," *Victoria News*, September 5, 2019, https://www.vicnews.com/news/unionized-rcmp-spells-increased-costs-for-municipalities/, accessed February 26, 2020.

5. See https://lop.parl.ca/sites/ParlInfo/default/en_CA/People/Salaries?ggCheckbox=false&senateCheckbox=false&HocCheckbox=true.

6. Morley Gunderson, Douglas Hyatt, and Craig Riddell, *Pay Differences Between the Government and Private Sectors: Labour Force Survey and Census Estimates*, Discussion Paper #W/10 (Ottawa: Canadian Policy Research Networks, 2000); Charles Lammam, Milagros Palacios, Feixue Ren, and Jason Clemens, *Comparing Government and Private Sector Compensation in Canada* (Fraser Institute, 2015).

7. Pay Equity Task Force, *Pay Equity: A New Approach to a Fundamental Right* (Ottawa: Department of Justice, 2004); Kate Elaine McInturff and Paul Tulloch, *Narrowing the Gap: The Difference That Public Sector Wages Make*. Canadian Centre for Policy Alternatives/Centre Canadien de Politiques Alternatives, 2014.

8. See S. Walsworth and R.J. Long, "Is the Union Employment Suppression Effect Diminishing? Further Evidence from Canada," *Relations industrielles/Industrial Relations* 67, no. 4 (2012): 654–80; T. Fang and A. Verma, "Union Wage Premium," *Perspectives* (Statistics Canada), September 2002, 13–19; Scott Walsworth and Richard Long, "Is the Union Employment Suppression Effect Diminishing? Further Evidence from Canada," *Relations Industrielles/Industrial Relations* 67, no. 4 (2012): 654–80.

9. See Kazi Stastna, "Canada's Working Moms Still Earning Less, Doing More than Dads," *CBC News Online*, May 10, 2012, http://www.cbc.ca/news/canada/story/2012/05/10/f-mothers-day.html, accessed September 29, 2016. Also see Morley Gunderson, "Male–Female Wage Differentials: How Can That Be?" *Canadian Journal of Economics* 39, no. 1 (2006): 1–21; and Force, Pay Equity.

10. See http://www.statcan.gc.ca/tables-tableaux/sum-som/l01/cst01/labr79-eng.htm.

11. Robert E. Sibson, *Compensation* (New York: American Management Association, 1990); Barry T. Hirsch, David A. Macpherson, and Edward J. Schumacher, "Measuring Union and Nonunion Wage Growth," *The Changing Role of Unions: New Forms of Representation: New Forms of Representation* (2016): 115.

12. Stanley E. Griffis, Thomas J. Goldsby, and Martha Cooper, "Web-Based and Mail Surveys: A Comparison of Response, Data, and Cost," *Journal of Business Logistics* 24 (2003): 237–57; Ron D. Hays, Honghu Liu, and Arie Kapteyn, "Use of Internet Panels to Conduct Surveys," *Behavior Research Methods* 47, no. 3 (2015): 685–90.

13. Jytte Seested Nielsen, "Use of the Internet for Willingness-to-Pay Surveys: A Comparison of Face-to-Face and Web-Based Interviews," *Resource and Energy Economics* 33 (2011): 119–29.

14. Edith D. de Leeuw, "Counting and Measuring Online: The Quality of Internet Surveys," *Bulletin of Sociological Methodology* 114 (2012): 68–78.

15. David E. Tyson, ed., *Carswell's Compensation Guide* (Toronto: Thomson Carswell, 2009).

16. Carolyn L. Weber and Sara L. Rynes, "Effects of Compensation Strategy on Job Pay Decisions," *Academy of Management Journal* 34, no. 1 (1991): 86–109.

# 10

# EVALUATING
# INDIVIDUALS

AFTER READING THIS CHAPTER, YOU
SHOULD BE ABLE TO:

- Identify and explain the main reasons for conducting performance appraisals.

- Explain why many performance appraisal systems fail to accurately measure employee performance.

- Identify and describe the different methods for appraising performance, along with their strengths and weaknesses.

- Identify the possible sources of performance appraisals and discuss the circumstances under which each would be appropriate.

- Explain the concept of "performance management."

- Discuss how to link merit pay to performance appraisals.

- Identify the key design issues in developing an effective merit pay system.

## MICROSOFT CHANGES ITS PERFORMANCE MANAGEMENT SYSTEM TO SUPPORT STRATEGY

For decades, performance management has been a core process that organizations use to align employee behaviour with organizational goals. The annual cycle of goal setting, midyear check-in, final review, and decisions on merit increase and annual (and long-term, in some cases) incentives has become part of the organization's routine business. However, as we entered the second decade of the new millennium, some organizations started to rethink and redesign their performance management processes. Microsoft is among those that did an overhaul of its performance management system.

The change was driven by external and internal factors. External factors included the fact that work was performed in a more collaborative way across multiple disciplines and locations; employees had different expectations as Millennials enter the workforce; and fresh perspectives from neuroscience indicated that employees responded better to reward stimuli than threat stimuli. Internally, Microsoft was transforming from the world's leading software provider to a provider of software, devices, and cloud-based services. To achieve this vision, Microsoft changed its organization to drive greater cross-group dependencies by abolishing the long-standing independent divisions with separate profit and loss statements (P&L) and creating a new "One Microsoft" with a single P&L.

To support this business and cultural transformation, Microsoft launched the new Performance and Development system in 2013 that focused employees' attention on contributing to team, business or customer impact, results that build on the work, ideas and effort of others, and contribution to the success of others. They eliminated traditional performance ratings and the ratings distribution, increased flexibility in allocating rewards based on impact, and enabled rewards decisions to be made lower in the organization.

Instead of the old process of allocating salary increases, bonuses and stock awards based on a forced rating distribution, where 20 percent of employees would receive a score of one, 20 percent of employees would receive a score of two, and so on until five. The new system differentiates between "top rewards" for those with exceptional performance, and the rest of the workforce. The old calibration meetings were replaced with "People Discussions for Reward Allocation," which serves as a benchmark opportunity for managers to understand how peer managers are considering impact and rewards decisions.

Microsoft also launched "Perspectives," which is a system that inspires employees to solicit feedback (though they hold off on using the word feedback for its negative connotation) from peers in a structured manner. The system then amalgamates and submits the responses to the employee and their manager. "Perspectives" is meant to encourage conversation and allow employees to feel like they are involved in a coaching session rather than a performance review.

A Microsoft spokesperson announced that the company would not publicly reveal information about how the changes in the performance review process has affected employee performance. Nonetheless, employees and managers have expressed a preference in the new approach and view the system as having a positive impact on how teams collaborate. The new system appears to have positively influenced employee engagement and satisfaction, as well as advanced the transformation of the company's business and culture. Perhaps the new performance management system, among many other culture changing initiatives (such as a paid leave policy, a focus on inclusion, and a stronger emphasis on addressing harassment complaints), is to thank for the significant positive change in corporate climate and a record year in financial performance in 2019.

Source: J. Ritchie, "Transforming a Company: How Microsoft's New Employee Performance System Supports Its Business and Cultural Transformation," *WorldatWork Journal* (Second Quarter 2016): 61–75; Sherin Sibu, "Microsoft Performance Reviews: How They Work Under Nadella," *Business Insider*, October 29, 2019; Herminia Ibarra and Anne Scourer, "The Leader as Coach," *Harvard Business Review*, November 2019; Jordan Novet, "Here Are the Most Important Execs at Microsoft Under Satya Nadella," *CNBC*, February 23, 2020; "A Kinder, Gentler Microsoft Is Replacing Feedback with 'Perspectives'," *Quartz at Work*, September 10, 2018.

# INTRODUCTION TO PERFORMANCE APPRAISAL AND PERFORMANCE MANAGEMENT

As the Microsoft case shows, performance management and performance appraisals are changing. There are many pros and cons of using "traditional" versus "new" systems. They key goal should be "fit" (discussed in Chapter 2); that is, an organization's performance management system should support its strategy. Microsoft has made changes to ensure that its management systems reflect its changing context and strategies.

Like Microsoft, approximately six percent of the Fortune 500 companies have gotten rid of their forced ranking system.[1] Accenture eliminated its forced ranking system as well as its annual performance review. Instead of yearly reviews, employees receive immediate feedback following assignments. The company is estimating that they will be making changes to 90 percent of their performance appraisals process.[2]

Many other companies are also changing their performance appraisal process and implementing more frequent check-ins, such as PwC, General Electric, and IBM. Amid a major business overhaul, IBM realized that the strategic actions of the business would necessitate employee engagement and that the antiquated and traditional performance management approach would no longer be effective. In the digital age, feedback is instant, and data is constantly changing.[3] Thus, IBM created a system called "Checkpoint." This program allows employees to give honest and continuous feedback to other employees, no matter what their position may be.[4] Employees meet with their supervisor at least four times a year to discuss and adjust their goals. Managers also manage performance through artificial intelligence. IBM's algorithm can predict which employees are likely to leave, which will excel with their capabilities and recommend action for managers to implement, usually regarding skill development.[5]

If you were an employee at Microsoft, IBM, or Accenture, how would you feel about the new performance management system? Your opinion would probably depend on how it works for you and your team.

Suppose that your organization uses merit pay to reward employees who display superior performance. How do you identify these employees in a fair and systematic way? And how can you fairly relate these judgments to actual pay decisions?

The success of merit pay systems depends on finding the right answers to these questions, and the purpose of this chapter is to help you find those answers. This chapter describes ways to evaluate the overall level of job performance displayed by individual employees (a process known as **performance appraisal**) and ways to link the resulting appraisals to financial rewards. We start by discussing some of the reasons for performance appraisals, and organizations' experiences with them, and then move on to the many pitfalls that may prevent accurate appraisal of employee performance.

**performance appraisal**
The process of assessing the overall performance levels of individual employees.

We then describe some of the commonly used performance appraisal methods and discuss who is best suited to conduct performance appraisals. We also discuss performance management, which is a broader process for managing employee performance in which the accurate measurement of employee performance plays an important role. Finally, we discuss how performance appraisal results can be linked to merit pay. This includes how to design a merit pay system as well as the thorny issue of whether and how to appraise individual performance in a team context.

# EXPERIENCE WITH AND REASONS FOR PERFORMANCE APPRAISAL

"I'd rather kick bricks with my bare feet than do appraisals!" says a manager at Digital Equipment Corporation.[6] Apparently, performance appraisal is not his favourite task—and many managers feel the same way. But what about their employers?

It turns out that many employers are no happier than their managers about their performance appraisal systems. For example, Pratt and Whitney, the giant manufacturer of jet engines, was dissatisfied with its performance appraisal system and made extensive changes to it. The following year, still unhappy with the system, the firm made more changes. The year after that, the firm abandoned its system altogether, replacing it with a completely different one.[7] Surveys have found that performance appraisal systems tend to be in constant flux as companies search for appraisal systems they are satisfied with.[8]

## EXPERIENCE WITH PERFORMANCE APPRAISAL

Despite all their efforts, companies have found it very hard to establish satisfactory appraisal systems. At the beginning of the 21st century, about 90 percent of Canadian human resource managers who were surveyed said that their company's performance appraisal system needed to be modified or abolished; even more—95 percent—of Canadian employees surveyed said the same thing.[9] In a U.S. study conducted in 2012, only three percent of organizations rated their systems for managing employee performance as "very effective."[10] Yet despite the disappointing history of performance appraisal, research suggest that 89 percent of Canadian organizations have mandatory performance appraisals, and 57 percent of organizations have repercussions for managers who do not complete their employees' performance reviews.[11]

Two findings stand out from this research. First, many companies can't seem to find a satisfying performance appraisal system. Second, despite their lack of success, they keep trying to make performance appraisal work. While performance appraisal is highly valued as a concept, translating that concept into effective practice is very difficult.

Some observers contend that translating the concept of performance appraisal into effective practice is virtually impossible. Some experts argue that, based on their experience, performance appraisals are incredibly inaccurate, costly, and have no impact on productivity. They contend that performance appraisal is a fundamentally flawed concept that cannot be made to work effectively.[12] Others agree that performance appraisal often does more harm than good but contend that performance appraisal can work effectively if applied in the right way and in the right circumstances.[13] In this book, we adopt the latter view, although we emphasize that the right circumstances for performance appraisal (particularly for the purposes of merit pay) are much less common than many employers think. (Those circumstances were described in our discussion of merit pay in Chapter 5 and are summarized in Compensation Notebook 5.1.)

# WHY DO PERFORMANCE APPRAISALS?

If performance appraisals are so difficult to do effectively, why do them at all? Organizations conduct performance appraisals for a variety of reasons, which tend to fall into four main categories: administrative, developmental, supervisory, and symbolic.

- Administrative reasons. Identify individuals who are not performing to required standards and for whom dismissal may be necessary, identify individuals who should be considered for promotion or merit increases, and monitor the overall quality of performance in the firm. A well-documented set of performance appraisals can help support legal arguments during unjust dismissal lawsuits. Moreover, a firm that cannot show that it attempts to manage employee performance may find itself liable in the event of errors or accidents caused by company employees. The key task is to measure individual performance accurately and consistently.

- Developmental reasons. Helping employees grasp the employer's expectations, the key performance dimensions of their jobs, the strengths and weaknesses in their performance, and the ways they can improve their performance. The key task is to provide useful feedback—an essential part of any learning process—that will help individuals change their behaviours in productive ways. This feedback is valuable to employees even if their performance does not need improvement because most employees want to know how their performance is regarded by their supervisors and the organization.

- Supervisory reasons. Improving the performance of supervisors by encouraging them to think systematically about employee performance and by encouraging communication with employees.

- Symbolic reasons. Creating the perception that management cares about good employee performance. Performance appraisals demonstrate this concern to employees (if they believe that performance is what the appraisal system truly measures, of course).

# PITFALLS IN PERFORMANCE APPRAISAL

Performance appraisals do not always accurately reflect employee performance. Two key aspects are crucial for accuracy. When an appraisal method has reliability, two different raters, judging independently, will come up with similar ratings of a given individual. When a method has validity, then the individuals identified by performance appraisal as the most effective employees are, in fact, the best performers.

Over the years, both academics and practitioners have expended an enormous amount of effort attempting to develop reliable and valid measures of employee performance. But despite this effort, performance appraisal often fails to achieve its goals. Part of the problem stems from the multiple objectives of most appraisal systems. Some experts have argued that there should be two separate performance appraisal processes—one for developmental purposes and one for administrative purposes. This makes a lot of sense in some ways because many firms do not want to use merit pay but may still want to evaluate individual performance to provide feedback about opportunities for performance improvement.

**performance appraisal reliability**
Occurs when a performance appraisal system produces the same scores even when applied by different appraisers.

**performance appraisal validity**
The process of assessing the overall performance levels of individual employees. Occurs when employees who receive the highest scores in a performance appraisal system are in fact the highest performers.

But for such feedback to be effective, it must be accepted by the employee as valid, it must identify specific behaviours that need to change (i.e., behaviours that are under the control of the employee), and it must occur in an environment where the person giving the feedback is seen as a trusted coach. However, when money is tied to appraisals, the appraiser is more likely to be seen as a feared judge than as a trusted coach.

One advantage of linking pay to appraisals is that doing so increases the likelihood that appraisals will be taken seriously by all parties. However, when appraisals are used for both pay and developmental purposes, the appraisal may end up focusing on judging, and the appraisers may have to justify and defend their decisions to grant or deny merit pay. As a result, instead of engaging in a candid discussion of their shortcomings, appraisees may attempt to portray their performance as favourably as possible ("Given the circumstances, my performance was actually pretty good") and to defend themselves when the appraiser does not award high performance ratings ("My performance may have been lower than expected, but it wasn't my fault").

Moreover, the most accurate systems for assessing performance may not be the best methods for generating useful feedback for the appraisee. Yet when merit pay is denied, employees expect to be told why and what they can do to correct the situation. Most organizations include a developmental (feedback) element in their administrative appraisals, even though this may make it more difficult to achieve either purpose.

There are two main reasons a performance appraisal system may not produce accurate evaluations. The first has to do with the appraisal system itself, which may not allow appraisers to accurately assess employee performance, no matter how hard they try and how much they may want to. The second—perhaps even more important—is that accurate performance measurement may not be the appraiser's main objective. This insight has emerged after many years of blaming performance appraisal problems on the appraisal systems themselves. Start by considering why appraisers may not want to produce accurate appraisals.

## INTENTIONAL INACCURACIES IN APPRAISALS

There is considerable evidence that when supervisors start the performance appraisal process, they often have in mind certain desired outcomes or consequences.[14] For example: Do I want Sally Jones to get a raise? Do I want Mike Ouimette to be promoted? Do I want Mudira Singh to quit? What impact will a low performance rating have on Yidari Woo? Will a high or low appraisal be most likely to improve Joan Baum's performance?

Supervisors may see performance appraisal as a tool to help them achieve their own goals or as a useless or even potentially damaging exercise. In any case, they are likely to keep the broader work context in mind when conducting appraisals, as this quote from one manager illustrates:

*As a manager, I will use the review process to do what is best for my people and the division . . . I've used it to get my people better raises in lean years, to kick a [person] in the pants if [he or she] really needed it, to pick up a [person] when he [or she] was down or even to tell him [or her] that he [or she] was no longer welcome here. It is a tool that the manager should use to help [her or him] do what it takes to get the job done . . . Accurately describing an employee's performance is not really as important as generating ratings that keep things cooking.*[15]

Another manager expresses concern for the possible interpersonal consequences of low performance ratings:

*There is really no getting around the fact that whenever I evaluate one of my people, I stop and think about the impact—the ramifications of my decisions on my relationship with the [person] and [his or her] future here. I'd be stupid not to. In the end I've got to live with [him or her], and I'm not going to rate a [person] without thinking about the fallout. There are a lot of games played in the rating process, and whether we admit it or not we are all guilty of playing them.*[16]

A common practice in performance appraisal is for supervisors to inflate ratings, known as the "leniency" problem. This can happen for reasons that, to the supervisor, are consistent with or supportive of organizational goals, or it can happen for other reasons. For example, supervisors may inflate ratings if they lack confidence in the appraisal instrument or process. They may believe that the appraisal does not measure the right things (it is not valid), that they have had insufficient opportunity to observe employee performance to make a valid assessment, or that they do not have the expertise to adequately appraise performance. In these cases, it would be difficult for the appraiser to defend poor ratings, so he or she avoids the problem by giving high ratings.

Supervisors may have other motives for giving high ratings. They may be concerned about damaging their relations with their subordinates or about the relationships among employees. Moreover, a supervisor may worry about damaging his or her own reputation if the subordinates are not performing well. Furthermore, some supervisors may believe that other supervisors are giving high ratings and that they must also do so in order to maintain a level playing field and to protect their department's "fair share" of the available merit money and promotional opportunities. Finally, supervisors may simply not want to put the necessary effort into producing accurate ratings; they give high ratings to prevent complaints about inaccuracy. (This tactic is not unknown in the university classroom, either, as you may have found!)

Supervisors may have specific motives for inflating the ratings of particular employees. For example, they may believe that an accurate rating would have a damaging effect on a subordinate's motivation and performance. Conversely, they may want to improve an employee's eligibility for a merit raise or a promotion if the employee has been unfairly treated in the past. They may want to protect a normally good performer whose performance is suffering because of a personal problem. They may want to reward employees who show great effort despite poor measurable results or who have other valued attributes not measured by the appraisal instrument. On a less noble plane, supervisors may wish to get rid of poor performers by promoting them out of the department. Finally, they may simply want to reward their friends.

Research has also found that managers sometimes (albeit much less often) deflate ratings.[17] For example, they may want to "scare" better performance out of an employee whom they believe could do much more or who is in danger of being fired. Or they may wish to punish a difficult or rebellious employee. They may also want to create a strong case to justify planned firings or to encourage problem employees to quit. In addition, they may be following a company order to achieve a certain distribution in ratings, and this may require deflating the ratings of some employees. Finally, they may simply be biased against some individuals.

# UNINTENTIONAL INACCURACIES IN APPRAISALS

Problems in the system itself can threaten the accuracy of appraisals. The most fundamental requirements for an accurate appraisal are an adequate opportunity to observe employee performance and an ability to draw valid conclusions from those observations. When a supervisor has many subordinates or when the supervisor and subordinates work separately, supervisors may have a very limited sample of behaviour on which to base their appraisals. Or the supervisor may lack the expertise to accurately gauge the quality of an employee's work, such as highly skilled or professional workers.

There are also many perceptual errors that can affect appraisal accuracy. These include central tendency, halo error, recency effect, contrast effect, similarity effect, and leniency/harshness. **Central tendency error** occurs when appraisers rate all employees as "average" in almost everything. Less commonly, some raters have the opposite tendency—to rate all individuals as either extremely good or extremely bad, with nobody in the middle. The **halo error** occurs when one characteristic for a given individual is judged to be either very good or very bad, which then prejudices the rater to rate all characteristics of that individual at the same level.

The **recency effect** refers to a tendency to place excessive weight on recent behaviour, with earlier employee behaviour having faded from memory. The **contrast effect** occurs when there is one employee who is either exceedingly good or exceedingly bad, which causes the appraiser to rate other employees either worse (or better) than they really deserve. The **similarity effect** describes a tendency for appraisers to rate individuals who are similar to themselves more highly than those who are different. Finally, some evaluators tend to be more lenient and rate all subordinates highly (the **leniency effect**), while others may be inherently harsh (the **harshness effect**), rating all subordinates poorly.

Finally, one rating error that has become increasingly apparent is the "**beauty effect**." This is the finding that performance appraisals can be biased by the perceived physical attractiveness of the appraisee. For example, attractive appraisees tend to receive higher performance ratings than their performance may justify, while unattractive appraisees tend to receive lower performance appraisals than their actual performance would warrant.[18] Taller appraisees are more likely to get promotions and raises than other employees.[19] Obese employees tend to receive lower performance ratings than they may deserve.[20] Compensation Today 10.1 explores this phenomenon in more depth.

These perceptual errors and inconsistencies across raters can be magnified by poor rating instruments, which provide insufficient definition of the characteristics being evaluated and of the scales used to rate these characteristics. Some rating instruments are better than others at controlling these errors. But despite 50 years of effort to develop valid appraisal processes, rater bias still has about twice the weight in determining performance ratings as does actual appraisee performance.[21]

A final problem with appraisals arises when they take place under inappropriate circumstances. For example, when work is highly interdependent, separating out individual behaviour may be virtually impossible, and it makes no sense to attempt to do so. Moreover, in some jobs, there is simply not much scope for individual performance to vary. Remember our chicken plant workers in Chapter 2 (Compensation Today 2.4)? It doesn't make sense to waste time attempting individual appraisals when so little performance variation is possible.

**central tendency error**
Occurs when appraisers rate all employees as "average" in everything.

**halo error**
Occurs when appraisers rate an individual either high or low on all characteristics because one characteristic is either high or low.

**recency effect**
The tendency of appraisers to overweight recent events when appraising employee performance.

**contrast effect**
The tendency for a set of performance appraisals to be influenced upward by the presence of a very low performer or downward by the presence of a very high performer.

**similarity effect**
The tendency of appraisers to inflate the appraisals of appraisees they see as similar to themselves.

**leniency effect**
The tendency of many appraisers to provide unduly high performance appraisals.

**harshness effect**
The tendency of some appraisers to provide unduly low performance appraisals.

**beauty effect**
The tendency for the physical attractiveness of a ratee to affect their performance appraisals.

Syda Productions/Shutterstock

What did I do wrong?

## THE BEAUTY EFFECT: DOES "HOTNESS" PAY?

Recent research has shown that people rated as "above average" in physical attractiveness earn $230 000 more over the course of their careers than people rated as "below average."[a] Interestingly, although people tend to think of "beauty" as a female characteristic, and therefore might assume that women benefit more from good looks—and suffer more from bad looks—than do men, research suggests that men can actually be more affected by a deficit or a surplus in physical attractiveness. For example, in the study cited above, men who were rated as "above average" in looks earned 17 percent more than men rated as "below average"; women rated "above average" earned 12 percent more than women rated "below average."

Well, you might say, you can see how people in professions such as acting and modelling might benefit from an attractiveness surplus, but surely this doesn't apply everywhere, especially not in the academic environment, where brains should be valued above all else. In fact, studies show that student evaluations of their professors are significantly affected by the perceived physical attractiveness of the professor.[b] What's more, so is professor pay.

But again, the findings regarding men and women are a bit counterintuitive. It turns out that, in a study of economics professors in Canadian universities, male professors who were rated as "hot" (those who received a hot chili pepper on the "RateMyProfessor" website) by students earned significantly more than male professors who were not rated as "hot"— with "hot" male professors about 20 percent more likely to earn more than $100 000 per year than were male professors not deemed "hot."[c] However, there was apparently no salary payoff at all for female economics professors rated as "hot." The study authors do note one caveat to these findings—very few female economics professors, especially those at senior levels (none at the full professor level) were rated as "hot" by students, so it is not clear how this may have affected results.

A U.S. study published in 2016 found similar results.[d] First, attractive individuals earn roughly 20 percent more than people of average attractiveness. Second, contrary to the research findings in previous studies, there are no significant gender differences in the returns to attractiveness. Attractiveness is no more or less important for women than for men when it comes to income earning. Third, grooming contributes significantly to higher income, especially for women. Good news for most of us who are not lucky to be born beautiful or handsome!

More recent research published in 2019 helps to explain the potential causes of the differential pay of attractive versus unattractive individuals. From an early age in life, attractive individuals receive special treatment from others. They, therefore, develop higher self-evaluations as compared to unattractive individuals, which thus supports their future career success. However, the authors found that other factors exist independent of high self-esteem ratings. The authors discovered that when attractive individuals start their careers, they receive increased career exposure and visibility as compared to nonattractive individuals. This means that attractive individuals have increased and better opportunities to work with prominent people in their organization that give them the ability to succeed because these established people are invaluable sources of organizational expertise. The attractive individuals are thus better able to build their social network. In the study, sponsorship was measured only six months after individuals started in the company, and differences between attractive and unattractive individuals already existed, accounting for significant variances in compensation 18 months later.[e]

Discrimination based on looks is not only unfair, but can also be a drag on productivity, if less competent employees are given opportunities, raises, or promotions over more competent (but less attractive) employees. As discussed in Chapter 3, we know that an unfair pay system has many negative consequences for the organization and can hurt productivity. For example, in the United States, it is estimated that discrimination against the unattractive costs the economy $20 billion per year.[f]

[a] Daniel Hamermesh, *Beauty Pays: Why Attractive People Are More Successful* (Princeton: Princeton University Press, 2011).

[b] Gabriella Montell, "Do Good Looks Equal Good Evaluations?" *Chronicle of Higher Education*, October 15, 2003, 1–4; Janie H. Wilson, Denise Beyer, and Heather Monteiro, "Professor Age Affects Student Ratings: Halo Effect for Younger Teachers," *College Teaching* 62, no. 1 (2014): 20–24.

[c] Frances Woolley, "The Hottie Factor: Why Some Profs Out-Earn Others," *The Globe and Mail Online*, October 28, 2010; see also Anindya Sen, Marcel Voia, and Frances Woolley, "The Effect of Hotness on Pay and Productivity," Department of Economics, Carleton University, unpublished paper, 2010.

[d] Jaclyn Wong and Andrew Penner, "Gender and the Returns to Attractiveness," *Research in Social Stratification and Mobility* 44 (2016): 113–23.

[e] Karyn Dossinger, Connie R. Wanberg, Yongjun Choi, and Lisa M. Leslie, "The Beauty Premium: The Role of Organizational Sponsorship in the Relationship Between Physical Attractiveness and Early Career Salaries," *Journal of Vocational Behavior* 112 (2019): 109–21.

[f] Daniel Hamermesh, *Beauty Pays: Why Attractive People Are More Successful* (Princeton: Princeton University Press, 2011).

# METHODS AND INSTRUMENTS FOR APPRAISAL

A number of appraisal systems have been developed over the years, but there is no widespread consensus that any of them work in every situation. As discussed in Chapter 5, this is partly because performance appraisals are often applied in circumstances where they do not fit and where no performance appraisal instrument would be effective.

However, depending on the setting and the objectives, some appraisal methods are more appropriate than others. This section discusses the relative merits of the best-known methods, in roughly the order in which they were developed:

- ranking and forced distribution graphic rating scale,
- behaviourally anchored rating scales,
- behavioural observation scales,
- objectives- and results-based systems,
- field review,
- continuous performance management, and
- combination approaches.

## RANKING AND FORCED DISTRIBUTION

Perhaps the simplest method of performance appraisal is just to rank the performance of all individuals engaged in similar jobs, from most effective to least effective. This method has the advantage that it does not require complicated forms and procedures. Furthermore, most supervisors generally have little difficulty in determining their best and worst performers. This approach also eliminates the problems of central tendency and leniency/harshness. In addition, it fits well with a system in which management decrees that only the top performers, say, 10 percent of employees, will receive merit pay.

However, this system has many drawbacks. It is highly subjective, does not allow for comparisons across departments, and provides little useful feedback to the individuals being rated. It is also subject to numerous perceptual errors, such as recency, halo, contrast, similarity, and bias, as well as inconsistency in application across supervisors because the bases for evaluating performance are usually not made explicit. The system also implies that the distances between the ranks are the same, when in fact there may be large gaps between, say, the third- and fourth-best performers.

It is also a win–lose system, in that the only way a person can improve her or his or ranking is to displace someone else. This may create conflict and lack of cooperation among employees. It is also highly unfair across departments because it does not recognize that some departments may be loaded with high performers, while other departments may have very few.

Finally, this kind of ranking is difficult to carry out. That is, it may be easy to pick out the best and worst performers but very difficult to rank the large middle group. For example, should an employee be ranked 10th or 11th out of 20 employees? It may also be very difficult to justify these fine differences to appraisees, and these fine differences are seldom needed for administrative purposes anyway.

One method for facilitating this ranking process is the paired comparison method. Each individual is compared with every other individual, one at a time. Then, the number of times each individual is judged the superior of the pair determines the rank of that employee. This method does simplify the ranking process; however, the number of comparisons that must be made increases geometrically with the number of employees being ranked.

A variation of the ranking method is the forced distribution method. This approach was popularized by Jack Welch, the highly successful former CEO of General Electric, who adopted it at GE. See Compensation Today 10.2 for a related discussion. Under this approach, the rater is presented with several categories and is required to place a certain percentage of the appraisees in each category. For example, Merck & Co. Inc., the large pharmaceuticals firm, adopted an approach that required supervisors to place five percent of employees in the top category ("exceptional"); 15 percent in the next ("with distinction"); 70 percent in the middle ("high Merck standard"); eight percent in the next to lowest ("room for improvement"); and two percent in the lowest ("not acceptable").[22] The company began using the system after it found that its previous rating scale was not discriminating between performance levels (almost everyone was rated at the highest level). For the same reason, IBM tried a similar approach in the 1990s, requiring each supervisor to place 10 percent of employees in the highest category and 10 percent in the lowest.

The U.S. Navy also uses a forced distribution method. They require that supervisors place employees in one of five categories: "significant problems," "progressing," "must promote," and "early promote." An "early promote" recommendation can only be awarded to 20 percent of individuals from each group and the combination of the "early promote" and "must promote" must not exceed 60 percent of any group.[23] However, the navy is now trying to move away from the forced distribution system. They feel that some sailors do not have the chance to progress and be promoted if other sailors from their group have already received the "early promote" score, yet each is equally as deserving. In contrast, other sailors are being promoted because there are less comparable excellent performers in their specific group.[24]

Even though forced distribution has almost all the deficiencies and problems of the ranking method, it does have this major advantage: it is not necessary to generate a specific rank for each employee, which can simplify the appraisal process greatly. This method, though, does not fit well with either human relations or high-involvement firms.

**forced distribution method**
A performance appraisal method that stipulates the distribution of employees across the performance categories.

## COMPENSATION TODAY 10.2

### CHANGING WITH THE TIMES

Jack Welch introduced the famous Vitality Curve to General Electric and led many of the Session C meetings where executives were ranked into A, B, and C players in a distribution of 20–70–10; that is, 20 percent were ranked as A players, 70 percent as B, and 10 percent as C. The C players were often terminated from the company. The process cascaded down the whole organization. Welch's tough management style turned GE from a bloated industrial conglomerate, struggling to compete with manufacturers globally, to an efficient and even more successful business. The company's value increased by more than $300 billion during Welch's tenure and *Fortune Magazine* named him the "manager of the century" in 1999. Vitality Curve, also called forced distribution, or stacked ranking, became a popular management process across industries.

Since Jack Welch left the helms of GE in 2001, a lot has changed at GE and in the world. According to a 2013 survey by WorldatWork, the forced distribution method is still used by about 12 percent of U.S. corporations; however, many organizations are changing their performance management systems to focus on employee development. At GE not only is the forced distribution discontinued, but also further changes to the performance management system are being piloted and

(*continued*)

implemented. While it is acknowledged that the forced distribution process made some sense in the 1980s and 1990s when managing cost and increasing efficiency were vital to the business, this management practice had become more a ritual than moving the company upward and forward, according to GE's current head of human resources.

A new app called "PD@GE" for "performance development at GE" was piloted to 80 000 employees in 2015 and 2016. The app enables employees set near-term goals, or priorities and have frequent discussions called "touchpoints" with the managers. Employees can ask for and provide feedback to anyone. The app can provide summaries on demand, through typed notes, photographs, or even voice recordings. The focus is not on rating, but on how employees can improve. Employees can request a meeting regarding their feedback at any time. Yet no direct manager has access to an employee's folder. Managers must still conduct an annual performance review with their employees where they look back at the year and set goals. Managers must also take part in compensation planning and identifying employees with high potential.

So far, employees seem to be embracing the change with open arms. Many employees like the new system and feel that PD@GE helps them concentrate on priorities and useful changes. Managers feel that they can focus on performance outcomes and employee development. It appears that GE has successfully managed to adapt to the changing business tech climate, which is a system of constant change, various inputs on performance, and continuous modifications. Nonetheless, similar to employees always receiving feedback and developing, GE will continue to gather feedback and amend the system.

Sources: Jack Welch, Straight from Gut (New York: Warner Books, 2001); Max Nisen, "Why GE Had to Kill Its Annual Performance Reviews," *Quartz*, August 13, 2015; Kate Linebaugh, "The New GE Way: Go Deep, Not Wide," *The Wall Street Journal*, March 7, 2012; Vitality Curve, *Wikipedia*, https://en.wikipedia.org/wiki/Vitality_curve; Martin Brit, "Why General Electric Moved Away from Traditional HR Review Practices," *Financial Post*, April 26, 2017.

## GRAPHIC RATING SCALE

**graphic rating scale**
An appraisal method in which appraisers use a numerical scale to rate employees on a series of characteristics.

For many decades, the **graphic rating scale** has been one of the most widely used performance appraisal methods. It is still, probably, the single most popular rating method, mainly because of its simplicity. First, the organization selects several traits judged relevant to job performance. These typically include things such as quantity and quality of work performed, initiative, responsibility, and cooperation with others. Then, immediate supervisors rate employees on the extent to which they possess each characteristic. In many cases, raters are required to make written comments in support of their ratings. These narrative comments are especially useful for feedback purposes and for justifying the ratings.

**Figure 10.1** shows a graphic rating scale that has been used by a police service in a western Canadian city. Seven characteristics are each rated in terms of six levels of performance. In this example, raters must depend on their own judgment to define both the characteristic being rated and the performance level. A more effective appraisal form would include brief descriptions of the traits and definitions of the performance levels; this would improve consistency of application. Some rating scales also weight the characteristics differentially.

Graphic rating scales have many shortcomings. First, the traits or characteristics are too often defined vaguely or not at all, as in Figure 10.1. As a result, different supervisors define and measure these traits differently. Second, some characteristics are very difficult for a supervisor to directly observe, which results in guesswork. Third, the traits being assessed are often simply someone's opinion of what is related to job performance and may not reflect actual job performance. Fourth, performance levels are usually

**FIGURE 10.1**

## Example of Graphic Rating Scale

Name _____  Type of Duty _____
Rank and Number _____  Rating Period: From _____
Date of Appointment _____            To _____
Promoted to Present Rank _____  Date of Rating _____

| Critical Standards of Performance | Inferior Performance | Acceptable Performance | | Superior Performance | | |
|---|---|---|---|---|---|---|
| | Below Standard 1 | Meets Minimum Standard 2 | Meets Standard 3 | Exceeds Standard 4 | Greatly Exceeds Standard 5 | Outstanding 6 |
| 1. Work performance | ☐ | ☐ | ☐ | ☐ | ☐ | ☐ |
| 2. Dependability | ☐ | ☐ | ☐ | ☐ | ☐ | ☐ |
| 3. Initiative | ☐ | ☐ | ☐ | ☐ | ☐ | ☐ |
| 4. Relationships | ☐ | ☐ | ☐ | ☐ | ☐ | ☐ |
| 5. Appearance | ☐ | ☐ | ☐ | ☐ | ☐ | ☐ |
| 6. Written communications | ☐ | ☐ | ☐ | ☐ | ☐ | ☐ |
| 7. Verbal communications | ☐ | ☐ | ☐ | ☐ | ☐ | ☐ |

Rater's Signature                    3. _____  Rank _____  Reviewing Officer's Signature
1. _____  Rank _____     4. _____  Rank _____  - - - - - - - - - - - - - - - - - - - -
2. _____  Rank _____     5. _____  Rank _____  Rank _____

defined in general terms, such as "excellent," "good," "satisfactory," or "unsatisfactory," and appraisers may differ significantly in their standards for each of these rating levels. Fifth, this method often fails to provide useful feedback to appraisees.

Moreover, the graphic rating scale is vulnerable to virtually all the perceptual errors in the rating process discussed earlier, especially leniency. Although some of these problems can be reduced by rater training and by careful definitions of rated characteristics and response scales, this method is generally considered one of the least reliable or valid approaches to performance evaluation. Indeed, many supervisors who are required to use this method are reluctant to put much effort into it or to place much reliance on it because of doubts about its validity.

Yet many organizations use this method because of its ease, low cost, and "face" validity—that is, it looks as if it should be a valid system. Because it is an absolute system (rather than a relative system, as in the case of ranking), it does avoid certain problems of ranking systems, such as the inability to make comparisons across departments. In some cases, it may be better than no system at all, especially if it is not used for pay purposes. Use of multiple raters may also improve the utility of this method.

## BEHAVIOURALLY ANCHORED RATING SCALES

**Behaviourally anchored rating scales (BARS)** are an attempt to improve on the graphic rating scale by providing specific descriptions of behaviours for each point on the rating scale for each job aspect. For example, take the job of "recruiting officer." This job has several different job aspects, such as identifying sources of good candidates, encouraging them

**behaviourally anchored rating scales (BARS)**
Appraisal method that provides specific descriptors for each point on the rating scale.

to apply for vacancies, gathering necessary information on each candidate, interviewing them, and recommending the best candidates. One aspect of the job involves soliciting and answering questions from applicants during the interview process. The following scale might be developed for appraising this aspect:

**Position**: Recruiting Officer.

**Name of Appraisee**: _____

**Job Aspect**: Soliciting and addressing questions from interviewees.

**Instructions**: Choose the statement below that is most typical of this individual:

1. Often fails to solicit questions from interviewee.
2. Attempts to solicit questions, but not very successful in generating questions.
3. Successfully generates questions, but often does not address them effectively.
4. Successfully generates questions and addresses most of them effectively.
5. Successfully generates questions and addresses virtually all effectively.

Similar scales would need to be developed for each aspect of the "recruiting officer" job.

Evidence that BARS results in an appreciable improvement in the reliability and validity of ratings is mixed, although there is some evidence that BARS provides better guidance to raters in defining degrees of effectiveness. BARS have the advantage of yielding a total score for purposes of pay decisions and an evaluation in specific behavioural terms that is useful in providing meaningful feedback for developmental purposes. The major disadvantage is that different scales need to be developed for each job aspect for each job in the organization, which can be both expensive and time consuming. Another problem is that supervisors may disagree with the ordering on the scale, or there may be two items that could be selected for a given scale.

## BEHAVIOURAL OBSERVATION SCALES

behavioural observation scales (BOS)
Appraisal method under which appraisers rate the frequency of occurrence of different employee behaviours

Behavioural observation scales (BOS) were developed to try to improve upon the BARS.[25] This method entails developing behavioural statements that reflect examples of positive behaviour for each job; each employee is then rated on the frequency with which each behaviour occurs (on a "1" to "5" scale from "almost never" to "almost always"). Overall ratings are developed by summing the individual scores. **Figure 10.2** illustrates some sample items in a BOS.

Proponents argue that this method preserves the advantages of BARS by specifically identifying the behaviours that will be rated, while eliminating some of their disadvantages. The major advantage of BOS over BARS is that once an item has been selected, there is no need to develop detailed definitions for each scale point. Furthermore, using frequency of behaviour as the rating scale ensures that two or more responses cannot be selected, as is possible for BARS.

Of course, this method also has its drawbacks. For example, the frequency of a given behaviour can be hard to judge, because most supervisors have only a limited number of observations on which to base this judgment. Furthermore, some research indicates that raters generalize from a global evaluation of the individual, instead of first determining frequencies for each item.[26] In fact, these researchers conclude that BOS may actually be more subjective than other scales, such as BARS.

## Sample Items from Behavioural Observation Scales

INSTRUCTIONS: Please consider the Sales Representative's behaviour on the job in the past rating period. Read each statement carefully, then circle the number that indicates the extent to which the employee has demonstrated this *effective* or *ineffective* behaviour.

For each behaviour observed, use the following scale:

| | |
|---|---|
| 5 represents almost always | 95–100% of the time |
| 4 represents frequently | 85–94% of the time |
| 3 represents sometimes | 75–84% of the time |
| 2 represents seldom | 65–74% of the time |
| 1 represents almost never | 0–64% of the time |

| Sales Productivity | Almost Never | | | | Almost Always |
|---|---|---|---|---|---|
| 1. Reviews individual productivity results with manager | 1 | 2 | 3 | 4 | 5 |
| 2. Suggests to peers ways of building sales | 1 | 2 | 3 | 4 | 5 |
| 3. Formulates specific objectives for each contact | 1 | 2 | 3 | 4 | 5 |
| 4. Focuses on product rather than customer problem | 1 | 2 | 3 | 4 | 5 |
| 5. Keeps account plans updated | 1 | 2 | 3 | 4 | 5 |
| 6. Keeps customer waiting for service | 1 | 2 | 3 | 4 | 5 |
| 7. Anticipates and prepares for customer concerns | 1 | 2 | 3 | 4 | 5 |
| 8. Follows up on customer leads | 1 | 2 | 3 | 4 | 5 |

Source: From Belcourt. *Managing Human Resources* Canadian Text, 3E. © 2002 Nelson Education Ltd. Reproduced by permission. www.cengage.com/permissions.

## OBJECTIVES-BASED AND RESULTS-BASED SYSTEMS

An approach that first gained prominence more than three decades ago involves establishing goals and objectives for each employee, usually on a joint basis, and then measuring actual performance against those objectives. This approach is known as **management by objectives (MBO)** or sometimes "management by results." MBO is regarded by many as a highly effective approach to employee motivation because of two key elements: participation by the employee in setting the goals, and frequent feedback on goal accomplishment. Research has consistently shown that setting goals and providing feedback on progress improves employee performance.[27] To be effective, goals must be significant yet realistic, and there must be a means of measuring the extent to which they have been achieved.

According to research conducted by one of the authors, most Canadian organizations use performance appraisals based on goal setting for their employees, and an even larger proportion use it for their managers. As will be discussed shortly, this change is likely due to a surge of interest in "performance management," which incorporates goal setting as a central feature.

**management by objectives (MBO)**
An approach to management that involves setting employee goals and providing feedback on goal accomplishment.

Although the motivational advantages of MBO systems can be significant, using them for determining pay levels can be difficult. One major difficulty is that not all significant goals can be easily measured in a concrete way, and goals that cannot be measured are often neglected.[28] Another problem is that different employees set different goal levels. Should an individual who sets high goals but falls slightly short be penalized, while an individual who achieves low goals is rewarded? The following example illustrates this problem:

*A high-level manager in the start-up operations of a paper products company set stringent goals to "shoot for" regarding start-up costs. Due to the inefficiencies of outside contractors, the targets were not attained. The manager was severely penalized at Christmas bonus time and again the following February at his annual performance review. He vowed that he would not repeat the same mistake.*[29]

Overall, the lesson this manager (and his subordinates) learned from this experience was to set specific, relatively easy goals. The manager subsequently became a senior vice president in his organization.

## FIELD REVIEW

The field review method involves a short period of direct observation of the job performance of the individual being rated, often by an individual from outside the department who is specially trained to conduct such reviews. This method is often used for jobs that are not normally under direct observation by the supervisor. Truck drivers and airline pilots are often appraised in this way. In the service sector, "mystery shoppers" are often used to assess the work performance of sales personnel and other service staff.

A major advantage of this method is that a small number of specially trained raters may be able to rate many employees, thus increasing the consistency and reliability of the appraisals. This method also provides the supervisor with a "second opinion" on the employee's performance and may reduce bias and other rating errors. Normally, this method is used in conjunction with other methods and provides supervisors with additional data for their appraisals. Its main disadvantages relate to the cost of training and using specialized raters and its limited application: field reviews are appropriate only in circumstances where the behaviour can be evaluated relatively quickly.

## CONTINUOUS PERFORMANCE MANAGEMENT

If you read business news often, you may be led to believe that performance management has become extinct. A large amount of recent research has been dedicated to analyzing why performance appraisals are futile or even detrimental. However, the appraisal system is not entirely abandoned, but rather the traditional annual appraisal is now increasingly being replaced with a continuous review process.

Continuous performance management is a novel way to view traditional employee review structures. Rather than bi-annual or quarterly reviews, continuous performance management involves aggregate information on employee outputs from various touchpoints. A significant factor of continuous performance management is the check-in. A check-in entails a one-on-one meeting with an employee and their manager/supervisor, in which they discuss the development in terms of predetermined objectives, priorities, concerns, and new goals to be established and mutually determined action points. The check-ins are usually every one-to-three months. Another major component of continuous performance management is real-time feedback.[30] Essentially, the appraisal meeting may be adjourned, but it is never done.

The specific features of the continuous performance management process may differ. However, the purpose is to establish appraisal and feedback as routine and ongoing elements of management practice. The amount of feedback involved may seem excessively labour-intensive. Yet, new software allows for an easier process.[31] Analytics and artificial intelligence can be incorporated into the system to allow for more data from various interactions. Thus, quantitative data can be coupled with ongoing qualitative data to allow for more knowledgeable decisions, precise feedback, and track the impact of various interventions on specific metrics. Managers can see which actions had a significant effect on employee performance.[32]

The continuous performance management is a cognisant exertion to reinforce positive behaviour and provide timely feedback as to an employee's performance. The outcome of the more frequent review is a more holistic and precise evaluation of employee performance with a decreased likelihood of bias.[33] Continuous feedback also meets the needs of millennial employees, who now want increased coaching and constant feedback.[34]

A critique of continuous performance management is that the aim is primarily the developmental component of appraisal, which is thought to fit inappropriately within the larger performance management system, which is often more punitive in nature.[35] Also, adjusting to this type of performance feedback would be a long journey requiring a complete overhaul of the system. New technology must be incorporated, new best practices must be learned, and employees and managers would require enough training.[36]

## COMBINATION APPROACHES

Of course, some of the methods described above can be used in combination with other methods. For example, at JPMorgan Chase, the financial services giant, the appraisal process has four components of their annual performance review: business results, client focus, teamwork, and risk controls. The firm is also developing a mobile tool that allows individuals to request and receive feedback only moments after a meeting or a project is completed, similar to an uber-rating.[37]

## SOURCES OF APPRAISALS

Who should conduct performance appraisals? In the past, the answer was obvious: the employee's immediate supervisor, often augmented by an overall review of appraisals by the next-higher level of management. Recent research, though, has shown that there may be value in including others in the appraisal process, including peers, subordinates, and even customers, and that use of these alternative sources of appraisal information has expanded. However, research by one of the authors indicates that supervisory appraisals are still the mainstay of the appraisal process; about three-quarters of Canadian employers use only supervisory appraisals.

## APPRAISAL BY SUPERIORS

The traditional approach to performance appraisal involves appraisals by the immediate superior. In a classical organization, supervisors are responsible for the performance of their units, so it seems logical to give them the responsibility for appraising the performance of the people within their units. Besides, this approach reinforces the authority of the supervisor—something that is important in classical organizations.

But relying on the supervisor as the sole source for performance appraisals can generate several problems. For example, supervisors may not have had sufficient opportunities to observe behaviour, or employees may skew their behaviour when they know a supervisor is observing. And as has been discussed, supervisors may distort ratings, intentionally or not.

The "solution" to these problems has traditionally been for the next-higher level of management to review the appraisals prepared by their subordinate managers. But while this practice may have some advantages, such as demonstrating that appraisers are accountable for their ratings, it does not solve all the performance appraisal problems noted earlier. Because the superior generally has even less knowledge about specific employee behaviour than the appraiser, the superior may be reluctant to question the results. For the same reason, the superior must resist the temptation to tinker with individual ratings.

## PEER APPRAISALS

To augment the information available to the manager, information is sometimes collected from employees who work at the same level as the appraisee. The rationale is that peers usually have much more contact with their coworkers than a supervisor does and thus are more likely in a position to observe typical behaviour (i.e., behaviour that is not skewed). Also, research has shown that rating errors are usually reduced when multiple raters are used.[38]

However, when appraisals are used for pay purposes, peers may be reluctant to "grade down" their colleagues, and the appraisal system may informally gravitate toward a mutual admiration society, in which all will benefit provided that they rate each other highly. Of course, the opposite may occur if there is only a limited amount of merit pay that can be awarded; that is, peers may give one another low ratings in an attempt to make their own performance look better, resulting in conflict and ill will among peers.

In general, research suggests that, if anything, peers are more lenient than superiors in making their ratings. As one observer put it: "In more than one team I studied, participants in peer appraisal routinely gave all their colleagues the highest rating on all dimensions. When I questioned this practice, the responses revealed just how perplexing and risky, both personally and professionally, evaluating peers can be."[39] Some employees in this example feared that providing negative feedback would damage their relationships with their peers and possibly hinder their own careers. Others felt that negative peer feedback was not in keeping with the supportive work environment in which they preferred to work.

## SUBORDINATE APPRAISALS

Appraisal of managers by their subordinates is playing an increasing role in the performance appraisal process. The logic is that subordinates can provide valid input regarding the effectiveness of a manager that may not be available from a different vantage point. For example, at Ernst & Young Canada, a professional services firm, all employees are asked to respond (anonymously) to this e-survey question: "How well does [your manager] foster a positive work environment and help our people grow?"[40] The company believes that only employees can tell them what the atmosphere is really like "down in the trenches."

However, supervisors often have serious concerns about subordinate appraisals. They may worry that their subordinates do not understand all the job demands placed on them or the constraints they are operating under. They may also fear that employees will downgrade them if they must make unpopular decisions.

For their part, employees may be reluctant to criticize their supervisor for fear of repercussions. In fact, a perverse situation can arise in which supervisors with good relationships with their subordinates—whose subordinates believe they are free to be candid in their comments—may actually receive less favourable evaluations than supervisors who are perceived as vindictive tyrants, as in the latter situation, employees may be afraid that any criticism could have negative repercussions.

In fact, research has shown that subordinate appraisals are actually much less accurate in assessing managerial performance than peer or supervisory appraisals (supervisory appraisals turned out to be the most accurate of the three, despite the finding that supervisory bias was twice as strong as employee performance as a determinant of appraisee ratings). It would seem that an easy solution to this dilemma would be to simply make subordinate results anonymous. However, one study found that anonymity does not produce accurate results as subordinates aren't held accountable for their ratings. The study found that the best way to make use of subordinate ratings was to have a third-party consultant made aware of subordinates' ratings of managers. However, the ratings would be anonymous to managers. The consultant could follow up with the subordinates to ask them to provide the reasoning behind each rating.[41]

Subordinate appraisals are only useful for certain workplaces. This model clearly does not fit well with classical organizations. Nor do they fit well with human relations organizations because nobody will want to provide any negative feedback about their well-liked supervisors. In short, subordinate appraisals can be expected to work well only in high-involvement organizations, where trust and open communication are key values.

## SELF-APPRAISALS

Including a self-appraisal component in the appraisal process may have several advantages—such as encouraging employees to critically examine their own performance and facilitating communication with superiors. However, self-appraisals are of very little value for pay purposes because they tend to be inflated. Not surprisingly, the poorest employees tend to inflate their performance the most (see Compensation Today 10.3), while some high performers may be overly self-critical.

Studies have also shown that self-appraisals are especially poor at identifying specific employee behaviours that impede productivity. In assessing these kinds of behaviours, peer appraisals were far superior to self-appraisals.[42] Indeed, rather than being used for assessing job performance in general, peer appraisals may be most helpful in identifying counterproductive employee behaviours.

## CUSTOMER APPRAISALS

Customers are sometimes included in the feedback process. This can be highly useful when customer satisfaction is a key factor in the organization's success. At Avis Rent-A-Car, for example, the Enterprise Service Quality index is a measurement of the percentage of customers who check the top box in a survey. This measurement is the foundation of employees' goals.[43] But this approach has limitations: not all employees come into contact with customers, and customers may not be able to single out the performance of individual employees.

## OTHER APPRAISERS

As with field reviews, professional raters may be useful for some organizations. Many firms in the service industry, including durable goods retailers, service retailers, car dealers,[44] restaurants,[45] banks,[46] and many other businesses, have full-time raters (known as "mystery shoppers" when they are not identified in advance) who visit specific sites and conduct detailed appraisals, which are then used to evaluate employee and managerial performance.[47]

## MULTISOURCE SYSTEMS/360-DEGREE FEEDBACK

**360-degree feedback**
An appraisal system that uses feedback from superiors, peers, subordinates, and possibly customers

But any combination of these sources is also possible. A relatively new method, the 360-degree feedback method, combines peer and subordinate appraisals (and sometimes even customer appraisals) with supervisory appraisals.[48] Because of dissatisfaction with existing appraisal systems, **360-degree feedback** expanded rapidly in the 1990s, although this expansion appears to have slowed as some of its shortcomings have become more apparent. Originally intended as a tool for providing developmental feedback, this system has since been used by many organizations for pay and promotion purposes.[49] According to research by one of the authors, perhaps one-fifth of Canadian firms are currently using 360-degree feedback for appraising their managers and employees (of course, for nonmanagers, it is really 270-degree feedback because they generally have no subordinates).

Multisource systems use standardized forms that provide numerical ratings of the appraisee along numerous dimensions. Individual raters (except the superior) are assured of anonymity so that they can feel free to be candid in their ratings. Importantly, the system employs several procedures to screen out invalid data. For example, in a set of ratings for a given appraisee, the extreme scores (i.e., the lowest and the highest) are dropped before the scores are averaged. And if a rater is more than 40 percent discrepant from other raters, that person's ratings may be eliminated entirely.

Advocates of this approach suggest that 360-degree systems have many advantages over traditional superior-only ratings.

1. They are fair, in that they have more safeguards to prevent bias, which results in less rating inflation.

2. They are more accurate, because they encompass the perspectives of many raters, who have different viewpoints from which to observe performance.

3. They are more credible to the recipient. Appraisees may believe a single rater to be wrong or biased, but could all these raters be wrong?

4. They may be more valuable for bringing about behaviour change because work associates are likely to be more specific in their behavioural feedback.

5. They may be more motivational because peer pressure may motivate constructive behaviour changes.[50]

However, multisource plans also have drawbacks. They are subject to most of the same problems faced by peer and subordinate ratings discussed earlier. Also, multisource systems can be complicated to set up. Forms (whether paper or electronic) must be developed that ask the right questions, and different forms may be necessary for different jobs.

Employees must be willing to fill out the forms voluntarily, and it may be difficult to track those who do not submit forms because the forms are submitted anonymously. To ensure anonymity, there must be at least four persons in each rating group (peers or subordinates), but this number of raters may not be available for all appraisees. Moreover, training needs to be provided to all raters, which is generally not practical given the number of potential raters in this system (i.e., virtually everybody!).

Are 360-degree systems effective? Unfortunately, there is very little evidence on this question. One early study indicated that 360-degree systems were somewhat more effective in fostering employee performance than other types of systems (68 percent of 360-degree users reported that their appraisal system had led to better employee performance, compared to 55 percent of users of traditional systems).[51] Moreover, 65 percent of 360-degree users believed that their systems produced valid information for promotions, compared to 55 percent of users of traditional systems. However, 360-degree systems had no real advantage over traditional systems in producing valid information for merit increases: 69 percent of 360-degree firms believed their systems produced valid information for merit raises, compared to 65 percent of other firms.

In a more recent study that reviewed the effectiveness of a 360-degree performance appraisal process for surgeons, 87 percent of surgeons and 80 percent of department heads agreed that reviewers offered accurate feedback of surgeons. In terms of identifying poor performing surgeons, 60 percent of department heads reported that the 360-degree evaluation pinpointed surgeons who had pre-existing concerns on their record, and 20 percent of department heads said that the review helped identify surgeons without a pre-existing history of poor performance. Of the surgeons participating in the 360-degree feedback system, 77 percent of surgeons were still willing to participate in a repeat evaluation. In comparison, 80 percent of department heads and 85 percent of reviewers were willing to participate in a similar process again. Furthermore, 63 percent of surgeons reported that they made changes to their performance based on the 360-degree evaluation results, and 60 percent of department heads noted improvement in the surgeon's behaviour. Yet only 32 percent of reviewers reported that they saw a significant change in staff behaviour.[52]

Other studies have found inconsistent results. In a meta-analysis reviewing the effects of 360-degree reviews, the authors found mixed results for its success. The authors believe that the reason for the widely different results can be due to the high amount of variation in design features.[53] Overall, current thinking is that 360-degree appraisal works better for feedback purposes than as a basis for merit pay.[54] The authors mentioned four characteristics of a 360-degree feedback process that is necessary to have a real impact on organizational change: relevant content, credible data, accountability, and census participation. It is also important, if employee behaviour is to actually change, that managers follow up the results of 360-degree feedback by discussing the results with appraisees and jointly developing plans for behaviour change.[55] It seems probable that, like subordinate appraisals, 360-degree systems are more likely to succeed in high-involvement organizations than in classical or human relations organizations.

## 720-DEGREE FEEDBACK

Critics make two common complaints surrounding the 360-degree feedback system: (1) it fosters defensiveness, which constrains development; and (2) it promotes action without providing the individual with the personal understanding and motivation to develop. Much of the complaints surrounding the 360-degree feedback system can be addressed with its successor, the 720-degree feedback system. The 720-degree feedback system, which is designed primarily to assess those in upper-level management, starts with a similar 360-degree process. However, this performance appraisal uses validated tools to highlight strengths, cognitions, motivations, personality, leadership style, and drive.[56] As compared to the 360-degree review process, the 720-degree review is more focused on ongoing development. Unlike the 360-degree review, the 720-degree performance appraisal is not an isolated event. Rather, the focus is on ongoing growth. At a minimum, there is both a pre-feedback and post-feedback meeting.[57] Once feedback is provided, a plan is developed, and measurable goals are established. Then, the individual receives ongoing support as the action plan unfolds.[58]

## PERFORMANCE MANAGEMENT

Although most practitioners and academics agreed that management by objectives (MBO) was a good concept, its use waned in the 1980s as the practical problems of making MBO work became more apparent. This decline in popularity was hastened by the emergence of the total quality management (TQM) movement in the 1980s, which eschewed the use of numerical goals, believing them to be counterproductive. However, in recent years, the concept of MBO has been resurrected under a new name—**performance management**—as part of the continuing quest to find a performance appraisal system that really works.[59]

Under performance management, the organization sets goals for individuals and groups, develops measures for goal achievement, provides feedback on progress, offers encouragement and support, and provides rewards for success.[60] When applied at the team level, performance management is really a type of goal-sharing plan (see Chapter 5).

Despite the vast majority of companies claiming to use a performance management system, less than one-fifth of Canadian Human Resources leaders feel that their performance management system is effective at achieving its main objective.[61] Furthermore, Deloitte's Global Human Capital Trends survey found that performance management systems do not often reward the right behaviour. For example, team performance is a major component of most jobs, yet only 28 percent of respondents claimed that their organizations provided performance awards based on "achievement of measurable team metrics."[62]

Because it has become such a widely adopted program, and because some companies do believe it to be effective, you need to understand its key elements, as listed in Compensation Notebook 10.1.[63] Although performance appraisal is an important aspect, when used properly, performance management is really more of a management system than an appraisal system.[64]

The first element of performance management is goals. These need to be "SMART"—that is, Specific, Measurable, Achievable, Relevant, and specified in Time. Goals need to be tied to key success factors for the firm, such as customer satisfaction or product quality. However, coming up with goals that apply to individual employees can be very difficult because results may depend on the collective efforts of a number of different employees. If this is the case, some type of group goal-sharing system may be preferable.

Organizations that use SMART goals need to develop measures that are both reliable and valid—which is not always easy to do. During the course of the year, employees need feedback on their progress toward goal accomplishment as well as specific guidance on ways to improve performance. They also need to be encouraged and reinforced as they make progress toward achieving their goals; and they must be appropriately rewarded when goal achievement occurs. Of course, all of this is easier said than done!

Recent research suggests that getting performance management right is neither easy nor common, that performance management is often used in circumstances where it does not fit, and that successful implementation of performance management is dependent on several key circumstances.[65] These include the quality of the employee–manager relationship, trust between the employee and the supervisor, and provision of both formal and informal feedback on performance and progress toward goal achievement.

**performance management** Method for improving employee performance based on goal setting, feedback, encouragement and support, and rewards for success.

---

## COMPENSATION NOTEBOOK 10.1

### KEY ELEMENTS OF PERFORMANCE MANAGEMENT

1. Goals are tied to the strategy and key success factors of the business.
2. Measures are the primary indicators of success.
3. Feedback is the data used to determine progress toward goals.
4. Reinforcement is the active encouragement and support for action.
5. Rewards are what the individual or team receives for achieving desired results.

# LINKING PAY TO PERFORMANCE APPRAISALS

The discussion so far has focused on performance management, in general. From a compensation perspective, the key is to establish methods to link an employee's performance with pay, if and when appropriate. In Chapter 5, we discussed some of these methods, including merit raises and bonuses.

That is, besides accurate measurement of performance, the other crucial aspect of merit pay is having an effective way of linking performance to pay.[66] There are several issues to consider here. First, should the link between performance appraisal and awarding a merit raise or bonus be fixed or discretionary? Second, should the amount of merit money each employee receives be fixed or discretionary? Third, how should the total amount of money available for merit pay be determined?

Regarding the first issue, whether or not an employee receives a merit increase can simply be left up to the supervisor, based on examination and comparison of performance appraisal results. However, this leaves the door open to supervisor bias and inconsistency, so most firms have a fixed link between performance appraisal results and whether a merit increase is granted.[67] For example, the firm may decide that nobody receiving less than a "very good" rating or a particular cutoff score will receive any merit increase. Or it may decide that merit pay will be restricted to the top 10 percent of employees in a department, based on their appraisal scores.

A second issue is whether the amount of the merit pay to be provided to each meritorious employee will be fixed or discretionary. In some cases, a supervisor simply receives a block of merit money to be allocated as he or she sees fit to the employees designated as meritorious, as long as pay ranges are not violated. However, research shows that this approach can lead to unfair allocation of merit money. For example, a recent study found that even when performance appraisals are fairly done, and even when there is no bias regarding which employees are selected to receive merit money, women and racial minority employees receive smaller raises than they deserve, relative to other meritorious employees.[68]

It makes sense to stipulate a fixed formula for the amount of merit money that meritorious employees will receive. In some instances, a forced distribution is stipulated. For example, the top one-quarter of employees in a department receive, say, a merit raise of 10 percent, the next quarter receive five percent, and the third and bottom quarters receive no merit increase at all.

One approach to linking merit pay to performance appraisal is the **merit pay grid** (sometimes referred to as a "**merit pay matrix**"). As **Table 10.1** shows, this grid has two dimensions. Across the top are employee performance ratings. Along the vertical axis are quartiles of the pay range for a particular set of employees. The numbers in each cell indicate the percentage increase employees in that cell receive as a merit raise. For example, an employee in the second quartile of the pay range with a "good" performance rating receives a five percent merit increase.

As in this example, a common practice is for employees in the lower quartiles of their pay range to receive a higher percentage increase to bring them up to the midpoint of the range quite quickly. (Of course, increments expressed in fixed dollar amounts also amount to a higher percentage increase for employees in the lower part of the range.) The example is also designed so that employees in the third and

**merit pay grid/merit pay matrix**
A tool for allocating merit raises, based on the performance level of the employee and the pay range quartile in which they fall.

TABLE 10.1

Example of A Merit Pay Grid

| | Employee Performance Level | | | |
|---|---|---|---|---|
| | Unsatisfactory | Satisfactory | Good | Excellent |
| Fourth (highest) quartile | — | — | 3% | 5% |
| Third quartile | — | — | 4% | 6% |
| Second quartile | — | 3% | 5% | 7% |
| First (lowest) quartile | — | 4% | 6% | 8% |

fourth quartiles receive no merit increase for simply doing satisfactory work, although employees in the first and second pay quartiles receive three or four percent. The logic of this is that employees paid above the midpoint in their pay are already being rewarded for "satisfactory" work, and that a higher rating is necessary to trigger a merit raise for them.

An alternative to the percentage approach to determining the amount of merit pay is to use a fixed increment method. Within every pay range, a fixed number of increments (with each increment normally having the same value) are made available for merit pay. For example, a job in a pay range of $50 000–$60 000 may have five "merit increments" of $2000 available, and if an employee proves meritorious in given year, that employee receives one increment. (Development of these increments was discussed in Chapter 8, in connection with developing a base pay structure.)

Note that individuals at the top of the pay range for their pay grade are not generally eligible for further merit raises, no matter how superior their performance. Motivational problems resulting from this situation can be eliminated by making merit bonuses available for those at the top of their range. Instead of providing a merit raise of $2000, a merit bonus of $2000 could be provided to meritorious performers who are at the top of their pay range.

A third issue is deciding how much money to make available for merit raises in a given year. There are two main approaches. A "bottom-up approach" does not set any arbitrary amount but simply adds up all the merit increments and pays them. The major disadvantage of this method is that the organization has no control over labour cost increases. Many organizations are not comfortable with that lack of control, so they set a maximum amount available for merit pay (the "top-down approach") and allocate it across departments. When this approach is used, the firm should ensure that it is making available sufficient funds to allow a reasonable number of merit increases.

Some firms gear the total amount of merit money available in a given year to the achievement of certain financial goals of the organization. Compensation Today 10.4 describes a system used by RBC Financial to determine how much money will be available for annual merit bonuses based on organizational performance. A problem here is that the entire merit pay system may become irrelevant when the firm is not meeting its financial goals. Is this really a time to signal to your top performers that merit will no longer be rewarded?

### [STOP] TYING BONUSES TO PERFORMANCE RATINGS AT RBC FINANCIAL

RBC Financial's merit bonus system—called the "quality performance incentive" or "QPI". Under this system, the total amount of the annual bonus pool is determined by the extent to which the bank achieves certain financial objectives in each year. The specific amount received by each employee depends on his or her annual performance rating.

The system works like this: If the company meets financial performance goals for the next year (in terms of return on equity and revenue growth), a specific sum—say $100 million—is placed in a bonus pool. This amount is increased by 25 percent if three other goals are met: if revenue growth, customer satisfaction, and employee commitment all exceed that of the competitors.

The amount each employee actually receives depends on the employee's individual performance rating. An employee who achieves less than a "satisfactory" performance rating normally receives none of the bonus. An employee who achieves a "satisfactory" rating receives 100 percent of the basic bonus amount available for that employee's salary band. If an employee achieves higher ratings, this amount goes to 130, 170, or 200 percent. For an employee in the lowest salary band, a standard payout could be $750, compared to $15 350 for an employee in the highest pay band. Depending on the type of work they do, some employees may be entitled to other bonuses, including sales incentives and commission-based compensation.

If you were an employee at RBC Financial, how would you feel about the "QPI" plan? Your opinion would probably depend on two considerations. First, is it likely that the bank will meet its performance criteria, thus creating a bonus pool? And second, will the performance ratings measure your performance fairly, so that you receive a merit bonus consistent with your performance? Without confidence that both of these are likely, you would find this combination individual and organizational performance pay plan irrelevant or even demotivating.

Source: Royal Bank of Canada, "2011 Corporate Responsibility Report and Public Accountability Statement," 2012.

---

Organizations must also decide whether persons performing at simply an adequate level should receive any merit increase. In general, the answer is "no." Some firms lump all their increases together, for cost of living, experience/seniority, and merit; in this way, everyone appears to get something. But this obscures the relationship between performance and merit pay.[69]

Instead, if cost of living increases are justified or if the labour market becomes highly competitive, increases should be provided across the board to all employees by raising base pay ranges or commission rates. If the organization wishes to reward seniority, seniority increases should also be kept separate from merit increases. One option is to provide inflation/market increases to all employees, seniority increases to all employees who are performing at a satisfactory or higher level, and an additional merit increase only to those persons who are clearly performing at a higher-than-satisfactory level. As discussed in Chapter 8, it is important for the amount of a merit increase to constitute a "just noticeable difference" in order for it to have impact.

Interestingly, conditions in the public sector may be more amenable to merit pay than they are in the private sector where business environments are rapidly changing and where alternatives, such as gain sharing and profit sharing, are available. In contrast, jobs in public sector organizations tend to be more stable and less subject to dramatic change. One occupational group that appears to fit many of the conditions for merit pay is university professors, as Compensation Today 10.5 illustrates.

## HOW WOULD YOU GRADE YOUR PROFESSOR?

Merit pay seems to be appropriate only in limited circumstances. However, university professors appear to meet many of the criteria. For the most part, they work independently and have control over their performance, and their accomplishments can usually be separated from those of others.

So how do you evaluate the performance of professors? In general, university professors are expected to perform in three main areas: teaching, research, and university and public service. Therefore, performance in each of these areas needs to be evaluated in some way.

The usual measure of research performance is the number of publications in high-quality academic journals. Why is this such a popular measure? Because it avoids virtually all the problems inherent in more subjective appraisal systems. When a professor believes that he or she has made a useful contribution to the state of knowledge in a particular field, that professor prepares a paper describing the research results and submits it to a journal that specializes in that type of research. This journal then has the article reviewed by two or more experts in the field, using what is known as a double-blind process. That is, the reviewers do not know whose work they are reviewing, and the researchers do not know who is reviewing their work. Thus, bias, halo, and the other major rating problems are avoided. Certainly, leniency is avoided because most reputable journals accept for publication only a small percentage of the work submitted to them—often as low as 5–10 percent of submissions. One could therefore argue that if there is any problem with this system, it is harshness.

Compare this practice with the evaluation of teaching. The usual process is to use feedback from superiors (e.g., the department head), peers (other professors), and customers (students). But superior and peer appraisals take place for only a small sample of teaching behaviour, perhaps one class per term, and it is usual practice to inform the professor well in advance of the appraisal. This, of course, allows the faculty member to alter behaviour to impress the appraisers. On the other hand, the presence of these appraisers could make the

What grade do you give me?

professor nervous and detract from her or his performance. But in any case, colleagues (department heads are normally considered as colleagues) are usually reluctant to be too critical of a colleague.

In addition, because no standardized rating form is usually used, the appraisals from peers are subject to all the errors discussed earlier in the chapter.

Students have the opportunity to attend all classes and so are in a better position to judge overall behaviour. But while they are qualified to judge things like preparation and organization of material, they are not well equipped to judge the rigour and academic validity of what is being taught, because they are (by definition) not experts in the subject matter. In addition, some faculty members attempt to influence student evaluations by combining lightweight material with easy tests and few assignments, in the hope of leading students to believe that they are learning a lot (as evidenced by their high grades), or simply to curry favour by making life as easy as possible for them.

With all these problems, it is difficult to place a high degree of confidence in evaluations of teaching. But evaluations of university and public service accomplishments are even less systematic and just as subjective. For example, what value should be placed on serving on the university budget committee or delivering a public lecture to the Rotary Club? Given the problems of accurately measuring teaching and university/public service, is it any wonder that research performance often carries the most weight in university appraisal processes?

# ISSUES IN DESIGNING AN EFFECTIVE MERIT SYSTEM

If the circumstances in an organization are judged to be right for an individual merit pay system, the next step is to design an effective system. This means addressing the following issues:

**1.** What should be the objectives of the system?
**2.** What is the most appropriate measurement system?
**3.** How frequently should appraisals be conducted?
**4.** How are appraisals to be linked to pay?
**5.** How should feedback be provided?
**6.** How is procedural justice to be achieved?
**7.** How are raters to be trained and evaluated?
**8.** How is the system to be evaluated?

We will discuss each of these issues in turn. We will conclude this section (and this chapter) with a discussion of the thorny issue of whether and how to evaluate the individual performance of employees who work in teams.

## DEFINE THE OBJECTIVES FOR MERIT PAY

The first issue is to define what the merit pay/performance appraisal system is supposed to accomplish. Is it intended primarily to stimulate performance, promote reward equity, retain valued performers, promote development/learning, or foster other desired behaviours? Is the focus to be on task behaviour, membership behaviour, or citizenship behaviour?

## DETERMINE THE MOST APPROPRIATE PERFORMANCE MEASUREMENT SYSTEM

The second issue is to determine the most appropriate performance measurement system. The appraisal method or process chosen should depend largely on the nature of the organization and of the jobs being appraised. For example, in jobs where employees do not work under close supervision, objectives-based and/or field review methods may be necessary. A 360-degree feedback system may also be useful.

As a general rule, ranking and forced distribution systems should not be used (because they foster a win–lose competitive environment among employees), except possibly when there is little or no interdependence among employees. These methods do not suit high-involvement or human relations organizations. Job-based systems, such as BARS, are probably not appropriate in organizations where jobs change rapidly. Ideally, whatever method is used, it should be systematic in approach, promote consistency across various raters, and be validated in some fashion.

## DETERMINE THE FREQUENCY OF APPRAISALS

Third, how often should appraisals be done? For accuracy and feedback, the more frequent, the better. From a practical point of view, an annual basis is usually best because merit raises are normally awarded once a year. One system that might be effective is to have two appraisals a year, with the intermediate appraisal used for feedback and development only, to give an indication of progress toward receiving a merit award.

## DETERMINE HOW TO LINK APPRAISALS TO PAY

Fourth, how should the appraisals be linked to pay? Several options were discussed in the previous section of this chapter. Overall, to be effective, merit pay systems need to provide some assurance that top-rated performance will be recognized in a significant way. The issue of whether and how to recognize employees at the top of their pay ranges needs to be dealt with here.

## DETERMINE HOW TO PROVIDE FEEDBACK

Fifth, how is feedback to be provided? To be useful, appraisal results should be fully communicated to employees, with concrete feedback on what can be done to improve individual performance. Also, employees should be encouraged to identify their own strengths and weaknesses and to communicate to the supervisor their view of the appraisal results and process. While appraisal interviews held at the time of each formal appraisal usually cover basic communication, the supervisor must also provide informal performance feedback on an ongoing basis to each subordinate.

For an appraisal interview to be effective, the supervisor must be highly familiar with the subordinate's job and performance, must take a supportive approach, and must encourage subordinates to present their views and perceptions. In general, a friendly approach that stresses strengths as well as weaknesses, and that enables subordinates to realize for themselves where their behaviour needs improvement, is most effective. The supervisor should focus on specific behaviours that are undesirable instead of simply making a general statement, such as "You have a bad attitude." A statement like that is guaranteed to generate defensiveness and resistance on the subordinate's part; furthermore, it provides no real guidance regarding exactly what behaviour needs to change. The appraisee should leave the interview with a description of specific, concrete steps that can be taken to improve performance.

Although it is important to use a systematic and valid appraisal method, effective performance appraisal goes far beyond the method used. The real key is the quality of the relationship between the supervisor and his or her subordinates. If a climate of trust and open communication does not exist between superior and subordinate, then the effectiveness of the appraisal process will be severely hampered, no matter how good the tools. One study found that a positive and supportive relationship with the supervisor was just as important as the performance score itself in determining appraisee satisfaction with the appraisal interview. A more recent study found that the relationship quality, including supervisor satisfaction, support, and trust, was strongly correlated with employees' reactions to performance appraisals. Relationship quality was even more strongly related to employees' reactions than appraisal participation or performance ratings.[70] Dissatisfaction with the appraisal interview led to lower job satisfaction and lower organizational commitment.

## DETERMINE MECHANISMS FOR PROCEDURAL JUSTICE

Sixth, there need to be mechanisms for ensuring procedural justice. Two key aspects are transparency (i.e., pay decisions are openly communicated to employees) and accountability (i.e., supervisors are held accountable for applying the merit pay system in a fair way).[71] One way of achieving transparency and greater employee confidence in the merit process is participation by employees in that process, although this may be viable only in high-involvement organizations. Another aspect of procedural justice is some type of review or appeals system. A highly developed process used by a Canadian university is illustrated in Compensation Today 10.6.

## DOES THIS SYSTEM HAVE ANY MERIT?

A major western Canadian university has used a complex system for merit increases. Each fall, faculty members in each academic department vote on whether to have an elected merit pay committee or to delegate this function to the department head. Then, faculty who wish to be considered for a merit increment (raise) are asked to submit evidence substantiating their case. The department committee or head then reviews these submissions, ranks them, and chooses which to submit to the College Review Committee, an elected body of faculty chaired by the dean of the college.

The College Review Committee reviews all submissions from the departments in the college and ranks them. The committee then awards merit increments (usually a half-increment, but occasionally a full increment) down the list until the available funds are exhausted. The funds available for merit increases are established through negotiations between the university and the faculty union, and they are usually sufficient to provide half-increments (which currently amount to about $1250) to approximately one-third of the faculty. There is also a special university-wide pool from which additional increments can be awarded to deserving faculty members. These funds are allocated by another elected faculty committee, the University Review Committee.

To ensure that teaching and university/public-service performance are not neglected because they are difficult to measure, most committees make a special effort to ensure that some awards are made on these bases. Once the awards are official, a report listing the faculty members who have received merit awards is provided to all faculty, along with a brief explanation of the basis for each award.

If an individual does not receive a merit increase, he or she has several avenues of appeal. If the department committee or head did not recommend an increase, that faculty member may appeal to the College Review Committee. If the College Review Committee does not grant an increment, the individual may then appeal to the University Review Committee.

It should also be noted that unless faculty members are at the top of the pay range for their rank, they will receive a full increment for each additional year of service, aside from whatever cost of living increase the faculty union is able to negotiate (which is not much these days). Thus, seniority usually counts about double the value of merit, even if one is among the fortunate one-third who receive merit increases.

You will recognize many elements of procedural justice in this system, including openness, the election of salary committees, the opportunity to make one's own case, and the two sets of appeal processes. Interestingly, despite all these elements of procedural justice, many faculties still feel slighted if they do not receive a merit increment and blame the system for "unfairness."

This system illustrates the difficulty inherent in developing a merit pay system that is perceived as fair by all employees. Part of the problem may be incomplete information: the brief report on merit awards that is provided to faculty typically does not portray the full spectrum of accomplishments on which the award is based, and many faculty members not receiving an award are able to point to somebody who appears to have done less than they have but were awarded a merit increment.

Is this merit system worthwhile? There is no clear answer, but it does accomplish several goals. It signals the behaviours that are important to the university, it attempts to provide some connection between contributions and rewards, it recognizes noteworthy accomplishments, and it serves as a mechanism for raising the pay of faculty members who might otherwise be lured to other universities.

## DETERMINE PROCEDURES FOR RATER TRAINING AND EVALUATION

Seventh, there need to be procedures for rater training, as well as for rater accountability. Raters need to be carefully trained to use the system, to make observations of employee behaviour, to relate these observations to the measurement system, and to provide effective feedback. In addition, a system needs to be in place for recognizing and rewarding those supervisors who take the appraisal process seriously and do it well. Supervisors need to know that appraisals of their own performance are partly based on how well they conduct performance appraisals for their subordinates.

## DEVELOP PROCEDURES FOR EVALUATING THE MERIT SYSTEM

Finally, how should the merit system be evaluated? Organizations need to develop a process for determining whether the system is achieving its objectives and whether it is causing any undesirable side effects. Rater and appraisee acceptance of the system can easily be evaluated through the use of surveys. If both raters and appraisees do not accept and believe in the system, then it doesn't stand a chance. However, even if both groups accept a particular appraisal system, its weaknesses may render it ineffective or dysfunctional. Employee satisfaction with the system and its results is a key check on how it is performing.

## EVALUATING INDIVIDUALS IN TEAMS

One final topic in performance appraisal is the issue of how (and whether) to evaluate the performance of individuals in teams. As tasks in organizations have become more complex and interrelated, and as the business environment has come to demand more speed and customer responsiveness, many organizations have come to depend on work teams. Research by one of the authors suggests that at least one-fifth of Canadian firms use work teams or project teams for their employees, although not every employee at these firms is necessarily included in a team.

### When Should Individuals in Teams Be Evaluated?

The topic of teamwork raises two questions: (1) Should you attempt to recognize individual performance when that individual spends most or all of his or her time in a team? And (2) if so, how can this be done? There are two schools of thought on the first question. One is that any attempt to single out individuals in a team context (except possibly on the basis of pay for knowledge) will likely do more harm than good. The argument here is that teams are so interdependent in accomplishing their goals that singling out individuals is inherently unfair. Singling out particular team members may lead to resentment and a less cohesive and cooperative team. There is also a risk that some members will devote more energy to looking good according to the appraisal system than to being effective team players. Thus, critics of individual pay believe that team-based reward systems—such as gain sharing or goal sharing—are the best means of rewarding performance in teams.

The second school of thought argues that it is inevitable that some team members will contribute more to team success than others, so it is unfair (and possibly demotivating) to high contributors not to have their contributions recognized financially. If the right behaviours are rewarded, if individual contribution levels are fairly determined, and if the system is used in conjunction with group-based and organization-based performance pay, then individual performance pay may play a useful role even in a team context.[72]

Which school is correct? Unfortunately, there is no definitive evidence on this issue. However, it is clear that work teams can be highly effective without the use of individual performance pay, as Toyota and Shell Sarnia have demonstrated. Whether teams at these companies would be even more successful with an element of individual performance pay is not clear. However, it is conceivable that if done right, individual performance pay might help a firm encourage and retain high contributors without negative repercussions for the team as a whole. But given the risks and possible pitfalls involved, it may well be that the risks usually outweigh the possible returns.

In some circumstances, identifying and rewarding individual contributions may be appropriate and even necessary for team success. For example:

1. when the members do not have strong intrinsic motivation,
2. when strong positive group norms do not exist,
3. when group sanctions against poor contributors are ineffective,
4. when little member commitment to overall team or organizational goals is evident, and/or
5. when teams are temporary and membership is part-time.

Under these conditions, recognizing individual contribution levels may be essential, not only to discourage free riding, but also to assure team members who are contributing that their rewards will be higher than those of the free riders. There is nothing more demoralizing to conscientious team members than the presence of free riders who benefit equally from the team's accomplishments. This can result in a downward performance spiral as all members "cut their losses" by competing to see who can get away with contributing the least.

### How Can Individuals in Teams Be Evaluated?

individual/team merit grid
A method for linking individual merit pay to both individual and team performance.

One way of avoiding a downward performance spiral by team members is through the use of an **individual/team merit grid** that recognizes individual contributions while providing incentives for team-oriented behaviour.[73] **Table 10.2** provides an example. The table shows three levels of team performance and four levels of individual performance (defined in terms of contribution to team success) to measure total performance. If the team does not meet its performance goals, there is no merit pay for anyone, regardless of individual performance. The message is that there can be no individual success without team success. However, even if the team does meet its performance goals, there will be no merit pay for individuals who did not make at least an "effective" contribution to team success. If the team meets its goals, "effective contributors" (the norm) will receive a four percent raise or bonus, "high contributors" will receive a six percent raise or bonus, and "exceptional contributors" (these will generally be quite rare) will receive eight percent. If the team exceeds its goals, these amounts will be doubled. Overall, this system creates a common goal for team members while recognizing individual contribution levels. Of course, the key to success for this system is to have some way of identifying individual contribution levels that is both accurate and accepted as fair.

### TABLE 10.2

Example of an Individual/Team Merit Grid

| | INDIVIDUAL MEMBER CONTRIBUTION TO TEAM | | | |
|---|---|---|---|---|
| | Unsatisfactory | Effective (%) | High (%) | Exceptional (%) |
| Team exceeds goals | — | 8 | 12 | 16 |
| Team meets goals | — | 4 | 6 | 8 |
| Team fails to meet goals | — | — | — | — |

**FIGURE 10.3**

## Comprehensive Assessment of Team Member Effectiveness—Behaviourally Anchored Rating Scale (BARS) Version

| | | | | | |
|---|---|---|---|---|---|
| | Your name | | | | ← Write the names of the people on your team including your own name.<br><br>**This self and peer evaluation asks about how you and each of your teammates contributed to the team during the time period you are evaluating. For each way of contributing, please read the behaviors that describe a "1," "3," and "5" rating. Then confidentially rate yourself and your teammates.** |

| | | | | | | |
|---|---|---|---|---|---|---|
| **Contributing to the Team's Work** | 5 | 5 | 5 | 5 | 5 | • Does more or higher-quality work than expected.<br>• Makes important contributions that improve the team's work.<br>• Helps to complete the work of teammates who are having difficulty. |
| | 4 | 4 | 4 | 4 | 4 | Demonstrates behaviors described in both 3 and 5. |
| | 3 | 3 | 3 | 3 | 3 | • Completes a fair share of the team's work with acceptable quality.<br>• Keeps commitments and completes assignments on time.<br>• Fills in for teammates when it is easy or important. |
| | 2 | 2 | 2 | 2 | 2 | Demonstrates behaviors described in both 1 and 3. |
| | 1 | 1 | 1 | 1 | 1 | • Does not do a fair share of the team's work. Delivers sloppy or incomplete work.<br>• Misses deadlines. Is late, unprepared, or absent for team meetings.<br>• Does not assist teammates. Quits if the work becomes difficult. |
| **Interacting with Teammates** | 5 | 5 | 5 | 5 | 5 | • Asks for and shows an interest in teammates' ideas and contributions.<br>• Improves communication among teammates. Provides encouragement or enthusiasm to the team.<br>• Asks teammates for feedback and uses their suggestions to improve. |
| | 4 | 4 | 4 | 4 | 4 | Demonstrates behaviors described in both 3 and 5. |
| | 3 | 3 | 3 | 3 | 3 | • Listens to teammates and respects their contributions.<br>• Communicates clearly. Shares information with teammates. Participates fully in team activities.<br>• Respects and responds to feedback from teammates. |
| | 2 | 2 | 2 | 2 | 2 | Demonstrates behaviors described in both 1 and 3. |
| | 1 | 1 | 1 | 1 | 1 | • Interrupts, ignores, bosses, or makes fun of teammates.<br>• Takes actions that affect teammates without their input. Does not share information.<br>• Complains, makes excuses, or does not interact with teammates. Accepts no help or advice. |
| **Keeping the Team on Track** | 5 | 5 | 5 | 5 | 5 | • Watches conditions affecting the team and monitors the team's progress.<br>• Makes sure that teammates are making appropriate progress.<br>• Gives teammates specific, timely, and constructive feedback. |
| | 4 | 4 | 4 | 4 | 4 | Demonstrates behaviors described in both 3 and 5. |
| | 3 | 3 | 3 | 3 | 3 | • Notices changes that influence the team's success.<br>• Knows what everyone on the team should be doing and notices problems.<br>• Alerts teammates or suggests solutions when the team's success is threatened. |
| | 2 | 2 | 2 | 2 | 2 | Demonstrates behaviors described in both 1 and 3. |
| | 1 | 1 | 1 | 1 | 1 | • Is unaware of whether the team is meeting its goals.<br>• Does not pay attention to teammates' progress.<br>• Avoids discussing team problems, even when they are obvious. |
| **Expecting Quality** | 5 | 5 | 5 | 5 | 5 | • Motivates the team to do excellent work.<br>• Cares that the team does outstanding work, even if there is no additional reward.<br>• Believes that the team can do excellent work. |
| | 4 | 4 | 4 | 4 | 4 | Demonstrates behaviors described in both 3 and 5. |
| | 3 | 3 | 3 | 3 | 3 | • Encourages the team to do good work that meets all requirements.<br>• Wants the team to perform well enough to earn all available rewards.<br>• Believes that the team can fully meet its responsibilities. |
| | 2 | 2 | 2 | 2 | 2 | Demonstrates behaviors described in both 1 and 3. |
| | 1 | 1 | 1 | 1 | 1 | • Satisfied even if the team does not meet assigned standards.<br>• Wants the team to avoid work, even if it hurts the team.<br>• Doubts that the team can meet its requirements. |
| **Having Relevant Knowledge, Skills, and Abilities** | 5 | 5 | 5 | 5 | 5 | • Demonstrates the knowledge, skills, and abilities to do excellent work.<br>• Acquires new knowledge or skills to improve the team's performance.<br>• Able to perform the role of any team member if necessary. |
| | 4 | 4 | 4 | 4 | 4 | Demonstrates behaviors described in both 3 and 5. |
| | 3 | 3 | 3 | 3 | 3 | • Has sufficient knowledge, skills, and abilities to contribute to the team's work.<br>• Acquires knowledge or skills needed to meet requirements.<br>• Able to perform some of the tasks normally done by other team members. |
| | 2 | 2 | 2 | 2 | 2 | Demonstrates behaviors described in both 1 and 3. |
| | 1 | 1 | 1 | 1 | 1 | • Missing basic qualifications needed to be a member of the team.<br>• Unable or unwilling to develop knowledge or skills to contribute to the team.<br>• Unable to perform any of the duties of other team members. |

Source: From Ohland, Matthew et al. 2012. "The Comprehensive Assessment of Team Member Effectiveness: Development of a Behaviorally Anchored Rating Scale for Self-and Peer Evaluation," *Academy of Management Learning and Education*, 11(4): 609–630. © 2012 Academy of Management.

If an organization cannot devise an appraisal system that the team accepts, it should not attempt to force the use of an unacceptable system because this will likely do more harm than good. However, a peer appraisal system could well be used to identify the performance of team members, so that weak members could take steps to improve their performance (or be removed from the team). Nothing is more damaging to team morale (and, ultimately, to team performance) than carrying a member who makes little or no contribution to team success (especially if that member will receive the same rewards as everyone else, or who could affect other team members' rewards!).

**Figure 10.3** provides a peer evaluation tool that has been tested for reliability and validity. It uses a behaviourally anchored rating scale format for assessing individual contribution to team success.[74]

## SUMMARY

The pay for a given employee is a function of the internal value of the employee's job (i.e., as determined by job evaluation), the external value of the job (i.e., as determined by market surveys), and the individual's contribution to the job (i.e., as determined by performance appraisal). Chapter 10 focused on the third element in determining compensation values.

Although most organizations believe that the *concept* of performance appraisal is a good thing, few organizations, managers, or employees seem happy with their actual performance appraisal systems. Part of the problem is that linking individual merit pay to performance appraisal is not appropriate in many circumstances. Performance appraisal can be applied effectively only where performance has scope to vary, where employees can control their performance levels, and where individual performance can be separated out and accurately assessed. In addition, you have learned that evaluating individual performance in a team context is an especially thorny matter.

There are many threats to the accuracy of performance appraisal, some of them intentional. Managers usually view performance appraisal in the context of their overall task objectives, and the accuracy of performance appraisal is often secondary to the achievement of managerial goals. Another potential source of problems is the appraisal method itself.

The key is to select the method that fits best with the purpose of the appraisal system, the nature of the behaviour being evaluated, and the organizational context in which it is applied. The same is true for selecting the most appropriate persons to actually conduct the appraisals.

When pay is based on performance appraisal, you must develop a method for effectively linking pay to the appraisal results. But you will still have to deal with other issues before completing the design of the merit system, including frequency of appraisals, feedback, mechanisms for procedural justice, procedures for rater training, and how to evaluate the merit system itself.

## KEY TERMS

360-degree feedback
beauty effect
behaviourally anchored rating scales (BARS)
behavioural observation scales (BOS)
central tendency error
contrast effect
forced distribution method

graphic rating scale
halo error
harshness effect
individual/team merit grid
leniency effect
management by objectives (MBO)
merit pay grid (merit pay matrix)

performance appraisal
performance appraisal reliability
performance appraisal validity

performance management
recency effect
similarity effect

## DISCUSSION QUESTIONS

1. Take several jobs that you or other members of your class have held or are currently holding and discuss whether and how you would go about designing a useful performance appraisal and merit system for them.

2. One alleged problem with performance appraisal is that most employees seem to think they are above average and do not like to be told otherwise. Do you think this is true, and, if so, how could you design an appraisal system that might avoid this problem?

3. What is continuous performance management? How is it different from traditional approaches?

4. What are the key issues related to merit pay for individuals in teams?

5. How are performance appraisals linked to merit pay in organizations?

## EXERCISES

1. On the website http://www.businessballs.com/performanceappraisalform.pdf, you will find a template for a performance appraisal form. Using the material in this chapter, assess the pros and cons of this form. Which type of performance appraisal method do you think it represents?

2. In groups of six to eight, share your experiences with performance appraisal. Group members who have been subject to a performance appraisal system should indicate whether they believe their performance was fairly evaluated and, if not, why not. After that, the groups should come together and discuss the overall experience of class members with performance appraisal. How many members believe they were fairly appraised, and how many believe they were not, and what were the differences between fair and unfair appraisal systems?

3. Assume you are the HR manager in a small firm with 10 employees; all the employees are eligible for merit pay. You have been allocated $10 000 to reward these employees. Design a performance management system to first evaluate the employees and then a system to link their performance with pay. Discuss your approach with members in the class. What are the pros and cons in the various approaches?

## CASE QUESTIONS

1. Refer to *Case 1—Henderson Printing* in the Appendix. The company currently has no formal performance appraisal system. The CEO, Georgette Henderson, thinks that a performance appraisal system might be useful, and she has hired you to assess the company and recommend whether to implement one. She also wants to know whether she should link pay to the appraisals. She expects your report to include the

pros and cons of each idea, along with a detailed justification for your recommendations.

2. The CEO at Henderson Printing (see Question 1) has decided to go ahead with a performance appraisal system, and she has decided to link it to merit pay. Impressed with your work, she has hired you to design the performance appraisal system and a merit pay system that will be linked to it. She expects your report to be sufficiently comprehensive so that it can serve as the blueprint for implementing these systems.

## SIMULATION CROSS-REFERENCE

If you are using *Strategic Compensation: A Simulation* in conjunction with this text, you will find that the concepts in Chapter 10 are helpful in preparing the simulation.

# ENDNOTES

1. Lillian Cunningham, "In Big Move, Accenture Will Get Rid of Annual Performance Reviews and Rankings," *The Washington Post*, https://www.washingtonpost.com/news/on-leadership/wp/2015/07/21/in-big-move-accenture-will-get-rid-of-annual-performance-reviews-and-rankings/, accessed March 10, 2020.

2. Lillian Cunningham, "In Big Move, Accenture Will Get Rid of Annual Performance Reviews and Rankings," *The Washington Post*, https://www.washingtonpost.com/news/on-leadership/wp/2015/07/21/in-big-move-accenture-will-get-rid-of-annual-performance-reviews-and-rankings/, accessed March 10, 2020.

3. Michael Schrage, David Kiron, Bryan Hancock, and Raffaele Breschi, "Performance Management's Digital Shift," *MIT Sloan*, February 26, 2019, https://sloanreview.mit.edu/projects/performance-managements-digital-shift/, accessed March 10, 2020.

4. Wes Gay, "How IBM Changed Its Feedback System to Engage Millennial Employees," *Forbes*, July 13, 2016, https://www.forbes.com/sites/under30network/2016/07/13/how-ibm-changed-its-feedback-system-to-suit-millennial-employees/#48d7d902ed9c, accessed March 10, 2020.

5. Michael Schrage, David Kiron, Bryan Hancock, and Raffaele Breschi, "Performance Management's Digital Shift," *MIT Sloan*, February 26, 2019, https://sloanreview.mit.edu/projects/performance-managements-digital-shift/, accessed March 10, 2020.

6. Jeffrey S. Kane and Kimberly F. Kane, "Performance Appraisal," in *Human Resource Management: An Experimental Approach*, ed. H.J. Bernardin and J.E.A. Russell (New York: McGraw-Hill, 1993), 378.

7. Kane and Kane, "Performance Appraisal," 377–404.

8. Don L. Bohl, "Minisurvey: 360-Degree Appraisals Yield Superior Results," *Compensation and Benefits Review* 28, no. 5 (1996); Peter Prowse and Julie Prowse, "The Dilemma of Performance Appraisal," *Measuring Business Excellence* 13, no. 4 (2009).

9. "Performance Appraisals Get Thumbs Down," *Human Resources Management in Canada*, Report Bulletin #208 (2004), 4.

10. Edward E. Lawler, George S. Benson, and Michael McDermott, *Performance Management and Rewards Systems* (Los Angeles: Center for Organizational Effectiveness, Marshall School of Business, University of Southern California, 2012).

11. Not surprisingly, use of formal performance appraisal is much lower in small firms; only 38 percent of firms with fewer than 100 employees reported having formal performance appraisal. See Terry H. Wagar and Lynn Langrock, "Performance Appraisal and Compensation in Small Firms," *Canadian HR Reporter* 17, no. 14 (2004): 10; Amanda Silliker, "Performance Appraisals Mandatory at Most Firms," *Canadian HR Reporter*, October 8, 2012, https://www.hrreporter.com/news/hr-news/performance-appraisals-mandatory-at-most-firms/314583, accessed March 5, 2020.

12. Tom Coens and Mary Jenkins, *Abolishing Performance Appraisals: Why They Backfire and What to Do Instead* (San Francisco: Berrett-Koehler, 2000); Chris Woolston, "Why Appraisals are Pointless for Most People," *BBC*, May 2, 2019, https://www.bbc.com/worklife/article/20190501-why-appraisals-are-pointless-for-most-people, accessed March 5, 2020.

13. Edward E. Lawler, *Rewarding Excellence: Pay Strategies for the New Economy* (San Francisco: Jossey-Bass, 2000); Chris Woolston, "Why Appraisals are Pointless for Most People," *BBC*, May 2, 2019, https://www.bbc.com/worklife/article/20190501-why-appraisals-are-pointless-for-most-people, accessed March 5, 2020.

14. Clinton O. Longenecker, H.P. Sims, and D.A. Gioia, "Behind the Mask: The Politics of Employee Appraisal," *Academy of Management Executive* 1 (1987): 183–93; Chris Woolston, "Why Appraisals are Pointless for Most People," *BBC*, May 2, 2019, https://www.bbc.com/worklife/article/20190501-why-appraisals-are-pointless-for-most-people, accessed March 5, 2020.

15. Ibid., 185.

16. Ibid., 183.

17. Clinton Longenecker and Dean Ludwig, "Ethical Dilemmas in Performance Appraisal Revisited," in *Performance Measurement and Evaluation*, ed. Jacky Holloway, Jenny Lewis, and Geoff Mallory (London: Sage, 1985), 66–77; Xiaoye May Wang, Kin Fai Ellick Wong, and Jessica YY Kwong, "The Roles of Rater Goals and Ratee Performance Levels in the Distortion of Performance Ratings," *Journal of Applied Psychology* 95, no. 3 (2010): 546.

18. Daniel Hamermesh, *Beauty Pays: Why Attractive People Are More Successful* (Princeton: Princeton University Press, 2011).

19. Daniel Hamermesh, *Tall or Taller, Pretty or Prettier: Is Discrimination Absolute or Relative?* (Cambridge, MA: National Bureau of Economic Research, 2012).

20. Rebecca Puhl and Kelly D. Brownell, "Bias, Discrimination, and Obesity," *Obesity Research* 9, no. 12 (2001): 788–805; Regina Ferreira Bento, Lourdes Ferreira White, and Susan Rawson Zacur, "The Stigma of Obesity and Discrimination in Performance Appraisal: A Theoretical Model," *The International Journal of Human Resource Management* 23, no. 15 (2012): 3196–224.

21. Steven E. Scullen, Michael K. Mount, and Maynard Goff, "Understanding the Latent Structure of Job Performance Ratings," *Journal of Applied Psychology* 85, no. 6 (2000): 956–70.

22. Kane and Kane, "Performance Appraisal."

23. Navy Personnel Command Public Affairs Office, "Navy Performance Evaluation Instruction Updated," *The Flagship*, April 22, 2011, https://www.militarynews.com/norfolk-navy-flagship/news/top_stories/navy-performance-evaluation-instruction-updated/article_24efa015-a59e-5595-a1b4-babe7bd07ab4.html, accessed March 5, 2020.

24. Joshua Karsten and Erik Salvin, "The End of Allcaps and !!!! in Performance Reviews Gains Supports from Sailors," *Stripes*, December 31, 2018, https://www.stripes.com/news/the-end-of-allcaps-and-in-performance-reviews-gains-support-from-sailors-1.562656, accessed March 5, 2020.

25. Gary P. Latham and Kenneth N. Wexley, *Increasing Productivity Through Performance Appraisal* (Reading: Addison-Wesley, 1994), 51.

26. Kevin R. Murphy and Jeanette N. Cleveland, *Understanding Performance Appraisal* (Thousand Oaks: Sage, 1995); Theresa J.B. Kline and Lorne M. Sulsky, "Measurement and Assessment Issues in Performance Appraisal," *Canadian Psychology/Psychologie Canadienne* 50, no. 3 (2009): 161.

27. Edwin A. Locke and Gary P. Latham, "Has Goal Setting Gone Wild, or Have Its Attackers Abandoned Good Scholarship?" *Academy of Management Perspectives* 23, no. 1 (2009): 17–23.

28. Lisa D. Ordonez, Maurice E. Schweitzer, Adam D. Galinsky, and Max H. Bazerman, "Goals Gone Wild: The Systematic Side Effects of Overprescribing Goal Setting," *Academy of Management Perspectives* 23, no. 1 (2009): 6–16.

29. Latham and Wexley, *Increasing Productivity*, 51.

30. Lin Grensing-Pophal, "How Does Continuous Performance Management Work, *HR Daily Advisor*, November 7, 2018, https://hrdailyadvisor.blr.com/2018/11/07/how-does-continuous-performance-management-work/, accessed March 15, 2020.

31. Glynne Williams and Vanessa Beck, "From Annual Ritual to Daily Routine: Continuous Performance Management and Its Consequences for Employment Security," *New Technology, Work and Employment* 33, no. 1 (2018): 30–43.

32. Abhinav Mathai, "The Rise of Continuous Feedback," *Thrive Global*, October 1, 2019, https://thriveglobal.com/stories/the-rise-of-continuous-feedback/, accessed March 16, 2020.

33. Lin Grensing-Pophal, "How Does Continuous Performance Management Work, *HR Daily Advisor*, November 7, 2018, https://hrdailyadvisor.blr.com/2018/11/07/how-does-continuous-performance-management-work/, accessed March 15, 2020.

34. Jeff Garton, "How's Your Job Going and What Are You Doing About It?" *The Epoch Times*, March 9, 2020, https://www.theepochtimes.com/hows-your-job-going-and-what-are-you-doing-about-it_3256019.html, accessed March 15, 2020.

35. Glynne Williams and Vanessa Beck, "From Annual Ritual to Daily Routine: Continuous Performance Management and Its Consequences for Employment Security," *New Technology, Work and Employment* 33, no. 1 (2018): 30–43.

36. Abhinav Mathai, "The Rise of Continuous Feedback," *Thrive Global*, October 1, 2019, https://thriveglobal.com/stories/the-rise-of-continuous-feedback/, accessed March 16, 2020.

37. Gary P. Latham and Soosan D. Latham, "The Importance of Performance Management to Productivity," *HR.com eBulletin*, June 11, 2001, http://www.hr.com; Hugh Son, "JPMorgan Opts for Real-Time Performance Reviews with Insight360 Software," *Financial Review*, March 10, 2017, https://www.afr.com/work-and-careers/management/jpmorgan-opts-for-realtime-performance-reviews-with-insight360-software-20170310-guux0y, accessed March 14, 2020.

38. Scullen et al., "Understanding the Latent Structure"; Steven H. Appelbaum, Michel Roy, and Terry Gilliland, "Globalization of Performance Appraisals: Theory and Applications," *Management Decision* 49, no. 4 (2011).

39. Maury A. Peiperl, "Getting 360° Feedback Right," *Harvard Business Review* 79, no. 1 (2001): 143.

40. Natalie Southworth, "Managers Crucial to Curbing Turnover," *Globe and Mail*, May 30, 2001, M1.

41. Scullen et al., "Understanding the Latent Structure"; Kevin M. Doyle and Richard D. Goffin, "Accountability and Accuracy in Subordinates' Ratings of Their Supervisors' Performance," *Social Behavior and Personality* 46, no. 9 (2018).

42. Sara L. Mann, Marie-Helene Budworth, and Afisi S. Ismaila, "Ratings of Counterproductive Performance: The Effect of Source and Rater Behavior," *International Journal of Productivity and Performance Management* 61, no. 2 (2012): 142–56.

43. Rob Markey, "The Dangers of Linking Pay to Customer Feedback," *Harvard Business Review*, September 8, 2011, https://hbr.org/2011/09/the-dangers-of-linking-pay-to, accessed March 8, 2020.

44. Gerald Blessing and Martin Natter, "Do Mystery Shoppers Really Predict Customer Satisfaction and Sales Performance?" *Journal of Retailing* 95, no. 3 (2019): 47–62.

45. A. Scott Rood and Joanna Dziadkowiec, "Cross Cultural Service Gap Analysis: Comparing SERVQUAL Customers and IPA Mystery Shoppers," *Journal of Foodservice Business Research* 16, no. 4 (2013): 359–77.

46. David Muturi, Sam Ho, Alexander Douglas, and Jacqueline Douglas, "Mystery Shoppers: An Evaluation of Their Use in Monitoring Performance," *The TQM Journal* 27, no. 6 (2015): 705–15.

47. Kane and Kane, "Performance Appraisal."

48. Mark R. Edwards and Ann J. Ewen, *360° Feedback* (New York: Amacom, 1996); Richard Lepsinger and Anntoinette D. Lucia, *The Art and Science of 360 Degree Feedback* (San Francisco: John Wiley & Sons, 2009).

49. Bohl, "Minisurvey"; Tracy Maylett, "360-Degree Feedback Revisited: The Transition from Development to Appraisal," *Compensation & Benefits Review* 41, no. 5 (2009): 52–59.

50. Edwards and Ewen, *360° Feedback*; Ding Ding Tee and Pervaiz K. Ahmed, "360 Degree Feedback: An Integrative Framework for Learning and Assessment," *Teaching in Higher Education* 19, no. 6 (2014): 579–91.

51. Bohl, "Minisurvey."

52. David W. Bracken, Carol W. Timmreck, John W. Fleenor, and Lynn Summers, "360 Degree Feedback from Another Angle," *Human Resource Management* 40, no. 1 (2001): 3–20; Suliat M. Nurudeen, Gifty Kwakye, William R. Berry, Elliot L. Chaikof, Keith D. Lillemoe, Frederick Millham, Marc Rubin, et al., "Can 360-Degree Reviews Help Surgeons? Evaluation of Multisource Feedback for Surgeons in a Multi-Institutional Quality Improvement Project," *Journal of the American College of Surgeons* 221, no. 4 (2015): 837–44.

53. David W. Bracken and Dale S. Rose, "When Does 360-Degree Feedback Create Behavior Change? And How Would We Know It When It Does?" *Journal of Business and Psychology* 26, no. 2 (2011): 183.

54. Angelo S. DeNisi, "360-Degree Feedback," in *Encyclopedia of Industrial and Organizational Psychology*, ed. Steven G. Rogelberg (Thousand Oaks: Sage, 2007), 809–12.

55. David W. Bracken and Dale S. Rose, "When Does 360-Degree Feedback Create Behavior Change? And How Would We Know When It Does?" *Journal of Business Psychology* 26 (2011): 183–92.

56. Kevin Cashman, "720 Development," *Leadership Excellence* 26, no. 11 (2009): 6.

57. James W. Smither and Manuel London, eds. *Performance Management: Putting Research into Action*. Vol. 21 (John Wiley & Sons, 2009).

58. Richard D. Galbreath, "Customer-Centric Evaluations," *Strategic HR Review* 6, no. 6 (2007): 4.

59. Tracey B. Weiss, "Performance Management," in *The Compensation Handbook*, ed. Lance Berger and Dorothy R. Berger (New York: McGraw-Hill, 2000), 429–42.

60. David E. Tyson, *Carswell's Compensation Guide* (Toronto: Thomson Carswell, 2009).

61. John Hilton, "Why Are Performance Management Initiatives Failing?" *Human Resources Director*, November 20, 2019, https://www.hcamag.com/ca/specialization/leadership/why-are-performance-management-initiatives-failing/192169, accessed March 8, 2020.

62. Declan Watson and Ron Harman, *Leading the Social Enterprise: Reinvent with a Human Focus: 2019 Deloitte Global Human Capital Trends* (Deloitte Insights, 2019).

63. Tyson, *Carswell's Compensation Guide*, 19–3.

64. John Shields, *Managing Employee Performance and Reward: Concepts, Practices, Strategies* (Cambridge: Cambridge University Press, 2007).

65. Elaine Pulakos and Ryan S. O'Leary, "Why Is Performance Management Broken?" *Industrial and Organizational Psychology* 4 (2011): 146–64; Marie-Helene Budworth, Garuy Latham, and Laxmikant Manroop, "Looking Forward to Performance Improvement: A Field Test of the Feedforward Interview for Performance," *Management, Human Resource Management* 54, no. 1 (2015): 45–54.

66. Mary Jo Ducharme, Mark Podolsky, and Parbudyal Singh, "Exploring the Links Between Performance Appraisal and Pay Satisfaction," *Compensation and Benefits Review* 37 (2005): 46–52.

67. Robert L. Heneman and Jon M. Werner, *Merit Pay: Linking Pay to Performance in a Changing World* (Greenwich: Information Age, 2005).

68. Emilio J. Castilla, "Gender, Race, and Meritocracy in Organizational Careers," *American Journal of Sociology* 113, no. 6 (2008): 1479–526.

69. Lawler, *Rewarding Excellence*.

70. I.M. Jawahar, "Antecedents and Potential Consequences of Satisfaction with Performance Appraisal Interview," *Proceedings of the Annual Conference of the Administrative*

*Sciences Association of Canada, Human Resources Division* 22, no. 9 (2001): 45–54; Shaun Pichler, "The Social Context of Performance Appraisal and Appraisal Reactions: A Meta⊠ Analysis," *Human Resource Management* 51, no. 5 (2012): 709–32.

71. Castilla, "Gender, Race, and Meritocracy."

72. Jack Zigon, "Measuring the Hard Stuff: Teams and Other Hard-to-Measure Work," in *The Compensation Handbook*, ed. Lance A. Berger and Dorothy R. Berger (New York: McGraw-Hill, 2000), 443–66; Bradley Kirkman, Ning Li, Xiaoming Zheng, Brad Harris, and Xin Liu, "Teamwork Works Best When Top Performers are Rewarded," *Harvard Business Review*, March 14, 2016, https://hbr. org/2016/03/teamwork-works-best-when-top-performers-are-rewarded, accessed March 9, 2020.

73. Tyson, *Carswell's Compensation Guide*.

74. Matthew Ohland, Misty L. Loughry, David J. Woehr, Lisa G. Bullard, Richard M. Felder, Cynthia J. Finelli, Richard A. Layton, Hal R. Pomeranz, and Douglas G. Schmucker, "The Comprehensive Assessment of Team Member Effectiveness: Development of a Behaviorally Anchored Rating Scale for Self-and Peer Evaluation," *Academy of Management Learning and Education* 11, no. 4 (2012): 609–30.

# DESIGNING
# PERFORMANCE
# PAY PLANS

## Learning Outcomes

AFTER READING THIS CHAPTER, YOU
SHOULD BE ABLE TO:

- Identify the main types of gain-sharing plans and key issues in their design.

- Identify the main types of goal-sharing plans and key issues in their design.

- Identify the main types of profit-sharing plans and key issues in their design.

- Identify the main types of employee stock plans and key issues in their design.

- Discuss the considerations in designing a nonmonetary rewards program.

## WHO WANTS TO BE A MILLIONAIRE?

In the 1980s, a young, aggressive software company wanted a tool to help it attract and motivate young, dedicated employees who would be willing to stick with the firm and do whatever it took to make the company successful. As part of its compensation strategy, the firm offered generous employee share plans, where employees would acquire significant holdings in the company. At the time, no one knew whether this would end up being a bonanza or a bust for the employees. In many cases like this, the company doesn't make it and the shares become virtually worthless.

In this case, the story had a very happy ending for the employees. The company was Microsoft, and by 1996 virtually all the company's original employees (and many of the later ones) had become millionaires. By 2015, it was estimated that Microsoft had created three billionaires and more than 12 000 millionaires through its employee share plans! Ironically, now that they are independently wealthy, many of these employees have left Microsoft to pursue a variety of life goals. Former employees now have very diverse careers, from starting independent businesses, to researching psychedelic drugs. Some previous employees own sports teams, while others pursued careers in photography, writing, making music, cooking, and philanthropy. Of the 11 original employees, Bill Gates was the only individual remained working for Microsoft. Bill sat on the board of directors and acted as a technical advisor to the current CEO, up until March 2020, when he decided to step down. However, many other long-term employees have stayed because Microsoft pays a lot of attention to providing jobs and a work environment that are intrinsically motivating.

Google has a similar story. Two Stanford PhD students that devised the concept of the search engine for a research project in 1996 created Google. The company was established in 1998 and became public in 2004. Once the company became public, experts estimate that approximately 900 employees turned into immediate millionaires. One of the multi-millionaires includes Bonnie Brown, who joined Google in 1999 as a part-time masseuse for the company's 40 employees. The company had offered her US$450 a week and Google stock options. Bonnie didn't think the shares would ever amount to much. She is now retired, has a personal masseuse and pilates instructor, and travels the world on money earned through Google.

Though both Microsoft and Google employees have had substantial success with employee share plans, current employees could fall victim to circumstance if they rely too heavily on stock options as their main source of income. Amid the COVID-19 panic in March 2020 (when this chapter was written), Microsoft's stock dropped more than 13 percent in one week, and Bill Gates lost US$6.6 billion of his net worth. The five most valuable American companies by market cap (Microsoft, Google-parent Alphabet, Apple, Amazon, and Facebook) lost a combined amount of US$238 billion in value in February 2020 as a result of a stock market plunge amid COVID-19 concerns. Yet experts remain assured that a recession will not significantly impact Microsoft or Google. Though both companies are well known for their influential cultures, only time will tell if current events will have an enduring impact on both employee stock options and, subsequently, company culture.

Microsoft has created thousands of millionaires among its employees.

© iStockphoto.com/NicolasMcComber

Sources: Julie Bick, "Microsoft Millionaires Branch Out," *Star Phoenix [Saskatoon]*, June 3, 2003, C10; Matt Weinberger, "Microsoft Millionaires Unleashed," *Business Insider*, August 8, 2015; Matt Weinberger, "The Weird and Wild Ways Microsoft's First Employees Spent the Millions They Made," *Business Insider*, December 29, 2017; Matt Weinberger, "Where are They Now? What Happened to the People in Microsoft's Iconic 1978 Company Photo," *Business Insider*, January 26, 2019; Will Jeakle, "In Praise of Bill Gates: Entrepreneur, Normal Guy, Potential Savior of the World," *Forbes*, March 19, 2020; Stefanie Olsen, "Life After Google, With Millions" *CNET*, January 23, 2008; Katie Hafner, "Google Options Make Masseuse a Multimillionaire," *The New York Times*, November 12, 2017; Jessica Bursztynsky, "Coronavirus Plunge Wipes More Than $230 Billion from Big Tech Stocks," *CNBC*, February 24, 2020.

# INTRODUCTION TO TYPES OF PLANS AND DESIGN ISSUES

Suppose that, based on all the considerations in the first half of this book, you have decided that an employee stock plan should be part of your compensation strategy. As you will see later in this chapter, not every employee stock plan works out as well as Microsoft's did. How can we design an employee stock plan that benefits both the company and its employees? What are the key issues to consider in designing a successful plan? Employee stock ownership may be a good fit for your firm, but many design issues will need to be dealt with effectively before such a plan can be launched, and you need to understand them.

This chapter addresses these design issues, not only for employee stock plans but also for three other important types of performance pay plans. In previous chapters we discussed individual employee performance plans. This chapter focuses on plans geared to the performance of work groups—notably gain-sharing and goal-sharing plans—and on plans geared to the performance of the organization as a whole—notably profit-sharing and employee stock plans. We end this chapter with a discussion of employee recognition programs that don't involve cash payments. As you understand by now, money is not the only valued reward an organization can offer!

## GAIN-SHARING PLANS

We'll start with gain-sharing plans. As you will recall, the defining feature of gain-sharing plans is that whenever employees in a particular work group are able to reduce costs or increase productivity, a portion of the resulting gains are shared in a systematic way among all the members of the work group. Cost savings can be brought about in a variety of ways, such as through improved quality, decreased waste, improved methods of working, and, of course, increased output per unit of labour.

## TYPES OF GAIN-SHARING PLANS

There are four main types of gain-sharing plans: the Scanlon plan, the Rucker plan, Improshare, and the family of measures plan. And there are countless permutations of these.

### The Scanlon Plan

**Scanlon plan**
A gain-sharing plan that creates mechanisms for employee participation in developing productivity improvements and that shares the financial benefits of those improvements with the employee group that generated them.

The **Scanlon plan** was developed by Joseph Scanlon, a United Steelworkers local president, at a financially troubled steel mill during the Great Depression. In a Scanlon plan, the organization first computes a "normal" labour cost, based on past experience and expressed as a percentage of the sales value of production. For example, labour costs may be 50 percent of the sales value of production. If workers lower this cost to 47 percent, they share this productivity gain (three percent of sales value) with the company according to a prearranged formula. For Scanlon plans, the share traditionally has been 25 percent for the company and 75 percent for employees, based on the notion that the workers are primarily responsible for the productivity gain; however, many gain-sharing plans use a 50/50 share.

The Scanlon plan is much more than a financial incentive plan. According to proponents, the key to its success is the development of a cooperative relationship among workers, union, and management, along with the establishment of a process through which workers can contribute to problem solving. Within each work unit, gain-sharing committees composed of management and worker representatives solicit and examine employees' suggestions for improvements and recommend either approval or rejection. If the proposal is outside the department's jurisdiction or involves large expenditures for implementation, the committee passes it on to a plant-wide committee, where top management and union officials (if the firm is unionized) discuss it. Typically, all members of the gain-sharing plan share in savings from any resulting improvements.

The Scanlon plan has been modified over time. A major modification has been the inclusion of additional costs besides labour.[1] There are two reasons for this change. First, many possible cost savings do not show up in labour costs, such as reductions in raw materials waste. Second, because it is usually possible to decrease labour costs by increasing other costs, a singular focus on reducing labour costs could spur a rise in other costs. For example, a worker may scrap slightly defective raw material instead of trying to work with it because using the poorer quality raw material would slow production and increase labour costs. As another example, a worker may discard tools that become somewhat dull because they slow down the work, even though replacements may be expensive. With the "multicost" approach, the share for employees is usually lower, perhaps by 50 percent, because potential savings are much higher with a broader cost base.

## The Rucker Plan

Another type of gain-sharing plan was developed in the 1930s by Alan Rucker, who modified the Scanlon plan in a small but very significant way by expressing labour costs as a percentage of value added (sales value of production less purchased inputs), rather than the sales value of production. The effect is that employees benefit from reductions in raw materials or any other purchased inputs and are therefore motivated to find ways to reduce these costs; like the Scanlon plan, the Rucker plan typically has a worker participation component.

**Rucker plan**
A gain-sharing plan similar to the Scanlon plan but that expresses labour costs as a percentage of value added.

## Improshare

A third type of gain-sharing plan, known as Improshare, was developed by industrial engineer Mitchell Fein in the 1970s.[2] This plan does not use dollar values of production but rather labour hours per unit of output, usually based on the previous year's output. The plan also takes into account indirect labour hours and includes them in the base productivity factor. When productivity exceeds the base productivity factor, a bonus is paid, usually 50 percent of the labour savings.

A disadvantage of Improshare is that it does not take other cost savings into account. Also, it does not make employee involvement integral to the system (something that classical firms might in fact regard as an advantage). Most experts believe that the participation element is vital to successful gain sharing; research has shown, however, that gain sharing can succeed even without mechanisms for employee participation.[3]

**Improshare**
A gain-sharing plan that focuses on labour hours per unit of output and that does not usually include worker participation.

## Family of Measures Plan

A family of measures plan describes any gain-sharing formula that uses multiple, independent measures. A gain (or loss) is calculated for each measure separately; the results are then aggregated to determine the size of the bonus pool.[4] The key attractions of this method are flexibility and focus. Flexibility comes from the ability to include performance measures that are especially important to the success of the business. Focus comes from the ability to specify the types of performance that lead to bonus payouts.

**family of measures plan**
A gain-sharing plan that uses a variety of measures to determine the extent to which a bonus payout is justified.

For example, the performance measures might include not only labour and materials efficiency but also production schedule attainment, quality levels, customer satisfaction measures, and even accident rates. Some of these additional measures can be based on historical records; others can be based on the achievement of targets or goals set by management. In addition, some measures (known as "modifiers") may subtract from rather than add to the bonus. For example, some firms subtract from labour savings if there are excessive accident levels. The logic here is that labour productivity should not increase at the expense of safety. Compensation Today 11.1 provides an example of a longstanding family of measures approach used at a service enterprise.

Family of measures plans have some disadvantages compared to the other types of plans. A major one is that some of the payouts are not based on calculated cost savings but rather on the achievement of certain goals. Thus, the payout for achieving these goals may bear little relation to actual cost savings because these cost savings are often hard to quantify. Consequently, employees may see the payouts as arbitrary (because there is no solid basis for them) and the goals as unrealistic. Where goals are seen as unrealistic, little effort will be made to attain them.

---

## COMPENSATION TODAY 11.1

### A GAIN-SHARING PLAN FOR NEUROSURGEONS

Gain sharing is a practice customarily frowned upon within the medical community. Nonetheless, somehow a group of neurosurgeons in the United States who conduct spinal fusion surgery has been approved to take part in a gain-sharing program. The gain-sharing plan is a three-year program designed to reward neurosurgeons with as much as 50 percent of the cost savings that have been accumulated from the neurosurgeons' use of specific products during surgery.

To determine the extent of the cost-savings, a Program Administrator thoroughly reviewed supply costs, quality of care, and application nationally, and then matched the results with the hospital's archival information. Then, both the Program Administrator and a committee of neurosurgeons pinpointed 24 potential cost-saving measures that can be classified into two groups. The first cost-saving category involves reducing the use of Bone Morphogenetic Protein to use in under four percent of surgeries (a product used in spinal fusion surgeries that is expensive). The second cost-saving category is using approved products (dependant on efficacy and cost).

To determine the cost-saving accomplished in a given year, the committee reviews the costs from the spinal surgeries that year compared to the expenses accrued from the previous year. The number of surgeries exceeding the amount performed in the last year is not considered in the savings calculation. Once the amount of savings is calculated, the hospital pays the group of neurosurgeons 50 percent of the savings on a per-capita basis after deducting Program Administrator costs and other administrative costs. The neurosurgeons' payout cannot exceed the potential savings first predicted by the Program Administrator.

Safeguards are put in place for consistent quality of care. Monitoring and reporting are significant components. Neurosurgeons cannot select which patients are part of the review. The selection of patients must be historically consistent. Patients are allowed to review the arrangement and ask the neurosurgeons how they enacted cost-saving measures. The incentive is collective to ensure that no individual neurosurgeon would attempt to cut costs for personal gain. Finally, in another strategy to ensure neurosurgeons do not cut corners, the Program Administrator determined the anticipated cost savings ahead of time.

Source: Ryan Cuthbertson and Nili S. Yoiln, "OIG Reaffirms Permissible Arrangements," *Mintz*, January 10, 2018.

---

# ISSUES IN DESIGNING GAIN-SHARING PLANS

There are key issues to consider when establishing gain-sharing plans.

1. Defining the group or work unit to be included in the plan.
2. Establishing the bonus formula.
3. Defining the baseline against which to measure improvement.
4. Deciding on the share between the company and the employees.
5. Deciding on the split among employees.
6. Deciding on the frequency of payout.
7. Developing procedures for communicating results.
8. Deciding whether and how to incorporate employee participation.

If each of these issues are not addressed appropriately, it could cause the plan to fail.

## Defining the Group

Defining the group or unit for a particular gain-sharing plan is not as easy as it sounds. In general, all employees who are in a position to significantly affect the results of the plan should be included.

For example, a company that distributed building materials (such as drywall) wanted to improve the productivity of its warehousing and delivery operations. It wanted to improve the efficiency of delivery and reduce wastage resulting from improperly loaded or carelessly handled material. It had warehouses in various cities across western Canada. At first, the company included just the warehouse staff and delivery drivers at each location in gain sharing. Thus, one gain-sharing group was the Winnipeg warehouse and delivery staff, another was the Regina warehouse and delivery staff, and so on.

In the beginning, the office staff at each location were not included in the gain-sharing groups. However, the company soon realized that these people had a significant impact on warehouse and delivery efficiency, depending on how quickly they responded to customers and passed the information on to the warehouse, whether they were precise about delivery locations, and how effectively they sorted out problems. Moreover, leaving office employees out caused them to think that the company did not consider them important. As a result, the plan was revised to include them in the gain-sharing groups, along with the warehouse managers, who had also been left out on the argument that they received other types of bonuses.

## Establishing the Bonus Formula

Because each gain-sharing program uses different criteria to establish its bonus formula, a company must determine which criteria are appropriate for its situation. In general, the simpler the formula, the better. But at the same time, the plan must capture all the factors that affect performance. Thus, most plans typically include a number of performance measures, along with some modifiers to constrain undesirable behaviour. For example, the performance measure for a mining team might be tonnes produced per person-hour. To avoid abuse of equipment (e.g., the changing of cutting bits more often than necessary to maximize production), any excess equipment replacement costs could be factored into the formula. And to avoid unsafe practices, a modifier stipulating no bonus for periods in which lost-time accidents occurred could be included.

## Defining the Baseline

Vital to a gain-sharing plan is a historical baseline against which to compare productivity to determine whether real productivity gains have actually taken place. Typically, a company can use its past two to three years of productivity results and compute an average. However, this procedure is valid only when the baseline over this period does not show a markedly upward or downward trend. In some cases, stable historical baselines don't exist, especially if the product/service mix is continually changing, if raw materials are improving (or declining) in quality or ease of use, or if the production/service technology frequently changes. If no valid historical benchmark can be set, then a gain-sharing plan is not viable and some other option (such as goal sharing) needs to be considered.

A key question is whether to change the baseline over time. A baseline that stays constant is known as a "fixed baseline," while baselines that change are known as "ratcheting" or "rolling" baselines. A ratcheting baseline goes up each year there is a productivity gain, so that last year's productivity becomes the new baseline. A rolling baseline uses a fixed period (say, a three-year period), dropping the oldest year off and adding the newest one. The result is similar to a ratcheting baseline, but it develops more slowly.

Management's rationale for ratcheting or rolling baselines is to keep pushing productivity up. However, employees may find that this kind of baseline just means working harder to maintain the same reward level. Moreover, depending on the measure, at some point it becomes very unrealistic to push the baseline up any further, unless the goal is to wipe out the gain-sharing plan without formally ending it. For example, if the measure is a reduction in defect rates, what happens when defect rates approach zero? Overall, ratcheting or rolling baselines are likely to be demotivational if employees start to see them as causing "long-term pain" for a "short-term gain."

This is not to say that baselines should never change. Changing them is reasonable if new capital equipment speeds up the production process without any increased worker effort, or if products are redesigned for easier production. However, in these cases, management must resist the temptation to take advantage of these changes to unduly raise the baseline. If workers are to have any trust in the plan, reasons for changes to the baseline must be clearly explained to them.

## Deciding the Share

The "share" is the formula for dividing the bonus pool generated by productivity gains between the employees and the company. Typically, the employee share ranges from 25 percent to 50 percent, although it can range as high as 75 percent in Scanlon plans, which defines productivity gains on a relatively small base.[5]

Three criteria must be considered when setting the share. First, the broader the bonus formula, the lower the share because there are more opportunities for productivity gains or cost savings with a broader formula. Second, the higher the capital intensity, the lower the share. Because there are relatively fewer employees in a capital-intensive firm, a lower share can still produce high bonuses for individual employees. Third, the more demanding the baseline (i.e., the greater the extent to which it increases), the higher the share needs to be to compensate for the increasing difficulty of achieving productivity gains.

## Deciding the Split

How should the bonus pool be split across the eligible employees? Should everyone receive an equal share? That sounds fair—but is it? What about employees who have been employed by the firm for only a few days during the bonus period? What about employees who are only part-time? What about employees who have performed exceptionally well during the bonus period? What about senior employees—do they deserve more of the pool?

The answers to these questions depend on the organization's goals for the gain-sharing plan. Some firms distribute the bonus according to the salary levels of employees, with those who have higher salaries receiving a greater share of the gain-sharing bonus, based on the assumption that the more highly paid employees have probably contributed more to the cost reductions. A major advantage of salary-based allocation is that it maintains the same proportion of goal-sharing compensation in the compensation mix for all employees.

However, the bonus allocation method that is most in keeping with the underlying philosophy of gain sharing is equal allocation across employees after adjusting for time worked during the bonus period. Gain sharing is intended to create cooperation and teamwork, and equality is an underlying condition of both. If singling out individuals for special treatment is necessary, companies should use other elements of the compensation system, rather than the gain-sharing plan.

## Deciding the Payout Frequency

On what period should the bonus calculations be based? Both technical and behavioural issues must be considered here. For example, if productivity results fluctuate widely on a weekly, monthly, or seasonal basis, longer payout periods will be required. But from a behavioural point of view, for maximum motivation, the receipt of rewards should closely follow the event that triggers the rewards. Also, the size of the reward should be at least enough to provide a "just noticeable difference." This suggests longer bonus periods, which would also reduce administrative costs. Overall, quarterly bonuses are often the best compromise.

## Communication

A compensation system will not have any impact if employees do not understand how it works and how their behaviour relates to rewards. Employees need to see whether they are making progress toward meeting the bonus criteria that have been set out, so frequent feedback about productivity results and cost savings is essential. However, communication does not happen without effort and planning, so procedures for communicating this information need to be planned and implemented carefully.

## Participatory Mechanisms

Some gain-sharing plans, such as Scanlon and Rucker, specifically incorporate a mechanism through which employees can participate in making productivity improvements. Participation is often achieved through an employee–management gain-sharing committee, which meets on a regular basis to solicit employee suggestions and feedback. Other plans, such as Improshare, carry no such requirements.

Research shows that Improshare systems can be effective even though they lack a participative element.[6] Research on group pay in general (including various types of group pay) indicates that such plans can be very successful in the absence of participatory mechanisms, although their success increases if they are accompanied by an employee suggestion program, which most gain-sharing plans include.[7] It is interesting, though, that the favourable results were not found in firms that pursued an innovator business strategy, only in firms that did not. Group pay had no impact—positive or negative—in innovator firms. This suggests that conditions in innovator firms are too unstable to provide the stable historical baselines necessary for successful gain sharing.

Considerable research has been conducted on the conditions necessary for gain-sharing plans to succeed.[8] First, employees must regard the gain-sharing system as fair and equitable in terms of both procedural and distributive justice. Employee participation in the development of the gain-sharing system can help achieve this goal. Because an organization needs to adjust these plans over time, it also needs a certain level of trust between management and employees, as well as a history of job security. Employees must have some assurance that they will not "work themselves out of a job." For example, when John Deere Corporation abandoned individual production bonuses for its employees and moved to gain sharing (see Compensation Today 11.2), it guaranteed that the only jobs that could be eliminated if productivity increased were those of retiring employees.

---

## COMPENSATION TODAY 11.2

### NOTHING RUNS LIKE A DEERE! ESPECIALLY A DEERE WITH GAIN SHARING!

In the 1980s, John Deere Corporation was in trouble. The long-time maker of agricultural equipment, including tractors and combines—as well as construction equipment and consumer products like riding lawnmowers—found sales in a deep slump due to economic circumstances. To survive, management had to come up with some way to increase productivity and cut costs. Previously, to motivate production employees, they had relied on a system of base pay plus an individual incentive based on whether the employee exceeded the production standard for his or her job.

However, while this system was believed to be effective in eliciting individual effort from the production employees, the company felt that it didn't promote teamwork or innovative production ideas. They saw three main problems with the current system. First, individual employees were not willing to spend any time training or helping new employees because this would cut into their own productivity. Second, the system led employees to conceal any methods for faster production from the industrial engineers, as employees were concerned that revealing these methods would result in a higher production standard, and less bonus for them (which is actually what would have happened). Third, the standard hours plan was very difficult and expensive to maintain—to maintain and update the production standards required more than 600 industrial engineers at a cost of over $30 million per year.

The company felt that replacing the standard hours system with gain sharing might alleviate these problems, and sought union approval to do so. After extensive consultation with the United Auto Workers, and having made a pledge that no existing employees would be laid off as a result of this change (the only jobs that could be eliminated were those of retiring employees), the union approved the change. First, all manufacturing employees were grouped into work teams, each of which was responsible for a particular part of the production process. This resulted in 240 work teams. Rather than individual performance, team performance was measured and rewarded. In addition to their hourly pay, each team was rewarded according to whether they had cut labour costs relative to standard costs, which were themselves based on historical costs. Team members would share equally whatever gain-sharing bonus the team had earned. John Deere has since found this system—which is really based on a transition from classical to high-involvement managerial strategy—to have substantially improved productivity not only in America but as well in the United Kingdom, Mexico, Uganda, Honduras, and Zambia.

In recent times, John Deere has faced obstacles and revenue loss. Most recently, in 2019, the Institute for Supply Management stated that the United States' manufacturing sector was in an economic recession. The trade war between the United States and China significantly impacted the United States farm produce, where China imported $19.5 billion of American farm produce in 2017, down to $9.1 billion in 2019. Not to mention, 2019 year had a record-setting wet spring that prohibited crop yields, and then a hot and dry summer that lessened corn and soybean yields. With fewer exports, American farmers bought less machinery.

One of the disadvantages of the gain-sharing plan is that it does not consider the changes in the company's prices,

---

revenue volume, client loyalty, and any other issues the organization may be facing. Paying out necessary gain-sharing amounts may not be sustainable. In 2015, John Deere laid off a thousand employees. As of March 2020, the company laid off 468 employees in the United States in less than a year.

The number of layoffs in the United States will likely increase, and layoffs will occur internationally in 2020 as well. If the situation becomes dire, the company may have to revisit its compensation strategy. Hopefully, current events do not hit employees like a Deere in the headlights.

Sources: Geoffrey B. Sprinkle and Michael G. Williamson, "The Evolution from Taylorism to Employee Gainsharing: A Case Study Examining John Deere's Continuous Improvement Pay Plan," *Issues in Accounting Education* 19, no. 4 (2004): 487–503; Alexander C. Gardner, "Goal Setting and Gainsharing: The Evidence on Effectiveness," *Compensation & Benefits Review* 43, no. 4 (2011): 236–44; Robert Connelly, "In the Last Year, Deere & Co. Has Laid Off 468 Employees. 340 Worked in Iowa," *Quad-City Times,* March 10, 2020; George Gallanis, "John Deere Announces Layoffs at Plants in Illinois and Iowa," *World Socialist Web Site,* October 4, 2019.

# GOAL-SHARING PLANS

Goal sharing gained popularity in the 1990s. However, like gain sharing and other group pay plans, it appears to have lost popularity over time. This is a bit surprising given that research shows that group-based plans can dramatically improve company profitability when adopted by firms that are not pursuing an innovator strategy.[9] Moreover, even in firms that do pursue an innovator strategy, these plans broke even on average, so there doesn't seem to be much to lose in trying them, especially when conditions are right.

The essence of goal sharing is that work groups or teams receive a bonus when specified performance goals are met. Goal-sharing plans differ from gain-sharing plans in several fundamental ways. In gain sharing, cost savings are quantified and then shared between the company and the group, whereas under goal sharing there is typically no systematic link between performance improvements and the goal-sharing bonus pool. How, for example, do you place a monetary value on achieving the goal of increased customer satisfaction?

There are no set goals with gain sharing other than to improve as much as possible relative to the historical baseline. In contrast, under goal sharing, goals on one or more performance indicators are set for each group or team, to be met within a specified time period, and a bonus is paid to all team members if the goal is achieved.

In gain sharing, there is an expectation of continuity—the gain-sharing system will not be changed arbitrarily, because procedures for calculating and sharing gains are so well spelled out. While goal-sharing plans are more flexible, the flip side of that is that continuity of goal-sharing plans is less assured than with gain sharing.

Finally, in most gain-sharing plans, there is usually an explicit expectation of employee involvement in suggesting ideas for productivity gains. Under goal sharing, employee participation is not necessarily a component, although it can be.

## TYPES OF GOAL-SHARING PLANS

Goal-sharing plans have not really evolved to the point where distinct types can be identified. However, one important distinction is whether they are single-goal plans, multigoal plans, or financially funded plans. Single-goal plans are the simplest and focus attention on one key goal, such as customer satisfaction. These plans may cause other important behaviours to be neglected,[10] so most firms typically use multigoal plans to better cover the range of desired behaviour.[11]

Financially funded plans combine two sets of criteria. The total amount of the goal-sharing bonus available is typically based on some indicator such as company profit, while the actual amount of the payout is based on the achievement of specified goals. This combination of criteria has the benefit of not paying out goal-sharing bonuses when the company is not profitable, but it also makes the performance-reward contingency less certain, which generally diminishes employees' motivation to meet goals.

## ISSUES IN DESIGNING GOAL-SHARING PLANS

Many issues need to be dealt with when designing a goal-sharing plan.

1. Defining the group to which goal sharing applies.
2. Deciding on the nature of the goals to be sought.
3. Determining levels and time frames for goal achievement.
4. Establishing bonus amounts.
5. Deciding on the split of the bonus among employees.

The first issue is defining the group to which a given goal-sharing plan will apply. In general, the smaller the group, the stronger the motivation; however, the group must include all employees who can play a significant role in goal achievement.

A critical variable is the nature of the goals to be set. They must be important to the organization and controllable by the work group, and they encompass the full range of desired behaviour. Care must be taken to ensure that the goals do not conflict. For example, Continental Airlines (that later merged with United Airlines) was suffering from a very poor on-time performance record. So the company established a goal-sharing plan in which all employees who affected on-time performance, such as baggage handlers, would receive a bonus if on-time performance improved to the point that Continental was among the five top airlines in this performance category. The plan worked: on-time performance improved and bonuses were paid out. Unfortunately, at the same time, customer complaints increased, as passenger baggage was often left behind in order to get flights out on time.[12]

Once the goals to be rewarded have been identified, the organization needs to determine the levels of achievement necessary to trigger a bonus payout. This is probably the single most important factor in the success of a goal-sharing plan. Goals that are seen as too difficult do not motivate behaviour. Goals that are too easy also do not motivate; such goals also carry the additional penalty of paying out bonuses for no real performance gain and may cause employees to ease off once the goal is achieved. When there is a single goal achievement level, there is no employee motivation to surpass the target goal; in fact, it may well be seen as undesirable to surpass the goal if so doing might result in a higher target goal the following year.

Many firms have now established several levels of achievement for each goal. At one firm, a goal level that exceeds current performance, but not by much, is called the "standard plus" goal; the next level is called the "goal level," which is viewed as realistic but not a sure thing; and the highest level, which employees have less than a 50 percent likelihood of achieving, is called the "goal plus" level. The "goal plus" level is an example of what is commonly known as a "stretch goal." Of course, bonus amounts increase substantially for each goal level that is met.

To establish goal levels to which employees will commit, many organizations involve employees in the goal-setting process. Research has shown that employees are more motivated to attempt goals they have played a role in developing.[13]

Goals also need to be bounded by some time period. Within what time frame does the goal need to be accomplished? For most goals, a year would seem a reasonable time period. At the end of the year, new goals can be established, depending on whether or not the goal was met.

Once an organization has established the target goal levels, it must set the dollar amount of bonus for each level of accomplishment. Sometimes it can find a cost basis for so doing. For example, if a company knows how much it costs to correct a particular type of error, it can use this number to calculate a reasonable bonus for achieving a particular reduction in the error rate. But in other cases, there may be no good basis for calculating the value of goal achievement—for example, the value of improved "on-time performance."

Another key issue is the basis for allocating the goal-sharing bonus among employees. The basis can be salary, seniority, individual performance, some combination of these, or equal distribution. Equal distribution is the most egalitarian, but is it really fair to more senior employees, who may feel that they have contributed more to company success and who have shown long-term commitment to the firm? The advantage of salary-based allocation is that it maintains the same proportion of goal-sharing compensation in the compensation mix for all employees. One advantage of allocating the bonus on individual performance is that it addresses the free-riding problem. But the challenge here is to create an individual performance appraisal system that employees accept as fair. Finally, even where equal allocation is used, adjustments typically have to be made based on the number of days or hours actually worked during the period in which goal accomplishment took place.

# PROFIT-SHARING PLANS

Research by one of the authors indicates that about one-quarter of medium to large Canadian firms use broad-based profit sharing. Profit-sharing plans are just as likely to be found in publicly traded as in privately held corporations. Studies have found that profit sharing is applicable to a wide variety of industries; the only commonality among profit-sharing firms is that they tend to be high-involvement organizations.[14]

## TYPES OF PROFIT-SHARING PLANS

As discussed in Chapter 5, there are three main types of profit-sharing plans: current distribution, deferred profit sharing, and combination. Research indicates that the majority of Canadian profit-sharing plans are current distribution (cash-based) plans and that most of the remainder are deferred plans. Alternatively, the majority of American profit-sharing plans are deferred plans. However, some firms may use a combination of cash and deferred, or pay the bonus in company stock.[15]

Establishing a current distribution plan does not require any approvals by government, unless the firm wants to register it as an employee profit-sharing plan (EPSP) under the federal Income Tax Act. The EPSP is not a tax-deferred plan, and these plans are really a type of unsheltered company-supported savings/investment plan. Their main purpose is to provide a vehicle for accumulating savings after the tax-deferred approaches have been exhausted. Registered EPSPs are rarely used because there are no real advantages to registering them with the federal government, and current distribution plans can be set up without government registration.

Because the deferred profit-sharing plan (DPSP) is a tax-deferred plan, registration with the federal government is required. A DPSP trust is set up, and both the employer contributions and the annual earnings of the trust are exempt from taxation until the employee actually cashes in the plan, usually at termination or retirement. Because of this feature, DPSPs are often used as a form of pension plan, especially in small- to medium-sized companies where no other pension plan exists. The maximum tax deduction for the DPSP is tied to the unused portion of the employee's registered retirement savings plan (RRSP) contribution. "Top hat" plans (those in which only senior management is eligible) are not eligible for registration as a DPSP, as DPSPs require wide employee eligibility.

Another taxation feature makes the DPSP even more attractive, if shares (rather than cash) are deposited in the trust. Instead of being taxed on the full market value of the shares at the time of withdrawal from the DPSP, the employee is taxed on "employment income" only on the original value of the shares when they were placed in the DPSP trust on behalf of the employee. When the shares are sold, the difference between the original value and the selling price is considered a capital gain rather than employment income. (Note that only publicly traded shares—including those of the employer—are eligible for purchase by a DPSP.)

Although there are some tax advantages, there is some risk to the employees, in that even if their shares have declined in value at the time of sale, they still have to pay income tax on the original amount of the profit-sharing bonus. However, the decline in share value is partially offset by the capital loss this creates, which can be used to offset any capital gains the employee may have.

To provide some idea of the diversity of profit-sharing plans, Compensation Today 11.3 gives examples of profit sharing that have been used at two prominent Canadian companies.

### PROFIT SHARING AT TWO PROMINENT CANADIAN COMPANIES

A company with one of the longest histories of profit sharing in Canada is ArcelorMittal Dofasco of Hamilton, Ontario. The only integrated steel company in the world that is not unionized, the company has always seen profit sharing as a major part of its human relations managerial philosophy. Their plan was Canada's first profit-sharing plan, which started in 1938 as a pension plan and continues as a Deferred Profit Sharing Plan (DPSP), Defined Contribution Pension Plan (DCPP), and a Supplemental Retirement Income Plan (SRIP).

ArcelorMittal Dofasco determines the DCPP amount to pay each employee by using a formula that considers an employee's age, years of service, and earnings. For those employees that are eligible for profit-sharing, 50 percent of their DPSP is directed towards their DCPP payment, and the company pays the remainder of the DCPP throughout the year to attain the Contribution Target. Employees may choose whether they would like the remaining 50 percent of the DPSP amount to be placed in their DCPP account, as in this case, it will be tax-deferred. The employee is encouraged to choose their investment strategy so it is aligned with their personal goals. However, if the employee does not make their own decision, their money is invested in a safe default investment that has typically low long-term returns.

The bonus pool for DPSP is 14 percent of pre-tax profits from operations, and it is allocated equally to eligible employees on an annual basis. All employees with at least two years of service are included in the plan. In 2000, the company made headlines when it split a bonus pool of $53.3 million—the highest payout ever—among employees, who each received $7906. Almost 15 years after becoming a subsidiary of ArcelorMittal, the employee profit-sharing plan is still going strong. The company employs around 5000 full-time employees in Canada and ships 4.5 million tons of high-quality steel every year for use in construction, automotive, tubular, packaging, appliance, and distribution industries. It won the Canada's Top 100 Employers 2016 Award and in 2018, the company was classified as one of the top employers for workers over 40 according to Mediacorp Canada.

Another company with a long-standing commitment to profit sharing is Canadian Tire. The founder of the chain, A.J. Billes, always believed in profit sharing in both a philosophical and a practical way. He believed that it was morally just that employees receive a portion of the profits they helped generate and that this would create employee commitment to the firm. The company has always had a profit-sharing plan that applies to the employees of the parent firm, and it strongly encourages profit sharing at its independently-owned associate stores and jointly sponsors the program with the dealers. Most stores see the importance of the plan, as 92 percent of such stores choose to participate.

The Canadian Tire plan is both a share plan as well as a profit-sharing plan. The company determines the amount that it will invest in the plan based on a minimum of one percent of the company's net profit. At the corporate level, the amount paid is based on a percentage of the employees' salary, whereas in a franchise the award is a fixed dollar amount.

A predetermined base amount is set based on limits determined by the Income Tax Act. This base amount is placed in a deferred profit-sharing account, which cannot be cashed out while the employee works for Canadian Tire. From the base amount, 10 percent must be reinvested into a Canadian Tire share (made up of Class A non-voting shares, Canadian Tire common shares, and a small cash amount), while 90 percent of the base amount can be invested in a variety of different options from which employees may choose.

The vesting schedule is 20 percent after the first year and 80 percent after the second year. If the profits exceed the target level (which they usually do), employees are paid an excess amount. The excess amount can be paid either through taxable cash, placing the money back into the plan for tax purposes, a group registered retirement savings plan or a tax-free savings account.

The company contributed $24.1 million to the plan in 2018 and $25.3 million in 2019. Employees at the corporate level are typically paid around 10 percent of their annual earnings. However, amid the COVID-19 pandemic in 2020, Canadian Tire announced that it would be closing "non-essential retail banners," including SportChek, Party City, Mark's Work Wearhouse, and others. Furthermore, at the Canadian Tire locations, store hours would be reduced. Profitability in 2020 is likely to be heavily impacted; therefore, Canadian Tire's contribution to the profit-sharing plan will likely be lower than in preceding years.

ArcelorMittal Dofasco has one of Canada's oldest profit-sharing plans.

Sources: Julie Slack, "'This is Unbelievable For Me,' Ben Ciprietti on Japanese Government Award," *Inside Halton*, May 29, 2019; David E. Tyson, *HR Manager's Guide to Profit Sharing in Canada* (Toronto: Thomson Carswell, 2006); Lina Stogiannis, "It's February and That Means Retirement Savings May Be Top of Mind," *Arcelor Mittal* 8, no. 1 (2016): 9; Ken Kilpatrick and Dawn Walton, "What a Joy to Work for Dofasco," *The Globe and Mail*, February 12, 2000, B1; ArcelorMittal, "Benefits & Pay at ArcelorMittal Dofasco," https://najobs.arcelormittal.com/dofasco/content/BenefitsAndPayDofasco/?locale=en_US; Diane Jermyn, "Canada's Top 100 Employers Rise to the Top for Their Focus on Mental Health, Social Impact and Work-Life Balance," *The Globe and Mail*, November 28, 2019; Richard Yerema and Kristina Leung, "Mediacorp Canada Inc. staff editors, Mediacorp Canada Inc.," *Canada's Top 100 Employers* (2016); "At a Glance," *ArcelorMittal Dofasco*, dofasco.arcelormittal.com/who-we-are/at-a-glance/about-dofasco.aspx; "ArcelorMittal Dofasco," *Forbes*, www.forbes.com/companies/arcelormittal-dofasco/#90d6b9533cba, January 28, 2020; "ArcelorMittal Dofasco Tops List of Leading Employers for Workers Over 40," *Benefits Canada*, November 15, 2017; Marg Bruineman, "How Canadian Tire Connects Retirement to Profits," *Benefits Canada*, April 15, 2016; Marg Bruineman, "How Canadian Tire Connects Retirement to Profits," *Benefits Canada*, April 15, 2016; Canadian Tire Corporation Limited, "Management's Discussion and Analysis: Fourth Quarter and Full-Year 2019," February 12, 2020; Canadian Tire Corporation Limited, "Management's Discussion and Analysis: Fourth Quarter and Full-Year 2019," February 12, 2020; Barret Wilson, "Breaking: Canadian Tire to Close Some Stores, Reduce Shopping Hours," *The Post Millennial*, March 19, 2020.

# ISSUES IN DESIGNING PROFIT-SHARING PLANS

Besides the form of the bonus payout (deferred, cash, stock, or a combination of these), profit-sharing plans have other design issues, including

- the formula for bonus determination (fixed or discretionary),
- employee eligibility,
- the basis for allocating the profit-sharing bonus across employees,
- payout frequency, and
- communicating financial results and profit sharing.

## Formula for Bonus Determination

Under a discretionary approach to bonus determination, management simply looks at the profitability at the end of the year and decides on an amount. The problem with discretionary plans is that the link between performance and reward becomes even more tenuous than otherwise because employees do not really know to what extent (if at all) better performance will be rewarded. For motivational reasons, fixed formula plans are strongly recommended. There are many possibilities. Two commonly used profit-sharing plans are straight profit-sharing plans and hurdle-rate profit sharing plans.

The straight profit-sharing plan is the most commonly used and simplest form of profit-sharing. A portion of pre-tax profit (say, 10 percent) goes into the profit-sharing bonus pool at the end of the year. Alternatively, the hurdle-rate profit-sharing plan can be a threshold (say, a return on investment of five percent), and no profit-sharing bonus is paid until this threshold is exceeded. The formula may also incorporate a step function, such that the percentage of profits going to the profit-sharing bonus increases as various thresholds or "steps" are exceeded. The purpose of the hurdle-rate profit-sharing plan is gain or profit improvement, and in this respect, it is similar to the gain-sharing plan. The higher the threshold established, the lower the risk to the organization, though the goal must still be attainable. If an organization wants to deliver a strong message about the importance of performance, they may freeze salaries and fund increases through its hurdle-rate profit-sharing plan, for example, after five percent increase on rate of sales. Otherwise, if a company pays at or above market in base pay, they may establish a higher threshold, such as distributing profit-sharing funds after a 10 percent increase on rate of sales.[16]

## Employee Eligibility

Another key issue is employee eligibility. In general, the more inclusive the better, although casual and contract employees are often excluded, as are unionized employees if the union does not agree to profit sharing. In most cases, there is a time period for eligibility (usually one year). Most firms offer the profit-sharing plan to all full-time employees. Many firms, such as Canadian Tire[17] and Ikea in Canada[18] offer the profit-sharing plan to part-time employees as well, although this is not done in the majority of companies. Other firms exclude unionized employees or part-time employees or restrict profit sharing to designated employees. Companies should review human rights legislation when considering excluding part-time employees. If all the employer's part-time employees are female, for example, and therefore only females are not included in the profit-sharing plan, this exclusion could be considered discriminatory, even if unintentional.[19]

## Basis for Allocating the Profit-Sharing Bonus

Allocation of the profit-sharing bonus can be based on salary, seniority, individual performance, some combination of these, or equal distribution. The advantage of salary-based allocation is that it maintains the same proportion of profit-sharing pay in the compensation mix for each employee. It also tends to provide a greater reward to those employees who are more able to influence profits. The advantage of allocating the bonus on individual performance is that it addresses the free-riding problem. But the key here is the availability of an individual performance appraisal system that employees accept as fair. Finally, even where equal allocation is used, adjustments have to be made based on the number of days or hours actually worked during the year in which the profit-sharing bonus was earned. Whichever allocation method the firm decides to use, total cash compensation for each position as compared to market rate should be considered.[20]

## Payout Frequency

Payout frequency is another issue. Results must be based on financial statements, which suggests that payouts should occur no more often than quarterly. In addition, where profits fluctuate by season, an annual basis is probably best to smooth out these fluctuations and to avoid paying profit sharing in an unprofitable year.

## Communicating Profit Sharing

As with other performance pay plans, communication is important to the success of profit sharing. Most profit-sharing firms distribute financial statements and profit-sharing newsletters on a regular basis, but some firms go beyond this. For example, WestJet holds a profit-sharing party every six months, at which employees receive their profit-sharing cheques and are treated to a company celebration.[21]

Research reveals that besides communications, various other factors exist that determine the effectiveness of the profit-sharing plan. For example, one study found that firms that pay above market rate before adopting the profit-sharing plan have higher success rates with profit sharing.[22] Another study found that firms that have open channels of communication so that employees can share thoughts or concerns pertaining to their peers' productivity are most successful with profit-sharing plans.[23] Rather surprisingly, company characteristics (such as company size), plan characteristics, and firm participatory practices were not found to have an impact on the effectiveness of the profit sharing plan.[24]

Research reveals that besides communications, two other factors significantly affect the success of profit sharing, as perceived by Canadian CEOs.[25] CEOs reported better results in firms that use high-involvement management and that allocate the bonus according to measures of individual performance. Note, however, that the measure of success used in this study is the CEO's perception of success, not financial data, so these are not definitive results.

Rather surprisingly, none of the other company characteristics or plan characteristics were very important influences on the results of profit sharing. It follows that profit sharing can be effective for most types of companies and that various plan designs can be effective as well. One interesting caveat to this finding, however, is that while there was no major difference in results between firms that used a fixed percentage for bonus determination and those that did not (except that industrial relations were more favourable in firms with a fixed percentage), for those with fixed percentage plans, success increased with the size of the bonus percentage. Overall, performance of the plan appears to improve when the bonus percentage exceeds 10 percent of profits.

# EMPLOYEE STOCK PLANS

As discussed in Chapter 5, an employee stock plan is any type of plan through which employees acquire shares in the firm that employs them. In some plans, employees receive shares at no cost, while in others, employees are given the opportunity to buy stock on favourable terms. This section describes the three main types of stock plans (stock bonus, share purchase, stock option), along with related plans that tie employee rewards to company stock performance but do not actually provide employees with the opportunity to acquire shares (phantom stock plans), as well as the issues to be addressed when designing these plans.

## EMPLOYEE STOCK BONUS PLANS

The essence of stock bonus plans is that employees receive company stock at no cost to themselves, through one of several methods. One approach is simply to make stock grants to employees at periodic intervals, often annually. Another approach is to tie stock grants to the profit-sharing plan, paying out in company stock instead of paying out in cash. The employee could then put this stock into a deferred profit-sharing plan, if desired. In some cases, stock bonuses are tied to certain company or individual performance criteria. As Compensation Today 11.4 shows, stock bonuses can be linked to almost any kind of criteria.

Stock bonus plans have experienced a decline in popularity in recent years, starting with the stock market downturn of 2001, which diminished interest in employee share ownership, and then due to the financial meltdown of 2008–09, which further reduced employee interest in share ownership. Of the three major stock plans, broad-based (i.e., not confined to just senior executives) employee stock bonus plans are the least common, with perhaps two percent of medium to large Canadian firms offering such plans to their employees. (By contrast, these plans are extremely common for executives.) Unlike other employee stock plans, these plans are equally common in publicly traded and privately held corporations.

A variation that merges the stock bonus plan with the stock option concept is **share appreciation rights**. Employees are first "allocated" a number of shares of company stock, although they do not actually receive any shares. If these "shares" appreciate within a fixed

THE CANADIAN PRESS/Larry MacDougal

WestJet's pay systems have turned employees into owners.

**share appreciation rights**
A plan through which employees are awarded shares in their employer at no cost to themselves if the price of employer shares rises during a specified period.

---

---

time period, employees receive as a bonus the number of actual company shares that this appreciation can purchase (although in some plans, they can opt to take the cash). For example, if an employee is "allocated" 1000 company shares and the share price is $20 at the outset and rises to the value of $25 each by the end of the specified period, then the employee will receive a bonus of 200 actual company shares (the $5000 appreciation will buy 200 shares at $25 each), at no cost to the employee.

Taxation is a major issue with employee stock plans and can be either a huge advantage (in an up market) or a huge disadvantage (in a down market). Employees who receive stock bonuses are deemed to have received employment income in the amount of whatever the value of the stock is when it is vested (which occurs when the employee receives full legal ownership of the shares), but it is taxed at the capital gains rate (which is half of the rate that applies to employment income). However, the income tax is not actually payable until such time as the employee sells the shares or the employer goes out of business. Any appreciation in share value (the difference between the initial value of the shares and the actual selling price of the shares, if positive) is taxed at the capital gains rate (which is half the normal rate that applies to employment income). Things are very rosy tax-wise for employee-owners in an up market.

However, things may not be so rosy in a down market. The problem in a down market is that the employee is liable to pay taxes (at the capital gains tax rate) on the value of the initial stock grant, regardless of the price the employee actually realizes from selling the shares. For example, let's suppose that an employee receives a stock grant of 1000 shares in 2010 and that those shares are selling at $10 per share when vested to the employee. That employee now has a tax liability based on $10 000 of deemed employment income (let us say a tax bill of about $2200, based on an average marginal tax rate of 44 percent); however, this tax does not need to be paid until the employee sells the shares or the company is wound up or sold. Let's suppose the down market causes the shares to fall and that the employee eventually sells at $1 per share. The employee realizes $1000 but faces a tax bill of $2200 on shares provided "free" to her or him by a seemingly benevolent employer! As Compensation Today 11.5 shows, this issue can even bankrupt employee-owners!

---

### COMPENSATION TODAY 11.5

#### "BARGAIN SHARES" BANKRUPT UNLUCKY EMPLOYEE-OWNERS

Shannon McLeod, a marketing manager at BC-based Creo—a digital imaging company—thought she knew a bargain when she saw one. Several years after the company had given her stock options—which confer the right to purchase a specified number of company shares at some point in the future at a fixed price—the value of those shares had risen dramatically. When they were trading at $53, McLeod borrowed money to purchase 10 000 shares at $17, which to her sounded like a terrific deal.

In purchasing those shares, she was deemed to have received employment income of $360 000—the difference between what she paid for them and what their market value was when she purchased them. At that time, she incurred a tax liability of $100 000 (taxed at the capital gains rate), which would not actually need to be paid to the Canada Revenue Agency until she sold the shares or the company was wound up or sold.

As it turned out, Creo was sold, and at the time of sale, her shares were actually worth slightly less than she had paid for them. She used the proceeds from the sale to repay the loan she had taken out to purchase the shares, but she was still left with the $100 000 tax bill, which was now due. She then had to take out another loan to pay her taxes. All in all, she ended up paying taxes of $100 000 on an investment that yielded her nothing.

(continued)

Although McLeod may not see it this way, she was actually luckier than some employees at other firms, who saw their shares plummet to almost zero. For example, a former Nortel manager, who was laid off in 1999, faced a tax bill of $204 000 on 1000 shares then-worth 25 cents each.

A number of employees who have encountered this problem banded together to form Canadians for Fair and Equitable Taxation, which lobbied the federal government for changes to the tax rules that put them in this situation. Their aim was to effect changes in line with those made to U.S. taxation rules in 2008 to deal with this problem. Changing the status of the initial share gain from employment income to capital gains income would allow employees to offset their capital gains with capital losses from the decline in share prices.

In 2010, the government amended the law so that taxes would be collected when options are exercised. Employers must withhold tax during the period in which employees exercise their stock options. The federal government has provided some taxation relief to employee-owners who have been affected in the taxation years 2000 and later, with regard to shares that were included in elections for deferral of taxable benefit income. However, other employee-owners remain out in the cold and cases such as Shannon's continue.

In a more current case, an executive in Alberta had his remission order rejected following his stock options plummeting in value after being exercised. The executive took this case to the federal court upon being denied. The executive had been granted stock options, which enabled him to purchase $75 000 shares at $0.95 per share. He had exercised his option when the shares were worth $13.70 per share. The taxable employment benefit was $956 250 as it was taxed at the capital gains rate. The executive had filed an appeal at this point because he explained that he was classified as an insider and was restricted from selling the shares right away. Therefore, the value of the shares could decrease. The court ruled in his favour, and his employment benefit was reduced to $648 000. However, when the Alberta executive sold his share later on, the shares were sold for $228 750. Thus, he had lost $419 250, and his employment benefit of $648 000 remained. He still had to pay income tax on the employment benefit. When the executive applied for remission at this point, his request was denied. The court contended that it had been in his control to buy, hold, and sell the shares.

Though amendments have been made to the tax law, employees must still be cautious and cognizant that if the company stock in which they own drops, this can result in a capital loss that is only used against capital gains. When an employee chooses to exercise their stock options and not immediately sell, they are now considered an investor, not an employee.

Sources: Kathy Tomlinson, "Thousands of Canadians Taxed on 'Phantom Income,'" *CBC News Online*, May 25, 2009; Canadians for Fair and Equitable Taxation, personal communication, January 2013; Jamie Golombek, "What You Need to Know About the Tax Consequences of Employee Stock Options," *Financial Post*, November 9, 2018.

## EMPLOYEE SHARE PURCHASE PLANS

In an employee share purchase plan, employees provide some kind of direct payment in return for company shares. But they often do not have to pay full market price for these shares, and firms offer many incentives to promote these purchases. Promotions include subsidized or discounted prices or matching programs in which the firm provides an additional share for each share purchased by an employee. In some cases, the company pays the brokerage fees, while in others, it provides low- or no-interest loans for stock purchase. In many cases, the company offers the convenience of payroll deduction.

Research by one of the authors suggests that these plans have apparently maintained their popularity—at least until mid-decade, the most recent period for which data are available. About one-fifth of medium to large Canadian firms have employee stock plans, with the proportion being higher in publicly traded corporations and lower in privately held corporations. Reasons for lower use in private corporations include more complicated mechanics (discussed shortly) and owners' reluctance to share ownership.

As for the tax status of employee stock purchase plans, the amount of the purchase discount (if any) is deemed to be employment income (but is taxed at the capital gains rate) and must be paid when the employee sells the shares or when the firm is wound up or sold. The tax rules for share appreciation also apply to stock bonus plans.

## EMPLOYEE STOCK OPTION PLANS

Under an employee stock option plan, employees receive options to purchase company stock at a future time at a fixed price. For example, if company stock is now trading at $10 a share, then 1000 options with an exercise price of $11 a share might be issued to each employee. Half of the options might be exercisable (when options become exercisable, they are considered "vested" in the hands of the employees) a year after they are granted, and the other half in two years with an exercise deadline (option expiry) of five years. What this means is that one year from now, the employee has the option of purchasing up to 500 shares of company stock at a price of $11 each. Obviously, if the stock is trading at that time at, say, $9 a share, there will be no reason to exercise the options. An employee who wants the stock could just purchase it through a stockbroker for $9 a share.

But if the stock is trading at, say, $12 a share, employees have a decision to make. They can exercise their options and purchase 500 shares at $11. But if they do purchase the shares, there is the possibility that these shares will go down in price. Of course, they might also go up in price. It's a gamble. But employees who don't want to gamble or who don't have the money with which to purchase the shares can simply cash out by purchasing the shares and then selling them immediately at $12, thus realizing a net gain of $500 (less any brokerage costs). The $500 would be deemed employment income (but taxed at the capital gains rate).

But they need not exercise their options at this time either. They could just continue to hold their options (for up to another four years because that is the expiry date) in the expectation that stock prices will go up over the next four years. But if the stock price sinks below the exercise price of $11 (when the stock price is below the exercise price, the stock options are said to be "under water") and never again rises above that price (during the next four years), employees will not realize any value from their options. On the other hand, they are not out of pocket any money, either, as they would be if they had purchased and held the shares as they dropped below the $11 mark.

In the early 2000s, excessive executive stock options were cited as a factor in the collapse of some major U.S. corporations and in the exorbitant increases in executive compensation that have been taking place for a number of years. Part of the problem was that due to a quirk in financial reporting systems, stock options appeared to be a virtually "costless" way of providing compensation to executives. However, stock options can exert a very real cost to shareholders by diluting share values. Recognizing this problem, the United States and Canada developed new accounting rules that require expensing of stock option grants.

When the Sarbanes-Oxley Act of 2002 was signed into law in the United States, one of its requirements was to explore the implications of moving from a rule-oriented system of GAAP to one that was more principle based.[26] The Sarbanes-Oxley Act was aimed at ensuring the accuracy of financial information submitted by firms, with more punitive penalties for firms that violate the Act. Canada became the first major jurisdiction to require that all public companies expense employee stock-based compensation awards as of January 1, 2004. The U.S. Financial Accounting Standards Board (FASB) subsequently issued the Revised Financial Accounting Standard 123 requiring companies to expense stock options.[27] The Sarbanes-Oxley Act also required companies to report all options grants within two days of the date of the grant, effectively eliminating options backdating. As a result of these legislative and accounting requirements, companies are now using fewer stock options and replacing them with incentives that are more closely tied to firm and individual performance. A Hay Group study shows that performance awards made up over half of the granted long-term incentive value provided to CEOs in 2012 while stock options dropped to about a quarter.[28]

In an even more recent survey by Willis Towers Watson of Canadian publicly traded companies with revenues over $2 billion, 100 percent of the companies offered CEOs and senior executives long-term incentive plans. Still, only 30 percent of salaried employees were eligible for long-term incentive plans. The survey found that 95 percent of the companies use performance share units, 85 percent use stock options, 55 percent use restricted share units, and 15 percent use other long-term incentive plans, including performance stock options or deferred share units. The study found that, though stock options are still commonly used, the number of such plans within long-term incentive plans and the number of individuals within a company that are entitled to this plan are declining. Another Willis Tower Watson study found that performance share units have surpassed stock options as the dominant long-term equity compensation incentive.[29]

Though recent information on private Canadian companies is less accessible, another Willis Towers Watson Survey of privately held U.S. companies found that around 50 percent of participants had long-term incentives and the incentives were mainly for larger companies. As compared to their public counterparts, long-term incentives amounts were 30 percent lower, 80 percent of long-term incentives were performance cash plans, and private companies were significantly less likely to use stock options. However, this data is general, and some industries such as oil and gas and energy or technology, where the company may be tight on cash, all employees may be eligible for stock options.[30]

## PHANTOM SHARE PLANS

**phantom share plan**
A plan through which employees participate in the appreciation of company shares and any associated dividends, without ever owning any company shares.

**phantom equity plan**
A plan that helps retain key employees by providing rewards based on the stock performance of a portfolio of promising new high-tech firms.

A **phantom share plan** ties an employee's bonus to the performance of company stock, but that employee never actually receives any stock. The employee is granted a certain number of "units," each corresponding to a share of stock. The employee is entitled to the same dividends that accrue to the actual stock and also to the appreciation in share value; both, however, are paid in cash at periodic intervals. Any payouts are considered employment income and are taxed at the full employment income rate.

A variation on a phantom stock plan is a **phantom equity plan**.[31] Professional service firms—such as management consulting giants McKinsey & Company and Accenture—developed this compensation method to help them retain staff who might otherwise be drawn to high-tech companies better able to offer stock options or equity shares (which professional services firms generally cannot do because they usually do not have a corporate ownership structure). The plan is not in fact an employee stock plan because the shares in question are not those of the employer; rather, it is a plan in which employees are granted participation units in a pool of equities of client firms. The value of the units varies with the value of the fund. Employees are allowed to cash out only at specified intervals and on termination, when they must do so.

Compensation Notebook 11.1 summarizes the main types of stock plans available as well as the other main types of group and organizational performance pay plans.

### TYPES OF GROUP AND ORGANIZATIONAL PAY PLANS

**Gain-Sharing Plans**
- Scanlon Plan
- Rucker Plan
- Improshare
- Family of Measures

**Goal-Sharing Plans**
- Single-Goal Plan
- Multigoal Plan
- Financially Funded Plan

**Profit-Sharing Plans**
- Deferred Profit-Sharing Plan (DPSP)
- Current Distribution Plan
- Combination Plan

**Employee Stock Plans**
- Share Bonus Plan
- Share Purchase Plan
- Stock Option Plan
- Phantom Share Plan

# ISSUES IN DESIGNING STOCK PLANS

The issues in designing an employee stock plan vary somewhat according to whether the employer is a publicly traded or a privately held corporation. However, for all companies, several factors differentiate more successful employee stock plans from less successful ones. The effectiveness of employee share ownership increases with the proportion of the employees who hold shares,[32] the proportion of the firm owned by employees,[33] and the degree of employee consultation in the development of the share plan.[34] Employees must feel that they own enough shares to make a difference to their financial well-being and must also feel a sense of real ownership in a corporate context where effective mechanisms for employee participation in decision making are in place.[35] Also essential are effective procedures for educating employees about the nature of the stock plan and communicating about company results.

## Design Issues for Stock Plans in Public Corporations

Employee stock plans are simpler to implement in publicly traded corporations than in privately held corporations because the public stock market provides a well-understood mechanism for the purchase and sale of company stock. However, organizations still must decide on a number of issues before implementing the plan:

- eligibility for inclusion,
- criteria for allocating stock among employees, and
- the type of holding period.

The first issue is eligibility for inclusion in the stock plan. In general, the more inclusive, the better, although temporary employees and contract employees are usually excluded. Often some minimal length of service is required, usually not exceeding one year.

Next, the criteria for allocating stock among employees must be decided. This allocation can be based on salary (probably the most common approach), seniority, employee performance, equal distribution, or some combination of these. Equal distribution is the most egalitarian, but is it really fair to more senior employees, who may feel that they are contributing more to the company's success or who have shown long-term commitment to the firm? Salary-based allocation has the advantage of maintaining the same proportion of stock in the compensation mix for all employees. Equal allocation is the simplest method, but adjustments typically still need to be made based on the number of days or hours each employee worked in the preceding year.

The holding period is another critical issue. If the objective is to create employee-owners, then some type of holding period should be imposed. Otherwise, it is very tempting to sell the shares immediately to realize the profit in so doing. In general, the more generous the stock plan, the longer the holding period. For example, if employees are purchasing the shares at only a small discount from the market price, then only a short holding period is justified, if any. But if employees are receiving the shares at no cost to themselves, they may be required to hold the shares for up to five years.

## Design Issues for Stock Plans in Private Corporations

Stock plans in private corporations must deal with the same issues as public corporations, and some others besides.[36] One key difference is that there is no external market to place a value on company shares and to serve as a mechanism for purchasing or selling the shares. Another difference is that the existing owners likely wish to prevent the unfettered sale of the shares to maintain control of the firm. Still another difference is that as minority shareholders in private corporations, employees may have very little control or influence over what goes on in the organization and no easy way to liquidate their shares if they are not happy with management or if they feel their interests are not being well represented. Employee-owners in public corporations may also have very little control, but at least they have the option of easily liquidating their holdings.

To deal with these issues, an artificial "market" is often set up. At regular intervals (usually quarterly or annually), company shares are priced by an outside auditor, and employees are allowed to purchase from or sell shares to other employees at these times. If the available shares exceed the demand, the company will often agree to buy back any shares up for sale. In general, when shares are issued, the company is given "right of first refusal" so that employees must offer their shares to the company before offering them to an outside buyer. In some cases, the board of directors is required to approve the sale of any of the employee shares to outside investors. In some cases, employees are not permitted to sell their shares except on termination or retirement from the firm. In many cases, employees are required to sell if they terminate their employment.

To help protect minority rights, employee shares should carry full rights to voting and information. There should be guaranteed board representation for employee shareholders and some legal protection for minority interests. For example, there could be a clause requiring a majority of employee-owners to agree to major changes that might materially affect their share value, such as sale or purchase of a plant or major asset, or issuance of new classes of stock to existing owners. These types of provisions are particularly important for share purchase plans, where employees must make a significant investment to purchase the shares.[37]

# NONMONETARY REWARD PLANS

"Dump the cash, load on the praise!" This is the advice of a well-known consultant who has come up with "1001 Ways to Reward Employees," many of which do not involve money.[38] He argues that what employees really want is recognition for their achievements and affirmation that they are valuable members of the organization. This recognition can take a variety of forms, ranging from simple praise to substantial prizes, such as an all-expenses-paid holiday.

Certainly, many employers find this attractive advice because not spending money is usually popular with employers. And as we have seen, there are many problems and difficulties with individually based financial incentive plans. It is not surprising that over half of medium to large Canadian firms now use formal noncash rewards to recognize individual employee performance. About one-fifth of firms have group-based recognition systems—in which all members of a team are recognized for the team's success—in addition to individual recognition. Some firms have noncash recognition programs that recognize only group performance, but this is quite rare.

However, while firms may be loading on the praise, they are certainly not "dumping the cash"; research shows that firms with noncash recognition plans actually have more performance pay plans than do firms without noncash recognition.[39]

What exactly is a nonmonetary recognition award? Perhaps one of the most famous examples is the "Golden Banana Award": "When a senior manager in one organization was trying to figure out a way to recognize an employee who had just done a great job, he spontaneously picked up a banana [which had been packed in his lunch], and handed it to the astonished employee with hearty congratulations. Now, one of the highest honours in that company has been dubbed the 'Golden Banana Award'."[40] Although some recognition rewards may have financial value (as in the case of a restaurant voucher or expenses-paid holiday), they are never provided as cash because the key to their importance is their symbolic value, as this example illustrates.

There are some important caveats regarding the use of nonmonetary rewards. First, such rewards are not a substitute for a fair and equitable pay system. Indeed, without an adequate pay system and a collaborative and trusting relationship between workers and management, employees will not likely attach much value to nonmonetary rewards. They will likely see such rewards as an attempt to manipulate them into working harder while withholding "real" (financial) rewards. And they will not value praise or recognition from managers whom they don't respect or trust.

But where there is equitable pay and employee–management trust, nonmonetary rewards can be effective, as the Toyota case illustrated (see Compensation Today 3.1). Overall, the arguments made by proponents of these reward systems are consistent with Maslow's theory: once lower-order needs are satisfied, then the needs for achievement and recognition for this achievement can come to the fore. But to be effective, praise must be grounded in actual achievement, follow accomplishment closely, and come from a credible and respected source.

Given all this, nonmonetary rewards seem most suited to high-involvement organizations, although they may also have applications in human relations organizations. Because the foundations for success do not exist in classical organizations, nonmonetary rewards will likely be of relatively little value there.

### NOT ONLY MONEY AT GOOGLE

Often employees choose to leave a company due to a lack of recognition at their current company. One study found that, on average, 66 percent of individuals confessed that they would leave a company if they felt unappreciated. When taking into account only Millennials, as many as 76 percent of individuals said that would look for another job. Google, being a forward-thinking company, considered this sentiment. They offered employees up to $1 million for top performance and high achievement. However, the company quickly discovered that monetary employee recognition programs were creating a toxic work environment and demotivating. The financial rewards were promoting envy and animosity. Thus, the cash reward was phased out and, instead, the company formed a new strategy that emphasized various nonmonetary rewards.

Rather than cash rewards, employees were rewarded with experiences, including dinners, new technology devices, and vacations to Hawaii. Google has created four programs to support their initiatives. The first recognition is a spot bonus program, which is a way for managers to recognize a particularly extraordinary accomplishment. The second recognition program is the peer bonus, in which employees acknowledge their peers' work and nominate that employee. Google's third program is gThanks, where employees can send online thank-you notes to coworkers. Lastly, employees are recognized by group performance through the "no name program." This program helps leaders identify teams for exceptional performance, and teams get to celebrate with celebrations or team trips. This recognition program has worked tremendously well. In a study by PayScale, 86 percent of Google employees expressed satisfaction with their jobs. Employees expressed that they find the new program more amusing, entertaining, and that the rewards were more considerate as compared to the cash awards.

Sources: Jane Lemons, "Best Employee Rewards and Recognition Programs. Reward and Recognize Employees Like Google," *Bucket List*, December 11, 2017; "Employee Recognition: The What, Why and How," *Employment Hero*, October 17, 2019.

## TYPES OF NONMONETARY REWARD PLANS

Two important dimensions on which noncash recognition programs can vary is whether they are formal or informal, and whether they recognize individual or group performance.[41] Informal programs, in which supervisors are encouraged to recognize employee performance as part of their day-to-day management approach, will not likely be effective without extensive managerial training and reinforcement by their superiors, and may end up being rather hit or miss across different supervisors. To be effective, an informal approach needs a supportive culture, such as a high-involvement managerial strategy would provide.

Formal programs can be more systematic and consistent across organizational units but even a formal program depends on the cooperation of supervisors for its success.

Regarding individual versus group recognition, if the organization depends on extensive cooperation within teams or units, then it is probably best to develop a program that provides recognition on both an individual and a group basis.

According to one expert, there are five types of nonmonetary awards—social reinforcers, merchandise awards, travel awards, symbolic awards, and earned time off.[42] Social reinforcers may range from a simple pat on the back to a valued training opportunity or a company picnic. The general purpose is to demonstrate the value the firm places on its employees.

Merchandise awards are given to individual employees to recognize performance accomplishments. Travel awards can be provided to recognize individuals or, more commonly, groups or teams for outstanding accomplishments. Symbolic awards are exemplified by the "Golden Banana" award. Earned time off can be used to recognize individuals or teams that have gone "above and beyond" the call of duty in finishing a project or assignment.

## ISSUES IN DESIGNING NONMONETARY REWARD PLANS

In any recognition system, the recognition must be truly deserved, and awards must not be handed out because they are relatively cheap. In general, the more inexpensive the reward, the more judiciously it must be provided if it is to be seen as having any value at all. In addition, it is important to avoid singling out individuals for recognition if their accomplishments have been achieved in a team context or with the help of other employees. This would lead to only divisiveness and discord.

It is best to structure these programs so that it is possible to recognize all deserving employees. For example, instead of saying that the employee with the highest sales will receive a recognition award, say that "all employees who achieve a 10 percent increase in sales" will receive a recognition award. Artificially "rationing" recognition goes against the principle of these programs, which is that any employee with a significant accomplishment should be recognized.

Another major issue is determining how to identify those individuals and teams deserving of formal recognition. Of course, any manager is free to provide recognition through praise and other informal means whenever he or she wishes. But for major recognition awards, many organizations use an elected committee of employees and managers.

At RBC, employees who wish to nominate a coworker can go online to do so. Then the nominee's immediate manager reviews the nomination. That manager may award a small recognition on the spot or may make a recommendation to the recognition committee.[43]

While a recognition program must focus at the grassroots level and become part of the corporate culture, keeping it alive and vibrant usually requires a champion who will take the lead in promoting the program. At RBC, a five-person unit is in charge of the recognition program, constantly monitoring its health and coordinating the recognition budget. To help promote and publicize the program, the bank uses a recognition intranet page. It also has 30 "recognition counterparts" scattered throughout the organization, from all functions and departments, who act as point persons for recognition in that part of the organization and who answer questions about the program. The recognition budgets for each area of the organization are funnelled through these people.

In terms of the awards themselves, the bank's recognition is in the form of "recognition points." Employees can redeem these points for a variety of awards (except cash), which enables them to select an award that is valuable to them. Employees can also accumulate recognition points in order to garner a larger recognition award.

Through this program, RBC is showing the importance it places on its employees as the key driver of business success. As earlier RBC examples interspersed throughout the book have shown, nonmonetary rewards are just part of the total reward program at the bank. The program as a whole is designed to help create a culture of employee commitment to the organization and its goals.

# SUMMARY

This chapter identified the key issues in the design of group and organizational performance pay plans as well as some of the key issues in designing noncash employee recognition plans.

There are four main types of gain-sharing plans—Scanlon, Rucker, Improshare, and family of measures—each of which uses a different formula for calculating productivity increases. You now understand the key issues in designing these plans and recognize that they suit stable organizations much better than more dynamic organizations.

Goal sharing is a more flexible system than gain sharing. It also has the potential to be more arbitrary, both in the criteria for goal achievement and in the amount of the bonus for goal achievement. When designing these programs, you need to create challenging but attainable goals; this may be more difficult in dynamic organizations.

Although simpler to develop than gain sharing or goal sharing, profit-sharing plans present a multitude of design choices. To succeed, these plans need extensive communications, implementation in a high-involvement setting, and allocation of the profit-sharing bonus by individual performance, where permitted by circumstances (i.e., availability of fair, accurate, and accepted individual performance measures).

The key issues in the design of employee stock plans and the major types (stock bonus plans, stock purchase plans, stock option plans, and phantom stock plans) were discussed. For an employee stock plan to succeed, it needs to incorporate widespread implementation, significant ownership for employees, and mechanisms for extensive employee participation within the enterprise.

Finally, you learned that nonmonetary recognition programs can play in a total rewards system. Effective noncash employee recognition program need to ensure that all deserving employees receive recognition, that the process for determining recognition is fair, that team-based recognition is provided when warranted, and that nonmonetary rewards are not used a substitute for equitable monetary rewards.

## KEY TERMS

family of measures plan
Improshare
phantom equity plan
phantom share plan

Rucker plan
Scanlon plan
share appreciation rights

## DISCUSSION QUESTIONS

1. What are the key issues to be considered when designing gain sharing plans?

2. When designing a profit-sharing plan, what design issues do you think would prove to be the most difficult to decide?

3. What issues should you consider when designing a goal sharing plan for a group of sales employees?

4. Discuss the pros and cons of nonmonetary reward programs.

5. Review expectancy theory from Chapter 3. Now, using expectancy theory, discuss the potential motivational impact of profit-sharing pay systems on employees.

## EXERCISES

1. Go to the National Center for Employee Ownership website (http://www.nceo.org) and identify the factors the Center suggests are important to the success of employee share ownership plans.

2. Examine the two profit-sharing plans described in Compensation Today 11.3. Evaluate the possible impact of each. Which do you think will be most effective, and why do you think so? What additional information would be useful in order to draw firm conclusions?

3. Assume you are an employee in a firm that is planning to implement profit sharing. As an employee, identify the design features you would like to see included.

Then, in a small group, compare your desired plans. How do they differ, and what do you think are the reasons for the differences?

## CASE QUESTIONS

1. You are a team of top-notch compensation consultants hired by Alliston Instruments (refer to *Case 6*, in the Appendix). After analyzing the various options available, you have decided that a group pay plan would be beneficial to this organization. Select the specific group plan that would seem to work best; then design it, describing specifically how you would deal with the various

design issues. When you are done, the plan should be ready for implementation.

2. You have decided that The Fit Stop (refer to *Case 2*, page xx in the Appendix) would be well suited to an organizational performance pay plan. Select the specific organization pay plan that would seem to work best; then design it, describing specifically how you would deal with the various design issues. When you are done, the plan should be ready for implementation.

## SIMULATION CROSS-REFERENCE

If you are using Strategic Compensation: A Simulation in conjunction with this text, you will find that the concepts in Chapter 11 are helpful in preparing the simulation.

# ENDNOTES

1. John G. Belcher, *Gain Sharing* (Houston: Gulf, 1991).

2. Mitchell Fein, *IMPROSHARE: An Alternative to Traditional Managing* (Hillsdale: Mitchell Fein, 1981).

3. R.T. Kaufman, "The Effects of IMPROSHARE on Productivity," *Industrial and Labor Relations Review* 45 (1992): 311–22; John Shields et al., *Managing Employee Performance & Reward: Concepts, Practices, Strategies* (Cambridge University Press, 2015).

4. Belcher, *Gain Sharing*.

5. Ibid.

6. Kaufman, "The Effects of IMPROSHARE."; John Shields et al., *Managing Employee Performance & Reward: Concepts, Practices, Strategies* (Cambridge University Press, 2015).

7. Richard J. Long, "Group-based Pay, Participatory Practices, and Workplace Performance." Paper presented at the Conference on the Evolving Workplace, Ottawa, September 2005, 28–29.

8. For example, see Kenneth Mericle and Dong-One Kim, *Gainsharing and Goalsharing: Aligning Pay and Strategic Goals* (Westport: Praeger, 2004). See also Christine Cooper, Bruno Dyck, and Norman Frohlich, "Improving the Effectiveness of Gainsharing: The Role of Fairness and Participation," *Administrative Science Quarterly* 37, no. 3 (1992), 471–90. See also Theresa M. Welbourne, David B. Balkin, and Luis Gomez–Mejia, "Gain Sharing and Mutual Monitoring: A Combined Agency–Organizational Justice Interpretation," *Academy of Management Journal* 38, no. 3 (1995): 881–99. See also Theresa M. Welbourne and Daniel M. Cable, "Group Incentives and Pay Satisfaction: Understanding the Relationship Through an Identity Theory Perspective," *Human Relations* 48, no. 6 (1995): 711–26. See also Dong-One Kim, "Factors Influencing Organizational Performance in Gainsharing Programs," *Industrial Relations* 35, no. 2 (1996): 227–44; Sachin H. Jain and Daniel Roble, "Gainsharing in Health Care Meeting the

Quality-of-Care Challenge: In Health Care, Gainsharing Carries Unique Challenges, but the Benefits are Worth the Effort," *Healthcare Financial Management* 62, no. 3 (2008): 72–79; Frances A. Kennedy, James M. Kohlmeyer, and Robert J. Parker, "The Roles of Organizational Justice and Trust in a Gain-Sharing Control System," in *Advances in Accounting Behavioral Research* (Emerald Group Publishing Limited, 2009).

9. Long, "Group-based Pay."

10. Lisa D. Ordonez, Maurice E. Schweitzer, Adam D. Galinsky, and Max H. Bazerman, "Goals Gone Wild: The Systematic Side Effects of Overprescribing Goal Setting," *Academy of Management Perspectives* 23, no. 1 (2009): 6–16.

11. Mericle and Kim, *Gainsharing and Goalsharing*; Angappa Gunasekaran, Amir M. Sharif, Chee Yew Wong, and Nuran Acur, "Understanding Inter-Organizational Decision Coordination," *Supply Chain Management: An International Journal* 15, no. 4 (2010): 332–43.

12. Edward E. Lawler, *Rewarding Excellence: Pay Strategies for the New Economy* (San Francisco: Jossey–Bass, 2000), 228.

13. K.M. Bartol and E.A. Locke, "Incentives and Motivation," in *Compensation in Organizations: Current Research and Practice*, ed. S.L. Rynes and B. Gerhart (San Francisco: Jossey-Bass, 2000), 104–50; Shikha Sahai and A.K. Srivastava, "Goal/Target Setting and Performance Assessment as Tool for Talent Management," *Procedia-Social and Behavioral Sciences* 37 (2012): 241–46.

14. Three Canadian studies found that profit sharing was more likely in high-involvement organizations than in classical and human relations organizations. See Terry H. Wagar and Richard J. Long, "Profit Sharing in Canada: Incidence and Predictors," *Proceedings of the Administrative Sciences Association of Canada, Human Resources Division* 16, no. 9 (1995): 97–105. See also Richard J. Long, "Motives for Profit Sharing: A Study of Canadian Chief Executive Officers," *Relations industrielles/Industrial Relations* 52, no. 4 (1997): 712–733. See also Richard J. Long, "Performance Pay in Canada," in *Paying for Performance: An International Comparison*, ed. Michelle Brown and John S. Heywood (Armonk: M.E. Sharpe, 2002); Kym Hambly, Rinu Vimal Kumar, Mark Harcourt, Helen Lam, and Geoffrey Wood, "Profit-Sharing as an Incentive," *The International Journal of Human Resource Management* 30, no. 20 (2019): 2855–75.

15. Richard Long and Tony Fang, "Do Strategic Factors Affect Adoption of Profit Sharing? Longitudinal Evidence from Canada," *The International Journal of Human Resource Management* 26, no. 7 (2015): 971–1001.

16. Stephen Bruce, "The Three Approaches to Profit-Sharing," *HR Daily Advisor*, April 30, 2014, https://hrdailyadvisor.blr.com/2014/04/30/the-3-approaches-to-profit-sharing/, accessed March 30, 2020.

17. "The Billes Family, Founders of Canadian Tire Corporation, Honoured with Retail Council of Canada's Lifetime Achievement Award," *Canada NewsWire*, May 13, 2015, http://ezproxy.library.yorku.ca/login?url=https://search-proquest-com.ezproxy.library.yorku.ca/docview/1680516933?accountid=15182, accessed March 30, 2020.

18. Michael McKiernan, "Keeping it Simple: Ikea's DPSP Reinforces Founder's Values," *Benefits Canada*, May 11, 2018, https://www.benefitscanada.com/news/ikeas-dpsp-reinforces-founders-focus-on-simplicity-114010, March 30, 2020.

19. "Part XIII—Benefit Plans," *Government of Ontario*, https://www.ontario.ca/document/employment-standard-act-policy-and-interpretation-manual/part-xiii-benefit-plans, accessed March 30, 2020.

20. Brad Cherniak, "How to Share Profits with Your Staff Without Running into Problems," *Financial Post*, October 15, 2013, https://business.financialpost.com/entrepreneur/how-to-share-profits-with-your-staff-without-running-into-problems, accessed March 30, 2020.

21. Richard Yerema, *Canada's Top 100 Employers* (Toronto: Mediacorp, 2005)

22. Richard J. Long and Tony Fang, "Do employees profit from profit sharing? Evidence from Canadian panel data," *ILR Review* 65, no. 4 (2012): 899–927.

23. Jeffrey Carpenter, Andrea Robbett, and Prottoy A. Akbar, "Profit Sharing and Peer Reporting," *Management Science* 64, no. 9 (2018): 4261–76.

24. Richard J. Long and Tony Fang, "Do employees profit from profit sharing? Evidence from Canadian panel data," *ILR Review* 65, no. 4 (2012): 899–927.

25. Richard J. Long, "Employee Profit Sharing: Consequences and Moderators," *Relations industrielles/Industrial Relations* 55, no. 3 (2000): 477–504.

26. Stephen Spector, "Expensing Stock Options." *CGA Magazine*, March–April 2004, at http://www.cga-canada.org/en-ca/AboutCGACanada/CGAMagazine/2004/Mar-Apr/Pages/ca_2004_03-04_dp_standards.aspx.

27. Summary of Statement No. 123 (revised 2004), *Financial Accounting Standards Board*, at http://www.fasb.org/summary/stsum123r.shtml, accessed October 2, 2016.

28. Executive compensation 2013: Data, trends and strategies. © 2014 *Hay Group*.

29. Julius Melnitzer, "A Look at Trends in Long-Term Incentives Plans," *Benefits Canada*, April 16, 2018, https://www.benefits-canada.com/news/a-look-at-trends-in-long-term-incentive-plans-113345, March 29, 2020.

30. Ibid.

31. Helen H. Morrison and Joseph S. Adams, "New Type of Phantom Equity Plan Used to Combat Employee Defections," *Journal of Employee Ownership Law and Finance* 13, no. 1 (2001): 109–26.

32. Alex Bryson, Andrew E. Clark, Richard B. Freeman, and Colin P. Green, "Share Capitalism and Worker Wellbeing," *Labour Economics* 42 (2016): 151–58.

33. Ernest H. O'Boyle, Pankaj C. Patel, and Erik Gonzalez-Mulé, "Employee Ownership and Firm Performance: A Meta-Analysis," *Human Resource Management Journal* 26, no. 4 (2016): 425–48.

34. Long, "Employee Profit Sharing."; Andrew Pendleton and Andrew Robinson, "Employee Stock Ownership, Involvement, and Productivity: An Interaction-Based Approach," *ILR Review* 64, no. 1 (2010): 3–29; Jennifer A. Harrison, Parbudyal Singh, and Shayna Frawley, "What Does Employee Ownership Effectiveness Look Like? The Case of a Canadian-Based Firm," *Canadian Journal of Administrative Sciences/Revue Canadienne des Sciences de l'Administration* 35, no. 1 (2018): 5–19.

35. Rosen et al., "Every Employee an Owner."

36. For examples of employee ownership systems in private Canadian corporations, see Carol Beatty and Harvey Schacter, *Employee Ownership: The New Source of Competitive Advantage* (Toronto: John Wiley and Sons, 2002); "Share Structure and Shareholders," *Government of Canada*, https://www.ic.gc.ca/eic/site/cd-dgc.nsf/eng/cs06644.html, accessed March 30, 2020; Richard Harroch, "How Employee Stock Options Work in Startup Companies," *Forbes*–February 27, 2016, https://www.forbes.com/sites/allbusiness/2016/02/27/how-employee-stock-options-work-in-startup-companies/#9c20c9e6633f.

37. An excellent source of information on the technical aspects of designing employee share plans in Canada is Perry Phillips, *Employee Share Ownership Plans* (Toronto: John Wiley and Sons, 2001).

38. Bob Nelson, "Dump the Cash, Load on the Praise," *Personnel Journal* 75, no. 7 (1996): 65–70. See also Bob Nelson, *1001 Ways to Reward Employees* (New York: Workman, 1994); or Bob Nelson, *1001 Ways to Reward Employees: 100s of New Ways to Praise* (New York: Workman, 2005).

39. Richard J. Long and John L. Shields, "From Pay to Praise? Non-Cash Employee Recognition in Canadian and Australian Firms," *International Journal of Human Resource Management* 21, no. 8 (2010): 1145–72.

40. Dean R. Spitzer, "Power Rewards: Rewards That Really Motivate," *Management Review* 85, no. 5 (1996): 48–49.

41. J.–P. Brun and N. Dugas, "An Analysis of Employee Recognition: Perspectives on Human Resources Practices," *International Journal of Human Resource Management* 19, no. 4 (2008): 716–30.

42. Jerry L. McAdams, "Nonmonetary Rewards: Cash Equivalents and Tangible Awards," in *The Compensation Handbook: A State-of-the-Art Guide to Compensation Strategy and Design*, ed. Lance A. Berger and Dorothy R. Berger (New York: McGraw–Hill, 2000), 241–59.

43. David Brown, "RBC's Recognition Department Oversees Rewarding Culture," *Canadian HR Reporter* 18, no. 5 (2005): 7–9.

# CHAPTER 12

# DESIGNING INDIRECT PAY PLANS

## Learning Outcomes

AFTER READING THIS CHAPTER, YOU SHOULD BE ABLE TO:

- Identify the six major categories of employee benefits and the specific types of benefits included in each category.
- Discuss the advantages and disadvantages of fixed versus flexible benefits plans and the circumstances in which each would be most appropriate.
- Describe the issues that must be addressed in designing a benefits system.

Something's always percolating at Digital Extremes. If not the free coffee (along with free meals—breakfast, lunch, and supper—prepared by full-time chefs employed by the firm), it's the interplay between employees as they work together to produce video games such as *Bioshock, Dark Sector, Warframe*, and the *Unreal Tournament* series. To keep things light in what can be a high-intensity work environment, the company has a "Fun Brigade" that organizes everything from ping-pong tournaments, to paintball and paper airplane contests, to pumpkin-carving competitions.

At this video games developer, based in London, Ontario, President Mike Schmalz believes it is important to keep things fun so that employees don't burn out. As Schmalz puts it, "As fun as it looks, it's a lot of hard work. There are big deadlines. We try to work hard, play hard, and ultimately we want to create something that everyone can be proud of." In addition to the food, fun, and stimulating work, the company offers a wide array of benefits to its employees, which include an in-house theatre, nap room, free parking, and free snacks. Digital Extremes allows for telecommuting and flexible work hours. The firm subsidizes tuition and professional accreditation and online training programs, tops up parental leave programs, offers matching RSP contributions, and has a company-paid health plan that covers everything from medicine and prescription coverage to eye and dental care for its employees and their families. Digital Extremes also covers fitness subsidies and developed a year-long wellness initiative to entice staff members to improve their fitness, diets, and overall health. The first prize winner received $1000 toward the purchase of a gym membership or fitness equipment and six months of online fitness training. The second-place winner received $600, and the third-place winner received $300 for the purchase of a gym membership or fitness equipment.

These benefits most likely play a role in attracting employees to a company in small-city London, Ontario, as opposed to its competitors in Toronto, Vancouver, or even California or Japan. All in all, it is no surprise that the firm has been consistently named one of "Canada's Top 100 Employers" from 2010 to 2020 and was nominated as a finalist for the Canadian HR Award's Venngo Award of Excellence for Financial, Physical and Mental Wellness in 2019.

Sources: Kira Vermond, "At Digital Extremes, Free Lunch Connects Workers," *The Globe and Mail Online*, October 10, 2012; Richard Yerema and Kristina Leung, *Canada's Top 100 Employers* (Toronto: Mediacorp, 2012), http://www.canadastop100.com/national; "DE Wins Company Honours" *Digital Extremes*, December 4, 2018; Richard Yerema and Kristina Leung, *Canada's Top 100 Employers* (Toronto: Mediacorp, 2019), https://reviews.canadastop100.com/top-employer-digital-extremes; Kira Vermond, "Video Game Maker Behind Warframe Gets Creative in Search for Specialized Talent," *The Globe and Mail*, October 24, 2018; "DE Tapped for Vengo Excellence Award," *Digital Extremes*, August 6, 2019.

# TYPES OF EMPLOYEE BENEFITS AND SERVICES

In 2020, because of their impressive array of benefits, Desjardins Group was awarded as one of Canada's top 100 employers, Canada's top family-friendly employers, and top employers for Canadians over 40. The company has a defined benefit pension plan, retirement planning assistance, and phased-in work options when reaching retirement. Once employees retire, they can permanently remain on the health benefit plan with shared contributions. Desjardins also offers a health benefits plan in which the company pays 80 percent of the premiums. The health plan has no waiting period for those who work a minimum of 10 hours a week at the company. Employees have access to an employee assistance program, a health spending account, wellness initiatives such as their smoking cessation program and a new sleep health program, and an on-site fitness facility at the head office in Montreal. Desjardins also has a generous parental leave plan, as well as an extensive program to subsidize tuition (whether the education is related or unrelated to their position) and apprenticeships. Lastly, the company offers flexible work hours, including a 35-hour workweek with full pay, shortened workweeks with fewer hours and less pay, compressed workweeks, and telecommuting.[1]

As discussed in Chapter 4, indirect pay is an important component of a firm's compensation strategy and can serve a variety of purposes. However, many issues affect the design of indirect pay, which is technically the most complex of the compensation components, not least because of all the legal and tax issues surrounding it. This chapter begins by discussing the six main categories of indirect pay and the specific employee benefits included in each. It then discusses fixed versus flexible benefits systems and concludes by outlining how to develop an effective employee benefits system.

There are six main categories of indirect pay are: mandatory benefits, retirement income, health benefits, pay for time not worked, employee services, and miscellaneous benefits. Within each of these categories, a multitude of specific benefits can be included. Compensation Notebook 12.1 provides an overview of the benefits that will be covered in this chapter.

Statistics Canada data[2] suggest that the most common nonmandatory benefits offered by Canadian private sector establishments with at least 10 employees are life insurance, supplemental medical benefits, and dental benefits (each of these is offered by about two-thirds of employers). About one-third of these employers offer group RRSPs, and about one-quarter offer a formal pension plan. About one in eight firms offer supplemental employment insurance. Most public sector employers, as well as unionized employers, offer all these benefits.

---

## COMPENSATION NOTEBOOK 12.1

### INDIRECT PAY CATEGORIES

**Mandatory Benefits**
- Canada/Quebec Pension Plan
- Employment Insurance
- Workers' Compensation

**Retirement Income**
- Defined benefit plans
- Defined contribution plans
- Hybrid pension plans

**Health Benefits**
- Supplemental health insurance
- Disability insurance
- Life and accident insurance
- Dental insurance
- Health care spending accounts

**Pay for Time Not Worked**
- Vacations, holidays, breaks
- Sickness, compassionate, and personal absences
- Supplemental unemployment benefits

- Parental leaves
- Educational and sabbatical leaves
- Severance pay

**Employee Services**
- Employee assistance programs
- Wellness and recreational services
- Child care/elder care
- Work/life balance
- Financial or legal services
- Food services
- Outplacement services

**Miscellaneous Benefits**
- Use of company vehicle
- Product/service discounts
- Housing/mortgage subsidies
- Employee savings plans
- Tuition reimbursements
- Work clothing/equipment

---

# MANDATORY BENEFITS

The federal and provincial governments require employers to contribute toward a number of government-provided employee benefits. That is, employers must participate in the following **mandatory benefits** on behalf of their employees: the Canada/Quebec Pension Plan (CPP/QPP), Employment Insurance (EI), and Workers' Compensation (which covers treatment expenses and other costs for workers who are injured on the job). Note, however, that employers do not have to contribute to these plans for independent contractors.

Employers must also provide minimum levels of holidays, rest breaks, and statutory vacation time. In some provinces they must also pay health care taxes. The amount the employer must contribute for each of these programs is based on the total cash compensation received by an employee. For lower-income employees, CPP/QPP, employment insurance, and workers' compensation premiums alone can amount to 10 percent of total compensation. However, because of caps on the premiums, these programs typically amount to a much smaller percentage of the compensation of more highly paid employees, so that the average is five to six percent.[3]

**mandatory benefits**
Government-provided employee benefits, such as pensions and employment insurance, to which employers must contribute on behalf of their employees.

# RETIREMENT INCOME

Because many employees are greatly concerned about securing a retirement income, many firms offer a pension plan that goes beyond the basic pension plan provided by the government. All Canadians are currently entitled to Old Age Security, which pays a small, fixed pension; low-income pensioners also receive a Guaranteed Income Supplement. All employees also qualify for the CPP or QPP, with the amount of their pension dependent on their credited contributions.

After mandatory benefits, pension and retirement plans are the costliest items in most company benefits packages. There are two main types of private pension plans: defined benefit and defined contribution. Hybrid pension plans, which combine the two, are used mainly to transition from one system (usually defined benefit) to the other (usually defined contribution).

## Defined Benefit Plans

**Defined benefit plans** provide a specified stream of income from the time of retirement until death. The amount is usually geared to some proportion of the employee's annual earnings, modified by the number of years the employee has been covered by the plan. At Imperial Oil, for example, employees receive 1.6 percent of the average of their best three years' earnings for each year of service. If an employee retires after 35 years and has averaged $50 000 per year during his or her three best years, that person receives an annual pension of $28 000 from Imperial ($50 000 × 0.016 × 35), in addition to payments from the CPP/QPP and Old Age Security.

**defined benefit plans**
Pension plans that provide retirement income based on a proportion of the employee's pay at the time of retirement.

## Defined Contribution Plans

With **defined contribution plans** (sometimes called "money purchase plans"), the employer commits to putting a certain amount of money in an investment trust on behalf of each employee; then, at the time of retirement, the amount of the annual pension is paid based on whatever amount of money is in that trust. Thus, there is no guarantee as to what amount the annual pension at retirement will actually be. Contributions can be defined in two ways: either as a fixed sum of money, with the amount established each year, or as a fixed proportion of company profits. In the latter case, the plan is known as a deferred profit-sharing plan (DPSP), which was discussed in Chapter 11.

**defined contribution plans**
Pension plans that provide retirement income based on the accrued value of employer and employee contributions to the plan.

Both defined benefit and defined contribution pension plans can be contributory (i.e., employees are required to make contributions) or noncontributory (i.e., employees make no contribution to the plan). The exception to this is deferred profit-sharing plans, all of which are noncontributory.

Defined benefit plans are still the most common type in Canada but there has been a trend away from them toward defined contribution plans, especially in the private sector. According to Statistics Canada, only 24 percent of private sector employees are covered by any kind of pension plan (in contrast, almost all public sector employees are covered).[4] As of 2012, 59 percent of private sector firms that offered employee pension plans offered defined contribution plans, whereas 85 percent of public sector organizations continued to offer defined benefit plans.[5] The same study reported that, overall, 37 percent of organizations with pension plans offered a group RRSP and that only three percent offered a hybrid plan (which combines features of both plans). However, the same StatsCan study found that these hybrid plans covered a significant number (about 10 percent) of the employees covered by pension plans.

Though some experts predict that defined benefit plans will continue to rise in the public sector, they also estimate that three percent or less of Canadians working in the private sector will be participating in a defined benefit plan by 2026. Many of the private sector employees still participating in a defined benefit plan are covered through a grandfathered plan while new hires are not offered a similar program.[6] Furthermore, various interest groups are also lobbying to have public sector pension plans converted to defined contribution plans.[7]

In recent years, the impetus for change has been the poor (or even negative) returns earned by pension funds. During the 2008–09 financial meltdown, most pension funds had a negative return, which led to defined benefit plans becoming seriously underfunded. To deal with this, firms had to make large extra payments to these funds—money that some firms had a hard time finding. In fact, 2008 was the worst year ever for pension funds—their value plunged by 15.9 percent.[8]

Another source of unexpected costs for defined benefit plans is increased life expectancies. This may pose a problem in fields in which more of the workforce is female because the life expectancy of women (83 years at birth) is four years longer than that of men (79 years at birth), according to Statistics Canada.[9] Some estimates suggest that the life expectancies figures are actually higher (89 years for women and 86 years for men).[10] A man who reaches the age of 65 can typically expect to live another 20.9 years; a woman, another 23.3.[11] This can make a big difference in the amount of money needed to fund these pensions. Moreover, if life spans continue to increase, then so will pension liability in defined benefit plans. Compensation Today 12.1 illustrates some interesting actuarial estimates for life expectancies and the way they relate to retirement income. Currently, organizations with defined benefit plans pay about 9.3 percent of total compensation to their pension plans, while organizations with defined contribution plans pay about 6.5 percent.[12]

The actuarial projections in Compensation Today 12.1 can vary for specific employee groups. Accountants have a better chance of surviving to a ripe old age than coal miners. Making accurate actuarial predictions for a particular employee group and then incorporating those predictions into the pension plan is a complex process, one that is not necessary for defined contribution plans. From an employer's perspective, defined contribution plans are much simpler than defined benefit plans.

### WOULD YOU TAKE THIS BET?

Project yourself far into the future. You are celebrating your 90th birthday. An obnoxious relative (how did he get invited to my party, you wonder) who always lords it over you because he is four years younger, has the poor taste to comment that he is glad to see you enjoying your birthday party so much, because it will probably be your last.

Hotly, you tell him that you plan to be around for a few more birthdays yet. He replies that if you are so sure about that, why don't you make some money from it? He offers to pay you $1000 if you make it to your 91st birthday, but you have to pay him $1000 if you don't (the money to be collected immediately and held by a third party until your demise or your 91st birthday, whichever comes first—he may be obnoxious, but he is no fool).

You stop to think. You are in good health for a 90-year-old but how likely is it that you will see your next birthday? Should you take the bet?

You should—in fact, you should try to raise the ante. According to actuarial statistics, your chances of making it to your 91st birthday are greater than 80 percent. In fact, you could be 105 and still have a better-than-even chance of making it to your next birthday.

Overall, Canadians enjoy one of the longest life expectancies in the world. This is good news from a health perspective, but bad news from a retirement income perspective.

Statistics indicate that 70 percent of Canadians feel that they are not saving enough to maintain their standard of living in retirement and 53 percent of Canadians are afraid that they will have to return to work after retirement.[a] Although 87.1 percent of employees in public sector organizations are covered by pensions, only 22.7 percent private sector Canadian employees are covered by company pension plans; overall coverage totals 37.1 percent of all working Canadians from both private and public sectors.[b] Many of those who are covered will not receive pensions adequate to maintain their standard of living over the 15–20 years (or more) of retirement they will enjoy.[c] Given that mandatory retirement has now been abolished in Canada, one possibility is that many employees without sufficient retirement income will continue to work well past normal retirement age, a trend that appears to have already started. In the private sector, retirement after age 70 is increasingly more prevalent and will especially be the case after the market crash following COVID-19.[d]

Of course, people vary in how much they value retirement income plans. Many young employees are especially prone to not worrying about retirement. Some say, why worry—I'll never even make it to retirement! But just what are the odds for a 25-year-old making it to age 65? In fact, better than 80 percent for males and about 90 percent for females. And if you are in normal health at age 25 and not in a hazardous occupation, the odds are much better than that. As this realization sinks in, it is likely that companies that offer pension plans will be increasingly favoured by potential employees.

[a] The Canadian Press, "More Than Half of Canadians Fear Not Having Enough for Retirement: Poll," *CTV News*, February 11, 2020.

[b] "Table 2 Percentage of Paid Workers Covered by a Registered Pension Plan." *Statistics Canada*, June 19, 2019.

[c] Steven Chase, "Canada's Growing Pension Puzzle," *The Globe and Mail*, June 1, 2009, A1; Derek W. Dobson, "Designing Retirement Schemes Canadians Want: Observations from a Modern DB Pension Plan," *Benefits Canada*, April 13, 2017.

[d] Martha Porado, "Retirement System Must Reflect Canadians Working Longer," *Benefits Canada*, March 24, 2020.

From an employee's perspective, defined contribution plans tend to be more portable than defined benefit plans. When employees move from one employer to another, their defined benefit plan is subject to commuted values, which reduces the value of their plan, compared to maintaining employment with the same firm.[13] Defined contribution plans are not subject to such commutations.

However, defined contribution plans have their own drawbacks. They are most beneficial to employees who enter them at a young age and thus contribute for a long time; conversely, defined contribution plans may result in seriously inadequate pensions for those who join up later in life. As long-term employment with a single employer becomes less common, many employees may face this problem. Furthermore, "the employee is saddled with the investment risk and the risk that annuity prices will be high at retirement."[14] In essence, defined contribution plans transfer the risk of retirement income accumulation from the employer to the employee.

One expert points out that firms are better able to manage retirement fund portfolios and their inherent risks than most employees. As she puts it: "Surely plan sponsors, with access to the various types of expertise required, investment, actuarial, and otherwise, are far better equipped to deal with these risks than are individuals."[15] This expert also points out that defined benefit plans offer the advantage of averaging risk over a large group of employees. Some members will terminate, die, or retire when the timing is bad for the fund, but others will do so when the timing is favourable. Such averaging is not possible under defined contribution plans.

## Hybrid Pension Plans

**hybrid pension plans**
Pension plans that combine features of the defined benefit pension plan and the defined contribution pension plan.

Hybrid pension plans combine elements of the defined benefit and defined contribution plans. For example, some firms have a defined benefit plan but also allow employees to contribute to a defined contribution plan. Some firms match employee contributions to a certain maximum level. These contributory plans are often set up as group registered retirement plans. Employees can deduct their contributions from their taxable income, and the plan's earnings accumulate on a tax-deferred basis. Employer and employee contributions to defined benefit and defined contribution plans (both of which must be registered with the government, and both of which are known as registered pension plans) are deducted from the amounts that may be contributed to a group RRSP. Group RRSPs have contribution limits established by the federal government. As discussed earlier, a large number of defined contribution plans are implemented in conjunction with defined benefit plans, most often as part of a process of transitioning away from the defined benefit plan. This finding can, in part, help explain the rapid rise in hybrid plans. According to Statistics Canada, between 2006 and 2010 alone, the hybrid plan increased by 880 percent, from only 40 000 people to 392 000.[16] As of 2019, there were more than 924 000 Canadian employees enrolled in a hybrid plan.[17]

## Experience with Pension Plans

Researchers have identified several important effects of pensions. For example, firms with pensions have lower employee turnover, and their employees retire earlier than those at firms without pension plans.[18] This can be beneficial to two types of firms: those for whom turnover is expensive, and those for whom employee productivity drops off (relative to their earnings) as employees near retirement. But recall from Chapter 3 that turnover can be low due to either affective or continuance commitment. Continuance commitment results in employees exerting only enough effort to meet the minimum standards necessary to avoid being fired, whereas affective commitment can lead to positive job attitudes and behaviour. If pension plans are reducing turnover by creating continuance commitment, this may not be much of a benefit to the firm.

This may help explain research findings suggesting that pensions have a negative impact in unionized firms: if continuance commitment is the only type of commitment generated by the firm, then high job security may allow employees to perform at the minimum standards necessary for job retention. For example, a study of a large Canadian unionized public utility organization found that "stayers" are employees that are a by-product of the selection effect. "Stayers" are attracted to the deferred wage contract and thus have a long-term commitment to the company. Such employees were not found to have an increased work effort because of the defined benefit pension plan. Alternatively, "savers," individuals who make real efforts to save for their retirement, we more likely to work harder, but were not found to be higher performers or partake in discretionary behaviours.[19] This suggests that many employees are putting in the minimum effort necessary to keep their jobs because of their employment and wage security. If this is what a pension plan achieves, is it actually of much value to the firm?

This helps explain why classical firms, especially unionized ones, are so reluctant to implement benefits such as pensions. First, the cost of turnover is often not high for them, so spending a lot of money on pension benefits is unlikely to pay off for the employer. Second, the job security provided by the union may make it difficult to terminate employees unless they are clearly below the minimum performance standards, so the pension system may result in dissatisfied employees who are able to get away with very low performance levels that the firm can do very little about.

In contrast, it is easy to see why pensions are an asset to human relations organizations, which depend on employee stability and on a sense of gratitude and obligation among employees. For these firms, positive social norms are sufficient to maintain employee productivity at acceptable levels. Also, because these firms are often not unionized, a generous benefits package can help forestall future unionization, which these firms regard as a threat to the close relationships that they like to cultivate between management and employees.

# HEALTH BENEFITS

One of the most highly valued employee benefits is health coverage, including disability and death benefits. These benefits are usually provided through some type of insurance program and may include supplemental health insurance, dental insurance, disability insurance, life and accident insurance, and health care spending accounts.

## Supplemental Health Insurance

Canadians enjoy many government-sponsored medical benefits under the system generally known as "medicare." In the United States, where government-sponsored universal medical coverage does not exist, employers are expected to bear the cost of medical insurance. This cost can be staggering in the United States. While recent changes with the introduction of the Affordable Care Act have benefitted many employees, the costs are still high for employers.[20]

However, because of medicare, health benefit costs for Canadian employers are much lower, resulting in much lower benefits costs than in the United States. Nonetheless, many medical expenses are not covered by Canadian medicare, including optical/vision care, chiropractic treatments, and prescription drugs. Until recently, the costs of these plans were rising quite sharply, mainly due to rising prescription drug costs. However, recent years have seen a slowdown in these increases as generic drugs have become more widely available.[21] Currently, extended health plans average about two percent of total compensation.[22]

## Disability Insurance

Many employers purchase long-term disability insurance for their employees to cover disabilities arising from non-work-related causes. (Work-related disabilities are covered under Workers' Compensation.) This coverage typically provides for 60–70 percent of normal pay and carries on until the employee is able to return to work, reaches retirement age, or dies (in which case, benefits are usually provided for the surviving spouse and/or dependent children).

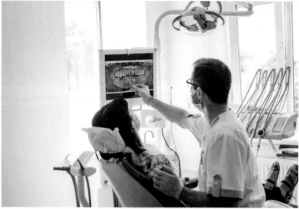

Dental insurance is a popular employee benefit.

Historically, most disability claims have been based on physical disabilities. However, it appears that this cause of disability has been declining and that mental disability is now driving higher disability claims.[23] One-third of disability claims in Canada are now related to mental illness, and mental illness claims account for 70 percent of Canadian disability claims costs.[24] By recent estimates, mental disorders now cost Canadian employers over $50 billion a year; this includes the cost of healthcare benefits and drug costs and disability programs. Also, employers indirectly spend an additional $6.3 billion annually; this consists of the cost of absenteeism, turnover, and "presenteeism," employees going to work while mentally unwell, thus reducing productivity.[25] To counter these problems, some of which may stem from workplace stress or work/life conflicts, many employers have launched employee assistance programs, wellness programs, and work/life balance programs.

## Life and Accident Insurance

One item included in almost all benefits plans is term life and accident insurance. This coverage is usually expressed in terms of a multiple of annual salary (e.g., two times annual salary). Employees are often given the option of increasing their coverage, either at their own expense or on a cost-shared basis. In some cases, insurance coverage is also available for family members, if the employee opts to pay the premiums for this coverage.

## Dental Insurance

Dental insurance has expanded rapidly in the past few years. It has become popular because dental coverage is not provided under medicare and can be a major expense (especially when it comes to orthodontic services for dependant children). It is also a highly tax-favoured benefit.

## Tax Status of Pension and Health Benefits

Registered pension plans receive favourable tax treatment (up to the limits imposed by the Canada Revenue Agency). Employees ultimately must pay taxes on the payouts from these plans, but not until retirement when they are likely to be in a much lower tax bracket. Moreover, at retirement, employees can use the funds to purchase annuities, so that income tax is spread over several years instead of being payable in the year of retirement. Also important for married couples in cases where one spouse has much higher pension income than the other, is that pension income can be split between spouses for tax purposes, which can dramatically reduce the overall amount of tax payable by the couple.

Note that because of RRSP legislation, individual employees can now create their own retirement plans that have tax benefits similar to those of company-provided plans. In the past, this was not the case, and company-provided pension plans had dramatic tax advantages over individual retirement plans.

Insurance plans enjoy favourable tax treatment as well, especially health/dental insurance and accidental death/dismemberment insurance. In both cases, employees do not pay tax either on the employer contributions for these plans or on the benefits that are paid out. Because employee contributions to these plans are not tax-deductible but employer contributions are, it makes sense for the company to provide these plans.

Suppose that an employer currently pays $800 per employee to purchase a dental plan. If the employer decided to instead give the $800 directly to each employee to purchase dental coverage, the employee would lose as much as $400 of this to federal and provincial income taxes, leaving only $400 to purchase the dental coverage, so the employee would receive much less coverage. On top of this, the employee would have to pay a higher price for the coverage purchased because individual plans typically cost much more than company plans. In fact, most employees would probably not find it feasible to purchase dental coverage at all, leaving them liable for major dental bills that may arise.

It is far more cost-effective for the employer to purchase dental coverage on behalf of employees. If an employer is not willing to provide the coverage, employees would be much better off to have their pay reduced by the $800 and have their employer pay this money toward health or dental coverage. Compared to purchasing their own coverage, employees would save up to $400 in income taxes and would also get better coverage.

In contrast, employer-provided long-term disability insurance is not as tax-favoured. Employees are not liable for income taxes on employer contributions to these plans, but they are liable for tax on any benefits received. (On the other hand, if the employees pay for these plans themselves, employee contributions are not tax-deductible but any benefits received are not taxable.) However, because the great majority of employees will be lucky enough never to receive these payments, it is far better for them to have the employer purchase the coverage with pretax money than for the employees to have to purchase the coverage with their after-tax money.

Another popular benefit, group life insurance, has become less tax-favoured over time as the tax rules have changed. It is the only benefit in which employer contributions are considered a taxable benefit, so there is no tax advantage for the employee in having the employer purchase the coverage. However, because employers receive much more favourable rates on purchase of this insurance than would employees, a company-provided group life insurance plan (whether the employer or the employee pays the premiums) is still beneficial to employees.

## Health Care Spending Accounts

Because of their tax-favoured status, **health care spending accounts** have become popular in recent years. In this benefit plan, employers place a certain amount of money (health care spending credits) in a separate account for each employee. Employees may then draw on their individual accounts to cover a wide variety of health care expenses not covered by their other plans, including nonprescription drugs; services that are only partly reimbursed under other plans; cosmetic surgery; and even the deductible amounts from other insurance plans. The key advantage of this benefit is that while employer contributions are still fully deductible for the employer, the funds paid to each employee are not taxable at any point—not when they are placed in the health care account and not when they are received by employees (except in Quebec, where reimbursements to employees are subject to provincial income tax). This is a very significant tax benefit.

Aside from the tax advantages, employers like the idea of a fixed amount set for health coverage. In conventional health insurance plans, as costs increase, the employer must either pay them, pass them along to employees, or reduce coverage—all unpopular choices. With a health care spending account, the employer has the option of not adjusting the health care credits as health costs increase, or of increasing the credits less than the full increases in health costs. However, this may result in employee discontent if the plan is no longer able to cover their needs.

**health care spending account**
A tax-favoured employee benefit that allows employees to use employer-provided health care spending credits to purchase a wide array of health care services.

# PAY FOR TIME NOT WORKED

pay for time not worked
An employee benefit that covers
a wide array of different types of
employee absences from work.

This awkward-sounding but descriptive term is used to cover a variety of circumstances in which employees receive pay even though they are not actually working. As discussed earlier, some **pay for time not worked** is mandatory, including basic vacations, statutory holidays, and rest breaks. But many firms go beyond these mandatory levels and provide pay for additional holidays, sickness and personal leave, educational and other types of leave, and severance pay.

## Vacations, Holidays, and Breaks

Most major employers go beyond the two or three weeks of vacation mandated by law (depending on the jurisdiction) and the nine statutory holidays, to give 11–13 paid holidays on fixed dates and up to three paid "floater" holidays that can be moved around from year to year. Most workplaces also give two paid rest breaks of 15–20 minutes (besides an unpaid lunch break) during a seven- or eight-hour day.

One new twist on vacations is the concept of "vacation buying or selling." Some firms allow employees to "buy" additional vacation days by forgoing the pay for these days. Conversely, employees can "sell" back to the employer any vacation days they don't intend to use. Essentially, vacation buying or selling simply provides some additional flexibility for employees. For some interesting benefits, including paid vacations, see Compensation Today 12.2.

---

## COMPENSATION TODAY 12.2

### GO WEST!

Have you ever been to Athabasca, Boyle, Lac La Biche, or Grassland in Alberta? Would you consider living and working in any of these communities? Well, if you would, Alberta-Pacific Forest Industries Inc. offers an interest-free loan of $25 000 to new employees. You will also start with four weeks paid vacation with the option to take the fourth week as time off or as additional income. With tenure, you will move up to 7.5 weeks of vacation. The company has a flexible personal time-off program as part of its health plan (with employees averaging 12 personal days off each year), and each employee receives an annual $3800 taxable lifestyle contribution that can be used toward alternative health coverage or even to purchase more vacation time. Alberta-Pacific Forest Industries Inc. offers up to 100 percent employer-sponsored health plan premiums and a health care spending account of $500 a year. The company also offers employees free membership to the on-site fitness facilities with treadmills, stationary bikes, stairmasters, instructor-led classes (boot camp held periodically), weights, shower facilities, weigh scales, and television and music system. The company has a defined-contribution pension and a matching RSP program. Furthermore, employees are offered parental benefits, with a maternity leave top-up of 100 percent for 18 weeks and an academic scholarship program for employees' children of $1250 per child per year.

Alberta-Pacific Forest Industries Inc. has also set up many training programs including an Aboriginal apprenticeship program, a leadership development program, a tuition reimbursement program up to 100 percent of the cost, as well as financial bonuses for the completion of certain accreditations ranging from $1500 to $10 000. The result is amazing. The company was recognized as one of the top employers in both Alberta and Canada in 2020. Alberta-Pacific Forest Industries also won the 2018 Leadership Award from the Forest Stewardship Council, the most reputable forest certification encouraging environmental, social, and economic governance. Among its over 400 full-time employees, the longest-serving has 30 years tenure!

Source: Richard Yerema and Kristina Leung, Mediacorp Canada Inc. staff editors, *Canada's Top 100 Employers*, November 8, 2015, http://content.eluta .ca/top-employer-alpac; Richard Yerema and Kristina Leung, *Alberta-Pacific Forest Industries Inc Recognized as One of Alberta's Top Employers*, Mediacorp Canada Inc., February 19, 2020, http://content.eluta .ca/top-employer-alpac; "Alberta-Pacific Forest Industries Inc. Receives 2018 Forest Stewardship Council Leadership Award for World Leading Practices," *NewsWire*, November 16, 2018; "Scholarships and Awards," *Alberta Pacific Forest Industries Inc*, https://alpac.ca/corporate-responsibility/community-investment/scholarships.

## Sickness, Compassionate, and Personal Absences

Most employers provide pay continuation for short-term absences from work due to illness or for other specified reasons, such as the death of a family member. Some firms have formal plans that allot a certain number of allowable sick days in a given period, beyond which wages will not be paid. In some cases, sick days can accumulate beyond a year; in most cases, they cannot. In other cases, employers do not formally provide sick leave, but neither do they dock absences if the missing time is made up at some future time. In still other cases, absences may be counted against the annual vacation allotment.

One issue is whether the only allowable paid absences are for personal illness, or whether other reasons (such as illness of a child) are allowable. Some firms refer to their "sick leave" days as "personal leave" days to avoid forcing employees to claim personal illness when the actual reason is an illness or personal emergency involving a family member. In other cases, employers roll all leave days together, including vacation and sick leave, and provide these as the total allowable number of paid absences. In a few cases, employers are willing to "buy back" unused leave days so that employees who do not use all their allotted days are not penalized relative to employees who do use all their leave days. However, it may not be wise to buy back all these days at full rates if this creates too strong an incentive for employees to come to work even when they are seriously ill.

Many firms also offer compassionate or bereavement leaves to permit employees to attend the funerals of close family members. All employers in the federal jurisdiction are required to provide unpaid compassionate care leave for employees who must be absent from work to provide support to a child, parent, spouse, or common-law partner who is gravely ill with a serious risk of death, and their jobs must be held for them until their return to work. Most major firms also provide paid leave for jury duty. Short-term absences to give birth or attend the birth of a child are also included here. (Longer-term maternity/paternity leaves will be discussed shortly.)

One way to help address the need for short-term absences is through a flexible-hours or a flexible-workplace program. For example, Cisco Canada allows its employees to work where, when, and how they want. Traditional working hours are not expected, as 48 percent of employees' work time is found to be outside of regular working hours. Also, 25 percent of the average employees' work is done at home.[26]

## Supplemental Unemployment Benefits

When an employee is temporarily laid off and must go on Employment Insurance, many firms offer **supplemental unemployment benefits (SUBs)**, which are designed to "top up" the EI benefits to some proportion of the employee's normal pay. The usual process is for the employer to set up a fund to which it contributes regular amounts based on the number of hours worked by employees. This fund is then used to provide the supplemental unemployment benefits to eligible employees; it may also include employees on maternity or paternity leave. But the firm's liability is limited to the amount in the fund. Note that these plans must be approved and registered with the Employment Insurance Commission.

**supplemental unemployment benefits (SUBs)**
An employer-provided benefit that extends government-provided unemployment benefits

## Parental Leaves

Some firms may also offer some period of paid maternity or paternity leave, usually in conjunction with Employment Insurance, which provides coverage for up to 50 weeks of maternity or paternity leave (but not both to the same couple at the same time). Firms may treat maternity or paternity leave in the same way as a temporary layoff and use funds from their supplemental unemployment fund to top up the employee's EI benefits to a certain proportion of normal income. Or if the firm does not have a SUB fund, it may simply have a policy for topping up EI in the case of maternity or paternity leave.

## Educational and Sabbatical Leaves

Some organizations have paid educational leave plans, in which employees are compensated while undertaking a full-time educational program. In some cases, full pay is provided, while in others some portion of normal pay is provided. There is normally an expectation that the employee will return to the employer after completing the educational program, and employees who don't return are usually expected to reimburse the employer for the cost of the leave. Because of their high cost, these plans are usually restricted to key individuals within the organization, and/or there may be some competitive process that awards a restricted number of paid leaves each year.

In some cases, firms offer unpaid sabbaticals. To facilitate sabbaticals, the Income Tax Act has created some opportunities for employees to defer income taxes while putting aside money for the sabbatical. Once an employer has registered a sabbatical leave plan with the Canada Revenue Agency, employees may put aside a portion of their earnings each year for a period of three to five years prior to the sabbatical. For example, schoolteachers in Toronto may set aside a fifth of their annual income for four years and then receive this money in the fifth (sabbatical) year. There are two tax advantages to this plan. First, the earnings from the deferred salary fund can accumulate tax-free until the funds are withdrawn. Second, the total amount of tax paid is reduced because income is being "smoothed." Instead of being taxed for four years at a higher marginal rate (and then having zero income in the sabbatical year), income is spread evenly over the five-year period.

## Severance Pay

The ultimate form of pay for time not worked is severance pay. The federal and provincial jurisdictions have statutory requirements either for notice to be provided when terminating employees without cause or for pay in lieu of this notice, but these requirements are quite minimal. For example, for employers covered by the federal jurisdiction, the only requirement is two weeks' notice, as long as an employee has been employed for at least three months. In Ontario, the requirement is generally a week's notice (or pay in lieu of notice) for each year of service up to eight years, to a maximum of eight weeks. Unionized firms typically have a formula that goes beyond these minimums for providing a lump-sum payment to employees who receive permanent termination. At the executive level, extensive severance packages ("golden parachutes") are often negotiated on an individual basis at the time of employment.

Technically, if an employee has been dismissed for cause, no notice or severance pay is required.[27] However, unless cause can be proven, an employer may end up with a wrongful dismissal suit against it and be required to pay a substantial severance award if it loses the suit. There are no hard and fast rules specifying the minimum notice for a given employee. However, based on court settlements, the following would seem to be the minimal notice amounts for fair severance in cases of termination without cause: for labourers, production workers, clerical workers, administrative support staff: two weeks per year of service, two-month minimum; for technical, professional, supervisory, and middle management: three weeks per year of service, three-month minimum; and for senior management: four weeks per year of service, four-month minimum. For all groups, the maximum is 24 months.

In setting notice periods (or severance amounts in lieu of notice), courts take several factors into account: (1) the employee's age, (2) the length of service, (3) the character of the employment, (4) the availability of similar employment, and (5) whether enticement was involved. Essentially, the more difficult it is for an employee to find similar employment, the longer the notice period. Beyond this, the notice period is extended dramatically if an employer had enticed the terminated employee away from secure employment in a different region or country, and this applies even to new employees and to employees who have not yet started their employment with the firm.[28] Though the general rule of thumb is one month per year, recently, Ontario courts have awarded far more than this for cases of enticement. The Ontario courts have considered the number of years worked at the previous place of employment as part of the severance pay calculation even to clerical employees or unskilled labour, and have made sizable awards even to employees with little or no seniority with the current firm. There has been no hard cap in notice periods in such cases.[29]

# EMPLOYEE SERVICES

Employee services are often not included in traditional surveys of employee benefits but are often of considerable value to employees and may produce some favourable spinoffs for the organization. A major advantage of these services is that most are tax-deductible to the employer and are not subject to income tax for employees. This section discusses several of the most common and important employee services.

## Employee Assistance Programs

Most large Canadian firms have established **employee assistance programs (EAPs)** to help employees deal with personal problems that have the potential to affect their work performance.[30] One problem covered by EAPs is substance abuse and addiction. In these cases, the firm may contract the services of professional counsellors or other specialists, who help employees to diagnose their problems and chart a course of action for dealing with them. This course of action may include paid leave to attend alcohol or drug treatment centres and coverage of the costs of these programs.

EAPs may also deal with other problems, such as stress; workplace conflict; and marital, family, or financial problems, either through the use of in-house counsellors or through referrals to outside specialists. (During the 2008–09 financial meltdown, the use of EAP services soared in firms that offered them, as a result of employee financial worries.[31]) Some organizations maintain 24-hour counselling hotlines.

There are obvious advantages to the employer if the EAP can help solve these problems because many of them have the potential to severely affect work performance or cause safety problems. Also, unresolved problems may cause valued employees to quit the firm. In some cases, EAPs provide an alternative to simply firing troubled employees, an act that may be seen as hardhearted and that may damage employee morale. Indeed, in order to effectively dismiss a problem employee and to avoid or win a wrongful dismissal suit, a company will need to show that it did all it could to solve the problem, and employee assistance programs can be used as evidence that the firm attempted to do so.

## Wellness Programs and Recreational Services

Some organizations sponsor company sports teams or help support other types of recreational programs. In addition, some firms provide on-site fitness centres or exercise rooms. Hamilton-based steelmaker ArcelorMittal Dofasco provides a recreation and learning

**employee assistance programs (EAPs)**
Employer-provided programs to help employees deal with a variety of personal problems.

Some firms provide wellness programs.

centre that includes two NHL-size arenas, a twin gym, a track, a golf driving range, tennis courts, baseball diamonds, and a playground.[32] Use of these facilities is typically nontaxable for the employees, as long as they are not operated as commercial ventures. Alternatively, some organizations purchase memberships in recreational clubs or sports facilities for employees and their families, but these do become taxable benefits for the employees if used.

Some firms provide these benefits in a broader context of a "wellness program," which typically deals with three main health issues: (1) individual health practices, such as smoking, inactivity, and unhealthy diets; (2) organizational health issues, such as lack of job satisfaction and stress; and (3) the physical work environment, such as ergonomics and musculoskeletal injury prevention.[33] Proponents argue that such programs can benefit the organization in a wide variety of ways, including reduced absenteeism, reduced health benefit costs, and higher employee productivity.[34] Overall, the trend toward such programs is gaining momentum—at least among medium to large employers—as the business case for investments in workplace health and wellness gets easier to make.[35] Compensation Today 12.3 illustrates an interesting wellness program.

## Child Care and Elder Care Services

As much as 44 percent of children in Canada that are not yet school-aged live in areas deemed, "child care deserts," regions in which there is one spot available per three or more children.[36] The high-quality child care that is available in Toronto can cost as much a $3400 a month for two children.[37] Some employers offer on-site daycares; however, most employers that have a program to support childcare use third-party services.[38] In Canada, eight percent of employers offer on-site child care, five percent of employers offer financial assistance for regular childcare, and 13 percent of employers offer emergency child care services.[39] In addition, Employee Assistance Programs offer child care information and referral services. These subsidies are not considered a taxable benefit.

### HUNGRY? GO HEALTHY!

At the Nature's Path home office in Richmond, British Columbia, employees are encouraged to enjoy healthy snacks with a fully stocked store available for them at significantly reduced costs. Apart from the matching RSP and health plans, which the company pays up to 50 percent of the premiums, the company provides a wide variety of benefits. The company offers an on-site fitness facility, instructor-led fitness classes, personal trainer services, and an annual $500 wellness subsidy toward the purchase of gym memberships or home fitness equipment. The company also organizes an annual health and wellness week, which includes meditation and yoga sessions, nutritionists, and biometric screening.

Employees also manage their own activity-based clubs, including running, walking, and even a juicing group. Nature's Path maintains a highly focused charitable program that is very much integrated into its core line of business, including the "Gardens for Good" and the longstanding "EnviroKidz 1% for the Planet" program. Their annual Live Green Week includes lunch and learns, movies, and initiatives to support the earth, such as garbage clean up. Nature's Path has established a zero-waste target and even has a unique employee-maintained on-site organic garden where employees can stroll outside and practise a little therapeutic gardening to unwind during a busy day.

Sources: *Canada's Top 100 Employers*, https://reviews.canadastop100.com/top-employer-natures-path-foods; Nature's Path website, https://www.naturespath.com/en-ca/

At the other end of the spectrum, some employees have the responsibility to care for aged parents or other elderly relatives. Most employer-sponsored elder care programs simply provide information and referral services through an employee assistance program.[40] Elder care support may be regarding topics such as outreach programs and transportation services, long-term accommodation options, and healthcare-related services. Given the demographic trends in Canada, the issue of elder care is of growing importance to many employees. If not dealt with effectively, it has the potential to lead to problems for both employees and employer, including stress-related problems and even withdrawal from the workplace.

Over eight million Canadians are caregivers, and 43 percent of employed caregivers have noted that they have arrived to work late, left work early, or had to take time off to care for ill family members.[41] Particularly under stress will be those employees who are responsible for both child care and elder care—the so-called "sandwich generation." Currently, 42 percent of Canadian parents with children under 15 years old are between 40 and 59 years old and are therefore often responsible for taking care of both their children and their elderly parents.[42]

Child care benefits are increasingly being demanded by families.

## Work/Life Balance Programs

Given all the stresses of balancing work and family life, many firms have created "work/life balance" programs to minimize these stresses as much as possible.[43] Work/life balance programs typically include many of the features discussed so far, such as flexible schedules, parental and personal leave programs, health care programs, child care and elder care programs, and wellness programs. However, while many organizations view work/life balance as an essential element of a total rewards program, a major survey tracking work/life balance among Canadian employees in 1991, 2001, and 2011–12 found that work/life balance had not improved over time; work demands were increasing, yet the availability of alternative work arrangements such as flextime had actually been declining since 2001.[44] Compensation Today 12.4 illustrates aspects of work/life balance (and other benefits).

## Financial or Legal Services

As retirement and financial planning becomes more and more complex, some firms are providing employees with access to financial planners to help them make good financial decisions. This service is most likely to be offered by firms with flexible benefit plans to help employees understand the ramifications of the choices they make.

In some companies, prepaid legal services are provided. There are two main types of legal plans. Access plans provide free telephone or office consultation, document review, and discounts on fees for more complex matters. Comprehensive plans cover matters such as real estate transactions, divorce cases, and civil and criminal cases.

---

### COMPENSATION TODAY 12.4

#### TAKING PRIDE IN HERITAGE

Aboriginal Peoples Television Network Inc. (APTN) is a television network for Aboriginal people and by Aboriginal people with programs in English, French, and Indigenous languages. While producing programming for both Aboriginal and non-Aboriginal audiences and employing a multicultural workforce, 66 percent of the employees self-declared as First Nations, Inuit, or Métis (in 2013). To instill pride among the employees, inside the downtown head office in Winnipeg, the walls are painted using an Aboriginal colour scheme of blue, red, and yellow, and custom-made boardroom tables reflect the traditional medicine wheel. The company offers a defined contribution pension plan and a variety of health and family-friendly benefits for employees working more than 21 hours a week. Some of the many benefits include an employee assistance program and employee and family assistance program, and northern living allowances and housing allowances for those located in Iqaluit. New mothers receive a parental leave top-up of 93 percent in the first week, and then 80 percent of salary for 16 weeks. New fathers and adoptive parents receive parental leave top-up of 80 percent for 16 weeks. Uniquely, the company offers an on-site reflexologist, massage therapist, and cranial sacral therapist bi-weekly as well as meditation once a week. In terms of personal development, employees are provided with the opportunity to be fully subsidized for their education or provide coverage of $1800 for job-related courses per year, as well as in-house career planning and leadership training. APTN encourages employees to actively volunteer and support community initiatives. Among the community organizations supported are United Way, Ma Maw Wi Chi Itata Centre, Alzheimer Society's Memory Walk, Christmas Cheer Board (sponsoring a family at Christmas), Broadway Neighbourhood Centre, Habitat for Humanity, Winnipeg Aboriginal Film Festival, Vision Quest Conference, and Soaring Indigenous Youth Career Conference. The company was recognized as one of Canada's top 100 employers and Manitoba's top employers in 2020.

Sources: APTN website, https://corporate.aptn.ca/; Richard Yerema and Kristina Leung, Mediacorp Canada Inc. staff editors, November 21, 2019, *Canada's Top 100 Employers*, https://reviews.canadastop100.com/top-employer-aboriginal-peoples-television-network.

---

## Food Services

Many organizations offer subsidized food services at company facilities. This program may be necessary on sites where food services are not readily available. An advantage of on-site food services is that employees do not need to waste scarce break time by leaving the company premises. In addition, subsidized food services constitute a taxable benefit for employees only if prices are set "unreasonably low." Employers can provide free food to employees without it becoming a taxable benefit to employees if business is conducted during the meal (i.e., a "lunch meeting") or if the food is provided in the context of over-time work, as long as the employee works at least three hours following his or her normal shift and it does not occur more than twice a week.

## Outplacement Services

Finally, some firms provide assistance to employees whose jobs are being terminated, beyond simply awarding severance pay. This assistance may include advice on how to secure new employment and how to manage financial affairs until new employment is found, as well as counselling to ease the shock of termination. Although these services will, by definition, not be used by continuing employees, employees notice whether terminated employees are being treated fairly, and this will condition their attitudes toward the employer; thus, provision of these services has a positive impact beyond the direct recipients.

# MISCELLANEOUS BENEFITS

Organizations can provide a wide array of other benefits, often related to the type of work an employee does or to the type of industry in which the firm operates.[45] For example, sales personnel who must travel extensively by automobile are often provided with a vehicle, which can also serve personal uses (although the personal use portion is taxable). Retailers may provide discounts on their products. Banks may provide subsidized loans. In general, businesses may provide their own products or services to their employees at a discounted rate, and these discounts will not constitute a taxable benefit to employees, unless they are provided at prices below cost. Other commonly offered benefits include tuition reimbursement and the provision of work equipment or clothing.

In the past, many firms have offered employee savings plans, where contributions by employees to company-sponsored savings plans are supplemented by employer contributions. However, with the development of RRSPs, many firms have converted these savings plans into group RRSP programs, which have significant tax advantages over nonregistered savings plans. With the introduction of the Tax-Free Savings Account (TFSA) by the federal government in 2009, some firms may elect to make these plans available as another savings option for their employees.[46] Contributions to TFSAs are not tax-deductible; however, the earnings on these accounts are not taxable at any time, unlike RRSPs, where the earnings are taxable on withdrawal.

# FIXED VERSUS FLEXIBLE BENEFIT SYSTEMS

How would you like to be able to pick and choose among the benefits your firm offers, selecting only the benefits of value to you, or possibly even forgoing some benefits and receiving the equivalent in cash? Some Canadian employers, such as IBM Canada, DuPont, and Husky Oil, are now giving employees this flexibility. These "flexible benefit plans" have become popular in recent years, in contrast to the fixed benefit plans that held sway for many years. Both plans have their advantages and disadvantages, and one of these plans may fit a given firm much better than the other plan.

## FIXED BENEFIT SYSTEMS

In **fixed benefit systems**, which have been the norm, all employees are covered by a standard package of benefits. The advantages of this approach include simplicity, economies of scale in purchasing the benefits, relatively low administrative costs, and ease in communicating the plan to employees. The key disadvantage of this approach is that it does not recognize differences among employees regarding how much they may value each benefit. Also, fixed benefit plans have a tendency to grow in cost as existing benefits escalate in cost or as new benefits are added to meet the diverse needs of the workforce. Existing benefits are seldom dropped to make way for new benefits.

## SEMI-FLEXIBLE BENEFIT SYSTEMS

Most benefits systems are not entirely fixed. When they are not fixed but don't meet the criteria to be considered a flexible benefit system, they are known as "semi-flexible benefit systems" or "simplified flex plans."[47]

There are a variety of ways to make fixed systems more flexible. The most common approach starts with a "core" set of benefits, to which employees "add on" additional levels of coverage or additional benefit options at their own expense, using after-tax dollars. (Note, however, that in some circumstances, the Canada Revenue Agency will permit employees to convert part or all of a performance bonus into flexible credits using pre-tax dollars.[48])

For some firms, the only flexible component is a health care spending account, which is becomingly increasingly popular as an "add-on" to traditional fixed benefit plans. Another approach is the "modular plan," in which employees are given the choice between two or more fixed benefit packages, each of which is designed to be of similar cost to the company. However, this type of modular plan is rarely used.

## FLEXIBLE BENEFIT SYSTEMS

The distinguishing feature of a **flexible benefit system** is employee control over the disposition of benefits funds provided by the employer, in addition to any funds that employees themselves provide. In a fully flexible approach, there is no "core" or "standard" benefits package. Instead, employees receive a set of "flexible credits" that they can use to "purchase" the combination of benefits that best suits them. An example of this approach is the "Beneflex®" system at telecommunications giant Telus, under which an employee can select several different levels of coverage (including none) for each of numerous benefits. Employees can also use real money (i.e., their after-tax earnings) to purchase higher levels of particular benefits after their "flexible credits" run out. If they have any unused flexible credits, they can take them in the form of cash (which, however, is then fully taxable as employment income).

Canada's first flexible benefit plan was introduced in 1984 by Cominco Mining (now Teck Resources Limited), based in Vancouver.[49] During the early 1990s, flexible benefit plans were the fastest growing pay innovation in Canada,[50] and by 2004, about 29 percent of firms were using them, according to research conducted by one of the authors. The popularity of these plans has since plateaued with about 29 percent of medium to large private sector firms using them in 2012, and about 20 percent of public sector organizations.[51] However, a 2013 Sun Life Financial study found that 70 percent of their Millennial plan members would prefer a flexible benefits plan over a traditional plan.[52]

Compensation Today 12.5 describes the flexible benefits program at KPMG Canada.

## Forces Promoting Adoption of Flexible Benefits

Flexible benefit plans began in the United States where employers found themselves subject to skyrocketing benefit costs, especially health insurance costs. The main impetus was benefits cost reduction or containment. Although Canadian firms have also been subject to increasing benefit costs, it has been much less due to government-funded medicare. While there is concern that rising prescription drug costs coupled with an aging workforce may increase health benefits costs in the future, there has been a much lower incentive for Canadian firms to adopt flexible benefits in comparison to the United States.

---

### COMPENSATION TODAY 12.5

#### FLEXIBLE BENEFITS AT KPMG CANADA

In 2016, KPMG Canada was at a crossroads with their benefits program. Several factors highlighted the need for a change. KPMG observed employees' evolving needs. Employees felt that the benefits program was arduous to comprehend and expressed concerns that their total rewards package was not competitive with the market. The new management team did not feel that the program had a high return on investment. Thus, management realized that the compensation system required redesigning.

Management first outlined their goals: agile and flexible to changing business needs; valuable to employees; all-encompassing to its multi-generational labour pool; simple to execute and uncomplicated for employees to access; easily assessed through key performance indicators.

The company revamped its compensation system in a two-stage process. The first stage involved significant changes to their direct compensation system. The second stage, which started in 2018, involved a change in their benefits offering.

Before the changes, KPMG had 20 lifestyle programs that were available on a use-it-or-lose-it plan. Also, employees had a fixed benefits plan for medical, dental, and drug coverage, and if employees were not using the benefit, the money was lost as well.

KPMG reconfigured the benefits plan to make it less complicated. They created a wellness pool. A set amount of money is accessible to each employee to be used toward a healthcare

spending account, a lifestyle spending account, flexible benefits, and savings alternatives, including a group tax-free savings account and a group registered retirement savings plan. The lifestyle and healthcare spending accounts include offerings such as elder care, backup childcare, nutrition, meditation, fitness, financial advisors, and many other options. If an employee selects coverage for dependants or a spouse as well, the program addresses the fact that the employee would have an added premium that would increase costs. Therefore, the system will give the employee extra money to cover such fees, and thus, such employees are given more in their wellness pool to finance the added cost.

The core medical, dental, and drug benefits were adjusted so that employees could tailor the plans to their needs. Employees are now able to either pull out from a specific benefit altogether, or select a basic, comprehensive, or premium level of coverage for medical, dental, and drug benefits. Employees can also place money from the wellness pool into their flexible benefits to increase their coverage.

The new benefit plan also offers free programs that are accessible to all employees, including an employee assistance program, adoption assistance, enhanced parental leave, and a defined contribution pension plan. Furthermore, all employees are granted $2000 toward mental-health coverage.

Thus far, the new benefits plan has been a hit with employees. Not only is the plan more flexible and tailored to individual needs, but employees feel that the program is more straightforward, and employees have a better understanding of the funding that they are receiving.

Source: Kelsey Rolfe, "How KPMG Canada Flexed Its Benefits Program with a Plan Redesign," *Insurable Interest*, August 16, 2019.

Firms that are the most concerned about benefit costs are those that, over time, have found themselves with very expensive benefit packages. As benefit costs increase, firms could simply reduce coverage, increase deductibles, or increase employee contributions, without recourse to a flexible benefit plan at all, and some firms have been doing this.[53] But flex plans allow employee preferences to play a major role in the evolution of the benefit package. At New Brunswick Power Corporation, a jointly developed flexible benefit plan reduced projected health benefit costs dramatically, to the benefit of both the employer and employees, as Compensation Today 12.6 describes.

Another possible reason for implementing flexible benefit plans is the increasing diversity of the workforce. Most traditional benefit systems were developed in an era when the typical employee was a married man with a spouse not employed outside the home and several dependant children. For example, in 1967, two-thirds of Canadian families fit this model.[54] Because of the homogeneity of this workforce, it was relatively easy to come up with a standard benefit package that would suit this "typical" employee. But by 1992, in 61 percent of married couples, both spouses were employed—in some cases by the same employer. Because benefit plans typically cover all members of a family, often the traditional benefits package unnecessarily duplicates benefit coverage. Research shows that, when employees are given various medical plan options, and they are married to someone who is insured under another plan, the employee typically opts for a minimum level of coverage.[55]

Moreover, as the workforce has become more diverse, there has been increased demand for additional types of benefits, such as child care or elder care, to supplement the traditional benefits. Flexible benefits are seen as one way of dealing with this diversity without

---

## COMPENSATION TODAY 12.6

### FLEXIBLE BENEFITS POWER SAVINGS AT THE POWER COMPANY

In 1999, projections at New Brunswick Power Corporation (NBPC) indicated that the annual costs of its health benefit plan would rise from $5.3 million in that year to $20 million in 2009–10. The company couldn't unilaterally change the benefit plan because 2200 of its 2700 workers were unionized. However, because of a good relationship with its union, the company was able to share this problem with the union leadership and ask for their help in solving it. Reduced health benefit costs would benefit union members, because under the collective agreement, benefit costs are shared 60–40 between the company and its workers.

Over the course of a year, management and the union worked together to create a voluntary flexible benefit plan that workers could opt into if they wished. From this new plan, employees would continue to be offered basic life, accidental death and dismemberment, long-term disability, dental, and medical. In addition, employees had the option of choosing to purchase further coverage from the optional benefits. By 2003, 68 percent of workers had opted for the flexible system. Combined with a plan redesign, the projected expenditure for health benefits in 2009–10 was reduced to $11.6 million. In 2013, the power company increased its contribution by an additional $7.69 biweekly to $16, and, as of 2016 and retroactive to 2015, the power company increased its contribution an additional $4 biweekly to $20. Nonetheless, NBPC continues to pay less relative to a fixed benefit system. Even more so, the company has received numerous awards for its positive work environment, including Waterstone Human Capitals' award as one of Canada's Most Admired Corporate Cultures in 2017 and Morneau Shepell's Employee Recommended Workplace Award in 2018 and 2019.

Sources: Todd Humber, "The Power to Change," *Canadian HR Reporter*, May 31, 2004, G1–G10; Collective Agreement (2012–5); http://www.ibew37.com/uploads/Generation_20130215.pdf, accessed October 3, 2016; Agreement Between New Brunswick Power Corporation and Local 37 of the International Brotherhood of Electrical Workers (2014–9), https://www.ibew37.com/wp-content/uploads/Nuclear.pdf

raising the costs of the benefits package to the employer. The company simply makes the new benefit available, and employees who want the benefit then re-deploy their benefits credits from other benefits less valuable to them until they come up with the combination that best suits their personal needs. As their needs and circumstances change, they can realign their benefits accordingly. Essentially, this plan allows employees to maximize the value of the benefits system for any given level of benefits expenditure by the employer.

Another impetus for flexible benefits is that employers may want to change the attitude among employees that benefits are an entitlement (i.e., something provided as a condition of employment). They may want to foster the idea that benefits are not granted but are actually a form of pay that must be earned. Flexible benefit systems can encourage employees to understand the cost and value of the benefits they are being provided.

Yet another factor in play is managerial strategy (see Chapter 2). When human relations organizations move toward the high-involvement model or the classical model, their attitudes toward benefits tend to change. Flexible benefits are attractive to both high-involvement and classical organizations, albeit for opposite reasons. For high-involvement organizations, flexible benefits fit with the concept of partnership, as well as with the belief that employees are responsible individuals capable of choosing their benefits more wisely than the firm could for them. Flexible benefit plans are simply one more way of increasing employee involvement and self-control in the workplace.

By contrast, classical organizations may simply see flexible benefits as an opportunity to cut benefits costs, although, as will be discussed shortly, such plans may actually be less successful in classical organizations than in other types of organizations. Research by one of the authors shows that high-involvement firms are much more likely to have flex plans than are other firms.

Firms that do not have a benefits package may find flexible benefits appealing. These employers may have stayed away from fixed benefit plans to avoid getting enmeshed in a program where costs can get out of hand. In this regard, a flex plan can be viewed as a type of defined contribution plan, in which the employer commits to making a limited sum of money available for benefits. Thus, there is less exposure for the employer if certain benefits escalate in cost.

Firms with flex plans may enjoy a competitive advantage in terms of employee recruitment and retention. First, prospective employees may find the idea of choosing their benefits appealing. Second, if the flex plan is designed and communicated properly, firms with these plans should be able to deliver more value to their employees than firms without flex plans for the same number of benefits dollars. Of course, this assumes that the flex plan is not so expensive to administer that the firm is forced to reduce the number of dollars it contributes to the plan, or to pay more for benefits because of loss of economies of scale (see below). It also assumes that flex plans are seen as attractive by prospective employees and not simply as code words for an inferior benefits plan.

Finally, as knowledge accumulates about any innovative practice, it becomes easier to apply. Many benefits consultants now have considerable experience working with flex plans and can guide and promote implementation of these plans. In addition, computer software makes the administration of a flex plan efficient and user-friendly.

## Forces Deterring Adoption of Flexible Benefits

Several factors can impede the adoption of flexible benefits plans. These include the cost of implementation and administration, the loss of economies of scale when benefits are purchased, possible confusion and poor decision making among employees, lack of fit with the organizational culture, and possible resistance from employees or unions.

One-time implementation costs in developing a flexible plan can be substantial. These include the costs of the personnel involved in the design process, as well as the costs of consultants. Few firms have the in-house expertise to develop such a plan without help from consultants.

In addition, administration and communication costs are likely to be much higher than with other benefits systems. Costing out the various options, predicting employee take-up, and pricing the benefits options fairly is a complex process. Additional tasks include informing employees about their options and the tradeoffs involved, and simply managing the paperwork. Add to this the fact that employees may be tinkering with their benefits packages every year, and it is clear that the additional administrative burden is substantial. However, this administrative burden can be reduced by new spreadsheet packages that allow employees to calculate their various options and costs and then submit their benefit choices. Outsourcing benefits administration to specialized firms may also reduce administrative costs.

Another problem with flex plans is the possible loss of economies of scale in purchasing benefits from suppliers. For example, most insurance is much cheaper if purchased in volume. If there is relatively low take-up on some benefits, the costs of these benefits will be higher. There is also the issue of adverse selection (adverse from the perspective of the insurance company, not the employee!), in the sense that, for example, employees with large families afflicted with many dental problems may load up on dental coverage, while those with no dental problems may forgo it entirely. Or people in ill health may be the only ones purchasing medical coverage. These situations drive up the costs of these benefits tremendously. To combat this problem, some firms impose mandatory minimum levels of some benefits, but this goes against the flexibility concept. Thus, for all these reasons, flex plans may actually increase benefits costs, to both the employer and the employee.

Another drawback is that employees can become confused by the array of choices. Research has found that more options can lead to stress. Individuals have restrictions as to the volume in which they can absorb, and if that amount is surpassed, cognitive costs ensue. The larger and more convoluted the choice is the increased capability for errors in decision making.[56] What are the odds that an employee will select the best possible combination for them? Critics of flex plans argue that this complexity can lead to poor benefits decisions and decreased satisfaction with benefits.

Another possible obstacle to flex plans is company culture. Human relations firms may be reluctant to move to flexible benefits for fear that the system will be too complex for employees, or that employees will make unwise benefits choices that leave them without coverage in the event of emergencies. And in classical organizations, flexible benefits may fail if such firms are unwilling to commit the resources necessary to effectively communicate their plans to employees and if the employees have little faith in the information they do receive because employees often have low trust of classical organizations. Employees and unions in classical organizations may have especially strong resistance to flex plans, fearing that such plans are simply a way to trick them into accepting reduced benefits.

Finally, some benefits consultants are starting to turn against completely flexible systems, arguing that they are too complex to serve employees well and that they don't serve many employers well because of their high administrative costs, which wipe out any savings.[57] These critics argue that semiflexible systems might be the best choice if the goal is to balance employee needs against administrative complexity. The advent of health care spending accounts may encourage semiflexible systems, by adding a flexible element to an otherwise fixed plan.

## Experience with Flexible Benefit Systems

Flexible benefits plans have been in use in Canada for over 20 years, yet there is very little research regarding their impact on benefits costs. Research conducted by one of the authors in the early 2000s compared firms that had flex plans with those that did not and found almost no difference in the percentage of benefits as a proportion of their total compensation. For both groups of firms, it averaged about 16 percent in 2004 (the last year for which data are available). Interestingly, four years earlier, firms with flex plans had devoted about 14 percent of total compensation to benefits, while firms without flex plans devoted about 15 percent. This suggested that flex plans did not reduce employer costs, although they may have increased the value of benefits to employees.

Although one must always be cautious when generalizing from a single study, the results suggest that flex plans in Canada may have had very little impact on benefits costs, consistent with the views of some consultants.[58] If so, this would help explain why the popularity of flex plans has apparently plateaued in Canada.

Leaving costs aside, have these plans had any impact on employee satisfaction with their compensation? Unfortunately, evidence is also sparse on this question. However, research has found that if a company switches to a flexible plan unless the plan is adequately communicated to its employees, employees may not reap its benefits. A survey from the United States found that 35 percent of employees have limited or no comprehension of their benefits coverage, and 62 percent of employees felt that their employer did not provide support for their benefits-related questions.[59] If the new flexible benefits plan is not adequately communicated and explained to employees, employees may select options similar to the coverage they had previously, and thus feel no more satisfied with the change in coverage.[60]

Other research indicates that employee satisfaction with flexible benefits plans depends on the level of benefits flexibility. Employees are less satisfied when employees are offered limited packages as opposed to a high degree of flexibility. This finding is consistent with the person-organization fit approach. Different benefit options have the potential to attract and retain employees. Thus, a flexible benefits plan allows for a wider variety of potential employees if their varying compensation needs could be met.[61] However, as stated previously from other research findings, too many benefit combinations can be detrimental. Thus, there is a need to find the correct balance, though there is limited research on the optimal number of combinations.[62]

As to what effects a flexible benefits system has on overall employee behaviour, almost nothing is known. To date, the few studies that have addressed this question are from publications outside of North America. The first study that reviewed the effects of the flexible benefits system was undertaken in Holland and Belgium, where majorities of HR managers believed that flexible benefits increased a firm's ability to attract and retain employees (86 percent for attraction; 65 percent for retention).[63] Another study that was undertaken in Spain found that a higher degree of flexibility (as compared to a flexible benefits system with limited packages), had a more significant positive effect on employee behaviour. A more flexible benefits plan positively affected retention rates. However, no significant impact was found for the attraction of potential employees to the company. The findings on retention make sense. Higher employee satisfaction with their compensation increases employee retention. However, the authors contributed to the lack of impact on attraction to the firm as being because the average Spanish employee may lack sufficient knowledge about this type of plan. Thus, perhaps a strategy hiring managers could use is to clearly communicate the advantages of a flexible benefits plan.[64]

## DESIGNING THE BENEFIT SYSTEM

To develop an effective benefits system, organizations need to address five questions. First, can the provision of benefits help achieve compensation objectives? If so, how? And what objectives should be set for indirect pay? Second, what will be the process for designing the plan? Third, what benefits system will be used, and what specific benefits will be included? Fourth, how should each individual benefit be structured regarding coverage, funding, eligibility, and flexibility? And fifth, what procedures for administering, communicating, evaluating, and adapting the benefits system are needed?

We will examine these issues to develop an understanding of benefits design. However, this chapter will make no attempt to deal with all the details involved in plan design. Benefits are the most technically complex aspect of the entire compensation system and dealing with all the technical details would require an entire book. Fortunately, some excellent sources of these technical details are available.[65]

### ISSUE 1: DETERMINE THE ROLE OF INDIRECT PAY IN THE COMPENSATION STRATEGY

The first issue in establishing an indirect pay system is to identify what compensation objectives it will serve beyond those that can be served by direct pay. (Ideally, this will have been done when formulating the compensation strategy as discussed in Chapter 6.) The role that indirect pay will play in generating the desired employee behaviour needs to be defined; this in turn will inform choices about the type of benefits system (if any) to be developed and the specific benefits to be included.

As discussed in Chapter 4, examples of possible roles to be served by indirect pay may include encouraging membership, retaining senior employees, satisfying lower-order needs for economic security, adding value to the compensation package, promoting specific behaviours of strategic importance to the firm (such as encouraging continuing education and training), and helping remove possible hindrances to productivity (through the use of employee assistance programs to address problems such as alcohol or drug abuse).

### ISSUE 2: CHOOSE THE PROCESS FOR PLAN DESIGN

Once an organization has decided that there is a significant role for indirect pay in its compensation system, and once it has defined the objectives for indirect pay, it then needs to establish a process for designing a benefits plan that will achieve these objectives. Most experts argue that employee participation in the process is highly desirable.[66] This participation can help achieve at least three important goals. First, it can provide a better understanding of employee needs. A benefits system that does not address real employee needs will be of little value to employees, yet it will still cost the employer money. Second, participation can result in stronger acceptance of the plan. Third, it can help communicate the plan. Without effective communication, any investment in benefits a firm makes could end up returning very little value to the employer.[67]

Firms vary enormously regarding employee participation. High-involvement firms probably have extensive employee participation on the design team, whereas human relations and classical firms are likely to rely more on staff specialists, management, and outside consultants. Besides direct employee representation on the design team, employee input can also be solicited through focus groups and benefits surveys.[68]

## ISSUE 3: IDENTIFY THE BENEFITS SYSTEM AND BENEFITS TO BE INCLUDED

After choosing the process for designing the benefits system, the organization needs to decide on the type of benefits system (i.e., flexible, semiflexible, fixed) and on the specific benefits to include in it. The design team must consider the extent to which a benefit contributes to the objectives of indirect pay, the extent to which it is valued by employees, the cost to the employer, and the net value it adds to the compensation package. Because firms have only a finite budget for benefits, these benefits must be prioritized in order of total value to the firm.

## ISSUE 4: DETERMINE THE STRUCTURE OF EACH BENEFIT

For each individual benefit, the organization must make decisions on four main structural issues: benefit coverage, funding of the benefit, eligibility for the benefit, and the flexibility of the benefit. In other words, what will the benefit provide? Who will pay for it? Who is eligible to receive it? And will it be required or optional?

### Coverage

A major decision for the design team is benefit coverage. How much coverage will be provided, on what will it be based, and how far will it extend? Take dental insurance, for example. Should a particular dental insurance plan cover all dental expenses, only certain types of dental expenses, or all dental expenses up to a certain prescribed limit in a given period? Will it cover all the expenses of a given procedure, or will the employee need to pay a portion—say, 20 percent—of each bill? Will there be a deductible, so that an employee must pay the first $10 of every claim? Will some employees receive a richer plan than others?

In addition to all that, will the coverage be restricted to the employee, or will it extend to family members? If it is going to be a family plan, how will "family member" be defined? In an era of blended families and nontraditional relationships, defining terms such as "family member" and "spouse" may not be as straightforward as it first appears. At what point, for example, is a common-law partner to be accepted as a "spouse" for the purposes of benefit coverage? What status will children of that "spouse" (but not of the employee) receive? Will they be considered dependant children of the employee?

Also, will coverage levels vary for different employees? For example, it is common for life insurance coverage to be provided as a multiple of salary. Pension contributions are also geared to salary. But other plans may be based on seniority, as in the case of Imperial Oil's savings plan, which matches one percent of salary the first year of employment and up to five percent of salary the fifth year. Will coverage continue after termination? Many firms do continue coverage of certain benefits for retirees and their immediate families.

A related issue is whether coverage will be geared to base pay only or to base pay plus performance pay. Many firms exclude performance pay as a basis for benefit calculations simply because they have never thought to include it.[69] Others exclude it because it raises benefits costs. But failure to include performance pay in benefits calculations actually weakens performance pay and penalizes employees with a large component of performance pay. By contrast, including performance pay in calculations of benefits entitlements is a way to link indirect pay to employee performance, thereby reinforcing performance pay and adding a performance element to indirect pay that is normally absent.

## Funding

The cost of the benefit (such as the premiums for health insurance) may be fully paid by the employer (noncontributory), or fully by the employee (fully contributory), or cost-shared (contributory). One option is for the basic level of the benefit to be employer-paid, and then higher levels of the benefit to be cost-shared or employee-paid. Under a flexible benefit system, the employee could have the choice of whether the benefit would be employer-paid or employee-paid.

## Eligibility

A key issue for each benefit is to define which employee groups will be eligible to receive it. Although firms typically cover all full-time employees, there is often a waiting period before new employees become eligible for all benefits.

A more complex issue is the treatment of part-time, temporary, or contract employees. In many firms, part-time employees (defined by Statistics Canada as anyone working less than 30 hours a week) are offered few or no benefits, even if they have been employees of the firm for many years. Only one province has legislation regarding benefits for part-time employees. In 1996, Saskatchewan passed legislation that all employees who work an average of at least 15 hours a week must receive the same benefits as a comparable full-time employee, although these benefits can be prorated according to hours worked. Temporary full-time employees can be excluded if they do not meet the minimum employment period for inclusion in the benefits plan, and contract employees are typically excluded. In fact, some firms use part-time, temporary, and contract workers for the express purpose of avoiding having to pay benefits.

Some firms distinguish between two categories of part-time employees. Casual part-time employees work entirely at the will of the employer when their services are required. They receive no guarantee of weekly hours and can be terminated at will. By contrast, permanent part-time employees are viewed as permanent employees of the firm, and the firm has committed itself to provide them with a minimum number of hours on a weekly basis. These employees are often included in the benefits program, although on a prorated basis. Part-time employees are commonly found today in organizations that want to enjoy scheduling flexibility but also want to encourage a permanent relationship with these employees. Permanent part-time arrangements are especially common in industries that depend on a large number of part-time employees on an ongoing basis, such as banking (e.g., for tellers) and health care (e.g., for nurses).

## Flexibility of Each Benefit

The next issue is the degree of flexibility for each benefit. Will the benefit be mandatory or optional? Even flex plans often include some benefits that all employees are required to take, such as long-term disability. And if a benefit is required, will there be a predetermined fixed level, or will there be a minimum compulsory level as well as optional levels? An organization that has decided on a flexible plan will need to decide whether the benefit will be included in the core area of coverage or in the optional area. In addition, what value of flexible credits will be offered? Will employees be able to take unused credits as cash?

# ISSUE 5: DEVELOP PROCEDURES FOR ADMINISTERING, COMMUNICATING, EVALUATING, AND ADAPTING THE SYSTEM

Once an organization has designed the benefits system, it must create a system for administering it and communicating it to employees. The complexity of these tasks depends on the complexity and flexibility of the system that has been designed.

## Administration of Benefits System

Benefits systems can be very complex to administer. The key administrative tasks include enrolling employees in the benefits system, updating changes to employee records and benefits packages, dealing with employees when they terminate and after they terminate, handling the tax issues associated with benefits, dealing with the fiduciary responsibilities of funds held in trust, calculating employer and employee contributions, determining the validity of benefit claims and overseeing benefit payouts, advising employees on their benefit status and answering questions, and monitoring and evaluating the program and recommending changes. Another periodic administrative task is to select and replace sources of the various benefit products.

Almost all organizations that offer benefits outsource some of this work. For some aspects, such as funds held in trust for pension plans, the law requires a separate trustee. Trust companies, banks, insurance companies, and investment firms are often used for this purpose. Most insurance firms handle the claims processing for insurance-based benefits. The degree to which the other aspects of the administrative process are outsourced varies dramatically, but as benefits systems have grown more complex, and as specialized providers of these services have emerged, use of outsourcing has been increasing.

An advantage of outsourcing routine benefits administration is that it frees the in-house HR staff to focus on the strategic issues of indirect pay and on the communications aspects. A disadvantage is that firms can lose touch with employees' needs and problems. That is why evaluation should be a key in-house function, as will be discussed shortly. Most firms believe that communication should also be an in-house function.

## Communication of Benefits Information

Ironically, although indirect pay may account for as much as one-quarter of an employee's total compensation, and although the company pension plan may represent the largest financial asset an employee will ever own, employee understanding of this aspect of their compensation is generally limited.[70] In one Canadian study of 1010 individuals aged 55–64, 69 percent of participants did not know what the maximum monthly payout would be from the Canadian Pension Plan, Quebec Pension Plan, and Old Age Security. Of the participants in the study, 60 percent said they have an employer-sponsored pension plan, and 55 percent of those participants did not know the amount of the monthly benefit.[71]

If a benefits system is to shape behaviour and attitudes, then employees have to understand it. As discussed earlier, research shows that satisfaction with benefits increases in direct proportion to how well the benefits are understood. There are two situations where communication and comprehension are especially important: when employees must make benefit selection decisions, and when they may be eligible to receive their benefits.

Among the traditional methods used to communicate benefits are employee handbooks and periodic newsletters, along with an annual statement of pension coverage, which is required under law. But these approaches have generally enjoyed little success, due to the arcane and legalistic language that usually prevails in these documents, combined with a lack of motivation on the part of most employees to wade through the material. However, two events may help improve employee comprehension of their benefits: the development of computer-based technology for communicating information on employee benefits, and the advent of benefits systems that require employees to make choices on their benefits, often on an annual basis.[72]

### Evaluating and Adapting the Benefits System

Once the system has been put into place, it needs to be evaluated on a regular basis to determine whether it is meeting its objectives in the most cost-effective way. There are three main types of analysis. Cost analysis examines the cost of each individual benefit and what is being received for that cost. Competitive analysis uses data from competitors to compare benefits plans. And benefits surveys examine employee satisfaction with each benefit and its value to them. Evaluation issues are covered in more detail in Chapter 13.

## SUMMARY

This chapter has examined the third component of a compensation system: indirect pay. Indirect pay is often a very large and growing component of many compensation systems, yet many employers have not carefully examined whether their mix of direct and indirect pay is optimal. Employers vary dramatically in the extent to which indirect pay is beneficial for them.

You are now familiar with the six main categories of benefits—mandatory benefits, retirement income, health benefits, pay for time not worked, employee services, and miscellaneous benefits—and the possible role of each type of benefit. You also understand the trend toward flexible benefit systems and the advantages and disadvantages of flexible systems.

Finally, you have learned about the five key issues in designing an effective indirect pay system: determining the role of indirect pay in the compensation strategy, choosing the process for plan design, identifying the benefits system and specific benefits to be included, determining the structure of each benefit, and developing procedures for administering, communicating, and evaluating the benefits system.

## KEY TERMS

defined benefit plans
defined contribution plans
employee assistance programs (EAPs)
fixed benefit system
flexible benefit system

health care spending account
hybrid pension plans
mandatory benefits
pay for time not worked
supplemental unemployment benefits (SUBs)

# DISCUSSION QUESTIONS

1. "Defined contribution pension plans are nothing more than an attempt by employers to shift risk from themselves to employees, who are much less able to bear this risk." Do you agree or disagree with this statement? Discuss why.

2. What are the key forces promoting the adoption of flexible benefits?

3. "Flexible benefits plans are beneficial to both employers and employees because they allow both groups to satisfy their needs." Do you agree with this statement? Discuss why or why not.

4. Assume that you have been hired to implement a benefits plan by your employer. What are the key steps you will advise your CEO to take?

5. Do you think the COVID-19 pandemic would lead to the adoption of new types of employee benefits? If so, what types and why? If not, why?

# EXERCISES

1. Go to the websites for the Benefits and Pension Monitor (http://www.bpmmagazine.com) and the Canadian Human Resources Reporter (http://www.hrreporter.com) and make a list of the key issues that came up most frequently in these publications in the past two months. Which of these issues do you think is the most important?

2. In a small group, discuss how important benefits will be to you in choosing your next job. Then identify the three specific benefits listed in Compensation Notebook 12.1 that are most important to you. Do choices vary in your group? If so, discuss why.

3. Three firms are described briefly below. For each firm, identify the role (if any) that you believe indirect pay should play in the compensation system, and the specific benefits that it would make the most sense to offer. Explain why.

   a. A company offers lawn maintenance and yard cleanup services in the summer and snow removal services in the winter. It employs about 600 people at peak season (in the summer) and has branches in major cities across the Prairies.

   b. A retail clothing chain offers personalized service and caters to upscale customers. It is located in major cities across Canada and employs approximately 600 sales staff.

   c. A computer software firm develops customized software for various specialized applications for individual clients. Located near Ottawa, it employs about 1000 people.

## CASE QUESTIONS

1. Analyze *Case 2—The Fit Stop Ltd.* (Appendix). Identify the benefits system (including specific benefits) that would make the most sense for this firm.

2. Analyze *Case 5—Plastco Packaging* (Appendix). Identify the benefits system (including specific benefits) that would make the most sense for this firm.

## SIMULATION CROSS-REFERENCE

If you are using Strategic Compensation: A Simulation in conjunction with this text, you will find that the concepts in Chapter 12 are helpful in preparing the simulation.

# ENDNOTES

1. Richard Yerema and Kristina Leung, *Canada's Top 100 Employers* (Toronto: Mediacorp, 2019), https://reviews.canadastop100.com/top-emp%20loyer-desjardins, accessed April 11, 2020.

2. Statistics Canada, *Workplace and Employee Survey* (2005), https://www150.statcan.gc.ca/n1/en/pub/71-585-x/71-585-x2008001-eng.pdf?st=lRQFGtBH, accessed April 11, 2020.

3. Conference Board of Canada, *Benefits Benchmarking 2012* (Ottawa: 2012).

4. Statistics Canada, "Pension Plans in Canada," *The Daily Online*, May 25, 2012.

5. Conference Board of Canada, *Compensation Planning Outlook 2013* (Ottawa: 2012).

6. Frederick Vettese, "The Extinction of Defined-Pension Plans is Almost Upon Us," *The Globe and Mail*, October 4, 2018, https://www.theglobeandmail.com/investing/personal-finance/retirement/article-the-extinction-of-defined-benefit-pension-plans-is-almost-upon-us/, accessed April 4, 2020.

7. Robert L. Brown and Craig McInnes, "Shifting Public Sector DC Plans to DC," *OP Trust*, October 2014, https://www.optrust.com/documents/DB-vs-DC-plans-research-paper.pdf, accessed April 4, 2020.

8. "2008: Worst Year Ever for Pensions," *Canadian HR Reporter*, February 9, 2009, 2.

9. Statistics Canada, "Life Expectancy," http://www.statcan.gc.ca/tables-tableaux/sum-som/l01/cst01/health26-eng.htm, accessed October 3, 2016.

10. Office of the Chief Actuary, *12th Actuarial Report on the Old Age Security Program as at 31 December 2012*, http://www.osfi-bsif.gc.ca/eng/oca-bac/ar-ra/oas-psv/pages/oas12.aspx#tbl-24, accessed October 3, 2016.

11. Statistics Canada, "Life Expectancy."

12. Conference Board of Canada, *Compensation Planning Outlook 2013*.

13. Charles Davies, "More DC Plans, More for Staff to Understand," *Canadian HR Reporter* 17, no. 11 (2004): G2–G8.

14. Laurence E. Coward, *Mercer Handbook of Canadian Pension and Benefit Plans* (Don Mills: CCH Canadian 1991).

15. H. Clare Pitcher, "In Defence of the Much-Maligned DB Plan," *Canadian HR Reporter* 17, no. 4 (2004): G4. See also Victoria Hubbell, "DB Pensions Best Option for Employers, Workers," Canadian HR Reporter 26, no. 1 (2013): 23.

16. Janet McFarland, "The Hidden Costs of Switching to a Cheaper Pension Plan," *The Globe and Mail,* July 18, 2011, https://www.theglobeandmail.com/report-on-business/the-hidden-costs-of-switching-to-a-cheaper-pension-plan/article555646/, accessed April 4, 2020.

17. "Pension Plans in Canada, as of January 1, 2018," *Statistics Canada*, June 19, 2019, https://www150.statcan.gc.ca/n1/daily-quotidien/190619/dq190619f-eng.htm, accessed April 4, 2020.

18. Steven G. Allen and Robert L. Clark, "Pensions and Firm Performance," in *Human Resources and Performance of the Firm*, ed. Morris M. Kleiner, Richard N. Block, Myron Roomkin, and Sidney W. Salsburg (Madison: Industrial Relations Research Association, 1987), 195–242; "A Fine Balance," Government of Ontario, 2008, https://www.fin.gov.on.ca/en/consultations/pension/report/Pensions_Report_Eng_web.pdf, accessed April 4, 2020.

19. Andrew A. Luchak and Dionne M. Pohler, "Pensions as Psychological Contracts: Implications for Work Outcomes," *Industrial Relations: A Journal of Economy and Society* 49, no. 1 (2010): 61–82.

20. Jeremy Quittner, "Business Owners Share How They Actually Chose Their Health Care Plans," *Fortune*, October 4, 2016, http://fortune.com/2016/10/04/business-owners-share-how-they-actually-chose-their-health-care-plans, accessed October 18, 2016.

21. *Canadian HR Reporter*, "Health Benefit Plan Cost Increases Slowing Significantly for Employ: Survey," July 24, 2012, http://www.hrreporter.com/article/13545-health-benefit-plan-cost-increases-slowing-significantly-for-employers-survey, accessed October 18, 2016.

22. Danielle Harder, "Generic Drugs Cheaper South of Border," *Canadian HR Reporter*, February 9, 2009, 17.

23. Paula Allen, "Mental Health Absenteeism Threatens to Break Disability Bank," *Canadian HR Reporter* 17, no. 6 (2004): 5–8; "CAA Shares Journey to a Healthy Workplace," *Benefits Canada*, September 7, 2018, https://www.benefitscanada.com/news/caa-shares-journey-to-a-healthy-workplace-118826, April 5, 2020.

24. Erika Alini, "'I Couldn't Believe It'—Why Disability Claims for Mental Health Are Often a Struggle," *Global News*, May 25, 2019, https://globalnews.ca/news/5306210/disability-insurance-mental-health/, accessed April 5, 2020.

25. Barbara Shecter, "Employers Who Spend More on Their Workers' Mental Health Make More Money, Deloitte Study Finds," *Financial Post*, November 9, 2019, https://business.financialpost.com/news/fp-street/employers-who-spend-more-on-their-workers-mental-health-make-more-money-deloitte-study-finds, accessed April 5, 2020.

26. Yaldaz Sadakova, "How Cisco Makes Flex Schedules Work," *Benefits Canada*, October 15, 2015, https://www.benefits-canada.com/news/coffee-with-david-heather-71116, accessed April 5, 2020.

27. Barry W. Kwasniewski, "Just Cause for Employee Dismissal: What Employers Need to Know," *Charity Law Bulletin* 175 (2009): 2–7.

28. For a full discussion of these issues and for awards by the courts, see Stacey R. Ball, *Canadian Employment Law* (Aurora: Canada Law Book, 2004); Dentons Canada LLP, "An Offer They Can't Refuse—The Dangers of Recruiting High Level Employees," *Martindale,* March 2, 2015, https://www.martindale.com/labor-employment-law/article_Dentons-Canada-LLP_2193644.htm, accessed April 5, 2020; "Avoiding the Pitfalls of Enticement," Pushor Mitchell LLP, March 8, 2009, https://www.pushormitchell.com/2009/03/avoiding-the-pitfalls-of-enticement/, accessed April 5, 2020; Paul McKeever, "Wrongful Dismissal," https://mckeever.com/dismissal.htm, accessed April 5, 2020.

29. Geoffrey J. Litherland, *An Employer's Guide to Dismissal* (Aurora: Aurora Professional Press, 2000); "Di Tomaso v. Crown Metal Packaging Canada LP," June 22, 2016, *ONCA,* https://www.canlii.org/en/on/onca/doc/2011/2011onca469/2011onca469.html.

30. Carolyn Baarda, *Compensation Planning Outlook 2001* (Ottawa: Conference Board of Canada, 2000).

31. Angela Scappatura, "EAP Use Soars as Economy Tanks," *Canadian HR Reporter,* March 23, 2009, 1–2.

32. Rappit, "Need Help . . . ?"; "Recreation and Learning Center," *ArcelorMittal Dofasco,* https://dofasco.arcelormittal.com/corporate-responsibility/recreation-and-learning-centre.aspx, accessed April 5, 2020.

33. Terry Martin, "Building the Business Case for Wellness," *Canadian HR Reporter* 18, no. 6 (2005): 7.

34. David Brown, "Benefits Providers Strive to Meet Clients' Wellness Needs," *Canadian HR Reporter* 18, no. 6 (2005): 5–6.

35. Conference Board of Canada, *Making the Business Case for Investments in Workplace Health and Wellness* (Ottawa: 2012).

36. Brianna Sharpe, "Is It Time for a Child-Care Uprising in Ontario?" *TVO,* February 12, 2020, https://www.tvo.org/article/is-it-time-for-a-child-care-uprising-in-ontario, accessed April 6, 2020.

37. Dan Healing, "Canadian Employers Content to Avoid Cost and Headache of Providing Daycare," *Global News,* May 28, 2018, https://globalnews.ca/news/4235943/daycare-employers-cost-suncor/?utm_source=GlobalNews&utm_medium=Facebook&fbclid=IwAR2dTXsqO7ymoukSHvWwpyaB8nTS1Caps6KUeM-ub41o_JY1X61BXU6j48g, accessed April 6, 2020.

38. Dan Healing, "Canadian Employers Content to Avoid Cost and Headache of Providing Daycare," *Global News,* May 28, 2018, https://globalnews.ca/news/4235943/daycare-employers-cost-suncor/?utm_source=GlobalNews&utm_medium=Facebook&fbclid=IwAR2dTXsqO7ymoukSHvWwpyaB8nTS1Caps6KUeM-ub41o_JY1X61BXU6j48g, accessed April 6, 2020.

39. Sandrine Devillard et al., "The Present and Future of Women at Work in Canada," *McKinsey & Company,* June 2019, https://www.mckinsey.com/~/media/mckinsey/featured%20insights/gender%20equality/the%20present%20and%20future%20of%20women%20at%20work%20in%20canada/the-present-and-future-of-women-at-work-in-canada-vf.ashx, accessed April 6, 2020.

40. Baarda, *Compensation Planning Outlook 2001*; Paula Allen, "Elder Care Increasingly Valuable," *HR Reporter,* September 6, 2010, https://www.hrreporter.com/news/hr-news/elder-care-increasingly-valuable/313072, accessed April 6, 2020.

41. Carolyn Tinglin, "How to Help Employers with Eldercare Responsibilities," *Benefits Canada,* April 3, 2014, https://www.benefitscanada.com/benefits/health-benefits/benefits-column-care-package-50185, accessed April 6, 2020.

42. Bonnie Schroeder, Jane MacDonald, and Judith Shamian, "Older Workers with Caregiving Responsibilities: A Canadian Perspective on Corporate Giving," *Aging International* 37 (2012): 39–56.

43. Chris Higgins and Linda Duxbury, *Reducing Work–Life Conflict: What Works? What Doesn't?* (2008), http://www.hc-sc.gc.ca/ewh-semt/pubs/occup-travail/balancing-equilibre/index-eng.php.

44. Linda Duxbury and Chris Higgins, "Revisiting Work-Life Issues in Canada: The 2012 National Study on Balancing Work and Caregiving in Canada" (2012), http://www.healthyworkplaces.info/wp-content/uploads/2012/11/2012-National-Work-Long-Summary.pdf.

45. Rappit, "Need Help . . . ?"

46. Angela Scappatura, "Support for Tax-Free Savings Account Limited," *Canadian Compensation and Benefits Reporter* 13, no. 3 (2009): 6.

47. Robert J. McKay, *Canadian Handbook of Flexible Benefits* (Mississauga: John Wiley and Sons, 2007).

48. McKay, *Canadian Handbook of Flexible Benefits.*

49. McKay, *Canadian Handbook of Flexible Benefits.*

50. Nathalie B. Carlyle, *Compensation Planning Outlook 1997* (Ottawa: Conference Board of Canada, 1996).

51. Conference Board of Canada, *Benefits Benchmarking 2012.*

52. "Gain the Advantage," *Sun Life Financial,* January 2013, https://www.sunlife.ca/static/canada/Sponsor/About%20Group%20Benefits/Group%20benefits%20products%20and%20services/Mental%20Health%20in%20the%20Workplace/files/Trends%20Brightpaper%202013%20GB10097%20E.pdf, accessed April 7, 2020.

53. David Brown, "Employers Approach Benefits Cost Containment with Caution," *Canadian HR Reporter,* 18, no. 2 (2005): 2–4.

54. McKay, *Canadian Handbook of Flexible Benefits.*

55. David E. Bloom and Jane T. Trahan, *Flexible Benefits and Employee Choice: Highlights of the Literature,* Elsevier (2016).

56. Lynn Quincy and Julie Silas, "The Evidence Is Clear: Too Many Health Insurance Choices Can Impair, Not Help, Consumer Decision Making," *Consumers Union,* November 2012, https://advocacy.consumerreports.org/wp-content/uploads/2012/11/Too_Much_Choice_Nov_2012.pdf, accessed April 7, 2020.

57. Daphne Woolf, "The Flux of Flex: How Flex Plans Are Faring," *Canadian HR Reporter* 18, no. 2 (2005): 15.

58. Woolf, "The Flux of Flex.

59. Amanda Aubin, 2019, "Making Employees More Comfortable with Open Enrollment," *Employee Benefit Adviser,* Oct 30, 2019, http://ezproxy.library.yorku.ca/login?url=https://search-proquest-com.ezproxy.library.yorku.ca/docview/2310682625?accountid=15182, accessed April 9, 2020.

60. Michel Tremblay, Bruno Sire, and Annie Pelchat, "A Study of the Determinants and of the Impact of Flexibility on Employee Benefit Satisfaction," *Human Relations* 51, no. 5 (1998): 667–88.; Kenneth MacDonald, "So You Think You Want a Flex Plan," *Benefits Canada,* January 23, 2014, https://www.benefitscanada.com/benefits/health-benefits/so-you-think-you-want-a-flex-plan-48671, accessed April 8, 2020.

61. M. Dolores Vidal-Salazar, Eulogio Cordón-Pozo, and M. José de la Torre-Ruiz, "Flexibility of Benefit Systems and Firms' Attraction and Retention Capacities," *Employee Relations* 38, no. 4 (2016): 487–504; Troy V. Mumford, Steven Hanks, and Cherissa Alldredge, "Strategically Managing Employee Benefits: Predictors of Benefit Choices," *International Journal of Business Management and Commerce* 4, no. 1 (2019): 39–51.

62. Sturman et al., "Computerized Decision Aids."

63. Xavier Baeten and Bart Verwaeren, "Flexible Rewards from a Strategic Rewards Perspective," *Compensation and Benefits Review* 44, no. 1 (2012): 40–9.

64. M. Dolores Vidal-Salazar, Eulogio Cordón-Pozo, and M. José, "Flexibility of Benefit Systems and Firms' Attraction and Retention Capacities," *Employee Relations* 38, no. 4 (2016): 487–504.

65. For the most up-to-date and comprehensive source of benefits information, see J. Bruce McDonald, *Carswell's Benefits Guide* (Toronto: Carswell, 2013). See also McKay, *Canadian Handbook of Flexible Benefits.*

66. John A. Haslinger and Donna Sheerin, "Employee Input: The Key to Successful Benefits Programs," *Compensation and Benefits Review* 26, no. 3 (1994): 61–70; Marc Neely, "Wellness Strategies for Smaller Businesses," *Benefits Quarterly* 28, no. 3 (2012): 16.

67. Robert Taylor, "The Benefits Are the Message," *Canadian HR Reporter,* January 12, 2009, 15.

68. Excellent guidance on the preparation of benefits surveys can be found in McDonald, *Carswell's Benefits Guide.*

69. John M. Burns and Diane Gherson, "Should Variable Pay Count Towards Benefits Calculations?" *Compensation and Benefits Review* 28, no. 5 (1996).

70. Andrew Luchak and Morley Gunderson, "What Do Employees Know about Their Pension Plan?" *Industrial Relations* 39, no. 4 (2000): 646–70; R.L. Clark, M.S. Morrill, and S.G. Allen, "The Role of Financial Literacy in Determining Retirement Plans," *Economic Inquiry* 50, no. 4 (2012): 851–66.

71. "Workers Nearing Retirement Don't Know How Much Retirement Income They Will Have—Or Need," *Canadian HR Reporter,* February 24, 2014, https://www.hrreporter.com/news/hr-news/workers-nearing-retirement-dont-know-how-much-retirement-income-they-will-have-or-need/279823, accessed April 11, 2020.

72. Sarah Dobson, "Benefits Consultations Make SFU Top Employer," *Canadian HR Reporter,* March 9, 2009, 12.

# ACTIVATING AND MAINTAINING AN EFFECTIVE COMPENSATION SYSTEM

## Learning Outcomes

AFTER READING THIS CHAPTER, YOU SHOULD BE ABLE TO:

- Identify the key issues in preparing to implement a compensation system.
- Develop an implementation plan for a new compensation system.
- Describe the steps necessary for implementing a compensation system.
- Develop a process for communicating the compensation system.
- Explain how to evaluate the effectiveness of a compensation system.
- Identify circumstances that may necessitate changes to the compensation system.
- Discuss the issues to be considered in adapting the compensation system.

A new compensation system has been blamed for the problems facing thousands of federal employees. More than 80 000 employees were affected by July 2016; some of them were not receiving any pay or were short-changed, others were not getting benefits or only some benefits, while many were not getting pay for overtime and supplemental pay for extra duties. A few employees were even overpaid! These problems forced many employees, among other strategies, to max out their credit cards, take loans to survive, and cash in RRSPs.

The problems started in early 2016 when the federal government replaced the 40-year old payroll system for its 300 000 personnel. The new multi-million-dollar payroll software, Phoenix, was supposed to integrate the payroll and management systems. However, it appears the scope of the task was underestimated. According to senior government officials, sufficient resources were not channelled into the implementation of the system. This resulted in a lack of training for the compensation staff. Those responsible for implementation may have also underestimated the time it would take to activate and maintain the new system.

A 2019 report concluded that 72 percent of public servants had been underpaid, overpaid, or not paid at all because of the Phoenix fiasco. Only 25 percent of employees were not affected, while 32 percent were only slightly affected. Meanwhile, 59 percent of employees had experienced significant hardship in 2018, and 56 percent of public servants still had unsettled pay issues. To make matters worse, in a severe breach of privacy, the federal government sent the personal information of 69 000 public servants to the wrong departments while trying to resolve the Phoenix payment issues.

The federal government continues to attempt to reconcile employees' compensation entitlement pursuant to their collective agreements and has offered further retribution for stress, aggravation, and lost time. In 2019, the federal government agreed to credit current employees with up to five paid vacation days over a four-year time frame. Later in 2019, previous employees were given the ability to file an electronic claim to request the cash equivalent of their vacation entitlement days. Many feel that a five-day leave is unreasonable given what employees had faced. Employees wanted a cash settlement substantial enough to make up for their pain and suffering.

Current and former employees can also request additional compensation for substantial costs and lost investments greater than $1500. Those who cashed investments such as RRSPs; were required to pay interest on a loan, mortgage, or credit card; had severance or pension payments postponed; and missed out on the interest on those earnings could be reimbursed.

As of January 2020, four years since the flawed system was rolled out, there remained a 209 000-case backlog. Many members remain unpaid. Victims are aggravated by how long a grievance takes to reach the hearing. People continue to suffer, whether it be with mental health, stress, loss of homes, and ruined credit ratings.

Most recent estimates propose that it will take an additional four years and $2.6 billion to repair the current system. The union was holding strike votes for affected workers. However, since the COVID-19 pandemic, strike votes have been suspended. The efforts to lessen the backlog is now of reduced priority at the time of writing this text; however, the government claims that the effort to replace the electronic pay system continues.

Sources: Kathleen Harris, "Phoenix Pay System Mess Affects 80,000, Government Officials Say," *CBC News*, July 18, 2016; Laura Payton, "Resolution in Pay Problems for 80,000 Civil Servants Still Months Away," *CTV News*, July 18, 2016; Michelle Zilio, "System Glitch Leaves 80,000 Public Servants Waiting for Pay," *Globe and Mail*, July 18, 2016; The Canadian Press, "Tax Collectors, Auditors to Help Field 'Historic' Numbers of Benefit-Seeking Callers," *Burnaby Now*, April 2, 2020; "Former Federal Employees Can Now Request Phoenix Compensation," *CBC News*, November 29, 2019; Andrew Duffy, "Public Service Employee Survey Finds 72 Per Cent Affected by Phoenix Pay Problems," *Ottawa Citizen*, January 15, 2020; Kevin King, "Union Rises Up Against Phoenix Pay System 'Fiasco'," *Windsor Star*, February 20, 2020; "Claim Damages Caused by Phoenix: Financial Cost and Lost Investment Income," Government of Canada; Catharine Tunney, "Information About 69,000 Phoenix Pay System Victims Sent in Error," *CBC*, February 18, 2020.

# INTRODUCTION: PUTTING THE SYSTEM IN PLACE

At last! Your final destination on the road to effective compensation is in sight. You have formulated your compensation strategy and designed the technical processes for converting this strategy into a compensation system. Now you must put the system into place. Once in place, the system needs to be communicated on an ongoing basis, evaluated to ensure that it is achieving its goals, and adapted to fit changing circumstances.

This chapter first outlines the important issues to be dealt with in preparing to implement a new compensation system, then discusses how to develop an implementation plan. Without adequate preparation, the difficulties in effectively implementing a new compensation system will be magnified dramatically. As the opening story shows, problems related to improper implementation can cause major headaches!

Next, you will learn the main steps in the implementation process itself and examine ways to communicate and evaluate the compensation system on an ongoing basis, after it is up and running. After that, key circumstances that may create needs for change to the compensation system are identified. The chapter concludes with a discussion of some of the key issues in adapting the compensation system.

# PREPARING FOR IMPLEMENTATION

Even after the compensation strategy has been established and the technical processes have been determined, there is still much to be done before the compensation system can be implemented. These tasks include preparing the compensation budget, planning the infrastructure for compensation administration, planning for information technology, and organizing for compensation administration.

## PREPARING THE COMPENSATION BUDGET

A compensation budget for the coming year is an essential part of the planning process for most organizations. A compensation budget is simply a forecast of what the firm expects to spend on compensation in the coming year. Such a budget can also serve as a way to control compensation costs (e.g., by requiring departments to secure authorization to exceed their budgeted allocations) and as a benchmark against which to evaluate whether the compensation system is behaving as expected.

Traditionally, compensation budgeting has been done in one of two ways—either bottom-up or top-down. In the bottom-up approach, the compensation rates for the coming year are applied to employees, factoring in probable merit and seniority increases as well as expected turnover (turnover reduces compensation costs because new employees usually start at a lower rate than those who are retiring or quitting), and the compensation budget for the coming year is based on the total dollar amount derived from this process. In the top-down approach, management sets a limit on the total amount of compensation available for the coming year (usually based on some adjustment of last year's compensation bill) and then divides the available funds among departments and units, which then divide them in turn among their employees.

The approach advocated in this book is top-down when compensation strategy is being formulated, to ensure that it dovetails with other key strategic aspects of the organization, but bottom-up for compensation budgeting. A top-down approach to budgeting, where an arbitrary amount is allocated to compensation, undermines the whole notion of strategic pay. Furthermore, with the top-down approach, top management may not possess the necessary awareness required to prepare the budget in every department of their firm. Managers at operating levels have a deeper understanding of their departments' operations. The creativity and commitment of the operating managers can be squelched if they are not involved in the process to determine what is necessary for their department. A budget requires guidance from the department level, while top management will understand the broader picture and therefore support the creation of the compensation strategy.[1]

# PLANNING FOR COMPENSATION ADMINISTRATION

There are four key issues to consider when planning for compensation administration: (1) documenting the compensation system, (2) administering compensation, (3) assigning compensation responsibilities and planning the infrastructure, and (4) developing ongoing communications about the system.

## Documenting the Compensation System

If an organization is to apply its compensation system uniformly, it must carefully document the system. Two aspects of documentation are particularly important. The first is the compensation system itself. If job evaluation is to be used, then manuals must be prepared that provide the compensable factors, the scales for measuring these, and the procedures for applying them. If pay for knowledge is to be used, then procedures for assessing skill levels and competencies must be documented. Benefits must also be described, along with application procedures, limits, and the like.

Second, the organization must document assigned responsibilities for carrying out the various compensation processes, spelling out which organizational units are responsible for which tasks. It also needs to negotiate and draw up contracts with service providers. These contracts need to describe the services to be provided, including minimum performance standards and penalties for failure to meet them, as well as the employer's responsibilities. Beyond addressing foreseeable tasks, contracts need to be flexible enough to deal with unknown future events. Quite a challenge for any document!

## Administering Compensation

For the compensation system to function, someone must collect the necessary information about time worked by each employee, whether any employees are eligible for overtime pay or bonuses, and which employees have been terminated or hired. Someone must calculate gross earnings and deductions from earnings, prepare and distribute the paycheques or notices of direct deposit for employees, and remit the proper amounts to various governmental agencies. In firms that offer employee benefits, someone must keep track of who is entitled to what and ensure that proper payouts are made. Taking care of these responsibilities is called **compensation administration**.

**compensation administration**
The process through which employee earnings are calculated and the appropriate remittances are paid to employees, governments, and other agencies.

## Assigning Responsibilities and Planning the Infrastructure

Once all the tasks and procedures for operating the compensation system have been identified, the organization needs to assign specific responsibilities for performing these tasks and plan the infrastructure to support the system. Who exactly will be responsible for inputting employee transactions? Who will develop the forms for recording these transactions and the computer systems for performing the pay calculations? Who will prepare the cheques: a payroll section in the human resources department, the accounting department, or an outside provider?

## Communicating Compensation Information

A process must be developed so that the ongoing communication that is necessary for effective operation of the compensation system takes place. Employees and their managers need to be made aware of any changes to compensation that affect them, and also be made aware of any responsibilities they have for providing information necessary for the compensation administration process. Any new managers or employees need to be briefed on compensation issues or responsibilities that are relevant to them. All employees must have a reliable source of compensation information available to them to address any questions or concerns. (We will devote more time to this issue later in this chapter because of the importance of ongoing communication.)

## PLANNING FOR INFORMATION TECHNOLOGY

Because it requires such a large number of mechanical calculations, payroll was one of the first functions to be computerized in most organizations. Since then, many firms have also introduced integrated human resource information systems, in which compensation is just one part. Computers facilitate compensation administration and can help transform complex compensation concepts—such as flexible benefit plans—into usable practices.

For most organizations, the question is not whether to use computers in compensation administration, but how far to extend their use. Possible uses include job documentation and evaluation, analysis of compensation survey data, communications, information collection, calculation of pay and remittances, record keeping, and compensation planning and research.[2] Firms must take steps to ensure that employees' privacy rights are secure when electronic systems are used. This imposes some restrictions on the types of IT systems that can be used.

### Job Documentation and Evaluation

Computers can be very useful in data collection for job analysis purposes, crafting job descriptions, generating job evaluations and pay structures,[3] and computing market lines and pay policy lines, as discussed earlier in the text.

### Labour Market Data Analysis

Analyses of labour market and compensation survey data can be facilitated by computers. Labour market data can be downloaded from a variety of governmental and other sources. As well, systems can be developed to store job matches from various surveys and then to generate various "market rates" based on several variables and assumptions.

### Communication

Computers are being used more and more to communicate compensation policies and information. An effective intranet can help firms deal with many of their compensation communication needs.[4]

### Information Collection

Online computer systems can be used to capture a wide variety of compensation information. Departments can use direct entry for transactions such as new hires, terminations, and pay rate changes, as well as for information such as hours worked and days absent. Appraisal and performance management systems, such as 360-degree feedback, can be greatly facilitated by online systems. Once the system has collected data and compiled employee information, it can also monitor the status of the performance management initiative and goal management capabilities can help organizations align individual goals with the firm's strategic goals.[5]

Computers can also be used to collect employees' choices regarding various aspects of compensation, especially benefits choices. Computers can guide employees through the benefits selection process and help them make the choices that are most consistent with their own needs (see Chapter 12).

## Pay and Remittance Calculation

Once properly programmed, computers excel at performing routine computations, such as calculating gross and net earnings and remittances to governmental agencies. Many off-the-shelf computer packages are available for such purposes, although many organizations find it necessary to customize the software to the needs of their particular organization. Compensation Today 13.1 describes how two hospitals cut costs by jointly purchasing the necessary software for their pay systems.

## Record Keeping

Accurate compensation records are essential for a wide variety of purposes, including internal control, financial reporting, and external reporting (e.g., for income tax or pension purposes).

## Compensation Planning and Research

Computers can be used to prepare compensation budgets and to make projections of future compensation costs under a variety of assumptions.[6] They can be used to analyze current pay structures or the distribution of merit money among departments. They can also be used to analyze labour productivity, absenteeism, and turnover rates. In addition, they are helpful for conducting online surveys of employee attitudes.

## Privacy and Legal Issues

Online computer systems can dramatically reduce the amount of paperwork in compensation administration, but firms must protect employee privacy rights in the process.

---

### COMPENSATION TODAY 13.1

#### HOSPITALS HARVEST HEALTHY SOFTWARE SAVINGS BY SHARING

In the fall of 2005, the payroll system at Queensway Carleton Hospital (QCH) in Ottawa—designed for handling 1000 employees but now struggling to handle twice that number—was already on life support when the technology provider announced that it would be pulling the plug on the system on April 1, 2008. Unfortunately, this turned out to be no April Fool's joke, and QCH had to scramble to find a new payroll system.

Because funds were scarce, QCH teamed up with Montfort Hospital, which was also in dire need of payroll system replacement. Working together, they were able to purchase one system (the VIP Integrated HR-Payroll System provided by Quebec-based DLGL) that would suit both hospitals—and split the nearly $1 million cost.

Besides its bargain price, the system has proved to be a good deal in other ways. For example, with the previous payroll system, many transactions—such as maternity and parental leaves—needed to be calculated manually, creating a considerable administrative burden. Now all these kinds of transactions are handled electronically by the system.

For the next phase of development, the hospitals plan to integrate employee scheduling and attendance with the system, thus eliminating the need for manual time sheets. This will also allow new applications such as research on patterns of absenteeism.

Source: Danielle Harder, "Resuscitating a Hospital Payroll System," *Canadian HR Reporter*, January 26, 2009.

In 2000, to protect employee privacy in the face of electronic access to employee data, the federal government passed Bill C-6, known as the Personal Information Protection and Electronic Documents Act (PIPEDA). Enacted in 2004, this legislation prohibits the release of "personal health information" (e.g., employee medical and dental claims) to anybody (including third-party benefits providers) without informed employee consent. This means that Web-based benefits systems must be careful to limit access to employee records to only a few authorized persons. For example, supervisors cannot be allowed access to detailed information about their employees' health claims. This legislation applies in all jurisdictions that do not have equivalent provincial legislation—Saskatchewan, Manitoba, Nova Scotia, Prince Edward Island, and the territories. Quebec, Alberta, British Columbia, Ontario, New Brunswick, and Newfoundland and Labrador have equivalent provincial legislation.

Another issue is the legality of electronic forms. For example, until 2000, Ontario employment standards legislation required that individualized employee pay statements be provided to each employee for every pay period in paper format. Since 2000, however, with the passage of provincial Bill 88 (the Electronic Commerce Act), employers in Ontario have been permitted to provide electronic pay statements, as long as these comply with certain conditions. For example, simply making the statements available on a website does not comply with the law; the statements must be personally sent to each employee (i.e., through email), and the employee must be able to keep (i.e., print or electronically save) a copy of the statement.

## ORGANIZING FOR COMPENSATION ADMINISTRATION

A major issue for employers is whether to perform all aspects of compensation administration in-house or to contract some or all of it to an outside agency.[7] When deciding whether to outsource compensation administration, organizations often distinguish between direct pay (payroll) and indirect pay (benefits).

| Sample Company Name, 3191 My Home Avenue, Regina, SK Canada S4N 0M3 | | | EARNINGS STATEMENT |
|---|---|---|---|

**Sarah Robertson**

| EMPLOYEE ID | PERIOD ENDING | PAY DATE | CHEQUE NUMBER |
|---|---|---|---|
| 8761 | 2020/09/24 | 2020/09/30 | 321654 |

| INCOME | RATE | HOURS | CURRENT TOTAL | DEDUCTIONS | CURRENT TOTAL | YEAR TO DATE |
|---|---|---|---|---|---|---|
| REGULAR | 20 | 80 | 1,600.00 | CPP | 65.03 | 1,495.69 |
| OVERTIME | 25 | 5 | 125.00 | EI | 28.62 | 658.26 |
| | | | | INCOME TAX | 305.90 | 7,035.70 |
| | | | | UNION DUES | 10.84 | 249.32 |
| | | | | LIFE INSURANCE | 4.94 | 113.62 |
| | | | | LONG TERM DISABILITY | 7.01 | 161.23 |
| | | | | CANADA SAVING BONDS | 8.00 | 184.00 |

| YTD GROSS | YTD DEDUCTIONS | YTD NET PAY | CURRENT TOTAL | DEDUCTIONS | NET PAY |
|---|---|---|---|---|---|
| 39,675.00 | 9,897.82 | 29,777.18 | 1,725.00 | 430.34 | 1,294.66 |

Pay stubs show gross pay and deductions.

Depending on the nature and extent of employee benefits offered, benefits administration can be very complex. Most organizations therefore outsource at least some of their benefits administration, often to the product provider, such as an insurance company. Although payroll processing is usually more straightforward than benefits administration, many companies outsource this work as well. Several large companies—such as Ceridian and ADP—and many smaller companies specialize in this type of service.

At one time, there were few if any firms capable of providing the full range of compensation administration services. That changed in 2001, when the Canadian Imperial Bank of Commerce outsourced nearly half of its human resources department, including payroll and benefits administration, to EDS (now a part of HP Enterprises). In the process, some 200 of the bank's HR employees were moved to EDS. According to bank officials, the primary motive for the move was not to save money but rather to free the bank's HR department from the detailed administrative work that could be done better by a specialized service provider.[8] In 2003, the Bank of Montreal followed suit, signing a 10-year deal with Exult Consulting (now a part of Aon Hewitt) to outsource most of its HR transactional work.[9]

The movement toward outsourcing may be losing momentum, however. As far back as 2004, a survey of the priorities of Canadian HR managers found that only three percent considered outsourcing of HR functions a priority—dead last on a list of 21 possibilities.[10] This may be at least partly due to the development of improved HRMS (human resources management system) software, as was demonstrated in the opening vignette. By 2013, one prominent commentator was asking aloud whether "the shine [has] come off HR outsourcing."[11] Many companies today (especially the larger ones) feel that they can handle HR functions more effectively in-house.

Moreover, outsourcing is not necessarily an all-or-nothing proposition. For example, payroll can be done entirely in-house, or it can be entirely outsourced, or it can be co-sourced, with the employer responsible for entering employee pay and attendance, and the outsourcer preparing the paycheques and other documentation.

The future of payroll will evolve with changes in demographics and advancements in technology. The younger generations entering the workforce are much more technologically astute and have more confidence that they can manage their technological processes and information. Thus, there will likely be a continued decrease in the need for a fully outsourced system. Instead, co-sourced options will continue to offer payroll services that can be run and submitted through an app on a mobile device or smartphone, as well as cloud source computing that can centralize data, ensure compliance, and offer trend data and analytics.[12]

## Advantages of Outsourcing

Outsourcing payroll and benefits administration has several advantages. The first is cost. Outside providers generally realize economies of scale that most employers cannot. For example, the costs of computerized benefits systems are very large for a single business, but an outside provider can spread these costs across numerous customers. Outside providers also achieve economies in terms of training, for their staff can specialize in compensation administration on a full-time basis, thereby also reducing costs.

A second advantage is expertise. Outside providers may be able to employ specialized legal and professional experts that a single employer—especially a small or medium-sized one—simply could not afford. Third, once freed of the responsibility for the day-to-day administration of the compensation system, in-house compensation managers may be able to spend more time on the strategic aspects of pay rather than on simply keeping the system running.[13] However, there is debate about whether that actually happens. One U.S. researcher found "no evidence that an HR department becomes 'more strategic' after outsourcing major parts of the HR function. In fact, I found the exact opposite."[14] In fact, as Canada Post realized, with better management of its HR systems, it made sense to bring the payroll function back in-house as illustrated in Compensation Today 13.2.

## Disadvantages of Outsourcing

One concern about outsourcing benefits administration is that the employer may lose touch with emerging problems and issues, or even lose the capacity to understand the benefits system. The firm may come to rely too heavily on advice from the service provider, who may not understand the organizational context, especially if changes to managerial strategy are taking place. Moreover, service providers may not be concerned about looking for the mix of benefits that best serves the particular compensation objectives of a given employer.

Managing the relationship with the vendor can be difficult and time consuming. If service contracts fail to specify all the details of who is responsible for what, within what time frame, and with what recourse if performance failures occur, then disagreements may materialize that take time and energy to resolve. For example, if paycheques are late, who covers the cost to employees of bounced cheques and late credit card payments?

Another potential drawback to outsourcing is the impact on employee morale if it is necessary to lay off employees when their functions are contracted out.[15] This is not much of an issue for classical firms, but for human relations and high-involvement firms, it is a serious consideration. Costs of severance and termination counselling also need to be considered. Although CIBC avoided this problem by transferring its in-house employees to the service provider, this option is not available to all firms.

---

### COMPENSATION TODAY 13.2

#### CANADA POST IMPROVES ITS INTEGRATED HR SYSTEM

As the century turned, Canada Post had a big dilemma. It was trying to cope in the electronic age with HR systems that had originated in the paper age. It seemed that every HR process had its own system, none of which communicated well with the other systems or with users. Supervisors and employees had trouble getting basic information about pay and benefits and making simple changes to employee hours or pay was an arduous process. Moreover, none of these systems connected well to the payroll function, which had been outsourced years before.

Like many firms, Canada Post decided to create a new HR system to integrate all its HR processes. But unlike many firms, it avoided what is known as the "customization trap," which is driven by the tendency of firms to want to customize commercial off-the-shelf systems to match their existing systems. Because customized systems are very complex, customization takes far longer than implementing an off-the-shelf system. Moreover, unanticipated difficulties emerge, costs are much higher, program elements don't work well together, and upgrades are expensive because they too have to be customized.

Instead, Canada Post went with an off-the-shelf integrated HR system from a major provider of HR software and customized only where absolutely necessary. This process was so successful that it even made economic sense to bring the payroll function back in-house, bucking a trend toward payroll outsourcing that had been evident for two decades or more.

Source: Todd Humber, "Through Wind, and Sleet, and the Internet," *Canadian HR Reporter*, November 8, 2004, G1–G8.

When should outsourcing be considered? Four factors are key:

- company size,
- internal capabilities,
- complexity and dynamism of the compensation system, and
- the strategic importance of compensation.

Regarding company size, research has shown that many large firms believe they can handle payroll and benefits more efficiently in-house because they can achieve economies of scale that are not available to smaller firms.[16] Internal capabilities can also influence outsourcing decisions: if the firm is already using a sophisticated human resources information system, and if computer systems and supports are already in place, separating payroll and benefits from the system by outsourcing them may make little sense.

The more complex, unique, and dynamic the compensation system is, the more preferable it is to develop in-house expertise for running it because an outside provider may be reluctant to devote specialized resources to an individual customer, for this would reduce the provider's economies of scale and drive up costs. Also, dynamic systems interfere with the provider's economies of scale if frequent changes are needed, which either drives up costs or generates provider resistance to system changes, thus causing compensation system rigidity.

A final consideration is the strategic importance of compensation. The more that compensation is regarded as a strategic variable, the more important it is to maintain in-house control of the compensation system. However, as discussed earlier, some observers believe that the strategic focus of the compensation function is enhanced when routine administrative functions are outsourced. The proper balance between outsourcing and in-house provision of compensation services probably differs for each firm.

© iStockphoto.com/Kritchanut

Outsourcing can help with pay administration.

# DEVELOPING THE IMPLEMENTATION PLAN

Once all these issues have been dealt with, an implementation plan needs to be developed. Key aspects include (1) the plan for managing the implementation process, (2) the training plan, (3) the plan for communicating the new system, and (4) the plan for evaluating the new system.

## DEVELOPING THE PLAN FOR MANAGING IMPLEMENTATION

Of course, someone or some group needs to be assigned responsibility for spearheading implementation. Depending on the magnitude and scope of the changes, several committees or task forces may be needed, each responsible for a particular aspect of the new compensation system, operating under the supervision of an umbrella group. For example, there may be one implementation task force for base pay, another for performance pay, and a third for indirect pay. There may even be separate task forces for specific programs, such as profit sharing. If the compensation plan is different for different employee groups, there may be a separate task force for each group.

The composition of these task forces is an important matter. Normally, the umbrella group is chaired by a senior executive, such as the head of Human Resources. It may even include the CEO if the changes are of sufficient magnitude. This could conceivably be the same body that developed the new compensation system. Whether or not it includes employee representatives will reflect the managerial strategy pursued by the organization. For example, the inclusion of a broad spectrum of employees, especially on the subsidiary committees or task forces, would certainly be expected for a high-involvement organization but not for a classical organization.

The schedule for implementation is a crucial matter. When will the system start? How long will it take to carry out the various implementation steps? It is crucial to develop an implementation timeline that details each step in the process and dates by which they will be completed.

When developing the implementation plan, it is important to identify any matters that will require attention before implementation can begin. For example, performance pay will be effective only if employees have control over performance. For there to be such control, it may be necessary to decentralize decision making. But that decentralization will be irresponsible unless employees have the information to make effective decisions and the training to interpret and use that information. When will this training be done? When will the information systems be revamped? All this must be considered when the implementation schedule is being developed. Of course, the greater the number of changes, the more complex this pre-implementation stage will be. But the more that an organization gets the stage properly set, the larger the payoff will be later.

Timing is another important implementation decision. If extensive changes are being made, should they be phased in? In theory, no. There is an old saying: "You can't leap a chasm in two jumps." To function effectively, all complementary parts of the system need to be in place at the same time. The reality, however, is that a single implementation date simply may not be feasible for all the needed changes. This timing dilemma is one reason that many compensation changes fail to produce the intended results.

But if everyone understands that all the pieces are coming, phasing in these changes may not be a problem. For example, if jobs are changed to make them more challenging and interesting, the intrinsic motivation from this alone may be enough to keep employees motivated, at least for a while. But if employees do become more productive and contribute more to the organization, this enthusiasm will fade if the promised financial recognition fails to follow promptly. Conversely, if group performance pay is introduced to promote teamwork, changes to the job structure to allow employees more control over their performance cannot lag too far behind.

If the organization is very large and is divided into separate business units, it may be possible to implement the new system in one of these units first, in order to assess the consequences and to identify any adjustments that need to be made.

## DEVELOPING THE TRAINING PLAN

Developing a training plan is important when implementing a new compensation system. First, key support people in the Human Resources department must be trained to fully understand the system and its components. They can then serve as trainers and advisers for the rest of the organization. Second, there must be sufficient training for managers and supervisors, who will play a key role in many aspects of the system, from job description, to job evaluation, to performance appraisal, to approving salary increases. The third step involves training all the other people who will play a role in operating the systems, ranging from secretaries (who must submit departmental time information) to recruiters (so that they will be able to explain the compensation system accurately to potential new employees).

## DEVELOPING THE COMMUNICATIONS PLAN

It is crucial to develop a plan to communicate the new system to all those who are affected by it. A pay system will not have the desired impact on employee attitudes and behaviour if it is not understood; indeed, it could have a negative impact on attitudes and behaviour if it is misunderstood.

Not only should the new system be well communicated, but so should the need for the new system. Employees are always sensitive about pay, so a misunderstanding of the motives underlying the new system may arouse suspicion, mistrust, and even resistance. Preventing this suspicion and mistrust is one reason that many experts recommend employee participation in compensation system development. Another advantage is that communicating information on the final system will be easier because employees have been kept informed as it was being developed.

When developing the communication plan, organizations need to carefully plan the media and processes, along with the timing. In some cases, the communication process starts with a presentation by the CEO regarding the general features of the new system, the reasons for its introduction, and its objectives. This may be followed by small-group meetings conducted by supervisors (once they have been trained in the new system) or by personnel from the Human Resources department. If the new system is complex, separate meetings may be planned for different aspects of the new system—one meeting for direct pay and another for indirect pay, for example. Some firms also prepare webcasts for employees who cannot attend these meetings and for employees hired later. Informational brochures (or websites) typically need to be developed for each plan aspect. In addition, a telephone or email hotline for questions should be set up.

If individual performance pay is part of the compensation package, then performance expectations also need to be communicated. If performance pay is to be linked to departmental or organizational indicators, then management must not only communicate what these indicators are but also provide status reports on these indicators. Some manufacturing plants actually have "electronic scoreboards" that provide immediate updates on the achievement of organizational goals.[17] At Saskatoon-based Cameco Corporation, one of the world's largest producers of uranium, charts showing progress toward meeting divisional and corporate goals are posted at every work unit and are updated throughout the year.

As discussed, effective communication is required not only when the compensation system is being implemented but also on an ongoing basis, whether or not the compensation system is new. Because of the importance of ongoing communication, we come back to this issue later in the chapter.

## DEVELOPING THE EVALUATION PLAN

Before implementation, the organization needs to develop a plan for evaluating the success of the compensation system, along with an approach to monitoring conditions that may warrant changes to it. Evaluation criteria need to be set out, as well as procedures for collecting the evaluation information. Depending on the criteria, organizations may need to collect some evaluation information (such as employee attitudes) prior to implementation, to serve as a benchmark for evaluating the consequences of the new system. The evaluation criteria should be based on the strategic objectives for the compensation system; ideally, they will have been developed during the compensation strategy formulation process. (Both of these crucial issues—evaluating the compensation system and monitoring organizational circumstances—are discussed in more depth later in the chapter.)

## IMPLEMENTING THE COMPENSATION SYSTEM

Relative to the preparation, actual implementation of the new compensation system is relatively straightforward. The implementation task forces need to be staffed and the administrative infrastructure put in place and tested. The key actors in the system need to be trained, and the system must be communicated. Finally, the new system needs to be launched, and the wrinkles smoothed out.

### STEP 1: ESTABLISH THE IMPLEMENTATION TASK FORCES

The first step in implementation is to appoint individuals to the implementation bodies and to provide technical and administrative support for those bodies. Task force members need to fully understand the new compensation system as well as the key issues and steps in the implementation process.

### STEP 2: PUT THE INFRASTRUCTURE INTO PLACE

Next, the compensation infrastructure must be put in place. Employees need to be hired or assigned to the compensation unit. Facilities need to be provided. The computer system must be developed and tested. Additional hardware may need to be purchased. Human resources personnel must be trained in the system. The forms, brochures, communications materials, and websites need to be developed. Trainers need to be selected and trained.

As well, necessary pre-implementation evaluation material needs to be collected. For example, it is often useful to conduct surveys of key employee attitudes before system implementation to have a baseline for future comparisons. Such a survey should ideally be done as early in the process as possible because information about the new system may affect these pre-existing attitudes.

## STEP 3: TEST THE SYSTEM

It is crucial that the compensation system be tested before implementation. One approach is to run a computer simulation. Employees would be put on the system, data collected and input into the system, pay calculated, and so on—all before the previous system is abandoned. This test allows flaws and bugs in the system to be identified and the accuracy of the calculations to be double-checked.

## STEP 4: CONDUCT THE TRAINING

Once the infrastructure is in place and debugged, it is time to train all those outside the HR department who will be playing a role in the new system. This normally includes managers, supervisors, and other personnel who administer the process. Training sessions must be scheduled, trainees informed, and the training conducted.

## STEP 5: COMMUNICATE INFORMATION ON THE SYSTEM

The communication program should now be activated. But simply making sure that everyone has sat through the webcast from the company president, has received the plan brochures, or has been referred to the website doesn't guarantee that communication has taken place. Communication does not actually occur until understanding passes from the sender to the receiver. Feedback is needed to check whether the key elements of the message were successfully communicated. Two-way communication greatly enhances the likelihood of effective communication.

## STEP 6: LAUNCH AND ADJUST THE SYSTEM

After all this preparation, the actual launch of the system may seem anticlimactic. However, it is likely that the first "cycle" of the new compensation system will be extremely hectic, with many unanticipated problems and issues arising. No matter how careful the preparation, some elements of the plan will not work. Adjustments will need to be made just to keep the system running. Many of these changes will be short-term fixes, which will later be incorporated into the system. For example, the computer system may not correctly calculate the holiday pay of permanent part-time employees who are on medical leave. But this adjustment can be calculated by hand until the computer system is reprogrammed.

## COMMUNICATING COMPENSATION SYSTEM INFORMATION

Two types of ongoing communication are important. One type focuses on ensuring that all who play a role in operating the compensation system understand their roles. The other type focuses on ensuring that all who are subject to the compensation system understand it. Research has found that employee satisfaction with their compensation is directly related to their understanding of the compensation system. For example, one study found that

75 percent of employees with a "very good" understanding of their compensation system thought themselves fairly paid, compared with 33 percent of those with a "poor" understanding of the pay system.[18]

## KEEPING MANAGERS INFORMED

An important part of compensation administration involves making sure that all those who help operate the system understand their roles. Some of these roles may seem obvious—such as reporting hours worked or employee absences—but new supervisors may not be aware of them. In addition, someone must keep track of overtime hours and report them, along with changes in job status, including terminations and new hires. When merit pay or bonuses are used, supervisors must understand the criteria and procedures for awarding these. Of course, they must also understand the compensation system well enough to be able to accurately answer employee questions about pay.

As an example of how to achieve this, a pharmaceutical company introduced new pay grades and pay ranges, based on a points system of job evaluation, which had never been used at that company before.[19] The company assembled all its managers for a day-long training session, during which the new job evaluation system was explained, including how compensation surveys would be used to create the pay ranges, as well as the principles for ensuring that pay would be equitable, competitive with the market, and performance based. Feedback indicated that managers felt that this session would really help them in dealing with employees regarding compensation issues.

Besides the "what" of the new compensation system, managers must also be given the tools and knowledge to explain the "why" of the new compensation system to their employees, including the reasons for the change and how it will contribute to the company's success. If the compensation system has been designed strategically, managers need to understand the intended links between compensation and organizational performance so that they can communicate this connection to their employees.

## KEEPING EMPLOYEES INFORMED

If compensation is to serve its intended role of shaping employee attitudes and behaviour, those employees have to understand the compensation that applies to them—that is, the types of compensation provided, the amount, and the procedures for determining the amount. In addition, employees need to be informed of the compensation and benefits options available to them and may need guidance in selecting the options that are best for them. Employees may have questions about their pay and the way it was calculated, and they must have some avenue to discuss their concerns about pay. Of course, if pay is based on certain performance indicators, as in the case of profit sharing or gain sharing, employees should be kept up to date on this information.

Employees' knowledge about their pension plans is especially weak.[20] This may cause employees to discount the value of this important component of the compensation system. Although certain types of information, such as an annual statement of pension contributions, are required by law, employers need to go beyond this minimal communication if they want employees to recognize the value of this reward.

As employee benefits choices become more complex, and as pensions move away from defined benefit plans toward defined contribution plans, the need for employee communication and education increases greatly. But most firms have been slow to respond to this need.

Social media is used to keep employees informed.

For example, many defined contribution pension plans have a matching employer contribution with decreased management fees and investments that are not accessible to individual retail investors. However, research findings show that employee contributions remain low, partly due to employees' lack of comprehension.[21] For this reason, in 2004, pension regulators published Guidelines for Capital Accumulation Plans which outlined employers' responsibilities for selecting and managing investments and for educating plan members.[22] While the extent to which employers can be held liable for poor pension choices by employees is unclear, making some effort to ensure that employees have the tools to make informed decisions in this very important matter is clearly in the employer's best interest.

Legal cases have found employers liable if they have failed to fully inform employees about benefits to which they may be entitled. In one case, an employee with behavioural problems quit his job after his employer threatened to fire him for unacceptable conduct.[23] Later, it was discovered that the employee's behaviour was due to mental illness. The court found that the employer was negligent in not informing the employee of his right to make a claim under the long-term disability policy that covered employees, and in failing to assist him in filing the claim.

This problem of keeping employees properly informed of their rights to benefits can be especially severe with flexible benefit plans, where there is much more potential for confusion than under fixed benefit plans. Based on court cases, the following steps should be taken, as a minimum, to avoid legal liability in this area.

- Have a competent benefits provider or lawyer certify that the employee benefits booklets are correct and divulge the necessary options of which employees should be cognizant. Keep a record of all versions of the benefits booklet on file.
- Provide clear, concise information concerning each employee's entitlement to benefits.
- Review benefits with each employee to identify his or her obligations under each benefit.
- Ensure each employee comprehends what has been communicated at each benefit meeting.
- Devise a written list of concerns, questions and answers, and details supplied to employees at benefits information training or discussions for both current and new employees. Outline and date in writing everything that has been discussed at benefit lunch-and-learns or meetings to have permanently on file.
- Understand that the benefits provider is acting as an agent for the employer. If the benefits provider presents inadequate or incorrect information to employees, the employer will be held legally accountable.[24]

## EVALUATING THE COMPENSATION SYSTEM

Evaluating the effectiveness of the compensation system is no simple matter, and this aspect of compensation management is probably the most neglected. There are two main reasons for this. The first is that separating out the precise impact of compensation on organizational performance with any degree of certainty is virtually impossible. There are just too many factors that affect overall organizational performance. The second reason is that most organizations don't even try to evaluate their compensation systems, either because they don't know how or because they consider it futile.

If the right information is collected, useful inferences about the effectiveness of the compensation system can be drawn. However, a thorough evaluation takes considerable effort using multiple indicators, and a slipshod attempt at evaluation that involves only a few indicators may be misleading and do more harm than good. Only with a comprehensive set of relevant indicators can useful conclusions about the success of a compensation system be drawn.

Evaluating the impact of the compensation system can be approached in three main ways: by examining its impact on compensation objectives, its impact on compensation costs, and its impact on employee behaviours and attitudes.

## IMPACT ON COMPENSATION OBJECTIVES

When formulating compensation strategy (see Chapter 6), the organization should establish objectives for the compensation system, as well as specific indicators of success in achieving those objectives. During the pre-implementation phase, the organization should develop procedures to collect the necessary data to assess these indicators. After implementation, the firm then needs to assess the extent to which these objectives have been met.

A key issue when assessing whether objectives have been accomplished is the time span over which the evaluation is to take place. The logical time for the first evaluation is one year after implementation, because one complete cycle will have been carried out. But is one year long enough to determine whether the desired consequences of the new system are materializing?

The answer: It depends on the magnitude of the changes being made and on the types of consequences that are desired. Some indicators, such as employee attitudes, can change fairly quickly (especially in a downward direction!), while other indicators, such as the ones that assess organizational performance, change much more slowly. A phenomenon known as the **initial dip** often occurs; this is a tendency for performance to decline during the initial stages of any change, until people start to understand and become proficient in the new system. Moreover, costs of changes are usually immediate, while benefits are gradual. For example, a change in compensation strategy to lead the market will increase costs immediately, but will increase productivity only gradually, as the turnover rate declines and as the firm is able to attract a higher calibre of employees.

Conversely, some changes—such as slashing pay rates—may bring immediate gain (in terms of reducing compensation costs) but long-term pain, as the company's best performers gradually leave. The key point is that it may take several years to really understand the impact of sweeping changes to the compensation system; therefore, evaluation needs to be carried out on a continuing basis.

Imagine that our compensation objectives have been fully achieved. We should pat ourselves on the back, right? Not necessarily. We still need to examine whether there have been any unintended negative consequences. The following examples illustrate actual cases where compensation objectives were achieved, but the net impact of the new compensation system on company performance was actually negative.

A Thai restaurant was, at one point, a hot spot. However, over the years, the restaurant became less popular, and waiting times dwindled. The restaurant then decided, to improve

**initial dip**
A tendency for performance to decline during the initial stages of any change.

their financial performance, they would have fewer waiting staff, decrease the portion sizes, increase the prices, and lower the quality. They were, in fact, able to cut costs. However, these efforts only lead to many more lost customers.[25]

A more disastrous example is Boeing, the aerospace company. The Boeing 737 Max was a defective plane model that caused two fatal accidents and was thus grounded for a substantial time. A former engineer claimed that the company had placed enormous stress on engineers to decrease production costs to circumvent close examination by the Federal Aviation Administration. Engineers were provided with strict cost targets and were supplied with scarce resources. The outcome was calamitous.[26]

In another case, a consumer electronics firm wanted to more rapidly reduce production costs of new products after their introduction. (Whenever a new product is introduced, production costs usually decrease over time.) The firm instituted bonuses to production managers based on how quickly after a product launch these cost reductions were achieved. The objective was achieved: after the bonus system was implemented, production costs fell much more rapidly than before. However, the company eventually discovered that managers were achieving this cost reduction by delaying product launches until they could work out ways of reducing production costs that could be quickly implemented after product launch. This slowed the introduction of new products and translated into losses in sales and market share.

The key point here is that it is important to put success in meeting compensation objectives in the context of broader organizational performance, and to carefully monitor a variety of indicators beyond only those associated with the compensation objectives.

## IMPACT ON COMPENSATION COSTS

One aspect of compensation that all firms will want to evaluate is the impact on compensation costs, as illustrated in Compensation Today 13.3. Compensation costs can be examined by comparing actual to budgeted costs, and by examining compensation cost indicators.

### Budgeted Versus Actual Compensation Costs

One way to examine the impact of the new system on compensation costs is by comparing actual to budgeted compensation costs. Imagine that you discover that actual compensation expenditures are much lower than budgeted. Great news, right? Not necessarily. Perhaps it means that senior employees hate the new system and are quitting in droves, only to be replaced by new employees who are paid much less—but are also much less experienced. This may make compensation costs look good but will probably have adverse consequences in terms of training costs and employee performance, which may well outweigh the compensation savings over the longer term.

Now, let us suppose the opposite has occurred and that total compensation expenditures are much higher than budgeted. This can only be bad news, right? Maybe not. In fact, this may be wonderful news, if these higher employee earnings are primarily a result of, say, a gain-sharing plan. Because cost savings are split between employer and employee in a gain-sharing plan, the more employees earn from it, the greater the savings for the company that the gain-sharing plan must be producing.

Or perhaps the higher-than-expected compensation expenditures stem from the fact that the compensation system is increasing retention of experienced employees more than expected. The result is fewer compensation savings from replacing senior employees with new employees, but also lower recruitment and training costs and a more productive workforce.

Higher-than-budgeted compensation expenditures, however, may not be wonderful news. Perhaps the job evaluation system has been overly generous in rating jobs, so that too many jobs are in high pay grades. Perhaps supervisors are granting merit increases too readily. Perhaps the performance thresholds for individual bonus plans have been set too low. Perhaps some employee benefits are costing much more than expected.

Another possibility is that the budgeted compensation figures were not realistic in the first place and if so, any comparisons to the budget are meaningless.

## Compensation Cost Indicators

When examining compensation costs, firms should at least examine two main indicators: compensation cost ratios and average earnings per employee. **Compensation cost ratios** are determined by taking total compensation costs as a percentage of total costs or as a percentage of revenues. **Average employee earnings** takes total compensation and divides it by the number of full-time-equivalent employees it covers. These two measures are not synonymous and tell us different things.

For example, it is possible for average employee earnings to go up but for the compensation cost ratio to go down. It is also possible for average employee earnings to go down but for the compensation cost ratio to go up. Finally, it is also possible for both average earnings and compensation cost ratio to go up and for company profits to go up at the same time. How can this be?

Average employee earnings takes the perspective of the individual employee. If average employee earnings go up, then the typical employee is earning more money; if it goes down, the typical employee is earning less money. Compensation cost ratio takes the total of all

**compensation cost ratio**
The ratio of total compensation costs to total costs or to revenues.

**average employee earnings**
Total compensation divided by the number of full-time equivalent employees.

compensation paid to all employees. It may change for one of three reasons: (1) if average employee earnings change, (2) if the total number of employees changes, or (3) if total costs or revenues change. Thus, it is possible for average employee earnings to increase but for the compensation cost ratio to decrease if fewer employees are required to perform the work of the organization.

It is also possible for the compensation cost ratio to increase, even without any increase in total compensation or average earnings, if total costs or revenues go down. If the increase in the compensation cost ratio is due to lower noncompensation costs, then the increase in the compensation cost ratio is not necessarily bad news at all. However, if the increase in the compensation cost ratio is due to declining revenues, then it is bad news, although not necessarily bad news caused by the compensation system. Conversely, a decrease in the compensation cost ratio is not good news if it is due to increases in noncompensation costs, but it is good news if it is due to increases in revenues. In the latter case, the decreased compensation cost ratio is a sign of greater productivity.

Clearly, what happens with employee earnings and total compensation costs is just part of the picture. Also important is what happens to employee performance and productivity. Employee performance may be instrumental in reducing noncompensation costs or in increasing revenue. Also, higher average earnings may increase the employee retention rate, thus reducing recruitment and training costs.

In medium to large organizations, it makes a lot of sense to examine compensation expenditures on a unit-by-unit basis. If one or two departments stand out from the others, this difference may warrant investigation. These differences may turn out to be justified, or they may indicate inconsistency in the application of the new system. Other ways to assess compensation costs are by comparing them with compensation expenditures in previous years or with those of competitors.

Unless the goal of the new system is only to reduce compensation costs, compensation costs alone do not give the whole picture. What is important is what the organization is receiving in return for its investment in compensation. Any evaluation that starts and ends with compensation costs may be worse than useless. Instead, the total impact of the system must be assessed.

## IMPACT ON EMPLOYEE BEHAVIOURS AND ATTITUDES

A variety of indicators can be used to assess the extent to which the desired employee behaviours and attitudes are occurring. As you know, three types of employee behaviour—membership, task, and citizenship—may be important to an organization, as well as three key job attitudes—job satisfaction, work motivation, and organizational identification. Additional attitudes that are highly relevant are employee attitudes toward compensation processes and compensation results.

### Membership Behaviour

Three key aspects of membership behaviour are attraction, retention, and attendance. Various indicators measure how effective the organization is at attracting new members. One indicator is simply the number of qualified applicants that job postings attract. Another is the percentage of offers made to potential new employees that are refused.

The main indicator of retention is employee turnover; however, some types of turnover are more serious than others. For example, is turnover spread across employees performing at different performance levels, or is it mainly high-performing employees who are quitting?

Is turnover concentrated in certain departments or units? Reasons for turnover are also important. Some employees quit because they have received a better offer from another employer; other employees quit because their spouses have been transferred to other cities. It is important to know the main reasons for employee turnover. Many organizations use exit interviews in an attempt to ascertain why employees are quitting the organization.

Another indicator of membership behaviour is absenteeism. Absenteeism can be measured in a variety of ways. One method is to simply tally up all the days missed by employees for any reason and divide by the number of employees. Note, however, that some absenteeism is unavoidable, due to reasons such as illness. That is why many experts argue that involuntary absenteeism should be excluded from the calculations. But while it might be theoretically correct to do this, actually doing it may be quite difficult. An alternative is to add up the number of occurrences and divide by the number of employees, thus yielding a statistic that is less likely to be skewed by long absences owing to serious illness.

## Task Behaviour

Employee performance has at least two dimensions: quantity and quality of work produced. Quantity of work can be measured in a variety of ways. For example, units produced or number of clients served can be divided by the number of employees, and compared over time or with competitors. Another measure is revenue divided by number of employees. Quality of performance can also be measured using indicators such as customer satisfaction, number of employee errors, or scrap losses.

## Citizenship Behaviour

Citizenship behaviour is the most difficult of the three key behaviours to measure in a quantitative way. One indicator might be the number of useful employee suggestions that are submitted. In addition, indicators such as "shrinkage"—employee theft—can be expected to decline if citizenship increases. Other departments or customers can be surveyed to determine the degree of cooperativeness and citizenship practised by members of a given department. Feedback from customers about employees who go above and beyond the call of duty can be gathered.

## Job Attitudes

Throughout this book, three key job attitudes have been discussed: job satisfaction, work motivation, and organizational identification. Over the years, many survey scales that measure these attitudes have been developed. In recent years, surveys have also included measures of "employee engagement,"[27] which is analogous to intrinsic motivation. Many firms conduct employee attitude surveys on an annual basis to track these attitudes over time.

## Compensation Attitudes

Employee attitudes toward the compensation system can also be surveyed. Two types of compensation attitudes need to be assessed: (1) satisfaction with the total amount of compensation received (distributive justice), and (2) satisfaction with the process by which compensation is determined (procedural justice). Both reflect the perceived fairness or equity of the system (see Chapter 3).

Attitudes toward individual components of compensation can also be examined. For example, are employees satisfied with the amount and fairness of their merit pay? What about the profit-sharing plan? Many organizations that use internal compensation surveys have a section dealing with employee benefits. Which benefits are employees most satisfied with? Least satisfied? Is the amount of the benefit satisfactory? Are benefits fairly allocated? Would employees prefer to replace certain benefits with other benefits?

Another important aspect to examine is employee understanding of the compensation system. Misunderstandings can cause dissatisfaction and complaints. Perhaps even more important, a system that is misunderstood will not have the desired effect on employee attitudes and behaviour, even if it is designed properly.

Organizations can also infer compensation understanding and attitudes toward compensation from employee behaviours. For example, the number of employee calls to the compensation office may provide an index of understanding. The number of complaints and grievances that pertain to compensation can also be tallied and examined. Or if there is a formal appeals process for compensation, the number of appeals initiated and the number granted can also be examined.

# MONITORING CHANGING CIRCUMSTANCES

"Compensation systems don't suddenly break; instead they gradually become obsolete."[28] In some cases, this obsolescence is so gradual that nobody notices that the compensation system is no longer adding value to the organization. To prevent obsolescence and ensure maximum value, organizations need to watch for changing circumstances that signal a need for adjustments to the system. These changing circumstances may be external or internal to the organization.

## CHANGES IN EXTERNAL CIRCUMSTANCES

External circumstances that may trigger a need for changes in the compensation system include legislative and tax changes, labour market changes, changes in competitive conditions, and socioeconomic changes. Crisis and pandemics may also trigger changes to compensation systems; these may be reflected in changes in all the external circumstances. For instance, the COVID-19 pandemic resulted in pay increases for several essential workers, grocery workers, and others. Others suffered pay cuts. Compensation Today 13.4 discusses one sector experiencing such cuts. While most of these pay changes may be temporal and cease once the pandemic is over, there may be longer term legal implications for hazard pay, as well as the pay determination process for essential workers.

### Legislative and Tax Changes

Provincial and federal laws have a significant impact on compensation systems. Moreover, these laws change quite often, because of revisions made by legislators or court decisions. Examples include employment standards laws, human rights laws, and pay equity laws. At the beginning of each year, organizations need to be aware of changes to RRSP limits, Canada/Quebec Pension Plan payments, Employment Insurance payments, and income tax and/or corporate tax provisions. Any of these changes may have implications for the compensation system.

### Labour Market Changes

As the demand or supply of particular categories of workers changes, attracting and retaining employees can become more—or less—difficult. The compensation system may need to change in response to either situation.

## Competitive Environment Changes

Changes in competitors' policies or the emergence of new competitors may have significant implications for compensation policies, either directly or indirectly. An example of a direct implication is when a competitor adds an attractive new benefit to its compensation package, so that it is difficult to attract employees without offering a similar benefit. An example of an indirect implication is when new competitors force existing firms to adopt a new managerial strategy, which then triggers a need for change in a variety of structural variables, including compensation.

## Socioeconomic Changes

Changes in either social attitudes or general economic conditions can also trigger a need for changes to the compensation system. For example, if economic conditions become more buoyant, an organization may decide to focus on noneconomic types of rewards, such as advancement opportunities or intrinsic rewards. If social attitudes toward a particular industry become less favourable, the organization may need to boost pay levels.

Demographic changes may also be important. For example, an aging workforce will likely trigger a much greater focus on pension plans and health benefits. Demographers point out that baby boomers (the generation born between 1947 and 1966) caused a major blockage to career advancement in organizations because the top end of hierarchies simply cannot accommodate so many people. However, this blockage should gradually diminish; the first of the boomers started to reach retirement age in 2012.[29]

This process will take a decade or more, so in the meantime, experts suggest that **spiral career paths** will continue to be important, with most employees taking at least two sideways

**spiral career paths**
Career advancement marked by a combination of sideways and vertical progression.

steps for each step up the hierarchy. This spiral pattern creates more pressure for firms to adopt pay-for-knowledge systems. However, whether or not a pay-for-knowledge system is implemented, employees will also value training and education opportunities highly as rewards (both for intrinsic reasons and because this makes employees more marketable), and organizations that offer these rewards will be much more attractive to employees than those that do not.

## CHANGES IN INTERNAL CIRCUMSTANCES

Internal changes that can trigger a need to change the compensation system include changes in managerial strategy, in the workforce, in the organization's financial circumstances, and in the scope of the organization.

### Changes in Managerial Strategy

Whenever the organization's fundamental managerial strategy changes, so must the compensation strategy. Factors that drive changes to managerial strategy have already been covered; they include changes in the organization's environment, its technology, its competitive strategy, its size, and its workforce. These changes themselves may also trigger a need for compensation changes.

### Changes in the Workforce

Changes in the organization's workforce affect reward and compensation systems in a variety of ways. If the type of employee recruited by the firm changes over time, then the needs of these employees may be different from those of previous employees, and the compensation system may have to change to recognize that. For example, if the workforce ages, compensation will need to be oriented more toward pension plans and retirement income. Conversely, if the workforce becomes younger, more cash and more family benefits, such as dental plans, may be needed.

A trend for most organizations in Canada is toward greater workforce diversity. This makes it more difficult to define a single reward system that meets everyone's needs. Some compensation elements, such as a flexible benefit plan, can accommodate diversity and changes in the workforce more easily than other systems.

### Changes in Financial Circumstances

A weakening of the organization's financial circumstances may trigger a need to cut costs, including compensation costs. The compensation strategy may be sound, but the organization may simply no longer have the funds to support it. In these circumstances, firms often ask for compensation concessions from their employees. As discussed later in the chapter, organizations have a variety of options for dealing with this problem. Firms with a greater degree of variable pay are less vulnerable to these changes than firms with less variable pay.

### Changes in Scope of the Organization

One obvious circumstance requiring adjustment of the compensation system is a company merger or acquisition. The two organizations will almost certainly have different compensation systems. Merging the systems can be a very complex process, and there are no hard and fast rules for doing so. Of course, in some cases, integrating the compensation systems may not be necessary if the organizations are to operate autonomously.

But when the units are to be integrated, a wide variety of compensation decisions will have to be made. The usual practice is to adopt the compensation system of the largest actor in the merger, but there are many constraints on this process, including legal obligations.

Furthermore, not merging the compensation systems where employees will be working together doing similar work is a formula for inequity and dissatisfaction as well as an ongoing administrative nightmare. This is just one of the reasons mergers often turn out to be much less successful than originally envisaged.

## ADAPTING THE COMPENSATION SYSTEM

What do you do when your evaluation has indicated that your compensation system is not achieving the expected results? How do you identify adaptations that will produce the desired results? Before you can answer this question, you will need to know exactly what is going wrong with your current system. The problems might not have anything to do with your compensation system at all, so you must first ascertain whether this is the case.

This final section of this chapter discusses some key considerations when making adaptations to the compensation system. Then it examines two specific situations that may call for making adaptations: financial crises and labour shortages. Finally, it deals with the thorny question of whether exceptions to compensation policy should be made for individual employees.

### IDENTIFYING WHAT TO ADAPT

Suppose your compensation system does not seem to be producing the desired results. Your first reaction may be to ask yourself what changes to the compensation system should be made to correct this problem. But this should not be your first question.

Your first question should be: Why are the desired results not occurring? There are many possible answers. Perhaps the wrong compensation strategy was adopted. But maybe not. Perhaps the compensation strategy is correct, but the technical processes for transforming the strategy into a compensation system were poorly designed. Or maybe these two aspects are fine but the system itself has been poorly implemented.

Maybe the necessary complementary policies have not been implemented. For example, a system for employee participation in decision making is necessary to realize the benefits of employee stock plans. Effective training programs are necessary for pay-for-knowledge systems to work. Or the lack of results could also simply be a problem of time: you are expecting too much too soon. Alternatively, maybe the problem is due to some cause completely unrelated to compensation, such as an aging plant or changes in the quality of raw materials. Finally, perhaps your expectations for the compensation system were not realistic in the first place.

How do you know which it is? All this shows that compensation is less a science than an art and that there is no substitute for understanding the organization and its people. This is why comprehensive evaluation data are so important. Evaluation data should allow you to rule out certain causes and perhaps pinpoint the problem. For example, if employees do not understand the compensation system, or if they misperceive it, this should be corrected before any changes are made to the compensation system itself.

The key point to remember here is that only when you have identified the cause of the perceived problem can you identify the proper adaptations. And when considering adaptations, they must be placed in the context of the system as a whole. Piecemeal changes to deal with specific problems may end up creating new problems, as will be seen shortly.

# ADAPTING TO FINANCIAL CRISES

As Compensation Today 13.4 shows, when a financial crisis hits an organization, compensation expenditures often look like a tempting target. The classical approach to cutting costs is to either lay off employees or to attempt to cut compensation or benefits. (Compensation Today 13.5 tells how one firm stirred its workers into a real lather by cutting a treasured benefit!) However, this approach may be shortsighted, depending on the cause of the crisis, its likely duration, and the nature of the organization. For example, if the crisis is not due to out-of-line compensation costs or is likely to be short in duration, cutting compensation may not be a good solution.

In fact, if the organization practises human relations or high-involvement management, cutting compensation should be the solution of last resort. Cutting compensation will cause problems for most organizations, but these problems will be least severe for classical organizations because they likely do not have positive job attitudes and citizenship behaviour to protect and the organization is geared toward making employees replaceable. But cutting compensation will likely cause serious problems for human relations and high-involvement organizations, because this action may be seen as violating the psychological contract between employees and the firm.

If there is no alternative to pay cuts, there are five measures that can minimize the damage to employee morale.

- First, provide full information on the crisis, showing that all other possible avenues for addressing the problem have been exhausted.
- Second, seek employee input on ways to deal with the crisis. In some cases, this may even produce a solution, but if not, communication creates an organization-wide understanding of the crisis.
- Third, ensure that compensation cuts are fairly shared throughout the organization.

## COMPENSATION TODAY 13.5

### REDUCED SUDS PUTS THESE WORKERS INTO A REAL LATHER!

The tough economic circumstances in 2009 caused many employers to look for ways to cut costs. Layoffs risk losing valuable workers and pay cuts are strongly resisted by workers, so many firms first chisel away at employee benefits. Surveys show that things such as fitness club memberships, tuition reimbursement, and subsidized dining are among the first to go.

But Molson Breweries has really hit its employees where it hurts. For many years, both employees and retirees have been entitled to up to six dozen free bottles of Molson beer every month for as long as they live. (The beer is, however, deemed a taxable benefit by the Canada Revenue Agency, so employees and retirees are not getting away scot-free.)

In a cost-cutting move, the brewery announced that the free beer "ration" would be cut back to two dozen bottles of beer a month for current workers, one dozen a month for retirees (to be phased out completely in five years), and none at all for new employees. The retirees were so frothed up that they demonstrated outside the brewery in St. John's, Newfoundland, and their union attempted to fight the changes to the free beer ration. Nonetheless, Molson Breweries followed through with their plans as the company estimated that this benefit cut would result in savings of over $1 million annually. Since 2014, the company has eliminated the free beer to retirees and decided that they would continue to give current workers a case of beer a week.

In a similar case, in 2016 Labatt Breweries followed suit and determined that they too would terminate the free beer benefit they previously had for retirees, claiming that it was too expensive to maintain. Labatt reduced the entitlement for existing retirees to half in 2018 and cut the entitlement off altogether in 2019.

Source: "Molson Free Beer Allocation Goes Flat for N.L. Retirees," *CBC News*, June 5, 2009; Marion Warnica, "Labatt Employees Mourn the End of Beer-for-Life Era," *CBC News*, November 13, 2016; Wyatt Marshall, "Why This Brewery is No Longer Giving Its Employees Free Beer for Life," *Vice*, November 15, 2016.

- Fourth, consult with employees on how best to achieve the necessary compensation reductions. For example, some employee groups may prefer reductions in certain benefits rather than decreases in base pay, while others may want to keep their benefits and reduce base pay. In some firms, early retirement programs may be preferred over layoffs. Another alternative to layoffs is to share the available work by going on a shortened workweek. As Compensation Today 13.6 describes, firms that opt for work-sharing programs can get federal support for so doing.
- Fifth, make commitments to provide future rewards when circumstances permit. For example, some firms have implemented employee stock bonus plans when cutting other compensation as one way of guaranteeing that employees receive rewards from any upturn in the firm's fortunes.

## COMPENSATION TODAY 13.6

### WORK-SHARING OR LAYOFFS: TO SHARE OR NOT TO SHARE?

As the economy went into a tailspin in 2008, Essar Steel Algoma in Sault Ste. Marie, Ontario faced a serious problem—a drastic reduction in the demand for steel. To survive, the firm needed to slash costs.

However, the firm wanted, as much as possible, to avoid layoffs in dealing with this problem. So, the firm looked for ways to cut costs and still keep people working. It curbed discretionary spending. It stopped outsourcing some work and used its own employees instead. It eliminated overtime. It offered early retirement incentives.

All these measures helped but were not enough. Layoffs loomed. But before going ahead with them, the firm approached its two locals of the United Steelworkers Union (one local for salaried employees and the other for hourly workers) to see whether they would consider entering into a work-sharing program, whereby employees would work 32 hours a week instead of 40 hours and receive Employment Insurance to cover the lost eight hours of work. The 600 salaried workers voted 54 percent in favour, while the 2700 hourly workers voted against the plan.

Under the federal work-sharing program (which must be approved by both employee and employer representatives and the Employment Insurance Commission), the company paid each of its salaried workers for four days of work a week at normal pay rates. On the day that employees didn't work,

Employment Insurance provided 55 percent of their normal daily pay. Overall, this amounted to a pay reduction of about 12 percent for working four days instead of five. Starting in February 2009, this arrangement was set to last for 26 weeks, with the option to extend it another 12 weeks if all parties agreed.

What happened with the hourly workers, who voted against work sharing? By the end of February 2009, 180 of them had been laid off. However, the company continued to experience financial difficulties. By late 2015, with steel prices and demand dropping across North America, production levels had to be curtailed and additional workers laid off as the company sought creditor protection. To restructure long-term debt, Essar Steel was able to secure US$200 million from investors to help support continued operations.

Three years later, in November 2018, Essar Steel was moved out of creditor protection and was purchased by new owners for $2 billion. The company was renamed Algoma Steel and announced that it would be engaging in a $300 million investment to broaden its capacity and grade capability. In a positive turn of events, the company also announced that it had plans to hire more employees. The company turned a page into a new growth strategy.

However, as of December 2019, the failed Essar Steel remains with a new name and under protection as it attempts to complete its bankruptcy proceedings. The company was provided with another six-month extension to complete various tasks before ending the four-year-old case. Furthermore, as the COVID-19 pandemic broke out, a major component of the $300 million endeavour was temporarily interrupted. The fate of the company and its newfound success remains unknown.

Sources: Shannon Klie, "EI Program Helps Employers Avoid Layoffs," *Canadian HR Reporter*, March 9, 2009, 1–2; Elaine Della-Mattia, "Layoffs at Essar Start Sunday," *Sault Star*, October 5, 2015; "Algoma Steel No Longer in Creditor Protection," *CBC News*, November 30, 2018; "One Year After Rebirth of Algoma Steel, Loose Ends Remain," *Northern Ontario Business*, December 2, 2019; The Canadian Press, "Essar Steel Algoma Seeks Creditor Protection," *CBC*, November 9, 2015; "COVID-19 Uncertainty Shuts Big Algoma Steel Construction Site," *Northern Ontario Business*, April 9, 2020.

Perhaps it is not necessary to actually cut compensation costs, but rather to contain them. Several possibilities are available.

- Enact a hiring freeze.
- Contain benefits costs.
- Replace fixed pay with variable pay.
- Replace some raises with bonuses.
- Tighten controls to slow progress through the pay range.
- Ensure that regional differences in wages are reflected in regional pay levels.
- Create a two-tiered pay system, under which new employees come in under new salary scales that are lower than the salary scales for existing employees.[30]

Of course, the best approach to financial crises is to avoid them, or failing that, to have a system in place that will adjust to financial problems. Financial problems are less likely to arise if the compensation system adds maximum value to the organization. Use of an appropriate variable pay component within the compensation system can promote employee performance and can also help make compensation adjust to the firm's financial circumstances. Some firms attempt to avoid having to cut compensation costs by maintaining production slightly below demand. Others keep a workforce of part-time employees or contingent employees to help protect core employees. There are many possibilities.

## ADAPTING TO LABOUR SHORTAGES

One problem organizations often encounter is a shortage of particular types of labour. For example, several years ago, Canada experienced shortages of technical employees, particularly those skilled in computer applications and software development. One way of coping with this problem is the use of **technical premiums**, through which technical employees receive extra compensation.

According to a survey of 1208 Canadian firms, 31 percent of companies with fewer than 20 employees, 56 percent of companies with 20–99 employees, and 64 percent of companies with 100 or more employees declared that they adjust their compensation practices in response to labour shortages. Subject matter experts stated that they are willing to pay their workers around seven percent higher salary than the industry standard to address such needs. However, other strategies include providing profit-sharing, stock options, commissions, and bonuses.[31]

The danger of making many of these adjustments is that they can undermine the overall integrity of the compensation system. Equity concerns can arise if this group of employees is being treated significantly differently from other groups of employees. Moreover, because of compounding, compensation costs for these employees can easily spin out of control, especially if incentives and benefits are calculated as a percentage of base pay. There is also the issue of how to deal with these salaries when there is no longer a shortage of the particular skill in question.

Of course, rather than attempting to lure away one another's employees, organizations can deal with a skills shortage through internal training. Although training may not be feasible for all employers, especially if they need quick expansion, this approach has numerous benefits. It provides opportunities for training and development to current employees, shows commitment by the organization, is more likely to create employees with skills specific to employer needs, avoids skewing the compensation system, and helps solve the labour shortage.

**technical premiums**
Compensation measures that increase the compensation of technical employees.

## SHOULD EXCEPTIONS BE MADE FOR INDIVIDUAL EMPLOYEES?

A dilemma every organization must deal with occurs when an individual employee demands special treatment. For example, an employee may brandish a job offer from another organization, asking her or his current employer to "meet it or beat it." Of course, frequent occurrences of this sort suggest that your compensation system needs to be reassessed. But what do you do about the individual employee? The temptation is to match the competitor's offer, even if it puts the individual outside the pay range for that job.

The problem with that solution is that it undermines the integrity and equity of the total compensation system. To avoid doing so, it may well be preferable to let the employee go to the other job. This individual may be more valuable to the other employer, justifying the higher rate of pay the other employer is offering. Or the other job may not really be comparable—it might include different job duties or duties not included in your company's job.

There may also be some other way of satisfying the employee, such as transferring the employee to more rewarding work or to work that has more opportunities for promotion or providing training opportunities. In fact, sometimes presentation of a job offer may represent a cry for recognition by the employee or some other problem, rather than a true desire to leave the firm.

A dilemma can also arise when recruiting new employees during brief, dramatic periods of shortage of certain kinds of expertise. If the firm responds by sweetening its offers to new employees, these employees may end up earning more than existing employees. Even if this inequity is subsequently corrected, this action may shake employees' confidence in the equity of the system. It is far better to address this issue before it becomes a problem or to address it in a comprehensive way, rather than in a piecemeal fashion.

## SUMMARY

This chapter has covered the final stretch along the road to an effective compensation system: the processes for implementing, managing, evaluating, and adapting the system. You now understand the issues in preparing for implementation, including preparing the compensation budget, planning for the mechanics of compensation administration, planning for information technology, and whether to do compensation administration in-house or to outsource some or all of it.

You have also learned the key components of an implementation plan, including development of a plan for managing implementation, for training, for communication, and for evaluation of the success of the new compensation system. You have learned the six steps in the implementation process: establishing the implementation bodies, putting the infrastructure in place, testing the system, conducting training, communicating the system, and launching and adjusting the system. And you have

learned the importance of communicating and evaluating the compensation—with strict attention to costs.

Compensation systems usually do not suddenly "break," but gradually become ineffective. To prevent this occurrence, you need to monitor changing circumstances external and internal to the firm and adapt the compensation system accordingly. External circumstances include legislative, labour market, competitive, and socioeconomic changes. Internal circumstances include changes in managerial strategies, the workforce, financial conditions, and organization scope.

You have now followed the entire road to compensation effectiveness. But that does not mean that your learning is at an end. Unlike reading a book, the journey to effective compensation has no end, because compensation needs to evolve as the organization and its circumstances change. The road to effective compensation is actually more like an ever-changing maze than a speedy expressway. But that's what makes compensation so challenging and interesting!

## KEY TERMS

average employee earnings
compensation administration
compensation cost ratio

initial dip
spiral career paths
technical premiums

## DISCUSSION QUESTIONS

1. Why is compensation communication such an important aspect of an effective compensation system?

2. What are the steps that should be taken to help mitigate legal liabilities related to benefits communications?

3. With the use of examples, discuss how organizations adapt the compensation system to financial crises.

4. What are the key forces that could trigger a need to adapt or modify the compensation system? Which of these do you think are the most important?

5. Discuss three ways in which an organization can evaluate the effectiveness of its compensation systems.

## EXERCISES

1. Go to the Office of the Privacy Commissioner of Canada website (https://www.priv.gc.ca/en/privacy-topics/employers-and-employees/02_05_d_67_tips/). Scroll down the page and review the 10 key privacy protection tips for federal human resource professionals under PIPEDA. Which of these apply to compensation? Management?

2. Form small groups. Each member of the group should check with a current or previous employer (or some other employer if this is not convenient) to determine whether the organization is outsourcing some or all of its compensation administration. Is the company happy with the current system? Why or why not?

### CASE QUESTION

1. In previous chapters, you may have prepared compensation strategies for The Fit Stop or one of the other cases in the Appendix. If so, develop a detailed plan for implementing the new compensation strategy at one of these firms. If not, prepare a compensation strategy for one of these firms, design the technical processes, and develop the implementation plan.

### SIMULATION CROSS-REFERENCE

If you are using Strategic Compensation: A Simulation in conjunction with this text, you will find that the concepts in Chapter 13 are helpful in preparing the simulation.

# ENDNOTES

1. Jae K. Shim and Joel G. Siegel, "The What and Why of Budgeting" in *Budgeting Basics and Beyond* (Hoboken, New Jersey: John Wiley & Sons, Inc., 2009), 1–20.

2. David M. van De Voort, Stephen W. McDonnell, Philip Drouillard, and David E. Tyson, "Computers in Compensation," in *Carswell's Compensation Guide*, ed. David E. Tyson (Toronto: Thomson Carswell, 2009), 14B-1–14B-26.

3. Dianna L. Stone, Diana L. Deadrick, Kimberly M. Lukaszewski, and Richard Johnson, "The Influence of Technology on the Future of Human Resource Management," *Human Resource Management Review* 25, no. 2 (2015): 216–31.

4. Cathy Ledden and Brenda McKinney, "Well-Made Intranet Offers Boundless Opportunity," *Canadian HR Reporter* 18, no. 2 (2005): 14.

5. Paul Loucks, "Plugging Into Performance Management," *HR Reporter*, February 6, 2007, https://www.hrreporter.com/news/hr-news/plugging-into-performance-management/311083, accessed April 13, 2020.

6. Ilsemann and Simms, "Using Information Technology"; Richard D. Johnson and Hal G. Gueutalm, "Transforming HR Through Technology: The Use of E-HR and HRIS in Organizations," *Society for Human Resource Management Effective Practice Guidelines Series* (Alexandria, VA, 2011).

7. Vic Murray, "Contracting Out HR Services: Passing Fad or Here to Stay?" *Human Resources Management in Canada*, July 1997, 637–41; Steve White and Penny Plante, "A Midsized Proposition: Benefits Outsourcing Is Not Just for Large Organizations," *Benefits Quarterly*, 27, no. 2 (2011): 19–23.

8. David Brown, "CIBC HR Department Halved as Non-Strategic Roles Outsourced," *Canadian HR Reporter* 14, no. 11 (2001): 1, 6.

9. Todd Humber, "Has the Shine Come Off HR Outsourcing?" *Canadian HR Reporter*, January 29, 2013, online.

10. Conference Board of Canada, *Compensation Outlook 2005* (Ottawa: 2005).

11. Humber, "Has the Shine Come Off HR Outsourcing?"

12. Shelly Ng, "Letting Go of that Paper Trail," *HR Reporter*, September 12, 2011, https://www.hrreporter.com/news/hr-news/letting-go-of-that-paper-trail/314015, accessed April 14, 2020.

13. Brian Hackett, Transforming the Benefit Function (New York: The Conference Board, 1995); Sarah Dobson, "Plowing Ahead with Payroll, HRIS," *Canadian HR Reporter* 27, no.1 (2014): 7, 9.

14. Statement by John Sullivan, Professor of Management at San Francisco State University, cited in Karen Beamon, ed., *Out of Site: An Inside Look at HR Outsourcing* (Burlington: IHRIM, 2004).

15. Monica Belcourt, "Outsourcing—The Benefits and the Risks," *Human Resource Management Review* 16 (2006): 269–279.

16. Suzanne Harrison, *Outsourcing and the "New" Human Resource Management* (Kingston: IRC Press, 1996); Allen Smith, "Small and Large Employers Outsource HR Duties Differently," *SHRM*, February 2, 2018, https://www.shrm.org/resourcesandtools/legal-and-compliance/employment-law/pages/small-and-large-employers-outsourcing.aspx, accessed April 15, 2020.

17. Claudio Belli, "Strategic Compensation Communication," in *The Compensation Handbook*, ed. M.L. Rock and L.A. Berger (New York: McGraw-Hill, 1991), 604–16; David T. Goomas, Stuart M. Smith, and Timothy D. Ludwig, "Business Activity Monitoring: Real-Time Group Goals and Feedback Using an Overhead Scoreboard in a Distribution Center," *Journal of Organizational Behavior Management* 31, no. 3 (2011): 196–209.

18. David E. Tyson, ed., *Carswell's Compensation Guide* (Toronto: Thomson Carswell, 2009).

19. Rob Lewis, Susan Hunter, and Marie Donnelly, 2012. "Getting Managers On Board with Total Rewards," *Canadian HR Reporter* 25, no. 14 (2012): 18.

20. Andrew A. Luchak and Morley Gunderson, "What Do Employees Know About Their Pension Plan?" *Industrial Relations* 39, no. 4 (2000): 646–70. Mary Picard, "Clarifying Benefits is Employer's Responsibility," *HR Reporter*, December 31, 2008, https://www.hrreporter.com/employment-law/news/clarifying-benefits-is-employers-responsibility/317863, accessed April 15, 2020.

21. David Brown, "Employees Ill-Equipped to Make Pension Choices," *Canadian HR Reporter* 14, no. 10 (2001): 1, 12; Barbara Shecter, "'Leaving Money on the Table': Many Canadians Not Taking    Advantage of Defined-Contribution Pensions," *Financial Post*, May 19, 2014, https://business.financialpost.com/personal-finance/retirement/leaving-money-on-the-table-how-many-canadians-arent-taking-advantage-of-defined-contribution-pension, accessed April 15, 2020.

22. Joe Nunes, "How Pensions Got Tangled in Total Rewards," *Canadian HR Reporter* 18, no. 3 (2005): R10.

23. Natalie C. MacDonald, "Going Flex Comes with Obligations for Employers," *Canadian HR Reporter* 17, no. 4 (2004): G5–G11.

24. Mary Picard, "Clarifying Benefits is Employer's Responsibility," *HR Reporter*, December 31, 2008, https://www.hrreporter.com/employment-law/news/clarifying-benefits-is-employers-responsibility/317863, accessed April 15, 2020.

25. Ian Altman, "The Good, the Bad, and the Ugly of Cost Cutting," *Forbes*, March 17, 2015, https://www.forbes.com/sites/ianaltman/2015/03/17/the-good-the-bad-and-the-ugly-of-cost-cutting/#1f313dc1377b, accessed April 16, 2020.

26. Alexandra Ma, "A Former Boeing 737 Max Engineer Said He Was 'Incredibly Pressurized' to Keep Costs Down and Downplay New Features to Avoid FAA Scrutiny," *Business Insider*, July 29, 2019, https://www.businessinsider.com/boeing-737-max-former-engineer-pressure-costs-avoid-faa-scrutiny-2019-7, accessed April 16, 2020.

27. Alan Saks, "Engagement: The Academic Perspective," *Canadian HR Reporter*, January 26, 2009, 31.

28. Paul B. Britton and Christian M. Ellis, "Designing and Implementing Reward Systems: Finding a Better Way," *Compensation and Benefits Review* 26, no. 4 (1994): 44.

29. David K. Foot and Rosemary A. Venne, "Population, Pyramids, and Promotional Prospects," *Canadian Public Policy* 16, no. 4 (1990): 387–98.

30. Although it is more than 20 years old, the most comprehensive source for learning about two-tier compensation systems remains James E. Martin and Thomas D. Heetderks, *Two-Tier Compensation Structures: Their Impacts on Unions, Employers, and Employees* (Kalamazoo: W.E. Upjohn Institute, 1990).

31. Michael Cocolakis-Wormstall, "Labour Shortage: Here to Stay," *Business Development Bank of Canada*, September 2018, https://www.bdc.ca/en/documents/analysis_research/labour-shortage.pdf?utm_campaign=Labour-Shortage-Study-2018--download--EN&utm_medium=email&utm_source=Eloqua, accessed April 17, 2020.

# APPENDIX

## CASES FOR ANALYSIS

The following cases, which reflect a range of compensation issues and organizational types, can be used in a variety of ways.

They are presented without questions attached, which allows instructors flexibility in their use. They can be used in conjunction with the end-of-chapter case questions to illustrate compensation issues relevant to that chapter and to provide opportunities for applying compensation concepts. They can also be used as a basis for major term assignments or group projects. Some cases are short enough to be used as exam cases. And, of course, they can serve as a basis for lively class discussions of many important compensation issues.

- Case 1—Henderson Printing
- Case 2—The Fit Stop
- Case 3—Multi-Products Corporation
- Case 4—Patriot Transportation Holding Inc.
- Case 5—Plastco Packaging
- Case 6—Alliston Instruments
- Case 7—Eastern Provincial University

## CASE 1—HENDERSON PRINTING

Henderson Printing is a small- to medium-sized manufacturer of account books, ledgers, and various types of record books used in business. Located in Halifax, the company has annual sales of about $12 million, mostly in the Atlantic provinces.

The owner, George Henderson, is a firm believer in making a high-quality product that will endure many years of use. He uses only high-grade paper, cover stock, and binding materials. Of course, this has led to high production costs and high prices. He also believes in a high level of customer service and is willing to make the products to customers' specifications whenever they so request. However, resetting the equipment for relatively short production runs of customized products takes considerable extra time and, of course, also drives up costs.

The firm employs about 80 people, most of whom work in production. The firm has a few supervisors to oversee production, but their responsibilities are not clearly spelled out, so the supervisors often contradict one another. There is no system for scheduling production; in fact, there are few systems of any kind. Whenever there is a problem, everyone knows that you have to go to George if you expect a definite answer.

The company also has several salespeople who travel throughout the Atlantic region; most of them are relatives of George or his wife. The company has one bookkeeper to keep records and issue the paycheques, and several office employees to handle routine administrative chores. The firm has no specialists in accounting, marketing, human resources, or production; George handles these areas himself, although he has no real training and little interest in any of them except production. He focuses most of his attention on ensuring product quality and on dealing with the countless problems that everyone brings to him every day. He has often been heard to exclaim, in his usual good-natured way, "Why am I the only one who can make decisions around this place?" as he deals with each of these problems.

When George was growing up, both his parents (his father was a printer and his mother was a seamstress in a garment factory) had to work hard in order to scratch out a living for their family. In those days, employers who showed little consideration for their employees were the norm, and George resolved that things would be different if he ever became an employer. Today, George tries hard to be a benevolent employer. Although he feels the organization cannot afford any formal employee benefits, he often keeps sick workers on payroll for a considerable time, especially if he knows the worker has a family to support. George is well liked by most employees, who have shown little interest in unionization during the few approaches made by union organizers.

George has no formal system for pay and tends to make all pay decisions on the spur of the moment, so almost everybody has a different pay rate. He has never gotten around to giving annual raises, so any employee who wants a raise has to approach him. He gives raises to most people who approach him, but the amount depends on his mood at the time and on how well he knows the employee. For example, if the firm has just lost a major customer, raises are lower, and if the firm has just booked a large order, they are higher. They are also higher if he knows the employee has a family to support, or if the employee's spouse has been laid off, or if the employee has added a new member to the family.

George believes that a good employer should recognize the contributions made by employees during the year. As a result, every Christmas—if profits allow—he gives merit bonuses to employees, which he says are based on their contributions to the firm. One day in early December, he sits down with his employee list, in alphabetical order, and pencils in an amount next to each name.

Everybody gets something, but the amounts vary greatly. If he can associate a face with the name (which is difficult sometimes because of high employee turnover), he tends to give larger bonuses. And if he can remember something such as a cheerful attitude, the bonuses are higher still. But if he remembers anyone complaining about that employee (he usually can't recall the exact reasons), the employee gets a smaller bonus. Not surprisingly, longer-term employees tend to receive much higher bonuses than new employees. He has noticed this tendency but assumes that if an employee has been with the firm longer, that person must be more productive, so this is fair. He personally distributes the bonus cheques on the last working day before Christmas.

Because he has just turned 60, George is planning to retire in the next year or two and turn the business over to his daughter, Georgette Henderson, who is just finishing her commerce degree at Dalhousie University. Ironically, it was on his 60th birthday that his bookkeeper informed him that there wasn't enough money in the bank account to meet payroll.

# CASE 2—THE FIT STOP LTD.

The Fit Stop Ltd. is a new firm that will open its doors exactly four months from today. Its business objective is to sell all types of training, fitness, conditioning, and exercise equipment to the general public. The Fit Stop plans to specialize in this equipment and to provide customers with personalized advice geared to a customer's specific training or conditioning needs (e.g., training for a particular sport, injury rehabilitation, strengthening of muscles to deal with back pain, general conditioning, and fitness), whether the customer is eight or 80 years of age.

In order to provide high-quality advice, each store will employ a physiotherapist (to provide advice on problems such as injuries or chronic back pain) and a person with a bachelor's degree in kinesiology (to provide advice on training for various sports or other physical activities). A staff member will even sit down with customers and develop a personalized training or conditioning program that meets their own specific objectives and needs, at no cost to the customer.

The remainder of the staff in the store will consist of a manager, with a Bachelor of Commerce degree, and sales staff, who will have at least high school diplomas. Due to the long opening hours, it is expected that between 8–12 salespeople will be needed for each store. Because the stores are located in shopping malls, they will operate on a seven-day-a-week basis, open 9:00–9:00 weekdays, 9:00–6:00 Saturdays, and noon to 6:00 on Sundays.

Aside from personally helping customers, the roles of the physiotherapist and kinesiologist will be to train other employees in how each type of equipment can be used for various conditioning and rehabilitation purposes. Initially, sales staff will be given general training, but as time goes by, each salesperson will be expected to learn in depth about all the different pieces of equipment, to help customers diagnose their needs accurately, and to be able to explain proper use of the equipment. Because of the high level of training required, all employees will be full-time.

The founder of the business is Susan Superfit, who has undergraduate degrees in kinesiology and commerce from the University of Saskatchewan. While at university, she participated in many sports (and suffered many injuries due to her all-out style of play). She came up with the idea for this business while laid up with one of her injuries. While there were businesses that sold fitness and conditioning equipment, she often found that the people selling it had very limited knowledge and often gave poor advice on what to buy and how to use it.

She has secured funding from private investors and from Growthworks, a large Canadian labour-sponsored investment fund. In order to get volume discounts on the equipment she will be purchasing and to beat competitors into the market, she wants to start off quite large, with stores in major cities in Ontario and the four western provinces, before expanding to Quebec and the Atlantic provinces. She knows that this is a risky strategy, and that cost control will be essential to keep the business going long enough to become well known and develop a stable clientele. She does not expect the business to make a profit for at least one year, or maybe even two.

Her main competitors will be sporting goods megastores and department and discount stores, each of which sells some of the same equipment. Some of these outlets will be able to price their equipment lower than The Fit Stop will be able to, but none have the range of equipment that The Fit Stop will have, and none provide the personalized services that The Fit Stop will.

Susan believes that the key to her business success will be highly motivated and knowledgeable employees who have a strong concern for their customers and who are able to work as a team with the other employees to provide the best possible customer service. Because no two customers are exactly alike, employees will have to be innovative in developing solutions that fit their needs. It will also be crucial to keep up with the latest fitness and training trends, as knowledge about fitness is continually increasing, along with new and different types of specialized equipment. A key aspect of company strategy is to be the most up-to-date and advanced supplier of new products and techniques.

Although Susan has given a lot of thought to her business, one thing she hasn't really given much thought to is how to compensate her employees. Because she doesn't really know much about compensation, she tends to feel that the safest thing would be to just do what her competitors are doing.

## CASE 3—MULTI-PRODUCTS CORPORATION

It is early February. Late last year, the firm you work for, Multi-Products Corporation, acquired the rights to a new type of golf club invented by a retired machinist who had been a lifelong golfer until his untimely demise (it turns out that golfing during a lightning storm is not such a great idea). The machinist had produced only a few sets of the clubs, but their superiority over existing clubs was so pronounced that word of his invention had spread far and wide. Fortunately for him (for his estate, actually), he had patented the design of these clubs, so nobody could copy them.

Multi-Products Corporation has numerous divisions, each producing different products in the sporting goods field. The company has never produced golf equipment of any kind and plans to set up a separate division to produce and distribute the new clubs. You found out yesterday that you have been selected to head the new division. Corporate management will provide you with all the financial resources you need to get the division going and will also help you staff the division with experienced managers from the parent corporation. Because of their confidence in you, management has given you complete freedom to organize and operate the division as you see fit, as long as you attain the financial goals that have been set for the division.

Your first task is to design the organization structure. But you recognize that before doing so, you need to understand some key aspects about the organization and its context. Market research suggests that the demand for your product will be strong and stable. This demand will not be very price-sensitive because golfers who want your product will generally be willing to pay what it takes to get it. Therefore, it will be relatively easy for you to secure distributors. In fact, one distributor is willing to agree to a four-year sales contract for your equipment, with a fixed volume and a fixed price. This distributor is confident enough to make this offer because it believes that nobody else will be able to manufacture a similar club, due to the patent protection.

The production side also looks straightforward. Your production process includes readily available materials and there are many possible suppliers. You expect to be able to negotiate long-term contracts with suppliers at a fixed price. Acquiring the production equipment will also be straightforward because the equipment is readily available in the marketplace.

The basic production technology, which will involve a sequential, step-by-step manufacturing process, has been in use for many years and has been refined to a high degree of efficiency. Because you know the likely volume of demand for your product, it is easy to decide on the optimum plant size, which will involve about 600 workers. The type of semiskilled worker that you need is readily available, and because unemployment is quite high in your region, acquiring employees should not be very difficult. Employees in this industry are usually unionized, but the main union in the industry has not been highly militant in recent years, so labour disruptions don't seem likely.

Government regulations represent another possible factor that might affect your operations. However, as long as your clubs meet CSA (Canadian Standards Association) standards, the government is unlikely to get involved with your product. Similarly, except for some groups opposed to the expansion of golf courses in ecologically sensitive areas (such as national parks), consumer and environmental groups are not likely to pose any concerns.

Future technological change is another possible issue, but it does not appear to be of great concern. You will start out with the most up-to-date production equipment, which has not changed much in recent years. The product itself (golf clubs) is not likely to be replaced by anything radically different. The pace of technological change for golf clubs is quite slow, and some of the most popular clubs have been virtually unchanged in 30 years.

# CASE 4—PATRIOT TRANSPORTATION HOLDING INC.

Ron Sandlin, President of Patriot Transportation Holding Inc., a trucking company located in Jacksonville, Florida, does not know what else to do. He increased base pay, increased vacation days, and decreased the age requirement from 25 to 23. He added a productivity-based pay system as well. He still cannot find enough people to hire as truck drivers for the company. Sandlin thinks that this issue is strictly due to a strengthening economy, which means higher demand and lower supply of workers. However, perhaps more can be done to attract the right workers.

The company is continuously growing its market footprint and therefore, a need for drivers is an ongoing concern. In fact, the lack of drivers is the company's top concern.

# CASE 5—PLASTCO PACKAGING LTD.

Plastco Packaging Ltd. is a medium-sized manufacturer of plastic bags, located on the West Coast. These bags are used in the retail sector for purposes ranging from groceries to clothing and other goods. These bags are made from a variety of types of plastic and in a variety of sizes, depending on the intended purpose. Usually the retailer's name is printed on them.

There are three main phases in the bag-manufacturing process: (1) producing the plastic sheeting (produced as rolls of tubing), (2) printing the retailer's name on the tubing, and (3) passing the rolls of tubing through bag-making machines that cut and seal the tubing into bag lengths.

This case focuses on the third step of the production process, the bag-making department. The department has 12 bag-making machines. Each machine operates semiautomatically but has to be manually loaded, set for the type of bag to be produced, started, monitored, and adjusted. The machines need frequent servicing to replace the cutting knives, adjust slipping belts, and lubricate the many moving parts. These functions and major repairs, when necessary, are carried out by mechanics from the maintenance department, a separate department reporting to the plant manager. The mechanics report machinery problems and future replacement and servicing needs to the maintenance supervisor, who reports significant problems to the plant manager. The plant manager then conveys any implications for production of bags to the bag-making supervisor.

There are six bag-making machine operators, with each operator tending two machines. There are also six inspectors/packers, who inspect the bags to ensure quality and pack them into boxes. Defective bags are thrown into waste bins, based on the type of plastic. They are then melted down and remanufactured. Whenever an inspector/packer discovers poor-quality output, she must notify the operator to correct the problem. If the inspector/packer deems waste to be excessive, she is expected to report the operator to the bag-making supervisor.

In addition, four utility workers handle miscellaneous tasks, such as delivering rolls of plastic tubing and hauling boxes of finished bags to the shipping department. Traditionally, operators and utility workers have always been male, while inspectors/packers have always been female.

When a new operator is needed, the bag-making supervisor selects one of the utility workers and assigns him to an experienced operator for on-the-job training. It takes up to six months before a new operator can consistently produce an acceptable-quality product without supervision because the machines are "finicky" to operate. The length of time needed to do bag changeovers also declines as the new operator gains experience.

The plant is unionized, and pay is based on an hourly wage. Operators receive approximately $28 per hour, utility workers $21 per hour, and inspectors/packers $14 per hour. Overall, benefits constitute about 20 percent of total compensation and increase with seniority.

The bag-making supervisor sees a number of problems at present. First is the high turnover among the inspectors/packers, as high as 100 percent a year. Turnover among the utility workers is about one-third of that, and lower than that among operators, who quit or retire at the rate of about one a year. Second, while the department usually meets the minimum production levels, the bag-making supervisor believes that productivity could be much higher.

He also believes there's a high level of waste. However, whenever he questions an operator about this, the operator either blames maintenance for doing a poor job servicing the machines or the inspectors/packers for being unnecessarily fussy. It is also difficult to pinpoint specific operators for performing poor-quality work because inspectors/packers seldom report an operator to the bag-making supervisor. When one does so, the operators usually accuse the inspectors/packer of incompetence. All in all, there are very poor interpersonal relationships among the operators, mechanics, and inspectors/packers. Few members of the department appear to enjoy being at work.

Another problem is that customers are complaining about inconsistent quality in the products they receive. Sometimes the bags are of very high quality, but at other times, many bags are defective. These complaints are a concern to the plant manager as a new competitor has recently opened up nearby and is competing aggressively for business. This competitor seems to be producing a product with fewer defects for a lower price. As if this weren't bad enough, the overall market for plastic bags has become more uncertain, as they have become the target of environmentalists; some communities have actually banned the use of plastic bags.

# CASE 6—ALLISTON INSTRUMENTS

Alliston Instruments is a manufacturer of specialty medical instruments located in southern Ontario. Manufacturing involves two types of processes. First, individual workers produce the components for the medical instruments in batches of various sizes, using a variety of machine tools and equipment. Then other workers assemble the components into finished products. Assembly is done sequentially, with each product passing through four to six workstations before completion. The quality of the products, which is crucial, depends on both the quality of the component parts that are produced and the quality of the assembly process.

It is late January 2020 and the financial statements for 2019 have just been released. They are grim. For the first time in the company's 50-year history, the firm has shown a loss. The company's chief executive officer believes a lot of this has to do with production problems. The 2019 production reports indicate that although the number of units produced per employee showed a slight increase last year, the number of defective units reached an all-time high. In addition, there was a high rate of wastage of raw materials and other supplies. Although total sales (and therefore total production) are down from the previous year, total labour costs are up. As a result, costs per unit are at an all-time high.

Because you are an expert in human resources management, the CEO has asked for your help. As background for your work, the CEO briefs you on industry conditions. Until two years ago, the firm had enjoyed increasing sales over many years. It also had increasing profits, with a record profit of over $3 million in 2016. However, in the last two years, the medical instruments industry has become more competitive. High-quality medical instruments are now being produced by several Asian firms, two of which entered the Canadian market in 2017. (Previously, the main competitors in the Canadian market were U.S. and European firms, but they are not much of a problem because their products are very high priced.)

Because of low labour costs, the Asian firms are able to price their products attractively; however, buyers initially held back, concerned about potential quality problems. For a while, it appeared as if Alliston's customers (mainly hospitals and health clinics) would remain loyal, even though they were themselves under pressure to cut costs, due to budget cuts. But in late 2017, an Asian competitor made a major sales push by slashing prices, and this cut dramatically into Alliston's 2018 sales. In mid-2018, Alliston laid off 50 employees. Although the firm had laid off employees from time to time in the past during production lulls, this was the largest layoff in company history.

To make up for the loss of sales, Alliston added a number of new products to its line. (Over the years, the company had tended to stick with the same set of products, although new products were being put into use in the hospitals.) While some of these new products sold well, they didn't really make money, because production costs were higher due to the need for new equipment and extensive employee training. Moreover, most employees preferred to work on the old products, so supervisors had to use a lot of pressure to get them to work on the new products.

Alliston's 250 production workers have been unionized since the 1960s. In 2016, they staged a short but bitter strike. Because product demand was so high, the company did not want a long work stoppage, and the union was able to win significant wage increases for 2017 and 2018 (a two-year contract was signed). Since then, union–management relations, never very good, have been quite strained. Relations between supervisors and workers are no better. Supervisors complain about lazy workers who don't care if they do a good job or not, and workers complain about overbearing supervisors who allocate work unfairly and spend all their time watching and harassing employees.

Interestingly, the employee turnover rate is low at Alliston. Pay at the firm is above average, and the benefits package, which increases with seniority, is very good, comprising about 25 percent of total compensation. Comparable alternative employment opportunities in the area are quite scarce.

In late 2018, in an effort to increase efficiency, the firm persuaded the union to accept an incentive system in which employees would receive, in addition to their hourly wages, a bonus based on individual output, rather than an increase in base pay for 2019. A standard per-hour production rate for each item or assembly operation was established, based on estimated 2018 production levels. (However, because the firm had never kept detailed records, these standards were simply based on the estimates of supervisors.)

Under the new system, if production per hour for a particular item exceeds 2018 levels, the employee receives a fixed sum for each piece produced over that level, in addition to the normal hourly pay. Of course, employees do not receive a bonus for items that are not of satisfactory quality, and supervisors are expected to deduct these from the employee totals. However, there are no set standards for quality, and each supervisor seems to set different standards.

There seem to be many problems with this new pay system. For example, workers complain that the production standards for some tasks are set too high and that they have no chance of earning a bonus on these items. Everybody tries to avoid these jobs, and productivity on them is poor. On the other hand, there are some jobs that everybody wants to do, because substantial bonuses can be earned, and productivity is up dramatically on these jobs. But the net effect is that overall units produced per employee have not really changed at all, while substantial sums are being paid out in bonuses.

In the past year, 10 production workers have retired or quit and not been replaced, but this workforce reduction was made possible by the drop in sales during the year, not by increased productivity. However, this reduction in the workforce has been partly offset by the need to hire two additional supervisors to handle the increased needs for supervision, inspection, and administration of the bonus system, plus one additional full-time clerical person in the payroll department just to handle the calculations for the new bonus system.

Supervisors have complained bitterly about the new system, saying it is placing additional pressure on them. They say it is causing increased conflict with employees because nobody wants the "bad" (i.e., poor-paying) jobs, and that employees resent it when these "bad" jobs are assigned to them. They find that employees don't care about quality as long as output meets minimum standards, nor do they care about the high wastage of raw materials. Supervisors have to supervise more closely to deal with these problems and try to keep quality and productivity up on the "bad" jobs.

And to top it off, supervisors are now making less money than some of the workers because they are not eligible for the bonus system. The fact that none of the non-union employees received any pay increase last year does not help their mood, either. During the year, three experienced supervisors have quit. The firm had never had more than one or two supervisors quit in a single year before.

Although the union is generally opposed to individual performance pay plans, it had accepted this one in return for a clause in the collective agreement ensuring job security for the current unionized workforce. Any workforce reductions occurring from greater efficiency will have to be achieved through attrition. Management had agreed to this condition because they did not expect to have to lay off employees. They had expected the new bonus system to reduce unit costs of production so that Alliston could lower its prices and win back the business that had been lost.

It hasn't worked out that way. Financial data for the last four years are shown below. They indicate that sales peaked two years ago at $31 million and have since fallen to $24 million. Customers are complaining about product price and quality. However, the company cannot afford to reduce prices, because unit costs are so high. It is clear to management that something needs to be done, and quickly, but exactly what should be done is not so clear!

| Year | Revenues | Total Employees | Labour Costs | Other Production Costs | Other Costs | Net Income (Loss) |
|------|----------|-----------------|--------------|------------------------|-------------|-------------------|
| 2016 | $27 000 000 | 320 | $ 9 000 000 | $13 500 000 | $1 350 000 | $3 150 000 |
| 2017 | 31 000 000 | 350 | 12 000 000 | 15 500 000 | 1 550 000 | $1 950 000 |
| 2018 | 25 000 000 | 300 | 11 000 000 | 12 500 000 | 1 500 000 | — |
| 2019 | 24 000 000 | 293 | 12 000 000 | 13 000 000 | 1 444 000 | ($2 444 000) |

# CASE 7—EASTERN PROVINCIAL UNIVERSITY

The following job descriptions are used for compensation purposes at Eastern Provincial University, which employs around 900 professors and 1500 nonacademic staff and has about 20 000 undergraduate and graduate students. Descriptions are provided for the job classes of clerk stenographer, draftsperson, grounds worker, and medical laboratory technologist.

## CLERK STENOGRAPHER I
### Kind and Level of Work

Employees of this class perform a variety of clerical tasks of limited complexity. These may include taking shorthand dictation and transcribing it. The vocabulary involved is usually free of technical terms and limited to the everyday language of business. Typing assignments, whether from hard copy, dictation, or machine transcription, require only normal speed and accuracy. The material copied may include scientific papers, theses, and special reports written in technical language from any of the university course subjects; the employee is responsible only for the accurate transcription of material already written or typed.

These employees maintain courteous and cooperative working relations with students and with faculty and other university staff, for whom they provide typing, simple duplicating, telephone reception, and other services. While some positions are located away from the supervisors, preliminary detailed instructions and established procedures leave little responsibility for the exercise of initiative or the formation of independent judgment.

### Typical Duties and Responsibilities

1. Type correspondence, class assignments, and technical papers using special vocabulary, from hard copy.
2. Act as receptionist at the counter and on the telephone, relaying calls, recording messages, and answering simple questions.

3. File and retrieve materials arranged in simple alphabetical, numerical, chronological, or geographical order.

4. Reproduce copies of materials by photocopy or other simple duplicating methods.

5. Transcribe correspondence and other materials containing everyday language, from dictating machines.

6. Prepare form letters by inserting appropriate material from files or other sources. Check forms for completeness.

7. Post figures to budget accounts or other simple statistical and accounting records.

8. Open, sort, route, and deliver mail according to predetermined patterns.

9. In some positions, take and transcribe correspondence and other materials; only a good vocabulary or grasp of ordinary language is required.

## Desirable Qualifications

Previous office experience desirable but not required. Grade 12 and completion of a standard course in word processing, spreadsheets, and shorthand. Ability to meet test standards in typing and shorthand (for those positions requiring the use of shorthand).

# CLERK STENOGRAPHER II

## Kind and Level of Work

Employees of this class perform a variety of moderately complex clerical tasks, which may include taking and transcribing shorthand dictation that requires knowledge of a technical vocabulary. Their work is supervised by academic, administrative, or senior clerical employees. This position is distinguished from Clerk Stenographer I in that it requires more knowledge of the organization, programs, and policies of the work unit; requires a higher degree of specialized clerical skills or knowledge of a technical vocabulary; carries independent responsibility for the maintenance of significant records; or some combination of these attributes. These workers maintain helpful and courteous relations with students and staff, for whom they provide information and services.

## Typical Duties and Responsibilities

1. From general instructions, compose and type routine correspondence, bulletins, and other materials requiring knowledge of the departments they serve.

2. Type from hard copy or dictating machine, class assignments, tests, research papers, and other materials requiring understanding of technical vocabulary, the use of special symbol keyboards, or judgment in the selection of format.

3. Answer students' inquiries concerning class schedules, timetables, general course content, class prerequisites, and similar matters requiring basic knowledge of calendars and departmental programs.

4. Train new employees by providing factual information on office routines, staff names and locations, work methods, and schedules.

5. Maintain records of budget expenditures, class attendance, class credits, grade distribution, and other data requiring accurate posting and simple calculations of totals, percentages, and balances, all subject to periodic review.

6. Compile simple statistical tables and graphs according to prescribed patterns, incorporating data flowing into or retained in their departments.

7. Organize, reorganize, and maintain filing systems based on alphabetic, numeric, or simple subject matter arrangement.

8. Act as receptionist for officials, screening telephone calls and visitors, providing answers to inquiries, making appointments, and referring callers to other officials.

9. Assist in the maintenance of counselling schedules at the time of student registration.

10. In some positions, take and transcribe shorthand dictation of correspondence, reports, research papers, and other materials containing technical language and concepts.

## Desirable Qualifications

Several years of office experience, preferably in a university setting. Grade 12 and completion of a standard course in word processing, spreadsheets, and shorthand. Ability to meet test standards in typing and shorthand (for those positions requiring the use of shorthand).

# CLERK STENOGRAPHER III

## Kind and Level of Work

Employees of this class perform responsible, varied, and complex clerical tasks, which may include taking and transcribing shorthand dictation. Typically, their assignments require a broad understanding of departmental structure and division of responsibility, functions, and programs. In most of these positions, they are secretaries to heads of larger departments and take initiative in relieving them of administrative details that do not require professional judgment. Their work is subject to supervision by academic or administrative supervisors, but they carry out a series of clerical operations calling for decisions without detailed instruction or review. The work of this class is distinguished from that of Clerk Stenographers I and II by broader knowledge requirements, greater latitude, and supervision of other clerk stenographers. In contacts with students, faculty and other staff, and the public at large, these employees attempt to promote public attitudes that support the work of the units.

## Typical Duties and Responsibilities

1. For their superiors, compose and type correspondence that requires good knowledge of departmental organization, functions, and policies.

2. Maintain records pertaining to students' marks, credits, and degree requirements, or supervise the maintenance of such records.

3. Maintain records on budget allotments, expenditures, commitments, and residual balances, and notify department office of over expenditures and balances, thus providing a measure of budget control.

4. Give elementary counselling services to students by advising them of degree requirements, class schedules, class prerequisites, and (in general terms) course content, using information from the calendars or from the faculty.

5. At the time of registration, schedule counselling interviews between students and professors and maintain records so that students are referred to the same counsellor each time.

6. Attend and record proceedings of faculty meetings or meetings between faculty and non-university groups, making shorthand notes summarizing discussions and transcribing the reports for the review of superiors.

7. Supervise assistants and participate in their selection, assign their duties, train them, reallocate work to meet deadlines, and exercise disciplinary control in minor matters.

8. Screen phone and office calls of visitors, setting up interviews with superiors as necessary, answering questions where possible, and referring visitors to other sources where appropriate.

9. Type tests and examinations for members of the faculty, ensuring that contents are kept confidential and that papers are properly secured.

## Desirable Qualifications

Approximately five years of office experience, including several years in a university setting and preferably including experience in a supervisory capacity. Grade 12 and completion of a standard course in word processing, spreadsheets, and shorthand. Ability to meet test standards in typing and shorthand (for those positions requiring the use of shorthand).

# DRAFTSPERSON I

## Kind and Level of Work

Employees of this classification use computer-aided design drafting (CADD) techniques to carry out assignments delegated by their supervisor, with direction from the project originator, where appropriate. They work from rough sketches and notes, verbal instructions, and other sources of information. While their day-to-day work is subject only to general supervision, completed assignments are reviewed. Although the projects on which they work may range across a variety of engineering and architectural fields, the more complex work is allocated to more senior positions. They may communicate with professional engineers and others who initiate the work they do to clarify certain requirements and details.

## Typical Duties and Responsibilities

1. Interpret existing records and information for the purpose of producing required CADD information.

2. Prepare finished CADD drawings from rough sketches, notes, and instructions.

3. Share in filing and managing inventory of records information.

4. Assist physical plant staff, professional engineers, and consultants in locating physical records information.

5. Use and be familiar with operating various equipment, including computer input/output devices, keyboards, digitizing equipment, and a blueprint machine.

6. Assist in site verification of existing campus buildings and facilities.

7. Periodically assist in making site surveys with senior or surveying staff.

8. Participate in training programs relative to the CADD system.

9. Interact and communicate in a professional manner with physical plant staff, the university community, consultants, contractors, etc.

### Desirable Qualifications

Previous related experience preferred. Grade 12 plus a two-year diploma in a related architectural/engineering-associated technical program. Completion of computer-assisted design and drafting course work or equivalent experience required. Eligibility for membership as an applied science technologist preferred.

# DRAFTSPERSON II
## Kind and Level of Work

Employees in this classification use more complex computer-aided design drafting techniques to carry out assignments delegated by their supervisor, with direction from the project originator where appropriate. Their work is differentiated from that of junior positions by the complexity of their assignments, the judgment they use in completing their work, and their degree of independence. Delegated projects may range across a variety of engineering and architectural fields. They develop and maintain cooperative working relations with professionals and tradespersons in fulfilling their tasks.

## Typical Duties and Responsibilities

1. Participate in production and design work of various projects as required.
2. Assist in the development, evaluation, implementation, and documentation of ongoing computer system procedures.
3. Assist in coordinating and supervising work of junior staff.
4. Complete site verification of existing campus buildings and facilities.
5. Participate in training in CADD system applications and in new and more complex portions of the system, and support other staff as required.
6. Interact and communicate in a professional manner with physical plant staff, the university community, consultants, contractors, etc.

## Desirable Qualifications

Minimum of two years' related experience in architectural and other engineering fields. An "operator" level of CADD and related computer operations is required. Grade 12 plus a two-year diploma in a related architectural/engineering-associated technical program. CADD course work or equivalent experience required. Eligibility for membership as an applied science technologist is also required.

# DRAFTSPERSON III
## Kind and Level of Work

Employees in this classification are responsible for directing the operation of a unit producing computer-aided design drafting information and drawings, under the general supervision of the Facilities Management Design and Information Systems manager. Their work is differentiated from that of other operational staff in the unit on the basis of the skill level involved and the responsibility to supervise others. They develop and maintain cooperative working relations with professionals and tradespersons to facilitate project completion.

## Typical Duties and Responsibilities

1. Supervise, allocate, assist, and participate in the work of subordinate staff.
2. Review work and ensure standards are maintained.
3. Assess incoming work, organize project priorities and flow, and plan and schedule workloads as appropriate.
4. Train and support physical plant staff in the use of system applications for records information access.
5. Assist in the design of computer system enhancements and general strategies.
6. Participate in the more complex design work of projects as required.
7. Interact and communicate in a professional manner with physical plant staff, the university community, consultants, contractors, etc.

## Desirable Qualifications

A minimum of five years' experience in the architectural field and a variety of engineering fields, including some experience in a supervisory capacity. Must have experience in CADD and related computer operations at an "operator" and "systems" level. Grade 12 plus a two-year diploma in a related architectural/engineering-associated technical program. CADD course work or equivalent experience required. Eligibility for membership as an applied science technologist is also required.

# GROUNDS WORKER I

## Kind and Level of Work

The employees in this classification carry out routine gardening by maintaining the grass, flowers, shrubs, and trees on the campus grounds. They either may be assigned an area on campus to look after or may work on a crew assigned to a task such as planting or pruning. These employees are responsible to a Grounds Worker II, who acts as a lead hand, assistant supervisor, or a supervisor.

## Typical Duties and Responsibilities

1. Water lawns and flowerbeds in a particular area.
2. Trim lawns in areas where larger mowers cannot cut.
3. Hoe weeds in flowerbeds, shrubbery beds, and gravel parking lots.
4. Perform general cleanup work in an area.
5. Prune broken branches on shrubs and trees.
6. Use hand clippers to trim areas of lawn not accessible to machines, such as along buildings and around ponds.
7. Assist in the planting of flowers, shrubs, trees, and grass.
8. Assist in sodding operations, which would involve removing old grass, preparing soil, laying new sod, spreading peat moss, and watering.
9. Do minor maintenance of small machinery.

## Desirable Qualifications

Gardening experience preferred but not required. Grade 9 education.

# GROUNDS WORKER II
## Kind and Level of Work

Employees in this class are responsible for a wide variety of gardening jobs involving many of those done by a Grounds Worker I. Generally, they are distinguished from the Grounds Worker I class in that they may be the lead person in a small group or may be a machine operator. These employees may be in charge of a specific operation, such as the greenhouse, a maintenance department, or the nursery. They are usually supervised by an assistant supervisor and supervisor.

## Typical Duties and Responsibilities

1. Supervise the grounds maintenance in a particular area.
2. Supervise a special work crew engaged in an activity, such as sodding, planting, or pruning.
3. Supervise the work done in the greenhouse and the stocking of indoor planters.
4. Operate a mower for cutting playing fields and large areas of grass.
5. Operate a rototiller around trees and shrubs to kill weeds.
6. Operate a tractor or other large machine and all attachments, such as front-end loader, grader blade, and backhoe.
7. Carry out maintenance on all equipment used in the department.
8. Train subordinates in all gardening operations.
9. Communicate instructions from the supervisor.

## Desirable Qualifications

Several years' experience as a grounds worker. Grade 9 education.

# GROUNDS WORKER III
## Kind and Level of Work

Employees in this classification collectively perform a wide variety of tasks related to the positions of ice making, machine operation, nursery management, irrigation, landscape maintenance, and tree and shrub pruning. Their work is distinguished from that of subordinate personnel by the degree of knowledge, skill, and understanding required to perform the duties, the extent of their supervisory and administrative responsibilities, or some combination of these factors. Their work is given general supervision and direction, usually by a supervisor or assistant supervisor, but these employees independently organize and supervise the work of the subordinates assigned to them.

## Typical Duties and Responsibilities

The incumbent is expected to be able to perform all the duties shown under the general listing below, and one of the specialties listed below that.

## General

1. Supervise subordinate employees in their unit by training, allocating their work, assessing their performance, and ensuring acceptable standards.
2. Perform administrative work related to their units, such as recording time, maintaining stocks of supplies, setting up work schedules, and arranging for replacements when necessary.

3. Be familiar with the operation and general maintenance of all machines and tools in their area of responsibility.

4. Act as a lead hand and be familiar with all duties of subordinates and be prepared to carry them out, including shift work, when appropriate.

5. Liaise with supervisors and subordinates on a regular basis to ensure effective communication and coordinated operation.

## Nursery/Landscaping/Pruning

1. Read and interpret blueprint information.

2. Supervise the application of herbicides or fungicides, or the landscaping of a specific area.

3. Perform a full range of skilled horticulture duties in areas such as pruning, tree surgery, landscaping, greenhouse, and nursery. Incumbents are expected to direct the work of and train subordinate staff in the operation of tree-pruning equipment, such as extension ladders, cranes, and pruners, and chemical applicators, such as hand-held sprayers, boom sprayers, and fertilizer spreaders.

4. Diagnose and treat various types of lawn and tree diseases in conjunction with the horticulture supervisor and assistant supervisor, using the proper application of appropriate chemicals.

5. Be familiar with all the duties required of a nursery person including all propagation practices, such as grafting, budding, seeding, transplanting, hardening, stratifying, etc.

## Facilities

1. Oversee the operation of the skating and curling facilities in a cooperative spirit with the College of Physical Education to promote optimum facility use and goodwill with patrons and staff.

2. Make ice in curling and skating rinks and paint markings on ice according to specifications.

3. Maintain ice surfaces with the use of appropriate equipment and tools.

4. Inspect mechanical rooms to ensure that ice-making equipment is functioning correctly, and call service people as required.

5. Ensure that patrons conform to regulations governing behaviour in the rinks and call for assistance from security personnel in case of serious problems.

6. Supervise personnel in ice maintenance and janitorial work.

7. Supervise gardening crews in the maintenance of playing fields, track-and-field facilities, and landscaped areas, parking lots, etc.

8. Be familiar with and supervise the operation of all gardening equipment used in the assigned area.

9. Inspect grounds and work areas regularly and take corrective action when required.

## Machine Operator

1. Operate all the mowers for cutting playing fields and open areas.

2. Operate tree spade for tree transplanting.

3. Operate equipment such as large dump truck, front-end loader, Bobcat, and snowplow.

4. Operate sanding truck in winter, including mixing sand and loading.

5. Do maintenance work on all equipment, but with primary emphasis on the maintenance of power machines (which this person normally operates).

## Irrigation

1. Read and interpret blueprint information.

2. Troubleshoot and repair electric and electronic components, and hydraulic controls of automated irrigation system as well as mechanical components.

3. Be responsible for opening and shutting down the irrigation system in spring and fall, including the blowing out of all lines.

4. Liaise with the supervisor and assistant supervisor for the scheduling of irrigation throughout the campus.

5. Through liaison with the foreman and supervisor, ensure optimum water use efficiency when setting irrigation run times and repeat cycles, considering factors such as soil capacities, turf usage, and sprinkler and line capacities and pressure, etc.

6. Repair and/or install lawn water service including cutting and fitting pipe (PVC and poly) and placing or replacing all types of fittings including galvanized, brass, PVC, and plastic.

## Desirable Qualifications

(A) Several years of work experience, including experience in supervision and in the specialty skill area that is pertinent. This must include considerable knowledge of horticultural identification of plant materials for the nursery position, and several years' experience with the installation and maintenance of manual and automatic irrigation systems for the irrigation position. Additionally, an aptitude in electrical and electronic applications would be of value in the irrigation position. (B) The ability to do rigorous manual labour. (C) Possession of a diploma in horticulture or a related field for the nursery and irrigation positions. (D) Completion of Grade 12. (E) Driver's licence. (F) Pesticide applicator's licence for those positions involved in the application of herbicides, insecticides, or fungicides.

# MEDICAL LABORATORY TECHNOLOGIST I

## Kind and Level of Work

This class comprises positions that require medical laboratory technologist certification and involves positions that are generally located in the medical, dental, and veterinary medical colleges of the university. These are full working-level technologists who are expected to conduct a variety of routine and semi-specialized tests and analyses in their areas of specialization, such as bacteriology, immunology, parasitology, virology, histology, etc. They are engaged in the examination of predominantly biological materials, such as blood, sera, tissue, urine, and feces, by chemical, bacteriological, or related techniques. After an initial orientation period, these employees work independently and are responsible for the accuracy of techniques and the reliability of results. Their work is subject to the general supervision of academic, technical, or administrative superiors.

## Typical Duties and Responsibilities

1. Perform routine and semi-specialized diagnostic analysis using manual and automated techniques.

2. Prepare and standardize reagents, solutions, media, and cultures for study requiring special techniques.

3. Operate basic scientific or technical equipment, maintain as necessary, and monitor quality-control procedures to ensure reliability of results.

4. Perform sample entry, recording, reporting, and filing of results.

5. Assist with the teaching program by preparing materials and providing demonstration or explanation of equipment and/or diagnostic techniques and procedures to students.

6. Assist students with material identification and with projects as required.

7. Assist in the orientation and instruction of new staff; may also supervise student assistants, technical assistants, or first-level technicians.

8. Assist with research experiments by carrying out a variety of standardized quantitative and qualitative analyses by performing assays, routine spectros-copy and chromatography, and microbiological and other standard test procedures.

9. Prepare purchase requisitions; order, receive, and store supplies, tools, and equipment; care for materials; and maintain required inventory and other records.

## Desirable Qualifications

A minimum of one year of experience related to the position assignment. Completion of Grade 12 plus a related technical school diploma from a recognized technical institute. Current certification as a registered technologist with the Canadian Society of Laboratory Technologists (CSLT).

# MEDICAL LABORATORY TECHNOLOGIST II

## Kind and Level of Work

This class comprises positions that require medical laboratory technologist certification and involves positions that are generally located in the medical, dental, and veterinary medical colleges of the university. Employees in positions allocated to this class are experienced technologists who conduct complex tests and/or provide supervision and training to technologists assisting with complex tests or performing common tests. Their work involves the analysis of predominantly biological materials and processes in support of a variety of specialized areas, such as bacteriology, immunology, parasitology, virology, etc. This class is distinguished from the Medical Laboratory Technologist I by the complexity of tasks performed, judgment factors involved, responsibility for work output, and the involvement in training and supervision of junior staff. Their work is subject to general supervision and direction, usually by a member of faculty, but these employees independently organize and supervise the work of their assistants and laboratories.

## Typical Duties and Responsibilities

1. Perform complex and specialized diagnostic analysis using manual and automated techniques.

2. Operate and maintain a variety of complex scientific equipment, ensuring accurate calibration and reliability of results.

3. Verify procedures, evaluate effectiveness of experiments, and modify or develop techniques and/or procedures as required.

4. Provide demonstration and problem-solving consultation involving complex equipment and/or diagnostic techniques and procedures to students in an undergraduate or graduate teaching environment, or on a one-to-one basis with students as required.

5. Participate in the selection and assume responsibility for the training, assigning, and reviewing of the work of subordinate staff or less experienced staff engaged in semi-skilled or skilled work; supervise students in the use of equipment and facilities.

6. Assist individual faculty members with research projects by carrying out experiments, usually involving relatively advanced techniques and procedures, and analyze and report on results.

7. Search published scientific papers for information relating to specific projects.

8. Perform administrative work related to the units such as budgeting, advising on the purchase of material and capital equipment, maintaining appropriate inventory and records, etc.

## Desirable Qualifications

Several years of work experience related to the position assignment including demonstrated supervisory experience. Grade 12 and either a technical school diploma in laboratory technology with ART standing, or a university degree relating to the position assignment. Current certification as a registered technologist with the Canadian Society of Laboratory Technologists (CSLT).

# GLOSSARY

## A

**360-degree feedback** An appraisal system that uses feedback from superiors, peers, subordinates, and possibly customers

**affective commitment** Attachment to an organization based on positive feelings toward the organization.

**agency theory** Agents (employees) will pursue their own self-interests rather than the interests of their principals (employers) unless they are closely monitored or their interests are aligned with the interests of their principals.

**aging the data** The process of adjusting compensation data to bring it up to date with the time period in which the new compensation will take effect.

**analyzer business strategy** Focuses on exploiting new opportunities at a relatively early stage while maintaining a base of traditional products or services.

**attribution theory** Theory of motivation arguing that humans often act without understanding their motives for their behaviour and afterward attempt to attribute motives for their actions.

**average employee earnings** Total compensation divided by the number of full-time equivalent employees.

## B

**balance sheet approach to expatriate pay** Approach to designing expatriate compensation that attempts to provide a standard of living comparable with the home country.

**base pay** The foundation pay component for most employees, usually based on some unit of time worked.

**base pay structure** The structure of pay grades and pay ranges, along with the criteria for movement within pay ranges, that applies to base pay.

**beauty effect** The tendency for the physical attractiveness of a ratee to affect their performance appraisals.

**behavioural observation scales (BOS)** Appraisal method under which appraisers rate the frequency of occurrence of different employee behaviours

**behaviourally anchored rating scales (BARS)** Appraisal method that provides specific descriptors for each point on the rating scale.

**benchmark job** A job in the firm's job evaluation system for which there is a good match in the labour market data.

**broad banding** The practice of reducing the number of pay grades by creating large or "fat" grades, sometimes known as "bands."

**business strategy** An organization's plan for how it will achieve its goals.

## C

**central tendency error** Occurs when appraisers rate all employees as "average" in everything.

**classical managerial strategy** An approach to management that assumes most employees inherently dislike work but can be induced to work in order to satisfy their economic needs.

**classification/grading method** The use of generic grade descriptions for various classes of jobs to assign pay grades to specific jobs.

**combination profit-sharing plan** A plan that combines the current distribution and deferred profit-sharing plans by paying some of the profit-sharing bonus on a current (cash) basis and deferring the remainder.

**communication and information structure** A dimension of organization structure that describes the nature of and methods for communication in an organization.

**compa-ratio** A measure of distribution of employees within their pay range calculated by dividing the mean base pay by the midpoint of the pay range.

**compensable factors** Characteristics of jobs that are valued by the organization and differentiate jobs from one another.

**compensating differential** A higher compensation level offered by an employer because of undesirable aspects of the employment.

**compensation administration** The process through which employee earnings are calculated and the appropriate remittances are paid to employees, governments, and other agencies.

**compensation cost ratio** The ratio of total compensation costs to total costs or to revenues.

**compensation strategy** The plan for the mix and total amount of base pay, performance pay, and indirect pay to be paid to various categories of employees.

**compensation system** The economic or monetary part of the reward system.

**competency-based pay** Pay that is based on the characteristics, rather than the performance, of individual employees; usually applied to managerial or professional employees.

**competitive bonus plan** A group pay plan that rewards work groups for outperforming other work groups.

**content theories of motivation** Theories that focus on understanding motivation by identifying underlying human needs.

**contextual variables** Factors in the firm's context that indicate the most appropriate managerial strategy and organizational structure.

**contingency approach to organizational design** An approach to organization design based on the premise that the best type of structure for an organization depends on the key contingencies (contextual variables) associated with that organization.

**contingent workers** Workers not employed on a permanent full-time basis.

**continuance commitment** Attachment to an organization based on perceived lack of better alternatives.

**contrast effect** The tendency for a set of performance appraisals to be influenced upward by the presence of a very low performer or downward by the presence of a very high performer.

**control structure** A dimension of organization structure that describes the nature of the processes used to control employee behaviour in an organization.

**conversion selling** Selling established products to new customers.

**coordination and departmentation** A dimension of organization structure that describes the methods used to coordinate the work of individual employees and subunits in an organization.

**correlation coefficient** A statistic that measures the extent to which plots of two variables on a graph fall in a straight line.

**current distribution profit-sharing plan** A profit-sharing plan that distributes the profit-sharing bonus to employees in the form of cash or shares, at least annually.

## D

**decision-making and leadership structure** A dimension of organization structure that describes the nature of the decision-making and leadership processes used in an organization.

**defender business strategy** Focuses on dominating a narrow product or service market segment.

**deferred profit-sharing plan (DPSP)** A profit-sharing plan in which the profit-sharing bonuses are allocated to employee accounts but not actually paid out until a later date, usually on termination or retirement.

**defined benefit plans** Pension plans that provide retirement income based on a proportion of the employee's pay at the time of retirement.

**defined contribution plans** Pension plans that provide retirement income based on the accrued value of employer and employee contributions to the plan.

**demographic characteristics** A person's age, gender, ethnicity, education, marital status, and similar characteristics.

**differential piece rate** A lower sum of money per piece is paid if employee production does not meet the production standard, and then a higher sum per piece is paid once the production standard is met.

**distributive justice** The perception that overall reward outcomes are fair.

**domain** Describes the specific products or services offered by a given organization.

## E

**employee assistance programs (EAPs)** Employer-provided programs to help employees deal with a variety of personal problems.

**employee profit-sharing plan** A formal pay program in which a firm provides bonus payments to employees based on the profitability of the firm.

**employee share purchase plan** A plan through which employees may purchase shares in their employer firm.

**employee stock bonus plan** A plan through which employees receive shares in their employer firm at no cost to the employee.

**employee stock option plan** A plan through which employees are provided with options to purchase shares in their employer at a fixed price within a limited time period.

**employee stock plan** Any type of plan through which employees acquire shares in the firm that employs them.

**employment standards legislation** Legislation that sets minimum standards for pay and other conditions of employment.

**equal increase approach** Method to establish pay grade sizes, in which each pay grade increases in width by a constant number of points from the preceding pay grade.

**equal interval approach** Method to establish pay grade widths, in which the point spreads are equal for all pay grades.

**equal percentage approach** Method to establish pay grade sizes, in which each pay grade increases in width by an equal percentage from the preceding pay grade.

**equity sensitivity** A personality trait that entails a high predisposition toward perceiving personal inequity.

**equity theory** Employees' base perceptions of equity (fairness) on a comparison of their rewards/contributions ratio to the ratios of others perceived as being similar.

**expectancy theory** A theory stating that individuals are more likely to exert effort to perform a particular behaviour if they believe that behaviour will lead to valued consequences and if they expect they can perform the behaviour.

**extrinsic rewards** Factors that satisfy basic human needs for survival and security, as well as social needs and needs for recognition.

## F

**factor comparison method** Assigns pay levels to jobs based on the extent to which they embody various job factors.

**family of measures plan** A gain-sharing plan that uses a variety of measures to determine the extent to which a bonus payout is justified.

**fixed benefit system** An employee benefit plan that provides a standard set of benefits to all those covered by the plan.

**flexible benefit system** An employee benefit plan that allows employees to allocate employer-provided credits to purchase the benefits of most value to them.

**forced distribution method** A performance appraisal method that stipulates the distribution of employees across the performance categories.

## G

**gain-sharing plan** Group performance pay plan that shares cost savings or productivity gains generated by a work group with all members of that group.

**goal-sharing plan** A group performance pay plan in which a work group receives a bonus when it meets prespecified performance goals.

**graphic rating scale** An appraisal method in which appraisers use a numerical scale to rate employees on a series of characteristics.

**group commissions** A performance pay plan in which the commissions of a group of sales workers are pooled and then shared equally among members of the group.

**group piece rates** A performance pay plan in which group members get paid based on the number of completed products produced by the group.

## H

**halo error** Occurs when appraisers rate an individual either high or low on all characteristics because one characteristic is either high or low.

**harshness effect** The tendency of some appraisers to provide unduly low performance appraisals.

**health care spending account** A tax-favoured employee benefit that allows employees to use employer-provided health care spending credits to purchase a wide array of health care services.

**high-involvement managerial strategy** An approach to management that assumes work can be intrinsically motivating if the organization is structured properly.

**high–low method** Determines entry-level and skill-block pay amounts by pricing comparable entry-level and top-level jobs in the market and allocating the difference to the various skill blocks.

**horizontal fit** Alignment of strategies at the same level.

**human relations managerial strategy** An approach to management that assumes most employees inherently dislike work but can be induced to work in order to satisfy their social needs.

**human rights legislation** Legislation that prohibits discrimination in hiring or employment on the basis of race, ethnic origin, religion, gender, marital status, age, or sexual orientation.

**hybrid compensation policy** A compensation-level strategy that varies across employee groups or compensation components.

**hybrid pension plans** Pension plans that combine features of the defined benefit pension plan and the defined contribution pension plan.

## I

**Improshare** A gain-sharing plan that focuses on labour hours per unit of output and that does not usually include worker participation.

**incentive** A promise that a specified reward will be provided if a specified employee behaviour is performed.

**indirect pay** Noncash items or services that satisfy a variety of specific employee needs, sometimes known as "employee benefits."

**individual/team merit grid** A method for linking individual merit pay to both individual and team performance.

**initial dip** A tendency for performance to decline during the initial stages of any change.

**intergrade differential percentage** Calculated by dividing the intergrade differential (expressed in dollars) of each pay grade by the midpoint (in dollars) of the previous pay grade.

**intergrade differentials** The differences between the range midpoints of adjacent pay grades in a pay structure, expressed in dollars.

**interquartile range** A measure of pay dispersion across employers, calculated by dividing the difference between the 25th and 75th percentile values by the value of the 25th percentile.

**intrinsic rewards** Factors that satisfy higher-order human needs for self-esteem, achievement, growth, and development.

## J

**job analysis** The process of collecting information on which job descriptions are based.

**job autonomy** The degree of freedom workers have in deciding how to perform their jobs.

**job description** A summary of the duties, responsibilities, and reporting relationships pertaining to a particular job.

**job design** A dimension of organization structure that describes the manner in which the total task of an organization is divided into separate jobs.

**job enrichment** The process of redesigning jobs to incorporate more of the five core dimensions of intrinsically satisfying work.

**job evaluation** Establishing base pay by ranking all jobs in the firm according to their value to that firm.

**job feedback** The extent to which the job itself provides feedback on worker performance.

**job satisfaction** The attitude one holds toward one's job and workplace.

**job specifications** The employee qualifications deemed necessary to successfully perform the duties for a given job.

**job-to-job method** Establishes pay equity by comparing a female job class to a male class that is comparable in terms of job evaluation criteria.

**just noticeable difference (JND)** The amount of pay increase necessary to be considered significant by employees receiving the increase.

## K

**key job matching** Including jobs on a compensation survey that are well understood and numerous in the labour market and asking respondents to supply compensation information for those jobs.

## L

**labour market** Constraints on compensation strategy flowing from the relative levels of demand and supply for particular occupational groups.

**lag compensation-level strategy** A compensation-level strategy based on paying below the average compensation level in a given labour market.

**lead compensation policy** A compensation level strategy based on paying above the average compensation level in a given labour market.

**leniency effect** The tendency of many appraisers to provide unduly high performance appraisals.

**leverage selling** Selling new products to existing customers.

**living wage** the minimum income necessary to help a worker enjoy a decent standard of living.

**localization approach to expatriate pay** Approach to designing expatriate compensation that entails paying expatriate employees the same compensation as local nationals in equivalent positions.

**long-term incentives (LTIs)** A type of performance pay in which the incentives are tied to an organization performance horizon that ranges beyond one year, often three to five years.

**lump-sum approach to expatriate pay** Approach to designing expatriate compensation in which various allowance amounts are paid directly in home-country currency.

## M

**maintenance selling** Selling established products to existing customers.

**management by objectives (MBO)** An approach to management that involves setting employee goals and providing feedback on goal accomplishment.

**managerial strategy** One of three main patterns or combinations of structural variables that can be adopted by an organization—namely, classical, human relations, or high involvement.

**mandatory benefits** Government-provided employee benefits, such as pensions and employment insurance, to which employers must contribute on behalf of their employees.

**market comparator firms** Firms selected as comparators when constructing a sample of market data.

**market comparator job** A job in the market data that matches a benchmark job within the firm's job evaluation system.

**market line** A regression line that relates job evaluation points to market pay (in dollars) for the benchmark jobs.

**market pricing** Establishing base pay by determining the average amount of pay other employers are offering for a given job.

**Maslow's hierarchy of needs** A content theory of motivation that groups human needs into five main levels and states that humans seek to satisfy the lowest order needs before satisfying higher order needs.

**match compensation policy** A compensation-level strategy based on paying at average compensation levels in a given labour market.

**mean or simple average** A measure of central tendency of a set of values derived by summing the values and dividing by the number of values.

**median** The middle value in an ordered list of values.

**membership behaviour** Occurs when employees decide to join and remain with a firm.

**merit bonus** A cash payment, provided to recognize good employee performance, that does not increase base pay.

**merit pay grid/merit pay matrix** A tool for allocating merit raises, based on the performance level of the employee and the pay range quartile in which they fall.

**merit raise** An increase to an employee's base pay in recognition of good job performance.

**mission** An organization's reason for existence.

## N

**negotiation approach to expatriate pay** Approach to designing expatriate compensation that entails negotiation between employer and employee to create a mutually acceptable compensation package.

**new market selling** Selling new products to new customers.

**noncash employee recognition programs** A program that provides noncash rewards to employees in recognition of employee accomplishments or actions that are valued by the organization.

## O

**optimal reward system** The reward system that adds the most value to the organization, after considering all its costs.

**organization structure** The means through which an organization generates the behaviours necessary to execute its business strategy.

**organizational citizenship behaviour** Occurs when employees voluntarily undertake special behaviours beneficial to the organization.

**organizational commitment** The strength of the individual's attachment to his or her organization.

**organizational culture** The set of core values and understandings shared by members of an organization.

**organizational identification** A sense of shared goals and belonging, and the desire to remain a member of the organization.

# P

**paired comparison method** Every job is compared with every other job, providing a basis for a ranking of jobs.

**pay-for-knowledge system (PKS)** Establishing base pay according to the total value of the skills and competencies an employee has acquired.

**pay for time not worked** An employee benefit that covers a wide array of different types of employee absences from work.

**pay grade** A grouping of jobs of similar value to the organization, typically grouped by point totals.

**pay policy line** The intended pay policy for the organization, generated by adjusting the market line for the intended pay level strategy of the organization.

**pay range** The minimum and maximum pay rates (in dollars) for jobs in a particular pay grade.

**performance appraisal** The process of assessing the overall performance levels of individual employees.

**performance appraisal reliability** Occurs when a performance appraisal system produces the same scores even when applied by different appraisers.

**performance appraisal validity** The process of assessing the overall performance levels of individual employees. Occurs when employees who receive the highest scores in a performance appraisal system are in fact the highest performers.

**performance management** Method for improving employee performance based on goal setting, feedback, encouragement and support, and rewards for success.

**performance pay** Relates employee monetary rewards to some measure of individual, group, or organizational performance.

**performance share plan** A long-term incentive in which the bonus amounts are expressed in company shares.

**performance unit plan** A long-term incentive in which the bonus amounts are expressed in units for which the monetary value will fluctuate, depending on degree of goal accomplishment.

**permissible differences** Pay differences between female and male job classes that are not considered inequitable because they stem from certain specified allowable circumstances, such as seniority.

**personal competencies** A person's physical, verbal, and mental skills.

**personal values** A person's core beliefs about appropriate and inappropriate behaviour.

**personality characteristics** A person's behavioural and emotional tendencies.

**phantom equity plan** A plan that helps retain key employees by providing rewards based on the stock performance of a portfolio of promising new high-tech firms.

**phantom share plan** A plan through which employees participate in the appreciation of company shares and any associated dividends, without ever owning any company shares.

**piece rates** A pay system under which individuals receive a specified sum of money for each unit of output they produce or process.

**point method** Establishes job values by the application of points to each job, based on compensable factors.

**pooled performance pay** A pay plan in which the performance results of a group are pooled and group members share equally in the performance bonus.

**procedural justice** The perception that the process for reward determination is fair.

**process theories of motivation** Theories that focus on understanding motivation by determining the processes humans use to make choices about the specific actions they will take.

**product/service market constraints** Constraints on compensation strategy caused by the nature of the product or service market in which the firm operates.

**proportional value method** Establishes pay equity where no comparator male job class exists by extrapolating a hypothetical male comparator job class based on other male job classes.

**prospector business strategy** Focuses on identifying and exploiting new opportunities quickly.

**proxy comparison method** Establishes pay equity in public sector organizations where neither the job-to-job method nor the proportional value method can be used.

**psychological contract** Expectations about the rewards offered by a given job and the contributions necessary to perform the job.

**purpose of a compensation system** To help create a willingness among qualified persons to join the organization and to perform the tasks needed by the organization.

# Q

**quartiles or deciles** Division of an ordered list of values into either four groups (quartiles) or 10 groups (deciles).

# R

**range spread** The difference between the maximum and the minimum pay level, in dollars, for a given pay range.

**range spread percentage** A percentage calculated by dividing the range spread for a given pay range by the minimum for that pay range.

**ranking method** The relative values of different jobs are determined by knowledgeable individuals.

**recency effect** The tendency of appraisers to overweight recent events when appraising employee performance.

**reinforcement theory** A theory that states a behaviour will be repeated if valued outcomes flow from that behaviour, or if performing the behaviour reduces undesirable outcomes.

**reliability** The extent to which a measuring instrument consistently produces the same measurement result when measuring the same thing.

**reward** Anything provided by the job or the organization that satisfies an employee need.

**reward strategy** The plan for the mix of rewards to be provided to members, along with the means through which they will be provided.

**reward system** The mix of intrinsic and extrinsic rewards that an organization provides to its members.

**Rucker plan** A gain-sharing plan similar to the Scanlon plan but that expresses labour costs as a percentage of value added.

# S

**salary** Pay based on a weekly, monthly, or annual time period.

**sales commissions** Pay that is geared to the dollar volume of sales or transactions conducted.

**Scanlon plan** A gain-sharing plan that creates mechanisms for employee participation in developing productivity improvements and that shares the financial benefits of those improvements with the employee group that generated them.

**share appreciation rights** A plan through which employees are awarded shares in their employer at no cost to themselves if the price of employer shares rises during a specified period.

**similarity effect** The tendency of appraisers to inflate the appraisals of appraisees they see as similar to themselves.

**skill-based pay (SBP)** Pay that is based on the specific skills and capabilities of individual employees, rather than on the specific tasks they are carrying out; usually applied to operational-level employees.

**skill block** The basic component of a skill-based pay system, containing a bundle of skills or knowledge necessary to carry out a specific production or service delivery task.

**skill certification** The testing process that determines whether an individual has mastered a given skill block and should be granted the pay raise associated with that skill block.

**skill variety** The variety of skills required for task completion.

**special-purpose incentive** An incentive designed to motivate a specific type of employee behaviour.

**spiral career paths** Career advancement marked by a combination of sideways and vertical progression.

**statistical/policy capturing method** Combines use of statistical methods and job questionnaires to derive job values based on prevailing external or internal pay rates.

**straight commission** Pay that is geared only to the volume of sales or transactions, with no base pay component.

**straight piece rate** The same specified sum of money is paid for each piece produced or processed, regardless of how many pieces are produced or processed.

**suggestion system** An incentive plan through which employees receive cash bonuses for submitting money-saving suggestions.

**supplemental unemployment benefits (SUBs)** An employer-provided benefit that extends government-provided unemployment benefits

## T

**task behaviour** Occurs when employees perform the tasks that have been assigned to them.

**task environment** The portion of the general environment that has direct relevance to a given organization.

**task identity** The extent to which a worker performs a complete cycle of job activities.

**task significance** The perceived importance or social value of a given task.

**technical ladder** Defined progression of skills development to keep work interesting and provide opportunities for higher compensation.

**technical premiums** Compensation measures that increase the compensation of technical employees.

**total rewards** A compensation philosophy that considers the entire spectrum of rewards that an organization may offer to employees.

**trade union legislation** Legislation that defines the rights of parties involved in a collective bargaining relationship.

**two-factor theory of motivation** Argues that intrinsic factors influence work motivation, while extrinsic factors influence job satisfaction.

## U

**utility analysis** A method used to analyze whether a lead, lag, or match compensation-level strategy is most efficient for a given organization.

## V

**validity** The extent to which a measuring instrument actually measures what we intend it to.

**values** Principles, beliefs, and attitudes that drive behaviour.

**vertical fit** Alignment of strategies at different levels.

**vision** An organization's desired future state.

## W

**wage** Pay based on an hourly time period.

**weighted mean or weighted average** A measure of central tendency of a set of values that adjusts the average based on the number of cases to which each value pertains.

**work motivation** The attitude one holds toward good job performance.

# INDEX